Simulated Annealing

Edited by

Cher Ming Tan

Simulated Annealing

Edited by Cher Ming Tan

Published by InTech

Janeza Trdine 9, 51000 Rijeka, Croatia

Additional hard copies can be obtained from orders@intechopen.com

Simulated Annealing, Edited by Cher Ming Tan
p. cm.
ISBN 978-953-7619-07-7

For EU product safety concerns:
IN TECH d.o.o., Prolaz Marije Krucifikse Kozulić 3, 51000 Rijeka, Croatia,
info@intechopen.com or visit our website at intechopen.com.

Preface

Optimization is important in all branches of engineering due to limited resources available. Through optimization, maximum usage of the resource can be achieved. However, global optimization can be difficult due to the requirement of the knowledge of the system behavior under analysis and the possible large solution space. Without this knowledge, the optimization thus obtained may only be a local optimization. Metaheuristic algorithms, on the other hand, are effective in exploring the solution space. Often, they are referred to as "black box" algorithms as they use very limited knowledge about the specific system to be tackled, and often it does not require a mathematical model of the system under study. Hence it can be used to solve a broad range of problem, and has thus receiving increasing attention.

One of the commonly used metaheuristic algorithms is the Simulated Annealing (SA). SA is an optimization algorithm that is not fool by false minima and is easy to implement. It is also superior as compared to many other metaheuristic algorithms as presented in this book. In this book, the different applications of the Simulated Annealing will be presented. The first 11 chapters are devoted to the applications in Industrial engineering such as the scheduling problem, decision making, allocation problem, routing problem and general optimization problem.

The subsequent chapters of this book will focus on the application of the Simulated Annealing in Material Engineering on porous material study, Electrical Engineering on integrated circuit technology, Mechanical Engineering on mechanical structure design, Structural Engineering on concrete structures, Computer Engineering on task mapping and Bio-engineering on protein structure. The last three Chapters will be on the methodology to optimize the Simulated Annealing, its comparison with other metaheuristic algorithms and the various practical considerations in the application of Simulated Annealing.

This book provides the readers with the knowledge of Simulated Annealing and its vast applications in the various branches of engineering. We encourage readers to explore the application of Simulated Annealing in their work for the task of optimization.

Editor

Cher Ming Tan
Nanyang Technological University
Singapore

Contents

1

Simulated Annealing as an Intensification Component in Hybrid Population-Based Metaheuristics

Davide Anghinolfi and Massimo Paolucci
Department of Communication, Computer and Systems Sciences
University of Genova
Italy

1. Introduction

The use of hybrid metaheuristics applied to combinatorial optimization problems received a continuously increasing attention in the literature. Metaheuristic algorithms differ from most of the classical optimization techniques since they aim at defining effective general purpose methods to explore the solution space, avoiding to tailor them on the specific problem at hand. Often metaheuristics are referred to as "black-box" algorithms as they use limited knowledge about the specific problem to be tackled, instead usually taking inspiration from concepts and behaviours far from the optimization field. This is exactly the case of metaheuristics like simulated annealing (SA), genetic algorithm (GA), ant colony optimization (ACO) or particle swarm optimization (PSO). Metaheuristics are based on a subset of features (e.g., the use of exploration history as short or long term memory, that of learning mechanisms or of candidate solution generation techniques) that represent a general algorithm fingerprint which usually can be easily adapted to face different complex real world problems. The effectiveness of any metaheuristic applied to a specific combinatorial problem may depend on a number of factors: most of the time no single dominating algorithm can be identified but several distinct mechanisms exploited by different metaheuristics appear to be profitable for searching high quality solutions. For this reason a growing number of metaheuristic approaches to combinatorial problems try to put together several techniques and concepts from different methods in order to design new and highly effective algorithms. Hybrid approaches in fact usually seem both to combine complementary strengths and to overcome the drawbacks of single methods by embedding in them one or more steps based on different techniques. As an example, in (Anghinolfi & Paolucci, 2007a) the SA probabilistic candidate solution acceptance rule is coupled with the tabu list and neighbourhood change mechanisms respectively characterizing tabu search (TS) and variable neighbourhood search (VNS) approaches to face parallel machine total tardiness scheduling problems. Several surveys exist proposing both classifications of metaheuristics and unified views of hybrid metaheuristics (e.g., (Blum & Roli, 2003), (Doerner et al., 2007), (Raidl, 2006) and (Talbi, 2002)). We would avoid to replicate here the various definitions and classifications through which the different approaches can be analysed and organized (the interested reader can for example refer to (Blum & Roli, 2003) for a valuable review). However, we should underline few basic concepts that allow us to focus on the different characteristics of the kinds of methods used in the hybrid algorithms presented in this chapter. SA, ACO and PSO are all stochastic algorithms, but SA is commonly classified as a *trajectory-based* method since it determines at each iteration a new single current solution, whereas ACO and PSO are *population-based* methods since they explore at each iteration a set of distinct solutions which they make evolve iteration after iteration. The concept behind these two *population-based* methods is that the overall exploration process can be improved by learning from the single exploring experiences of a population of very simple agents (the ants or the particles). As will be cleared in the following of the chapter, ACO explicitly exploits a learning mechanism in order to identify, iteration after iteration, which features should characterize good, i.e., the most promising, solutions. If in ACO the communication among the exploring agents (the ants) is indirect, PSO, on the other hand, drives the search of the population of agents (the swarm of particles) on the basis of simple pieces of information (e.g., where the current best is located), making the agents moving towards promising solutions. Therefore, both ACO and PSO use memory structures, more complex in ACO, simpler in PSO, to elaborate their exploration strategies; agents in ACO and PSO perform a learning or information driven sampling of the solution space that could in general be considered wide but also quite coarse, and that can be trapped in local optima (the so-called *stagnation* (Dorigo & Stutzle, 2004)). SA, on the other hand, is a memoryless method which combines the local search aptitude of exploring in depth regions in the solution space with the ability, ruled by the *cooling schedule* mechanism, of escaping from local optima. From this brief overview the possible advantage of coupling the different complementary abilities of the two types of metaheuristics should begin to emerge. Therefore in this chapter our purpose is to focus the attention on hybrid population-based metaheuristic algorithms with a specific reference to the use of SA as a hybridizing component. Then, according to the classification proposed in (Raidl, 2006), the kind of hybrid algorithms here considered result from the combination of two distinct metaheuristics (the "what is hybridized" aspect) among which a low-level strong coupling is established (the "level of hybridization" aspect), in particular the execution of SA is interleaved with the iterations of the population-based metaheuristics (the "order of execution" aspect) so that SA can be viewed as an integrated component of these latter (the "control strategy" aspect).

Several works recently appeared in the literature show the interest of embedding SA into population-based approaches as ACO, PSO and GA. Examples of PSO hybridized by incorporating SA intensification can be found in (Liu et al., 2008), where the proposed hybrid PSO (HPSO), which includes a probabilistically applied local search (LS) and a learning-guided multi-neighbourhood SA, is applied to makespan minimization in a permutation flow shop scheduling problem with the limited buffers between consecutive machines; in (He & Wang, 2007), where constrained optimization problems are faced by a HPSO which applies the SA search from the best solution found by the swarm in order to avoid the premature convergence; in (Li et al., 2006), where the hybrid algorithm, named PSOSA, is used for non-linear systems parameter estimation; in (Ge et al., 2007) where the HPSO is used to face the job shop scheduling. Differently, in (Xia & Wu, 2005) multi-objective flexible job shop scheduling problems are confronted by a hierarchical approach exploiting PSO to assign operations to machines and then SA to schedule operations on each machine. Hybrid ACO approaches, which combine pheromone trail based learning mechanism with the SA search ability of escaping from local optima, are proposed for example in (Demirel & Toksarı, 2006) for the quadratic assignment problem and in (Yuanjing & Zuren, 2004) for flow-shop scheduling problems. Finally, in (Yogeswaran et al., 2007) a hybrid metaheuristic named GASA, which combines GA and SA, is used to solve a bi-criterion machine loading problem in flexible manufacturing system.

In this chapter we would highlight the effectiveness of embedding a trajectory method, i.e., SA, as intensification method of population-based algorithms, i.e., ACO and PSO. Many works in the literature witnessed the fundamental role for population-based approaches, as ACO, PSO or GA, of an intensification phase which usually corresponds to a local search (LS) exploration (Blum & Roli, 2003). However, a well-known and common characteristic of trajectory methods, as SA, VNS or TS, is their ability of overcoming the LS limitation of being trapped in local optima. For this reason the role of this class of powerful methods goes beyond that of a local intensification procedure, since they allow the calling population-based method to be "re-directed" towards portions of the solution space which may not be confined to the basin of attraction of a local optimizer. Then, we can view the hybrid algorithms discussed in this chapter as composed by a main population-based component which exploits a second level subordinate SA procedure in order to deeply explore (intensify) the neighbourhood of one (or more) promising solution, as well as escaping from such a neighbourhood when it includes a local optima attractor (diversify). On a symmetric standpoint, we could also consider these hybrid metaheuristics as an *iterated* trajectory method, i.e., an iterated SA, whose (promising) starting solutions are determined at the beginning of each iteration by a population-based algorithm. This latter algorithm in fact, exploiting memory and/or learning mechanisms, performs a sort of solution perturbation or shaking, possibly driving the SA search to focus on alternative promising regions of the solution space. In this case we can consider the population-based algorithm as an effective memory and learning based diversification device for SA. Whatever standpoint one would prefer, we believe that the effectiveness of the overall resulting algorithm emerges from the interaction of the complementary capabilities of the methods of the two different classes, that is, according to (He & Wang, 2007), from the balance of the intensification and diversification components included in them. An important aspect to be taken into account when designing the interaction mechanism between the population-based and the trajectory (i.e., SA) components of the hybrid algorithm regards how to identify the solutions which are worth to intensify; therefore in this chapter, we will also discuss several alternative strategies available to this end, pointing out their possible different effectiveness and computational burden.

The rest of this chapter is organized as follows. First in the Section 2 we briefly present the two scheduling problems used as reference to analyse the behaviour of the hybrid metaheuristics. Note that, even if different, the solutions of these two problems share the common property of being represented by sequences of jobs, i.e., by permutations of a given number of integers. Then in the Section 3 we illustrate the two hybrid metaheuristics considered, first introducing the main features of the pure population-based metaheuristics, respectively ACO and PSO, then showing how these are combined with SA, as well as discussing alternative triggering rules that can be used to determine the SA starting solutions. In the Section 4 we report the experimental test performed, comparing the obtained results with the ones of other algorithms from the literature. Finally, in the Section 5 we draw the chapter conclusions.

2. The referenced scheduling problems

In this section we briefly introduce the characteristics of the two scheduling problems faced by the two hybrid metaheuristics presented in the following, reporting also some literature review for them. These problems are the Single Machine Total Weighted Tardiness with Sequence-Dependent Setups (STWTSDS) problem and the Permutation Flowshop Scheduling (PFS) problem. Even if apparently different, the solutions to such problems have a common structure since they can both represented by permutation. For this reason, we introduced here some common notation. In general a solution x to one of the two scheduling problems involving a set of n jobs can be represented by a permutation or sequence $\sigma(x)=([1],..., [n])$, where $[j]$ indicates the index of the job sequenced in the j-th place. In addition we denote with $\varphi_\sigma:\{1,..., n\}\rightarrow\{1,..., n\}$, the mapping between the places in a sequence σ and the indexes of the sequenced jobs; for example, if job j is sequenced in the h-th place of σ we have $j=\varphi_\sigma(h)$.

2.1 The single machine total weighted tardiness problem with sequence-dependent setups

The STWTSDS problem consists in scheduling n independent jobs on a single machine. All the jobs are released simultaneously, i.e., they are ready at time zero, the machine is continuously available and it can process only one job at a time. For each job $j=1,..., n$, the following quantities are given: a processing time p_j, a due date d_j and a weight w_j. A sequence-dependent setup time s_{ij} must be waited before starting the processing of job j if it is immediately sequenced after job i. Setup operations are necessary to prepare production resources (e.g., machines) for the job to be executed next, and whenever they depend, as in this case, on the (type of) preceding job just completed they are called sequence-dependent setups. The tardiness of a job j is defined as $T_j=max(0, C_j-d_j)$, being C_j the job j completion time. The scheduling objective is the minimization of the total weighted tardiness expressed as $\sum_{j=1}^{n} w_j T_j$. This problem, denoted as $1/s_{ij}/\Sigma w_j T_j$, is strongly NP-hard since it is a special case of the $1//\Sigma w_j T_j$ that has been proven to be strongly NP-hard in (Lawler, 1997) (note that also the $1//\Sigma T_j$ special case is still NP-hard (Du & Leung, 1990)). Apart from its complexity, the choice of the STWTSDS as reference problem is also motivated by its relevance for manufacturing industries; in particular, the importance of performance criteria involving due dates, such as (weighted) total tardiness or total earliness and tardiness (E-T), as well as the explicit consideration of sequence-dependent setups, has been widely recognized in many real industrial contexts. In the literature both exact algorithms and heuristic algorithms have been proposed for the STWTSDS problem or for a slightly different version disregarding the job weights. However, since only instances of small dimensions can be solved by exact approaches, recent research efforts have been focused on the design of heuristics. The apparent tardiness cost with setups (ATCS) heuristic (Lee et al., 1997) is currently the best *constructive* approach for the STWTSDS problem. However, constructive heuristics, even if requiring smaller computational efforts, are generally outperformed by improvement, i.e., local search, and metaheuristics approaches. The effectiveness of stochastic search procedures for the STWTSDS is shown in (Cicirello & Smith, 2005), where the authors compare a value-biased stochastic sampling (VBSS), a VBSS with hill-climbing (VBSS-HC) and a simulated annealing (SA), to limited discrepancy search (LDS) and heuristic-biased stochastic sampling (HBSS) on a 120 benchmark problem instances for the STWTSDS problem defined by Cicirello in (Cicirello, 2003). The literature about applications of metaheuristics to scheduling is quite extended. In (Liao & Juan, 2007) an ACO algorithm for the STWTSDS is proposed, which is able to improve about 86% of the best known results for the Cicirello's benchmark previously found by stochastic search procedures in (Cicirello & Smith, 2005) Recently the Cicirello's best known solutions have been further independently improved in (Cicirello, 2006) by means of a GA approach, in (Lin & Ying, 2006) with three SA, GA and TS algorithms, in (Anghinolfi & Paolucci, 2008) using an ACO approach and in (Anghinolfi & Paolucci, 2007b) with PSO.

2.2 The permutation flowshop scheduling problem

The PFS problem requires to schedule a set of n jobs on a set of m machines so that each job is processed by each machine and the sequence of jobs is the same for all the machines. Then, a permutation of the n jobs identifies a solution to the PFS problem which consists in finding an optimal permutation for the jobs. For each job j and machine h the processing time p_{jh} is given; then, the completion times of the jobs on the machines can be computed for any given permutation σ=([1],..., [n]) of n jobs as follows

$$C_{[1]}^{1} = p_{[1],1} \tag{1}$$

$$C_{[j]}^{1} = C_{[j-1]}^{1} + p_{[j],1} \quad \forall j = 2,\dots,n \tag{2}$$

$$C_{[1]}^{h} = C_{[1]}^{h-1} + p_{[1],h} \quad \forall h = 2,\dots,m \tag{3}$$

$$C_{[j]}^{h} = \max\{C_{[j-1]}^{h}, C_{[j]}^{h-1}\} + p_{[j],h} \quad \forall h = 2,\dots,m; j = 2,\dots,n \tag{4}$$

where $C_{[j]}^{h}$ represents the completion time of the j-th job in the permutation on machine h. The scheduling problem is to find the job permutation σ^* that minimizes the *makespan* $C_{\max}$, corresponding to the completion time of the last job on the m-th machine, i.e., $C_{\max} = C_{[n]}^{m}$. The makespan minimization for the PFS problem, denoted as $n/m/P/C_{\max}$, was originally proposed in (Johnson, 1954) and afterwards it has been widely investigated in the literature. This problem is NP-hard in the strong sense (Garey et al., 1976) for $m \geq 3$ and only instances of limited size can be solved by exact solution methods in an acceptable computation time. Therefore numerous heuristics approaches have been proposed in the literature, among which constructive heuristics (e.g., (Palmer, 1965), (Campbell et al., 1970), (Taillard, 1990)) improvement heuristics (e.g, (Ho & Chang, 1991), (Woo & Yim, 1998), (Suliman, 2000)) and metaheuristics as SA ((Osman & Potts, 1989), (Ishibuchi et al., 1995)), TS ((Nowicki & Smutnicki, 1996), (Grabowski and Wodecki, 2004)), GA ((Reeves, 1995), (Ruiz et al., 2006)), ACO ((Rajendran & Ziegler, 2004)) and PSO algorithms ((Liao et al., 2007), (Lian et al., 2006a), (Tasgetiren et al., 2007), (Jarboui et al., 2007)), some of which are taken as reference for the performance evaluation of the PSO-SA proposed in the following.

3. Two hybrid population-based metaheuristics

In this section we introduce the main concepts of ACO and PSO and we show how two hybrid algorithms, respectively ACO-SA and PSO-SA, can be derived through the interaction with SA. Note that in order to illustrate the specific characteristics of the algorithms we refer to the STWTSDS problem for ACO-SA and to the PFS one for PSO-SA.

3.1 The hybrid ant colony optimization algorithm

The ACO metaheuristic aims at exploiting the successful behaviour of real ants in cooperating to find shortest paths to food for solving combinatorial problems (Dorigo & Stützle, 2002), (Dorigo & Blum, 2005). Most of the real ants use *stigmergy* during food search, i.e., they have an effective indirect way to communicate each other which is the most promising trail, and finally the optimal one, towards food. Ants produce a natural essence, called pheromone, which is left on the followed path to food in order to mark it. The pheromone trail evaporates over time, finally disappearing on the abandoned paths. On the other hand, the pheromone trail can be reinforced by the passage of further ants; due to this fact effective (i.e., shortest) paths leading to food are finally characterized by a strong pheromone trail, and they are followed by most of ants. The ACO metaheuristic was first introduced in (Dorigo et al., 1991), (Dorigo et al., 1996) and (Dorigo, 1992), and since then it has been the subject of both theoretical studies and applications. ACO combines both *Reinforcement Learning* (RL) (Sutton & Barto, 1998) and *Swarm Intelligence* (SI) (Kennedy & Eberhart, 2001) concepts:

- each single agent (an ant) takes decisions and receives a reward from the environment, so that the agent's policy aims at maximizing the cumulative reward received (RL);
- the agents exchange information to share experiences and the performance of the overall system (the ant colony) emerges from the collection of the simple agents' interactions and actions (SI).

ACO has been successfully applied to several combinatorial optimization problems, from the first travelling salesman problem applications (Dorigo et al., 1991), (Dorigo et al., 1996), to vehicle routing problems (Bullnheimer et al., 1999), (Reinmann et al., 2004), and to single machine and flow shop scheduling problems (den Besten et al., 2000), (Gagné et al., 2002) and (Ying & Liao, 2004).

In this section we present a new hybrid ACO-SA approach to face the STWTSDS problem. In (Anghinolfi & Paolucci, 2008) we recently introduced the main characteristics of the pure ACO component of ACO-SA, which mainly differ from previous approaches in the literature for the following aspects: (a) we use a new pheromone trail model whose pheromone values are independent of the problem cost (or quality) function and they are bounded within an arbitrarily chosen and fixed interval; (b) we adopt a new global pheromone update (GPU) rule which makes the pheromone values asymptotically increase (decrease) towards the upper (lower) bound, without requiring any explicit cut-off as in the *Max-Min* Ant System (MMAS) (Stützle & Hoos, 2000); (c) we use a diversification strategy based on a temporary perturbation of the pheromone values performed by a local pheromone update (LPU) rule within any single iteration. The ACO that we proposed in (Anghinolfi & Paolucci, 2008) is mainly based on the Ant Colony System (ACS) (Dorigo & Gambardella, 1997), and it includes concepts inspired to the MMAS (Stützle & Hoos, 2000) and to the approaches in (Merkle & Middendorf, 2000), (Merkle & Middendorf, 2003), even if such concepts are encapsulated in a new pheromone model and exploited in a real different manner. We report in Figure 1 the very high level structure of the ACO-SA algorithm. In the following we will detail all the involved steps apart from *SA intensification* that we will describe in a separate subsection as this step is in common with the PSO-SA algorithm.

```
Initialization;
k=1;
While <termination condition not met>
{
  For each ant a∈A
  {
    Construction of solution xa^k;
    Local pheromone update;
  }
  SA intensification;
  Global pheromone update;
  k=k+1;
}
```

Figure 1. The overall ACO-SA algorithm

We consider a set A of na artificial ants. At each iteration k, every ant a identifies a solution x_a^k building a sequence $\sigma(x_a^k)$ of the n jobs, whose objective value $Z(x_a^k)$ is then simply computed by executing each job at its feasible earliest start time for that sequence. Every ant a builds the sequence $\sigma(x_a^k)$ by iterating n selection stages: first, the set of not sequenced jobs for ant a, U_a^0, is initialized as $U_a^0 = \{1,...,n\}$; then, at stage h=1,..., n, the ant a selects one job j from the set U_a^{h-1} to be inserted in the position h of the partial sequence, and updates $U_a^h = U_a^{h-1} \setminus \{j\}$; at stage h=n all the jobs are sequenced and $U_a^n = \varnothing$. The job selection at each stage h of the construction procedure at iteration k is based on a rule that is influenced by the pheromone trail $\tau_k(h,j)$ associated with the possible *solution components*, i.e., position-job pairs, (h, j), where $j \in U_a^{h-1}$. Differently from other approaches in the literature, the pheromone values assigned to $\tau_k(h,j)$ are independent of the objective or quality function values associated with previously explored solutions including the component (h, j). In particular, we adopt an arbitrary range $[\tau_{Min}, \tau_{Max}]$ for the pheromone values, which is independent of the specific problem or instance considered; therefore any pair of values, such that $\tau_{Min} < \tau_{Max}$, can be chosen so that τ_{Max} and τ_{Min} are not included in the set of parameters that must be specified for the algorithm. In addition, the GPU rule controlling the ant colony learning mechanism imposes a smooth variation of $\tau_k(h,j) \in [\tau_{Min}, \tau_{Max}]$ such that both the bounds are only asymptotically reached. Note that also in MMAS lower and upper bounds are imposed for $\tau_k(h,j)$, but they must be appropriately selected, dynamically updated each time a new best solution is found, taking into account the objective function values, and they are used as cut-off thresholds. In the following we consider relative pheromone values $\tau'_k(h,j) = \tau_k(h,j) - \tau_{Min}$ such that $\tau'_k(h,j) \in [0, \tau'_{Max}]$, where $\tau'_{Max} = \tau_{Max} - \tau_{Min}$, whenever this makes simpler and more readable the expressions introduced.

Initialization. For each solution component (h, j), h, j=1,..., n, we assign an initial value of the pheromone trail by fixing $\tau_0(h,j) = (\tau_{Max} + \tau_{Min})/2$; in addition, we initialize the best current solution x^* as an empty solution, fixing the associated objective value $Z(x^*)$ to infinity.

Job selection rule. At a selection stage h of iteration k, an ant a determines which job $j \in U_a^{h-1}$ is inserted in the h-th position of the sequence as follows. First, similarly to the ACS, the ant chooses which job selection rule to use between *exploitation* and *exploration*: a random number q is extracted from the uniform distribution $U[0, 1]$ and if $q \leq q_0$ the ant uses the exploitation rule, otherwise the exploration one. The parameter q_0 (fixed such that $0 \leq q_0 \leq 1$) directs the ants' behaviour towards either the exploration of new paths or the exploitation of the best paths previously emerged. The *exploitation* rule selects the job j in a deterministic way as

$$j = \arg\max_{u \in U_a^{h-1}} \{\tau'_k(h,j) \cdot [\eta(h,j)]^{\beta}\} \tag{5}$$

whereas the *exploration* rule according to a *selection probability* $p(h, j)$ computed as

$$p(h,j) = \frac{\tau'_k(h,j) \cdot [\eta(h,j)]^{\beta}}{\sum_{u \in U_a^{h-1}} \tau'_k(h,j) \cdot [\eta(h,j)]^{\beta}} \tag{6}$$

The quantity $\eta(h, j)$, associated with the solution component (h, j), is an heuristic value computed equal to the priority $I_t(h, j)$ of assigning job j in position h at time t according to the ATCS rule (Lee et al., 1997)

$$\eta(h,j) = I_t(h,j) = \frac{w_j}{p_j} \exp\left[\frac{\max(d_j - p_j - t, 0)}{k_1 \overline{p}}\right] \exp\left[-\frac{s_{\varphi_\sigma(h-1)j}}{k_2 \overline{s}}\right] \tag{7}$$

where

$$t = \sum_{i=1}^{h-1} (s_{\varphi_\sigma(i-1)\varphi_\sigma(i)} + p_{\varphi_\sigma(i)}) + s_{\varphi_\sigma(h-1)j} \tag{8}$$

$\overline{p}$ and $\overline{s}$ are respectively the average processing time and the average setup time, and k_1 and k_2 are the lookahead parameters fixed as originally suggested in (Lee et al., 1997). Therefore, in the ACO-SA algorithm the influence of the sequence-dependent setups is encapsulated in the heuristic values used in the job selection rule. The parameter β in (5) and (6) is the relative importance of the heuristic value with respect to the pheromone trail one.

Local pheromone update (*intra-iteration diversification*). As often done in ACO approaches to avoid premature convergence of the algorithm, a LPU is performed after any single ant a completed the construction of a solution x_a in order to make more unlike the selection of the same sequence by the following ants. In the ACO-SA we adopt the following the local pheromone update rule

$$\tau'_k(h,j) = (1-\rho) \cdot \tau'_k(h,j) \quad \forall h = 1,\dots,n; j = \phi_\sigma(h) \tag{9}$$

where ρ is a parameter fixed in [0, 1]. We must remark that such kind of update strictly *local*, i.e., we use it to favour the diversification of the sequences produced by the ants within the same iteration and (9) temporarily modifies the pheromone values only in the single iteration scope, since such changes are deleted before executing the *global pheromone update phase* and starting the next iteration. We denoted in (Anghinolfi & Paolucci, 2008) this feature is as *reset of the local pheromone update* (RLPU).

Global pheromone update. The (relative) pheromone values $\tau'_k(h, j)$ are varied within the range $[0, \tau'_{Max}]$ during the GPU phase with a rule, called *Unbiased Pheromone Update* (UPU), that we introduced in (Anghinolfi & Paolucci, 2008). The UPU rule does not uses cost or quality function values, but smoothly updates of pheromone trails associated with a set of quality solution components. We denote with Ω_k^* the *best component set* determined after the completion of iteration *k*; then, the UPU rule consists of the three following steps:

1. pheromone evaporation for the solution components not included in Ω_k^*

$$\tau'_{k+1}(h, j) = (1-\alpha)\cdot\tau'_k(h, j) \quad \forall (h, j) \notin \Omega_k^* \tag{10}$$

   where $0 \le \alpha \le 1$ is a parameter establishing the evaporation rate;
2. computation of the maximum pheromone reinforcement $\Delta\tau'_k(h, j)$ for the solution components in Ω_k^*

$$\Delta\tau'_k(h, j) = \tau'_{Max} - \tau'_k(h, j) \quad \forall (h, j) \in \Omega_k^* \tag{11}$$

3. update of the pheromone trails to be used in the next iteration for the solution components in Ω_k^*

$$\tau'_{k+1}(h, j) = \tau'_k(h, j) + \alpha\cdot\Delta\tau'_k(h, j) \quad \forall (h, j) \in \Omega_k^* \tag{12}$$

The UPU rule guarantees that $\tau'_k(h, j) \in [0, \tau'_{Max}]$ and that $\tau'_k(h, j)$ converges towards the bounds asymptotically ($\Delta\tau'_k(h, j)$ is progressively reduced as much as $\tau'_k(h, j)$ approaches to τ'_{Max}, as well as the decrease of $\tau'_k(h, j)$ towards 0 in (10)) with a law similar to the most frequently used cooling schedule for SA. The set Ω_k^* adopted in the ACO-SA is the one defined in (Anghinolfi & Paolucci, 2008) as the *Best-so-far* (BS) solution component set, that is, it includes only the solution components associated with the best sequence σ^* find so far

$$\Omega_k^* = \{ (h, j) : h = 1, \ldots, n; j = \phi_{\sigma^*}(h) \} \tag{13}$$

Termination conditions. The algorithm is stopped when a maximum number of iterations, or a maximum number of iterations without improvements, is reached.

3.2 The hybrid particle swarm optimization algorithm

PSO is a recent metaheuristic approach motivated by the observation of the social behaviour of composed organisms, such as bird flocking and fish schooling, and it tries to exploit the concept that the knowledge to drive the search for optimum is amplified by social interaction. PSO executes a population-based search in which the exploring agents, the *particles*, modify their positions during time according not only to their own experience, but also to the experience of other particles. In particular, a particle p may change its position with a velocity that in general includes a component moving p towards the best position so far achieved by p to take into account the particle experience, and a component moving p towards the best solution so far achieved by any among a set of neighbouring particles (*local neighbourhood*) or by any of the exploring particles (*global neighbourhood*). Note that, differently from GA, the PSO population is maintained and not filtered. PSO is based on the *Swarm Intelligence* (SI) concept (Kennedy & Eberhart, 2001): the agents are able to exchange information in order to share experiences, and the performance of the overall multi-agent system (the swarm) emerges from the collection of the simple agents' interactions and actions. PSO has been originally developed for continuous nonlinear optimization (Kennedy & Eberhart, 1995), (Abraham et al., 2006). The basic algorithm for a global optimization problem, corresponding to the minimization of a real objective function $f(x)$ of a variable vector x defined on a n-dimensional space, uses a population (*swarm*) of np particles; each particle i of the swarm is associated with a position in the continuous n-dimensional search space, $x_i=(x_{i1},\dots, x_{in})$ and with the correspondent objective value $f(x_i)$ (*fitness*). For each particle i, the best previous position, i.e. the one where the particle found the lowest objective value (*personal best*), and the last particle position change (*velocity*) are recorded and represented respectively as $p_i=(p_{i1},\dots, p_{in})$ and $v_i=(v_{i1},\dots, v_{in})$. The position associated with the current smallest function value is denoted as $g=(g_1,\dots, g_n)$ (*global best*). Denoting with x_i^k and v_i^k respectively the position and velocity of particle i at iteration k of the PSO algorithm, the following equations are usually used to iteratively modify the particles' velocities and positions:

$$v_i^{k+1} = w \cdot v_i^k + c_1 r_1 \cdot (p_i - x_i^k) + c_2 r_2 \cdot (g - x_i^k) \tag{14}$$

$$x_i^{k+1} = x_i^k + v_i^{k+1} \tag{15}$$

where w is the *inertia* parameter that weights the previous particle's velocity; c_1 and c_2, respectively called *cognitive* and *social* parameter, multiplied by two random numbers r_1 and r_2 uniformly distributed in [0, 1], weight the velocity towards the particle's personal best, $(p_i - x_i^k)$, and the velocity towards the global best solution, $(g - x_i^k)$, found so far by the whole swarm. The new particle position is determined in (15) by adding to the particle's current position the new velocity computed in (14). The PSO velocity model given by (14) and (15) is called *gbest*, but also a *lbest* model is introduced in (Kennedy & Eberhart, 2001): in this latter model the information about the global best position found so far by the whole group of particles is replaced by the local best position for each particle i, $l_i=(l_{i1},\dots,l_{in})$, i.e., the position of the best particle found so far among a subset of particles nearest to i. The PSO parameters that we need to fix are the inertia w, the cognitive and social parameters c_1 and c_2, and finally the dimension of the swarm np; taking into account that in the standard PSO for continuous optimization $c_1+c_2=4.1$ (Clerc & Kennedy, 2002), the number of parameters needed by this metaheuristic is quite reduced.

In recent years many there is an increasing attention in the literature for application of the PSO approach to discrete combinatorial optimization problems. For example, PSO has been applied to the traveling salesman problem (TSP) (Pang et al., 2004), the vehicle routing problem (Chen et al., 2006), and scheduling problems (Tasgetiren et al., 2004), (Liao et al.,

2007), (Lian et al., 2006a), (Lian et al., 2006b), (Allahverdi & Al-Anzi, 2006) and (Parsopoulos & Vrahatis, 2006). Discrete PSO (DPSO) approaches differ both for the way they associate a particle position with a discrete solution and for the velocity model used; in particular, since here we consider a combinatorial problem whose solutions are represented by permutations, we could classify the DPSO approaches in the literature according to three kinds of solution-particle mapping, i.e., binary, real-valued and permutation-based, and three kinds of velocity model used, i.e., real-valued, stochastic or based on a list of moves. The first DPSO algorithm proposed in (Kennedy & Eberhart, 1997) used a binary solution representation and a stochastic velocity model since it associates the particles with *n*-dimensional binary variables and the velocity with the probability for each binary dimension to take value one. In (Tasgetiren et al., 2007), (Tasgetiren et al., 2004), (Parsopoulos & Vrahatis, 2006) real values are associated with the particle dimensions to represent the job place in the scheduling sequence according to a *random key representation* (Bean, 1994), and a *smallest position value* (SPV) rule is exploited to transform the particle positions into job permutations. Permutation-based solution-particle mappings are used in (Hu et al., 2003) for the *n*-queens problem together with a stochastic velocity model, representing the probability of swapping items between two permutation places, and a mutation operator, consisting of a random swap executed whenever a particle coincides with the *local* (*global*) *best* one. In (Lian et al., 2006a) particles are associated with job sequences and velocities are implemented as *crossover* and *mutation* operators borrowed from the genetic algorithm approach. Generally the velocity models adopted in DPSO approaches are either stochastic or real-valued. To our best knowledge the unique examples of velocity models based on a list of moves can be found in the DPSO approach for the TSP in (Clerc, 2004), together with the new DPSO approach that we very recently presented in (Anghinolfi & Paolucci, 2007b) to face the STWTSDS problem. This velocity model is quite difficult to be used as it needs the definition of an appropriate set of operators to extend the PSO computations in a discrete solution space.

In the following we illustrate the main features of the hybrid PSO-SA which extends the DPSO approach introduced in (Anghinolfi & Paolucci, 2007b) to face the PFS problem. As for the algorithm in (Anghinolfi & Paolucci, 2007b), PSO-SA is based on both a permutation solution-particle representation and on a list-of-moves velocity model, but differently we here introduce a new restart mechanism to avoid the stagnation of particles. In Figure 2 we report the overall structure of the PSO-SA algorithm. Then, similarly to what done for ACO-SA, we will detail the main PSO steps, finally dealing with the *SA intensification* in the last subsection.

```
Initialization;
While <termination condition not met>
{
  For each particle
  {
    Velocity update;
    Position update;
    Fitness computation;
  }
  SA intensification;
  Group restart;
  Best references update;
}
```

Figure 2. The PSO-SA algorithm.

We use a set of np particles, each one associated with a permutation σ, that is, with a schedule x whose fitness is given by the cost value $Z(x)$. To define the particle behaviour we need to introduce a metric for the permutation space and a set of operators to compute velocities and to update particles' positions consistently. As illustrated in (Anghinolfi & Paolucci, 2007b) we define a velocity as a set of moves, called *pseudo-insertion* (PI) moves, that, if applied to a given particle or permutation, change the position of the particle, generating a different permutation. Velocities are produced as difference between particle positions. For example, given a pair of particles p and q, the velocity v moving particle p from its current position to the one of particle q is a list of PI moves computed as the difference $v=\sigma_q-\sigma_p$. A PI move is a pair (j, d), where d is an integer displacement that is applied to job j within the permutation. Assuming for example that $j=\varphi(h)$, a PI move (j, d), which delays a job j in the permutation σ, extracts j from its current place h in σ and reinserts it generating a new permutation such that $j=\varphi(\min(h+d, n))$; analogously, a PI move $(j, -d)$, which instead anticipates a job j, produces a new sequence such that $j=\varphi(\max(h-d, 0))$. If for example we consider two particles associated with two permutations of n=4 jobs, σ_p=(1,2,3,4) and σ_q=(2,3,1,4), then, we compute the velocity $v=\sigma_q-\sigma_p$={(1,2),(2, 1),(3,-1)}. The list of PI moves representing a velocity can include at most a single PI move for a given job.

We define a *position-velocity sum* operator to change the particle positions in the permutation space, which applies the PI moves included in a velocity list one at a time by extracting the involved job from the permutation and reinserting it in the new place. We call these moves as pseudo-insertion since in general they do not produce feasible permutations but what we called *pseudo-permutations*. We illustrate this point with an example: if we apply to the permutation σ_p=(1,2,3,4) the first move in the velocity v={(1,2),(2, -1),(3,-1)}, then we extract job 1 from the first place and reinsert it in the third place obtaining the pseudo-permutation (-,2,[3,1],4), where symbol "-" denotes that no job is now assigned to the first place, whereas [3,1] represents the ordered list of the two jobs 3 and 1 both assigned to the third place. Hence, PI moves produce in general not feasible permutations but pseudo-permutations characterized by one or more empty places and by others places containing a list of jobs. Then, we introduce the *permutation completion procedure* reported in Figure 3 to transform a pseudo-permutation into a feasible permutation. In Figure 3 $\pi(h)$ denotes the ordered set of items in the h-th place of the pseudo-permutation π, *pull*(s) the function that extracts the first element from an ordered set s, and *push*(i, s) the function that inserts the element i at the bottom of the set s. Hence, the permutation completion procedure manages $\pi(h)$ as a first-in-first-out (FIFO) list. As an example, starting from the pseudo-permutation π=([1,3],-,-,[4,2]) the permutation completion procedure produces the feasible permutation (3,1,4,2).

We define a *velocity sum* operator $\oplus$ which generates the list of PI moves for a velocity $w=v\oplus v'$ from the union of the PI moves in v and v'; in addition, since any job can appear only once in the PI list associated with a velocity, if v and v' include respectively the PI moves (j, d) and (j, d'), then w must include $(j, d+d')$ only if $d+d'\neq 0$. Finally, we define the *constant-velocity multiplication* so that the velocity computed as $w=c\cdot v$, where c is a real positive constant, includes the same PI moves of v whose displacement values have been multiplied by c.

```
Input: π a pseudo-sequence
Output: σ a feasible sequence
for each h=1,...,n
  {
    if |π(h)|=1 skip;
    else if |π(h)|=0
     {
       repeat
              k=h+1;
         while k<n and |π(k)|=0
         π(h)=pull(π(k));
     }
    else if |π(h)|>1
     {
         while |π(h)|>1
            push(pull(π(h), π(h+1));
        }
  }
σ=π;
```

Figure 3. The sequence completion procedure.

We can now consider the main steps of PSO-SA.

Initialization. A set of initial solutions, i=1,..., np, is assigned to the np particles by randomly generating a set of np permutations. This initialization procedure is similar to the one adopted for the discrete PSO approach in (Tasgetiren et al., 2007). Analogously, a set of np initial velocities is randomly produced and associated with the particles. In particular these velocities are generated first randomly extracting the number of PI moves composing a velocity from the discrete uniform distribution $U[[\lfloor n/4 \rfloor, \lfloor n/2 \rfloor]$, then, for each move, randomly generating the involved job and the integer displacement are respectively from $U[1, n]$ and from $U[\lfloor -n/3 \rfloor, \lfloor n/3 \rfloor]$. The set of particles is partitioned into n_c clusters G_{cl}, cl=1,..., n_c, randomly associating each particle to one of them, and the *local best* position l_i (i.e., the related solution x_{li}), computed as $l_i = \arg\min_{j \in G_{cl}} Z(x_j^0)$, is associated with each particle $i \in G_{cl}$. The quantity n_c is an input parameter of the algorithm. Finally, the global best position, that is the position associated with the best permutation found by any of the particles, is denoted with g (whose related solution is x_g).

Velocity and position update. At iteration k, we define for each particle i three velocity components, inertial (iv), directed to local best velocity (lv), and directed to global best velocity (gv), as follows:

$$iv_i^k = w \cdot v_i^{k-1} \tag{16}$$

$$lv_i^k = c_1 r_1 \cdot (l_i - \sigma_i^{k-1}) \tag{17}$$

$$gv_i^k = c_2 r_2 \cdot (g - \sigma_i^{k-1}) \tag{18}$$

Parameters w, c_1 and c_2 respectively represent the *inertia* parameter that weights the previous particle's velocity, and two kinds of *social* parameters, multiplied by two random numbers r_1 and r_2 extracted from $U[0,1]$, weighting the velocities towards the best position in the clusters (*local best*) and the *global best* position of the whole set of particles. Then, we update the particles' velocities by summing the three components (16), (17) and (18). The velocity model adopted for the PFS problem is the one called *glbest* in (Anghinolfi & Paolucci, 2007b) that does not include any velocity component directed towards the particle's personal best solution. In addition, differently from the standard PSO procedure, we compute the new position separately summing to the current particle position the three velocity components (16), (17) and (18) one at a time, so moving the particle through a set of intermediate feasible permutations obtained by the permutation completion procedure.

Restart of a group of particles. Differently from the DPSO in (Anghinolfi & Paolucci, 2007b), we restart all the particles in a group to avoid a premature convergence of the algorithm due to the stagnation of all the particles in one single position of the permutation space and to differentiate exploration. In particular, the positions of the particles belonging to the group whose local best solution is coincident with the global best solution of the swarm are reinitialized with a random solution and the local best is reset. Moreover, after such a reset, for the same group of particles we substitute for r iterations the weight of the global best velocity component c_2 with the value c_2^k computed according to the following rule

$$c_2^k = c_2\left(\frac{k-k'}{r}\right) \qquad k = k',...k'+r \tag{19}$$

Since k' is the iteration at which the reset of the positions takes place and r is a parameter to be fixed, (19) corresponds to set for all the involved particles the value of the weight c_2 to 0 and then to make it linearly increase to its original value in r iterations. In this way the diversification effect of this group restart is reinforced since the particles in this group are not driven to immediately follow the direction towards the global best position but they can search for other good solutions independently.

3.3 The SA intensification

The *SA intensification* step included in the overall structures of both the ACO-SA and PSO-SA algorithms respectively in Figure 1 and 2 is performed using a SA procedure similar to the one adopted for the H-CPSO algorithm presented in (Jarboui et al., 2007). The SA algorithm, which originally took its inspiration from the simulation of the physical annealing of melted metals (Kirkpatric et al., 1983), iterates exploring the neighbourhood $N(x)$ of the current solution x accepting a stochastically generated candidate $x' \in N(x)$ with the following probabilistic rule: if $\Delta Z = Z(x) - Z(x') \leq 0$ then x' becomes the new current solution, otherwise x' is randomly accepted according to the probability distribution $P(\Delta Z, T) = e^{(\frac{-\Delta Z}{T})}$, where T is a control parameter playing the role of the temperature in the physical annealing process. This algorithm is usually initialized with a high value T_0 of the control parameter and it iterates progressively decreasing it until a termination condition is met according to a rule, called *cooling schedule*, which is critical for the algorithm convergence (Kirkpatric et al., 1983). In both the proposed hybrid algorithms to update T we adopt the exponential rule $T_k = T_0 \cdot \theta^k$, where θ is a constant positive parameter. Similarly to (Jarboui et al., 2007) we use a stochastic definition of the neighbourhood $N(x)$ of the current solution x based on the random selection of insert and swap moves. In particular, we apply either an insert or a swap move on the permutation associated with x to generate the solution candidates at each SA iteration: first the algorithm randomly chooses with probability 0.5 between the two kinds of move, then it randomly selects the job to be moved and its insertion point or the pair of jobs to be swapped. The SA terminates when it reaches a maximum number of non improving iterations.

An important aspect to be considered whenever we embed an intensification procedure into a main metaheuristic is when such procedure is fired and which triggering rule is used. Designing a (hybrid) metaheuristic we should find an acceptable balance between exploration thoroughness and computational burden. Apparently, intensification steps greatly improve the accuracy of the search but also increase the time of computation. A quite straightforward choice for the two algorithms considered in this chapter is to perform intensification after all the exploring agents complete an iteration. Then, in ACO-SA the SA intensification takes place after all the ants generate a solution and in PSO-SA after all the particles have updated their position. Triggering rules specify which set X_{SA} of solutions in the current population have to be intensified, i.e., which solutions are chosen as starting point of SA. Even in this case a balance between accuracy and computation workload must be usually found. We can adopt rules selecting one or more starting points for intensification as detailed in the following.

a) The *best in iteration* (BI) rule: the SA is started from the (single) best solution found by the ants (particles) in the current iteration, i.e., $X_{SA} = \{x_{i^*}^k : i^* = \arg\min_{i=1,\ldots,na} Z(x_i^k)\}$.
b) The *random* (RND) rule: the SA is started from a single solution that is randomly extracted from the solutions determined by the ants or particles in the current iteration k.
c) The *improved solution without intensification* (ISWI) rule: to implement this rule we need to define x_{WI}^* as the best solution found by any ant (particle) in the previous iterations without using the SA intensification. Then, the set X_{SA} may include one or more solutions found in the current iteration k improving x_{WI}^*, i.e. $X_{SA} = \{x_i^k : Z(x_i^k) < Z(x_{WLS}^*), i = 1,\ldots,na\}$. Apparently, the number of solutions that can be subject to intensification at the end of an iteration with this rule can vary from zero to the number of ants *na* (or to the number of particles, *np*), even if the upper bound appear very unlikely.
d) The *all* (ALL) rule: the intensification is started from all the solutions found by the ants or particles in the current iteration k.

Independently of the used rule, if the solution produced by SA improves the starting $x_{i^*}^k$, then in ACO-SA the new solution may become the new current best and their relevant pheromone trails are updated accordingly, whereas in PSO-SA the new solution is associated with the particle i^*, so updating its relevant position, and the *lbest* solution for the cluster including particle i^*, as well as the *gbest* solution are possibly updated.

The BI and RND rules clearly outperform the ALL rule, and they are very likely to outperform also the ISWI one, under the computational time aspect as they both intensify a single solution. The ALL rule apparently should allow to produce solutions with the same quality of the other rules (we must keep in mind that intensification is executed with a stochastic algorithm) if we grant it a sufficiently long computation time, since it is a superset of them; on the other hand the ALL computational requirement is so high to make such rule hard to be accepted. Our experience also pointed out that the quality of the solutions yielded using RND are on the average dominated by the ones form the BI one. Therefore, we believe that in general the BI and ISWI may represent good compromise choices for triggering rules: the decision between these two rules can finally depend on the different time and quality requirements of the case under concern.

4. Experimental results

In this section we present some experimental results with the purpose of providing evidence on the possible benefit of combining SA with the two population-based metaheuristics considered. To this end we compared the behaviour of ACO-SA and PSO-SA with the one of the two same algorithms when LS is used instead of SA as intensification component. In particular, we adopted the deterministic LS procedure, reported in Figure 4, that, similarly to the SA algorithm described in the previous section, explores a mixed type of solution neighbourhood obtained by insert and swap moves.

```
x_b=x_c=x_0;
non_impr=0;
neigh_type=1;

repeat
  {
   x_c=x_b;

   x_c=best_in_neigh(x_b,neigh_type);

   if Z(x_c)<Z(x_b)
     {
      x_b=x_c;
      neigh_type=1;
     }
   else
     {
      non_impr++;
      neigh_type++;
     }
  }  until  (non_impr  >  max_non_impr)  and
neigh_type<=2;
```

Figure 4. The LS algorithm

We must observe that the LS in Figure 4 implements a kind of variable neighbourhood descent procedure (VND) (Hansen & Mladenovic, 1999), which for each current solution completely explores the neighbourhood generated by insert moves and, if no improvement is found, the one produced the swap moves. Then, in the following we report first the experimental tests performed for ACO-SA, giving greater emphasis to the analysis of the behaviour and relative effectiveness of the alternative triggering rules introduced in Section 3.3, whereas we limit the successive discussion on PSO-SA only on the comparison with the LS intensified version of algorithm. All the versions of the two algorithms analysed were coded in C++ and the experimental tests were executed on an Intel Core 2 6600, 2.4 GHz, 2 Gb PC (note however that our implementations do not exploit the dual processor architecture). During all the experimental campaign we adopted as termination criterion the maximum number of fitness (objective) function evaluations, that we fixed = 20,000,000. This choice follows the recommendation in (Taillard, 2005) suggesting the use of absolute computational burden measures (i.e., independent of the kind of computer) in order to obtain results easier to be compared in the scientific community. As regards the values of the parameters characterizing the SA procedure included in both the hybrid algorithms here considered, we fixed θ=0.95, the initial temperature $T_0 = -(0.2 \cdot Z_0)/\log(0.5)$ (such value is chosen to impose that at the initial iteration the probability of accepting a solution with a 20% deviation from objective value of the starting solution is 0.5), and imposing $10 \cdot n^2$ non improving iterations, where n is the number of jobs of the considered scheduling problem, as SA stopping criterion (note that similar settings are used in (Jarboui et al., 2007)).

4.1 The tests on ACO-SA

The benchmark that we adopted to analyse ACO-SA is the set of 120 problem instances for the STWTSDS with 60 jobs provided in (Cicirello, 2003) and available online at http://www.cs.drexel.edu/~cicirello/benchmarks.html. Note that this benchmark was used for testing various metaheuristic approaches recently appeared in the literature as (Cicirello & Smith, 2005), (Liao & Juan, 2007), (Cicirello, 2006), (Lin & Ying, 2006), (Anghinolfi & Paolucci, 2008) and (Anghinolfi & Paolucci, 2007b). The benchmark was produced by generating 10 instances for each combination of three different factors usually referenced in the literature (for a definition and discussion see, e.g., (Pinedo, 1995)): the due date tightness δ, the due date range R, and the setup time severity ξ, selected as follows: $\delta \in \{0.3, 0.6, 0.9\}$, $R \in \{0.25, 0.75\}$, $\xi \in \{0.25, 0.75\}$. For this set of tests we fixed the parameters characterizing the ACO as follows: na=30, α=0.09, β=0.5, ρ=0.05, q_0=0.7.

We conducted first a test in order to compare the possible triggering rules, i.e., BI, RND, ISWI and ALL, for ACO-SA. For each configuration of the algorithm c and for each instance i in the benchmark we executed 5 runs then computing the average result $\overline{Z}_{ci}$; after that, we obtained the best average result for each instance i as $\overline{Z}_i^* = \min_c \overline{Z}_{ci}$, and we computed for each configuration c and instance i the average percentage deviation Δ_{ci} from the best average $\overline{Z}_i^*$ as

$$\Delta_{ci} = \frac{\overline{Z}_{ci} - \overline{Z}_i^*}{\overline{Z}_i^*} \tag{20}$$

finally obtaining the overall average percentage deviation Δ_c for each configuration c as

$$\Delta_c = \frac{1}{I} \sum_{i=1}^{I} \Delta_{ci} \tag{21}$$

where I is the total number of instances considered. In Table 1 we summarise the obtained results. The columns of Table 1 report the overall average percentage deviations (Δ_c) and the relevant standard deviations (*Std*) for the four tested triggering rules, with and without the elimination of possible outliers; in fact, since in the objective values in the benchmark we observed differences of several orders of magnitude, the elimination of the outliers would reduce the possible influence of very slight absolute differences in the objectives for instances with small reference values. In particular, excluding the outliers we eliminated from the computation of the averages the instances with a percentage deviation not in the interval (-40%, 40%). In the last column of Table 1 we also show the average computational time (*CPU*) in seconds needed to terminate the runs.

			Without outliers (5 over 120)		
	Δ_c	Std	Δ_c	Std	CPU (sec.)
BI	0.14%	0.44%	0.10%	0.20%	23.8
RND	2.18%	6.10%	1.49%	4.89%	22.5
ISWI	7.51%	20.53%	4.21%	13.22%	20.8
ALL	7.99%	23.89%	4.41%	15.15%	20.6

Table 1. The comparison of intensification triggering rules for ACO-SA.

As we can observe, there are relevant differences both in the average percentage deviations and in the standard deviations for the tested rules. Then we executed the well-known non-parametric *Friedman's test* with 5% significance level obtaining that the differences between two groups of rules, one consisting of BI and RND, and the other ISWI and ALL, are significant from a statistical standpoint, both including and excluding the outliers. Therefore, at least for the kind of termination condition here considered, the two rules that execute a single SA intensification for iteration of the algorithm dominates the others. This may be due to the fact that the fixed maximum number of fitness function evaluations is better exploited by allowing fewer, here specifically one, SA search for iteration, so letting the whole algorithm execute a greater number of iterations. This behaviour is also suggested by the slightly larger computation time spent using the BI and RND configurations. Since we noted that the overall results for BI and RND in the first two rows of Table 1 were rather distant, we repeated the statistical test for a lower significance level, finding that the hypothesis that samples are not significantly different can be rejected when fixing a 4% level. In the second test performed we compared the ACO-SA results produced with the BI rule, with the one generated substituting SA with the LS described in Figure 4. In particular, we compared this latter configuration, denoted as ACO-LS, with ACO-SA in Table 2 (whose structure is analogous to Table 1).

			Without outliers (5 over 120)		
	Δ_c	Std	Δ_c	Std	CPU (sec.)
ACO-SA	0.15%	0.45%	0.11%	0.22%	23.8
ACO-LS	8.25%	22.33%	4.23%	10.05%	16.6

Table 2. The comparison of ACO-SA and ACO-LS.

The differences between the performance (both with and without outliers) of the two algorithms are apparent and also in this case their significance was confirmed by the statistical test with 5% significance level. Observing the computational times in the *CPU* column, we again could explain the worst behaviour of ACO-LS with the attitude of LS of being trapped in local optima: LS spent more fitness function evaluations than SA at each iteration as it deeply explores the basin of attraction of the intensified solution; then, the whole algorithm performed a smaller number of iterations. On the other hand, the ability of SA of escaping from local optima, i.e., its ability of diversifying the search, clearly turns out to be more effective.

Even if the evaluation of the performance of stochastic algorithms should always be based on average results, to complete the tests with the Cicirello's benchmark for the STWTSDS we report also the comparison of the best results over 5 runs obtained with ACO-SA and ACO-LS with a set of best known results. In particular, we consider an aggregate set of best known solutions combining the best solutions yielded by the following approaches: the ACO algorithm in (Liao & Juan, 2007), the GA in (Cicirello, 2006) and the SA, GA and TS algorithms in (Lin & Ying, 2006). Table 3 basically reproduces the same picture of Table 2, but here the possible presence of good solutions produced by chance for some instances should appear from the higher standard deviation values.

			Without outliers (8 over 120)	
	Δ_c	**Std**	Δ_c	**Std**
ACO-SA	1.18%	11.50%	0.99%	3.43%
ACO-LS	8.20%	21.74%	3.41%	6.04%

Table 3. The comparison of ACO-SA and ACO-LS with the best known solution.

4.2 The tests on PSO-SA

In order to evaluate the performance of PSO-SA compared to the one of the PSO algorithm with the LS presented in Figure 4 (denoted in the following as PSO-LS), we considered the well-known set of benchmark instances for the PFS problem with makespan criterion provided by Taillard (Taillard, 1993). In particular, we considered the benchmark set that includes 10 instances for n=20, 50, 100, 200, 500 jobs and m=5, 10, 20 machines (such classes of instances are denoted in the following with the n x m notation). For this test we used a set of $np=2 \cdot n$ particles and a number of particle clusters $n_c=np/10$, fixing the values of the parameters needed by PSO as w=0.5, c_1=1 and c_2=2, setting r=40 for the instances with 20 and 50 jobs and r=20 for the ones with 100, 200 and 500 jobs. Similarly to the campaign for ACO-SA, we executed 5 runs for each benchmark instance, computing the average results, the best average results as previously described, finally the overall average percentage deviations as (21). In this case we directly compared PSO-SA and PSO-LS adopting BI as intensification firing rule. Table 4 summarizes the results produced by the two algorithms highlighting the outcomes for the different classes of instances as specified in the first column (*Problem*).

	Avg vs Avg (Δ_c)		Avg vs BK ($\Delta^{BK}{}_c$)		Total CPU		CPU for finding best	
Problem	**PSO-SA**	**PSO-LS**	**PSO-SA**	**PSO-LS**	**PSO-SA**	**PSO-LS**	**PSO-SA**	**PSO-LS**
20x5	0.00%	0.00%	0.04%	0.04%	23.5	26.5	0.1	0.2
20x10	0.00%	0.03%	0.00%	0.03%	41.2	42.0	3.7	4.4
20x20	0.01%	0.01%	0.02%	0.02%	76.5	79.0	16.7	18.3
50x5	0.00%	0.02%	0.00%	0.02%	39.8	39.5	3.2	4.0
50x10	0.00%	0.37%	0.54%	0.91%	79.3	71.7	29.7	29.8
50x20	0.00%	0.36%	1.04%	1.41%	149.3	154.9	78.4	77.9
100x5	0.02%	0.02%	0.11%	0.11%	76.9	65.8	17.2	17.7
100x10	0.03%	0.11%	0.70%	0.78%	146.7	126.3	55.9	42.9
100x20	0.03%	0.16%	2.41%	2.54%	242.3	275.0	138.7	185.1
200x10	0.00%	0.49%	0.16%	0.65%	253.6	212.7	105.8	106.2
200x20	0.00%	1.42%	1.34%	2.78%	377.2	462.8	270.3	416.8
500x20	0.00%	4.06%	0.75%	4.85%	900.0	1112.2	737.4	1104.2

Table 4. The comparison of PSO-SA with PSO-L1 for benchmark instance classes.

The first pair of columns in Table 4 reports the comparison between the overall average percentage deviations (Δ_c) from the best average; as it appears, PSO-SA outcomes are on the average never worse than the PSO-LS ones for each class of instances and also the Friedman's test with 5% significance level confirmed the statistical significance of this result. We must remark that we report here also the runs for the greatest instances with 500 jobs even if for such cases the value of maximum fitness function evaluations adopted as termination criterion turned out to be too restrictive: such value in fact allowed a too small number of iterations to really appreciate the behaviour of the whole hybrid approach (actually, we could consider the test for the 500x20 only a comparison between SA and LS). Nevertheless, we verified the statistical significance of the results even excluding the 500x20 instances. The second pair of columns in Table 4 shows the overall average percentage deviations ($\Delta^{BK}{}_c$) of the average PSO-SA and PSO-LS results from the best know solutions (BK) for the Taillard's PSP benchmark (we suggest the readers interested to BK to refer to Taillard's web site where this set is maintained and updated). The third pair of columns reports the total average CPU time needed by the compared algorithms to terminate, whereas the last pair of columns the average CPU needed to find the best solution produced in the runs (both values are in seconds). As we can observe, the differences among computational times are not really significant for this benchmark.

We show in Table 5 the overall comparison between PSO-SA and PSO-LS for the benchmark, including also the standard deviations.

	Avg vs Avg		**Avg vs BK**		**CPU**	
	Δ_c	**Std**	$\Delta^{BK}{}_c$	**Std**	**Total**	**For best**
PSO-SA	0.01%	0.03%	0.59%	0.73%	200.5	121.4
PSO-LS	0.59%	1.14%	1.18%	1.47%	222.4	167.3

Table 5. The overall comparison of PSO-SA and PSO-LS algorithms.

Finally, we can comment that also in the case of a hybrid PSO based algorithm, the presence of the SA search resulted apparently more effective than a LS one (we must recall that the LS used here has also a VND flavour), due to its powerful intensification ability but specifically to its attitude to smoothly diversify the exploration according to the reduction of the value of the parameter T ruled by the cooling schedule.

5. Conclusions

In this chapter we illustrated how SA can be exploited to embed in two alternative population-based metaheuristics a trajectory search component. Population-based metaheuristics need intensification procedures as LS to reach peak performances for discrete combinatorial problems. The effectiveness of using SA instead of LS to this end emerged from the experimental tests reported in this chapter. We considered ACO and PSO and we analysed the performance of the resulting hybrid algorithms on two scheduling problems quite extensively faced in the literature, the STWTSDS and the PSP problems. However, even different, the combinatorial structure of such problems is the same, as their relevant solutions can be represented by permutations. Actually, we compared two "structurally" similar trajectory methods, LS and SA: in particular we adopted a deterministic LS which explores a combination of two neighbourhoods generated respectively by insert and swap moves, with a VND fashion; similarly, the stochastic SA procedure at each iteration derives the next candidate solution first randomly selecting between an insert and a swap move. In other words we tried to use the same kind of ingredients in the two trajectory methods in order to measure their relative strength. Hence the results that we showed allow to conclude that the principles in SA can lead to superior solution improvement procedures than LS when the same level of sophistication is used in both of them, without implying the obviously wrong claim that "any" SA procedure is better than "any" LS.

Hybridization by combining a population-based algorithm, provided with memory, learning and/or swarm intelligence mechanisms, with SA is a viable strategy to produce in a simple way high quality metaheuristics. Therefore, we would recommend to consider also this possibility when tackling complex combinatorial problems: the intensification (the attitude of operating as a LS) and diversification (the attitude of not limit the search to a confined region) features that are blended in SA in a dynamic fashion (ruled by the cooling schedule) are certainly good ingredients for powerful hybrid methods.

6. References

Blum, C., Roli, A.: Metaheuristics in combinatorial optimization: Overview and conceptual comparison. ACM Computing Surveys 35(3) (2003) 268–308

Doerner, K.F.; Gendreau, M.; Greistorfer, P.; Gutjahr, W.; Hartl, R.F.; Reimann, M. (Eds.). Metaheuristics - Progress in Complex Systems Optimization. Springer. Series: Operations Research/Computer Science Interfaces Series , Vol. 39. 2007.

Raidl G.R. A unified view on hybrid metaheuristics. In Francisco Almeida et al., editors, Proceedings of the Hybrid Metaheuristics Workshop, volume 4030 of LNCS, pages 1-12. Springer, 2006.

Talbi, E.G.: A taxonomy of hybrid metaheuristics. Journal of Heuristics 8(5) (2002) 541–565.

Dorigo M., Stutzle T. Ant Colony Optimization. MIT Press. 2004.

Anghinolfi D., Paolucci M. Parallel machine total tardiness scheduling with a new hybrid metaheuristic approach. Computers & Operations Research, Volume 34, Issue 11, November 2007, Pages 3471-3490

Liu B, Wang L, Jin Y-H. An effective hybrid PSO-based algorithm for flow shop scheduling with limited buffers. Computers & Operations Research. 2008; 35: 2791-2806.

Qie He and Ling Wang. A hybrid particle swarm optimization with a feasibility-based rule for constrained optimization. Applied Mathematics and Computation, Volume 186, Issue 2, 15 March 2007, Pages 1407-1422.

Ling-lai Li, Ling Wang and Li-heng Liu. An effective hybrid PSOSA strategy for optimization and its application to parameter estimation. Applied Mathematics and Computation, Volume 179, Issue 1, 1 August 2006, Pages 135-146.

Ge, Hongwei Du, Wenli Qian, Feng A Hybrid Algorithm Based on Particle Swarm Optimization and Simulated Annealing for Job Shop Scheduling. Proceedings of ICNC 2007. Third International Conference on Natural Computation 2007. Volume: 3

Weijun Xia and Zhiming Wu. An effective hybrid optimization approach for multi-objective flexible job-shop scheduling problems. Computers & Industrial Engineering, Volume 48, Issue 2, March 2005, Pages 409-425

Nihan Çetin Demirel and M. Duran Toksarı. Optimization of the quadratic assignment problem using an ant colony algorithm. Applied Mathematics and Computation, Volume 183, Issue 1, 1 December 2006, Pages 427-435

Feng, Yuanjing; Feng, Zuren. Ant colony system hybridized with simulated annealing for flow-shop scheduling problems. WSEAS Transactions on Business and Econonomics. Vol. 1, no. 1, pp. 133-138. Jan. 2004.

Yogeswaran, M. Ponnambalam, S. G. Tiwari, M. K. An hybrid heuristic using genetic algorithm and simulated annealing algorithm to solve machine loading problem in FMS. Proc. of International Conference on Automation Science and Engineering, 2007. CASE 2007. IEEE On page(s): 182-187.

Lawler, E.L. (1997). A 'pseudopolynomial' algorithm for sequencing jobs to minimize total tardiness. Annals of Discrete Mathematics, 1: 331–342.

Du, J. and Leung, J.Y-T. (1990). Minimizing total tardiness on one machine is NP-hard. Mathematics of Operations Research, 15: 483–495.

Lee, Y.H., Bhaskaran, K. and Pinedo, M. (1997). A heuristic to minimize the total weighted tardiness with sequence-dependent setups. IIE Transaction, 29: 45-52.

Cicirello, V.A. and Smith S.F. (2005). Enhancing stochastic search performance by value-based randomization of heuristics. Journal of Heuristics, 11: 5–34.

Cicirello, V.A. (2003). Weighted tardiness scheduling with sequence-dependent setups: a benchmark library. Technical Report, Intelligent Coordination and Logistics Laboratory, Robotics Institute, Carnegie Mellon University, USA.

Liao C-J, Juan HC. An ant colony optimization for single-machine tardiness scheduling with sequence-dependent setups. Computers & Operations Research 2007; 34; 1899-1909.

Cicirello VA. Non-Wrapping Order Crossover: An Order Preserving Crossover Operator that Respects Absolute Position. In: Proceeding of GECCO'06 Conference, Seattle, Washington, USA; 2006. p. 1125-1131.

Lin S-W, Ying K-C. Solving single-machine total weighted tardiness problems with sequence-dependent setup times by meta-heuristics. The International Journal of Advanced Manufacturing Technology 2006; Available online (www.springerlink.com).

Anghinolfi D., Paolucci M., A new ant colony optimization approach for the single machine total weighted tardiness scheduling problem, International Journal of Operations Research, Vol. 5, No. 1, 44-60. 2008.

Anghinolfi D., Paolucci M., A new discrete particle swarm optimization approach for the single-machine total weighted tardiness scheduling problem with sequence-dependent setup times. European Journal of Operational Research (avaliable online) 2007.

Johnson SM. Optimal two-and three-stage production schedules. Naval Research Logistics Quarterly. 1954; 1: 61-68.

Garey MR, Johnson DS, Sethi R. The complexity of flowshop and jobshop scheduling. Mathematics of Operations Research. 1976; 1: 117-129.

Palmer DS. Sequencing jobs through a multistage process in the minimum total time: A quick method of obtaining a near-optimum. Operational Research Quarterly. 1965; 16: 101-107.

Campbell HG, Dudek RA, Smith ML. A heuristic algorithm for the n job, m machine sequencing problem. Management Science. 1970; 16(10): B630-B637.

Taillard E. Some efficient heuristic methods for the flowshop sequencing problems. European Journal of Operational Research. 1990; 47: 65-74.

Ho JC, Chang Y-L. A new heuristic for the n-job, m-machine flow-shop problem. European Journal of Operational Research. 1991; 52: 194-202.

Woo HS, Yim DS. A heuristic algorithm for mean flowtime objective in flowshop scheduling. Computers and Operations Research. 1998; 25: 175-182.

Suliman SMA. A two-phase heuristic approach to the permutation flow-shop scheduling problem. International Journal of Production Economics. 2000; 64: 143-152.

Osman I, Potts C. Simulated annealing for permutation flow shop scheduling. OMEGA. 1989; 17(6): 551-557.

Ishibuchi H, Misaki S, Tanaka H. Modified simulated annealing algorithms for the flow shop sequencing problem. European Journal of Operational Research. 1995; 81: 388-398.

Nowicki E, Smutnicki C. A fast tabu search algorithm for the permutation flowshop problem. European Journal of Operational Research. 1996; 91: 160-175.

Grabowski J, Wodecki M. A very fast tabu search algorithm for the permutation flowshop problem with makespan criterion. Computers and Operations Research. 2004; 31(11): 1891-1909.

Reeves C. A genetic algorithm for flowshop sequencing. Computers and Operations Research. 1995; 22(1): 5-13.

Ruiz R, Maroto C, Alcaraz J. Two new robust genetic algorithms for the flowshop scheduling problem. OMEGA. 2006; 34: 461-476.

Rajendran C, Ziegler H. Ant-colony algorithms for permutation flowshop scheduling to minimize makespan/total flowtime of jobs. European Journal of Operational Research. 2004; 155(2): 426-438.

Liao C-J, Tseng C-T, Luarn P. A discrete version of particle swarm optimization for flowshop scheduling problems. Computers & Operations Research. 2007; 34: 3099-3111.

Lian Z, Gu X, Jiao B: A similar particle swarm optimization algorithm for job-shop scheduling to minimize makespan. Applied Mathematics and Computation. 2006; 183: 1008-1017.

Tasgetiren MF, Liang Y-C, Sevkli M, Gencyilmaz G. A particle swarm optimization algorithm for makespan and total flowtime minimization in the permutation flowshop sequencing problem. European Journal of Operational Research. 2007; 177: 1930-1947.

Jarboui B, Ibrahim S, Siarry P, Rebai A. A combinatorial Particle Swarm Optimisation for solving permutation flowshop problems. Computers & Industrial Engineering. 2007; doi: 10.1016/j.cie. 2007.09.006.

Dorigo, M. and Stützle, T. (2002). The ant colony optimization metaheuristics: algorithms, applications and advances. In Handbooks of metaheuristics (Ed.: Glover, F. and Kochenberger, G). Int. Series in Operations Research & Management Science, Kluver, Dordrech, 57: 252-285.

Dorigo, M. and Blum, C. (2005). Ant colony optimization theory: A survey. Theoretical Computer Science, 344: 243-278.

Dorigo, M., Maniezzo, V. and Colorni, A. (1991). Positive feedback as a search strategy. Tech Report 91-016. Dipartimento di Elettronica, Politecnico di Milano, Italy.

Dorigo, M., Maniezzo, V. and Colorni, A. (1996). Ant system: optimization by a colony of cooperating agents. IEEE Trans. Systems, Man, Cybernet.-Part B, 26: 29-41.

Dorigo, M. (1992). Optimization, learning and natural algorithms (in Italian). PhD Thesis, Dipartimento di Elettronica, Politecnico di Milano, Italy.

Sutton, R.S. and Barto, A.G. (1998). Reinforcement Learning: An Introduction. MIT Press, Cambridge.

Kennedy, J. and Eberhart, R.C. (2001). Swarm Intelligence. Morgan Kaufmann Publishers.

Bullnheimer, B., Hartl, R.F. and Strauss, C. (1999). An improved ant system algorithm for the vehicle routing problem. Annals of Operations Research, 89: 319-328.

Reinmann, M., Doerner, K. and Hartl, R.F. (2004). D-ants: savings based ants divide and conquer the vehicle routing problems. Computers & Operations Research, 31(4): 563-591.

den Besten, M., Stützle, T. and Dorigo, M. (2000). Ant colony optimization for the total weighted tardiness problem. Proceeding PPSN VI, Sixth International Conference Parallel Problem Solving from Nature, Lecture Notes in Computer Science, Berlin, Springer, 1917: 611–20.

Gagné, C., Price, W.L. and Gravel, M. (2002). Comparing an ACO algorithm with other heuristics for the single machine scheduling problem with sequence-dependent setup times. Journal of the Operational Research Society, 53: 895–906.

Ying, G.C. and Liao, C.J. (2004). Ant colony system for permutation flow-shop sequencing. Computers & Operations Research, 31: 791–801.

Stützle, T. and Hoos, H.H. (2000). Max-min ant system. Future Generation Computer System, 16: 889–914.

Dorigo, M. and Gambardella, L.M. (1997). Ant colony system: a cooperative learning approach to the traveling salesman problem. IEEE Transactions on Evolutionary Computation, 1: 53–66.

Merkle, D. and Middendorf, M. (2000). An ant algorithm with a new pheromone evaluation rule for total tardiness problems. Proceedings of the EvoWorkshops 2000, Springer Verlag LNCS 1803: 287–296.

Merkle, D. and Middendorf, M. (2003). Ant Colony Optimization with Global Pheromone Evaluation for Scheduling a Single Machine. Applied Intelligence, 18: 105–111.

Kennedy J, Eberhart R. Particle Swarm Optimization. Proceeding of the 1995 IEEE International Conference on Neural Network 1995; 1942-1948.

Abraham A, Guo H, Liu H. Swarm Intelligence: Foundations, Perspectives and Applications. In: Abraham A, Grosan C, Ramos V (Eds), Swarm Intelligence in Data Mining, Studies in Computational Intelligence (series). Springer-Verlag: Berlin; 2006.

Clerc M, Kennedy J. The particle swarm: Explosion, stability, and convergence in a multi-dimensional complex space. IEEE Transactions on Evolutionary Computation 2002; 6; 58-73.

Pang W, Wang KP, Zhou CG, Dong L-J. Fuzzy discrete particle swarm optimization for solving traveling salesman problem. In: Proceedings of the 4th International Conference on Computer and Information Technology. IEEE CS Press; 2004. p. 796 - 800.

Chen A, Yang G, Wu Z. Hybrid discrete particle swarm optimization algorithm for capacitated vehicle routing problem. Journal of Zhejiang Univ. SCIENCE A 2006; 7: 607-614.

Tasgetiren MF, Sevkli M, Liang YC, Gencyilmaz G. Particle swarm optimization algorithm for single machine total weighted tardiness problem. In: Proceedings of the IEEE congress on evolutionary computation, vol.2. Portland; 2004. p. 1412–1419.

Liao C-J, Tseng C-T, Luarn P. A discrete version of particle swarm optimization for flowshop scheduling problems. Computers & Operations Research 2007; 34; 3099-3111.

Lian Z, Gu X, Jiao B. A similar particle swarm optimization algorithm for permutation flowshop scheduling to minimize makespan. Applied Mathematics and Computation 2006a; 175; 773-785.

Lian Z, Gu X, Jiao B. A similar particle swarm optimization algorithm for job-shop scheduling to minimize makespan. Applied Mathematics and Computation 2006b; 183; 1008-1017.

Allahverdi A, Al-Anzi FS. A PSO and a Tabu search heuristics for the assembly scheduling problem of the two-stage distributed database application. Computers & Operations Research 2006; 33; 1056–1080.

Parsopoulos KE, Vrahatis MN. Studying the Performance of Unified Particle Swarm Optimization on the Single Machine Total Weighted Tardiness Problem, Lecture Notes in Artificial Intelligence (LNAI) 2006; 4304; 760-769.

Kennedy J, Eberhart R. A discrete binary version of the particle swarm algorithm. In: Proceedings of the International Conference on Systems, Man, and Cybernetics, vol.5. IEEE Press; 1997. p. 4104–4108.

Bean JC. Genetic algorithm and random keys for sequencing and optimization. ORSA Journal on Computing 1994; 6; 154-160.

Hu X, Eberhart R, Shi Y. Swarm intelligence for permutation optimization: a case study of n-queens problem. In: Proceedings of the 2003 IEEE Conference on Swarm Intelligence Symposium (SIS '03). IEEE Press; 2003. p. 243-246.

Clerc M. Discrete Particle Swarm Optimization. In: Onwubolu GC, Babu BV (Eds), New Optimization Techniques in Engineering. Springer-Verlag: Berlin; 2004; 219-240.

Kirkpatric S, Gelatt Jr. CD, Vecci MP. Optimization by simulated annealing. Science 1983; 220: 671-80.

Hansen P., Mladenovic N. Variable neighborhood search: Methods and recent applications. In Proceedings of MIC'99, pages 275–280, 1999.

Taillard E., Few guidelines for analyzing methods. in Tutorial, 6th Metaheuristics Int. Conf., 2005.

Pinedo M. Scheduling: Theory, Algorithms, and Systems. Prentice Hall: Englewood Cliffs, NJ; 1995.

Taillard E. Benchmarks for basic scheduling problems. European Journal of Operational Research. 1993; 64: 278-285.

2

Multi-objective Simulated Annealing for a Maintenance Workforce Scheduling Problem: A case Study

Nima Safaei, Dragan Banjevic and Andrew K.S. Jardine
C-MORE Lab, Department of Mechanical and Industrial Engineering, University of Toronto Canada

1. Introduction

A multi-objective simulated annealing (MOSA) algorithm is described in this chapter to solve a real maintenance workforce scheduling problem (MWSP) aimed at simultaneously minimizing the workforce cost and maximizing the equipment availability. Heavy industry maintenance facilities at aircraft service centres, railroad yards and steel companies must contend with scheduling Preventive Maintenance (PM) tasks to ensure critical equipment remains available (Quan et al., 2007). PM tasks are labour intensive and the workforce that performs those tasks are often highly-paid and highly skilled with different proficiencies, which means the PM tasks scheduling should minimize the workforce costs. Therein lies a dilemma: a small labour force would help control costs, but a small labour force cannot perform many PM tasks per hour—and equipment that is not available does not generate revenue. A long completion time is not cost effective but neither is having too many workforce costs. A proper balance would minimize labour costs while simultaneously finishing all PM tasks in a timely manner. In other words, a trade-off must be made between the workforce costs and a timely completion of all PM tasks. Hence, in most real PM tasks scheduling problems, we encounter the multi-objective optimization.
There are very few previous papers focusing on the maintenance workforce scheduling problem. Higgins (1998) formulated the railway track maintenance crew problem as a mathematical program, and then used tabu search algorithms to solve the problem. Ahire et al., (2000) examined the utility of the evolution strategies to solve a MWSP with the aim of minimizing Makespan considering multiple-skills labour and workforce availability constraints. Yanga et al., (2003) formulated an airline maintenance manpower planning problem under a one week planning cycle considering various flexible strategies such as short-term or temporary contracts, trainee, part-time and subcontracted workers. They considered workforces with different types of skills that are grouped into a number of so-called "squads" with different numbers of members (or size). The objective was to minimize the total required manpower while satisfying the demand for every time slot. Quan et al., (2007) used the evolutionary algorithms to solve a multi-objective PM task scheduling problem with the aim of simultaneously minimizing workforce costs and Makespan. Workforce costs consist of the hiring cost of workers required to complete all PM tasks on time as well as the idle time cost. Makespan refers to the total amount of time it takes to

complete all PM tasks. Notice that these two objectives are conflicting because minimizing the workforce increases the Makespan. They assumed that workers have two different skills, i.e., mechanic and electric and each worker can perform only one skill.
The rest of the chapter is organized as follows. Section 2 presents the problem description. In Section 3, the preliminary definition and concepts of the multi-objective optimization as well as MOSA's literature are presented. The MOSA to solve the considered problem is developed in Section 4. Experimental results are presented and discussed in Section 5. Finally, Section 6 mentions the conclusion and some future work.

2. Problem description

The considered problem is related to a steel company which has recently moved to a plant wide scheduling approach, through a central department, called Central Services (CS), to respond to the maintenance requirements of manufacturing areas or Business Units (BUs). The aim of this department is to minimize the workforce costs as well as avoid long-term disruptions and shutdowns of the critical equipments within BUs. Each BU schedules their work requests and then submits them to CS which attempts to schedule the workforce on those work requests to meet the needs across the plant. Work requests represent PM tasks to return the associated equipment to the as-good-as-new condition (throughout this paper, we use the phrase 'work request' or briefly 'work' and PM task interchangeably). Given the number and variety of the work requests, and the number of workers and the variety of their skills, the CS department has found it very difficult to optimally schedule works in a reasonable time.
The CS department satisfies labour requirements through internal and external resources, as regular time, overtime, and contract. The internal resource consists of a number of specialized groups with certain proficiency/skill for PM tasks, called field groups (FGs) such as mechanical, electrical, pipefitting and lubrication proficiencies. FGs are mobile groups, variable in size (number of members), which are responsible for PM/repair tasks at BUs. The external workforce is provided by contractors. Obviously, CS prefers to use the internal workforce in regular time and overtime (including weekends) and to use the contractors when they encounter the workforce shortage. CS manages the FGs to meet the demand of BUs, and supplements them with external forces. The PM schedule for each BU may be different for different periods depending upon the variety and failure nature of the existing assets and equipments. Thus, CS always encounters a new set of work requests in each period that must be scheduled, however, the required information of the work requests is known for CS in advance. In Figure 1, the relationship between CS, BUs and labour resources are shown schematically.

2.1 Mapping the MWSP as a generalized job shop scheduling problem

The MWSP can be considered as an extended job shop scheduling problem in which each FG represents a machine type and each work request represents a job with a number of operations that must be processed on the predetermined machines according to certain precedence relations. The capacity of machines is limited in the given planning horizon. Each job has a known ready/submission time and must be completed before its due date. The conflicting objectives are the workforce cost minimization versus the BU/equipment availability maximization. The workforce cost can be interpreted as machine operating/idle costs and the BU/equipment availability can be interpreted as the flow time of the associated job (see Section 2.2 for more details). A schematic mapping of MWSP into a job shop scheduling problem with 4 FGs and 5 work requests is shown in Figure 2. Symbol "W*i*" represents work *i*. Each work may be done by different FGs according to certain precedence relations.

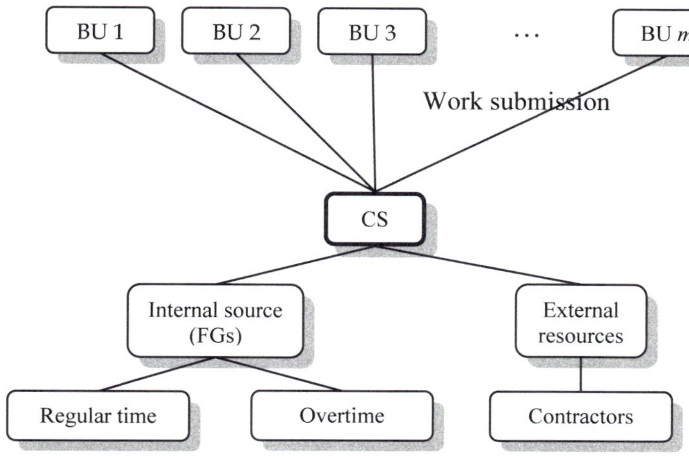

Fig. 1. Maintenance workforce management by Central Service

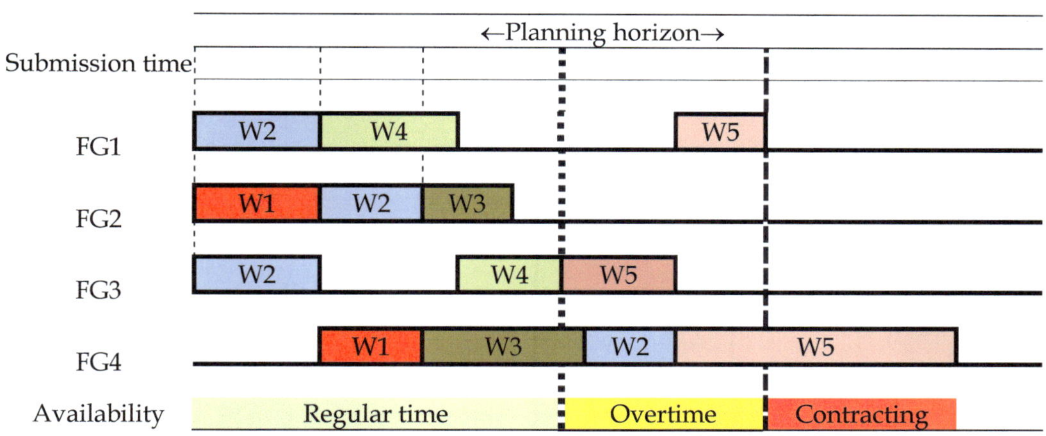

Fig. 2. Typical mapping of MWSP into job shop scheduling problem

A typical example of precedence relations associated with work 2 is shown in Figure 3. As shown in this figure, FGs 1 and 3 can operate simultaneously; however, both FGs are preceding operations for FG 2, and also FG 2 is a preceding operation for FG 4. From mathematical point of view, the precedence relations shown in Figure 3 can be presented as a 0-1 matrix as shown in Figure 4. As Figure 4 indicates, we need overtime for FGs 1, 3 and 4 to complete works 2, 3, and 5. Also, we need the external workforce as subcontracted workers for FG 4 to complete work 5. Moreover, the interference constraint between FGs causes some idle times during the operation time of FGs 1, 3 and 4.

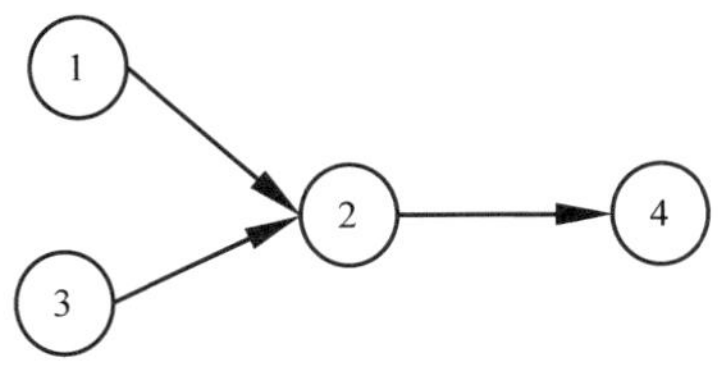

Fig. 3. Precedence relations between FGs for doing work 2

FG	1	2	3	4
1	0	1	0	0
2	0	0	0	1
3	0	1	0	0
4	0	0	0	0

Fig. 4. Matrix form presentation for the precedence relations of Work 2

2.2 Scheduled and unscheduled shutdowns

As pointed out earlier, each work i is submitted to CS at time r_i and must be finished before due date d_i. r_i is typically called submission time or earliest start (ES) time, and d_i is typically called the latest request (LR) or latest finish (LF) date. After submission, the process of the work will start in s_i where $ES \leq s_i$ and completed in c_i, where $c_i \leq LF$. s_i is called the starting time, or "Time in", and c_i is called the completion time, or "Time out" of work i. Thus, the duration or processing time of work i is determined as s_i - c_i (see Figure 5). This duration is also known as scheduled shutdown in which the asset or equipment will not be available in interval $[s_i, c_i]$. However, sometimes an unscheduled shutdown is also considered for the work request which depends on the starting time of the work. Unscheduled shutdown is an approximated time interval that is estimated in terms of the magnitude of s_i. That is, by increasing s_i, the processing time of the work request (or equivalently the unavailability of the asset) will increase progressively because of the nature/mode of the failure. The unscheduled shutdown can be used to determine the importance degree (or weight) of the work request. The local objective of each BU is to minimize the flow time of corresponding work requests, i.e., to minimize $f_i = c_i - LE$. However, solely meeting this objective increases the workforce costs.

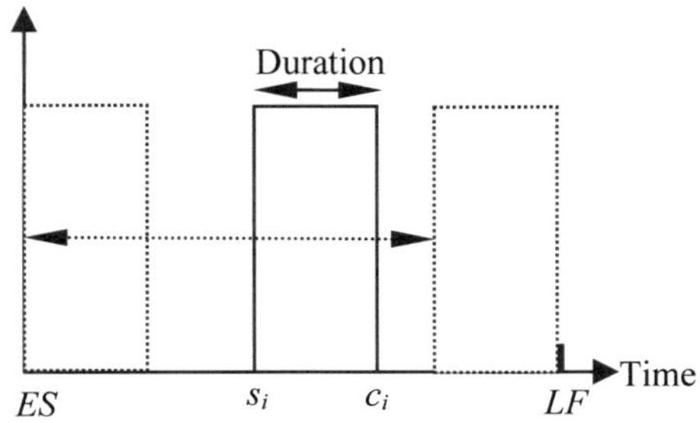

Fig. 5. Scheduled and Unscheduled Shutdowns

According to the above explanation, the MWSP considered in this study deals with two conflicting objectives:

1. Minimization of the total weighted flow time (TWFT) of works (BUs ultimate objective).
2. Minimization of the workforce costs (WfCs) consisting of fixed, overtime and contracting costs (one of the CS objectives)

2.3 Man-hour unit to measure the labour requirements

The processing time of a work request is often a function of the number of assigned workers. That is, by increasing the number of assigned workers, the processing time of the work decreases with a decreasing slope. In such cases, we need a proper unit to measure work done. Man-hour is a common time unit used in industry for measuring work. For example, if the size of a FG is 5 and the number of working hours per day is 8, then 5×8=40 man-hours are available per day for that FG. Thus, if a work request needs 10 man-hours, it can be done by one worker in 10 hours, or 2 workers in 5 hours, etc. Man-hour integrates the time and size of the labour requirements together. A number of studies can be found in which the labour requirements are estimated in terms of man-hour unit. For instance, in (Yanga et al., 2003), the maintenance department estimates that the short-term layover maintenance manpower demand in terms of man-hours, based on the available ground holding time slots, the different aircraft types, and the tasks required.

2.4 Assumptions

The assumptions of the problem can be summarized as follows:

1. The length of the planning horizon is fixed and the work requests submitted in the current planning horizon will be scheduled for succeeding planning horizon.
2. All work requests are submitted to CS during the current planning horizon with a known submission time.
3. The labour requirement and the processing time (duration) of each work request by each FG are known in advance.
4. Each work request has a known due date.
5. Each FG has a certain proficiency which is provided by the internal resources as regular and overtime, or the external resources as contract.
6. The number of members (size) of each FG in regular time, overtime and contacting is known in advance.
7. The labour requirement for work requests is measured in terms of the "man-hour" unit.
8. Workforce availability: The available man-hours for each FG as regular time, overtime and contract are known in advance.
9. Workforce costs consist of fixed cost, overtime cost and contracting cost per man-hour. Obviously, the unit cost of contracting is greater than one of overtime.
10. A fixed cost per man-hour is considered irrespective of the type of the workforce (i.e., internal or external). This cost can be interpreted as to include the transportation, tools, lunch and idle costs.
11. Each FG can operate only one work request at a time.
12. The scheduled shutdown of each work request is represented by its flow time. Flow time is defined as the difference between the completion time (time out) and submission time of the work request.
13. A weight is also associated with each work request which measures the importance degree of the work request. This weight is determined in terms of the unscheduled shutdowns of the work request.

After detailed explanation of the problem, it is worthwhile to briefly highlight how this study differs from previous works:

1. We consider the total weighted flow time instead of Makespan.
2. We consider the precedence relations between FGs to do a given work.

3. We consider workforces with different proficiencies, and overtime and subcontracted workers simultaneously.

2.5 Typical data set

For illustration, a typical data set with 10 work requests and 4 Field groups (mechanical, electrical, pipefitting and lubrication proficiencies) inspired by the real data is presented in this section. Consider a one-week planning horizon with 5 workdays and 2 holidays (weekend). Each workday consists of 8 hours regular time and 4 hours overtime and each holiday includes 4 hours overtime for each internal worker. Moreover, 4 hours in each workday is available for each subcontracted worker as an external labour. Subcontracted workers don't work on weekends. Other information related to work requests and FGs are presented in Tables 1 to 3. The expected duration of each work request by each FG (in terms of man-hour), submission time and unscheduled shutdown (in terms of hours), and also the weight of work requests are shown in Table 1. Table 2 shows the workforce availability in regular time, overtime and contracting. In Table 3, the precedence relations between FGs associated to each work are shown (in all tables FG stands for field group).

Man-hour	W1	W2	W3	W4	W5	W6	W7	W8	W9	W10
FG1	0	0	19	8	6	0	0	0	8	0
FG2	18	13	15	0	11	4	11	13	10	4
FG3	15	2	17	11	18	15	3	0	12	0
FG4	6	5	18	0	0	3	0	12	0	0
Submission time	57.6	43.3	16.21	49.82	4.86	31.49	8.73	39.17	1.94	45.32
Due date	170.86	109.78	214.26	115.12	117.11	102.81	99.94	119.49	112.41	113.51
Shutdown	0.21	0.36	0.12	0.37	0.21	0.34	0.26	0.3	0.22	0.35
Weight	0.58	0.98	0.33	1	0.58	0.92	0.72	0.81	0.59	0.96

Table 1. Work request Information

	Size			Cost per hour per man ($)			Availability per day per man (hours)		
	Regular time	Overtime	Contracting	Fixed Cost	Overtime	Contracting	Regular time	Overtime	Contracting
FG1	9	8	3	2	22	29	8	4	4
FG2	9	5	3	4	24	27	8	4	4
FG3	10	7	3	4	20	28	8	4	4
FG4	8	6	2	4	24	28	8	4	4

Table 2. Field group Information

FG	W1				W2				W3				W4				W5			
	1	2	3	4	1	2	3	4	1	2	3	4	1	2	3	4	1	2	3	4
1	0	0	0	0	0	0	0	0	0	0	1	0	0	0	0	0	0	1	1	0
2	0	0	0	0	0	0	0	1	0	0	1	0	0	0	0	0	0	0	0	0
3	0	1	0	0	0	0	0	0	0	0	0	1	1	0	0	0	0	0	0	0
4	0	0	1	0	0	0	1	0	0	0	0	0	0	0	0	0	0	0	0	0

FG	W6				W7				W8				W9				W10			
	1	2	3	4	1	2	3	4	1	2	3	4	1	2	3	4	1	2	3	4
1	0	0	0	0	0	0	0	0	0	0	0	0	0	0	0	0	0	0	0	0
2	0	0	0	1	0	0	0	0	0	0	0	1	0	0	1	0	0	0	0	0
3	0	0	0	1	0	1	0	0	0	0	0	0	1	0	0	0	0	0	0	0
4	0	0	0	0	0	0	0	0	0	0	0	0	0	0	0	0	0	0	0	0

Table 3. Precedence relations

3. Multi-objective simulated annealing

As depicted earlier, MWSP is an extended version of the job shop scheduling problem and obviously it is NP-hard and cannot be solved in a reasonable time using an exact approach for the real-sized problems. This reasoning was a motivation to develop a MOSA approach to solve the MWSP. In this section, the preliminary definitions and concepts of the multi-objective optimization are presented to illustrate the performance of the MOSA. Also, the MOSA's literature is completely reviewed.

3.1 Multi-objective optimization

In multi-objective optimization problems, we attempt to simultaneously optimize a number of conflicting objective functions in which the objectives are non-commensurable and the decision-maker has no clear preference for the objectives relative to each other. Without loss of generality, we will assume that all objectives are of the minimization type. A minimization multi-objective decision problem with K objectives is defined as follows: Given an n-dimensional solution space S of decision variables vectors $X=\{x_1,\ldots,x_n\}$, find a vector X^* that satisfies a given set of criteria depending on K objective functions $Z(X)=\{Z_1(X),\ldots Z_K(X)\}$. We wish to find an "ideal" vector X^* that minimizes all objective functions simultaneously which is usually not possible. The solution space S is generally restricted by a series of constraints, such as $g_j(X^*) = b_j$ for $j= 1,\ldots,m$, and bounds on the decision variables. In many real-life problems, objectives under consideration conflict with each other. Hence, optimizing vector X with respect to a single objective often results in unacceptable results with respect to the other objectives. Therefore, a perfect multi-objective solution that simultaneously optimizes each objective function is almost impossible. A reasonable solution to a multi-objective problem is to investigate a set of solutions, each of which satisfies the objectives at an acceptable level, and without being dominated by any other solution. We summarize the multi-objective optimization area within the following definitions (Zitzler & Thiele., 1998):

- ***Dominant solution***: If all objective functions are used for minimization, a feasible solution X is said to dominate another feasible solution Y ($X \succ Y$), if $Z_i(X) \leq Z_i(Y)$ for $i=1,\ldots,K$ and $Z_i(X) < Z_i(Y)$ for at least one objective function j.
- ***Pareto optimal (Efficient) solution***: A solution is said to be Pareto optimal if it is not dominated by any other solution in the solution space. A Pareto optimal solution cannot be improved with respect to any objective without worsening at least one of other objective.
- ***Pareto optimal set***: The set of all feasible non-dominated solutions in S is referred to as the Pareto optimal set. For many problems, the number of Pareto optimal solutions is enormous (perhaps infinite).
- ***Pareto front***: For a given Pareto optimal set, the corresponding objective function vector values in the objective space are called the Pareto front.

The ultimate goal of a multi-objective optimization algorithm is to identify solutions in the Pareto optimal set.

3.2 Literature on MOSA

Numerous approaches have been developed in the literature with the aim of determining the Pareto optimal set using SA. A comprehensive review of SA based optimization algorithms to tackle multi-objective problems can be found in Suman & Kumar (2006). The first MOSA method has been proposed by Serafini (1992). The algorithm of the method is almost the same as the algorithm of single objective SA. The method uses a modification of the acceptance criteria of solutions in the original algorithm. Various alternative criteria have been investigated in order to increase the probability of accepting non-dominated solutions. A special rule given by the combination of several criteria has been proposed in order to concentrate the search almost exclusively on the non-dominated solutions.

Suppapitnarm & Parks (1999) proposed a multi objective SA method, namely Suppapitnarm-MOSA, in which only one solution is used and the annealing process adjusts each temperature independently according to the performance of the solution in each criterion during the search. The concept of archiving the Pareto optimal solutions with SA has been initially used by Suppapitnarm et al., (2000). In their study, an archive set stores all the non-dominated solutions between each of the multiple objectives. A new acceptance probability formulation based on an annealing schedule with multiple temperatures (one for each objective) has also been used. The acceptance probability of a new solution depends on whether or not it is added to the set of potentially Pareto-optimal solutions. If it is added to this set, it is accepted to be the current solution with probability equal to one. Otherwise, a multi-objective acceptance rule is used.

Ulungo et al., (1999) proposed another MOSA method in which for a multi-objective problem, a move from the present position to a new position can result in three different possibilities:

a) Improving moves with respect to all objectives is always accepted with probability one.
b) Simultaneous improvement and deterioration with respect to different objectives. In this case neither the new move nor the current solution dominate. Therefore, the strategy devised must be sound enough to discriminate between the new and the current solutions.
c) Deterioration with respect to all objectives is accepted with a given probability.

Their method uses a strategy called the *criterion scalarizing strategy* since probability to accept the new solution must take into account the distance between the old and the new move. This strategy maps the multi-dimensional criteria space into a one-dimensional space. Thus, this strategy works with a predefined diversified weight vector. This set of weights is uniformly generated. Two scalarizing functions have also been used: the weighted sum of objectives and the Chebyshev norm (Teghem et al., 2000).

Czyzak, & Jaszkiewicz (2000) proposed a MOSA approach by combining SA with a genetic algorithm (GA). This method uses the concept of neighborhood, acceptance of new solutions with some probability and annealing schedule from SA and the concept of using a sample population of interacting solutions from GA. Their method uses scalarizing functions based on probabilities for accepting new solutions. In each iteration of the procedure, a set of solutions called generating samples controls the objective weights used in the acceptance probability. This assures that the generating solutions cover the whole set of efficient solutions. One can increase or decrease the probability of improving values of a particular objective by controlling the weights. The higher the weight associated with a given objective, the lower the probability of accepting moves that decrease the value of this objective and the greater the probability of improving the value of this objective.

Suman (2002) proposed a MOSA approach to tackle the constraint violations. The proposed MOSA attempts to handle constraints within its main algorithm by using a weight vector in the acceptance criterion by directing the move towards the feasible solutions. It does not use any extra techniques such as the penalty function approach to handle constraints. It has been shown that the substantial reduction in computational time can be achieved without worsening the quality of solution with this method. The weight vector depends on the number of constraints violated by the given solution and the objective function. Suman (2005) proposed a MOSA approach using Pareto-domination-based acceptance criterion. He uses an idea that a strategy of Pareto-domination based fitness can easily be adapted to simulate annealing in the acceptance criterion. Here, fitness of a solution is defined as one plus the number of dominating solutions in Pareto-optimal set (containing both feasible as well as infeasible solutions). The larger the value of fitness, the worse the solution. Initially, the fitness difference between the current and the generated solution is small and the temperature is high so any move is accepted. This gives us a way to explore the full solution space. As the number of iterations increases, temperature decreases and fitness difference between the current and generated solutions may increase. Both make the acceptance move more selective and it results in a well-diversified solution in true Pareto-optimal solutions.

Most of the proposed MOSA approaches, except Suppapitnarm-MOSA, use a kind of scalarizing function for combining the objectives into a weighted summation term as fitness/energy function to evaluate the solutions. However, it is unclear how to choose the weights in advance. Indeed, one of the principal advantages of multi-objective optimization is that the relative importance of the objectives can be decided with the Pareto front on hand. To overcome this disadvantage, Smit et al., (2004) proposed a dominance based energy function. According to this function, the energy value of solution x is equal to the cardinality of set $F_x \subset F$ where F is the best Pareto front obtained so far (archive of the estimated Pareto front) and subset F_x contains all solutions belong to F that dominate x. This function ensures that the new solutions that move the estimated front towards the true (ultimate) Pareto front are always accepted. As the authors claim, a benefit of this energy function is that it encourages exploration of sparsely populated regions of the front.

However, the performance of this function highly depends on the cardinality of set F. That is, when F is small the resolution in the energies can be very coarse, leading to a low resolution in acceptance probabilities. To overcome this disadvantage, they artificially increased the size of F using three methods: conditional removal of dominated points, linear interpolation and attainment surface sampling.

4. MOSA to solve MWSP

The consideration of precedence relations in addition to interference relations causes the size of the feasible space to decrease; however, it doesn't mean the Pareto optimal set will be achieved simply. Contrariwise, the ultimate Pareto optimal set will be difficult to access, especially when the size of the problem increases. In this case, the population-based algorithms such as Genetic Algorithms lead to infeasible solutions most of the time. This reasoning became a motivation to select a single solution-based meta-heuristics such as SA to solve the considered problem.

In our opinion, the method proposed by Suppapitnarm et al., (2000) is one of the best in the context of the MOSA. In this method, we don't need to determine a weight for each objective function while all objectives affect the acceptance probability of the non-improver solutions. Moreover, a new solution is accepted if it can be added to the best Pareto archive set obtained so far. This strategy guarantees the continuous improvement of the current Pareto front toward the ultimate one. Thus, we use Suppapitnarm-MOSA to solve the MWSP. The specialization of the Suppapitnarm-MOSA to solve the MWSP is presented in the following subsections, using the nomenclature presented in the Appendix.

4.1 Initial Temperature

According to the fundamental concepts of SA, non-improver solutions are accepted in the primary iterations with high probability. Thus, we set the initial temperature (for each objective) in such a way that the non-improver solutions are accepted with a probability of about 95 percent in the primary iterations. The related pseudo code is shown in Figure 9 (Safaei et al., 2008). Parameter Q represents the number of samples.

Sub Initial_Temperature( )
 For k=1 to K
  For q=1 to Q
   Do
    Generate two solutions X_1 and X_2 at random
    LOOP UNTIL $(Z(X_1) \neq Z(X_2))$
    Set $T_q^0 = \dfrac{|Z_k(X_1) - Z_k(X_2)|}{-\ln(0.95)}$
   Next q
  Set $T_0^k = (1/Q)\sum_{q=1}^{Q} T_q^0$
 Next k
 End Sub

Fig. 9. Pseudo code of the initial temperature generation subroutine

4.2. Solution representation

The main objective of the MWSP in this study is to determine the sequence of work requests (works, for short) that must be done by each FG in such a way that some objectives are optimized. Thus, the solution representation must determine the sequence of operating works for each FG. To this propose, we consider a matrix consisting of K rows (number of FGs) and M columns (number of works) to represent the solution to the MWSP. The solution representation is shown in Figure 10 for typical solution $X=[x_{i[j]}]_{K\times M}$ where $x_{i[j]}=w$ means that work w must be scheduled on j^{th} position (i.e., $[j]$) in the sequence of works associated with FG i. It should be noted that some of the entries in the solution representation are inherently zero/null because all works need not be done by all FGs. For more clarity, an example solution related to the data set presented in section 2.5 is shown in Figure 11.

	W[1]	W[2]	...	W[j]	...	W[M]
FG1	$x_{1[1]}$	$x_{1[2]}$		$x_{1[j]}$		$x_{1[M]}$
FG2	$x_{2[1]}$	$x_{2[2]}$		$x_{2[j]}$		$x_{2[M]}$
⋮						
FGi	$x_{i[1]}$	$x_{i[2]}$		$x_{i[j]}$		$x_{i[M]}$
⋮						
FGK	$x_{K[1]}$	$x_{K[2]}$		$x_{K[j]}$		$x_{K[M]}$

Fig. 10. Solution Representation

	W1	W2	W3	W4	W5	W6	W7	W8	W9	W10
FG1	4	5	3	9	-	-	-	-	-	-
FG2	5	8	2	10	6	7	3	9	1	-
FG3	4	5	7	3	6	2	9	1	-	-
FG4	3	8	1	6	2	-	-	-	-	-

Fig 11. An example solution for data set presented in section 2.5

4.3 Initial solution generation

In general, for better exploration of the feasible space, the initial solution is generated at random. However, as discussed in Section 2, MWSP is actually a generalized job shop scheduling problem with precedence constraints in addition to interference constraints inherently embedded in the scheduling problems. Thus, the generating of a random solution which simultaneously satisfies both precedence and interference constraints is one of the most important portions of this research that makes it different from workforce scheduling problems described in the literature. In this case, the applied approach for generating the initial solution must maintain the CPU time on an acceptable level and use advantages of the random generation.

To overcome this drawback, we introduce a recursive-sequential approach in which at each iteration i, the sequence of works corresponding to FGi is randomly generated considering the history of assignments in previous FGs 1,..., i-1 as well as the precedence relations. The recursive procedure verifies the feasibility of the current assignment. This procedure uses the information given in the matrix $S=[s_{il}]_{K\times K}$ where $S=R\oplus R^2\oplus\ldots\oplus R^{K-1}$, in which $s_{il}\in\{0,1\}$, $R=[r_{il}]_{K\times K}$; $r_{il}\in\{0,1\}$ is the precedence relation matrix for a given work (see Figure 3) and $\oplus$ represents the Boolean summation operator (Seyed-Hosseini et al., 2006). Matrix S

consists of all direct and indirect precedence relations between FGs to do a given work. In other words, s_{il} =1 means FG*i* is prior to FG*l* directly ($i \rightarrow l$) or indirectly ($i \rightarrow \ldots \rightarrow l$). This recursive procedure prevents the creation of the infinite loop during the sequential assignment process. An infinite loop is a sequence of the precedence and interference relations that loops endlessly. A typical example of the infinite loop is shown in Figure 12. In this figure, both works A and B must be done by both FGs *i* and *l*. However, FG*l* is directly prior to FG*i*, i.e., $l \rightarrow i$, for work A and contrariwise FG*i* is indirectly prior to FG*l* for work B, i.e., $i \rightarrow k \rightarrow l$, where $i<l<k$. Assume that the sequence of works for FG*i* is already created according to the sequential phase of the approach. Moreover, the sequence of works for FG*l* is being preceded and for FG*k* has not created yet. Currently, work A is randomly selected and would be scheduled immediately after work C on FG*l*. We want to check the feasibility of this assignment. The completion time of work A on FG*l* is obtained as $ct_{lA} = pt_{lA} + ct_{lC}$. Without loss of generality, we define the term $a \subset b$ that means for obtaining parameter *a*, parameter *b* must already be determined. Thus, we have $ct_{lA} \subset ct_{lC}$. Using the backward recursive algorithm, the following infinite loop is obtained: $ct_{lC} \subset ct_{lB} \subset ct_{iB} \subset ct_{iA} \subset ct_{lA} \subset ct_{lC}$. Thus, the assignment presented in Figure 11 is infeasible. Consequently, the proposed approach doesn't allow that work A is scheduled after work B on FG*l* and so it must be scheduled before work B.

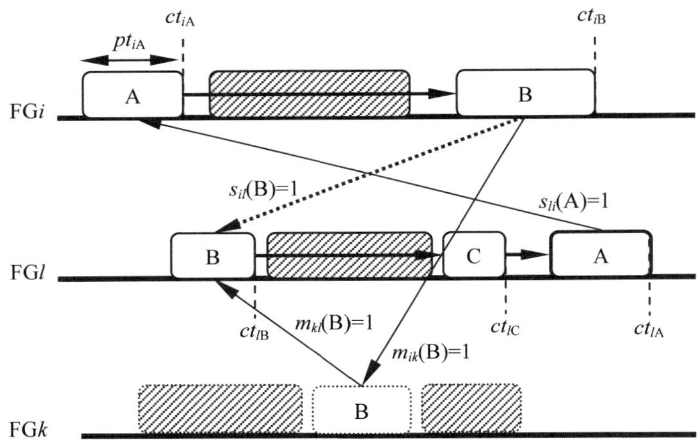

Fig 12. Typical infinite loop

As an example, according to the precedence relations given in Table 3, for work 3, we have ($1 \rightarrow 3$) and for work 4, we have ($3 \rightarrow 1$). Assume that works 3 and 4 are swapped together on FG 3 in the solution presented in Figure 11. Thus, we encounter an infinite loop as: $ct_{34} \subset ct_{37} \subset ct_{35} \subset ct_{33} \subset ct_{13} \subset ct_{15} \subset ct_{14} \subset ct_{34}$. Thus, work 4 cannot be scheduled anywhere after work 3 on FG 3, if the sequence of works for FG 1 has already been fixed.

4.4 Neighbourhood solution generation

The swapping adjacent pair method is used to generate the neighbourhood solutions. At first, two adjacent works on a FG are randomly selected and then are swapped together. The feasibility of this change is checked by the recursive procedure explained in the previous section.

A stochastic sampling scheme of size 1000 within the objective function space is used to verify the efficiency of the applied strategy. The scatter diagram corresponding to this sampling is shown in Figure 13. Point A represents the initial solution and other points are generated by the swapping adjacent pair method. Point B is associated with the best obtained solution. As it can be seen in this figure, this method can correctly navigate the solution space. Our reason for it is that the generated solutions have an improvement trend in terms of the objective function values as the best obtained solution (Point B) improves each objective function by about 50% compared with the initial solution (Point A). It should be noted that this sampling is completely random, without using an improvement criterion. In other words, the results indicate that the probability of the improver movements is significantly greater than non-improver ones and hence the strategy used is a proper one to explore the solution space.

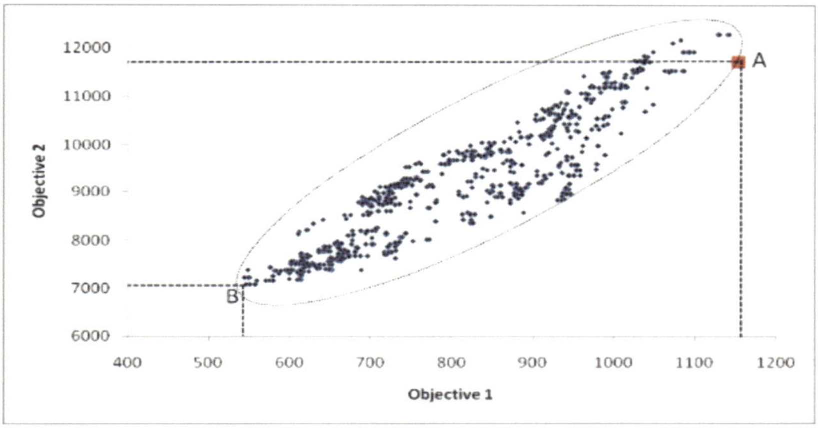

Fig 13. Scatter diagram related to the stochastic sampling of the neighbourhood solution generation method

4.5. Cooling schedule

The classical cooling schedule of SA is used for each temperature (one for each objective) as $T_t^k = \alpha T_{t-1}^k$ where α is the cooling rate or decrement factor and k=1,2.

4.6 Fitness function

As mentioned in Section 3, the MWSP involves two conflicting objectives: minimizing the TWFT versus minimizing the WfC. Even though, the generated solutions satisfy the precedence and interference constraints, there are still two restrictions which must be considered by the generated solutions. These two restrictions are the due date of the works and the workforce resource limitations in regular time, overtime and contracting. To this end, we consider two penalty functions, one for each objective. The first penalty function (PF_1) that is added to the first objective as Z_1=TWFT+λPF_1 penalizes the solutions violating the due date of some works. Parameter λ represents the penalty coefficient which is a large positive number. Likewise, the second penalty function (PF_2) that is added to the second objective as Z_2=WfC+λPF_2 penalizes the solutions violating the workforce limitations. These penalty functions lead the infeasible solutions toward feasible space. The mathematical expressions of the obtained fitness functions are given in Eq. (1) and (2):

$$Z_1 = \min \sum_{m=1}^{M} w_m \left(rw_m - r_m \right) + \lambda \sum_{m=1}^{M} \max\left\{ rw_m - d_m, 0 \right\}, \tag{1}$$

$$Z_2 = \min \sum_{k=1}^{K} \Big(c_k rf_k + c'_k \max\left\{ \min\left(rf_k, s_k h_k + s'_k h'_k \right) - s_k h_k, 0 \right\}$$

$$+ c''_k \max\left\{ \min\left(rf_k, s_k h_k + s'_k h' + s''_k h''_k \right) - s_k h_k - s'_k h'_k, 0 \right\} \Big)$$

$$+ \lambda \sum_{k=1}^{K} \max\left\{ rf_k - \left(s_k h_k + s'_k h' + s''_k h'' \right), 0 \right\}, \tag{2}$$

The release time of work m is recursively computed as follows:

$$rw_m = \max_{1 \le k \le K} \left\{ ct_{km} \right\};\ ct_{km} = pt_{km} + \max\left\{ \max_{l;\, p_{mlk}=1} \left\{ ct_{lm} \right\}, ct_{kn}, r_m \right\},\ m = 1, 2, \ldots, M, \tag{3}$$

where n represents the work that must be scheduled immediately before work m for FG k. Initial values are $ct_{k1} = pt_{k1}$ for each k.

4.7 Acceptance strategy

Similar to the SMOSA, an archive set stores all the non-dominated/Pareto solutions between each of the multiple objectives. The acceptance probability of a new solution depends on whether or not it is added to the set of potentially Pareto-optimal solutions. If it is added to this set, it is accepted to be the current solution with probability equal to one. Otherwise, it is accepted with the following probability.

$$p = \min\left\{ 1, \exp\left(\frac{-\Delta Z_1}{T_1} \right) \times \exp\left(\frac{-\Delta Z_2}{T_2} \right) \right\}. \tag{4}$$

In Eq. (4), $\Delta Z_k = Z_k(Y) - Z_k(X)$ in which X is the current solution and Y is a neighbourhood solution resulting from X using the neighbourhood solution generation method.

4.8 Stoppage criteria

The MOSA algorithm is stopped when one of the following criteria is satisfied:

1. Maximum number of consecutive temperature trails (R).
2. Minimum allowable value of temperatures (final temperature) (T_f).
3. Maximum elapsed time after the last updating of Pareto archive set ($t_{\max}$).

4.9 Lower bounds for objective functions

As mentioned before, a large amount of time is needed to obtain the Pareto optimal set for MWSP. Hence, due to unavailability of Pareto optimal set for comparison and having an idea about the quality of the obtained Pareto solutions, a traditional methodology is to compare the lower bound of the objective functions with the obtained Pareto front. In this study, we use two different methods to obtain the lower bound of TWFT and WfC. The lower bound of the first objective function, $TWFT_{LB}$, is computed assuming the processing of each work by each FG is started immediately after submission or equivalently after completion by the preceding FGs (no-wait strategy). The mathematical expression of $TWFT_{LB}$ is given in Eq. (5):

$$TWFT_{LB} = \sum_{m=1}^{M} w_m \left(rw_m^{LB} - r_m \right),$$

$$rw_m^{LB} = \max_{1 \le k \le K} \left\{ ct_{km}^{LB} \right\};\ ct_{km}^{LB} = pt_{km} + \max \left\{ \max_{l:\, p_{mkl}=1} \left\{ ct_{lm}^{LB} \right\}, r_m \right\}, \tag{5}$$

where ct_{km}^{LB} represents the possible earliest time of completing processing of work m by FGk. The possible earliest time occurs when the processing of work m is started immediately after submission by BU or completion by the preceding FGs. Initial values are $ct_{k1}^{LB} = pt_{k1}$ for each k. The lower bound for the second objective function, WfC_{LB}, is computed according to the FIFO strategy in which the works are scheduled for each FG in increasing order of their arriving times. In this case, FGs are scheduled independently as a single-machine scheduling problem.

Although, the solutions under the obtained lower bounds are not necessarily feasible, the obtained lower bounds can be considered as a criterion to measure the goodness of the obtained Pareto front. In this case, we say the performance of the solution method is acceptable, if under the same conditions, the relative gap (distance) between lower bounds and obtained Pareto front is relatively small or at least does not increase significantly, while the size of the problem increases. It is worth noting that the difference between $TWFT_{LB}$ and its optimal value will increase while the size of the problem increases. It is because the precedence relations cause the waiting time of the in-process works to increase significantly.

5. Computational results

In this section, we verify the performance of the developed MOSA to solve the MWSP using a number of numerical examples. Numerical examples are inspired by the real data and generated randomly in pre-defined intervals. Ten numerical examples with 10, …, 100, works and 4 FGs are generated and solved by the developed MOSA. The details of these examples are not given here. The number of FGs is constant for all problems, as in the real case. MOSA is developed by Visual Basic 2008 on an x64-based multi-processor personal computer with 8 Intel Xeon processors and 2 GB memory. Each numerical example is solved 10 times and the best Pareto solutions obtained are reported and then the corresponding Pareto front is compared with the lower bound of the objectives. The parameter setting of the developed MOSA is shown in Table 4. For tuning the MOSA's parameters, some examples with different sets of parameters were solved. In the end, we found that the following parameter setting was effective to solve the MWSP. As it is evident from Table 4, parameters N and R are considered as linear functions in terms of the problem size.

Parameter	Q	α	N	R	T_f	$t_{\max}$	λ
Value	$M/2$	0.95	$10M$	$10M$	0.01	120 Sec.	10

Table 4. MOSA parameter setting

In the first step, the numerical example presented in Section 2.5 is solved and the best Pareto solutions are reported in Table 5. The average and standard deviation (SD) of *TWFT* and *WfC* values associated with the obtained Pareto solutions are also presented in this table. As it is evident from Table 5, the small values of SD imply that the algorithm converges to a small region of the objective space. That means that the distance between the obtained Pareto solutions is insignificant and the solutions have a relatively identical importance degree from the decision making point of view. The small values of SD can be the necessary condition for efficiency of the proposed method. However, the sufficient condition for efficiency is that the ultimate/optimal Pareto front is also in this small region. This issue will be discussed in below this section. For more clarity, the Pareto front associated with the Pareto set indicated in Table 5 is shown in Figure 14.

Pareto No.	*TWFT*	*WfC*
1	244.17	1531.48
2	259.76	1441.06
3	268.88	1433.06
4	247.18	1491.48
5	251.96	1453.36
6	265.99	1435.16
7	248.95	1469.92
8	254.39	1443.16
Average	255.16	1462.33
S.D	8.94	34.19

Table 5. Best Pareto solutions associated with the data set from Section 2.5

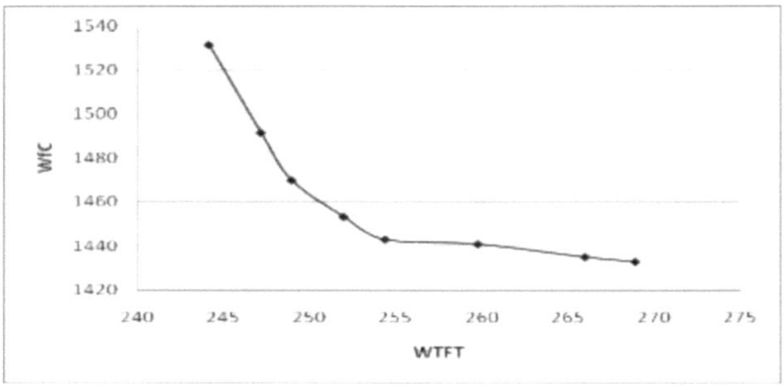

Fig 14. Pareto front associated with the Pareto set indicated in Table 5

Likewise, the information related to the obtained Pareto solutions and Pareto front for the numerical example with 20 works, i.e., 20×4, is provided in Table 6 and Figure 15. The same reasoning applicable to the first test problem is also applicable to the second one.

Pareto No.	*TWFT*	*WfC*
1	147.77	1173.10
2	148.31	1171.42
3	149.30	1171.42
4	149.90	1157.10
5	151.10	1139.42
6	152.63	1129.74
7	155.84	1127.42
8	156.13	1123.58
9	157.86	1121.26
10	158.09	1117.26
11	158.66	1115.34
Average	153.24	1140.64
S.D	4.18	23.16

Table 6. Best Pareto solutions associated to problem 20×4

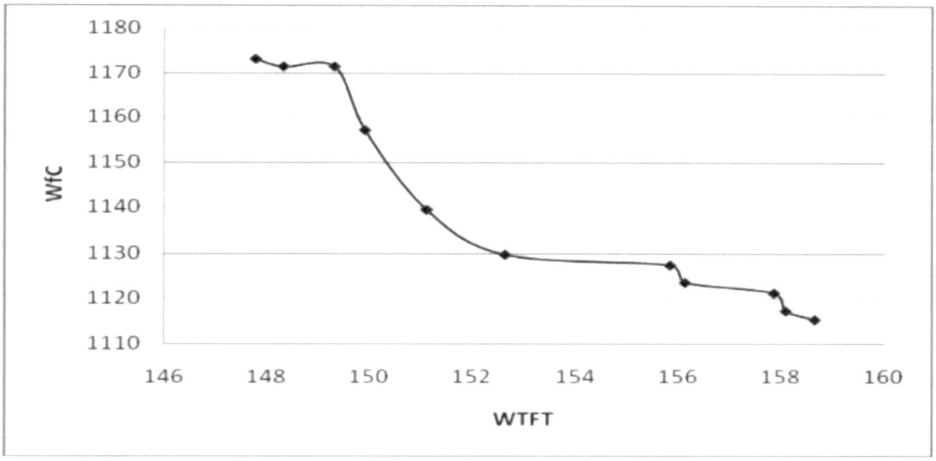

Fig 15. Pareto front associated with the Pareto set indicated in Table 6

The obtained results associated with the different real-sized problems are summarized in Table 7 in terms of the mean of objective values, i.e., $TWFT_M$ and WfC_M, corresponding to Pareto solutions, lower bounds, CPU time, and relative gaps. The relative gap between $TWFT_M$ and $TWFT_{LB}$ is computed as their ratio. The relative gap between WfC_M and WfC_{LB} is computed as the relative difference between WfC_M and WfC_{LB}, that is $[(WfC_M-WfC_{LB})/WfC_{LB}]\times 100$. As shown in Table 7, by increasing the size of the problems, TWFT_Gap doesn't necessarily increase. Moreover, WfC_Gap is significantly small, which means that the obtained WfC_M values are very close to the optimal ones. Thus, according to the discussion presented in Section 4.9 and earlier in this section, we can conclude the developed MOSA is a proper and robust approach to solve the considered MWSP. The trend of the CPU time shown in Figure 16 can be estimated by the formula $CPUtime=51.21M^2-216M+400$, with $R^2= 0.97$, which means the developed MOSA algorithm is of a polynomial order, with a complexity degree $O(M^2)$.

Test Problem		Objective mean		Lower bound		CPU time (Sec.)	Gap	
Size	Planning cycle (week)	$TWFT_M$	WfC_M	$TWFT_{LB}$	WfC_{LB}		$\frac{TWFT_M}{TWFT_{LB}}$	WfC (%)
10×4	1	255.16	1462.33	161.39	1321	34	1.58	10.69
20×4	1	153.24	1140.64	64.56	1080.70	252	2.37	5.54
30×4	1	637.53	1065.14	95.5	1005.84	329	6.67	5.89
40×4	2	173.72	2064.66	66.9	2062.5	528	2.59	0.10
50×4	2	186.97	1699.55	67.48	1680.34	648	2.77	1.14
60×4	2	179.86	1820.8	59.17	1800.88	978	3.03	1.10
70×4	2	572.18	2193.2	92.31	2117.34	1136	6.19	3.58
80×4	2	248.07	2047.41	34.66	1991	1866	7.15	2.83
90×4	2	280.09	2618.21	34.69	2568.7	2416	8.07	1.92
100×4	2	386.45	1614.55	59.89	1539	3612	6.45	4.90

Table 7. Comparison between Pareto fronts and lower bound values

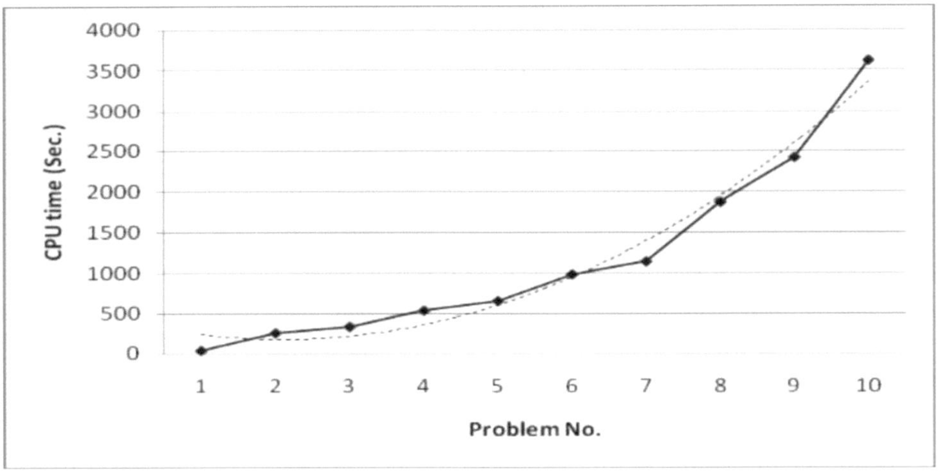

Fig 16. Trend of CPU times according to the information provided in Table 7

6. Conclusion

In this chapter, we proposed a multi-objective simulated annealing (MOSA) algorithm to solve a real maintenance workforce scheduling problem (MWSP) with the aim of simultaneously minimizing the workforce cost and the flow time of the work requests. The latter objective is equivalent to the maximization of the equipment availability because by increasing the flow time of a work request the unscheduled shutdown of the corresponding asset will increase too. Workforces have different proficiencies and are grouped into a number of teams called "Field Groups" (or FG for short). Labour requirements are provided from internal and external resources as regular time, overtime and contract.

We use a MOSA algorithm introduced in the literature namely Suppapitnarm-MOSA to solve the MWSP. In this method, an archive set stores all the non-dominated/Pareto solutions between each of the multiple objectives. The acceptance probability of a new solution depends on whether or not it is added to the set of potentially Pareto optimal set. However, all objectives affect the acceptance probability of a non-improver solution. The developed MOSA uses the swapping adjacent pair strategy to explore the feasible solution.

One of the main differences between the current study and previous ones is that we consider the precedence relations between FGs to do a given work request, in addition to the traditional interference relations between work requests that must be scheduled for a given FG. This extra assumption is a big obstacle to generating the feasible or neighbourhood solutions. Hence, the single solution-based meta-heuristics such as SA or Tabu search seem to be the unique alternatives to solve this problem. This is because population-based operators, such as crossover in Genetic Algorithm, lead to infeasible solutions most of the time.

To overcome this drawback, we introduce a recursive-sequential approach to construct the sequence of works for each FG with the aim of identifying the infinite loops resulting from consecutive interference and precedence relations.

Because the Pareto optimal set cannot be obtained in real-sized problems, a lower bound was developed separately for each objective function and the obtained Pareto front is compared with these lower bounds.

The obtained results show that the developed MOSA is a robust method to solve the MWSP. Our reasoning is that the developed MOSA always converges to a small region of the feasible space, very close to the lower bound of one of the objective functions while the relative difference between the obtained results and the lower bound of another objective function doesn't increase significantly when the size of the problem increases.

7. References

Ahire, S.; Greenwood, G.; Gupta, A. & Terwilliger, M. (2000). Workforce-constrained preventive maintenance scheduling using evolution strategies, *Decision Science Journal*, vol. 31 (4), pp. 833–859.

Czyzak, P. & Jaszkiewicz, A. (1998). Pareto simulated annealing - a metaheuristic technique for multiple-objective combinatorial optimization, *Journal of Multi-Criteria Decision Analysis*, vol. 7, pp. 34-47.

Quan, G.; Greenwood, G.W.; Liu, D. & Hu, S. (2007). Searching for multiobjective preventive maintenance schedules: Combining preferences with evolutionary algorithms, European Journal of Operational Research, vol. 177, pp. 1969–1984.

Safaei, N.; Saidi-Mehrabad, M. & Jabal-Ameli, M.S. (2008). A hybrid simulated annealing for solving an extended model of dynamic cellular manufacturing system, *European Journal of Operational Research*, vol. 185 (2), pp 563-592.

Serafini, P. (1992). Simulated annealing for multiple objective optimization problems, *Proceedings of the Tenth International Conference on Multiple Criteria Decision Making*, pp 87–96, Taiwan, 19–24 July 1, 1992, Taipei.

Seyed-Hosseini, S.M.; Safaei, N. & Asgharpour, M.J. (2006). Reprioritization of failures in a system failure mode and effeCS analysis by decision making trial and evaluation laboratory technique, *Reliability Engineering and System Safety*, Vol. 91(8), pp. 872-881.

Smith, K.I.; Everson, R.M. & Fieldsend, J.E. (2004). Dominance measures for multi-objective simulated annealing, *Congress on Evolutionary Computation (CEC2004)*, vol. 1, pp.23 - 30.

Suman, B. (2002). Multiobjective simulated annealing—a metaheuristic technique for multiobjective optimization of a constrained problem, *Foundations of Comput Decision Science*, vol. 27, pp. 171–191.

Suman, B. (2005). Self-stopping PDMOSA and performance measure in simulated annealing based multiobjective optimization algorithms, *Computs and Chemical Engineering*, vol. 29, pp. 1131–1147.

Suman, B. & Kumar, P. (2006). A survey of simulated annealing as a tool for single and multiobjective optimization, *Journal of the Operational Research Society*, vol. 57, pp, 1143–1160.

Suppapitnarm, A. & Parks, T. (1999). Simulated annealing: an alternative approach to true multiobjective optimization. *Proceeding of Genetic and Evolutionary Computation Conference. Conference Workshop Program*, pp 406–407, Florida, Orlando.

Suppapitnarm, A.; Seffen, K.A.; Parks, G.T. & Clarkson., P.J. (2000). A simulated annealing algorithm for multiobjective optimization, *Engineering Optimization*, vol. 33. pp. 59-85, 2000.

Teghem, J.; Tuyttens, D. & Ulungu, E.L. (2000). An interactive heuristic method for multiobjective combinatorial optimization, *Journal of Comput and Operations Research*, vol. 27, pp. 621–634.

Ulungu, E.L.; Teghaem, l.; Fottemps, Ph. & Tuyttens, D. (1999). MOSA method : a tool for solving multiobjective combinatorial decision problems, *Journal of multi-criteria decision analysis*, vol. 8. pp. 221-236.

Zitzler, E. & Thiele, L. (1998). Multiobjective optimization using evolutionary algorithms: a comperative case study. In: Eiben., AE., Back, T., Schoenauer, M. & Schwefel, H.P. (eds). Parallel Problem Solving from Nature V. Springer, Berlin, Germany, pp 292–301.

Yanga, T-H.; Yanb, S. & Chen H-H. (2003). An airline maintenance manpower planning model with flexible strategies, *Journal of Air Transport Management*, vol. 9, pp. 233–239.

Appendix: Nomenclature

MWSP:

M number of work requests (m=1,2,…,M)

K number of FGs (k = 1,2,…,K)

r_m submission (ready) time of work m

pt_{mk} man-hours required for FGk to process work m. This parameter is interpreted as the duration or processing time of work m by FGk

a_{mk} =1 if work m must be operated by FGk; and =0 otherwise

p_{mkl} =1 if FGl must operate immediately before FGk on work m; and =0 otherwise (precedence relations)

h_k hours available for FGk in regular time during the planning horizon

h'_k hours available for FGk in overtime during the planning horizon

h''_k hours available for FGk in contracting time during the planning horizon

s_k size of FGk in regular time during the planning horizon

s'_k size of FGk in overtime during the planning horizon

s''_k size of FGk as contract during the planning horizon

c_k fixed cost of FGk per hour

c'_k unit cost of FGk per hour in overtime

c''_k unit cost of FGk per hour in contracting time

w_m weight (or importance degree) of work request w. We assume that $w_m = \tau_m / \max_m\{\tau_m\}$, where τ_m represents the unscheduled shutdown of work m

ct_{mk} completion time of work m by FGk

rw_m release time of work m. The difference between rw_m and r_m is interpreted as shutdown of work m

rf_m release time of FGk

MOSA:

α rate of cooling (decrement factor)

T_0^k initial temperature for objective k

T_t^k system temperature in iteration t associated with objective k

T_f final temperature

$Z_k(X)$	value of objective function k (or fitness function) for solution X. Here, k=1,2
N	number of accepted solutions in each temperature (Epoch Length)
R	maximum number of consecutive temperature trails

3

Using Simulated Annealing for Open Shop Scheduling with Sum Criteria

Michael Andresen, Heidemarie Bräsel, Mathias Plauschin and Frank Werner
Otto-von-Guericke-Universität Magdeburg, Fakultät für Mathematik
Germany

1. Introduction

In this chapter, we consider the open shop scheduling problem which can be described as follows. A set of n jobs $J_1, J_2, \ldots, J_n$ has to be processed on a set of m machines $M_1, M_2, \ldots, M_m$. The processing of job J_i on machine M_j is denoted as operation (i, j), and the sequence in which the operations of a job are processed on the machines is arbitrary. Moreover, each machine can process at most one job at a time and each job can be processed on at most one machine at a time.

Such an open shop environment arises in many industrial applications. For example, consider a large aircraft garage with specialized work-centers. An airplane may require repairs on its engine and electrical circuit system. These two tasks may be carried out in any order but it is not possible to do these tasks on the same plane simultaneously. Further applications of open shop scheduling problems in automobile repair, quality control centers, semiconductor manufacturing, teacher-class assignments, examination scheduling, and satellite communications are described by Kubiak et al. (1991), Liu and Bulfin (1987) and Prins (1994).

For each job J_i, $i = 1, 2, \ldots, n$, there may be given a release date $r_i \geq 0$ which is the earliest possible time when the first operation of this job may start, a weight w_i and a due date $d_i \geq 0$ by which the job should be completed. The processing time of operation (i, j) is denoted as t_{ij}. It is assumed that the processing times of all operations are assumed to be given in advance.

Let C_i be the completion time of job J_i, i.e. the time when the last operation of this job is completed. Traditional optimization criteria are basically partitioned into two types: either the minimization of the maximum term $\max_{1 \leq i \leq n} \{f_i(C_i)\}$ or of the sum $\sum_{i=1}^{n} f_i(C_i)$ is considered, where $f_i(C_i)$ denotes the cost arising when job J_i is completed at time C_i. A typical example of an optimization criterion of the first type is the minimization of makespan $C_{max} = \max_{1 \leq i \leq n} \{C_i\}$, while a rather general example of a criterion of the second type is the minimization of total weighted tardiness $\sum_{i=1}^{n} w_i T_i = \sum_{i=1}^{n} w_i \max\{0, C_i - d_i\}$. If release dates of the jobs are given, the latter problem is also denoted as $O|r_i \geq 0|\sum w_i T_i$ which is the most general problem considered in this study.

In the following, we first give a few comments on the open shop problem with minimizing the makespan C_{max} and then a literature review on such problems with sum optimization criteria. Here we discuss only some papers dealing with arbitrary processing times.
Most papers in the literature dealt with the minimization of makespan. In view of the NP-hardness of problem $O \mid \mid C_{max}$, branch and bound as well as heuristic algorithms have been developed for this problem. Among the exact algorithms, we only mention those given by Laborie (2005) and Tamura et al. (2006) which were able to solve open benchmark instances from the recent literature. In Laborie (2005), a complete search for cumulative scheduling based on the detection and resolution of minimal critical sets was performed. The heuristic for selecting such sets relied on an estimation of the related reduction of the search space, where additionally an extension of the search procedure using a selfadapted shaving was proposed. This approach was implemented on the top of classical constraint propagation algorithms. The algorithm was able to solve the remaining 34 open instances out of the 80 instances with up to 10 jobs and 10 machines given by Gueret and Prins (1999). In Tamura et al. (2006), a method to encode constraint satisfaction problems with integer linear constraints into Boolean satisfiability problems was proposed. The effectiveness of this approach was tested on several benchmark instances for the open shop problem. In particular, this algorithm was able to solve all the 192 benchmark instances of three sets from the literature (Brucker et al. (1997), Gueret & Prins (1999), Taillard (1993)).
Among metaheuristic algorithms, we only discuss two papers presenting simulated annealing algorithms. The first algorithm by Liaw (1999) used particular neighborhoods based on up to three pairwise interchanges of two adjacent operations belonging to the same job or being processed on the same machine such that the resulting neighbor satisfies a necessary condition for an improvement of the objective function value. The cooling scheme was of the geometric type and used an initial temperature of 15. The recommended variant had a low temperature reduction scheme (it used a reduction factor of 0.995 for the temperature). The number of iterations with a constant temperature was set to be equal to $30 \cdot n \cdot m$. Taking into account that at least 100 epochs with constant temperatures have been considered per run in Liaw (1999) (usually even substantially more epochs), this means that e.g. for problems with 20 jobs and 20 machines, at least $30 \cdot 20 \cdot 20 \cdot 100 = 1,200,000$ iterations had to be performed. Moreover, since five runs were made for each instance and in one iteration of the algorithm, up to four neighbors were checked (see neighborhood NH_1 in Liaw (1999)) and the best neighbor among them was then taken, much more than 6, 000, 000 feasible solutions had to be evaluated per instance to get the results presented in Liaw (1999). Thus, extremely long runs of simulated annealing were considered in that paper (up to 3.5 hours per single run of an instance with $n = m = 30$). On the other side, the quality of the solutions obtained was comparable to the results obtained by the insertion algorithm combined with beam search given in Bräsel et al. (1993). In particular, comparing the best results of some beam-insert variant from Bräsel et al. (1993) with the best of the five runs of the simulated annealing algorithm from Liaw (1999) on the 30 benchmark instances with $n = m \in \{10, 20, 30\}$ given by Taillard (1993), the results were equal for 18 instances, 8 times the simulated annealing algorithm was better and four times the beam-insert algorithm was better. A particle swarm algorithm combined with simulated annealing has been given by Yang et al. (2006). For the simulated annealing routine, a very small initial temperature of 2 was used. Computational results have been presented for some benchmark instances with up to 20 jobs and machines given by Taillard (1993) (however, the values

stated as best known solutions in Yang et al. (2006) are rather far away from the real best known solutions so that also the results presented in that paper are not competitive). For a discussion of further exact and heuristic algorithms for open shop problems with minimizing the makespan, the reader is referred to Andresen et al. (2008).

There exist only a few papers considering sum criteria. First, we discuss the papers dealing with minimization of mean flow time (or what is the same, total completion time) in an open shop. If preemptions are allowed, the two-machine problem is NP-hard in the ordinary sense (Du & Leung (1990)) while the three-machine preemptive problem is NP-hard in the strong sense (Liu & Bulfin (1985)). For problem $O|pmtn|\sum C_i$, Bräsel & Hennes (2004) derived lower bounds and heuristics which have been tested on problems with up to 50 jobs and 50 machines. For problems with a small number of jobs, the results with the heuristics have been compared to the optimal solutions found by an exact algorithm.

Concerning non-preemptive problems, Achugbue & Chin (1982) proved that problem $O2\|\sum C_i$ is NP-hard in the strong sense. Liaw et al. (2002) considered the problem of minimizing total completion time with a given sequence of jobs on one machine. This problem is NP-hard in the strong sense even in the case of two machines. A lower bound has been derived based on the optimal solution of a relaxed problem in which the operations on every machine may overlap except for the machine with a given sequence of jobs. Although the relaxed problem is NP-hard in the ordinary sense, it can nevertheless be rather quickly solved via a decomposition into subset-sum problems. Moreover, a branch and bound algorithm has been presented and tested on problems with $n = m$. The algorithm was able to solve all problems with 6 jobs in 15 minutes on average and most problems with 7 jobs within a time limit of 50 hours with an average computation time of about 15 hours for the solved problems. A heuristic algorithm has been given which consists of two major components: a one-pass heuristic generating a complete schedule at each iteration, and an adjustment strategy to adjust the parameter used in each iteration. This algorithm has been tested on square problems with up to 30 jobs and 30 machines. For the small problems with at most 7 jobs, the average percentage deviation from the optimal value was about 4 % while for larger problems, the average percentage deviation from the lower bound was about 8 %.

Bräsel et al. (2008) presented a computational study of heuristic constructive algorithms for mean flow time open shop scheduling. They compared matching heuristics, priority dispatching rules as well as insertion and appending algorithms combined with beam search on problems with up to 50 jobs and 50 machines, respectively. From Bräsel et al. (2008), it followed that the choice of an appropriate constructive algorithm strongly depends on the ratio n/m. In particular, it turned out that for problems with $n > m$, the rather fast algorithm beam-append was superior while for problems with $n < m$, the more time-consuming algorithm beam-insert gave the best results. For the square problems with $n = m$, an overlapping has been observed: For small problems, the beam-insert algorithm was slightly superior while for larger problems, variants of the beam-append algorithm were better. However, the algorithms were rather sensitive with respect to parameter settings.

Andresen et al. (2008) presented a simulated annealing and a genetic algorithm for the problem of minimizing mean flow time. They tested their algorithms on problems with up to 50 jobs when performing short runs, where every algorithm may generate 30,000 solutions. It has been found that in contrast to makespan minimization, the hardest problems are those with $n > m$, while for problems with $n < m$, often a lower bound for the

corresponding preemptive open shop problem (Bräsel & Hennes (2008)) was reached. For the hard problems, it was essential to use a good constructive initial solution and to start the simulated annealing algorithm with an extremely small temperature.
Concerning approximation algorithms with a performance guarantee, the currently best result has been given by Queyranne and Sviridenko (2000, 2002). They presented a 5.83-approximation algorithm for the non-preemptive open shop problem of minimizing weighted mean flow time which was based on linear programming relaxations in the operation completion times. This was used to generate precedence constraints. For the preemptive version of this problem, a 3-approximation algorithm has been given.
There exist some papers dealing with open shop problems and other optimization criteria than makespan and mean flow time. Liaw (2004) gave a dynamic programming algorithm for the two-machine preemptive problem of minimizing total weighted completion time. Moreover, a restricted variant was given as a heuristic which was based on pairwise interchanges in the job completion time sequence, i.e. the sequence in which the jobs are ordered according to non-decreasing completion times. Computational experience has shown that the dynamic programming algorithm can handle problems with up to 30 jobs and that the heuristic has an average percentage deviation of less than 0.5 % from the optimal value for these problems.
Liaw (2005) presented a branch and bound algorithm for the preemptive open shop problem to minimize total tardiness. Computational results for the two-machine problem showed that the algorithm can handle problems with up to 30 jobs. A heuristic procedure was also given which determined in the q-th iteration the job to be placed in position q in the sequence of the jobs ordered according to non-decreasing completion times. This was done by means of the repeated solution of linear programs. The solutions obtained by the heuristic algorithm had an average deviation of less than 2 % from the optimal value.
Blazewicz et al. (2004) considered open shop problems with a common due date, where the goal is to minimize total weighted late work, i.e. the weighted portion processed after the common due date. In addition to some complexity results, a polynomial algorithm for the two-machine problem of minimizing total late work and a pseudo-polynomial algorithm for the corresponding weighted case have been given.
In this chapter, we investigate the application of simulated annealing to open shop scheduling problems with different sum criteria. The most general problem considered in this work deals with the minimization of total weighted tardiness subject to given release dates. Preemptions of operations are forbidden. The remainder of the chapter is organized as follows. In Section 2, we introduce the mathematical model used for describing feasible solutions. In Section 3, we discuss the components of the simulated annealing algorithms considered in our study. A detailed comparative study for the different types of problems is presented in Section 4. In particular, we discuss the influence of the initial solution, the parameters of the algorithms and the problem type in terms of n and m, release dates, processing times, weights and due dates of the jobs and compare the results for short and longer runs. Moreover, a comparison with a genetic algorithm is performed to test the influence of the use of a population. Section 5 contains some conclusions and summarizing recommendations.

2. Basic notions

Next, we describe the mathematical model for representing feasible solutions for the open shop problem. In the following, we use the digraph $G(MO, JO)$ with operations as vertices and arcs between two immediately succeeding operations of a job or on a machine. If we place the operations in a rectangular array, where the operations of job J_i are sequenced in row i and the operations on machine M_j in column j and draw an arc between immediately succeeding operations of the same job or on the same machine, we get the graph $G(MO, JO) = G(MO) \cup G(JO)$, where $G(MO)$ contains only horizontal arcs (describing the machine order of the jobs) and $G(JO)$ contains only vertical arcs (describing the job orders on the machines).

Example 1: *Let the machine orders of the jobs be chosen as*

$$J_1 : M_3 \rightarrow M_1; \qquad J_2 : M_1 \rightarrow M_3 \rightarrow M_2; \qquad J_3 : M_2 \rightarrow M_3 \rightarrow M_1$$

and, moreover, let the job orders on the machines be as follows:

$$M_1 : J_2 \rightarrow J_1 \rightarrow J_3; \qquad M_2 : J_3 \rightarrow J_2; \qquad M_3 : J_1 \rightarrow J_3 \rightarrow J_2.$$

Figure 1 shows the graphs G(MO), G(JO) and G(MO, JO) (with the pair ij of job and machine indices of the operations given inside the vertices).

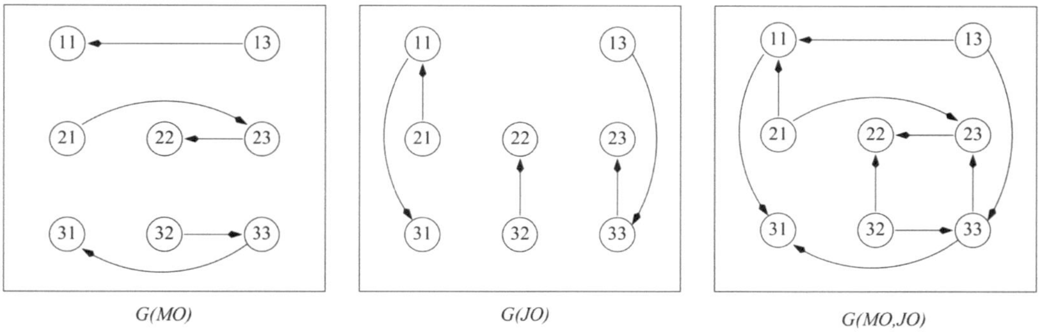

Figure 1. $G(MO)$, $G(JO)$ and $G(MO, JO)$

A combination of machine orders and job orders (MO, JO) is feasible, if $G(MO, JO)$ is acyclic. We call such an acyclic digraph $G(MO, JO)$ a *sequence graph*. Note that all above graphs represent partial orders on the set of operations. Similarly as in (Bräsel (2006), Bräsel et al. (1993), Werner & Winkler (1995)), we describe a sequence graph $G(MO, JO)$ by its *rank matrix* $A = (a_{ij})$, i.e., the entry $a_{ij} = k$ means that a path to operation (i, j) with a maximal number of operations includes k operations. Due to this property, equality $a_{ij} = k$ implies that there is no other operation with rank k in row i and column j, and the so-called *sequence property* is satisfied: 'For each $a_{ij} = k > 1$, the integer $k - 1$ occurs as entry in row i or column j (or both).' Now we assign the processing time t_{ij} as the weight to operation (i, j) in $G(MO, JO)$. The computation of a longest path to the vertex (i, j) with (i, j) included in an acyclic digraph $G(MO, JO)$, i.e. a path for which the sum of the vertex weights is maximal, gives the completion time c_{ij} of operation (i, j) in the semiactive schedule $C = (c_{ij})$. We remind that a schedule is called *semiactive* if no operation can start earlier without changing the underlying sequence graph.

Example 2: *Consider an open shop problem with* $n = 3$ *jobs and* $m = 3$ *machines. Let the release dates of the jobs be given as follows:* $r_1 = 3$, $r_2 = 1$, $r_3 = 6$. *The job weights are* $w_1 = 1, w_2 = 4, w_3 = 2$. *Moreover, the due dates of the jobs are given as follows:* $d_1 = 10$, $d_2 = 13$, $d_3 = 18$. *The matrix T of the processing times of the operations is given as*

$$T = \begin{pmatrix} 4 & \cdot & 5 \\ 2 & 3 & 3 \\ 5 & 1 & 2 \end{pmatrix}$$

(note that job J_1 has to be processed only on machines M_1 and M_3). Assume that the job and machine orders are chosen as in Example 1. The resulting graph G(MO, JO) corresponds to the rank matrix

$$A = \begin{pmatrix} 2 & \cdot & 1 \\ 1 & 4 & 3 \\ 3 & 1 & 2 \end{pmatrix}.$$

For this instance, we obtain the following schedule C from the given matrix of processing times $T = (t_{ij})$ and the rank matrix $A = (a_{ij})$:

$$C = \begin{pmatrix} 12 & \cdot & 8 \\ 3 & 16 & 13 \\ 17 & 7 & 10 \end{pmatrix}.$$

Thus, we obtain the completion times $C_1 = 12, C_2 = 16$ and $C_3 = 17$. For the optimization criterion $F = \Sigma w_i T_i$, we get the objective function value

$$\begin{aligned} F &= w_1 \cdot \max\{0, C_1 - d_1\} + w_2 \cdot \max\{0, C_2 - d_2\} + w_3 \cdot \max\{0, C_3 - d_3\} \\ &= 1 \cdot \max\{0, 12 - 10\} + 4 \cdot \max\{0, 16 - 13\} + 2 \cdot \max\{0, 17 - 18\} \\ &= 1 \cdot 2 + 4 \cdot 3 + 2 \cdot 0 = 14. \end{aligned}$$

It can be noted that the advantage of the use of the rank matrix in contrast to the usual description of a solution by a permutation (i.e. sequence) of the operations is the exclusion of redundancy: different rank matrices describe different solutions while different operation sequences may describe the same solution. For example, both the permutations

$$OP^1 = \Big((1,3),(3,2),(2,1),(1,1),(3,3),(2,3),(3,1),(2,2)\Big)$$

and

$$OP^2 = \Big((2,1),(3,2),(1,3),(3,3),(1,1),(3,1),(2,3),(2,2)\Big)$$

represent the same sequence graph given as *G(MO, JO)* in Fig. 1. Considering e.g. the operations to be processed on machine M_3, we have in both permutations OP^1 and OP^2 the same sequence

$$((1, 3), (3, 3), (2, 3)),$$

i.e. both permutations represent the same chosen job order on $M_3 : J_1 \rightarrow J_3 \rightarrow J_2$. This is also true for the remaining job orders and all machine orders of the jobs. Moreover, there exist at least $3! \cdot 2! \cdot 2! \cdot 1! = 24$ permutations of the operations which represent the same job and machine orders as the rank matrix *A* since there are three operations with rank 1, two operations with rank 2, two operations with rank 3 and one operation with rank 4 in *A*. In general, the problem of counting possible extensions of a partial order (as it is given e.g. by a rank matrix of a sequence graph) is #*P*-complete (see Brightwell & Winkler (1991)).

3. Simulated annealing algorithms

In this chapter, we focus on the application of simulated annealing algorithms for solving open shop problems with different sum criteria. One of the major goals of this study consists in finding similarities and differences in the recommendations for the parameters of the algorithms for the different types of problems.
It is well-known that simulated annealing is an enhanced version of local search. Annealing refers to the process when physical substances are raised to a high energy level and then gradually cooled until some solid state is reached. The goal of this process is to reach the lowest energy state. In this process physical substances usually move from higher energy states to lower ones if the cooling process is sufficiently slow. However, there is some probability at each stage of the cooling process that a transition to a higher energy state will occur, but this probability of moving to a higher energy state decreases in this process.
In terms of our open shop model, a basic simulated annealing algorithm starts with generating an initial solution (rank matrix) A. Then a neighbor (rank matrix) A^* of rank matrix A is generated and the difference $\Delta = F(A^*) - F(A)$ in the objective function values of both schedules is calculated. If $\Delta < 0$, the neighbor A^* is accepted as the new starting solution in the next iteration since it has a better function value. If the objective function value does not decrease (i.e. $\Delta \geq 0$), the generated neighbor may also be accepted with a probability $\exp(-\Delta / T)$, where T is a control parameter called temperature. This temperature is periodically reduced by a cooling scheme every EL iterations, where EL is a preset parameter called the *epoch length*. As a stopping criterion, one may use e.g. a given number of iterations, a time limit or a given number of iterations without an improvement of the best objective function value. In the first two cases, one must adjust the cooling scheme in such a way that the algorithm stops with a sufficiently small temperature. In our tests, we investigate in particular the influence of the chosen neighborhood and the cooling scheme.

3.1 Neighborhoods

First, we briefly discuss the generation of neighbors of a current solution described by the rank matrix A of a sequence graph $G(MO, JO)$. In the case of a job shop problem, often a neighbor is generated by interchanging two adjacent jobs in exactly one machine order (this means that the ranks in the current rank matrix are changed in such a way that in exactly one machine order two adjacent jobs have been interchanged). We denote this neighborhood as machine oriented API neighborhood, abbreviated as API(MO). In an open shop problem we can, due to symmetry, also consider a neighborhood based on adjacent pairwise interchanges in the job order on a machine, abbreviated as API(JO). In our algorithms, we use the union of both neighborhoods, abbreviated as API. This means that, in order to generate a neighbor, the rank matrix is modified such that exactly in one job or machine order, two adjacent operations are interchanged. Thus, in order to generate a neighbor, an operation (i, j) is randomly selected and then it is interchanged with the predecessor or successor operation on machine M_j or of job J_i. One of these (at most) four possibilities is randomly chosen. If the pairwise interchange leads to a feasible schedule, it is accepted as the generated neighbor, otherwise another second operation is chosen to perform an adjacent pairwise interchange in a job or machine order. Note that the adjacent pairwise interchange always leads to a feasible solution if the ranks of the two chosen operations differ only by one. As a consequence, if the first operation has been chosen, one of the at most four possibilities for generating a neighbor in the API neighborhood always leads to a feasible solution which follows from the sequence property stated in Section 2.

Moreover, we consider the neighborhood k-API, in which a neighbor is generated from the current sequence graph $G(MO, JO)$, respectively the corresponding rank matrix A, by generating consecutively up to k neighbors in the API neighborhood (i.e. a path containing up to k arcs in the resulting neighborhood graph is generated). When generating a neighbor, the number $s \in \{1, 2, \ldots, k\}$ of interchanges of two adjacent operations of a job or on a machine is randomly chosen. Note also that the neighborhood used in Liaw (1999) is a subneighborhood of the 3-API neighborhood, where one or up to four neighbors with specific properties have been generated per iteration.

As a generalization of the shift neighborhood for permutation problems we use a neighborhood SHIFT, where exactly one operation is changed in the relative order of operations, namely in such a way that either in the job order on one machine or in the machine order of one job exactly one operation is shifted left or right. In order to generate a neighbor, an operation (i, j) is randomly chosen. Then another operation belonging to the same job or to be processed on the same machine is selected. Consider the first case (the second one is analogue), and let (i, k) be the other chosen operation. If the rank a_{ik} is smaller than a_{ij} , the rank a_{ij} is modified such that operation (i, j) appears immediately before operation (i, k) (it corresponds to a left shift of machine M_j in the machine order of job J_i). If the rank a_{ik} is larger than a_{ij} , the rank a_{ij} is modified such that operation (i, j) appears immediately after operation (i, k) (it corresponds to a right shift of machine M_j in the machine order of job J_i). Notice that usually the ranks of some other operations have to be modified in order to maintain all established precedence relations. If the chosen shift leads to an infeasible solution, this shift is not performed, and two other operations for performing a shift are randomly chosen.

Another neighborhood considered is a restricted SHIFT neighborhood denoted as crit-SHIFT. Here only such neighbors in the SHIFT neighborhood are considered which satisfy a necessary condition for an improvement of the makespan value, namely a critical path (i.e. a longest path among all paths ending in a sink of the corresponding sequence graph) in the starting solution is 'destroyed', and there does not exist a path in the graph describing the generated neighbor which contains the same vertices as this critical path of the current starting solution. This neighborhood is based on the so-called block approach originally introduced for shop scheduling problems with makespan minimization. Clearly, the crit-SHIFT neighborhood is a subneighborhood of the complete SHIFT neighborhood.

In our experiments, we always randomly generate one neighbor in the chosen neighborhood in each iteration. In particular, we do not consider such variants which investigate in one iteration all or several neighbors of the current starting solution in a particular neighborhood and select the best neighbor as the generated one to which the acceptance criterion of simulated annealing is applied.

Example 3: *We illustrate the API, SHIFT and crit-SHIFT neighborhoods discussed above by the following example with* $n = 3$ *and* $m = 4$. *Let the current sequence graph be described by the rank matrix*

$$A = \begin{pmatrix} 2 & 1 & 7 & 3 \\ 3 & 2 & 6 & 1 \\ 4 & 3 & \mathbf{5} & 2 \end{pmatrix}.$$

Assume that operation $(3, 3)$ *with* $a_{33} = 5$ *(given in bold face above) has been chosen randomly for generating a neighbor in the API neighborhood. This operation* $(3, 3)$ *is contained*

a) *in the machine order of job J_3: $M_4 \rightarrow M_2 \rightarrow M_1 \rightarrow M_3$ and*
b) *in the job order on machine M_3: $J_3 \rightarrow J_2 \rightarrow J_1$.*

Using this operation (3, 3), *one can generate two neighbors in the API neighborhood (note that we cannot generate four neighbors since machine* M_3 is *the last one in the machine order of J_3 and J_3 is the first job in the job order on machine M_3). If we interchange the machines M_1 and M_3 in the machine order of job J_3 (see a) above), we get the rank matrix*

$$A^1 = \begin{pmatrix} 2 & 1 & 6 & 3 \\ 3 & 2 & 5 & 1 \\ \mathbf{5} & 3 & \mathbf{4} & 2 \end{pmatrix}$$

as the generated neighbor in the API neighborhood. If we interchange the jobs J_3 and J_2 in the job order on machine M_3 (see b) above), we get the rank matrix

$$A^2 = \begin{pmatrix} 2 & 1 & 6 & 3 \\ 3 & 2 & \mathbf{4} & 1 \\ 4 & 3 & \mathbf{5} & 2 \end{pmatrix}$$

as the generated neighbor.

Next, we consider the generation of a neighbor in the SHIFT neighborhood. Let again (3, 3) be the operation chosen first and assume that operation (3, 2) is selected as the second operation. Operation (3, 2) is performed earlier and belongs to job J_3 too. This means that operation (3, 3) will be shifted left in the machine order of job J_3 so that it is rescheduled directly before operation (3, 2). This gives the rank matrix

$$A^3 = \begin{pmatrix} 2 & 1 & 5 & 3 \\ 3 & 2 & 4 & 1 \\ 5 & \mathbf{4} & \mathbf{3} & 2 \end{pmatrix}$$

of the generated neighbor (notice that the entries of some operations have to be changed in order to maintain all precedence relations). Assume now that operation (1, 3) *is chosen as the second operation. This operation is performed later than* (3, 3) *on the same machine which means that operation* (3, 3) *is shifted right in the job order on machine M_3 so that it is rescheduled directly after operation* (1, 3). *This gives the rank matrix*

$$A^4 = \begin{pmatrix} 2 & 1 & \mathbf{5} & 3 \\ 3 & 2 & 4 & 1 \\ 4 & 3 & \mathbf{6} & 2 \end{pmatrix}$$

of the generated neighbor. So both rank matrices A^3 and A^4 describe feasible neighbors of rank matrix A in the SHIFT neighborhood.

Now assume that the processing times of all operations are equal to one. In this case, the makespan value of rank matrix A is equal to 7, and a critical path contains e.g. the vertices

$$(1,3), (2,3), (3,3), (3,1), (2,1), (2,2), (2,4)$$

(note that the critical path is not uniquely determined for this instance). In this case, both rank matrices A^3 and A^4 are also a neighbor of rank matrix A in the crit-SHIFT neighborhood (because in

both cases operation (3, 3) is shifted to a position 'outside' the chosen critical path). In fact, both neighbors lead indeed to an improvement of the makespan value: $C_{max}(A^3) = 5$ *and* $C_{max}(A^4) = 6$. *Considering e.g. the objective function* $F = \sum C_i$ *and assuming that all release dates are equal to zero, the starting solution described by A has the function value* $F = 7 + 6 + 5 = 18$, *and both generated neighbors lead to an improvement of the objective function value:* $F(A^3) = 5+4+5 = 14$ *and* $F(A^4) = 5 + 4 + 6 = 15$.

3.2 Cooling schemes

Typical cooling schemes used in a simulated annealing algorithm are a geometric, a Lundy-Mees and a linear reduction scheme. The three cooling schemes have been tested for open shop problems with mean flow time minimization in Andresen et al. (2008). It has been found that often the geometric scheme is slightly superior. In most other applications to scheduling problems, a geometric cooling scheme is also preferred. Therefore, in the following we test exclusively geometric schemes.

The geometric cooling scheme reduces the current temperature T^{old} to the new temperature T^{new} in the next epoch according to

$$T^{new} = \alpha \cdot T^{old},$$

where $0 < \alpha < 1$.

In our experiments we fix the initial temperature T^0, the epoch length EL and set the temperature reduction factor α in such a way that the final temperature is close to zero (we always use $T^{end} = 0.01$ as the final temperature) taking into account that in our study, the maximal number of generated solutions is settled in advance and therefore, the maximal number of epochs with a constant temperature is fixed. Based on the experiments in Andresen et al. (2008), we fix the epoch length as $EL = 100$.

In addition to the usual procedure of one cooling cycle, we also consider variants of simulated annealing with several cooling cycles in one run, where the temperature reduction is done faster within one run such that, if the final temperature is reached, the procedure is restarted again with the initial temperature. This requires that the (maximal) number of solutions to be generated in one run is settled in advance. The number CC denotes the number of cooling cycles in one run of the algorithm.

4. Computational results

In this section, we present the computational results with the tested algorithms. First, we describe the generation of the open shop instances in Section 4.1. Then we give some comments on the generation of the initial solution in Section 4.2. In Section 4.3, we describe the design of the comparative study. A detailed comparison of the simulated annealing algorithms is made in Section 4.4. Finally, we compare the fast simulated annealing algorithms with genetic algorithms from Andresen et al. (2008) in Section 4.5.

4.1 Generation of instances

For the comparative study, we consider all pairs (n,m), with $n \in \{10, 15, 20, 30\}$ and $m \in \{10, 15, 20, 30\}$ yielding a total of 16 combinations of m and n. In particular, there are four pairs (n,m) with $n = m$, six pairs with $n > m$ and six pairs with $n < m$.

For each pair (n,m), we generated several problem types differing in the job weights, the processing times, the release dates and the due dates.
For the job weights, we considered the following two variants:
w1: All weights are equal to one: $w_i = 1$ for $i = 1, 2, \ldots, n$.
w2: The weights are uniformly distributed integers from the interval [1, 10].
For the processing times of the operations, we also consider two variants:
t1: The processing times are uniformly distributed integers from the interval [1, 100].
t2: The processing times are uniformly distributed integers from the interval [35, 66].
For the above two cases, we have chosen two uniform distributions having the same expectation value of 50.5, but in the second case the standard deviation is substantially smaller, namely a bit less than one third of the standard deviation in the first case.
For the release dates, we consider two different variants:
r1: All release dates are equal to zero: $r_i = 0$ for $i = 1, 2, \ldots, n$.
r2: The release dates are uniformly distributed integers from the interval $[0, r_{max}]$, where

$$r_{max} = \frac{1}{2n} \cdot \sum_{i=1}^{n} \sum_{j=1}^{m} t_{ij}.$$

In case r2, the value of r_{max} has been settled in such a way that it is equal to the half of the average total processing time of a job.
For the due dates of the jobs, we considered the following three variants:
d1: The due dates of all jobs are equal to zero: $d_i = 0$ for $i = 1, 2, \ldots, n$ (in this case, we have the objective function $\sum w_i C_i$ or its special case $\sum C_i$).
d2: The due dates of the jobs are generated as follows:

$$d_i = r_i + TF \cdot \sum_{j=1}^{m} t_{ij}, \quad i = 1, 2, \ldots, n$$

with the tightness factor $TF = 1.0$ for problems with $n \leq m$ and $TF = 1.25$ for the problems with $n > m$.
d3: The due dates of the jobs are generated as follows:

$$d_i = r_i + TF \cdot \sum_{j=1}^{m} t_{ij}, \quad i = 1, 2, \ldots, n$$

with the tightness factor $TF = 1.1$ for the problems with $n \leq m$ and $TF = 1.5$ for the problems with $n > m$.
While for the second variant d2 due dates are more tight, they are more lose for the third variant d3. We have found that problems with $n \leq m$ and $TF \geq 1.2$ tend to become rather easy in the sense that often the best of the constructive procedures has an objective function value of zero which means that the optimal solution has already been found. On the other hand, larger tightness factors are of interest for the problems with $n > m$. So we decided to use different tightness factors for the problem types with $n \leq m$ and $n > m$ under consideration.
Each problem type is described by a 4-tuple (w,t,r,d), For instance, the 4-tuple (w1,t1,r1,d1) characterizes the open shop problem $O\|\sum C_i$ of minimizing mean flow time when all

release dates are equal to zero and processing times are taken from the interval [1, 100] (this was the only problem type investigated in Andresen et al. (2008)). In our tests, we considered problems of all possible 4-tuples. This gives altogether $2^3 \cdot 3 = 24$ different types of problems. For each of these types and any of the 16 pairs (n,m), we generated 20 instances, giving a total of $24 \cdot 16 \cdot 20 = 7,680$ instances.

4.2 Generation of the initial solution

Often initial solutions for shop scheduling problems are obtained by generating active or nondelay schedules. A schedule is called *active* if no operation can be started earlier without changing the underlying sequence graph and delaying some other operation. A schedule is called *nondelay* if no machine is left idle provided that it is possible to process some job. Obviously, any nondelay schedule is an active schedule, and any active schedule is a semiactive one. Similarly as in Bräsel et al. (2008) for mean flow time minimization, we have found in initial tests that nondelay schedules are superior to active schedules for the problems under consideration. Therefore, we exclusively used the generation of nondelay schedules as fast constructive procedures.

The algorithms for constructing a nondelay schedule repeatedly append operations to a partial schedule. Starting with an empty schedule (which is obviously a nondelay one), operations are appended as follows: we determine the minimal head r of all unscheduled operations. At time r, there exist both a free machine and an available job. To maintain the nondelay property of the schedule, we have to append an operation which can start at time r. Among all operations (i, j) with $r_{ij} = r$, choose one according to some priority dispatching rule.

In our tests, we have used the following priority dispatching rules for generating a nondelay schedule:

- RND (an operation is randomly selected)
- FCFS (first come first served, i.e. the operation that entered the queue first is chosen),
- SPT (shortest processing time),
- WSPT (weighted shortest processing time, i.e. the operation with smallest quotient t_{ij}/w_i is chosen) and
- LPT (longest processing time),
- EDD (earliest due date)

4.3 Design of the comparative study

For each of the instances generated as described in Section 4.1, we first tested the different simulated annealing variants. In particular, we have used the following simulated annealing algorithms, differing in the construction of the initial solution, the stopping criterion, the neighborhood and the cooling scheme.

Initial Solution: We consider one variant with a weak initial solution and one variant with a better initial solution:

I1: The initial solution is determined by the generation of a nondelay schedule according to the rule RND.

I2: The initial solution is determined as the best nondelay schedule obtained by the application of all priority dispatching rules mentioned in Section 4.2.

Stopping criterion: We consider two variants with an a priori fixed number of iterations (i.e. the number of generated solutions) and additionally one variant, where the algorithm stops

if no improvement of the best function value has been obtained for a certain number of iterations. In particular, we use the following stopping criteria:
S1: The algorithm performs 30,000 iterations.
S2: The algorithm performs 200,000 iterations.
S3: The algorithm performs at most 200,000 iteration but stops, if no improvement of the best objective function value has been obtained for 10,000 iterations.
Neighborhoods: The simulated annealing algorithm uses one of the four neighborhoods discussed in Section 3:
N1: The algorithm uses the API neighborhood.
N2: The algorithm uses the 3-API neighborhood.
N3: The algorithm uses the SHIFT neighborhood.
N4: The algorithm uses the crit-SHIFT neighborhood.
Cooling Scheme: The geometric cooling scheme tested in our algorithms is characterized by the initial temperature and the number of cooling cycles. For the initial temperature, we used the following two variants:
IT1: The initial temperature is equal to 2.
IT2: The initial temperature is equal to 15.
For the number of cooling cycles, we considered the following two variants:
CC1: The number of cooling cycles is equal to 1.
CC2: The number of cooling cycles is equal to 5.
In our tests, we considered any possible combination of an initial temperature and the number of cooling cycles, yielding four different cooling schemes.
Since we fixed the epoch length as $EL = 100$, this means that for variant CC1, the number of epochs is equal to 300 for stopping criterion S1. Moreover, since we fixed the final temperature as $T^{end} = 0.01$, the reduction factor α in the geometric scheme is equal to $\alpha = 0.983$ for an initial temperature of 2 corresponding to IT1 and $\alpha = 0.976$ for an initial temperature of 15 corresponding to IT2. For variant CC2, the number of epochs per cooling cycle is equal to 60. As a consequence, in each run the reduction factor α is equal to $\alpha = 0.916$ for an initial temperature of 2 and $\alpha = 0.887$ for an initial temperature of 15.
For the long runs with stopping criterion S2, the number of epochs is 2,000 (for S3, the maximal number of epochs is 2,000). Therefore, for variant CC1, the reduction factor α is equal to $\alpha = 0.998$ for an initial temperature of 2 and $\alpha = 0.997$ for an initial temperature of 15. For variant CC2, the number of epochs per cooling cycle is equal to 400. As a consequence, the reduction factor α is equal to $\alpha = 0.987$ for an initial temperature of 2 and $\alpha = 0.982$ for an initial temperature of 15.
A particular simulated annealing variant is described by a 5-tuple. For instance, algorithm (I2,S2,N3,IT1,CC2) means that the best constructive solution is taken as initial solution, 200,000 iterations are performed, the SHIFT neighborhood is used and the cooling scheme is characterized by an initial temperature of 2 and five cooling cycles. We have run simulated annealing for any possible combination of a stopping criterion, use of a particular initial solution, a neighborhood and a cooling scheme. This yields $3 \cdot 2 \cdot 4 \cdot 4 = 96$ different simulated annealing algorithms.
Concerning computational times we only mention that for the large problems with $n = m = 30$, the average computational time per instance for a variant with stopping criterion S2 is 198.3 s on an AMD Athlon XP 3200+. For smaller problems with $n = 10$ and $m = 20$, this average computational time for a long run per instance is 19.8 s while for the corresponding problems with $n = 20$ and $m = 10$, this average time is 22.2 s. We also note that one computer of this type would require about 4,250 hours to perform all runs done in our study.

4.4 Comparative study of simulated annealing

Before comparing the simulated annealing variants, we give a few comments on the performance of the constructive algorithms. For $n < m$, we have found that the LPT rule is clearly the best algorithm. It is followed by the rules RND, SPT and WSPT which yield solutions of approximately the same quality. In particular, the rather good quality of the RND rule is surprising. This rule is clearly better than the ECT and FCFS rules which are the weakest constructive algorithms for problems with $n < m$. Problems with d3 tend to become easy. In this case, the majority of the dispatching rules yield the best constructive solutions, and many objective function values are equal or very close to zero. For the problems with $n > m$, the LPT rule works bad. The best results have been obtained with the EDD, WSPT and FCFS rules. If $n = 30$ and $m = 10$, the WSPT rule works good for problems with w2. However, for problems with w1, the FCFS rule is clearly the best for problems with d1 and the EDD rule is superior for the problems with d2 and d3. The observed trends are most obvious for a large ratio of n/m (although, if the ratio n/m decreases, the observations are similar but not so strong). For problems with $n = m$, all dispatching rules contribute best values. In general, there is an overlapping of the observations for the problems with $n < m$ and $n > m$. We observed that the EDD rule is good for problems with r1 and d3 while the LPT rule works well for problems with r2.

For evaluating the 96 simulated annealing variants, we use a *performance index* defined as follows. Let F^A be the heuristic function value obtained for a particular instance by algorithm A, F^{CON} be the best function value obtained by some of the constructive procedures mentioned in Section 4.2, and F^{BEST} be the best function value obtained by one or several of the 96 tested simulated annealing variants. In the case of $F^{CON} > 0$, the performance index PI of algorithm A for this particular instance is given by

$$PI = \begin{cases} \frac{F^{CON} - F^A}{F^{CON} - F^{BEST}} \cdot 100 & \text{if } F^{BEST} \leq F^A < F^{CON} \\ 0 & \text{if } F^A \geq F^{CON} \end{cases}$$

If $F^{CON} = 0$, we define the performance indices of all simulated annealing algorithms with the corresponding constructive initial solution to be equal to 100. Moreover, let $PI(k)$ be the percentage of the instances, for which a particular algorithm has obtained a performance index of at least k. That is, $PI(95) = 80$ means that the algorithm under consideration has obtained a performance index greater than or equal to 95 for 80 % of the instances. In the following evaluations, we consider the performance indices $PI(95)$ (which stands for an excellent performance) and $PI(75)$ (which stands for a good performance of the particular algorithm).

First, we give some general observations from our study. Then we discuss separately the results for the problems with $n < m$, $n = m$ and $n > m$ in more detail.

General Observations:

As a general observation we have found that the ratio of n and m influences the hardness of the problems. Among the problem data, the range of the processing times and the job weights have in particular an influence on the selection of an appropriate algorithm or the quality of the results, while release dates and due dates have only minor influence. Therefore, the recommendations in the following sections do not strongly depend on different due dates and release dates. Hence, at most four algorithms (for any combination of weights and processing times) are suggested for every stopping criterion S1, S2 and S3, respectively. On the other side, the range of due dates influences the range of the objective function values and their possible percentage improvements.

The use of the best constructive algorithm leads to better results with the simulated annealing algorithms than the use of only a randomly generated initial solution. The choice of an appropriate neighborhood turns out to be substantial for the quality of the results. An appropriate initial temperature is at least for certain problem types important. In particular, some problems with unit weights require a low initial temperature when using short runs while for most problems with w2, the results with the different initial temperatures do not differ very much. From an overall point of view, the number of cooling cycles per run has only a small influence on the quality of the results. In general, algorithms with variant CC2 turn out to be a bit superior to those with CC1.

If one looks for an overall variant that performs well, we can recommend the algorithms with a good initial solution, the use of the SHIFT neighborhood and a cooling scheme with a low initial temperature and one or five cooling cycles.

Problems with n < m:

In Table 1, we summarize some results for the problems with $n < m$. The rows refer to the 24 different problem types described by a 4-tuple (w,t,r,d). In column 2, we present the average objective function value F^{CON} (rounded to integers) of the best constructive algorithm taken over all instances of the six pairs (n,m) with $n < m$. In column 3, the average percentage improvement PERC of the best function value obtained by the 96 simulated annealing variants over the function value of the initial solution is given. In the remaining columns, we present first the average performance index (columns AVG) of the corresponding algorithm and then the values $PI(95)$ and $PI(75)$ (columns 95/75) for the recommended variants with stopping criterion S1 (Alg 1), criterion S2 (Alg 2) and criterion S3 (Alg 3), respectively. In particular, based on the experiments and the discussion below, we have chosen the following algorithms:

Alg 1: algorithm (I2,**S1**,N3,IT1,CC2) for problems with t1; algorithm (I2,**S1**,N1,IT2,CC2) for problems with t2;

Alg 2: algorithm (I2,**S2**,N3,IT1,CC1) for problems with w1; algorithm (I2,**S2**,N3,IT2,CC2) for problems with w2;

Alg 3: algorithm (I2,**S3**,N3,IT1,CC2) for problems with t1; algorithm (I2,**S3**,N1,IT1,CC1) for problems with w1 and t2; algorithm (I2,**S3**,N1,IT2,CC2) for problems with w2 and t2.

From Table 1 we see that there is a large range of percentage improvements over the constructive algorithm for the particular types of problems. For problems with d1 (i.e. minimization of mean flow time or its weighted version), the average percentage improvements are very small (always less than 1 %). This corresponds to the observation for problem type (w1,t1,r1,d1) in Andresen et al. (2008), where it has been found that the solutions obtained by constructive algorithms are already almost optimal and often even a lower bound for the corresponding preemptive problem has been reached. On the other hand, problems with d3 tend to be easy in the sense that the initial solution has already a function value close to zero. Note that for these problems, the performance indices of Alg 1 - Alg 3 are strongly influenced by the large number of instances with $F^{CON} = 0$, where the performance index is 100 per definition. For problems with d2, substantial average percentage improvements over the initial solution have been obtained. For these problems, it is remarkable that rather small objective function values have been obtained by the best simulated annealing algorithms although the tightness factor $TF = 1$ leads to tight due dates.

As a consequence, there are only short waiting times of the jobs in the best solutions found. Among all particular combinations of a problem type (w,t,r,d) and a pair (*n*,*m*), we observe that the absolute improvements of the average function values obtained by the best simulated annealing variant over the average values of the initial solutions are up to 130 units for problems with w1 and up to 800 units for problems with w2. For problems with w1 and d1, they are typically around 50 units. However, from Andresen et al. (2008) it follows that often the heuristic solution is equal or close to a lower bound for the optimal value of a problem of type (w1,t1,r1,d1).

(w,t,r,d)	F^{CON}	PERC	Alg 1		Alg 2		Alg 3	
			AVG	95/75	AVG	95/75	AVG	95/75
(w1,t1,r1,d1)	17,041	0.32	71	25/53	93	72/91	71	21/55
(w1,t1,r1,d2)	160	36.2	70	22/49	93	66/91	71	22/51
(w1,t1,r1,d3)	2	97.5	100	100/100	100	100/100	100	100/100
(w1,t1,r2,d1)	21,238	0.23	71	22/50	90	63/88	69	22/58
(w1,t1,r2,d2)	166	39.3	70	21/48	90	60/87	70	23/53
(w1,t1,r2,d3)	0.3	98.3	100	100/100	100	100/100	100	100/100
(w1,t2,r1,d1)	17,009	0.55	56	13/30	78	46/64	49	15/29
(w1,t2,r1,d2)	161	62.9	54	14/28	75	40/63	50	16/28
(w1,t2,r1,d3)	0	100	100	100/100	100	100/100	100	100/100
(w1,t2,r2,d1)	21,156	0.33	58	20/41	78	45/70	53	24/33
(w1,t2,r2,d2)	118	69.8	54	21/35	77	44/67	51	19/31
(w1,t2,r2,d3)	0	100	100	100/100	100	100/100	100	100/100
(w2,t1,r1,d1)	94,637	0.32	68	20/45	90	58/88	70	18/58
(w2,t1,r1,d2)	835	41.6	68	21/47	91	63/88	71	22/60
(w2,t1,r1,d3)	8	98.0	99	98/98	100	99/100	100	99/100
(w2,t1,r2,d1)	118,132	0.22	66	19/45	88	53/81	67	22/47
(w2,t1,r2,d2)	838	39.7	66	23/45	88	56/81	64	20/45
(w2,t1,r2,d3)	1	100	100	100/100	100	100/100	100	100/100
(w2,t2,r1,d1)	94,475	0.56	61	18/41	82	45/73	58	15/38
(w2,t2,r1,d2)	847	68.8	56	18/33	83	43/75	53	13/31
(w2,t2,r1,d3)	0	100	100	100/100	100	100/100	100	100/100
(w2,t2,r2,d1)	117,665	0.32	58	26/40	83	51/73	55	21/38
(w2,t2,r2,d2)	594	73.7	56	24/39	79	43/73	55	23/38
(w2,t2,r2,d3)	0	100	100	100/100	100	100/100	100	100/100
average			75.1	47/61	90.0	69/85	74.1	46/62

Table 1. Results for problems with $n < m$

Moreover, the use of the SHIFT neighborhood is clearly superior for the problems with t1. In contrast, for most problem types with t2, both the API and 3-API neighborhoods are superior to the SHIFT neighborhood when using shorter runs with stopping criteria S1 and S3, and this tendency increases with the problem size. In addition, the API neighborhood is slightly superior to the 3-API neighborhood. We observed that the superiority of the SHIFT neighborhood in comparison with the two API-based neighborhoods is larger for problems with t1 than the superiority of the API-based neighborhoods over the SHIFT neighborhood for those with t2 for short runs. However, the SHIFT neighborhood becomes the single best for the long runs with stopping criterion S2. The variants with stopping criterion S2 yield the best results, often followed by the algorithms with S1 and finally those with S3 (an explanation is given in the next paragraph). Variants with an initial temperature IT1 tend to be superior to those with the initial temperature IT2, in particular for problems with w1, t1, for which they are substantially better (for an arbitrary stopping criterion). Moreover, for most problems algorithms with five cooling cycles work slightly better than variants using only one cooling cycle. However, for the long runs with stopping criterion S2, the use of one cooling cycle is slightly better for the problems with w1.

Next, we discuss the number of iterations executed in the case of stopping criterion S3. First, taking the average number of generated solutions over all problems with $n < m$, this number is up to 25 % for algorithms with N3 and only up to 12 % for algorithms with N1, N2 and N4. In particular, for neighborhood N4 the algorithm stops very quickly. For problems with w1, even for neighborhood N3 the algorithm stops after 5 % when using the larger initial temperature IT2 and CC1. This means that for an initial temperature of 15, usually no improvements over the function value of the initial solution are obtained. The percentage of generated solutions is also larger for problems with t1 in comparison with the problems with t2. The largest percentage of generated solutions was obtained for problem type (w2,t1,r1,d1) as well as $n = 20$ and $m = 30$ using N3, IT1, CC2 and a random initial solution, where 48 % of the iterations were executed. Comparing stopping criteria S1 and S3, we observe that only for the SHIFT neighborhood usually more than 30,000 solutions were generated for S3 while for the other neighborhoods, typically only around 20,000 solutions have been generated.

Problems with n = m:

Some results for the problems with $n = m$ are given in Table 2. The meaning of the rows and columns is the same as in Table 1. Based on the experiments and the discussion below, the following algorithms for the stopping criteria S1, S2 and S3, respectively, are included in Table 2:

Alg 1: algorithm (I2,**S1**,N1,IT2,CC2) for problems with w1 and t2; algorithm (I2,**S1**,N3,IT1, CC2) for all other problems;

Alg 2: algorithm (I2,**S2**,N3,IT1,CC1) for problems with w1, algorithm (I2,**S2**,N3,IT1,CC2) for problems with w2 and t1; algorithm (I2,**S2**,N3,IT2,CC2) for problems with w2 and t2.

Alg 3: algorithm (I2,**S3**,N1,IT2,CC1) for problems with t2; algorithm (I2,**S3**,N3,IT1,CC2) for problems with w1 and t1; algorithm (I2,**S3**,N3,IT1,CC1) for problems with w2 and t1.

For the problems with w1 and d1, the average percentage improvements are smaller than 1 %. These percentage improvements are larger for problems with w2 and t2. Here they are up to 2.53 % for problem type (w2,t2,r1,d1) and $n = m = 10$. For problem type (w1,t2,r2,d3), average percentage improvements of more than 90 % have been obtained and the final average objective function values for the instances of the particular pairs (n,m) are between 0 and 10 so that many problems have been solved to optimality. When comparing the average function values of the initial solutions with the average values by the best simulated annealing solutions, the absolute improvements are up to 200 units for problems with w1 and up to 1,500 units for the problems with w2.

Among the neighborhoods, the SHIFT neighborhood is clearly on the first place followed by the 3-API neighborhood (which is, however, substantially worse) when considering the results for all pairs (n,m). The crit-SHIFT neighborhood works extremely weak. The use of a small initial temperature is slightly superior. In particular, for the long runs with neighborhood N3 and stopping criterion S2, often the large initial temperature combined with one cooling cycle works weak for problems with w1. In general, the use of five cooling cycles is slightly superior in most cases. As for the problems with $n < m$, for the long runs with stopping criterion S2, the use of one cooling cycle is better for the problems with w1 while the use of five cooling cycles is better for w2.

(w,t,r,d)	F^{CON}	PERC	Alg 1		Alg 2		Alg 3	
			AVG	95/75	AVG	95/75	AVG	95/75
(w1,t1,r1,d1)	22,362	0.60	39	0/1	68	14/38	41	1/10
(w1,t1,r1,d2)	1,690	7.1	46	4/15	76	30/54	46	3/15
(w1,t1,r1,d3)	241	27.2	46	5/10	73	24/59	43	1/15
(w1,t1,r2,d1)	26,962	0.55	46	4/11	77	30/55	52	8/19
(w1,t1,r2,d2)	1,314	8.3	45	3/9	77	23/61	47	1/16
(w1,t1,r2,d3)	171	41.3	50	4/18	76	30/59	52	4/25
(w1,t2,r1,d1)	21,928	0.80	40	4/14	60	21/35	42	8/18
(w1,t2,r1,d2)	1,360	9.4	40	3/9	66	25/45	44	14/20
(w1,t2,r1,d3)	53	79.3	45	24/34	69	35/53	40	20/26
(w1,t2,r2,d1)	26,682	0.73	35	1/6	61	19/35	38	4/11
(w1,t2,r2,d2)	1,106	13.4	33	1/9	59	20/33	31	3/10
(w1,t2,r2,d3)	51	93.7	57	25/31	73	36/54	38	11/23
(w2,t1,r1,d1)	124,053	0.77	45	1/13	78	28/61	50	5/20
(w2,t1,r1,d2)	8,974	9.0	44	0/9	76	19/55	52	4/24
(w2,t1,r1,d3)	1,122	36.0	55	4/26	78	28/61	51	8/33
(w2,t1,r2,d1)	150,066	0.53	46	1/11	76	23/59	56	3/25
(w2,t1,r2,d2)	7,140	8.9	43	0/9	75	19/58	51	0/20
(w2,t1,r2,d3)	790	40.9	57	4/29	84	40/78	57	5/35
(w2,t2,r1,d1)	121,967	1.33	45	1/16	80	26/63	39	5/14
(w2,t2,r1,d2)	7,404	17.1	48	4/15	79	41/68	42	3/19
(w2,t2,r1,d3)	258	78.0	54	24/34	74	38/58	49	26/38
(w2,t2,r2,d1)	148,458	1.09	45	4/18	80	33/68	34	4/15
(w2,t2,r2,d2)	5,965	20.8	46	5/18	82	38/63	32	0/9
(w2,t2,r2,d3)	237	94.7	50	11/30	72	34/64	44	15/25
average			45.7	6/16	73.6	28/56	44.6	6/20

Table 2. Results for problems with $n = m$

When looking at the instances of the particular pairs (n,m), we can note that there is a tendency that with an increasing number of jobs, the API neighborhood becomes more and more competitive to the SHIFT neighborhood. For the problems with $n = m = 20$, the API neighborhood becomes superior for the problems with w1 when using short runs. For the problems with $n = m = 30$, the API neighborhood is also superior for most problem types when using short runs and even for problems with w1 when using long runs. This

corresponds to the observation in Andresen et al. (2008), where the API neighborhood became superior for the short runs with problem type (w1,t1,r1,d1) and $n \geq 20$.
Moreover, for most problems with w1 and t2, it turned out that in the case of short runs with stopping criterion S1, the recommended variant (I2,S1,N1,IT2,CC2) works not so good for small problems with $n = 10$ while the use of the API neighborhood is clearly superior for the larger problems with $n \geq 20$.
In addition, the variant (I2,S3,N1,IT2,CC1) was recommended for problems with w2 and t2 from an overall point of view when using S3. However, for these problems the performance depends also on the existence of release dates. In general, the API neighborhood is better for the problems with r1 while the SHIFT neighborhood is better for the problems with r2 when using S3 (the latter differs from the recommendation for Alg 3 made from an overall point of view for the corresponding group of problem types). Nevertheless, in contrast to the above comment, for the small problems with $n = m = 10$ and r1, the SHIFT neighborhood is superior while for the large problems with $n \geq 20$ and r2, the API neighborhood is clearly superior. This coincides with the general observation that the SHIFT neighborhood is often substantially better for small problems while the API neighborhood becomes better for the large problems.
For stopping criterion S3, the number of performed iterations slightly increases with the problem size. For problems with $n = m = 20$, up to 44 % of the iterations have been performed when using the SHIFT neighborhood. The largest number of iterations were performed for problems with t1. However, these numbers are substantially smaller for the other neighborhoods. In particular, for the small problems with $n = m = 10$, the number of performed iterations is roughly only the half of those for the large problems but in general, these percentages for the large problems are still rather low. For a substantial number of problems with d3, an objective function value of zero has been obtained for the long runs with the SHIFT neighborhood.

Problems with n > m:

Some results for the problems with $n > m$ are summarized in Table 3. The meaning of the rows and columns is the same as in Table 1. Based on the experiments and the discussion below, we have chosen the following algorithms for the stopping criteria S1, S2 and S3, respectively:

Alg 1: algorithm (I2,**S1**,N3,IT2,CC2) for problems with w2 and t1, algorithm (I2,**S1**,N3,IT1, CC1) for all other problems;

Alg 2: (I2,**S2**,N3,IT2,CC2) for problems with w2; algorithm (I2,**S2**,N3,IT1,CC2) for problems with w1 and t1, algorithm (I2,**S2**,N3,IT1,CC1) for problems with w1 and t2;

Alg 3: algorithm (I2,**S3**,N3,IT1,CC1) for problems with w1 and t2 as well as w2 and t1; algorithm (I2,**S3**,N3,IT1,CC2) for all other problems.

For the problems with d2 and d3, the average percentage improvements are much smaller than for the problems with $n \leq m$. In particular, for the problems with $n = 30$ and $m = 10$, these percentages are less than 1.4 % for the problems with w1. For the corresponding problems with w2, these average percentages are between 3.2 and 4.8 %. In terms of the objective function values, the absolute improvements of the function values are larger than for the problems with $n \leq m$. More precisely, the absolute improvement of the average function value obtained by the best simulated annealing variant over the average value of the initial solution among all particular combinations of a problem type (w,t,r,d) and a pair (n,m) is up to 230 units for problems with w1 and up to 2,800 units for problems with w2. In

particular, for problem type (w1,t2,r2,d3) and the instances with n = 30 and m = 20, the average function value of the initial solution is 233.5, but the average function value of the best simulated annealing solution is only 3.4.
In general, it can be observed that the performance indices of the algorithms using the SHIFT neighborhood and stopping criterion S2 are consistently rather large. One can also note that long runs with the API-based and crit-SHIFT neighborhoods do not reach the quality of short runs with the SHIFT neighborhood. As an exception, the crit-SHIFT neighborhood works (surprisingly) good for the problems with n = 15 and m = 10 as well as n = 30 and m = 20 for the problems with d3 (sometimes even better than the SHIFT neighborhood). Variants with a low initial temperature ar mostly superior, and this superiority is stronger than for the problems with $n \le m$. This becomes particularly obvious for the problems with w1. For the short runs with stopping criteria S1 and S3, often the use of one cooling cycle can be recommended.

(w,t,r,d)	F^{CON}	PERC	Alg 1		Alg 2		Alg 3	
			AVG	95/75	AVG	95/75	AVG	95/75
(w1,t1,r1,d1)	26,932	0.69	49	0/9	86	41/76	59	3/22
(w1,t1,r1,d2)	5,142	2.9	48	3/13	86	45/78	53	8/24
(w1,t1,r1,d3)	2,935	13.6	54	16/25	86	51/75	62	21/35
(w1,t1,r2,d1)	29,207	0.63	52	0/10	87	37/80	65	8/28
(w1,t1,r2,d2)	3,953	5.2	50	1/13	85	43/77	57	5/24
(w1,t1,r2,d3)	2,070	28.4	63	27/39	91	63/83	68	32/47
(w1,t2,r1,d1)	26,417	0.75	44	1/13	78	33/68	37	0/11
(w1,t2,r1,d2)	5,558	4.4	46	5/19	72	32/56	35	5/12
(w1,t2,r1,d3)	3,180	32.9	44	18/23	71	36/54	38	18/22
(w1,t2,r2,d1)	28,692	0.66	44	5/11	73	23/58	38	3/7
(w1,t2,r2,d2)	4,069	12.2	38	3/10	73	27/53	28	1/9
(w1,t2,r2,d3)	2,304	51.9	60	31/38	87	64/75	54	30/38
(w2,t1,r1,d1)	133,174	1.03	56	0/16	88	35/85	73	8/46
(w2,t1,r1,d2)	21,466	6.9	50	0/10	82	32/73	65	11/45
(w2,t1,r1,d3)	11,848	16.1	52	13/21	85	43/72	64	18/38
(w2,t1,r2,d1)	151,172	0.98	52	0/8	87	32/84	67	5/40
(w2,t1,r2,d2)	17,471	8.4	49	0/9	80	23/63	60	7/28
(w2,t1,r2,d3)	9,025	31.5	59	26/36	85	50/74	68	31/43
(w2,t2,r1,d1)	126,784	2.03	61	4/28	87	42/83	68	8/44
(w2,t2,r1,d2)	17,057	10.9	52	3/18	83	38/73	53	4/26
(w2,t2,r1,d3)	9,829	38.7	52	17/24	79	41/62	52	18/26
(w2,t2,r2,d1)	145,917	1.64	56	4/15	86	44/81	62	9/30
(w2,t2,r2,d2)	13,994	17.6	50	3/13	81	35/71	48	3/18
(w2,t2,r2,d3)	7,686	55.5	59	26/35	88	59/78	62	28/38
average			51.6	8/19	82.8	40/72	55.6	12/29

Table 3: Results for problems with $n > m$

When looking at the instances of the particular pairs (n,m), we observe for the problems with $n = 30$ and $m = 20$, that the API neighborhood and also the 3-API neighborhood become superior to the SHIFT neighborhood for short runs. This tendency is stronger for the problems with w1. We note that this also corresponds to the observation in Andresen et al. (2008), where the API neighborhood became superior for problems of the type (w1,t1,r1,d1) with $n > m \geq 20$. One can conjecture that such a trend becomes even stronger for larger problems not considered in this study (see also Andresen et al. (2008)). For the long runs with S2, the SHIFT neighborhood is still superior to the API neighborhood for almost all problem types with $n = 30$ and $m = 20$. This observation is particularly obvious for the problems with w2. An exception are problems of the types (w1,t2,r1,d3) and (w2,t2,r1,d3), where both the API and the 3-API neighborhoods are clearly superior to the SHIFT neighborhood. For stopping criterion S3, sometimes the SHIFT and in other cases the API neighborhood works better. On the other side, for problems with $n = 30$ and $m = 15$ and short runs with S1, the API neighborhood is only superior for some problem types with w1 and t2.

When using stopping criterion S3, the largest number of performed iterations can be observed for algorithms with the SHIFT neighborhood and a randomly generated initial solution when $n = 30$ (the largest numbers of iterations have been executed for problems with w2 and t1). In this case, up to more than 90 % of the maximal number of generations have been generated. On the other side, in the case of a good initial solution the percentage of performed iterations is mostly less than 30 %, and for the API-based neighborhoods both with a weak and a good initial solution, these percentages are always less than 30 %, often even substantially less. Nevertheless, on average, only for these problems with $n > m$, the performance indices of the recommended algorithms with S3 are better than those of the recommended algorithms with S1.

From an overall point of view it turned out that problems with $n > m$ are the hardest ones, in particular those with a large ratio n/m.

4.5 Comparison with a genetic algorithm

Genetic algorithms belong to the class of artificial intelligence techniques and they are based on Darwin's theory about 'survival of the fittest and natural selection'. This type of algorithms has been developed by Holland (1975), and one of the first genetic algorithms for scheduling problems has been given by Werner (1984). A genetic algorithm is characterized by a parallel search of the state space by keeping a set of possible solutions under consideration, called a population. A new generation is obtained from the current population by applying genetic operators such as mutation and crossover to produce new offspring. The application of a genetic algorithm requires an encoding scheme for a solution (also denoted as an individual), the choice of genetic operators, a selection mechanism and the determination of genetic parameters such as the population size and probabilities of applying the genetic operators.

In our tests, we use the genetic algorithm tested in Andresen et al. (2008) on the mean flow time open shop scheduling problem. For a more detailed description of this algorithm, the reader is referred to Andresen et al. (2008). Here, we use the recommended parameters, in particular we use a mutation probability of 0.8 and a crossover probability of 0.2. The initial population includes the best constructive solution of the algorithms described in Section 4.2 as one solution. We consider three variants of this genetic algorithm, denoted by

GA(*popsize*), differing only in the population size *popsize*. In particular, we apply the variants *GA*(10),*GA*(50) and *GA*(100).

We mainly compare the genetic algorithm with the short runs of simulated annealing (stopping criterion S1). In Andresen et al. (2008), both the simulated annealing and the genetic algorithms generated 30,000 solutions. However, the genetic algorithms needed substantially larger computational times. In the following, for the genetic algorithms we allow a time limit of two times the required average running times for the simulated annealing algorithms with 30,000 generated solutions (estimated in advance).

For evaluating the genetic algorithms, we also use the performance index *PI* introduced in Section 4.4. However, since we refer to the best value obtained by some simulated annealing variant, the performance index can be greater than 100 for a particular instance, if a genetic algorithm generates a better solution than the best one obtained among all simulated annealing variants.

In Table 4, we present the average performance indices of the three genetic algorithms for the 24 problem types, where again all pairs (n,m) of the corresponding relation between n and m are considered. For $n < m$, it can be seen that in most cases a large population size of 100 is superior. Algorithm *GA*(10) is better than the recommended variant Alg 1 (but we remind that the time limit for the genetic algorithms is roughly twice the time limit for Alg 1). However, on average, the performance of the long simulated annealing algorithms is not reached. Moreover, the performance indices of the genetic algorithms depend on the problem size. Sometimes the genetic algorithm reaches clearly a better performance (even than the long runs of simulated annealing with stopping criterion S2). The largest performance indices have been obtained as 143 for problem type (w2,t2,r2,d1) and as 137 for problem type (w2,t2,r1,d2) for the problems with $n = 10$ and $m = 15$ both with algorithm GA(100). On the other side, the performance index of algorithm *GA*(100) for the problems with $n = 20$ and $m = 30$ and type (w1,t1,r1,d1) is only 14.

For $n = m$, it can be observed that an average performance index of more than 100 has been obtained for 10 problem types both by algorithms *GA*(50) and *GA*(100). However, a large range of the performance indices can be observed. The smallest index of algorithm *GA*(100), namely 33, has been obtained for problem type (w1,t1,r1,d3) for the instances with $n = m = 30$. Concerning the large performance indices for problem type (w2,t2,r2,d2), we note that these two values for the algorithms *GA*(50) and *GA*(100) are strongly influenced by one outlier instance, where simulated annealing works bad and the function value of the initial solution is only improved by two units with the best simulated annealing algorithm while the genetic algorithm with a large population size can improve the function value by some hundreds of units. (On the other side, there are also instances for this type, where simulated annealing is better then the best genetic algorithm by several hundreds of units.) In a weaker form, this also holds for problem type (w2,t2,r2,d1). Excluding these outlier instances, the results of the genetic algorithms improve with the population size and particularly algorithm *GA*(100) can be recommended for problems with $n = m$. However, from an overall point of view, all three genetic algorithms are superior to fast simulated annealing runs (see also Andresen et al. (2008) for mean flow time minimization).

A different behavior can be obtained for the problems with $n > m$. For these problems, the quality of the solutions of the genetic algorithm decreases with increasing population size in terms of the performance index. Moreover, the performance indices of the genetic algorithms are smaller than those obtained for fast simulated annealing algorithms (and they are substantially smaller than those for the best simulated annealing algorithms). For the best genetic algorithm *GA*(10), the largest performance index for the problems with d1 and d2 is 84 for problem type (w2,t2,r1,d2) for the instances with n = 15 and m = 10 (note that some of the problems with d3 are easy so that larger indices have been obtained) while small performance indices have been obtained in particular for the problems with n = 30.

(w,t,r,d)	$n < m$			$n = m$			$n > m$		
	10	50	100	10	50	100	10	50	100
(w1,t1,r1,d1)	67	65	63	83	104	111	37	25	12
(w1,t1,r1,d2)	67	67	64	64	80	89	34	24	13
(w1,t1,r1,d3)	100	100	100	60	66	62	42	34	24
(w1,t1,r2,d1)	68	73	76	77	103	100	38	27	16
(w1,t1,r2,d2)	67	74	76	82	103	105	38	27	17
(w1,t1,r2,d3)	100	100	100	74	78	88	54	43	36
(w1,t2,r1,d1)	67	77	84	94	145	149	43	31	19
(w1,t2,r1,d2)	60	75	74	66	111	122	42	33	21
(w1,t2,r1,d3)	100	100	100	74	93	101	49	47	38
(w1,t2,r2,d1)	76	98	99	107	150	166	47	39	21
(w1,t2,r2,d2)	73	98	102	96	146	166	43	38	26
(w1,t2,r2,d3)	100	100	100	78	92	101	62	59	55
(w2,t1,r1,d1)	67	67	65	60	72	76	46	25	12
(w2,t1,r1,d2)	62	66	63	45	52	60	49	30	14
(w2,t1,r1,d3)	100	100	100	55	57	60	49	35	22
(w2,t1,r2,d1)	70	74	75	77	83	86	42	25	13
(w2,t1,r2,d2)	68	81	78	71	79	88	44	28	14
(w2,t1,r2,d3)	100	100	100	72	79	81	55	43	34
(w2,t2,r1,d1)	61	75	70	81	92	90	55	35	18
(w2,t2,r1,d2)	70	76	83	76	87	99	55	39	20
(w2,t2,r1,d3)	100	100	100	84	104	97	57	46	41
(w2,t2,r2,d1)	78	97	100	108	139	227	59	37	20
(w2,t2,r2,d2)	80	94	102	93	577	363	56	43	25
(w2,t2,r2,d3)	100	100	100	86	96	97	66	62	57
average	79.2	85.6	86.5	77.5	116.1	115.9	48.3	36.5	24.5

Table 4. Results of the genetic algorithms

More precisely, even for the best genetic algorithm *GA*(10), for the problems with n = 30 and m = 20 a smallest performance index of 15 is obtained for problem type (w1,t2,r2,d2), for the problems with n = 30 and m = 15 the smallest index is 21 for problem type (w1,t1,r1,d3) and for the problems with n = 30 and m = 10 the smallest index is 29 for problem type (w1,t2,r1,d3). In general, among all 72 combinations of a problem type and one of the pairs

(n,m) with $n = 30$, the indices of algorithm $GA(10)$ are smaller than 40 for 48 of the 72 cases, among them 32 cases with w1. Moreover, the smallest performance index of algorithm $GA(100)$ is even only 3 for the problems with $n = 30$ and $m = 15$ and type (w1,t1,r1,d2). The superiority of good simulated annealing variants becomes stronger for problems with an increasing number of jobs.

The results of the comparison of simulated annealing and genetic algorithms correspond to those obtained in Andresen et al. (2008) for problem type (w1,t1,r1,d1), where genetic algorithms are competitive for problems with $n \leq m$ while simulated annealing was clearly better for instances with $n > m$ and a large ratio of n/m.

5. Concluding remarks

Often in the literature, a particular type of a problem is considered (e.g. processing times are uniformly distributed in the interval [1, 100]) and then the parameters of a simulated annealing algorithm are tuned for this concrete situation. The use of such an algorithm is then recommended for arbitrary instances of the problem under consideration. However, in general it is not a priori clear that this particular tuning is also recommendable for other types of instances of the problem when, for instance, processing times have a substantially different range, due dates are set in another way, or job weights are very different, etc. One of the major goals of this study was to find out which parameters of open shop problems with the minimization of total weighted tardiness have a strong influence and which have a smaller influence on the selection of an appropriate simulated annealing algorithm.

From our computational study for problems with up to 30 jobs and 30 machines, we can give the following conclusions and recommendations:

- The concrete data of the problems have a substantial influence on the design of an appropriate simulated annealing algorithm. While for makespan minimization in an open shop only square problems with $n = m$ have been considered in the literature (because they are the hardest problems), the ratio of n and m has an influence on the performance of particular simulated annealing and genetic algorithms for problems with sum criteria. As in Andresen et al. (2008), we have evaluated the results separately for the cases $n < m$, $n = m$ and $n > m$.
- For problems with $n \leq m$ including positive due dates, only instances with a tightness factor up to approximately 1.1 are of interest. Even for the problems with a tightness factor between 1.0 and 1.1, the final function values are rather small and therefore, the corresponding solutions are close to the optimal ones. For larger tightness factors, problems are very easy in the sense that already simple dispatching rules construct solutions with a function value equal or close to zero. For problems with $n > m$, instances with larger tightness factors are of interest. If $n = 30$ and $m = 10$ and due dates according to d3 are considered, the objective function values of the best solution are still around 10,000 for the problems with w1 and around 30,000 for the problems with w2.
- In terms of the objective function value, the absolute improvements of the average function values of the final solution over the average values of the initial solutions are usually larger for the problems with $n > m$ (where these improvements are even up to 2,800 units) while for problems with $n < m$, these improvements are smaller (always less than 130 units for all problem types and pairs (n,m)). It appears that problems with $n <$

m are easier to solve while problems with $n > m$ are the hardest ones. This coincides with the observations made in Andresen et al. (2008), where it has been found for the problems of type (w1,t1,r1,d1) that the objective function values of the heuristic solutions are close to a lower bound for problems with $n < m$. If we consider percentage improvements of the objective function values, they are higher for the problems with d2 and d3 (where the function values of the initial solutions are considerably smaller).

- In general, the choice of a good initial solution strongly influences the quality of the iterative solution finally obtained. One possibility is to generate nondelay schedules by priority dispatching rules. Among the six rules used in our study, the LPT rule can be recommended for problems with $n < m$, the WSPT, EDD and FCFS rules are good for particular types of problems with $n > m$, and for problems with $n = m$, all the six rules considered in our study contribute good initial solutions. This confirms and generalizes the results from Bräsel et al. (2008). Since these algorithms are very fast, the application of several rules and the selection of the best solution can be recommended to generate appropriate initial solutions.
- The choice of an appropriate neighborhood has probably the largest influence on the quality of a simulated annealing algorithm. For most problem types considered in this study, the use of the SHIFT neighborhood is strongly recommended and superior to API-based neighborhoods. An exception are the following situations when using short runs with stopping criterion S1 or S3. For problems with $n < m$ and t2, the results both with the API- and the 3-API neighborhoods are better than with the SHIFT neighborhood. In addition, for large problems with $n \geq m \geq 20$, the API neighborhood and also the 3-API neighborhood become superior for more and more problem types. On the other side, for long runs with stopping criterion S2, the API neighborhood becomes superior to the SHIFT neighborhood only for the large square problems with $n = m = 30$, in particular for the problems with w1 and also for most problems with w2 and d3. Moreover, the algorithms using the crit-SHIFT neighborhood are not competitive for almost all problems.
- The selection of an appropriate simulated annealing algorithm does not essentially depend on the concrete pair (n,m) within each of the three groups $n < m$, $n = m$ and $n > m$ with the exceptions discussed in the previous item. However, the observed trends for the problems with $n < m$ are stronger if n/m is small, and the trends for the problems with $n > m$ are stronger if n/m is large. On the other side, if n/m is close to one, the observations are more similar to the case $n = m$. This corresponds to the results in Andresen et al. (2008) for problems with minimizing mean flow time.
- For some problems it is essential to start with an extremely small temperature. This is particularly true for problems with w1, especially for short runs. On the other side, the choice of an appropriate initial temperature is not so important for the problems with w2. In particular, for the long runs with stopping criterion S2, the use of a small initial temperature is advantageous for problems with w1 while for problems with w2, variants with a larger initial temperature become more competitive. Moreover, the use of a low initial temperature is superior for most problems with $n > m$ as well as for the problems with w1, t1, arbitrary values of n and m and arbitrary stopping criterion.

- The number of cooling cycles does not have a substantial influence on the quality of the simulated annealing algorithms. Among the recommended algorithms, there are variants with one and five cooling cycles. From an overall point of view, the use of five cooling cycles leads to slightly better results, in particular for the problems with $n \le m$.
- As one can expect, the long runs with stopping criterion S2 obtain the best results. However, when using long runs with the API and 3-API neighborhoods, for most problem types the results are nevertheless worse than in the case of short runs with the SHIFT neighborhood. This is partially opposite for problems with $n < m$ and t2. Variants with the flexible stopping criterion S3 are not superior to short runs with stopping criterion S1 for the majority of problem types. An exception are most types of the hard problems with $n > m$, in particular problems with w2.
- From an overall point of view, a variant using a good initial solution and the SHIFT neighborhood with a small initial temperature of two and one or five cooling cycles can be recommended among the simulated annealing algorithms for problems with up to 30 jobs and 30 machines. However, as mentioned above, for the problems with $n \ge m \ge 20$, the API neighborhood becomes better. It can be conjectured that this trend becomes even stronger for problems with $n \ge m$ as the number of machines increases further.
- When comparing fast simulated annealing and the genetic algorithms used in our study, we have to distinguish the cases $n \le m$ and $n > m$. While for problems with $n \le m$ the genetic algorithm with a large population size often gets a better solution than short and sometimes even the best simulated annealing algorithm, this is not true for the problems with $n > m$. Here a good fast simulated annealing algorithm is usually superior to the best genetic algorithm (and the genetic algorithms perform extremely poor in comparison to the long simulated annealing algorithms).

The algorithms presented in this paper are included into the program package LiSA - A Library of Scheduling Algorithms, version 3.0 (see http://lisa.math.uni-magdeburg.de). For a free use of the algorithms discussed in this paper and the whole package, the interested reader can contact the LiSA team under the above website. A table with the seeds for generating the open shop instances used in this paper can also be obtained.

6. References

Achugbue, J.O.; Chin, F.Y.: Scheduling the Open Shop to Minimize Mean Flow Time, SIAM J. on Computing, Vol. 11, 1982, 709 - 720.

Andresen, M.; Bräsel, H.; Mörig, M.; Tusch, J.; Werner, F.; Willenius, P.: Simulated Annealing and Genetic Algorithms for Minimizing Mean Flow Time in an Open Shop, Math. Comp. Modelling (to appear, doi 10.1016/j.mcm.2008.01.002).

Blazewicz, J.; Pesch, E.; Sterna, M.; Werner, F.: Open Shop Scheduling with Late Work Criteria, Discrete Appl. Math., Vol. 134, 2004, 1 - 24.

Bräsel, H.: Matrices in Shop Scheduling Problems, in: Perspectives on Operations Research - Essays in Honor of Klaus Neumann (ed. by M. Morlock, C. Schwindt, N. Trautmann and J. Zimmermann), Deutscher Universitäts-Verlag, Wiesbaden, 2006, 17 - 43.

Bräsel, H.; Herms, A.; Mörig, M.; Tautenhahn, T.; Tusch, J.; Werner, F.: Heuristic Constructive Algorithms for Open Shop Scheduling to Minimize Mean Flow Time, European J. Oper. Res., Vol. 189, 2008, 856 - 870.

Bräsel, H.; Tautenhahn, T.; Werner, F.: Constructive Heuristic Algorithms for the Open-Shop Problem, Computing, Vol. 51, 1993, 95 - 110.

Brightwell, G.; Winkler, P.: Counting Linear Extensions, Order, Vol. 8, 1991, 225 - 242.

Bräsel, H.; Hennes, H.: On the Open-Shop Problem with Preemption and Minimizing the Average Completion Time, European J. Oper. Res., Vol. 157, 2004, 607 - 619.

Brucker, P.; Hurink, J.; Jurisch, B.; Wöstmann, B.: A Branch-and-Bound Algorithm for the Open-Shop Problem, Discrete Appl. Math., Vol. 76, 1997, 43 - 59.

Du, J.; Leung, J.Y.T.: Minimizing Mean Flow Time in Two-Machine Open-Shops and Flow-Shops, Journal of Algorithms, Vol. 14, 1990, 24 - 44.

Gueret, C.; Prins, C.: A New Lower Bound for the Open-Shop Problem, Annals Oper. Res., Vol. 92, 1999, 165 - 183.

Holland, J.A.: Adaptation in Natural and Artificial Systems, Ann Arbor, University of Michigan, 1975.

Kubiak, W.; Sriskandarajah, C.; Zaras, K.: A Note on the Complexity of Open Shop Scheduling Problems, INFOR, Vol. 29, 1991, 284 - 294.

Laborie, P.: Complete MCS-Based Search, Application to Resource Constrained Project Scheduling, Proceedings of International Joint Conference on Artificial Intelligence, Vol. 19, 2005, 181 - 186.

Liaw, C.-F.: Applying Simulated Annealing to the Open Shop Scheduling Problem, IEE Transactions, Vol. 31, 1999, 457 - 465.

Liaw, C.-F.: Scheduling Two-Machine Preemptive Open Shop Shops to Minimize Total Completion Time, Comput. Oper. Res., Vol. 31, 2004, 1349 - 1363.

Liaw, C.-F.: Scheduling Preemptive Open Shops to Minimize Total Tardiness, European J. Oper. Res., Vol. 162, 2005, 175 - 183.

Liaw, C.-F.; Cheng, C.-Y.; Chen, M.: The Total Completion Time Open Shop Scheduling Problem with a Given Sequence of Jobs on One Machine, Comput. Oper. Res., Vol. 29, 2002, 1251 - 1266.

Liu, C.Y.; Bulfin, R.L.: On the Complexity of Preemptive Open-Shop Scheduling Problems, Oper. Res. Lett., Vol. 4, 1985, 71 - 74.

Liu, C.Y.; Bulfin, R.L.: Scheduling Ordered Open Shops, Comput. Oper. Res., Vol. 14, 1987, 257 - 264.

Prins, C.: An Overview of Scheduling Problems Arising in Satellite Communications, Journal Oper. Res. Soc., Vol. 40, 1994, 611 - 623.

Queyranne, M.; Sviridenko, M.: New and Improved Algorithms for Minsum Shop Scheduling, Proceedings of the 11th annual ACM-SIAM Symposium on Discrete Algorithms, San Francisco/ USA, 2000, 871 - 878.

Queyranne, M.; Sviridenko, M.: Approximation Algorithms for Shop Scheduling Problems with Minsum Objective, Journal of Scheduling, Vol. 5, 2002, 287 - 305.

Taillard, E.: Benchmarks for Basic Scheduling Problems, European J. Oper. Res., Vol. 64, 1993, 278 - 285.

Tamura, N.; Taga, A.; Kitagawa, S.; Banbara, M.: Compiling Finite Linear CSP into SAT, Proceeding of the 12th International Conference on Principles and Practice of

Constraint Programming (CP'06), Lecture Notes in Computer Science, Vol. 4204, Springer, 2006, 590 - 603.

Werner, F.: On the Solution of Special Sequencing Problems, Ph.D. Thesis, TU Magdeburg, 1984 (in German).

Werner, F.; Winkler, A.: Insertion Techniques for the Heuristic Solution of the Job Shop Problem, Discrete Appl. Math., Vol. 50, 1995, 191 - 211.

Yang, Q; Sun, J.; Zhang, J.; Wang C. : A Hybrid Discrete Particle Swarm Algorithm for Open-Shop Problems, Lecture Notes in Computer Science, Vol. 4247, 2006, 158 - 165.

4

Real Time Multiagent Decision Making by Simulated Annealing

[1]Dawei Jiang and [2]Jingyu Han
[1]*National University of Singapore,*
[2]*Nanjing University of Posts and Telecommunications,*
[1]*Singapore*
[2]*China*

1. Introduction

In this chapter, the application of Simulated Annealing (SA) algorithm in real time multiagent coordination problem is described. A **M**ulti**a**gent **S**ystem (MAS) consists of a group of agents that interact with each other. Research in MAS aims to provide theories and techniques for agents' behavior management. The focus of this chapter is on fully cooperative MAS, where all the agents share a common long-term goal. Examples include a team of robots who play football against another team or a group of rescue robots that, after an earthquake, must safely rescue the victims as soon as possible. The challenging issue in such systems is ***Coordination***: the policy to insure that the individual action of each agent can generate the optimal joint action as a whole.

Coordination in MAS has been explored from many aspects such as game theory (Osborne & Rubinstein , 1999), communications (Carrier & Gelernter, 1989), social conversions (Boutilier, 1996) and learning(Tan, 1997). Unfortunately these approaches have some flaws. First, in the worst case, these approaches degrade to a naïve solution which searches the whole joint action space whose size grows exponentially with the number of agents (It is called "curse of dimensionality"). Therefore, they do not scale well for large systems. Second, many of the approaches report an answer only when all the possible statuses have been considered. This is not suitable for real time case. In many real time scenarios such as robot football, rescue robots, etc., it is often needed that decision making algorithm returns a well enough answer at any time.

Recently, there is some work on how to decrease the joint action space by *coordination graph* (CG) (Guestrin & Venkataraman , 2002). The insight in CG is that in MAS only a small part of agents need to coordinate their actions while others can still act individually. Thus, the global joint payoff function, the representation of the global joint coordination dependencies among all agents, is approximated as a sum of local payoff functions, each of which represents the local coordination dependencies between a small sub-group of the agents. Then, the agents use a *variable elimination* (VE) algorithm to determine their optimal joint action. Unfortunately, the worst time complexity of VE grows exponentially with the number of agents. Moreover, VE only reports results when the whole algorithm terminates, therefore it is unsuitable for real-time systems. Max-plus (MP) algorithm is proposed as an

approximate alternative to VE (Kok & Vlassis, 2005). MP can converge to the optimal solution for tree-structured graphs and also find near optimal solutions in graphs with cycles, but it limits the local payoff functions to contain at most 2 agents.
In this chapter, An **S**imulate **A**nnealing (SA) based algorithms to address aforementioned coordination problem is presented. This approach has two main benefits. First, the time taken by the algorithm grows polynomial with the number of agents. Second, the algorithm can report a near-optimal answer at any time.
The chapter is organized as follows. Section 2 describes the problem setting and representative work on how to solve multiagent decision problem, especially on **V**ariable **E**limination (VE) approach. Section 3 introduces the general steps and key elements of SA algorithms, which is employed in later sections. Section 4 gives how to effectively find a satisfactory answer in any time for multiagent decision problem by SA algorithm. In Section 5, the performance of SA algorithm on multiagent decision problem is evaluated by comparing it with comparable approaches followed by conclusion and future work.

2. Problem setting and variable elimination approach

Multiagent decision making problem can be formally describe as follows.
Given a group of agents $G=\{G_1,G_2,\ldots,G_n\}$*, they are interacting with each other together during a long time sequence* $\{t_1,t_2,\ldots,t_n\}$ *to reach final goal . At each time* t_i*, each agent* G_i *selects an individual action* a_i *from his own action set* A_i *(Thus the joint policy space is* $A=\times A_i$ *) based on payoff function* $v(a)$ *and goes into next time* t_{i+1}*. At each time, the decision making problem is to find the optimal joint action* a^* *that maximize the global payoff function* $v(a)$*. That is to say,* $a^*=\max\arg_a v(a)$*.*
To overcome the curse of dimensionality, the global joint payoff function is decomposed into a linear combination of s set of local payoff functions, each of which is only related to a small number of agents. For example, in RoboCup, only the players that are close to each other have to coordinate their actions to perform a pass or a defend. In some situations, this approach can get a very compact representation for coordination dependencies among agents. Furthermore, such representation can be mapped onto a coordination graph $G=(V,E)$ according to the following rules: each agent is mapped to a node in V, and each coordination dependency is mapped to an edge in E. Then **V**ariable **E**limination (VE) can be used on G to determine the optimal joint actions.
Variable Elimination is also called bucket elimination. It is first used for reasoning in Bayes network. It can also be effectively used to solve the multiagent decision making problem. The technical steps include two passes. In the first pass, by enumerating all the possible combinatorial joint actions of his neighborhood, each agent conditionally computes his own optimal action and sends the result to the entire neighborhood. Then, the agent will be eliminated from the system. This process will continue until only one agent remains in the system. In the second pass, all agents do the entire process in reverse elimination order. In the process every agent can find his own optimal decision based on his neighborhood agent's behavior. An example is taken to illustrate the execution of VE algorithm. Suppose that the system has 4 agents with each one having 4 different actions, then the number of joint actions is $4^4=256$, and global joint payoff function can be decomposed as:

$$V(a)=v_1(a_1,a_2)+v_2(a_2,a_4)+v_3(a_1,a_3) \quad (1)$$

Fig.1 shows the initial corresponding coordination graph. The key idea in VE is that, rather than enumerating all possible joint actions and summing up all functions to do maximization, each time only one variable is optimized. The example begins with optimization for agent 1. Agent 1 collects all local payoff functions including its own, i.e., v_1 and v_3 then does maximization. Hence, it can be obtained that

$$\max_a v(a) = \max_{a2,a3,a4} \{v_2(a_2,a_4) + \max_{a1} [v_1(a_1,a_2)+v_3(a_1,a_3)]\} \tag{2}$$

After enumeration of possible action combinations of his neighbors, i.e., agent 2 and agent 3, agent 1 conditionally returns his best response and yield a new function $e_1(a_2,a_3) = \max_{a1}[v_1(a_1,a_2)+v_3(a_1,a_3)]$. Its value at the point a_2, a_3 is the value of the internal max expression in equation (2). At this time, agent 1 is eliminated from G. The global joint payoff function is rewritten as:

$$\max_a v(a) = \max_{a2,a3,a4} \{v_2(a_2,a_4)+e_1(a_2,a_3)\} \tag{3}$$

Now fewer agents remain. Next, agent 2 does the same procedure. After collecting $v_2(a_2,a_4)$

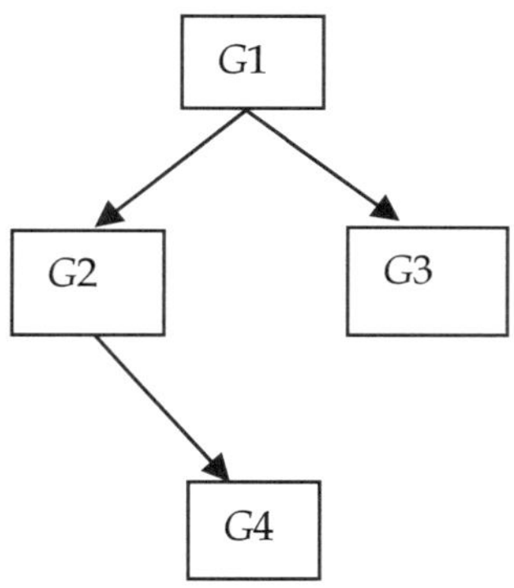

Fig.1. Initial coordination graph

and $e_1(a_2,a_3)$, agent 2 produces a conditional strategy based on the possible actions of agent 3 and agent 4, and returns his choice, i.e., $e_2(a_3,a_4) = \max_{a2} \{v_2(a_2,a_4)+e_1(a_2,a_3)\}$ to the system, then is eliminated. The global payoff function only contains 2 agents now:

$$\max_a v(a) = \max_{a3,a4} \{e_2(a_3,a_4)\} \tag{4}$$

Agent 3 begins to do optimization. Enumerating actions of agent 4, he reports his own choice and gives a conditional payoff $e_3(a_4) = \max_{a3} e_2(a_3,a_4)$. Finally, the only remaining agent 4 can simply choose his optimal action: $a_4^* = \arg\max_{a4} e_3(a_4)$.

In the second pass, all agents do the entire process in reverse elimination order. To fulfill agent 4's optimal action a_4^*, agent 3 must select $a_3^* = \arg\max_{a3} e_3(a_4^*)$. Then agent 2 can make a decision $a_2^* = \arg\max_{a2} e_2(a_3^*,a_4^*)$. Finally, agent 1 does $a_1^* = \arg\max_{a1} e_1(a_2^*,a_3^*)$ to choose his optimal action appropriately. The whole procedure needs only 4×4+4×4+4=36 iterations which is much smaller than 256 iterations of the whole joint action space.

The outcome of VE is independent of the elimination order and always gives the optimal joint action (Guestrin, 2003). However, the running speed of VE is depended on the elimination order and exponential in the induced width of the coordination graph (Guestrin

& Venkataraman, 2002) (Dechter,1999). Finding the optimal elimination order for VE is a well known NP-complete problem (Arnborg et al., 1987). Thus, in some cases and especially in the worse case, the time consumed by VE grows exponentially with the number of agents. Furthermore, VE can not give any useful results until the termination of the complete algorithm. Therefore, it is not suitable for real time multiagent decision making scenario. So in the following graph how to use simulated annealing (SA) approach to circumvent such limitations is addressed in detail.

3. Simulated annealing algorithms

The simulated annealing algorithm (also called as monte carlo annealing or probabilistic hill-climber), inspired by statistical mechanics, is very popular for combinatorial optimization. In this area efficient methods are developed to find minimal or maximal values for a function of a number of independent variables. The simulated annealing process executes by 'melting' the system being optimized at a high effective temperature at first, and then lowering the temperature by slow stages until the system 'freezes' and no further change occurs. In the following subsection the generic procedure to solve combinatorial optimization is introduced first, and then the essential factors in designing SA algorithm are analyzed.

3.1 Generic procedure to solve combinatorial optimization by SA

Given a generic function to be optimized f: $(x_1,x_2,\ldots,x_j,\ldots x_n)\rightarrow R+$, where $x_j \in S$ (here S is the domain) is a component of vector X and $N(x_j)\in S$ is the neighborhood of x_j. To find the maximal or minimal result, SA algorithm executes as the following 4 steps.

1. Initial temperature T_{max} and initial answer X (0) is given.
2. Based on X (i), a new resultant X' which contains a certain newly produced component $x' \in N(x(j))$ is obtained.
3. Whether X' will be accepted as a new answer X (i+1) depends on the probability

$$P(X(i)\rightarrow X')=\begin{cases} 1 & \text{if } f(X') < f(X(i)) \\ e^{-\frac{f(X')-f(X(i))}{T_i}} & \text{otherwise} \end{cases} \quad (5)$$

In other words, If $f(X')$ is less than $f(X(i))$ then $X(i+1)=X'$, otherwise X' will be accepted as X (i+1) with the probability of $e^{-\frac{f(X')-f(X(i))}{T_i}}$. If X' is rejected, the control flow goes to step 2 again until an acceptable X (i+1) is found.

4. Step 2 and 3 is repeated until a final status defined before reached.

It can be seen that the process of SA is a discrete status sequence. At each temperature T_i, its new status X ($i+1$) only depends on X (i) and has no relevance with X (i-1), X (i-2)…, X (0). Thus it is a Markov process.

3.2 Essential factors for designing simulated annealing algorithm

When a simulated annealing algorithm is designed, six essential factors should be taken into consideration.

3.2.1 Neighbor function (status production function)

A neighbor function is used to generate a new candidate answer based on current status. When a neighbor function is designed, it should ensure that all the candidate answers in the state space can be reachable. In general, designing a neighbor function focuses on two key aspects, which are the rule of producing candidate answers and the distribution of candidate answers. The former determines how to produce a candidate answer based on current answer. The latter determines the probability of newly produced different candidate answers. Usually production rule of neighbor function is devised according to concrete problem and distribution of candidate answers takes uniform distribution, normal distribution, exponential distribution and Cauchy distribution .etc.

3.2.2 Status transition probability (acceptance probability)

Status transition probability is the likelihood that one feasible answer, denoted as x_{old}, transits to another feasible answer, denoted as x_{new} . In other words, it is the chance that a new feasible answer will be accepted as current answer. As a rule, the status transition probability observes the followings.

1. At the same temperature, the chance to accept the candidate answer which will decrease objective function value is larger than that which will increase objective function value.
2. As the temperature declines, the chance to accept the answers that will decrease objective function value should gradually become smaller and smaller.
3. As the temperature is approaching zero, only the answers that make objective function value decrease can be accepted.

In most of the cases, Metropolis rule as equation (5) is used.

3.2.3 Cooling function

Cooling function determines how the simulated annealing proceeds from a high temperature T_{max} to lower temperature by stages. If the temperature decreases slow enough, the objective function value can concentrate on the global minima or maxima with an expensive cost. If the temperature decreases too fast, the global minima or maxima will not be reachable. Let $T(t)$ be the temperature at time t. The classical cooling function usually takes $T(t) = T_{\max}/lg(1+t)$ and the fast cooling function usually takes $T(t) = T_{\max}/(1+t)$. These two types of cooling function can gurantee the algorithm converge to the global minima or maxima.

3.2.4 Initial temperature

Many experiments show that the higher the initial temperature $T(0)$ is, the greater the chance of obtaining high quality final answer is. But the time consumed is also longer. Therefore, to get a better initial temperature $T_{\max}$, both optimization effectiveness and efficiency should be taken into consideration. Usually, the following several approaches can be applied.

1. At first, a group of statuses is obtained by uniform sampling. Then, the initial temperature T_{max} is defined as the variance of all the statuses' objective function values.
2. At first, a group of statuses is random obtained. Then, the biggest difference of objective function values, denoted as $|\triangle_{\max}|$, is obtained by comparing every two statues.

Finally, the initial temperature T_{max} is determined by a function which takes $|\triangle_{\max}|$ as parameter.

3. The initial temperature T_{max} is determined based on engineering experience for some specific problems.

3.2.5 Metropolis sampling rule

This rule is used to determine how many candidate answers will be produced at a certain temperature. The following policies are widely used.

1. Test whether the average of object function values is stable or not. If so, the sampling will continue, otherwise the sampling will stop.
2. Test whether objective function value difference in continuous steps is small enough. If so, the sampling will continue, otherwise, the sampling will stop.
3. The sampling is constrained by fixed number of steps.

3.2.6 Termination rule

It is used to determine when the simulated annealing algorithm ends. It includes the following approaches.

1. An ending temperature threshold is set. If the current temperature is below the threshold, the simulated annealing stops.
2. The number of iteration is set. The simulated annealing process will proceed according to the times of iterations.
3. The simulated annealing will end if the objective values do not change in a series of continuous steps.
4. The termination depends on whether the system entropy is stable or not.

4. Multiagent decision making by simulated annealing algorithm

It is natural to apply SA to multiagent decision making problem since the global payoff function needs to be optimized via a number of independent action variables of each agent. The process works as follows. First, the global payoff function is decomposed into a number of local terms. Then, global payoff function will be rewritten as the linear combination of the local terms to avoid the curse of dimensionality. That is to say, given n agents, its global payoff function can be decomposed as follows:

$$v(\mathrm{a})=\sum_{i\in G} v_i(a_i)+\sum_{i,j\in G} v_{ij}(a_i,a_j)+\ldots+\sum_{i,j,k} v_{i,j,k}(a_i,a_j,a_k)+\ldots. \quad (6)$$

Here $v_i(a_i)$ represents the payoff that an agent contributes to the system when acting individually, e.g. dribbling with the ball. $v_{ij}(i,j)$ denotes the payoff of a joint action between agent i and j, and $v_{ijk}(a_i,a_j,a_k)$ depicts another coordination action involving three agents, e.g. pass from i to j, then j to k . Coordination among more agents can be added similarly if needed. This decomposition approach is different from MP for the number of agents is not limited while MP does. In MP algorithm, the global joint payoff function can only be decomposed into $\sum_{i\in G} v_i(a_i)+\sum_{i,j\in G} v_{ij}(a_i,a_j)$.

Now SA can be smoothly applied to solve the multiagent decision problem. The goal is to find the optimal joint action, i.e., $a^{*}= \arg\max_a v(a)$. The pseudo-code of SA is presented in

Alg.1. The SA algorithm is implemented in a centralized version and performed by the agents in parallel, without assuming the availability of communications. The idea behind the algorithm is very straightforward. In each iteration (called an independent try), the algorithm starts with a random choice of joint action for the agents, then loop over all the agents. Each agent optimizes the global payoff function with his own action while all of the other agents stay the same. If the agent's local optimization can yield a better joint action than the initial one, the new solution is accepted. Otherwise, the new solution is accepted with a probability of $\frac{1}{1+e^{-(\Delta/T)}}$. The looping continues until the temperature T decayed from T_{max} to a predefined threshold T_{min}. Then a new random starting position is selected and the whole process is repeated. When an agent should send action to the server, he returns his own action from the optimal joint action found so far.

Basically, what the SA does is to seek the global maximum of the global joint payoff function. As a stochastic algorithm, although SA can not guarantee the convergence to optimal joint action, in a rather short time it can find an approximately optimal solution. It has the following attractive features. First, SA is an anytime algorithm that can report an answer at any time. Secondly, in each independent try, agent i only has to iterate his own actions instead of all combinatorial actions of his neighbors, thus makes the algorithm tractable.

Algorithm 1. Pseudo-code of the simulated annealing algorithm

Define: $G = \{G_1, G_2, \ldots, G_n\}$ the agents who want to coordinate their actions
Define: $v(a)$ the global joint payoff function
Define: a^* the optimal joint action so far
Define: a_i the action of agent i
Define: a_i^* the optimal action of agent i found so far
Define: a_{-i} the actions of all agents but agent i

```
g←0
t←0
While t<MaxTries do
 a = random joint action
 T← Tmax
  repeat
  for each agent i in G do
        a′=argmax_ai (a-i∪ai)
        △←v(a′)-v(a)
        if (△>0) then
        a←a′
        else
        a←a′ with probability 1/(1+e^(-(Δ/T)))
        end if
        if v(a)>v(a*) then
        a*←a
        g←v(a*)
```

```
        choose a_i* from a*
        end if
        if should send action to server then
        send a_i* to server
        end if
  end for
  T←T.decay
 until T<T_min
 t←t+1
end while
```

5. Experiments

In this section, the simulated annealing algorithm is evaluated by comparing it with other algorithms, especially with variable elimination algorithm. The following subsections include three parts. The first subsection describes the test bed of experiment since there is no standard benchmark to use. The remaining two subsections give the details of the experiment. It runs in two stages. In the first stage, the number of agents and the number of different actions per agent are fixed to test the scalability of the two algorithms when the number of neighbors per agent grows. In the second stage, the relative payoff SA returned and the optimal payoff produced by VE is compared to evaluate SA algorithm's performance.

5.1 Test bed setting

Since there is no standard benchmark to evaluate multiagent decision algorithm, a *random generator* (RG) is used to generate all test sets. The inputs of RG include the number of agents $|\boldsymbol{G}|$, the number of different actions per agent $|A|$, maximum number of neighbors per agent nr_s, and the number of payoff functions each agent has nr_ρ. It is believed that these aspects should be sufficient to describe the difficulty of the coordination problem. The output of RG is a set of payoff functions. Each function is a value rule $<\rho : \upsilon>$, which is first used by literature (Guestrin & Venkataraman , 2002) and proved suitable for many real-world applications. The global joint payoff function is thus represented by the sum of value rules of all agents. A sample output of RG with $|G| = 4$, $|A| = 4$, $nr_s = 3$, $nr_\rho = 1$ is shown in table 1.

$<\rho : \upsilon>$
$< a_1 = 3 \wedge a_3 = 3 \wedge a_4 = 4 : 7.19085 >$
$< a_2 = 4 \wedge a_3 = 4 : 4.67774 >$
$< a_1 = 1 \wedge a_2 = 1 \wedge a_3 = 2 \wedge a_4 = 2 : 4.67774 >$
$< a_1 = 4 \wedge a_3 = 2 \wedge a_4 = 1 : 4.67774 >$

Table 1. Sample output of RG

Here the integer value of a_i is an action index and is mapped to a predefined action in real MAS such as dribbling, pass .etc. in a real RoboCup. The details will not be addressed here for the focus is concentrated on the performance of multiagent decision. The following two subsections give how to evaluate the performance of SA algorithms in details. All the programs are implemented in C++, and the results are generated on a 2.2GHz/512MB IBM notebook computer.

5.2 Scalability of SA algorithm

In this stage, 120 coordination problems are generated and each one is assigned with 4 test sets based on different actions per agent. The aim of this experiment is to evaluate the scalability of SA algorithm. For the problem in each test set, the settings are as follows. The number of the agents is set to $|G| = 15$. Each agent has $nr_{\rho} = 8$ value rules with different number of neighbors. The payoff in each value rule is generated from a uniform random variable U [1, 10]. The number of neighbors k in each value rule is in the range $k \in [1, nr_s]$. Each value has a chance of $\binom{Nr_{ne}}{k} / 2^{Nr_{ne}}$.

When applying VE, the algorithm is speed up by eliminating the agent with the minimum number of neighbors. When running SA, *MaxTries* is set to 20, the highest temperature T_{max} is 0.3, and lowest temperature T_{min} is 0.05. The temperature *decay* of this algorithm is in proportion to nr_s. Therefore, if certain value rule contains a large number of agents, the SA algorithm will search deeply in an independent try, vice versa. To weaken the side effect of hardware and operating system the experiment is repeated 10 times and the average is adopted as the measure. Fig. 2(a)–2(d) gives a clear picture of the timing results for the four

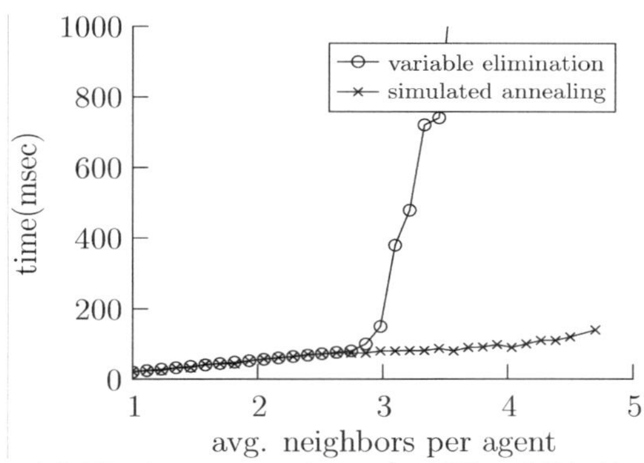

(a) Timing comparisons for VE and SA (4 actions per agent).

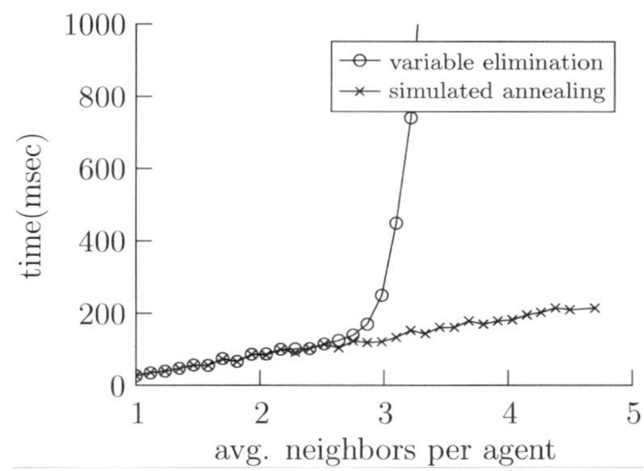

(b) Timing comparisons for VE and SA (6 actions per agent).

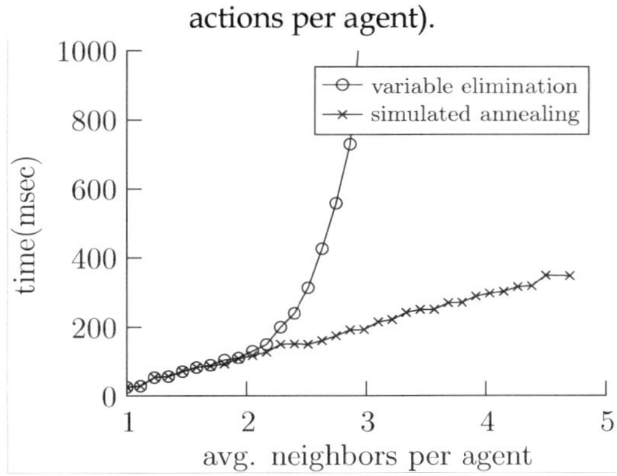

(c) Timing comparisons for VE and SA (8 actions per agent).

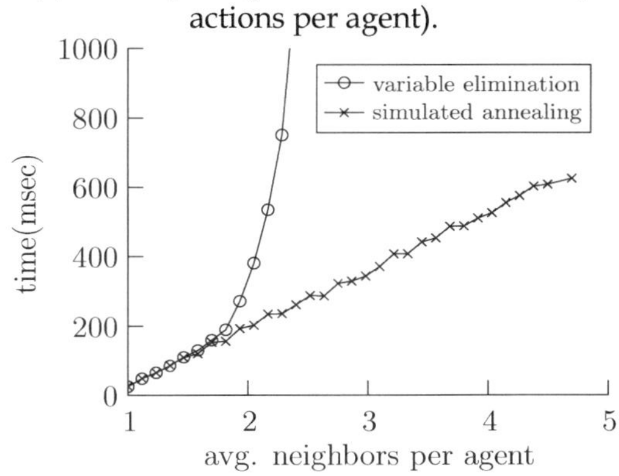

(d) Timing comparisons for VE and SA (4 actions per agent).

Fig.2. Time consumed comparisons for both VE and SA

test sets. It can be easily seen that the running time of SA algorithm grows linearly as the number of the neighbors per agent increases. In contrast, the time of VE algorithm grows exponentially, since it must enumerate all neighbors' possible combination actions in each iteration.

Furthermore, when the average number of neighbors per agent is more than 3.5, VE can not always compute the optimal joint action so these tests are removed from the test sets. In sum, the SA algorithm outperforms the VE algorithm with respect to scalability and this is especially meaningful in multiagent decision scenario.

5.3 Relative payoff comparison

In the second stage, 6 coordination problems are generated. Each problem has its own settings such as number of agents, number of neighbors per agent .etc.. VE and SA are both employed to solve them. When SA is applied, instead of starting with a random choice for all agents, in i^{th} independent try, the agent selects action according to the ith highest value rule if he is involved; otherwise the action is selected randomly. The *MaxTries* is set to 200, so that SA has enough time to run. Other settings are the same as the first stage.

To give a clear comparison of VE and SA, the payoff axis is scaled so that the global maximum payoff is 1. The time axis is also scaled so that the whole time taken by VE to terminate is 1. Thus the points in the figure can be seen as the fraction of the payoff and the running time of VE. The results of SA will be scaled to its VE companion. The experiment is also repeated 10 times to weaken hardware and software's side effect.

The relative payoff found by the SA with respect to VE is plotted in Fig. 3(a)–3(f). It can be seen SA performed very well. It is obvious that the near optimal result is found in all tests. In loosely connected coordination problem with few actions, i.e., Fig. 3(a), SA converges to the maximum payoff with only the 60% time that VE takes. However, if the number of actions is big as Fig. 3(b), SA can not reach the optimal result although it can find near optimal solution (96% payoff) quickly. Further experiments show that if the joint action space is huge (more than 15 agents, and each agent has more than 10 actions) the acceptable probability should be increased to speed up the convergence to optimal result. This is because in such situations, a little higher acceptable probability can increase the chance of stochastic movement of SA. This technique help SA jump away from local optimizations and cover the joint action space as possible as it can. But the exact relationship between acceptable probability and the convergence speed is still not very clear. For the medium connected problems (Fig. 3(c)–3(d)), SA can compute the optimal policy with a little fraction of time (2%–6%) that variable elimination needs to solve the same problem. Fig. 3(e) and Fig. 2(f) give us a strong impression that SA can compute more than 98% payoff within the time ranges between 0.015% to 0.2% of the time VE takes in the densely connected problems. Other unpublished tests are also carried out. For example, SA is compared with max-plus algorithm informally. The experiment shows that when reaching the same relative payoff, the time difference between the two algorithms is at most 5%. Although SA algorithm is not much faster than max-plus, it is still believed that SA approach is more appropriate for complex coordination problems, since in these problems the coordination dependencies in the value rule is often more than two, therefore max-plus can not be applied directly.

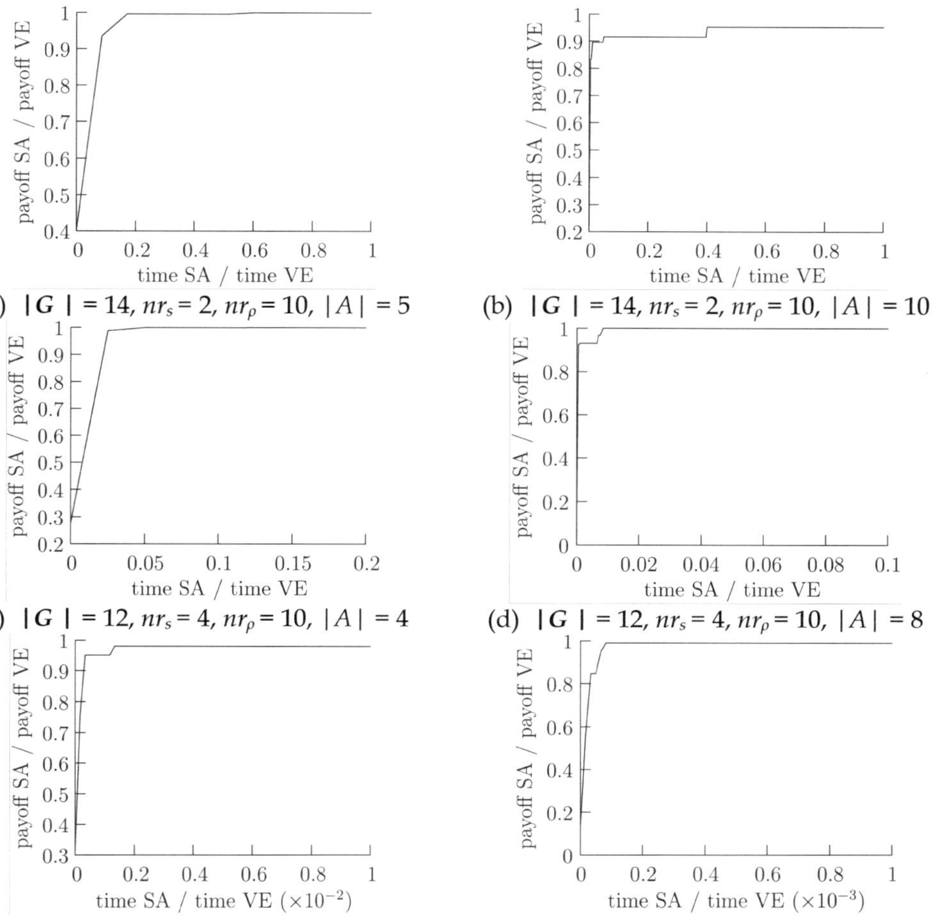

(a) $|G| = 14, nr_s = 2, nr_p = 10, |A| = 5$

(b) $|G| = 14, nr_s = 2, nr_p = 10, |A| = 10$

(c) $|G| = 12, nr_s = 4, nr_p = 10, |A| = 4$

(d) $|G| = 12, nr_s = 4, nr_p = 10, |A| = 8$

(e) $|G| = 10, nr_s = 8, nr_p = 10, |A| = 4$

(f) $|G| = 10, nr_s = 8, nr_p = 10, |A| = 8$

Fig. 3. Relative payoff found by SA with respect to VE.

6. Conclusion

In this chapter, SA algorithm is employed to solve real time multiagent decision making problem. Compared with exact method this chapter's empirical evidences show that (1) this method is almost optimal with a small fraction of the time that VE takes to compute the policy of the same coordination problem; (2) the running time of SA grows linearly with the increasing number of neighbors per agent;(3) it is an anytime algorithm which return result at any time. For above reasons, it is believed that SA is a feasible approach for action selection in large complex cooperative autonomous systems.

As future research, an appropriate setting of the acceptable probability will be figured out, especially the decay rate in SA. Some recent work shows that neural network algorithm can produce a good decay rate for larger problems. Such techniques may be employed to solve multiagent decision making problem. Furthermore, whether reinforcement learning algorithms can be applied to automatically learn the payoff in each value rule is to be investigated

7. References

Arnborg,S.; Corneil,D.G. & Proskurowski,A. (1987). Complexity of finding embeddings in a K-tree. *SIAM Journal on Algebraic Discrete Methods*, vol.8, no.2, (1987) page number (277-284), ISSN: 0196-5212

Boutilier,C.(1996). Planning, learning and coordination in multiagent decision processes, *Proceedings of the 6th conference on theoretical aspects of rationality and knowledge*,pp.195-210,ISBN:1-55860-417-9,the Netherlands,1996, Morgan Kaufmann publisher Inc., San Francisco,CA, USA

Carrier,N.; Gelernter,D.(1989). Linda in context. *Communications of the ACM*, vol.32, no.4,(1989)page number(444-458),ISSN: 0001-0782

Dechter,R.(1999). Bucket elimination: a unifying framework for reasoning. *Artificial Intelligence*, vol.113,No.(1-2),(1999)page number(41-85),ISSN: 0004-3702

Guestrin, C. ,Venkataraman (2002). Context specific multiagent coordination and planning with factored MDPs, *Proceedings of the eighteenth national conference on artificial*, pp.253-259,ISBN: 0-262-51129-0, Edmonton Canada, July 2002, American Association for Artificial Intelligence, Menlo Park, CA, USA

Guestrin,C. (2003).Planning Under Uncertainty in Complex Structured Environments .PhD thesis ,Stanford University

Jiang,D.W;Wang,S.Y.(2007). Using the simulated annealing algorithm for multiagent decision making, proceedings of the 10th annual RoboCup international symposium,pp.109-120,ISBN: 978-3-540-74023-0, Bremen Germany, June 2006,Springer, Berlin Heidelberg Germany

Kok,J.R.; Vlassis,N.(2005).Using the max-plus algorithm for multiagent decision making in coordination graphs, *Proceedings of RoboCup 2005*, pp.1-12,ISBN: 978-3-540-35437-6,Osaka, Japan, 2005, Springer Berlin, Heidelberg

Osborne,M.J.;Rubinstein,A.(1999). *A course in game theory*, MIT Press, ISBN: 978-0262650403, Cambridge of USA

S.Kirkpatrick, C.D.Gelatt, Jr., M.P.Vecchi (1983). Optimization by Simulated Annealing. *Science*, vol.4598,no.220, (May 1983)page number(671-681),ISSN: 220.4598.671

Tan,M.(1997). Multi-agent reinforcement learning: independent vs. cooperative learning. *Proceedings of Readings in agents*,pp.487-494,ISBN:1-55860-495-2,Morgan Kaufmann Inc., San Francisco, USA

5

Learning FCM with Simulated Annealing

M.Ghazanfari and S. Alizadeh
Industrial Engineering Department, Iran University of Science and Technology (IUST) Narmak, Tehran, Iran

1. Introduction

In decision making process, there are some critical components. In most of the time, numbers of these critical components are numerous and they affect each other, so analyzing them is not easy. The efficiency of decision-making depends largely on the ability of decision-makers to analyze the complex cause and effect relationships and take productive actions based on the analysis. In complex systems, different components affect each other, and these cause and effect relations show system behavior. Cause and effect are two different concepts. Causes tell the reason why something happened, whereas effects are the results of that happening. In most of the systems, managers draw a system conceptualization graph to understand all of the system aspect. This diagram shows the cause and effect relations between system components. The information about these relations generated and enriched over time with the experience of managers who are expert in that field. There are two big challenges, at first, if there is no expert to construct the above mental model how this must be drawn and secondly, if there is a way to construct that diagram with more components, how they could be analyzed. Therefore, a new mechanism must be used to bridge these two gaps and constituted with experts in first case and cluster the components into similar categories based on their behaviors for the second one. This article organized as follows: This paper is organized as follows: section 2 states some basic concepts and definitions of Fuzzy Cognitive Map (FCM) and history of FCM Automatic construction. The proposed learning model is presented in section 3. While, section 4 presents the experimental evaluation and discussion of the achieved results and model effectiveness. Finally, Section 5 covers conclusions and future research directions.

2. Theoretical background

2.1 Fuzzy cognitive map

Cognitive Maps contain components and their corresponding relations, which may be positive, negative, or neutral. A cognitive Map is a directed graph that its nodes correspond to relevant concepts and the edges state the relation between these two nodes by a sign. A positive sign implies a positive relation; moreover, any increase in its source value leads to increase in its target value. A negative sign presents negative relation and any increase or decrease in its source value leads to reverse effect to its target value. In a cognitive map if there is no edge between two nodes it means that, there is no relation between them.

Cognitive Maps were initially introduced by Robert Axelrod in 1976 and applied in political science [1]. Also it was used in numerous areas of application such as analysis of electrical circuits [2], medicine [3], supervisory systems [4, 5, 6], organization and strategy planning [7], [8], analysis of business performance indicators [9], software project management [10,11], Information retrievals[12], modeling of plant control [13], system dynamics and complex systems [14, 15, 16, 17, 18, 19, 20, 21] and modeling virtual world [22], etc.
In 1988, Kosko introduced a new extension concept for Cognitive Map and named it fuzzy cognitive maps (FCM) [23, 24, 25, 26]. In a FCM, the relation between two nodes is determined by taking a value in interval [-1, 1]. While -1 corresponds to the strongest negative, +1 corresponds to strongest positive one. The other values express different levels of influence. This model can be presented by a square matrix called *connection matrix*. The value of relation between two nodes is set in their corresponding cell. In the connection matrix, row and column are associated with a source node and a target node, respectively.
An FCM consists of nodes, Ci, $i = 1 \ldots N$, where N is the total number of concepts Each arc between two nodes Ci and Cj , has a weight Fij , which is the strength of the causal link between Ci and Cj . The sign of Fij indicates whether the relation between two concepts is direct or inverse. The direction of causality indicates whether the concept Ci causes the concept Cj or vice versa. Thus, there are three types of weights:
$Fij > 0$ express positive causality,
$Fij < 0$ express negative causality,
$Fij = 0$ express no relation,
A simple FCM with five nodes and ten weighted arcs is depicted in Fig.1.

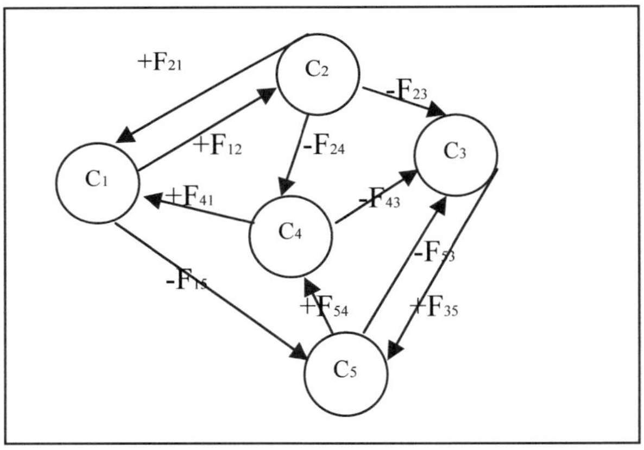

Fig. 1. A simple Fuzzy Cognitive Map (FCM)

Experts develop a FCM or a mental model manually based on their knowledge in the area under study. At first, they identify key domain issues or concepts. Secondly, they identify the causal relationships among these concepts and thirdly, they estimate causal relationships strengths. The achieved graph (FCM) shows not only the components and their relations but also the strengths.
A group of experts can be utilized to improve the results. All experts are asked to determine the relevant factors in a brain storm meeting. They discuss about main characteristics of the system, for example, number and kinds of concepts and relation between nodes, which are in the FCM. Then, they determine the structure and the interconnections of the network

using fuzzy conditional statements or fuzzy rules. Each expert may draw his own individual FCM, which can be different from the others. In order to deal with these diagrams, the assigned weights by each expert can be considered and a new FCM will be constructed by all experts. Thus, this constructed FCM will represent the knowledge and experience of all related experts. [27], [28]

FCMs can be produced by expert manually or generated by other source of information computationally. They named manual FCMs and automated FCMs.

In Fuzzy Cognitive Maps like Cognitive Map, the influence of a concept on the others is considered as "negative", "positive" or "neutral", but all relations are expressed in fuzzy terms, e.g. very weak, weak, medium, strong and very strong. The following set of linguistic variables is also considered:

{negatively very strong, negatively strong, negatively medium, negatively weak, zero, positively weak, medium, positively strong and positively very strong}.

The corresponding membership functions for these terms are shown in Fig. 2:

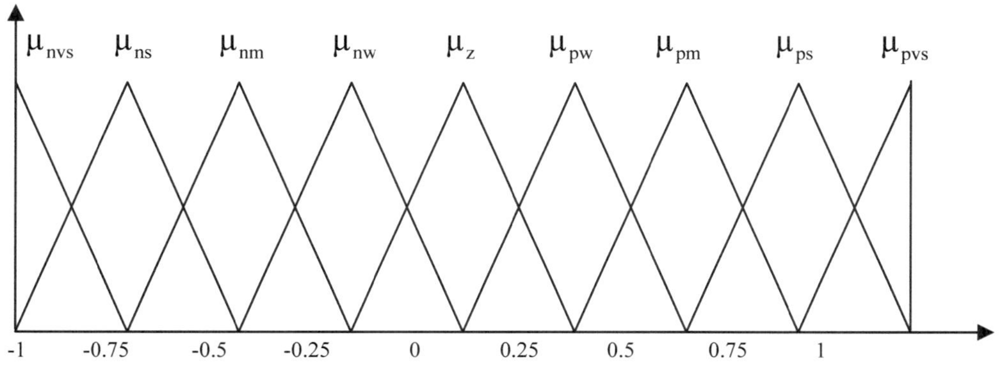

Fig. 2. Membership functions

In a FCM, all fuzzy variables are mapped into interval [-1, 1]. A simple way is to map fuzzy expression to numerical value in a range of [-1, 1]. For example, positively weak is mapped to 0.25, negatively medium to -0.5, positively strong to 0.75. [29] Then, all the suggested linguistic variables, are considered and an overall linguistic weight is obtained, with the defuzzification method of Centre of Gravity (COG) [30], is transformed to a numerical weight belonging to the interval [-1, 1].

In general, the manual procedures for developing FCM have occurred, when at least there is one expert who has expertise in the area under study. In some situations, a FCM could not be constructed manually such as:

- There is no expert to define a FCM.
- The experts' knowledge is different with each other and they draw different FCM.
- There are large amount of concepts and connections between them, which could not be drawn without mistakes.

The above situation shows that in many cases, to develop a FCM manually becomes very difficult and experts' intervention could not resolve the problem. Therefore, a systematic way should be found in order to bridge this gap. For example designing a new method could eliminate the existing weakness. The related knowledge can be extracted by analyzing past information about the given systems.

2.2 Automated FCM constructin (related works)

When the experts are not able to express their expertise or even there is no expert in the area under studied to add some expression based on her/his expertise, therefore a new way should be defined. For these reasons, the development of computational methods for learning FCM is necessary [31]. In this method, not only casual relations between nodes, but also the strength on each edge must be achieved based on historical data. The required knowledge is extracted from historical data by means and new computational procedures. Many methods for learning FCM model structure have been recently proposed. In general, these methods are categorized in two min groups:

- Hebbian algorithm
- Genetic algorithm

Soft computing approach such as neural networks and genetic algorithm can be used to discover appropriate knowledge from historical data in the form of a graph or a FCM. Many researches worked on these areas by investigating FCM learning methods using historical data.

Kosko proposed a new model by use of simple Differential Hebbian Learning law (DHL) in 1994, but he used this model to learning FCMs without any applications [32]. This learning process modified weights of edges existing in a FCM in order to find the desired connection matrix. In general, when the corresponding concept changes, the value of the related edges for that nodes will be modified too.

In 2002, Vazquez introduced a new extension to DHL algorithm presented by Kosko. He used a new idea to update edge values in a new formula [33]. Another method of learning FCMs based on the first approach (Hebbian algorithm), was introduced in 2003 by Papageorgiou et al. He developed another extension to Hebbian algorithm, called Nonlinear Hebbian Learning (NHL) [34]. Active Hebbian Algorithm (AHL) introduced by Papageorgiu et al. in 2004. In the recent method, experts not only determined the desired set of concepts, initial structure and the interconnections of the FCM structure, but also identified the sequence of activation concepts [35].

Another category in learning connection matrix of FCM is application of genetic algorithms or evolutionary algorithms. Koulouriotis et al. applied the Genetic Strategy (GS) to learn FCM's structure In 2001 [36]. In mentioned model, they focused on the development of an ES-based procedure that determines the values of the cause-effect relationships (causality). Parsopoulos et al also published other related papers in 2003. They tried to apply Particle Swarm Optimization (PSO) method, which belongs to the class of Swarm Intelligence algorithms, to learn FCM structure [37, 38]. Khan and Chong worked on learning initial state vector of FCM in 2003. They performed a goal-oriented analysis of FCM and their learning method did not aim to compute the connection matrix, and their model focused on finding initial state vector for FCM [39]. In 2005, Stach et al. applied real-coded genetic algorithm (RCGA) to develop FCM model from a set of historical data in 2005 [28].

Other work to train a FCM was done by Konar in 2005. He worked on reasoning and unsupervised learning in a FCM. In this paper, a new model was introduced for unsupervised learning and reasoning on a special type of cognitive maps realized with Petri nets [40]. In 2006, Parsopoulos et al combined these two categories and published a paper about using evolutionary algorithms to train Fuzzy Cognitive Maps. In their model, they investigated a coupling of differential evolution algorithm and unsupervised Hebbian learning algorithm [29]. Our model based on Simulated Annealing and genetic algorithm is a new method to learn connection matrix rapidly. Table 1 shows a comparison between some existing methods. The table compares the methods based on several factors, such as learning goal, kind of input historical data, type of transformation function, size of FCM model, type of learning strategy and whether experts are involved in model or not. In this table *Single* historical data consisting of one sequence of state vectors and *multiple* historical data consisting of several sequences of state vectors, for different initial conditions. When initial human intervention is equal "Yes&No" it means that human interaction is necessary but later when applying the algorithm there is no human intervention needed.

This study aims to provide a learning method, which avoids disadvantages of the existing methods. It uses Simulated Annealing to develop FCM connection matrix based on data consisting of one sequence of state vectors. In contrast, the approach introduced in [36], requires a set of such sequences. The proposed method is fully automatic, i.e. in contrast to NHL and AHL methods it does not require input from a domain expert. This algorithm learns the connection matrix for a FCM that uses continuous transformation function, which is a more general problem that the one considered in [33]. The quality of RCGA algorithm [28] deteriorates with the increasing size of the maps. In general, the RCGA method achieved maps up to 6 nodes while; our algorithm is satisfied for learning FCM with nodes more than 6 with excellent quality. In next section, it shows that this algorithm is better than RCGA algorithm which proposed by Stach in learning FCM.

Algorithm	learning goal	Human Intervention	type of data used	transformation Function	NO of node	learning algorithm
DHL	Connection matrix	No	Single	N/A	N/A	Hebbian
BDA	Connection matrix	No	Single	Binary	5 7 9	Modified Hebbian
NHL	Connection matrix	Yes&No	Single	Continuous	5	Modified Hebbian
AHL	Connection matrix	Yes&No	Single	Continuous	8	Modified Hebbian
GS	Connection matrix	No	Multiple	Continuous	7	Genetic
PSO	Connection matrix	No	Multiple	Continuous	5	Swarm
GA	Initial vector	N/A	N/A	Continuous	11	Genetic
RCGA	Connection matrix	No	Single	Continuous	4,6,8,10	Genetic
SA (This paper)	Connection matrix	No	Single	Continuous	Any Number	SA

Table 1. Overview of some learning approaches applied to FCMs

3. The proposed learning method by SA

This new method proposed a solution for automatic construction of Fuzzy Cognitive Map by using Simulated Annealing. The focus of this model is to determine cause-effect relationships (causality) and their strength.

3.1 Problem definition

As mentioned before, a cause-effect relation is specified by a related Connection matrix. The elements of this matrix are the values of edges in the FCM. The aim of the proposed method is to find these elements. The relations between nodes and edges are calculated as:

$$C_i(t+1) = f\left(\sum_{i=1}^{n} e_{ji} C_j(t)\right)$$

where e_{ij}'s are the elements of the matrix and f is a transform function which includes recurring relation on t >=0 between C(t + 1) and C(t) that can be presented by a logistic function like:

$$f(x) = \frac{1}{1+e^{-cx}}$$

Eq. (1) and Eq. (2) can be expressed by Eq.(3):

$$Output_i(t_{n+1}) = E \times Input_i(t_n)$$

$Input_i(t_n)$ is input data for node i, $Output_i(t_{n+1})$ is its corresponding output data and E is the Connection matrix of FCM. Eq. (3) implies that for each node i its corresponding output can be calculated. E (Related connection Matrix) is a vital factor in Eq. (3) which should be determined in the FCM learning process. The proposed FCM learning methods forms structure of a FCM and is able to generate state vector sequences that transform the input vectors into the output vectors. When all real input and output values of a FCM are in hand, the most important step is to find a new solution for the FCM and calculate the estimated output related to this new FCM.

$$Output_i^{estimated}(t_{n+1}) = E^{proposed} \times Input_i(t_n)$$

According to Eq. (4), $Output_i^{estimated}(t_{n+1})$ is the estimated output and $Input_i(t_n)$ is its corresponding input for the ith node. $E^{proposed}$ is the new proposed matrix. The real output is $Output_i^{real}(t_{n+1})$ and the difference between real and estimated outputs is calculated by:

$$Error = Output_i^{estimated}(t_{n+1}) - Output_i^{real}(t_{n+1})$$

By using the later two equations, the objective is defined as minimizing the difference between real and estimated outputs. This objective is defined for all nodes as:

$$Total\_Error = \sum_{n=1}^{K}\sum_{i=1}^{N} Output_i^{estimated}(t_{n+1}) - Output_i^{real}(t_{n+1})$$

Where N is the number of nodes and K is the iteration.

$$Input_i(t_n) \rightarrow Output_i(t_{n+1}) \qquad \forall\ t = 0, \ldots, K-1$$

If $Input_i(t_n)$ defined as an *initial vector*, and $Output_i(t_{n+1})$ as *system response*, *K-1* pairs in the form of {*initial vector, system response*} can be generated from the input data.
As mentioned in section 3, there are many methods for automatic constructing FCM matrix, for example, Stach et al. constructed this matrix by a Real Code Genetic Algorithm (RCGA) with simple operators. In this paper, we concentrate on simulated annealing as a heuristic model in learning FCM. Fig.3 shows the outline of the proposed method:

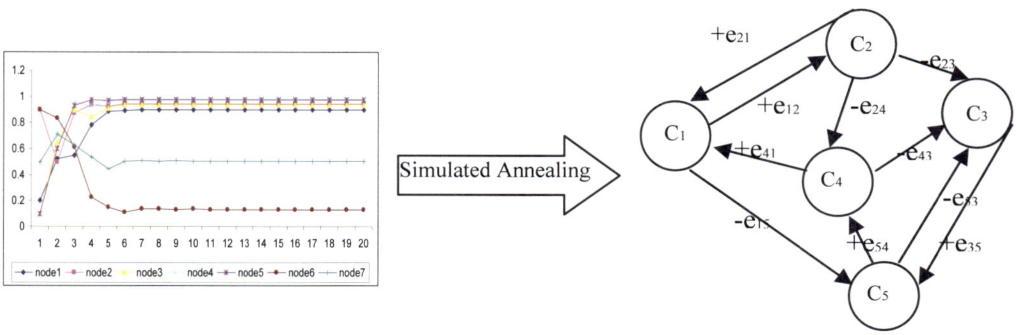

Fig. 3. the diagram of new model

The proposed learning model uses simulated annealing is used to escape the local minimum solution and to improve the optimum solution. The following sections provide details about simulated annealing and compare it with GA. It assumed that readers are familiar with GA and SA. A useful summary about relevant GA and SA can be found in [41, 42, 43]. Also, it is tried to demonstrate all essential elements of propose method, including structure of solution coding (chromosomes), generation of initial solution, initial temperature, fitness function, stopping condition, genetic operators in GA, Neighboring solutions in SA, and selection strategy.

3.2 A proposed SA method for learning FCM

In this section, SA algorithm for learning FCM is introduced. Simulated annealing is an algorithm for discrete optimization backs to the early 1980s. It was originally developed as a simulation model for a physical annealing process and hence it is referred to as simulated annealing. In simulated annealing, a problem starts at an initial solution, and a series of moves (i.e., changing the values of decision variables) are made according to a user-define annealing schedule. It terminates, when either the optimal solution is attained or the problem becomes frozen at a local optimum that cannot be improved. To avoid freezing at a local optimum, the algorithm moves slowly (with respect to the objective value) through the solution space. This controlled improvement of the objective value is accomplished by accepting non-improving moves with a certain probability that decrease as the algorithm progresses. Important parts of the simulated annealing algorithm for learning FCM are explained as follows:

SA algorithm

* Initialization: Select an initial solution x_1 in X

Initialize the best value F^{best} of F and the corresponding solution x^{best} :

$F^{best} = F(x_1)$

$x^{best} = x_1$

Initialize N, T, α

Do while not stopping condition is fulfilled $T_{n+1} > \alpha$

Do (n < N) and (Not Change)

n=n+1

Consider $x^{neighbour}$ at random in the neighbourhood

If $F(x^{neighbour}) = F(x)$ then *counter=counter+1* and *change=false*

If $F(x^{neighbour}) < F(x)$ then $x \leftarrow x^{neighbour}$

If $F(x^{neighbour}) < F^{best}$ the $F^{best} \leftarrow F(x^{neighbour})$ and $x^{best} \leftarrow x^{neighbour}$

If $F(x^{neighbour}) > F(x^{best})$

Consider R= a random number in [0 , 1],

$\Delta = F(x^{neighbour}) - F^{best}$

$$\alpha = \frac{1}{1 + e^{\frac{-\Delta}{T}}}$$

If R < α Then $x \leftarrow x^{neighbour}$

End loop

$T_{n+1} = \frac{1}{1 + e^{\frac{-\Delta}{T}}} * T_n$, N=0 , Change=false

End loop

For designing the SA algorithm, many principle factors considered and introduced here:

Solution coding

The solution coding for SA is considered in Figure (4).

e11	e12	E13	E14	E15
e21	e22	E23	E24	E25
e31	e32	E33	E34	E35
e41	e42	E43	E44	E45
e51	e52	E53	E54	E55

Fig. 4. the solution code structure

Fitness function

As mentioned before, the total difference between real and estimated outputs for all nodes is defined in Eq(7). This error can be used as the core of fitness function.

$$\text{Fitness function}= \mathrm{h}\left(\alpha\left(\sum_{n=1}^{K}\sum_{i=1}^{N} Output_i^{estimated}(p_{n+1}) - Output_i^{real}(p_{n+1})\right)^2\right)$$

α is the parameter used to normalize error rate, which equal to $1/(\mathrm{K}-1).\mathrm{N}$ (K and N were explained before) *h* is an auxiliary function. The auxiliary function *h* was introduced for two main reasons:

- To ensure that better individuals correspond to greater fitness function values. Argument of this function is the summed error rate, and thus needs to be inversed.
- To embed non-linearity that aims to reward solution code, which are closer to the desired solution.

The following function *h* was proposed: $\mathrm{h(x)} = \dfrac{1}{\mathrm{ax}+1}$ where parameter *a* is established experimentally. The fitness function is normalized to the (0, 1] where It is zero for worse case or it is equal to one for an ideal chromosome, which results is exactly the same state vector sequence as the input data. The mathematical modeling of this problem is presented here: *Max Z = h(x)*

Initial solution

An initial solution is a starting solution (point) that will be used in the search process and considered as a random solution. In this research, the initial solution generates randomly.

Initial temperature and cooling schedule

An initial temperature T_0 and a cooling schedule (α) are used to control the series of moves in the SA search process. In general, the initial temperature should be high enough to allow all candidate solutions to be accepted. Cooling schedule (α) is the rate at which temperature is reduced. In this paper, a classical schedule is represented in figure (5). Starting from T0, the temperature is decreased through multiplication by a fixed factor (α) ($0<\alpha<1$).

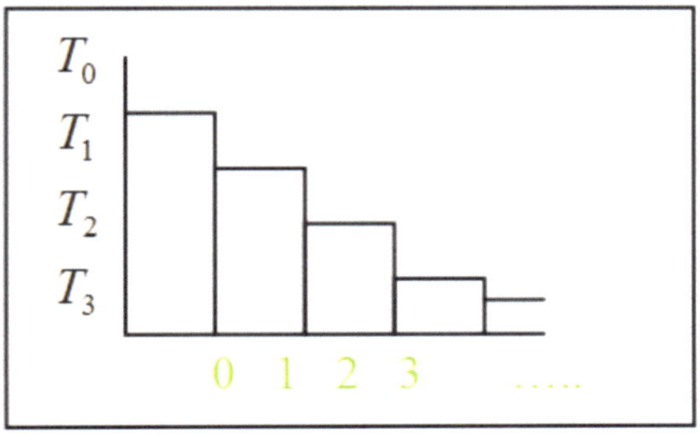

Fig. 5. temperature schedule

Neighboring solutions
Neighboring solutions are the set of feasible solutions that can be generated from the current solution. Each feasible solution can be directly reached from current solution by a move (like genetic operations mutation or inversion) and resulted neighboring solution.
Stopping criteria
Here are four criteria for stopping the algorithms (GA, SA) as follows:

- Maximum number of the established generation (G).
- Least variance of the generation (μ)
- Maximum run time for the algorithm (MRT).
- The number of temperature transitions is used as a stopping criterion. Furthermore the SA algorithm can be terminated, when the term ($T_{n+1} > \varepsilon$) or stopping condition is satisfied. ε can be a constant or calculated by other parameters.

4. Computational results

In our experiment, the problem data were used to construct FCM by using SA on a PC Pentium IV, 1.6 GHz. The meta-heuristic algorithms were developed using Visual Basic 6. Two algorithms, the genetic algorithm which used by the others and Simulated Annealing ran with mentioned data and the Error and time consuming saved. Table 2 shows the essential parameters for these algorithms. The aim of the experiments is to assess quality of the proposed method for learning FCMs. Two algorithms, the genetic algorithm, Simulated Annealing ran with different Node numbers: 2, 3, 4, 5, 6, 7, 8, 9, 10, 11, 12, 13, 14, 15 and for every run the Error and time consuming saved. Each considered FCM, in terms of the number of nodes, was simulated 100 times with the two algorithms. The obtained results are shown in table 3.

Parameter name	Value	Comments
Generation	300	The Max Number of Generation
Population	1000	The Number of population in each Generation
p_c	0.95	Probability of crossover
p_m	0.90	Probability of mutation
δ	0.1	For stopping criterion (when algorithm $T_{n+1} > \delta$ stops)
T_n	$T_{n+1} = \alpha * T_n$	Value of temperature in transition (n)
T_0	5000	The first temperature
α	$\alpha = \frac{1}{1+e^{\frac{-\Delta}{T}}}$	α denotes the temperature and cooling schedule in SA $\Delta = F(x^{neighbour}) - F^{best}$
μ	10	Least variance of the generation
MRT	0.5 hour	Maximum run time for the algorithm
a	10000	$h(x) = \frac{1}{ax+1}$ parameter a is established experimentally

Table 2. Parameters in two algorithms

NO Node	Genetic algorithm Fitness Function L2 (Error)	Genetic algorithm Time(sec)	Simulated Annealing Fitness Function L2 (Error)	Simulated Annealing Time(sec)
2	1.7998E-06	40	3.5000E-05	2.96
3	1.8308E-06	40	3.8308E-05	2.68
4	3.0140E-06	40	4.8140E-05	2.39
5	5.6714E-06	40	5.2714E-05	2.18
6	1.5381E-05	40	5.4381E-05	1.85
7	2.4262E-05	40	6.4262E-05	1.64
8	3.1149E-05	40	7.1432E-05	1.51
9	6.4874E-05	40	7.4320E-05	1.25
10	1.0917E-04	40	7.6345E-05	1.09
11	1.5211E-04	40	8.2345E-05	0.96
12	1.9053E-04	40	8.7432E-05	0.75
13	2.6694E-04	40	1.0060E-04	0.6
14	3.2980E-04	40	1.0604E-04	0.48
15	4.0198E-04	40	1.2029E-04	0.43

Table 3. Experiment results with different fitness functions and times

The results of these experiments show that these algorithms gradually converge into a high-quality candidate FCM. Two examples of FCM learning experiments based on GA and SA are plotted in Fig.6-1 and Fig.6-2.

Fig. 6-1. An example of SA fitness Function which show that error coverges to near zero

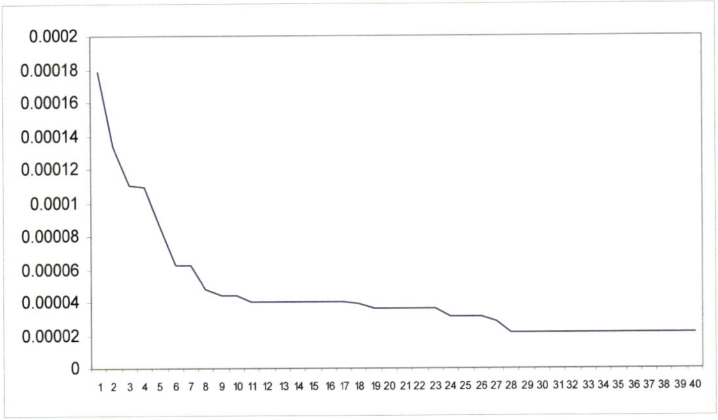

Fig. 6-2. An example of GA fitness Function which show that error coverges to near zero

Fig. 7. shows the error of GA and SA algorithms. This figure shows that SA algorithm produce better solution with less error for FCM with node number more than 10. That means SA is appropriate for learning FCM with nodes more than 10.

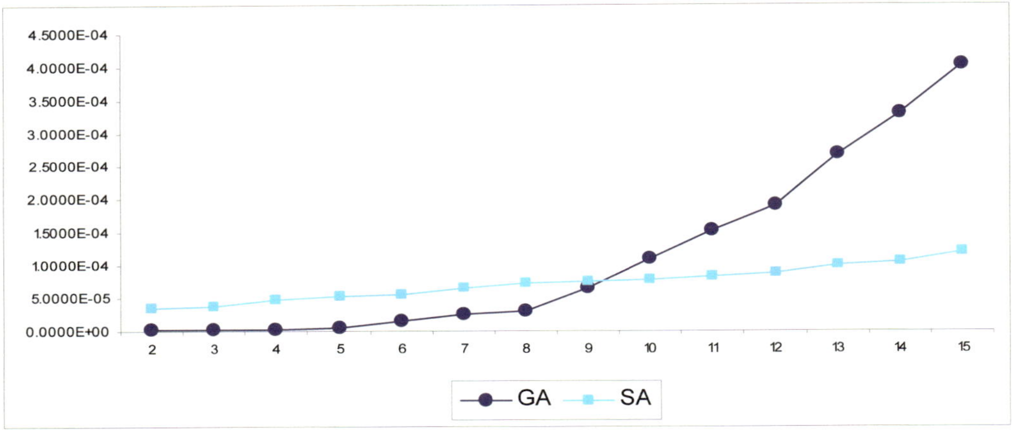

Fig. 7. GA and SA errors for different nodes

Fig. 7. compares the time consuming with GA and SA algorithms. This figure shows that simulated annealing algorithm, as a learning algorithm for FCM is faster than genetic algorithms in the same problem. Therefore, The SA algorithm found related solutions in less computational times than GA.

In these two algorithms, the error of GA in FCM with little Node is less that Simulated annealing. However, in FCM with more nodes the error of SA as a new learning algorithm is less that GA. Considering the results of Tables (3) shows that the presented metaheuristic algorithms are able to find and report the near-optimal and promising solutions in a reasonable computational time. This indicates the success of the proposed method in learning FCM. In general, we can conclude that the SA algorithm meanly found better solutions than GA in less computational times for nodes more than 10.

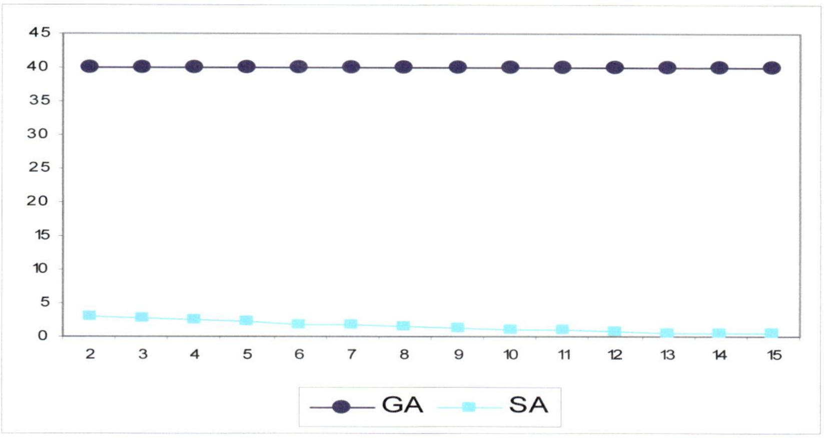

Fig. 8. Time consuming with GA and SA algorithms

5. Conclusion

In this paper, we have developed a new method for learning FCMs by SA algorithm. It has been shown that SA not only can improve the speed of learning process, but also can improve the quality of learning FCMs with nodes more than 10. The quality of learning method based on GA deteriorates with the increasing size of the maps but SA over comes this difficulty and when the size of maps increase the GA algorithms replaced with SA algorithms. According to these properties, a new method proposed. The results show this new method is very effective, and generates FCM models that can almost perfectly represent the input data. In general, the proposed method achieves excellent quality for maps in every size of FCM. The produced results could provide some guidelines for other learning methods. The future work will concern on the improvement of the proposed learning method. One of interesting and open issues is using the other heuristic methods for learning FCMs and comparing them with the others.

6. References

R.Axelrod, Structure of Decision: The Cognitive Maps of Political Elites, Princeton University Press, Princeton, NJ, 1976.

M.A. Styblinski, B.D. Meyer, Signal flow graphs versus fuzzy cognitive maps in application to qualitative circuit analysis, Internet. J. Man Mach. Studies 35 (1991) 175–186.

V.C. Georgopoulos, G.A. Malandraki, C.D. Stylios, A fuzzy cognitive map approach to differential diagnosis of specific language impairment, J. Artif. Intel. Med. 29 (3) (2003) 261–278.

C.D. Stylios, P.P. Groumpos, The challenge of modeling supervisory systems using fuzzy cognitive maps, J.Intel. Manuf. 9 (4) (1998) 339–345.

C.D. Stylios, P.P. Groumpos, Fuzzy cognitive maps: a model for intelligent supervisory control systems, Comput. Ind. 39 (3) (1999) 229–238.

C.D. Stylios, P.P. Groumpos, Fuzzy cognitive map in modeling supervisory control systems, J. Intel. & Fuzzy Systems 8 (2) (2000) 83–98.

M. G. Bougon, "Congregate Cognitive Maps: a Unified Dynamic Theory of Organization and Strategy," Journal of Management Studies, 29:369-389, (1992)

K.C. Lee,W.J. Lee, O.B. Kwon, J.H. Han, P.I.Yu, Strategic planning simulation based on fuzzy cognitive map knowledge and differential game, Simulation 71 (5) (1998) 316–327.

D. Kardaras, G. Mentzas, Using fuzzy cognitive maps to model and analyze business performance assessment, in: J. Chen, A. Mital (Eds.), Advances in Industrial Engineering Applications and Practice II, 1997, pp. 63–68.

W. Stach, L. Kurgan, Modeling software development project using fuzzy cognitive maps, Proc. 4th ASERC Workshop on Quantitative and Soft Software Engineering (QSSE'04), 2004, pp. 55–60.

W. Stach, L. Kurgan,W. Pedrycz, M. Reformat, Parallel fuzzy cognitive maps as a tool for modeling software development project, Proc. 2004 North American Fuzzy Information Processing Society Conf. (NAFIPS'04), Banff, AB, 2004, pp. 28–33.

A. R. Montazemi, D. W. Conrath, "The Use of Cognitive Mapping for Information Requirements Analysis," MIS Quarterly, 10:44-55, (1986)

K. Gotoh, J. Murakami, T.Yamaguchi, Y.Yamanaka, Application of fuzzy cognitive maps to supporting for plant control, Proc. SICE Joint Symp. 15th Systems Symp. and Tenth Knowledge Engineering Symp., 1989, pp. 99–104.

Carvalho, J.P.,Tomé, J.A.,"Rule Based Fuzzy Cognitive Maps and Fuzzy Cognitive Maps - A Comparative Study", Proceedings of the 18th International Conference of the North American Fuzzy Information Processing Society, NAFIPS99, New York

Carvalho, J.P., Tomé, J.A.,"Rule Based Fuzzy Cognitive Maps- Fuzzy Causal Relations", Computational Intelligence for Modelling, Control and Automation, Edited by M. Mohammadian, 1999

Carvalho, J.P., Tomé, J.A., "Fuzzy Mechanisms for Causal Relations", Proceedings of the Eighth International Fuzzy Systems Association World Congress, IFSA'99, Taiwan

Carvalho,J.P.,Tomé, J.A.,"Rule Based Fuzzy Cognitive Maps – Qualitative Systems Dynamics", Proceedings of the 19th International Conference of the North American Fuzzy Information Processing Society, NAFIPS2000, Atlanta

S.Alizadeh, M.Ghazanfari, M.Jafari, "An approach for solving fuzzy system dynamics problems", 21st International system dynamics conference, U.S.A, July 2003.

D.E. Koulouriotis, I.E. Diakoulakis, D.M. Emiris, E.N. Antonidakis, I.A. Kaliakatsos, Efficiently modeling and controlling complex dynamic systems using evolutionary fuzzy cognitive maps (Invited Paper), Internat. J. Comput. Cognition 1 (2) (2003) 41–65.

D.E. Koulouriotis, I.E. Diakoulakis, D.M. Emiris, C.D.Zopounidis, Development of dynamic cognitive networks as complex systems approximators: validation in financial time series, Applied Soft Computing 5 (2005) 157–179

C.D. Stylios, P.P. Groumpos, Modeling complex systems using fuzzy cognitive maps, IEEE Trans. Systems Man, Cybern. Part A: Systems Humans 34 (1) (2004).

D.E. Koulouriotis, I.E. Diakoulakis, D.M. Emiris, Anamorphosis of fuzzy cognitive maps for operation in ambiguous and multi-stimulus real world environments, 10th IEEE Internet. Conf. on Fuzzy Systems, 2001, pp. 1156–1159.

B. Kosko, Hidden patterns in combined and adaptive knowledge networks, Internet. J.Approx. Reason.2 (1988) 377–393.

B. Kosko, Fuzzy cognitive maps, Internat. J. Man-Mach. Studies 24 (1986) 65–75.

B. Kosko, Neural Networks and Fuzzy Systems, Prentice-Hall, Englewood Cliffs, NJ, 1992.

B. Kosko, Fuzzy Engineering, Prentice-Hall, Englewood Cliffs, NJ, 1997.

M. Khan, M.Quaddus, Group decision support using fuzzy cognitive maps for causal reasoning, Group Decision Negotiation J. 13 (5) (2004) 463–480.

Wojciech Stach, Lukasz Kurgan,Witold Pedrycz, Marek Reformat Genetic learning off uzzy cognitive maps, Fuzzy Sets and Systems 153 (2005) 371–401

E Papageorgiou, C.Stylios P. Groumpos, Unsupervised learning techniques for fine-tuning fuzzy cognitive map causal links, Int. J. Human-Computer Studies 64 (2006) 727–743

Lee C. C, Fuzzy logic in control systems: Fuzzy logic controller, Part 1, 2 IEEE Trans.Syst.Man Cybernet, 20 (2), 404-435.

M. Schneider, E. Shnaider, A. Kandel, G. Chew, Automatic construction of FCMs, Fuzzy Sets and Systems 93 (2) (1998) 161–172.

J.A. Dickerson, B. Kosko, Fuzzy virtual worlds, Artif.Intel. Expert 7 (1994) 25–31.

A. Vazquez, A balanced differential learning algorithm in fuzzy cognitive maps, Technical Report, Departament de Llenguatges I Sistemes Informatics, Universitat Politecnica de Catalunya (UPC), 2002.

E. Papageorgiou, C.D. Stylios, P.P. Groumpos, Fuzzy cognitive map learning based on nonlinear Hebbian rule, Australian Conf. on Artificial Intelligence, 2003, pp. 256–268.

E. Papageorgiou, C.D. Stylios, P.P. Groumpos, Active Hebbian learning algorithm to train fuzzy cognitive maps, Internat. J.Approx.Reason.37 (3) (2004) 219–249.

D.E. Koulouriotis, I.E. Diakoulakis, D.M. Emiris, Learning fuzzy cognitive maps using evolution strategies: a novel schema for modeling and simulating high-level behavior, IEEE Congr. On Evolutionary Computation (CEC2001), 2001, pp. 364–371.

E. Papageorgiou, K.E. Parsopoulos, C.D. Stylios, P.P. Groumpos, M.N. Vrahatis, Fuzzy cognitive maps learning using particle swarm optimization, J. Intel. Inform.Systems. 2005

K.E. Parsopoulos, E.I. Papageorgiou, P.P. Groumpos, M.N. Vrahatis, A first study of fuzzy cognitive maps learning using particle swarm optimization, Proc. IEEE 2003 Congr. On Evolutionary Computation, 2003, pp. 1440–1447.

M. Khan, A. Chong, Fuzzy cognitive map analysis with genetic algorithm, Proc. 1st Indian Internat. Conf. on Artificial Intelligence (IICAI-03), 2003

Amit Konar, Uday K. Chakraborty , Reasoning and unsupervised learning in a fuzzy cognitive map , Information Sciences 170 (2005) 419–441

Duc Truong Pham, Intelligent Optimisation Techniques: Genetic Algorithms, Tabu Search, Simulated Annealing and Neural Networks.

Marc Pirlot, General local search methods, European journal of operational research 92, 1996 , 493-511

van Laarhoven, and Aarts, E. (1987): Simulated Annealing: Theory and Applications. Dordrect: Reidel.

R.Tavakkoli-Moghaddam, M.B. Aryanezhad, N.Safaei, A. Azaron, Solving a dynamic cell formation problem using metaheuristics, Applied Mathematics and Computation 170 (2005) 761–780

6

Knowledge-Informed Simulated Annealing for Spatial Allocation Problems

Jiunn-Der Duh
Department of Geography, Portland State University
Portland, Oregon, USA

1. Introduction

Generating prescribed patterns in spatial allocation is a difficult and complex optimization task. Many spatial allocation problems require the arrangement of resources in ways that their patterns promote some desirable landscape functions (e.g., Taylor et al.,2007; De Clercq et al., 2007; Milder et al., 2008). The complexity of the optimization task comes from the simultaneous effects of siting multiple spatial entities that usually require complex formulae to quantify (Tomlin, 1990; Brookes, 2001). Such spatial allocation problems are combinatorial in nature, and often require the use of global optimization algorithms such as simulated annealing or genetic algorithms (Revees, 1993) to find good solutions. Furthermore, spatial allocation problems often exhibit substantial complexity, especially when analyses must consider multiple, often conflicting, objectives (Malczewski, 1999). Despite successful examples of using global optimization algorithms in solving spatial allocation problems (Brookes, 2001; Aerts & Heuvelink, 2002; Xiao et al., 2002), however, an increase in the number of spatial entities involved in allocation deteriorates the performance of the trial-and-error mechanism of meta-heuristic algorithms.

Recent efforts to solve spatial optimization have been made by developing approaches that use auxiliary rules (i.e., heuristics; e.g., Church et al., 2003; Duh & Brown, 2005; Duh & Brown, 2007). Heuristic approaches, if used appropriately, can greatly improve the performance and utility of spatial optimization algorithms in spatial allocation and interactive spatial decision-making. This chapter describes the design, implementation, and evaluation of a knowledge-informed simulated annealing (KISA) algorithm that applies heuristics in single and multi-objective spatial allocation problems. The discussion at the end of the chapter addresses the potential applications and limitations of the approaches presented.

2. Spatial allocation problems

Spatial allocation is to arrange spatial entities in a two dimensional space so that the resulting arrangement exhibits certain preferred characteristics. The spatial entities involved in spatial allocation problems have been represented either as cells in a gridded coordinate system or as two dimensional geometric objects (i.e., polygons). These representations correspond to the raster and vector data models in Geographic Information Systems (GIS), which usually are used to model geographic phenomena as continuous fields and discrete objects respectively (Longley et al., 2005). The allocation problems discussed in this chapter was to assign cells in a raster data model with different land-cover types (e.g., trees and built-up areas). Contiguous cells of the same land-cover types form landscape *patches*. Mathematic formulae quantifying the patterns of landscape patches were used as objective functions of the spatial allocation problems. The approach introduced here can be implemented in vector-based data model with modifications.

There are various ways of quantifying patterns. Some examples are wavelet analysis (De Bonet & Viola, 1997), semivariance (Deutsch & Journel, 1992), Markov random field (Cross & Jain, 1983; German & German, 1984), and lacunarity (Dale, 2000; McIntyre & Wien, 2000). Recent development in landscape ecology provides a systematic way of understanding and quantifying landscape patterns in order to relate them to ecological or socioeconomic processes (e.g., Vos et al., 2001; Schmid-Holmes & Drickamer, 2001; McAlpine & Eyre, 2002; and Liu et al., 2003). The quantitative indices, also called landscape pattern metrics, provide ways of characterizing the composition or configuration, or both, of landscape patches on categorical maps (McGarigal & Marks, 1995). Because of the ecological implications of landscape pattern metrics, they could be used as the objective functions in spatial allocation problems that are intended to achieve ecological goals. I used a pattern metric that measures patch fragmentation as the pattern objective function of the optimization problem. The metric, PFF, developed by Riitters et al. (2000), is defined as the average proportion of cells among the eight neighboring cells of any cell of the same type (Equation 1).

$$\mathrm{PFF} = \frac{\sum_{i=1}^{N}\left[w_i \times \sum_{j=1}^{8} d_{ij} \right] / 8}{\sum_{i=1}^{N} w_i} \tag{1}$$

where d_{ij}, a neighborhood dummy variable, equals 1 when cell i and its neighbor j are of the same cover types, otherwise 0, w_i equals 1 when cell i is of the cover type currently measured, otherwise 0, and N is the number of pixels present in the landscape. PFF equals 0 when all pixels of a cover type, if there are any, are isolated, and 1 when the landscape is completely covered by a seamless cover of that cover type. Examples of landscapes with different PFF values are shown in Fig. 1.

Fig. 1. Example 18 by 18 landscape maps with 50% patch cells (dark color)

The single objective spatial allocation is formulated in a two dimensional space that is composed of N cells, of which K cells ($K < N$) are foreground whose pattern is to be measured and $N - K$ cells are background. The goal of the spatial allocation is to find the least fragmented landscape formed by a given number of patch cells. The problem is structured as follows:

$$\text{Maximize} \qquad \mathrm{PFF} \tag{2}$$

Subject to $$\sum_{i=1}^{N} w_i = K \tag{3}$$

In the multi-objective spatial allocation problem, in addition to the PFF pattern metric, a cost surfaces (C) was used to define a second objective function. The objective function was evaluated by summing the cell values on the cost surface if the location was occupied by foreground cells. The two-objective optimization problem is expressed as follows:

Maximize $$\text{PFF} \tag{4}$$

Minimize $$\sum_{i=1}^{N} c_i \times w_i \tag{5}$$

Subject to $$\sum_{i=1}^{N} w_i = K \tag{6}$$

where c_i is the cost value at cell location i, w_i equals 1 when cell i is a foreground cell. When multiple objectives are specified in an optimization problem, finding one best solution that optimizes all objectives is often impossible, especially when the objectives to be achieved conflict with each other. Earlier generations of optimization algorithms dealt with multi-objective problems using a technique called scalarization, which collapses the multiple objectives to form a single objective (Sawaragi, Nakayama, et al., 1985; Eastman, Jin, et al., 1995). Such an approach involves the conversion of multiple objectives into commensurate criteria, which usually requires direct consultation with decision makers in finding the final solutions. This technique has several significant weaknesses: 1) it can only be applied to problems that are mathematically formulated; 2) it is inefficient when applied to large problems; and 3) it may fail to find important solutions (Miettinen, 1999). With the improvement of computers and algorithms, CPU-intensive approaches have been developed to find multiple compromise solutions (i.e., Pareto optimal solutions) that represent the trade-offs between conflicting objectives.

3. Knowledge-informed simulated annealing

3.1 Knowledge-informed algorithms

The term *knowledge-informed* optimization (Duh & Brown, 2005) is referred to as the algorithm that uses auxiliary knowledge (i.e., heuristics) of the nature and structure of spatial configuration to control the local search process in a global optimization algorithm. The main purpose of using auxiliary knowledge in a local-search algorithm is twofold: the auxiliary knowledge can reduce the search space, preventing unproductive search, or it can alter the structure of the solution space, making it easier to navigate to areas in the solution space where global optima are located. Empirical evidence indicates that optimization problems can thus be solved faster and easier (Pressey, Ferrier, et al., 1995; Sorensen & Church, 1996; Glover & Laguna, 1997). However, excessive use of inappropriate knowledge can generate significant errors in solving location problems and, very often, can result in sub-optimal solutions with different initial conditions (Church & Sorensen, 1996).

A simple but effective way to generate neighboring solutions in the local search process used in simulated annealing is by swapping cells randomly selected from the current best-solution. Knowledge-informed simulated annealing (KISA) uses some rules, instead of complete random selections, to guide the generation of neighboring selections. The *compactness rule* (Duh & Brown, 2005) was used here to solve the spatial allocation problem whose goal was to find the least fragmented landscape. The KISA compactness rule preferentially move a randomly selected patch (i.e., foreground) cell to a location that promotes patch compactness, i.e., one with a high number of neighboring patch cells. PFF increases greatly when a patch cell is placed on a location where most neighbors are of the same cover type. Such an allocation not only increases the individual PFF for the patch cells being moved but also increases the individual PFF of the neighboring cells.

3.2 Multi-objective optimization

In recent decades, many techniques have been developed to address the needs of multi-objective decision-making. The most popular is the method of generating the efficient frontier, also known as the Pareto front. A Pareto front is formed by solutions whose performance on one objective cannot be improved without sacrificing performance on at least one other, a condition known as Pareto optimality (Pareto, 1971). A common way to determine Pareto optimality is using the concept of Pareto dominance. A Pareto optimal solution is referred to as a non-dominated solution.

In an optimization problem with D objectives, a solution x is said to dominate another x' (denoted $x \succ x'$) if and only if

$$f_i(x) \geq f_i(x') \; \forall i = 1, \ldots, D \text{ and } f_i(x) > f_i(x') \text{ for some } i, \tag{7}$$

where $f_i(x)$ is the objective function value of objective i for a solution x. This formulation has assumed the problem is one of maximization, but the modifications necessary for a minimization problem are clear.

A set of solutions is said to be a non-dominated set (or Pareto set) if no member of the set is dominated by any other member. A non-dominated set is usually used as an approximation of the true Pareto front. The Automatic Accumulated Ranking Strategy (AARS) proposed by Goldberg (1989) provides a way to identify the non-dominated set in a set of solutions. AARS ensures that all the non-dominated solutions in the population are assigned rank 1 and removed from the population temporarily, then a new set of non-dominated solutions are assigned rank 2, and so forth. After all solutions have been assigned a rank, the solutions that have a Pareto ranking of 1 are non-dominated solutions. The pseudo-code of AARS algorithm is illustrated in Algorithm 1.

```
SUBROUTINE Set_Pareto_Ranking
BEGIN:
    Mark each solution in the solution set as not evaluated
    Set Current Ranking to 1
    EVALUATION:
    IF there are any not-evaluated solutions, THEN
        FOR EACH not-evaluated solution, check If_solution_is_dominated
            IF it's not dominated, THEN
                Set its Pareto Ranking as the Current Ranking
                Mark the solution as evaluated
        After checking all solutions, increase Current Ranking by 1
    REPEAT EVALUATION
END
```

```
SUBROUTINE If_solution_is_dominated
BEGIN:
    FOR all other solutions in the solution set that are not evaluated or
    have a Pareto Ranking that equals the Current Ranking,
        Check if there exists at least one solution that has at least one objective function value
        that is larger (in the case of maximization) or smaller (in the case of minimization) than
        that of the target solution
    IF "Yes", THEN the solution is dominated, ELSE, the solution is not dominated
END
```

Algorithm 1. The pseudo-code of the Automatic Accumulated Ranking Strategy (Goldberg, 1989)

3.3 Multi-objective pareto simulated annealing

Multi-objective simulated annealing is conceptually identical to a single-objective simulated annealing algorithm. Czyzak & Jaszkiewicz (1998) modified simulated annealing algorithm for multi-objective optimization problems and developed Pareto simulated annealing (PSA). Instead of using just one candidate for the final solution, as done in the single-objective simulated annealing algorithm, PSA uses a set of interacting solutions, called the generating set *S*, at each iteration to propagate new solutions. The initial set of generating solutions is normally generated randomly. The subsequent sets of generating solutions are generated using a random swapping method based on the results at the prior stage. Any solution *y* generated that is not dominated by its preceding solution *x* in the generating set is checked for Pareto dominance among solutions in a non-dominated set *M*. The newly generated solution is added to the non-dominated set if it is non-dominated. All solutions originally in the non-dominated set that are dominated by the added solution are removed from the non-dominated set. PSA preserves some solutions based on a probability function *P*. The probability of preserving a new solution *y* in the generating set equals one when *y* dominates or is equal to the current solution *x*. Otherwise,

$$P(x, y, T, \Lambda^x) = \min\{1, \exp(\sum_{j=1}^{D} \lambda_j^x (f_j(x) - f_j(y)) / T)\} \tag{8}$$

where $f_j(x) - f_j(y)$ is the change of the objective function values of objective *j* for solutions *x* and *y*, *D* is the number of objectives, *T* is the annealing temperature, and Λ^x is the weighting vector ($\Lambda^x = [\lambda_1^x, \lambda_2^x, ..., \lambda_D^x]$) used in the previous iteration for solution *x*. The weighting vector is used to assure dispersion of the generating solutions over the whole set of non-dominated solutions (i.e., the complete Pareto front). The higher the weight associated with a given objective, the lower the probability of accepting swappings that decrease the value on this objective and the greater is the probability of improving the value of this objective. For a given solution $x \in S$, the weights are changed in order to increase the probability of moving away from its closest neighbor in *S* denoted by *x'*. This is obtained by increasing the weights of the objectives with a factor of α ($\alpha > 1$ and is a constant close to 1) on which *x* is better than *x'* and decreasing the weights of the objective with a factor of $1/\alpha$ on which *x* is worse than *x'*. The general scheme of PSA is shown in Algorithm 2.
The PSA process is stopped when stop conditions are fulfilled. Several commonly used stop conditions include: 1) predetermined number of solutions (i.e., iterations) is generated and evaluated and 2) the accepting ratio of solutions falls below a threshold. When PSA stops, the non-dominated set *M* contains solutions that form the approximated Pareto front.

```
Select a starting set of generating solutions S
FOR each solution x ∈ S DO
    Update the set M of potentially non-dominated solutions with x
Set current temperature T to initial temperature T0

REPEAT
    For each x ∈ S do
        Construct a feasible solution y
        IF y is not dominated by x THEN Update the set M with y
        Select the solution x' ∈ S closest to x and non-dominated with respect to x
        IF there is no such x' or it's the 1st iteration with x THEN Set random weights such that
```

$$\forall j, \lambda_j^{x'} \geq 0 \text{ and } \sum_j \lambda_j^{x'} = 1$$

```
        Else
            For each objective fj
```

$$\lambda_j^{x'} = \begin{cases} \alpha \lambda_j^x & \text{if } f_j(x) \geq f_j(x') \\ \lambda_j^x / \alpha & \text{if } f_j(x) < f_j(x') \end{cases}$$

```
            Normalize the weights such that
```

$$\sum_j \lambda_j^{x'} = 1$$

```
        Update x with y with acceptance probability P(x,y,T, Λx')
    If the conditions of changing the temperature are fulfilled then
    Decrease T according to cooling schedule T(k)
UNTIL the stop conditions are fulfilled
```

Algorithm 2. The pseudo-code of the Pareto simulated annealing algorithm (Czyzak & Jaszkiewicz, 1998)

3.4 Knowledge-informed pareto simulated annealing

There are two complementary knowledge-informed PSA strategies for improving the performance of PSA in solving multi-objective spatial allocation problems (Duh & Brown, 2007). First, similar to the single objective approach, auxiliary rules are used to preferentially generate subsequent solutions. Second, the Extended Initial Generating Set (EIGS) approach, which uses solutions optimized by single-objective simulated annealing as the initial solutions of PSA. This makes the initial generating set more diverse. The first strategy should result in an improvement in the effectiveness and efficiency of approximating the Pareto front. The second strategy, which extends the spread of the initial PSA generating set, is expected to encourage the diversity of Pareto solutions generated by PSA.

4. Performance evaluations

Multiple experiments were conducted to compare the performance of KISA against simulated annealing and Pareto simulated annealing in single and multi-objective spatial allocation problems. The allocation was carried out on a hypothetic 18 rows by 18 columns landscape (N = 324) with 50% of patch (i.e., foreground) cells (K = 162). K remained unchanged throughtout the simulation process. Quantitative performance indices were used for comparisons.

4.1 Single objective benchmark

In single objective experiments, ten random landscapes (K = 162) were used as initial maps. Each initial map was optimized ten times under each of four cooling schedules by simulated annealing (SA) and KISA with the compactness rule. The objective was to maximize PFF (see Section 2). Four cooling schedules used were: Boltzmann, Cauchy, Exponential, and Greedy. Their definitions are:
Boltzmann (logarithmic) schedule:

$$T(k) = \frac{T_0}{\ln k},\ k > 1\,. \tag{9}$$

Cauchy (modified logarithmic) schedule:

$$T(k) = \frac{T_0}{k},\ k > 0\,. \tag{10}$$

Quenching (exponential) schedule:

$$T(k) = T_0 \exp((c-1)k)\,,\ c = 0.9966. \tag{11}$$

Greedy:

$$T(k) = 0 \tag{12}$$

In the equations above, T_0 is the initial temperature and k is an index of annealing time, which was defined as the number of processed iterations. The initial temperature was determined to allow about 80% of the deteriorated solutions be accepted initially (Laarhoven, 1987).
Two indices, Max Objective Function Value (MAXOFV) and Weighted Performance Index (WPI) (Duh & Brown, 2005), were respectively used to compare the effectiveness and efficiency between algorithms. MAXOFV is the best objecitve function value (OFV) ever achieved in each run. WPI is the average of weighted OFVs using a linearly decreasing weighting scheme, which gives more weight to the OFVs in the earlier stage of runs. These indices were calculated based on an arbitrary cutoff annealing time of 25000 iterations.

4.2 Multi-objective benchmark

For multi-objective experiments, the pattern metric, PFF, and two different cost surfaces, a uniform random and a conical surface (Fig. 2) were used as the objective functions. The random and conical cost surfaces exhibit low and high spatial autocorrelation of the distribution of cost, respectively. They were created as non-pattern objectives to contrast the PFF pattern objective. Costs are incurred when any location on the cost surface is occupied by a cell of the patch cover type. These objective functions formed two types of benchmark problems. The two types of problems represent the cases in which there are conflicting or concordant objectives. The first type (MOP1), maximizing PFF, which produces compact landscape, and minimizing the cost defined by the uniform random cost surface, which produces fragmented landscape, represents the case where the two optimization objectives are conflicting. The second type (MOP2), maximizing PFF and minimizing the cost defined by the conical cost surface, represents the case where the two objectives are concordant.

Fig. 2. Cost surfaces defined for multi-objective experiments: (A) uniform random and (B) conical (light color indicates higher costs if the location is occupied by patch cells).

Ten different initial landscape maps were used as the initial input to the multi-objective Pareto optimization. Four simulated annealing algorithms were tested. They are Pareto simulated annealing (PSA), knowledge-informed PSA (KIPSA), PSA with extended initial generating set (EIGS), and knowledge-informed PSA with extended initial generating set (KIPSA+EIGS). The size of generating set was ten. The ten generating solutions were created by randomly shuffling the initial map. For the Extended Initial Generating Set algorithm, only eight out of ten initial maps were randomly generated. Two additional initial maps were created to optimize each of the individual objectives specified in the problems and added to the generating set. I used the standard Boltzmann cooling schedule with an initial annealing temperature of 0.01. The values of both objectives were rescaled to the range 0 to 100 using their theoretical upper and lower bounds. Five repeated runs were conducted on each set of initial solutions, a total of 50 runs for each algorithm.

Two indices, Average Rank Value (RANK) and Average Spread Value (SPREAD), were used to measure the effectiveness of algorithms. RANK provides a relative comparison of the effectiveness of the algorithms for approximating the true Pareto front. It was calculated using the AARS method described earlier. The calculation first involved pooling the Pareto sets generated by different algorithms and assigning a Pareto ranking to every solution in the pool. The ranking values were then averaged for each algorithm to get the RANK index (i.e., average rank) of the corresponding algorithm. The closer the rank index value is to 1, the closer the corresponding Pareto set is to the true Pareto front. SPREAD is calculated based on the density evaluation scheme developed by Lu and Yen (2003). They calculated the density value by imposing a cell system, which is formed by partitioning the solution range of each objective into equally spaced cells, and counting the density of individual solutions within each cell. SPREAD is the quotient of the total number of solutions in a Pareto set and the average density value of the set. I randomly coupled individual runs of the four algorithms to create 50 combinations. Each of the 50 runs for a given algorithm was used exactly once. The two performance indices were calculated based on the 50 combinations of runs.

4.3 Random number generators

The simulated annealing algorithms use a random number generator (RNG) to control the stochastic process of local search. The inherent biases of RNGs could affect the outcomes of stochastic experiments (Van Neil & Laffan, 2003). Therefore, the validity of stochastic experiments is reliant on the RNG used. I tested the RNGs on the single-objective spatial allocation problem using, in addition to the rnd function in Microsoft Visual Basic (Microsoft, 1999), three other RNGs: Mother of All (MOA) (Marsaglia, 1994), Ranshi (Gutbrod, 1995), and Taus (L'Ecuyer, 1996, 1999) and found no systematic biases in performance. The results presented in this chapter were all derived from simulations based on the Visual Basic rnd RNG.

5. Results

A total of 800 runs were carried out in the single objective benchmark, 100 runs for each of the 8 combinations of the four cooling schedules and two algorithms. Both algorithms, simulated annealing (SA) and knowledge-informed simulated annealing (KISA), found near-optimal solutions (PFF > 0.94) and conspicuous sub-optimal solutions (PFF < 0.88) in some runs (Fig. 3). The average PFF at 25000 iterations was about 95% of the best PFF ever achieved at the maximal number of iterations (Table 1). The data confirm that most runs had converged at 25000 iterations and the use of 25000 iterations as the cutoff range for measuring MAXOFV and WPI was reasonable. KISA converged faster than SA in maximizing PFF (Fig. 4). When using the same cooling schedule, KISA performed better than SA, i.e., with higher MAXOFV values (Fig. 5a). The Boltzmann and the Exponential schedules were most effective but least efficient in generating the (near-)optimal solutions, whereas Cauchy and Greedy schedules, though more efficient in converging to optimal solutions, were not generating solutions as good as those generated using Boltzmann or Exponential schedules (Fig. 5b). The data suggest that using KISA with a Boltzmann or an Exponential cooling schedule is the most effective and efficient annealing setting for maximizing PFF.

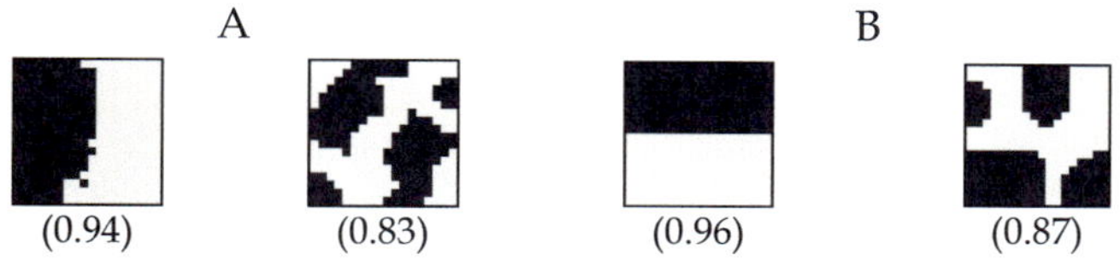

Fig. 3. Better and worse solutions and their PFF values (in parentheses) of maximizing PFF of patch class (dark color). These solutions are generated using (A) SA and (B) KISA.

Schedule \ *Algorithm*	*SA*	*KISA*
Boltzmann	0.892 (0.945)	0.939 (0.958)
Cauchy	0.914 (0.914)	0.934 (0.956)
Exponential	0.896 (0.934)	0.944 (0.957)
Greedy	0.905 (0.917)	0.954 (0.958)

Table 1. The averaged maximal PFF reached in 25,000 iterations versus the maximal PFF ever reached in 150,000 iterations (in parentheses).

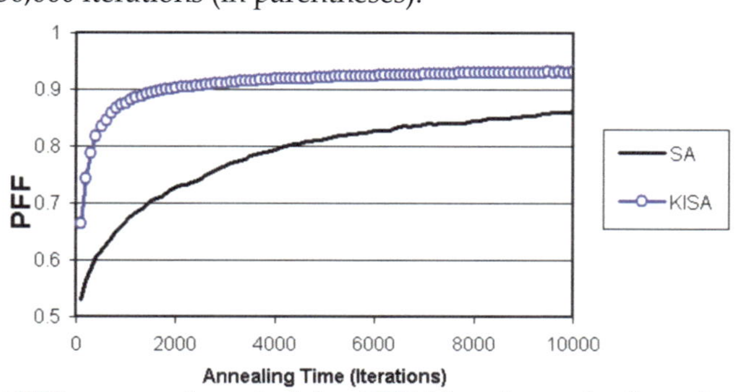

Fig. 4. Averaged OFV curves of maximizing PFF (showing only the solutions solved using the Boltzmann cooling schedule).

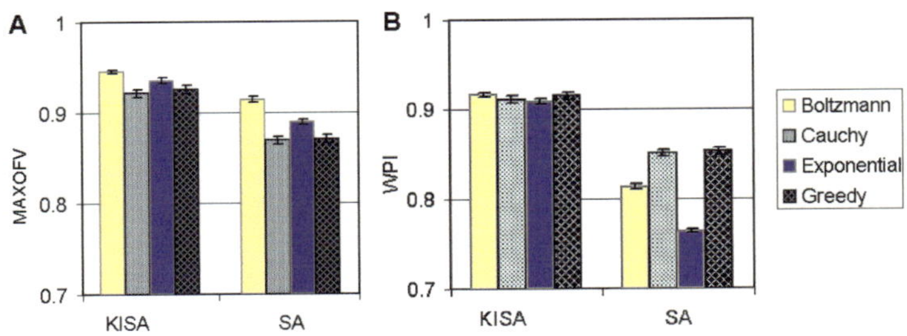

Fig. 5. Performance indices of maximizing PFF: (A) MAXOFV, (B) WPI. The error bars of ± 2 standard errors of the mean are included.

For multi-objective experiments, a total of 400 runs were carried out, 50 runs for each of the four algorithms in solving two types of multi-objective spatial allocation problems. The problems with conflicting objectives (i.e., MOP1) formed outstretched Pareto fronts (Fig. 6), while problems with concordant objectives (MOP2) formed compact Pareto fronts (Fig. 7). Approaches with extended initial generating set (i.e., EIGS and KIPSA+EIGS) have more outstretched Pareto fronts than those without EIGS (Fig. 6, 7). When look closely, in MOP1, KIPSA improved the approximations of the pattern objective but sacrificed by not exploiting the non-pattern objective (y-axis) as well as the PSA approach. Such sacrifices did not exist in MOP2 where the objectives were concordant.

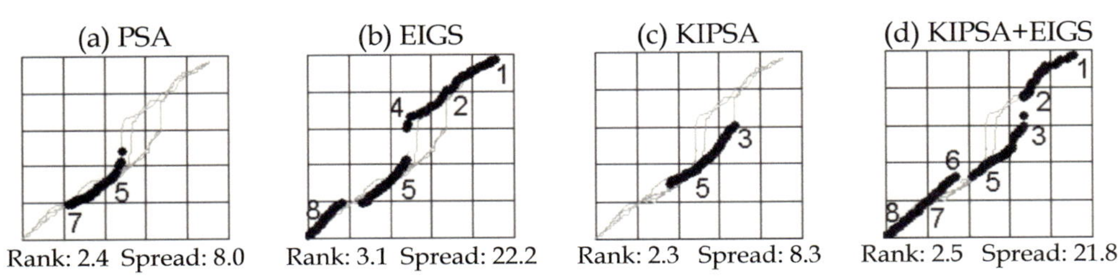

Fig. 6. Approximated Pareto fronts (gray lines) and Pareto solutions (black dots) derived using 4 PSA algorithms for MOP1. The Pareto set in each scatter plot represents the outcome of one run. The x-axis is the OFV for maximizing PFF and y-axis is the OFV for minimizing cost on the uniform random cost surface. Numbers indicate the locations of individual solutions shown in Fig. 8.

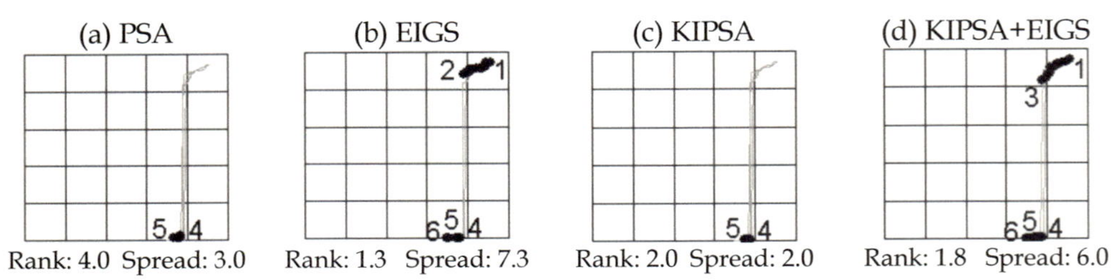

Fig. 7. Approximated Pareto fronts (gray lines) and Pareto solutions (black dots) derived using 4 PSA algorithms for MOP2. The Pareto fronts are superimposed as visual references. The Pareto set in each scatter plot represents the outcome of one run. The x-axis is the OFV for maximizing PFF and y-axis is the OFV for minimizing cost on the conical cost surface. Numbers indicate the locations of individual solutions shown in Fig. 9.

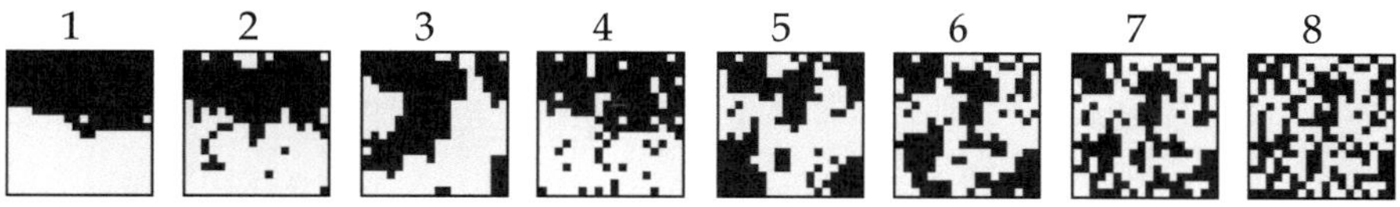

Fig. 8. Sample solutions of MOP1, each illustrates a particular combination of objective function values on a location indicated by a number shown in Fig. 6. These numbers do not connote that a solution was generated by a particular algorithm.

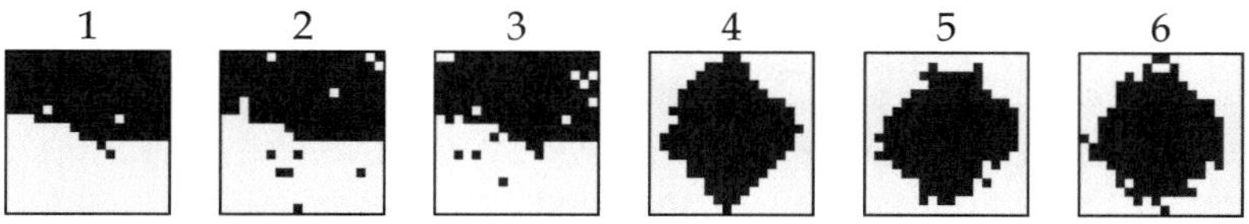

Fig. 9. Sample solutions of MOP2, each illustrates a particular combination of objective function values on a location indicated by a number shown in Fig. 7. These numbers do not connote that a solution was generated by a particular algorithm.

Sampled solutions for MOP1 (Fig. 8) illustrate the versatility of Pareto simulated annealing in solving multi-objective spatial allocation problems with conflicting objectives. Each map, 1 through 8, represents a (near-)optimal solution solved with different weightings of objectives in a single-objective optimization problem, with map 1 having a full weighting on maximizing PFF and with map 8 having a full weighting on minimizing the cost on the uniform random cost surface. The weighting on maximizing PFF diminishes from maps 1 to 8. Sample solutions for MOP2 (Fig. 9) indicate that, despite the capability of Pareto simulated annealing of generating diverse Pareto solutions, the diversity is intrinsic to the multi-objective optimization problems. Problems with concordant objectives have less diverse Pareto solutions.

The measures of performance indices reinforce and confirm the performance relationships alluded to above. Knowledge-informed algorithms (KIPSA and KIPSA+EIGS), in most cases, had significantly smaller average Pareto rankings (RANK) (Fig. 10a & 11a), indicating that KISA rule was more effective in generating Pareto solutions closer to the true Pareto front than PSA. However, knowledge-informed rules were not as effective in promoting diversity in Pareto solutions (Fig. 10b & 11b). The incorporation of EIGS greatly increased the spread of solutions (Fig. 10b & 11b).

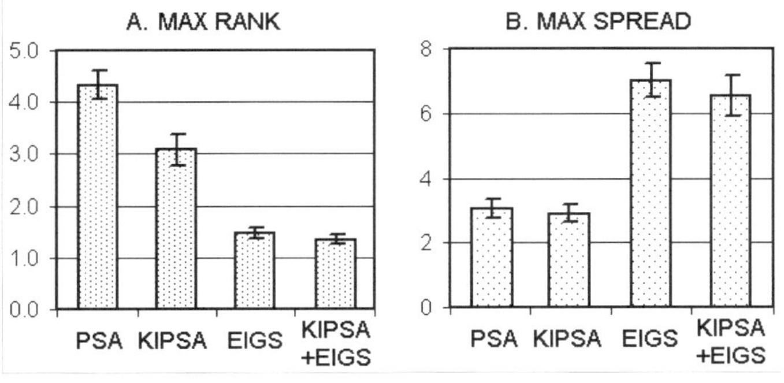

Fig. 10. Multi-objective performance indices for MOP1: (a) RANK, (b) SPREAD. The error bars of ±2 standard errors of the mean are included.

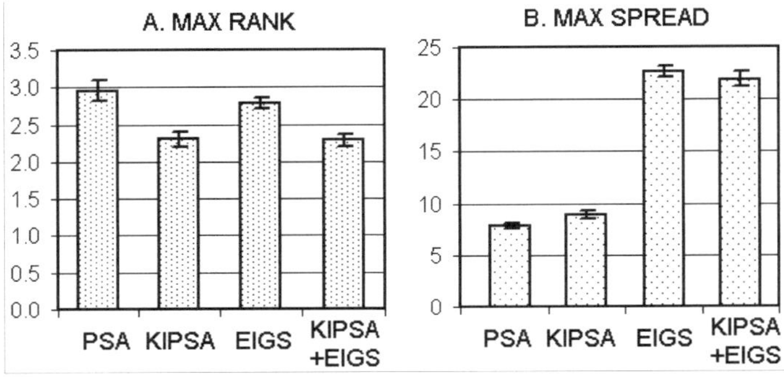

Fig. 11. Multi-objective performance indices for MOP2: (a) RANK, (b) SPREAD. The error bars of ±2 standard errors of the mean are included.

5. Discussion and conclusions

This chapter presents a knowledge-informed simulated annealing (KISA) approach to improving the performance of solving single and multi-objective spatial allocation problems. Simulated annealing is flexible and versatile in dealing with complex pattern objective functions, and empirical results indicate that KISA further improved its performance, making the approach of combining auxiliary information and simulated annealing desirable for similar applications. In addition to the compactness objective characterized by the PFF metric, there are other pattern objectives, such as connectivity. Corresponding KISA rules for these pattern objectives need to be designed, implemented, and evaluated.

The multi-objective benchmark shows that PSA algorithm is improved by various approaches, including using the KISA rule and extended initial generating sets (EIGS) strategy. The KISA rule improved the approximation of the Pareto front. EIGS greatly increased the diversity of Pareto solutions in problems with conflicting objectives. In these problems, efforts to approximate the Pareto front shifted toward the maximization of PFF when using the KISA rule, resulting in inferior approximations of the Pareto front toward the other objective, yet an overall improvement of the approximated Pareto front. One should use these strategies in multi-objective spatial optimization problems that emphasize pattern objectives.

The performance comparison in multi-objective benchmark did not measure the improvements in computation time. There is no predictable relation between the number of solutions evaluated and the CPU-time consumed for the algorithms used. This was because I did not set a maximal size of the Pareto set, so as the number of solutions in the Pareto set increases the required computation time for checking Pareto dominance also increases. It turned out that the PSA approaches that generated more diverse Pareto solutions used more CPU time and problems with conflicting objectives required more time to solve.

This research illustrates that knowledge-informed rules, which promote the formation of desirable pattern characteristics at an individual-cell level by acting through uncoordinated discrete steps, could eventually generate the desirable landscape patterns. Knowledge-informed simulated annealing should have the same performance improvement for other pattern metrics that were not tested in this research if the associated rules are tailored to capture the desirable pattern characteristics.

7. References

Aerts, J. C. J. H. & Heuvelink, G. B. M. (2002). Using simulated annealing for resource allocation. International Journal of Geographic Information Science, 16: 571-587.
Brookes, C.J. (2001). A genetic algorithm for designing optimal patch configurations in GIS. International Journal of Geographic Information Science, 15 (6): 539-559.
Church, R. L & Sorensen, P. (1996). Integrating normative location models into GIS, problems and prospects with the p-median model. In P. Longley & M. Batty (Eds.), Spatial Analysis: Modeling in a GIS Environment. Cambridge, UK: GeoInformation International.
Church, R. L., Gerrard, R. A., Gilpin, M., & Stine, P. (2003). Constructing cell-based habitat patches useful in conservation planning. Annals of the Association of American Geographers, 93 (4): 814-827.
Cross, G. R. and Jain, A. K. (1983). Markov random field texture models. IEEE Transactions on Pattern Analysis and Machine Intelligence, PAMI-5(1): 25-39.
Czyzak, P. & Jaszkiewicz, A. (1998). Pareto simulated annealing - A metaheuristic technique for multiple-objective combinatorial optimization. Journal of Multi-Criteria Decision Analysis, 7: 34-47.
Dale, M. R. T. (2000). Lacunarity analysis of spatial pattern: A comparison. Landscape Ecology, 15 (5): 467-478.
De Clercq, E. M., De Wulf, R., and Van Herzele, A. (2007). Relating spatial pattern of forest cover to accessibility. Landscape and Urban Planning, 80 (1-2): 14-22.
De Bonet, J. and Viola, P. (1997). A non-parametric multi-scale statistical model for natural images. In. Advance in Neural Information Processing, Vol 9. MIT Press.
Deutsch, C. V. and Journel, A. C. (1992). GSLIB: Geostatistical Software Library and User's Guide. Oxford University Press, Oxford.
Duh, J. D. & Brown, D. G. (2005). Generating prescribed patterns in landscape models. In D. J. Maguire, M. F. Goodchild, & M. Batty (Eds.), GIS, Spatial Analysis and Modeling (pp. 423-444), ESRI Press.
Duh, J. D. and Brown, D. G. (2007). Knowledge-Informed Pareto Simulated Annealing for Multi-Objective Spatial Allocation. Computers, Environment and Urban Systems, 31(3): 253-281.
Eastman, J. R., Jin, W. G., Kyem, P. A. K., & Toledano, J. (1995). Raster procedures for multi-criteria/multi-objective decisions. PE&RS, 61 (5): 539-547.
Geman, S. and Geman, D. (1984). Stochastic relaxation, Gibbs distribution and the Bayesian restoration in images. IEEE Trans. Patt. Anal. Mac. Int., 6(6): 721-741.
Glover, F and Laguna, M. (1997). Tabu search. Boston: Kluwer Academic Publishers.
Goldberg, D. E. (1989). Genetic Algorithms in Search, Optimization, and Machine Learning. Reading, MA: Addison-Wesley.
Gutbrod, F. (1995). A fast random number generator for the Intel Paragon supercomputer. Computer Physics Communications, 87 (3): 291-306.
Laarhoven Van, P. J. M. (1987). Theoretical and Computational Aspects of Simulated Annealing. PhD Thesis, Erasmus University Rotterdam.
L'Ecuyer, P. (1996). Maximally Equidistributed Combined Tausworthe Generators. Mathematics of Computation, 65 (213): 203-213.
L'Ecuyer, P. (1999). Tables of Maximally-Equidistributed Combined LFSR Generators. Mathematics of Computation, 68 (225): 261-269.
Liu, Y. B., Nishiyama, S., and Kusaka, T. (2003). Examining landscape dynamics at a watershed scale using landsat TM imagery for detection of wintering hooded crane decline in Yashiro, Japan. Environmental Management, 31 (3): 365-376.

Longley, P. Goodchild, M. F., Maguire, D. and Rhind, D. (2005). Geographical Information Systems and Science. 2nd Edition. John Wiley and Sons, pp: 493-502.
Lu, H. M. & Yen, G. G. (2003). Rank-density-based multiobjective genetic algorithm and benchmark test function study. IEEE Transactions on Evolutionary Computation, 7 (4): 325-343.
Malczewski, J. (1999). GIS and Multicriteria Decision Analysis. John Wiley & Sons, Inc.
Marsaglia, G. (1994). The Mother of All Random Generators. Posted by Bob Wheeler to sci.stat.consult and sci.math.num-analysis on behalf of George Marsaglia on October 28, 1994. The code is available at ftp.taygeta.com.
McAlpine, C.A. and Eyre, T.J. (2002). Testing landscape metrics as indicators of habitat loss and fragmentation in continuous eucalypt forests (Queensland, Australia). Landscape Ecology, 17 (8): 711-728.
McGarigal, K. and Marks, B. J. (1995). FRAGSTATS: Spatial Pattern Analysis Program for Quantifying Landscape Structure. Gen. Tech. Report PNW-GTR-351, USDA Forest Service, Pacific Northwest Research Station, Portland, OR.
McIntyre, N. E. and Wiens, J. A. (2000). A novel use of the lacunarity index to discern landscape function. Landscape Ecology, 15: 313-321.
Microsoft (1999). MSDN Library Visual Studio 6.0 Release. Microsoft.
Milder, J. C., Lassoie, J. P., Bedford, B. L. (2008). Conserving biodiversity and ecosystem function through limited development: An empirical evaluation. Conservation Biology, 22 (1): 70-79.
Miettinen, K. M. (1999). Nonlinear Multiobjective Optimization. Kluwer Academic: Boston, MA.
Pareto, V. (1971). Manual of Political Economy (Augustus M. Kelley, New York) translated from French edition of 1927 by Ann S. Schwier, first published in 1896.
Pressey, R. L., Ferrier, S., Hutchinson, C. D., Sivertsen, D. P., & Manion, G. (1995). Planning for negotiation: using an interactive geographic information system to explore alternative protected area networks. In D.A. Saunders, J.L. Craig, & E.M. Mattiska (Eds.), Nature Conservation 4: The Role of Networks (pp. 23-33), Surrey Beatty, Sydney.
Revees, C.R. (1993). Modern Heuristic Techniques for Combinatorial Problems. John Wiley & Sons, Inc.
Riitters, K., Wickham, H., O'Neill, R., Jones, B., & Smith, E. (2000). Global-scale patterns of forest fragmentation. Conservation Ecology, 4 (2): 3.
Sawaragi, Y., Nakayama, H, & Tanino, T. (1985). Theory of Multiobjective Optimization. Academic Press: Orlando, FL.
Schmid-Holmes, S. and Drickamer, L. C. (2001). Impact of forest patch characteristics on small mammal communities: a multivariate approach. Biological Conservation, 99:293-305.
Sorensen, P. A. & Church, R. L. (1996). A comparison of strategies for data storage reduction in location-allocation problems. Geographical Systems, 3: 221-242.
Taylor J. J. Brown, D. G. and Larsen, L. (2007). Preserving natural features: A GIS-based evaluation of a local open-space ordinance. Landscape and Urban Planning, 82: 1–16.
Tomlin, C.D. (1990). Geographic Information Systems and Cartographic Modelling. New Jersey: Prentice Hall.
Van Neil, K. & Laffan, S. W. (2003). Gambling with randomness: the use of pseudo-random number generators in GIS. International Journal of Geographic Information Science, 17 (1): 49-68.
Vos, C. C., Verboom, J., Opdam, P. F. M., and Ter Braak, C. J. F. (2001). Towards ecologically scaled landscape indices. American Naturist, 157(1): 24-51.
Xiao, N., Bennett, D.A., & Armstrong, M.P. (2002). Using evolutionary algorithms to generate alternatives for multiobjective site-search problems. Environment and Planning A, 34: 639-656.

An Efficient Quasi-Human Heuristic Algorithm for Solving the Rectangle-Packing Problem

Wenqi Huang [1] and Duanbing Chen[2]
[1] *School of Computer Science, Huazhong University of Science and Technology, Wuhan 430074, P.R. China*
[2] *School of Computer Science, University of Electronic Science and Technology of China, Chengdu 610054, P.R. China*

1. Introduction

Rectangle-packing problem involves many industrial applications. For example, in shipping industry, various size boxes have to be loaded as many as possible in a larger container. In wood or glass industries, rectangular components have to be cut from large sheets of material. In very large scale integration (VLSI) floor planning, various chips have to be laid on the chip board, and so on. The rectangle-packing problem belongs to a subset of classical cutting and packing problems and has shown to be NP hard (Leung *et al.*, 1990). For more extensive and detailed descriptions of packing problem, please refer to Lodi *et al.* (2002) and Pisinger (2002). Various algorithms based on different strategies have been suggested to solve this problem. In general, these algorithms can be classified into two major categories: non-deterministic algorithms and deterministic algorithms. The key aspect of non-deterministic algorithms, such as simulated annealing and genetic algorithm (Hopper & Turton, 1999; Bortfeldt, 2006), is to design data structure that can represent the topological relations among the rectangles. The key aspect of deterministic algorithms is to determine the packing rules, such as *less flexibility first* principle (Wu *et al.*, 2002).

Optimal algorithm for orthogonal two-dimensional cutting is proposed in Beasley (1985), but it might not be practical for large scale problems. In order to improve the quality of solution, some scholars combine genetic algorithm or simulated annealing with deterministic method and obtain hybrid algorithms (Liu & Teng, 1999; Leung *et al.*, 2003). Some heuristic and meta-heuristic algorithms are also presented in literatures(Lodi *et al.*, 1999; Hopper & Turton, 2001; Zhang *et al.*, 2005; Burke *et al.*, 2004). In recent years, some people began to formalize the wisdom and experience of human being and obtain the quasi-human heuristic algorithms (Huang & Jin, 1997; Huang & Xu, 1999; Wu *et al.*, 2002; Huang *et al.*, 2007). The "quasi-human" tries to simulate the behavior of human being in related special work such as bricklaying.

Huang et al. (2007) presented a heuristic algorithm based on two important concepts, namely, the corner-occupying action and caving degree. Based on Huang et al. (2007), an efficient quasi-human heuristic algorithm (QHA) for solving rectangle-packing problem is proposed on the basis of the wisdom and experience of human being in this paper. The objective is to maximize the area usage of the box. The key point of this algorithm is that the rectangle packed into the box always occupies a corner, even a cave, if possible. Furthermore, the rectangle should occupy as many corners and overlap as many edges with other previously packed rectangles as possible. In this way, the rectangles will be close to each other wisely, and the spare space is decreased. As compared with reviewed literatures, the results from QHA are much improved. For 21 rectangle-packing test instances taken from Hopper & Turton (2001), optimal solutions of 19 instances are achieved by QHA, and two, three and sixteen ones by the algorithm in Wu et al. (2002), Zhang et al. (2005) and Huang et al. (2007), respectively. For each of 13 random instances taken from Burke et al. (2004), the container height obtained by QHA is smaller than that by best fit (BF) heuristic (Burke et al., 2004). Furthermore, optimal solutions of three instances are achieved by QHA. Experimental results show that QHA is rather efficient for solving the rectangle-packing problem.

2. Problem description

Given an empty box B_0 with width w_0 and height h_0, and a series of rectangles R_i with width w_i and height h_i (i=1, 2,..., n). The task is to pack as many rectangles into the box B_0 as possible, where the measurement of "many" is the total area of the already packed rectangles. The constraints for packing rectangles are:

1. Each edge of a packed rectangle should be parallel to an edge of the box.
2. There is no overlapping area for any two already packed rectangles, and any packed rectangle should not exceed the box boundary.
3. The rectangle should be packed horizontally or vertically.

Without significant loss of generality, it is usual to assume that all w_i and h_i (i=0, 1,..., n) are integers.

3. Algorithm description

3.1. Main idea

If some rectangles have been packed into the box without overlapping, that is, the overlapping area is zero, the question is which rectangle is the best candidate for the remainder, and which position is the best one to be filled. There is an aphorism in ancient China: "*Golden corners, silvery edges, and strawy voids*". It means that the empty corner inside the box is the best place to be filled, then the boundary line of the empty space, and the void space is the worst. And more, if the rectangle not only occupies a corner, but also touches some other rectangles, the action for packing this rectangle is perfect. We may call the corresponding action as cave-occupying action. Therefore, we can develop foresaid aphorism into "*Golden corners, silvery edges, strawy voids, and highly valuable diamond cave*". In addition, we hope that the rectangle occupies as many corners and overlaps as many edges with previously packed rectangles as possible. Thus, the following packing principle is natural: The rectangle to be packed into the box always occupies a corner, and the caving degree of the packing action should be as large as possible, where the caving degree reflects the closeness between the rectangle to be packed and the previously packed rectangles, the details about caving degree will be described in 3.2(6). Furthermore, the rectangle should occupy as many corners and overlap as many edges with other previously packed rectangles as possible. Thus, the rectangles are close to each other wisely. Actually, this strategy describes a quasi-human idea, that is, to simulate the behavior of human being in related special work such as bricklaying.

3.2. Definitions

The concepts of corner-occupying action, cave-occupying action and caving degree are presented in Huang et al. (2007). We summarize them in this paper again. For more details, the readers are referred to Huang et al. (2007). In this paper, other two important concepts, i.e., corner degree and edge degree, are presented.

(1) Corner-occupying action (COA)

A packing action is called a *corner-occupying action* (COA), if the edges of the rectangle to be packed overlap the different directional edges with other two previously packed rectangles including the box (we can regard the 4 edges of the box as 4 rectangles with very small height which have been packed at the prespecified positions), and the overlapping lengths are longer than zero. Note that the two rectangles are not necessarily touching each other. A COA is called a feasible one, if the rectangle to be packed does not overlap with any previously packed rectangle, i.e., the overlapping area is zero, and does not exceed the box boundary. For example, in Fig. 1, the shadowed rectangles have been packed, and the rectangle "1" is outside the box. The packing action is a feasible COA, if rectangle "1" is situated at place *A*, *B*, *C* or *D*; it is a non-feasible COA if situated at place *E* or *F*; it is not a COA if situated at place *G* or *H*.

(2) Cave-occupying action

A packing action is called a cave-occupying action if the rectangle to be packed not only occupies a corner, but also touches some other previously packed rectangles including the box. For example, in Fig. 2, the shadowy rectangles have been packed. Rectangle *A* occupies the corner formed by rectangles *a* and *b*. Furthermore, it touches rectangle *c*. Thus, rectangle *A* occupies a cave formed by rectangles *a*, *b* and *c*. The action of packing rectangle *A* is a cave-occupying action. Actually, a cave-occupying action is a special COA.

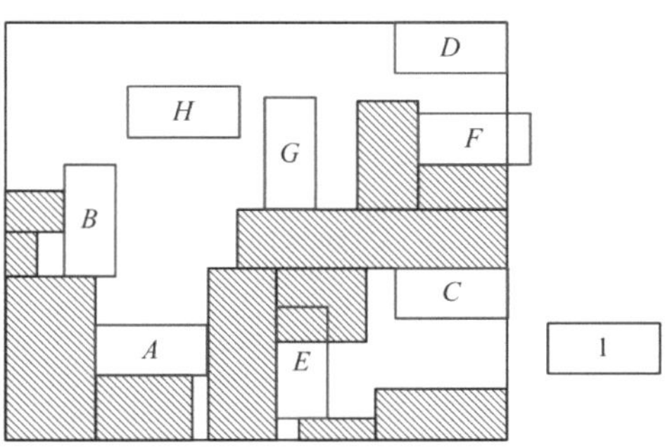

Fig. 1 Corner-occupying action

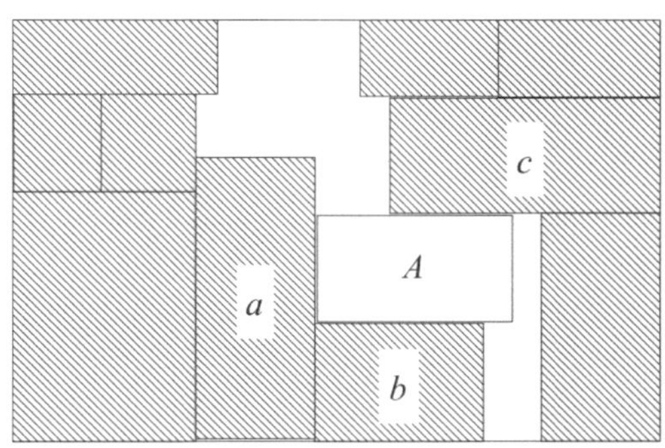

Fig. 2 Cave-occupying action

(3) Configuration

Fig. 3 shows a configuration. Some rectangles have been packed into the box without overlapping area and some remain outside. A configuration is called an initial one if there is no rectangle in the box. A configuration is called an end one if all n rectangles have been packed into the box without overlapping area or, no feasible COA can be done although some rectangles remain outside.

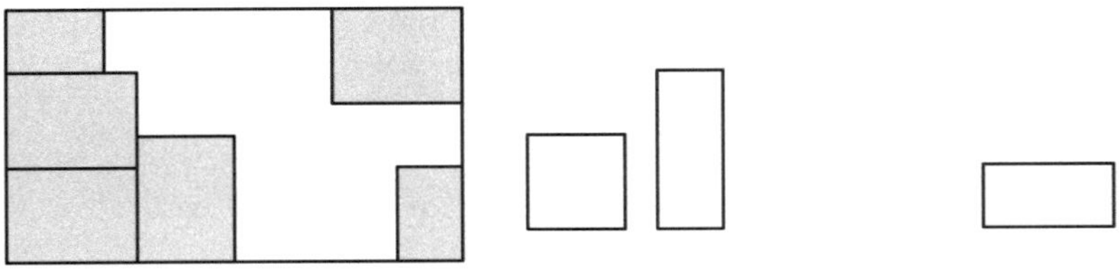

Fig. 3 Configuration

(4) Distance between two rectangles

For two given rectangles R_i with width w_i and height h_i and R_j with width w_j and height h_j, the central coordinate of rectangle R_i and R_j is (x_i, y_i) and (x_j, y_j), respectively. These two rectangles do not overlap (i.e., the overlapping area is zero) if $|x_i - x_j| \geq \frac{1}{2}(w_i + w_j)$ or $|y_i - y_j| \geq \frac{1}{2}(h_i + h_j)$, and more, the distance d_{ij} between rectangle R_i and R_j is defined as follows:

$$d_{ij} = \max\left(|x_i - x_j| - \tfrac{1}{2}(w_i + w_j), 0\right) + \max\left(|y_i - y_j| - \tfrac{1}{2}(h_i + h_j), 0\right).$$

In fact, d_{ij} is the Manhattan distance between two rectangles which is an extension of Manhattan distance between two points.

(5) Distance between one rectangle and several other rectangles

For a given rectangle R and a set of rectangles $\{R_i \mid i=1, 2,\ldots, m\}$. Let the distance between R and R_i (i=1, 2,…, m) be d_i. The minimum of d_i (i=1, 2,…, m) is defined as the distance between rectangle R and m rectangles $R_1, R_2,\ldots, R_m$.

(6) Caving degree of COA

As shown in Fig. 4, if a rectangle R_i is packed into the box according to a feasible COA, let the distance between rectangle R_i and all the previously packed rectangles including the box (except the rectangles a and b those form this corner) be $d_{\min}$. The caving degree C_i of the corresponding COA is defined as follows:

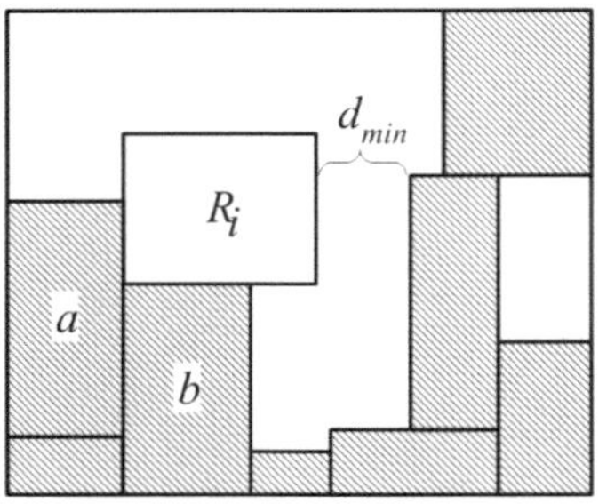

Fig. 4. Caving degree of COA.

$$C_i = 1 - \frac{d_{\min}}{\sqrt{w_i \cdot h_i}},$$

where w_i and h_i is the width and height of R_i respectively. The caving degree reflects the closeness between the rectangle to be packed and the previously packed rectangles including the box (except the rectangles that form this corner). It is equal to 1 when the corresponding rectangle occupies a cave formed by three or more previously packed rectangles, and less than 1 when just occupies a corner formed by two previously packed rectangles.

(7) Corner degree of COA

For a given COA, the number of corners occupied by the related rectangle is defined as *corner degree* of the corresponding COA. For example, as shown in Fig. 5, the shadowy rectangles have been packed. If rectangle "1" is situated at place *A*, it occupies the corner formed by rectangles *a* and *b*. Then, the corner degree of the corresponding COA equals 1. If situated at place *B*, it occupies two corners. One is formed by rectangle *b* and the bottom boundary and, the other is formed by rectangle *c* and the bottom boundary. Thus, the corner degree of the corresponding COA equals 2. If situated at place *C*, it occupies 4 corners which are formed by rectangle *d* and *e*, *d* and *f*, *e* and right boundary, *f* and right boundary. In this situation, the corner degree of the corresponding COA becomes 4.

(8) Edge degree of COA

For a given COA, the number of edges that overlap with the related rectangle is defined as *edge degree* of the corresponding COA. For example, as shown in Fig. 6, the shadowy rectangles have been packed. If rectangle "1" is situated at place *A*, since it overlaps the left and top boundary and one edge of rectangle *a*, the edge degree of the corresponding COA equals 3. If situated at place *B*, the edge degree of the corresponding COA equals 2 for overlapping one edge of rectangle *b* and *c*, respectively. If situated at place *C*, the edge degree of the corresponding COA equals 5 for overlapping the bottom boundary and one edge of rectangle *c*, *d*, *e* and *f*, respectively.

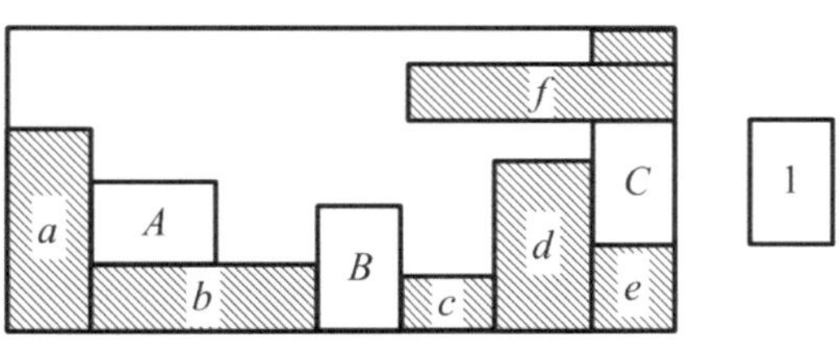

Fig. 5. Corner degree

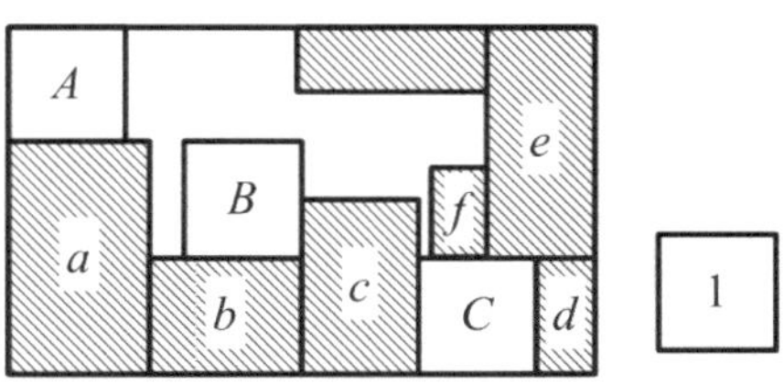

Fig. 6. Edge degree

(9) Precedence of point

Let P_1 (x_1, y_1) and P_2 (x_2, y_2) be two points in the plane rectangular coordinates *o-xy*. P_1 has precedence over P_2 if $x_1 < x_2$, or if $x_1 = x_2$ and $y_1 < y_2$.

3.3. Sketch of the algorithm

At each step, do the COA with the largest caving degree (if there are more than one COA with the largest caving degree, do the COA with the largest corner degree, if there are still multiple choices, do the COA with the largest edge degree) until no rectangle is left outside the box or no feasible COA can be done according to the current configuration.

In fact, this describes a greedy packing process. On the basis of greedy packing process, we introduce backtracking process, and so, develop the greedy packing algorithm into a new algorithm which can achieve better solution than greedy packing algorithm.

4. Computing program

4.1. Selecting rule

Rule 1. Select the COA with the largest caving degree, if there is more than one COA satisfying the condition, then:

Rule 2. Select the COA with the largest corner degree based on rule 1, if there is more than one COA satisfying the condition, then:

Rule 3. Select the COA with the largest edge degree on the basis of rule 2, if there is more than one COA satisfying the condition, then:

Rule 4. Select the COA with the highest precedence of the left-bottom vertex of the corresponding rectangle, if there is more than one COA satisfying the condition, then:

Rule 5. Select the COA with the corresponding rectangle packed with the longer sides horizontal if both the horizontal and vertical packings are feasible, if there is more than one COA satisfying the condition, then:

Rule 5. Select the COA with the smallest index of the corresponding rectangle.

4.2. Basic program

Step 1. If there is no feasible COA under the current configuration, output the unpacked area and stop the program. Otherwise, enumerate all feasible COAs, and then calculate the caving degree, corner degree and edge degree for each COA.

Step 2. Select a COA according to the selecting rule (see section 4.1) and pack the corresponding rectangle. Then reach a new configuration.

Step 3. If all rectangles have been packed into the box, output the packing result and stop successfully. Otherwise, return to step 1.

4.3. Strengthened program

Step 1. If there is no feasible COA under the current configuration, stop the program. Otherwise, enumerate all feasible COAs as candidates.

Step 2. For each candidate COA, pseudo-pack ("pseudo-pack" means to pack the rectangle into the box temporarily which will be removed from the box in the future) the corresponding rectangle and reach a new configuration. Based on this new configuration, pseudo-pack the remainder rectangles according to the *basic program*. If all rectangles have already been packed, output the packing result and stop successfully. Otherwise, calculate the area usage of the box according to the tentative end configuration as the score of the corresponding candidate COA.

Step 3. Select the COA with the highest score and pack the corresponding rectangle. Then reach a new configuration and return to step 1. If there are multiple COAs with the highest score, go to step 4.

Step 4. Select the COA according to the selecting rule (see section 4.1) and pack the corresponding rectangle. Then reach a new configuration and return to step 1.

4.4. Computational complexity

As each iteration of packing will occupy one or more corners and generate some new corners.The number of corners left should be proportional to n^2. Therefore, for each rectangle to be packed, the number of COAs generated will be bounded by $O(n^3)$. For *basic program*, the process is repeated once for each rectangle packed. As a result, the worst-case time complexity of *basic program* will be $O(n^3 \times n) = O(n^4)$. For *strengthened program*, the *basic program* is repeated $O(n^3)$ times for each rectangle packed. So the worst-case time complexity of *strengthened program* will be $O(n^4 \times n^3 \times n) = O(n^8)$. It should be noted that the time complexity of our algorithm is polynomial and relative small compared with the exponential time complexity of the original problem.

5. Experimental results

Two group benchmarks taken from Hopper & Turton (2001) and Burke et al. (2004) are used to test the performance of the algorithm proposed in this paper. The first group has 21 instances with the number of rectangles ranging from 16 to 197. The second group includes 13 instances with the number of rectangles ranging from 10 to 3152. The optimal solutions of these two groups are known.

5.1 21 rectangle-packing instances provided by Hopper and Turton

The performance of QHA has been tested with 21 rectangle-packing test instances taken from Hopper & Turton (2001). For each instance, the optimal solution is perfect, i.e., all rectangles can be packed into the box without overlapping area, the area usage of the box is 100%, and the unutilized area is zero. For more details about these instances, please refer to Hopper & Turton (2001).

Wu et al. (2002), Hopper & Turton (2001), Zhang et al. (2005) and Huang et al. (2007) reflect the most advanced algorithms that have already been published up to now. Heuristic1 (Wu *et al.*, 2002) is based on the conception of flexibility; SA+BLF (Hopper & Turton, 2001) means simulated annealing+bottom left fill, GA+BLF (Hopper & Turton, 2001) means genetic algorithm+bottom left fill; hybrid heuristic (HH) (Zhang *et al.*, 2005) is based on divide-and-conquer; and heuristic for rectangle packing (HRP) (Huang *et al.*, 2007) is based on corner-occupying action and caving degree. Heuristic1, SA+BLF, GA+BLF, HH and HRP are not implemented in this paper, so the results are directly taken from Wu et al. (2002), Hopper & Turton (2001), Zhang et al. (2005) and Huang et al. (2007). Heuristic1 is run on a SUN Sparc20/71 with a 71MHz SuperSparc CPU and 64MB RAM; SA+BLF and GA+BLF are run on a Pentium pro with a 200MHz processor and 65MB RAM; HH is run on a Dell GX260 with a 2.4GHz CPU; QHA and HRP are run on IBM notebook PC with a 2.0GHz processor and 256MB memory. As an example, the packing results of instances 2, 5, 8, 14, 17 and 20 achieved by QHA are shown in Fig. 7.

For 21 rectangle-packing test instances, optimal solutions of 19 ones are achieved by QHA, i.e., all rectangles are packed into the box without overlapping area, the area usage of the box is 100%, and percent (%) of unpacked area, which is defined by 100(*box area - total area of already packed rectangles*)/*box area*, is 0%. And optimal solutions of 2, 3 and 16 ones are achieved by heuristic1, HH and HRP, respectively. The comparisons of the results of 21 instances between HRP, heuristic1, HH and QHA are listed in table 1. From table 1, we see that the runtime of QHA on some larger instances is shorter than that on some smaller instances because the program stops successfully when all rectangles are packed into the box without overlapping. As a result, it is natural that the runtime of QHA on instance 20 is much shorter than that on instance 19 and 21, as shown in table 1.

The original problem can be equivalently described as to minimize the container height under packing all rectangles without overlapping into a fixed width rectangular container.

This is so-called strip packing. In this paper, the minimal container height is calculated by QHA for each of 21 instances. The optimal solutions of all 21 ones except instances 19 and 21 are achieved by QHA. The best solution (i.e., the minimal box height) of instance 19 and 21 achieved by QHA is listed in table 2. Comparisons of the relative distance of the best solution to optimal solution (%) which is defined by 100(*best solution - optimal solution*)/*optimal solution* and the runtime (min) between SA+BLF (Hopper & Turton, 2001), GA+BLF (Hopper & Turton, 2001) and QHA are listed in table 3, where the relative distance and runtime is the average value of three instances, as shown in table 3.

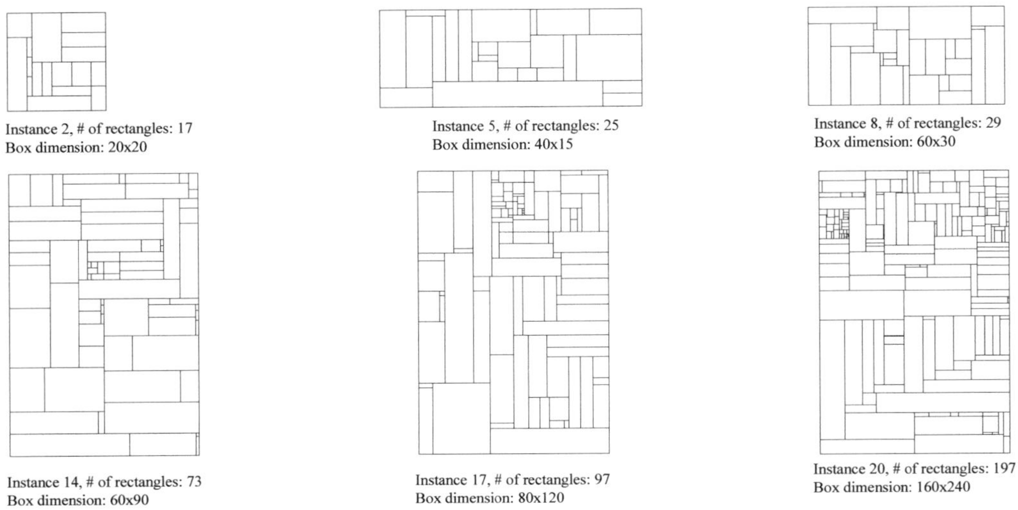

Fig. 7. The packing results of instances 2, 5, 8, 14, 17 and 20

5.2 13 random instances provided by Burke et al

We also use 13 random instances[1] provided by Burke et al. (2004) to test our algorithm. The comparisons of the box height and runtime between BF heuristic (Burke et al., 2004) and QHA are listed in table 4. For these 13 instances, optimal solutions of 3 ones are achieved by QHA, but none of them by BF heuristic. For each of the 13 instances, the container height obtained by QHA is smaller than that by BF heuristic, as shown in columns 4 and 6 of table 4. From table 4, we can see that the integrated performance of QHA is also rather satisfying for random instances. As an example, the packing result of instance N13 is shown in Fig. 8.

6. Conclusion

In this paper, an efficient quasi-human heuristic algorithm (QHA) for solving rectangle-packing problem is proposed. High area usage of the box can be obtained by this algorithm. Optimal solutions of 19 of 21 test instances taken from Hopper & Turton (2001) and 3 of 13 instances taken from Burke et al. (2004) are achieved by QHA. The experimental results demonstrate that QHA is rather efficient for solving the rectangle-packing problem. We guess the quasi-human approach will be fruitful for solving other NP-hard problems.

---

[1] The 13th instance N13 is generated on the basis of the 20th instance in Hopper & Turton (2001).

Instance	# of rectangles	Box dimensions (wxh)	QHA		HRP (Huang et al., 2007)		heuristic1 (Wu et al., 2002)		HH (Zhang et al., 2005)	
			% of unpacked area	Runtime (sec)	% of unpacked area	Runtime (sec)	% of unpacked area	Runtime (sec)	% of unpacked area	Runtime (sec)
1	16	20 x 20	0	0.02	0	0.05	2	1.48	2	0
2	17	20 x 20	0	0.22	0	0.23	2	2.42	3.5	0
3	16	20 x 20	0	0.04	0	1.12	2.5	2.63	0	0
4	25	40 x 15	0	0.3	0	0.08	0.67	13.35	0.67	0.05
5	25	40 x 15	0	0.09	0	0.1	0	10.88	0	0.05
6	25	40 x 15	0	0.05	0	0.28	0	7.92	0	0
7	28	60 x 30	0	1.16	0	2.58	0.67	23.72	0.67	0.05
8	29	60 x 30	0	7.77	0	4.19	0.83	34.02	2.44	0.05
9	28	60 x 30	0	2.51	0	2.5	0.78	30.97	1.56	0.05
10	49	60 x 60	0	265.58	0	327.12	0.97	438.18	1.36	0.44
11	49	60 x 60	0	20.13	0	36.59	0.22	354.47	0.78	0.44
12	49	60 x 60	0	20.78	0	135.6	No report	No report	0.44	0.33
13	73	60 x 90	0	72.09	0	55.44	0.3	1417.52	0.44	1.54
14	73	60 x 90	0	5.25	0	29.17	0.04	1507.52	0.44	1.81
15	73	60 x 90	0	38.34	0	51.13	0.83	1466.15	0.37	2.25
16	97	80 x 120	0	1610	0.15	873.38	0.25	7005.73	0.66	5.16
17	97	80 x 120	0	86.29	0	327.61	3.74	5537.88	0.26	5.33
18	97	80 x 120	0	490.81	0.06	577.59	0.54	5604.7	0.5	5.6
19	196	160 x 240	0.04	8303.13	0.24	4276.82	No report	No report	1.25	94.62
20	197	160 x 240	0	1520.27	0.12	3038.6	No report	No report	0.55	87.25
21	196	160 x 240	0.13	9288.21	0.16	3980.65	No report	No report	0.69	78.02

Table 1. Experimental results of 21 instances provided by Hopper & Turton (2001) on HRP, heuristic1, HH and QHA

Instance	# of rectangles	Box width	Optimal solution	Best solution	Runtime(sec)
19	196	160	240	241	8304.89
21	196	160	240	241	9291.44

Table 2. The best solution of instance 19 and 21 under packing all rectangles into the box

Instance	1, 2, 3	4, 5, 6	7, 8, 9	10, 11, 12	13, 14, 15	16, 17, 18	19, 20, 21
QHA (Relative distance, %/ runtime, min)	0/<0.01	0/<0.01	0/0.06	0/1.70	0/0.64	0/12.15	0.28/ 106.20
SA+BLF (Hopper & Turton, 2001) (Relative distance, %/ runtime, min)	4/0.7	6/2.4	5/4	3/33	3/115	3/382	4/4181
GA+BLF (Hopper & Turton, 2001) (Relative distance, %/ runtime, min)	4/1	7/2	5/3	3/13	4/36	4/86	5/777

Table 3. Comparisons of the relative distance of best solution to optimal solution (%) and the runtime (min) between SA+BLF, GA+BLF and QHA

Instance	# of rectangles	Optimal height	BF heuristic (Burke et al., 2004)		QHA	
			Box height	Runtime (sec)	Box height	Runtime (sec)
N1	10	40	45	<0.01	40	0.17
N2	20	50	53	<0.01	50	1.73
N3	30	50	52	<0.01	50	2.91
N4	40	80	83	<0.01	81	105.53
N5	50	100	105	0.01	102	134.04
N6	60	100	103	0.01	101	137.92
N7	70	100	107	0.01	101	423.73
N8	80	80	84	0.01	81	865.96
N9	100	150	152	0.01	151	1242.77
N10	200	150	152	0.02	151	7912.36
N11	300	150	152	0.03	151	1.5×10^4
N12	500	300	306	0.06	303	4.4×10^4
N13	3152	960	964	1.37	962	5.2×10^5

Table 4. Comparisons of the box height and runtime between BF heuristic and QHA

7. Acknowledgments

This work was partially supported by National Natural Science Foundation of China under Grant No. 10471051, by NKBRPC (2004CB318000), by National High-tech R&D Program (2006AA01Z414, 2007AA01Z440), by Research and Development Project on Application Technology of Sichuan under Grant No. 2008GZ0009. and by Chinese Information Security Research Plan under Grant No. (242)2007B27.

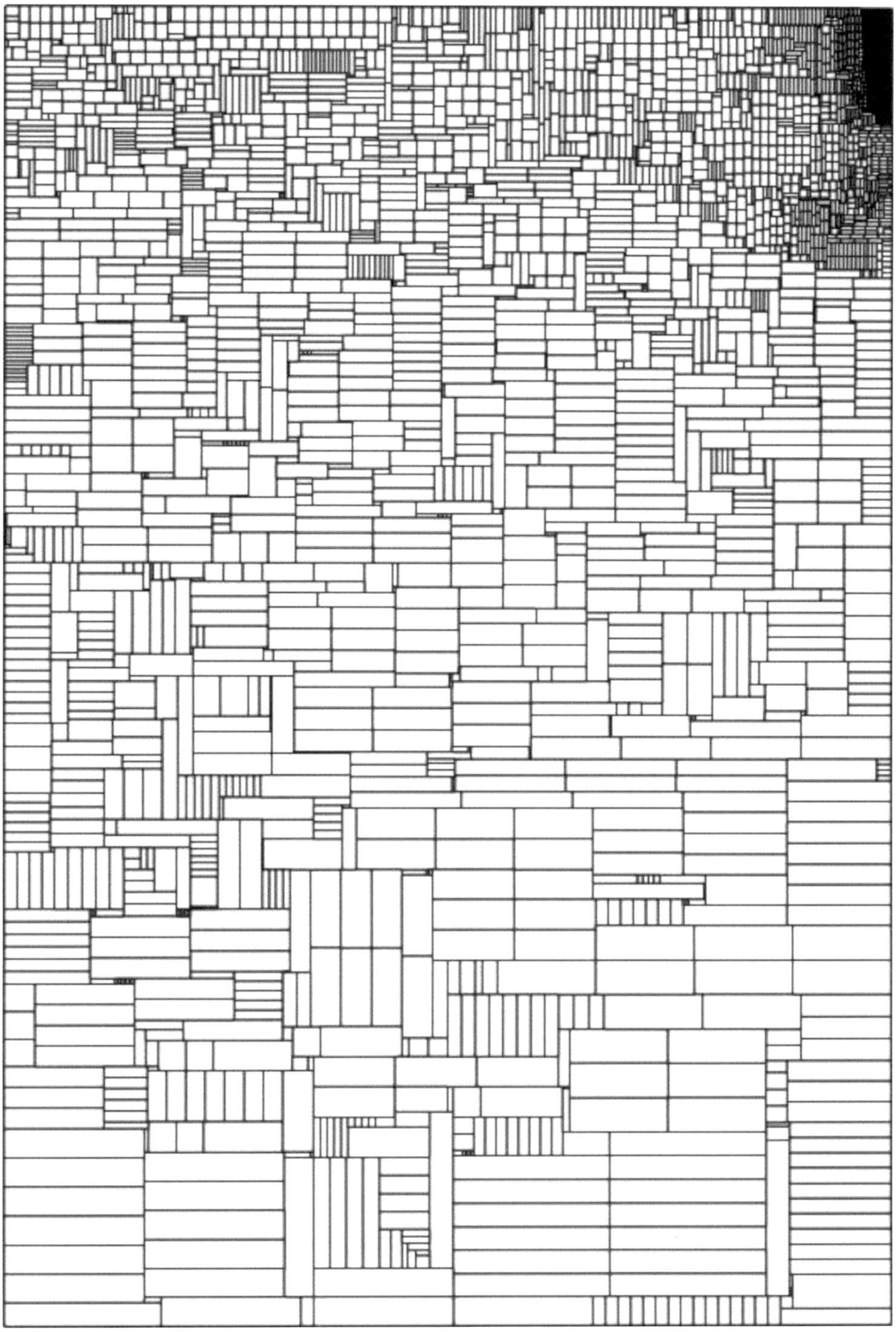

Fig. 8. The packing result of instance N13 by QHA

8. References

Leung J., Tam T., Wong C.S., Young G. & Chin F. (1990), Packing squares into a square, *Journal of Parallel and Distributed Computing*, Vol. 10, No. 3, November 1990, pp. 271-275.

Lodi A., Martello S. & Monaci M. (2002), Two-dimensional packing problems: A survey, *European Journal of Operational Research*, Vol.141, No. 2, September 2002, pp. 241-252.

Pisinger D. (2002), Heuristic for the container loading problem, *European Journal of Operational Research*, Vol. 141, No. 2, September 2002, pp. 382-392.

Hopper E. & Turton B. (1999), A genetic algorithm for a 2D industrial packing problem, *Computers & Industrial Engineering*, Vol. 37, No. 1-2, October 1999, pp. 375-378.

Bortfeldt A. (2006), A genetic algorithm for the two-dimensional strip packing problem with rectangular pieces, *European Journal of Operational Research*, Vol. 172, No. 3, August 2006, pp. 814-837.

Wu Y. L., Huang W., Lau S., Wong C. K. & Young G. H. (2002), An effective quasi-human based heuristic for solving the rectangle packing problem, *European Journal of Operational Research*, Vol. 141, No. 2, September 2002, pp. 341-358.

Beasley J. E. (1985), An exact two-dimensional non-guillotine cutting tree search procedure, *Operations Research*, Vol. 33, No. 1, January 1985, pp. 49-64.

Liu D. & Teng H. (1999), An improved BL-algorithm for genetic algorithm of the orthogonal packing of rectangles, *European Journal of Operational Research*, Vol. 112, No.2, January 1999, pp. 413-420.

Leung T. W., Chan C.K. & Troutt M. D. (2003), Application of a mixed simulated annealing-genetic algorithm heuristic for the two-dimensional orthogonal packing problem, *European Journal of Operational Research*, Vol. 145, No. 3, March 2003, pp. 530-542.

Lodi A., Martello S. & Vigo D. (1999), Heuristic and metaheuristic approaches for a class of two-dimensional bin packing problems, *INFORMS Journal on Computing*, Vol. 11, No.4, April 1999, pp. 345-357.

Hopper E. & Turton B. (2001), An empirical investigation of meta-heuristic and heuristic algorithm for a 2D packing problem, *European Journal of Operational Research*, Vol. 128, No.1, January 2001, pp. 34-57.

Zhang D., Deng A. & Kang Y. (2005), A hybrid heuristic algorithm for the rectangular packing problem, *in: Proceedings of the 5th International Conference on Computational Science, Atlanta, GA, USA, May 22-25, 2005, part I, Lecture Notes in Computer Science*, Vol. 3514, pp. 783-791.

Burke E. K., Kendall G. & Whitwell G. (2004), A new placement heuristic for the orthogonal stock-cutting problem, *Operations Research*, Vol. 52, No. 4, July/August 2004, pp. 655-671.

Huang W. & Jin R. (1997), The quasi-physical and quasi-sociological algorithm solar for solving SAT problem, *Science in China, Series E (Technological Sciences)*, Vol. 27, No.2, April 1997, pp. 179-186.

Huang W. & Xu R. (1999), Two personification strategies for solving circles packing problem, *Science in China, Series E (Technological Sciences)*, Vol. 42, No. 6, December 1999, pp. 595-602.

Huang W., Li Y., Akeb H. & Li C. (2005), Greedy algorithms for packing unequal circles into a rectangular container, *Journal of the Operational Research Society*, Vol. 56, No. 5, May 2005, pp. 539-548.

Huang W., Chen D. & Xu R. (2007), A new heuristic algorithm for rectangle packing, *Computers & Operations Research*, Vol.34, No.11, November 2007, pp. 3270-3280.

8

Application of Simulated Annealing to Routing Problems in City Logistics

Hisafumi Kokubugata and Hironao Kawashima
Department of Administration Engineering, Keio University
Japan

1. Introduction

The R & D activities to realize systems which provide road traffic information and route guidance have been conducted as core systems of Intelligent Transport Systems (ITS). However, the implementation of these systems will have less effect on freight transport unless logistics operation is rationalized in parallel to the development of ITS. On the other hand, according to the expansion of internet, information has been exchanged with extremely high speed and low cost. Nevertheless, goods must be moved in the real space. E-commerce has caused the increase of door-to-door deliveries. The demands for high-quality delivery services such as small-amount high frequency deliveries with time windows have been made by many clients (including companies and individuals). The loading rate of trucks has decreased and the rate of freight transportation in total road traffic has increased. The rationalization in terms of increasing the loading rate and decreasing the total travel time is aimed not only for reducing operational costs in each freight carrier but also for relieving traffic congestion, saving energy and reducing the amount of CO_2. Freight transportation in urban areas that is described above is called city logistics (Taniguchi et al. 2001).

Many researches on routing problems have been appeared in the literature. Comprehensive and detailed explanations of theoretical models and solutions of them are given by Toth & Vigo (Toth & Vigo, 2002). On the other hand, in the context of city logistics, real routing problems should not be based under the assumption on the symmetry of the link costs of visiting customer j after customer i or customer i after customer j, $p_{ij}=p_{ji}$, and other related mathematical properties, as triangular property etc. This is due to the fact that in an urban environment routes using the streets have to account for one way streets, issues related to regulations at intersections. In addition, travel time might vary according to traffic conditions, that is to say, it might be time dependent. Moreover, in urban road networks, demands might be located on not only spots on streets but also streets themselves. This chapter is aimed for describing the original solution, which has been invented by the authors of this chapter, to routing problems in city logistics.

At the beginning of this chapter, a variety of routing problems will be introduced and followed by the explanation of features of routing problems in city logistics. And then, a practical solution method, which is composed of a data model, transformation rules of a solution on the data model and an overall algorithm using Simulated Annealing for solving a variety of routing problems in city logistics, is proposed in this chapter. Evaluation of the proposed method is conducted by comparisons on computational results with those derived from other heuristics.

2. Typical routing problems in city logistics

Typical routing problems are abstracted from actual logistics operations in urban areas and formalized as mathematical problems. They are categorized as the combinatorial optimization problems. In this section, according to the type of the place that demand belongs, three problems are distinguished. They are introduced as follows.

2.1 Vehicle Routing Problem (VRP)

The Vehicle Routing Problem (VRP) is the most popular problem in routing problems. It involves the design of a set of minimum cost vehicle trips, originating and ending at a depot, for a fleet of vehicles with loading capacity that services a set of client spots with required demands. The problems studied in this chapter can be described in the style used by Crescenzi & Kann (Crescenzi & Kann, 2000) for their compendium of *NP* optimization problems. Although VRP is not listed in the compendium, it is given by Prins & Bouchenoua (Prins & Bouchenoua, 2004) as follows.

- INSTANCE: Complete undirected graph $G = (V,E)$, initial vertex $s \in V$, vehicle capacity $W \in IN$, length $c(e) \in IN$ for each $e \in E$, demand $q(i) \in IN$ for each $i \in V$.
- SOLUTION: A set of cycles (trips), each containing the initial vertex s, that collectively traverses every node at least once. A node must be serviced by one single trip and the total demand processed by any trip cannot exceed W.
- MEASURE: The total cost of the trips, to be minimized. The cost of a trip is the sum of its traversed edges.

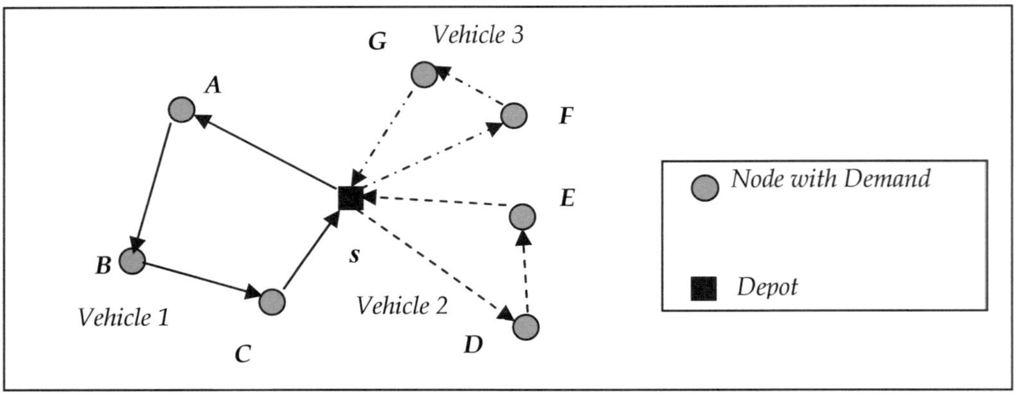

Fig. 1. Vehicle Routing Problem (VRP)

Although the VRP in a narrow sense is defined above, the VRP in a broader sense includes the more comprehensive class of routing problems related to various conditions in which demands are located on nodes. It includes VRP with time windows imposed by clients, VRP with multiple depots, periodic VRP and etc. In this case, the simplest VRP defined above is called capacitated VRP (CVRP).

2.2 Capacitated Arc Routing Problem (CARP)

When people observe deliveries in urban area, it is understood that some delivery or pickup demands belong not to spots but to streets. This circumstance contains the case where the demands are densely located along a street such as postal deliveries, and the case where the demand belongs to a street itself such as garbage collections and snow removals. In these cases, they are more suitable to be formulated as the Capacitated Arc Routing Problem (CARP) rather than as VRP. CARP was introduced by Golden & Wong (Golden & Wong, 1981). It consists of determining a set of vehicle trips at minimum total cost, such that each trip starts and ends at a depot, each required undirected edge is serviced by one single trip, and the total demand handled by any vehicle does not exceed its loading capacity. The definition of CARP is also given by Prins & Bouchenoua in the Crescenzi & Kann's style.

- INSTANCE: Undirected graph $G = (V,E)$, initial vertex $s \in V$, vehicle capacity $W \in IN$, subset $E_R \subseteq E$, length $c(e) \in IN$ and demand $q(e) \in IN$ for each edge $e \in E_R$.
- SOLUTION: A set of cycles (trips), each containing the initial vertex s, that collectively traverses each edge of E_R at least once. Each edge of E_R must be serviced by one single trip and the total demand processed by any trip cannot exceed W.
- MEASURE: The total cost of the trips, to be minimized. The cost of a trip comprises the costs of its traversed edges, serviced or not.

However, when the actual city logistics is considered, the original CARP is merely able to express arc routing operations in the real world imperfectly. To take waste collection as an example, there are many one-way streets in urban areas. Besides, even in two-way streets, vehicles often collect waste along one side of the street only, because broad streets are often split by central reservations. Therefore, the extended CARP introduced by Lacomme et al. (Lacomme et al., 2001) that takes account of both undirected edges and directed arcs is dealt with in this chapter.

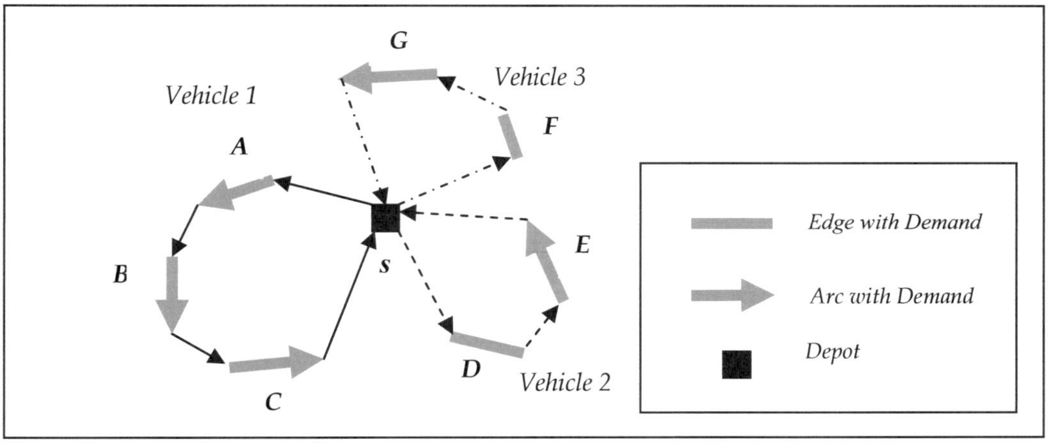

Fig. 2. The Extended Capacitated Arc Routing Problem (The Extended CARP)

2.3 General Routing Problem with Nodes, Edges, and Arcs (NEARP)

To take waste collection as an example of city logistics, there are some punctual dumps (such as factories, schools, and hospitals) that put out a large amount of waste, while other small waste dumps along a street are considered as the grouped arc demand. In order to fit the model more closely to the routing situations in the real world, Prins & Bouchenoua defined a general routing problem with nodes, edges, and arcs (NEARP) that handles demands which belong to any of nodes, (undirected) edges and (directed) arcs (Prins & Bouchenoua, 2004).

- INSTANCE: Mixed graph $G = (V, E, A)$, initial vertex $s \in V$, vehicle capacity $W \in IN$, subset $V_R \subseteq V$, subset $E_R \subseteq E$, subset $A_R \subseteq A$, traversal cost $c(u) \in IN$ for each "entity" $u \in V \cup E \cup A$, demand $q(u) \in IN$ and processing cost $p(u) \in IN$ for each required entity (task) $u \in V_R \cup E_R \cup A_R$.
- SOLUTION: A set of cycles (trips), each containing the initial vertex s, that may traverse each entity any number of times but process each task exactly once. The total demand processed by any trip cannot exceed W.
- MEASURE: The total cost of the trips, to be minimized. The cost of a trip comprises the processing costs of its serviced tasks and the traversal costs of the entities used for connecting these tasks.

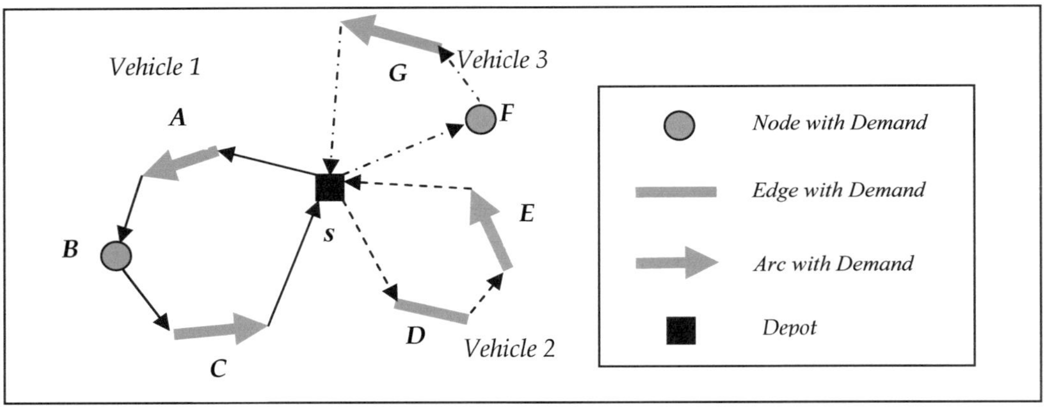

Fig. 3. Node, Edge and Arc Routing Problem (NEARP)

3. Precedent studies on heuristics for routing problems

The VRP belongs to *NP*-hard problems. Even concerning the simple VRP, exact methods are not fit for large problems. Therefore, heuristics have been important in the application of the VRP. Before the proposed method will be explained, precedent studies on heuristics for VRP are introduced briefly. The heuristics for solving routing problems are classified into two major classes (Toth & Vigo, 2002). One is the family of classical heuristics and the other is the family of metaheuristics including Simulated Annealing.

3.1 Classical heuristics for VRP

The heuristics belong to the first class have been specially invented for solving routing problems. They utilize the proper characteristics of routing problems. They are called classical heuristics. They are further classified into three types.

The first one is the type of constructive heuristics that produce vehicle routes by merging existing routes or inserting nodes into existing routes. The famous saving method (Clark & Wright, 1964) that made the beginning of the studies on VRP belongs to this subtype.

Chistofides, Mingozzi & Toth Insertion Heuristic (Chistofides et al., 1979) also belongs to this subtype.

The second one is the type of two-phase heuristics. Most of them assign nodes with demands to vehicles in the first phase, and then decide routing order of nodes for each vehicle in the second phase. These are called cluster-first, route-second methods. Fisher & Jaikumar Algorithm (Fisher & Jaikumar, 1981) is the typical method which belongs to this type. The optimization in the second phase which is applied to the result of optimization in the first phase is not guaranteed to derive global optimum. There are also route-first cluster-second methods which produce a giant tour including entire nodes in the first phase, and then cut and divide into vehicle routes in the second phase.

The last one is the type of improvement heuristics which make changes in one vehicle route or between several vehicle routes. Lin & Kernighan (Lin & Kernighan, 1973) method is the typical method which belongs to this type. Many methods of this type are based on λ-opt mechanism in which λ edges connecting nodes are exchanged in routes.

3.2 Metaheuristics for VRP

Metaheuristics have been introduced into the solutions for VRP in the last two decades. Because metaheuristics are generally recognized to fit combinatorial optimizations, Simulated Annealing (SA), Tabu Search (TS), Genetic Algorithm (GA) and Ant Colony Optimization (ACO) have been tried to apply to VRP.

Among the methods incorporating TS, Taburoute algorithm of Gendreau et al., (Gendreau et al., 1994) has had an established reputation. In each repetition in the method, one node is deleted from a vehicle route and inserted into the best position in other routes.

Among the methods incorporating GA, the method proposed by Prins (Prins, 2001) is reported to get good results. It adopts a hybrid strategy that consists of GA procedure in the giant tour without route delimiters, and local search procedures carried out in a route or between two vehicle routes.

With respect to ACO, not so many works on VRP are appeared in the literature.

Among VRP solutions using SA, the method proposed by Osman (Osman, 1993) is popular. In its main procedure, one node or two nodes are exchanged between existing two vehicle routes. The move of one node or two nodes from one vehicle route to another is also allowed.

In a comprehensive survey on metaheuristics for VRP given by Gendreau et al. (Gendreau et al., 2002), it is described that the methods based on TS are the most effective. It is also said that existing methods based on SA are not competitive with TS; while those based on GA and ACO have possibility to be competitive in future studies because they have not been fully exploited.

Most of the procedures for solving the extended routing problems are developed by making use of the procedures for VRP.

4. Data model and generating neighbours in searching process of the proposed method for VRP

Although some precedent methods based on metaheuristics mentioned above show good performance, their procedures are considerably complex. In particular, the local search procedures incorporated into them are rather complicated. The original solution of VRP which is composed of a simpler data model and a one phase algorithm, incorporated with original methods of generating neighbours, has been proposed by the authors of this chapter.

4.1 Data model for VRP

The model to express a state of solution of VRP is realized as a sequence of integers, i.e., a string. In the string, the position of a number, which is a symbol of the node with demand, implies not only which vehicle tours the node but also the routing order of it. An example of the string model is illustrated in Fig.4. In the string, a node with demand is expressed by a positive number. The special number '0' should be interpreted not only as the depot but also as the delimiter which partitions the trips. If the number of vehicles is denoted by m, $(m-1)$ '0's are provided in the string. If there is no number between '0' and '0', the relevant vehicle is not in use.

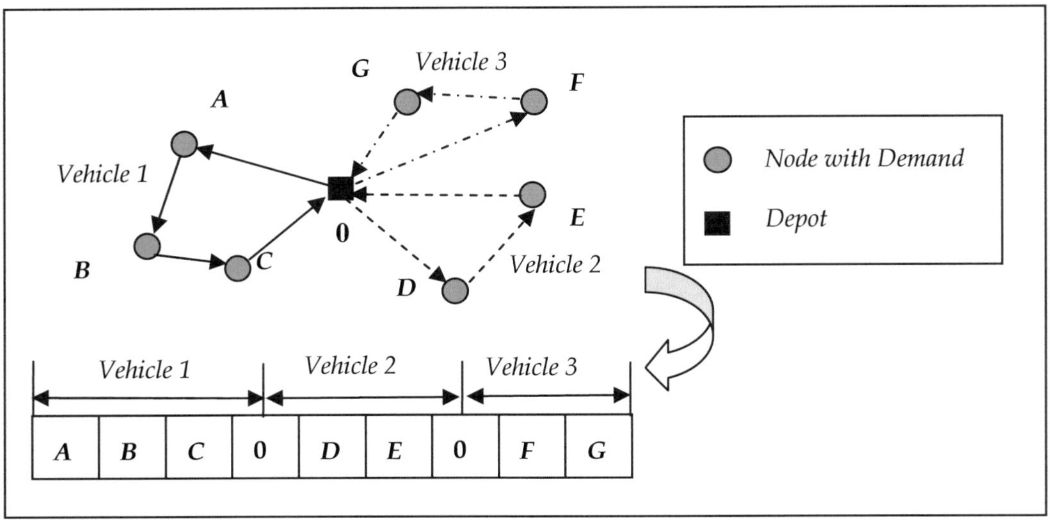

Fig. 4. Proposed Data Model for VRP

This data model is coincidentally similar to that invented for the solution based on a kind of GA. It was introduced by Gendreau et al. (Gendreau et al. 2002) as the original idea was given by Van Breedam (Van Breedam, 1996). However, the proposed transformation rules in this chapter based on the data model are quite different from those of precedent methods as they will be described in the following section.

4.2 Transformation rules for generating neighbors

In a repetition in the proposed procedure, a new state of solution is generated from the present state by one of the following three types of transformation rules for generating neighbours. The first rule is to exchange a number with another one in the string. The second rule is to delete an arbitrary number and then insert it to another position in the string. The third rule is that after a part of the string is taken out temporally, the direction of the partial string is reversed, and then embedded in the place where the string is taken out. These three transformation rules are illustrated in Fig. 5.

Note that the rules are also applied to the special number '0' in the string data model illustrated in Fig.4. In other words, '0' is treated impartially with other numbers.

If 'one-to-one exchange' is executed within a substring partitioned by '0', only a vehicle route is changed. An example of the case is illustrated in Fig. 6. If 'one-to-one exchange' is executed between two non-zeros striding over '0', two tasks are exchanged between two vehicle routes. An example of this case is illustrated in Fig. 7. If 'one-to-one exchange' is executed between a non-zero number and '0', two vehicle routes are merged, while another vehicle route is divided into two vehicle routes. An example is illustrated in Fig. 8.

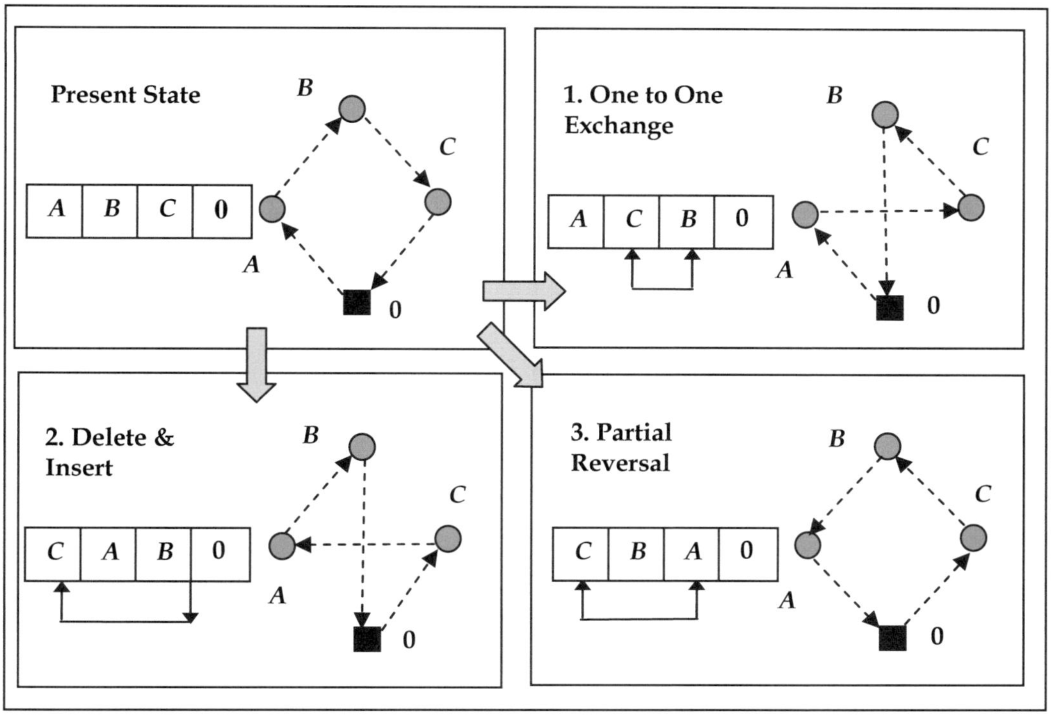

Fig. 5. Three Transformation Rules for Generating Neighbours

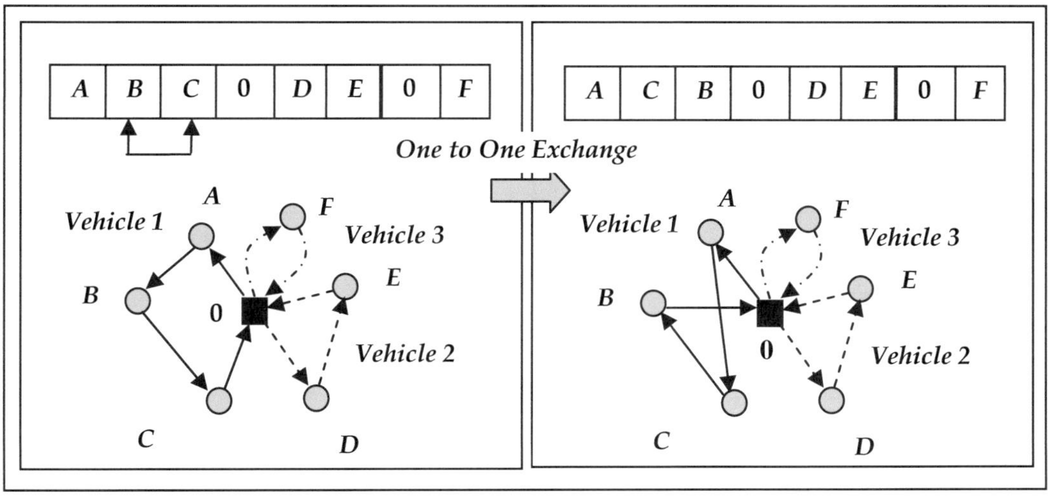

Fig. 6. A Result of 'One-to-One Exchange' within a Vehicle Route

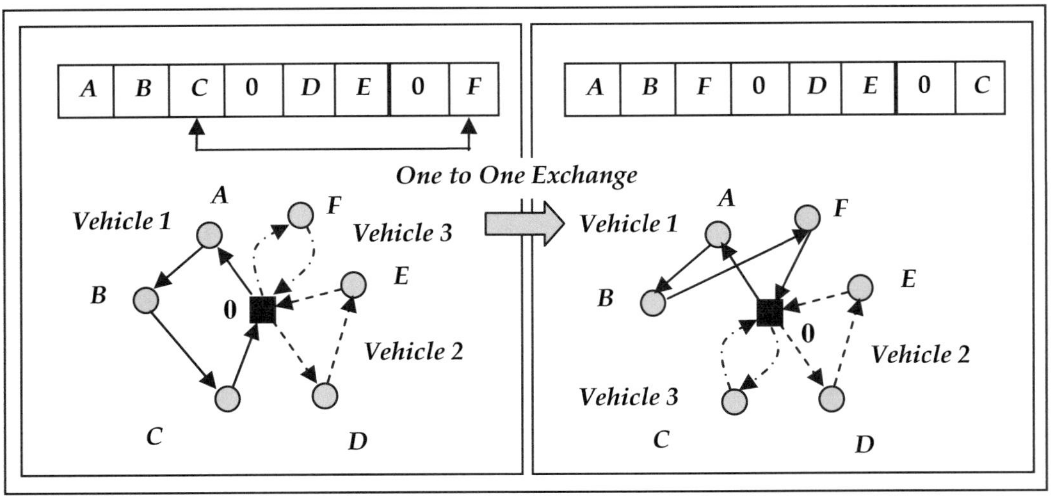

Fig. 7. A Result of 'One-to-One Exchange' between Two Non-Zeros Striding over '0'

When the second transformations rule 'delete and insert' is applied, several different cases also arise. If a non-zero number is deleted and inserted at '0', a task is moved to another vehicle route. An example is illustrated in Fig. 9.

When the third transformations rule 'partial reversal' is applied, several different cases also arise. If a substring including '0' is reversed, the relevant plural vehicle routes are changed. An example is illustrated in Fig.10.

These transformation rules were originally presented by the authors of this chapter (Kokubugata et al., 1997).

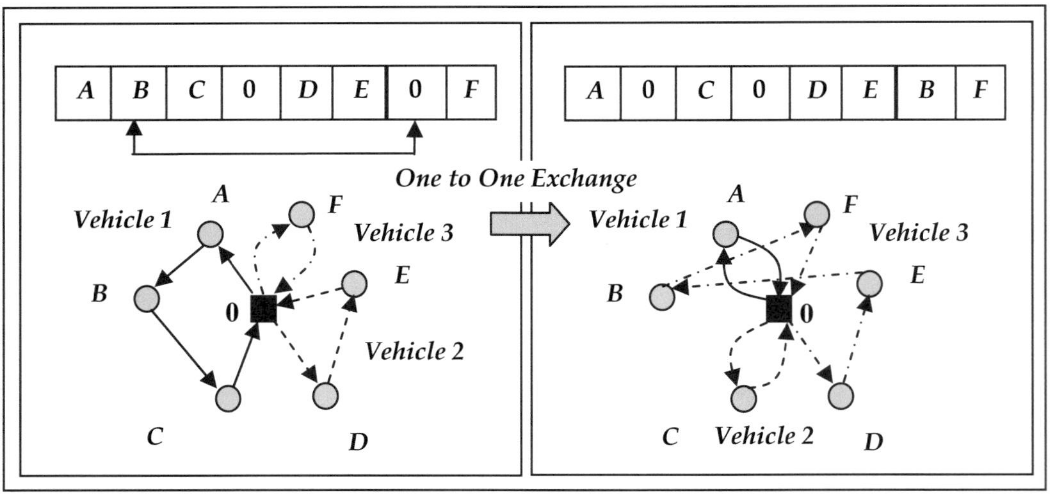

Fig. 8. A Result of 'One-to-One Exchange' between Non-Zero and '0'

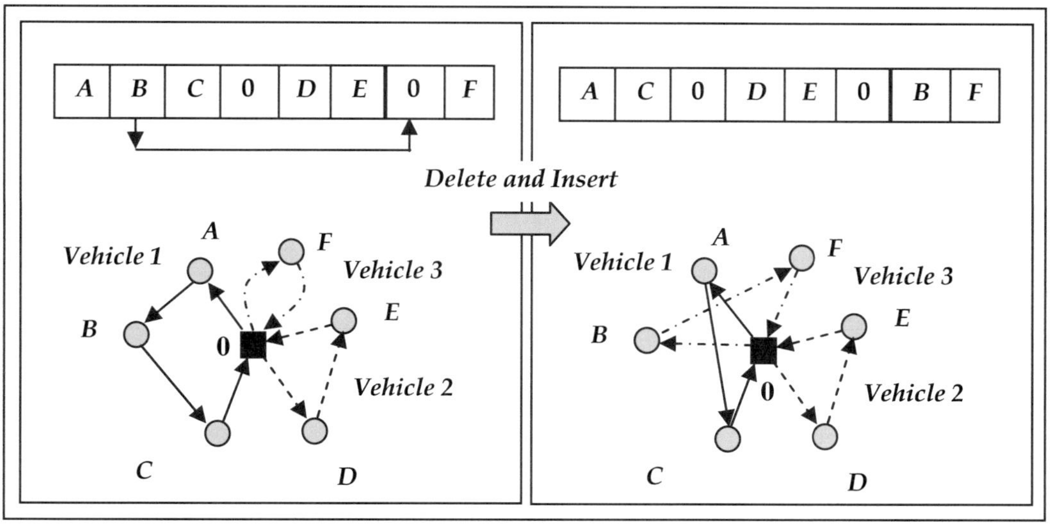

Fig. 9. A Result of Deleting Non-Zero and Inserting It at '0'

4.3 Objective function

The objective of the VRP is the minimization of total cost which is subject to constraints including the loading capacity of each vehicle. The objective function of the VRP is formulated as follows.

$$E = \sum_{i=1}^{n} c_{s_i} + \sum_{i=0}^{n} p_{s_i, s_{i+1}} \tag{1}$$

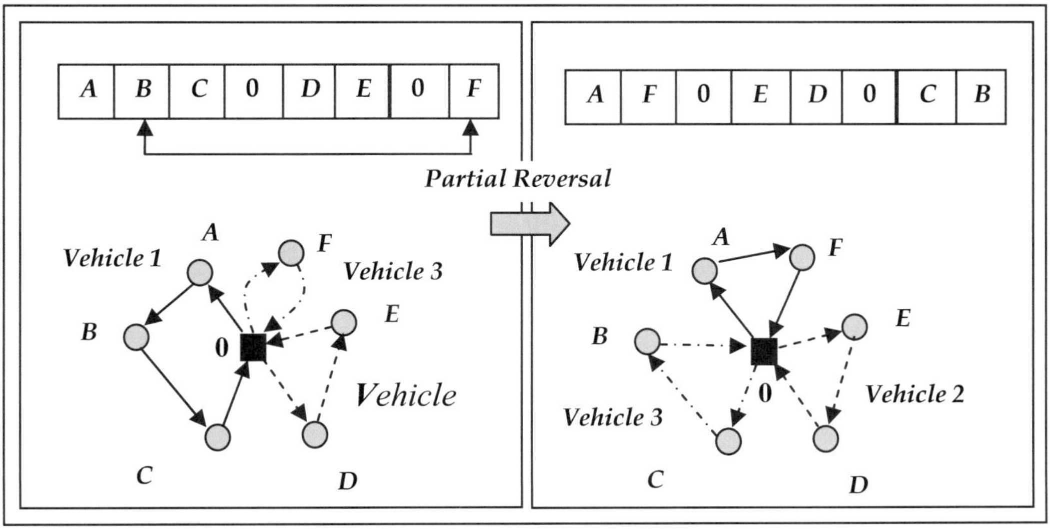

Fig. 10. A Result of 'Partial Reversal' Striding over '0'

where $s = (s_1, s_2, \cdots, s_n)$ is a string that consists of the nodes with demands and a depot; s_0 and s_{n+1} are the implicit expressions of the depot omitted in the string s; c_k is the servicing cost at the node k (if $k = 0$,then $c_k = 0$); $p_{k,l}$ is the minimal traversing cost from the node k to the node l.

Each value of $p_{k,l}$ might be given by input data; or calculated as the Euclidean distances between a pair of coordinates of nodes; or calculated by the shortest path search algorithm (Warshall-Floyd's algorithm) when road network is given and vehicles must are follow the roads in the network.

4.4 Optimization algorithm using simulated annealing

Simulated Annealing (Metropolis method) is adopted as the optimization technique for the proposed method since it is characterized by simple stochastic procedures and by global searching scope.

Starting with a random initial state, it is expected to approach an equilibrium point. In the proposed method, the three transformation rules described in Sec. 4.2 are applied randomly to the string model. The entire algorithm for the VRP is described as follows.

{ I. Preparation}
Read input data;
If the link cost are not given from the input data, calculate the minimum path cost $p_{k,l}$
between all pair of tasks k, l including the depot 0;
{II. Initialization} Generate a random initial feasible solution x_0; $x := x_0$; $x^* := x$; (2)
$T :=$ *INITTEMP; Set N as the averaged neighbourhood size;*
{III. Optimization by SA} Minimize E by repetition of applying randomly one of the three transformation rules to the string model corresponding to x in the framework of SA;
{IV. Output} Output the best solution x^*.

Step III, that is the main part of this algorithm, is detailed as follows.

```
Repeat
    trials := 0; changes := 0;
   Repeat
       trials := trials + 1;
       Generate a new state x´from the current state x by applying randomly
       one of the three transformation rules to the string model of x;
       If x´is feasible Then
           Calculate ΔE = E(x´) − E(x);
           If ΔE < 0 Then
               x´is accepted as a new state;                                    (3)
               If E(x´) < E(x*) Then x* := x´
           Else x´is accepted with probability exp(−ΔE/T )
           If x´is accepted Then changes := changes + 1; x := x´
   Until trials ≥ SIZEFACTOR · N or changes ≥ CUTOFF · N;
   T := T · TEMPFACTOR
Until T ≤ INITTEMP / FINDIVISOR
```

As sketched in Sec. 3.2, in the existing methods using metaheuristics including SA, the transformation procedure of a solution is carried out intentionally between two existing vehicle routes. However, as descibed in Sec. 4.2, the transformation procedure of a solution of the proposed method is carried out randomly to all over the string data model. Hence, the transformation might derive changes in a vehicle route on one occation, it might derive changes over several vehicle routes on other occation.

5. Analysis of generating neighbours in searching process of the proposed method for VRP

As described in the previous section, the proposed method is based on the stochastic creation of neighbours on the string data model in searching process. In this section, the effects of transformations are classified and analyzed experimentally.

5.1 The instance of VRP for the analysis

An instance of VRP for the analysis is taken from the famous Solomon's bench mark problem sets produced by Solomon (Solomon, 1987) and provided from Solomon's own website (Solomon, 2005). c101 is chosen as an instance among them. In c101, the number of nodes is 100, the maximum number of vehicles is 25. Moreover, the amount of demand, coordinates, time window and service time are given for each node. Although these sets are provided for VRP with Time Windows (VRPTW), time window and service time in c101 are neglected for dealing with simple VRP.

5.2 Frequencies of three transformations

Frequencies of each of three transformations are counted in computational experiments. In the computations, according to the preliminary experiments and the reference to the recommended values by Johnson et al. (Johnson et al., 1989; 1991), the values of the parameters that appear in the proposed SA algorithm are set as follows.

$$
\begin{aligned}
&N = 2L^2 \ (L: \text{length of string}) \\
&SIZEFACTOR = 8 \\
&CUTOFF = 0.2 \ (\text{Repeat iterations in the same temperature } T, \\
&\qquad\qquad \text{until } (trials \geq SIZEFACTOR \cdot N \text{ or } changes \geq CUTOFF \cdot N)) \qquad (4) \\
&INITTEMP = 20 \ (\text{Initial temperature}) \\
&TEMPFACTOR = 0.95 \ (T_{n+1} = 0.95\, T_n) \\
&FINDIVISOR = 50 \ (\text{If } T \leq INITTEMP \,/\, FINDIVISOR, \text{ terminate the whole of the iterations.})
\end{aligned}
$$

Each of the three transformation rules mentioned in Sec.4.2 should be applied equally probably to produce a new feasible state of solution. However, the feasibility rates of the results generated from three transformations are not equal. Hence, in order to produce a feasible solution generated by each transformation with almost equal probability, applying rates of these three transformations at creating neighbours are adjusted, taking account of the feasibility rates computed in the preliminary experiment.

Frequencies of three transformations at creating neighbours are shown by the top bar in Fig. 11. Those in feasible solutions are shown by the second bar. Frequencies of feasible solutions bringing cost reduction are shown by the third bar. In the procedure of SA, a transformation is executed not only in the case of cost reduction but also in the case of cost increase at certain probability. Frequencies of three transformations which are really executed are shown by the fourth bar.

When the proportions of three transformations are focused on, the result of the experiment is shown as in Fig. 12. The sum of the amount of cost reduction brought by the

transformations with cost reduction is shown by the fifth bar. Moreover, the amount of cost reduction par frequencies is shown by the sixth bar.
As the result of the experiment, the fact that all of the three kinds of transformation are effective is presented.

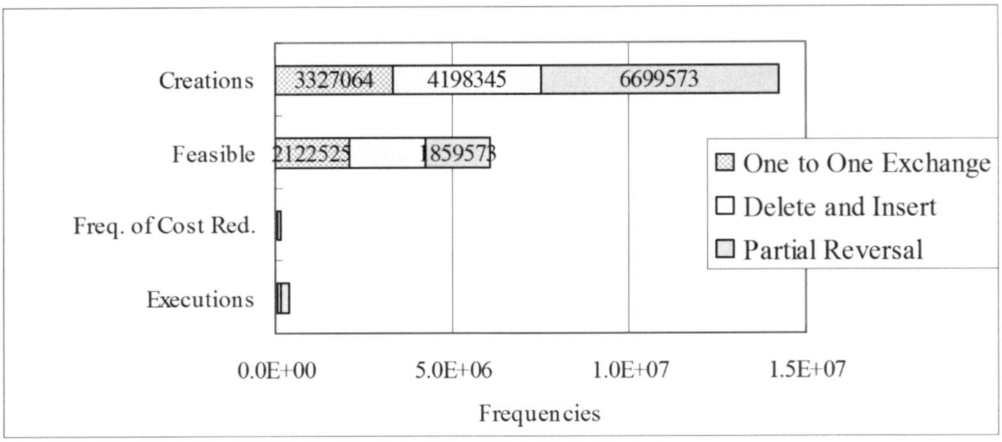

Fig.11. Frequencies of Three Transformations

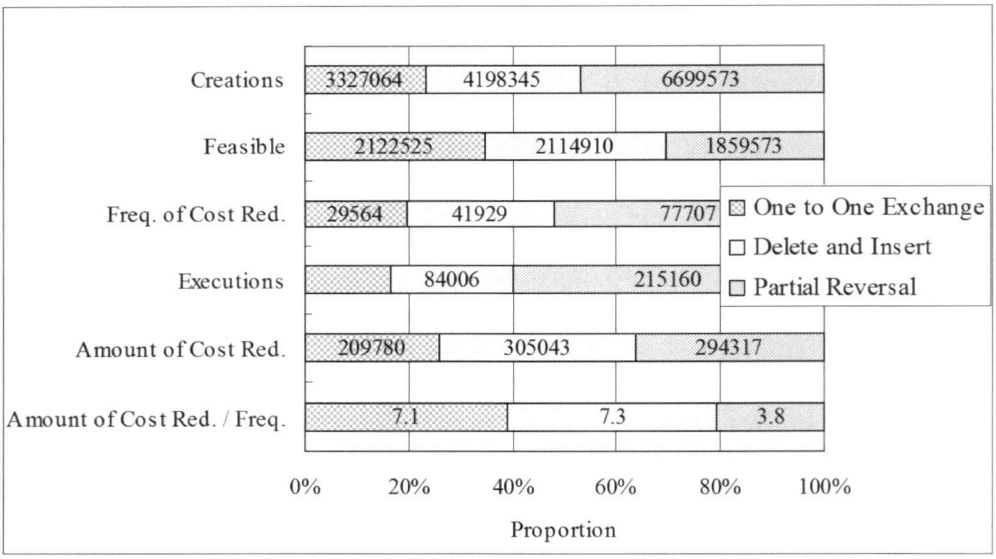

Fig.12. Proportions of Three Transformations

5.3 Classification of effects of each transformation

The core mechanism of the proposed method is based on the stochastic creation of neighbours on the string data model in searching process. Even the result of 'one-to-one exchange' varies as shown in Fig. 6-Fig. 8 according to the two positions selected randomly in the string data model. In this section, the effects of transformations are classified according to magnitude of the move.

5.3.1 Classification of effects of 'One to One Exchange'

First of all, classification of effects of 'one to one exchange' is considered. Let p be the first selected position, and q be the second selected position in the string data model. The number s_p at p is exchanged with the number s_q at q in the string s. The effects of 'one-to-one exchange' are classified as follows.

P_1 : when $p = q$. In this case, the exchange is meaningless, hence no exchange is executed.

P_2 : when $s_p = s_q = 0$. In this case, the exchange is meaningless, hence no exchange is executed.

P_3 : when ($s_p = 0$ & $s_q \neq 0$) or ($s_p \neq 0$ & $s_q = 0$). In this case, two vehicle routes are merged, while another vehicle route is divided into two vehicle routes; hence magnitude of the move might be large. An example of this case is illustrated in Fig.8 in Sec. 4.2.

P_4 : when ($s_p \neq 0$ & $s_q \neq 0$) & (there is at least one '0' between s_p and s_q). In this case, two nodes belonging to different vehicle routes are exchanged; hence magnitude of the move may be medium. An example of this case is illustrated in Fig.7 in Sec. 4.2.

P_5 : when ($s_p \neq 0$ & $s_q \neq 0$) & (s_p is not adjacent to s_q) & (there is no '0' between s_p and s_q). In this case, two nodes belonging to the same vehicle route are exchanged; hence magnitude of the move may be small.

P_6 : when ($s_p \neq 0$ & $s_q \neq 0$) & (s_p is adjacent to s_q). In this case, two adjacent nodes belonging to the same vehicle route are exchanged; hence magnitude of the move may be small. An example of this case is illustrated in Fig.6 in Sec. 4.2.

A result of computational experiment is illustrated in Fig.13.

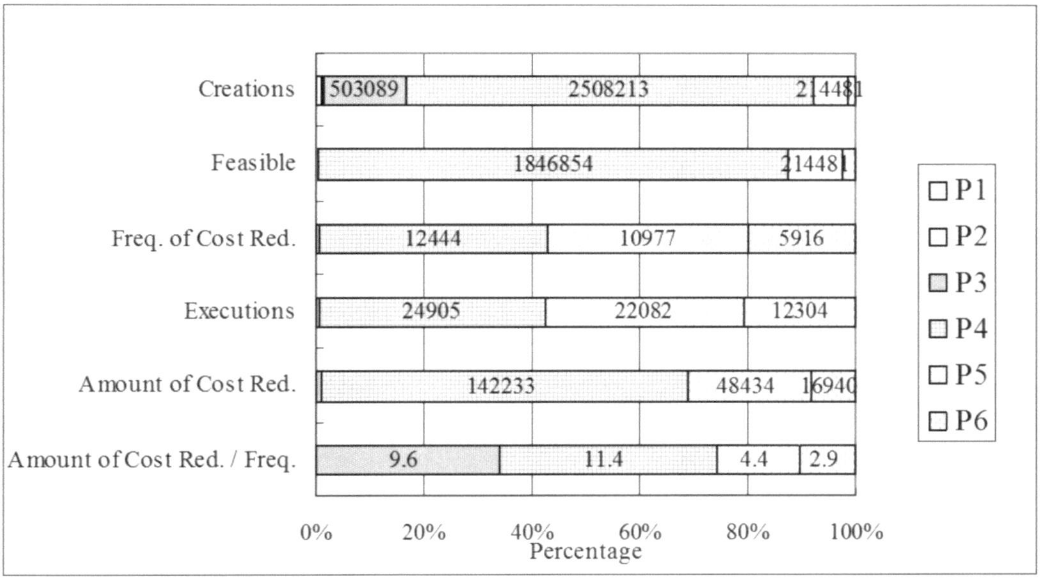

Fig.13. Effect of Each Class Related to 'One to One Exchange'

In this figure, dark parts in the bars are expressed as the moves with large effect, while light parts as the moves with small effect. As the result of the experiment, the fact that the move with medium effect (P_4) is dominant in the SA execution is presented.

5.3.2 Classification of effects of 'Delete and Insert'

The effects of 'delete and insert' are classified as follows.

Q_1 : when $p = q$. In this case, the transformation is meaningless, hence no move is executed.

Q_2 : when $s_p = s_q = 0$. In this case, '0'is moved to the adjacent position to another '0' in the string. As the result of this transformation, two vehicle routes are merged; hence magnitude of the move might be large.

Q_{31}: when $s_p = 0$ & $s_q \neq 0$. In this case, two vehicle routes are merged; hence magnitude of the move might be large.

Q_{32}: when $s_p \neq 0$ & $s_q = 0$. In this case, a node with demand is moved from a vehicles route to the tail or the end of another vehicle route; hence magnitude of the move may be medium. An example of this case is illustrated in Fig. 9 in Sec. 4.2.

Q_4 : when ($s_p \neq 0$ & $s_q \neq 0$) & (there is at least one '0' between s_p and s_q). In this case, a node with demand is moved from a vehicle route into another vehicle route; hence magnitude of the move may be medium.

Q_5 : when ($s_p \neq 0$ & $s_q \neq 0$) & (s_p is not adjacent to s_q) & (there is no '0' between s_p and s_q). In this case, a node with demand is moved to another position within the same vehicle route; hence magnitude of the move may be small.

Q_6 : when ($s_p \neq 0$ & $s_q \neq 0$) & (s_p is adjacent to s_q) . In this case, two adjacent nodes belonging to the same vehicle route are exchanged; hence magnitude of the move may be small.

A result of computational experiment is illustrated in Fig.14.

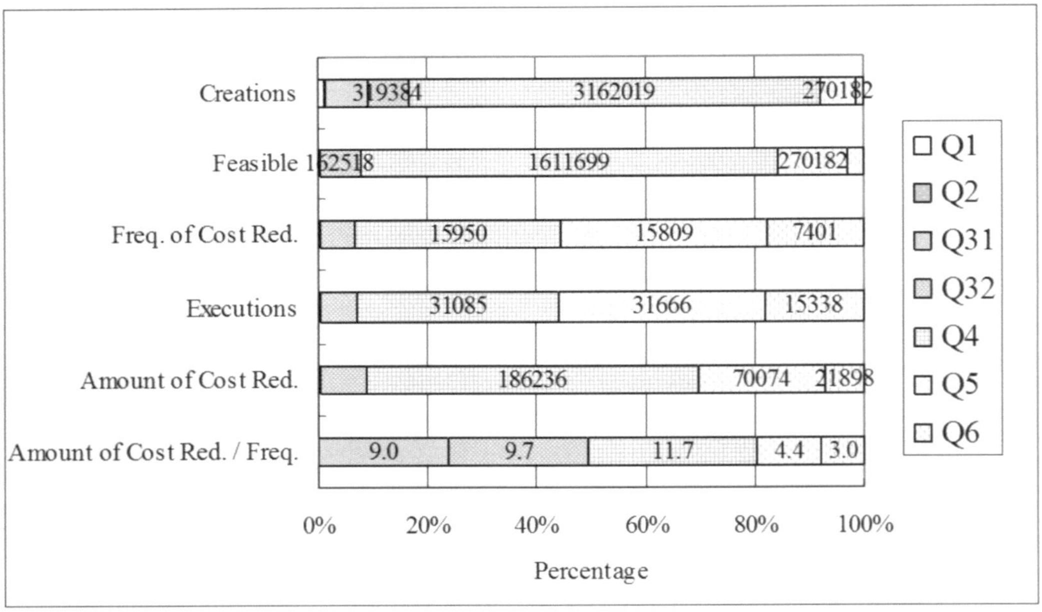

Fig.14. Effect of Each Class Related to 'Delete and Insert'

As the result of the experiment, the fact that the move with medium effect (Q_4) is dominant in the SA execution is presented.

5.3.3 Classification of effects of 'Partial Reversal'

The effects of 'partial reversal' are classified as follows.

R_1 : when $p = q$. In this case, the transformation is meaningless, hence no move is executed.

R_2 : when $s_p = s_q = 0$. In this case, a substring partitioned by two '0's is reversed. As the result, vehicle routes are reversed but vehicle assignments are not changed; hence magnitude of the move may be medium.

R_3 : when ($s_p = 0$ & $s_q \neq 0$) or ($s_p \neq 0$ & $s_q = 0$). In this case, more than one vehicle route is changed. Moreover, in the relevant vehicle routes, both composition and routing order are changed; hence magnitude of the move might be large.

R_4 : when ($s_p \neq 0$ & $s_q \neq 0$) & (there is at least one '0' between s_p and s_q). In this case, more than one vehicle route is changed. Moreover, in the relevant vehicle routes, both composition and routing order are changed; hence magnitude of the move might be large.

R_5 : when ($s_p \neq 0$ & $s_q \neq 0$) & (s_p is not adjacent to s_q) & (there is no '0' between s_p and s_q). In this case, a sub route in a vehicle route is reversed; hence magnitude of the move may be small.

R_6 : when ($s_p \neq 0$ & $s_q \neq 0$) & (s_p is adjacent to s_q). In this case, two adjacent nodes belonging route to the same vehicle are exchanged; hence magnitude of the move may be small.

A result of computational experiment is illustrated in Fig.15.

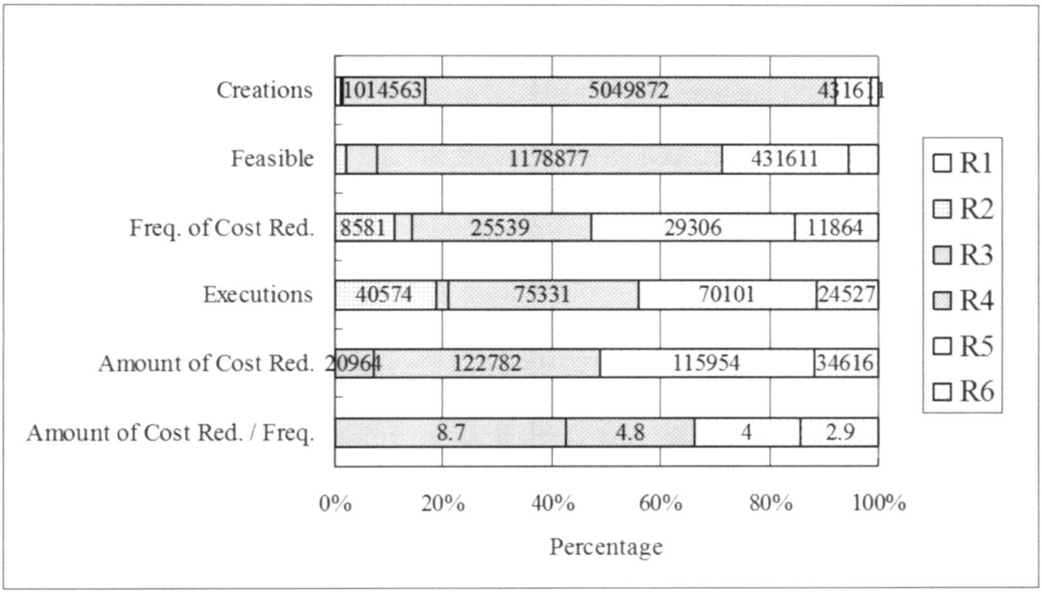

Fig. 15. Effect of Each Class Related to 'Partial Reversal'

As the result of the experiment, the fact that the move with possible large effect (R_4) and the move with small effect (R_5) are dominant in the SA procedure is presented.

Through the entire observation of the effects of moves related to three transformations, it seems that each move works appropriately and achieves the expected effects in SA executions.

The tendency for the move with large effect to be dominant at higher temperature and that for the move with small effect to be dominant at lower temperature are recognized in the closer inspection over total experiments; the detailed explanation of this topic has not been presented yet by the authors of this chapter.

6. Computational experiments on the proposed method

Computational experiments have been attempted for testing the performance of the proposed method. They have been tried on typical instances for VRPTW, CARP and NEARP.

6.1 Experiments on Solomon's benchmark problems for VRPTW

In Vehicle Routing Problem with Time Windows (VRPTW), the earliest arriving time e_i and the latest arriving time l_i are specified for each client i, that is to say, the node with demand, in addition to the definition of simple VRP. Solomon's benchmark problems are extremely popular VRPTW instances, and have been used for testing performance of methods by many researchers. Although in some of instances, optimum solutions have been already found by using exact methods, in others, they have not found yet. In both cases, the best solutions found by heuristics have been presented in the literature.

Instances including 25, 50, and 100 clients have been provided from Solomon. In this chapter, 7 instances are chosen for computational experiments among 26 instances including 100 clients and 25 available vehicles. In the instance, each position of clients is given as x-coordinate and y-coordinate. Link cost between client i and client j is calculated with the Euclidian distance. Service time is also given to each client i, in addition to the earliest arriving time e_i and the latest arriving time l_i. The geographical data are randomly generated in problem instances R101, R102 and R108, clustered in instances C101 and C102, and a mix of random and clustered structures in instances RC101 and RC102. Because time windows are included in the constraints of the problem, objective function and the relevant procedure in the algorithm are modified in order to fit for VRPTW. Time window constraints and load capacities are treated as the penalty terms to be added to the objective function (1) as follows:

$$E = \left(\sum_{i=1}^{n} c_{s_i} + \sum_{i=0}^{n} p_{s_i, s_{i+1}} \right) + \alpha \left(\sum_{i=1}^{n+1} \max\left(0, a_{s_i} - l_{s_i}\right) \right) + \beta \left(\sum_{k=1}^{m} \max\left(0, \sum_{i=z_{k-1}+1}^{z_k} d_{s_i} - W_k \right) \right) \qquad (5)$$

where a_{s_i} is arriving time at node s_i; m is the number of vehicles; d_{s_i} is the amount of demand of node s_i; z_k is the position of k th '0' in the string $s = (s_1, s_2, \cdots, s_n)$ (let $z_0 = 0$; $z_m = n+1$) and W_k is the loading capacity of vehicle k. According to the modification, the position on the check of feasibility in the algorithm (3) must be changed as shown in the algorithm (6).

Repeat
    trials := 0; changes := 0;
    Repeat
        trials := trials + 1;
        Generate a new state x´ from the current state x by applying randomly one of the three transformation rules to the string model of x;

Calculate $\Delta E = E(x') - E(x)$;
If $\Delta E < 0$ *Then*
x′ is accepted as a new state; (6)
If $(E(x') < E(x^*)$ *and* x' *is feasible) Then* $x^* := x'$
Else x′ is accepted with probability $\exp(-\Delta E/T)$
If x′ is accepted Then changes := changes + 1; $x := x'$
Until trials ≥ SIZEFACTOR · N or changes ≥ CUTOFF · N;
T := T · TEMPFACTOR
Until T ≤ INITTEMP/FINDIVISOR

In the computations, according to the preliminary experiments and the reference to the recommended values by Johnson et al. (Johnson et al., 1989, 1991), the values of the parameters that appear in the proposed SA algorithm are set as follows.

$N = 2L^2$ (L : length of string)
SIZEFACTOR = 8
CUTOFF = 0.2 (Repeat iterations in the same temperature *T*,
until (trials ≥ SIZEFACTOR · N or changes ≥ CUTOFF · N))
INITTEMP = 20 (Initial temperature)
TEMPFACTOR = 0.95 ($T_{n+1} = 0.95\ T_n$) (7)
FINDIVISOR = 50 (If *T* ≤ *INITTEMP* / *FINDIVISOR*, terminate the whole of the iterations.)
α = 20 to 100 (to be adjusted according to the tightness of time windows), $\beta = 1$
(In the experiment on C101 and C102, *INITTEMP* = 20 and *FINDIVISOR* = 5 are set exceptionally, because these instances are extremely easy to find the best known solutions.)

The procedure related to the creation of an initial solution in step II in the algorithm (2) should be modified in order to fit for VRPTW. The initial solution is produced by assigning nodes to vehicles in ascending order of the specified earliest arriving time; the initial solution might be infeasible.
The best solutions found by the proposed method are compared with optimum solutions obtained by exact methods and best known solutions obtained by existing heuristics. The relevant data to be compared are provided by Solomon (Solomon, 2005) and Díaz (Díaz, 2007). The computation of the proposed method is executed on Windows Vista, with Core 2 Duo, 2.0GHz CPU.

Instance	Optimum (Year Published)	Best Known by Heuristics (Year Published)	Proposed Method	Computing Time (sec)
C101	827.3 (1999)	828.94 (1999)	828.94	76
C102	827.3 (1999)	828.94 (1995)	828.94	73
R101	1637.7 (1999)	1645.79 (2000)	1644.33	194
R102	1466.6 (1999)	1486.12 (1995)	1476.12	189
R108	Not found yet	960.88 (2001)	958.98	131
RC101	1619.8 (1999)	1696.94 (1997)	1644.82	189
RC102	1457.4 (1999)	1554.75 (1997)	1480.46	188

Table 1. Computational Results on Solomon's Benchmark Problems

As shown in the Table 1, in all instances tested, the best solutions found by the proposed method are better than or equal to the best known solutions found by existing heuristics. Moreover, it seems that computing time is suited to practical use.

6.2 Experiments on instances for CARP

The proposed data model and algorithm are able to apply to the extended CARP defined in Sec. 2.2. According to the original paper by the authors of this chapter (Kokubugata et al. 2006), the outline of it is explained in this section. The data used in this method is based on an internal network coding. In the coding, entities (edges, arcs) are stored in a form which is embodied as a three dimensional array. The first component of it expresses the head node of the entity and the second expresses the tail node. The third is the Boolean value that attains 1, if and only if the entity is a directed arc. The model to express a state of solution of the extended CARP is realized as a sequence of integers, i.e., a string.

A new state of solution is generated from the present state by one of the following three types of transformation rules. The first rule is to exchange a number with another one in the string. It is the same rule as that in VRP. The second rule is to delete an arbitrary number and then insert it to another position in the string. It is also the same rule as that in VRP. However, the third rule 'partial reversion' for VRP is not adopted in the extended CARP, because 'partial reversion' likely makes infeasible neighbours in this problem. Instead, the new rule that reverse the traversing direction of an undirected edge is adopted as the third transformation rule. This rule is illustrated in Fig. 16. Of course, 'direction reversal' can not be applied to directed arcs.

Note that three rules are also applied to the special number '0' in the method for the extended CARP.

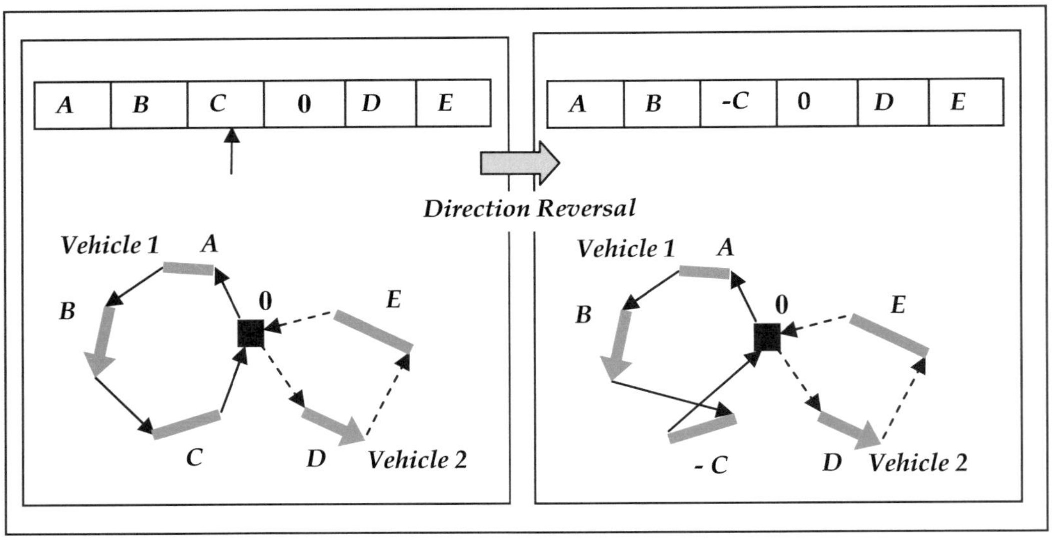

Fig. 16. A Result of 'Direction Reversal'

Instances for CARP can be obtained from the web site named CARPLIB that is supported by Belenguer (Belenguer, 2005). In the CARPLIB, some series of CARP are provided. The GDB series includes 21 small size problems, each of which contains 19-55 undirected required

arcs. The BCCM series includes 34 medium size problems, each of which contains 39-97 undirected required arcs. Link cost in these instances is not given by Euclidean distance between a pair of clients. Cost of both arc with demand and arc without demand is given directly from input data. (Edges are treated as bidirectional arcs.) Therefore, link cost between the tail of demand arc i and the head of demand arc j is obtained by calculating the shortest path traversing intermediate arcs (with demand or without demand) connecting arc i and arc j using Warshall-Floyd's algorithm.
Computational experiments are attempted to compare the proposed method with two existing heuristics. The method of Hertz et al. (Hertz et al., 2000) is based on Tabu Search, which is extended from Tabu Search used for VRP solution by Gendreau et al. (Gendreau et al., 1994) introduced in Sec. 3.2. The method of Lacomme et al. (Lacomme et al., 2001) is based on Genetic Algorithm, which is extended from Genetic Algorithm used for VRP solution by Prins (Prins, 2001) introduced in Sec. 3.2. The computation of the proposed method is executed on Windows XP, with Pentium IV, 1.8GHz CPU. In the computations, according to the preliminary experiments and the reference to the recommended values by Johnson et al. (Johnson et al., 1989; 1991), the values of the parameters that appear in the proposed SA algorithm are set as follows

$N = 2L^2$ (L : length of string)
$SIZEFACTOR = 4$
$CUTOFF = 0.1$ (Repeat iterations in the same temperature T,
until ($trials \geq SIZEFACTOR \cdot N$ or $changes \geq CUTOFF \cdot N$))
$INITPROB = 0.4$ (Initial acceptance probability) (8)
$TEMPFACTOR = 0.99$ ($T_{n+1} = 0.99\ T_n$)
$FINDIVISOR = 10$ (If $T \leq INITTEMP\ /\ FINDIVISOR$, terminate the whole of the iterations.)
$INITTEMP$ must be calculated by exploratory SA executions, so as to make $changes/trials = INITPROB$ (= 0.4).

Instance number	Num. of vehicles	Num. of Required arcs	Hertz *et al.*	Lacomme *et al.*	Proposed Method	Computing Time (sec)
GDB1	5	22	316	316	316	3.4
GDB3	5	22	275	275	275	3.3
GDB9	10	51	317	303	309	29.6
GDB23	10	55	235	235	233	59.9
BCCM1A	2	39	173	173	173	6.6
BCCM3B	3	35	87	87	87	15.1
BCCM6C	10	50	329	317	317	22.1
BCCM9B	4	92	329	326	326	55.6

Table 2. Computational Results on CARP Instances

As shown in the Table 2, the proposed method has performance almost equal to the existing two heuristics. Moreover, it seems that computing time is satisfactorily short for the practical use.

6.3 Experiments on instances for NEARP

The proposed data model and algorithm are also able to apply to NEARP defined in Sec. 2.3. According to the original paper by the authors of this chapter (Kokubugata et al. 2007), the outline of it is explained in this section. The data used in this method is based on an internal network coding as same as that used for the extended CARP. In the coding, all entities (nodes, edges, arcs) are stored in a common form which is embodied as a three dimensional array. The first component of it expresses the head node of the entity and the second expresses the tail node. The third is the Boolean value that attains 1, if and only if the entity is an arc. If the head and the tail are the same node, the entity is understood as a single node. The model to express a state of solution of NEARP is also realized as a sequence of integers, i.e., a string.

A new state of solution is generated from the present state by one of three types of transformation rules as same as those used for the extended CARP. These are 'one to one exchange', 'delete and insert' and 'direction reversal'. Note that three rules are also applied to the special number '0' in the method for NEARP.

Prins & Bouchenoua have provided 23 instances of NEARP (Prins & Bouchenoua, 2004). These instances were produced by their original generator accompanied with randomization. They include 1-93 required nodes, 0-94 required edges and 0-149 required arcs, among 11-150 nodes and 71-311 links (integrated alias with edges and arcs). As mentioned by them, the lower bounds have not been found for their NEARP instances. The data files of NEARP instances were sent by them at the authors' request.

In the computations, all the same parameter values as used for the extended CARP (8) are used again.

Comparison between the solutions generated by the proposed method and the solutions given by Prins & Bouchenoua are conducted for 23 NEARP instances. In Table 3, the average deviations over the best value and the averaged computing time are shown. In the column of *MA*, the result of Memetic algorithm given by Prins & Bouchenoua (Prins & Bouchenoua, 2004) is shown. In the column of *Best*MA*, the performance of the best solution found with various parameter settings during their experiments is shown. $Avg_{10}SA$ is the averaged result of ten computations, while $Best_{10}SA$ is the best result of them. Note that the $Best_{10}SA$ is obtained by computations with the standard parameter setting and it is quite different from the *Best*MA* in spite of using the same word '*Best*'.

The computation of the proposed method was executed on Windows XP, with Pentium IV, 1.8GHz CPU, while the computation by Prins & Bouchenoua was executed on Windows 98, with Pentium III, 1GHz CPU.

	MA	*MATime* (sec)	*Best*MA*	$Avg_{10}SA$	*SATime* (sec)	$Best_{10}SA$
Average	1.65%	452.9 (s)	0.38%	1.51%	176.6 (s)	0.22%

Table 3. Averaged Computational Results on NEARP Instances

As shown in Table. 3, $Avg_{10}SA$ is superior to *MA*, and $Best_{10}SA$ obtains better results than *Best*MA*.

As a result, it is shown that the proposed method has good performance on NEARP.

7. Applications to varieties of routing problems

The proposed method is adaptable to varieties of routing problems abstracted from actual city logistics operations. In this section, three examples of varieties are explained briefly.

7.1 Routing problem with repeated trips

The case in which repetitive trips of a vehicle are allowed is frequently appeared in actual city logistics operations. After the first trip returns to the depot, unloading and loading are operated at the depot. Then, the second trip starts. This problem is also dealt with by the proposed method. In order to cope with it, another delimiter, for example '999', is introduced in the string model (Fig.17). In the transformation procedure of a solution, '999' is treated evenly with '0' as well as other numbers which represent nodes with demand.

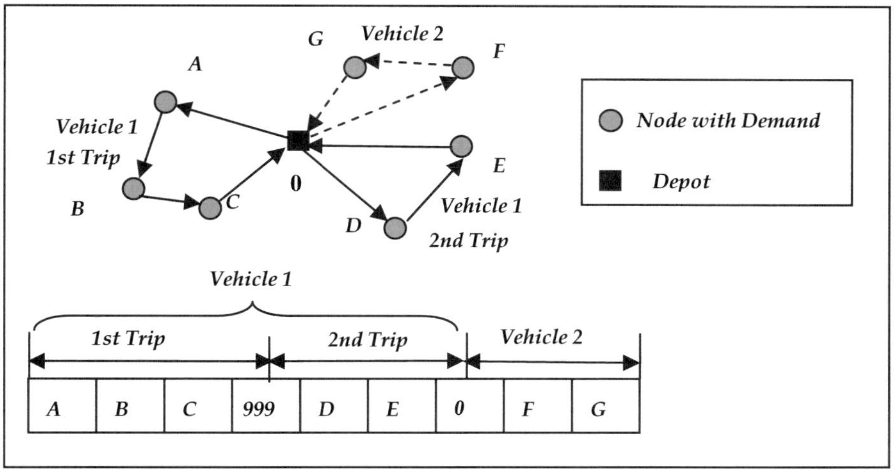

Fig. 17. VRP with Repeated Trips

This method was presented by the authors of this chapter (Hasama et al., 1999). It can be applied to the extended CARP and NEARP in the same way as VRP (Kokubugata et al., 2007).

7.2 Routing problem with plural depots

Planning of vehicle routing related to vehicles belonging to plural depots is required in actual city logistics operations. Routing problem in which plural depots are managed at a time could be also dealt with by the proposed method. The other delimiter, for example '−999', is introduced in the string model (Fig.18). In the transformation procedure of a solution, '−999' is treated evenly with '0' and other numbers.

This method was also presented by the authors of this chapter (Hasama et al., 1999). It can be applied to the extended CARP and NEARP in the same way as VRP (Kokubugata et al., 2007).

7.3 Routing problem with backhauls

In some cases of the freight transport operations, goods are delivered from the depot and empty pallets are retrieved to the depot.

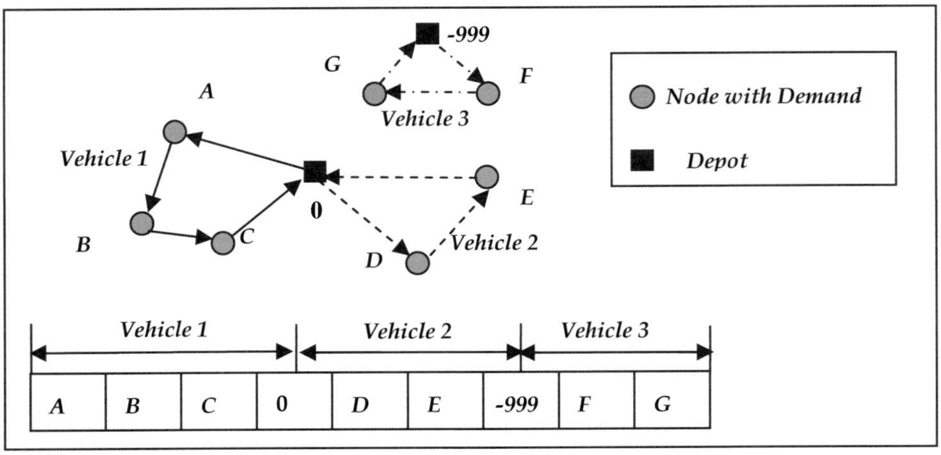

Fig. 18. VRP with Plural Depots

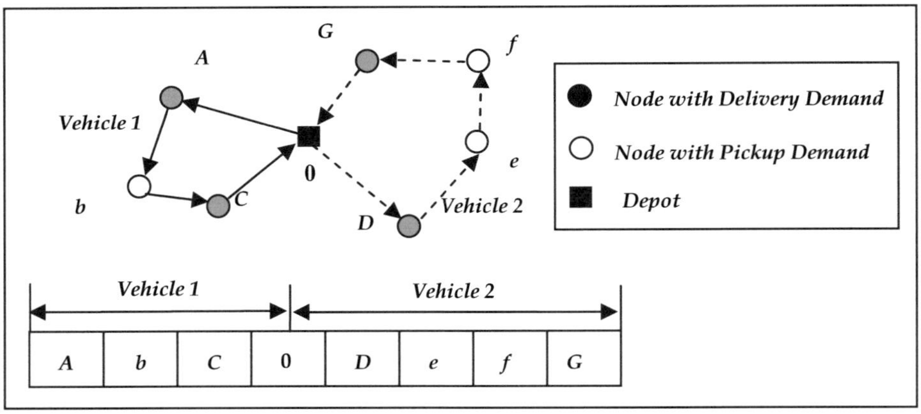

Fig. 19. VRP with Backhauls

In home-delivery service operations, both pickup and delivery services are carried out. A problem related to both deliveries and pickups is considered. Vehicles are loaded with goods at a central depot in order to service the delivery points. New goods are collected at the pickup points and brought back to the depot (backhauls). This type of problem is called the vehicle routing problem with backhauls (VRPB).The proposed method can be applied to VRPB.
In the string model corresponding to this problem, positive numbers are used for expressing delivery points, while negative numbers are used for expressing pickup points. In Fig.19, positive numbers are indicated by capital letters, while negative numbers are indicated by small letters. Each letter including '0' is treated evenly in the transformation procedure of a solution. This method was presented by the authors of this chapter (Hasama et al., 1998).

8. Conclusion

As introduced in Sec. 3.2, the applications of Simulated Annealing (SA) to routing problems have been evaluated not highly in the literature as compared with those of Tabu Search (TS) and Genetic Algorithm (GA) etc. In the core procedure of the prominent method making use of SA, only one or two nodes are exchanged between existing two vehicle routes at a time.

The descriptions written in this chapter have revealed that the proposed method making use of SA for routing problems has superior to other method based on other metaheuristics. The explanations made in this chapter are summarized as follows.

- The proposed method for solving the routing problems consists of simple transformation procedures applied over the entire string data model. In the framework of SA, each random application of one of transformation rules may cause the exchange of tasks between two trips, the move of a set of tasks from one trip to another trip, the exchange of tasks in the same trip, the changes in routing order in some trips and so on. Because transitions of a solution in the string data model may occasionally cause drastic changes in solutions, fast convergence to an equilibrium point might be achieved.
- The solutions generated by the proposed method are compared with the solutions given by other methods by making computational experiments on VRPTW, CARP and NEARP instances. In most cases, the proposed method shows superior performance to other methods.
- The proposed method is adaptable varieties of routing problems abstracted from practical logistics operations. The case in which repetitive trips of a vehicle are allowed, the case in which plural depots are managed at a time and routing problem with backhaul are dealt with.
- Although the proposed method is advantageous to complicated logistics operations, the following topics should be considered in order to apply the method to practical use in city logistics.
    - Applications of TS and GA to the proposed string model and the transformation rules should be attempted to compare with the proposed method making use of SA. The supposition that SA is the fittest for the string model and the transformation rules should be confirmed.
    - The proposed data model can be applied to complicated problems such as NEARP with time windows, multiple depots cases and pickup and delivery cases. The application to these cases should be examined. However, the necessary data of actual delivery cases have not been obtained yet.
    - Actual travel time may vary according to traffic conditions. Dynamic routing planning system taking account of time dependent link cost should be studied.

9. References

Belenguer, J.M. (2005). Web site: http://www.uv.es/~belengue/carp/

Clarke, G. & Wright, W. (1964). Scheduling of Vehicles from a Central Depot to a Number of Delivery Points, *Operations research*, Vol. 12, pp. 564-581

Chistofides, N.; Mingozzi, A. & Toth, P. (1979). The Vehicle Routing Problem, In: *Combinatorial Optimization,* Chistofides, N. ; Mingozzi, A. ; Toth, P. & Sandi, C. (Eds.), pp. 315-338, Wiley, Chichester

Crescenzi, P. & Kann, V. (2000). A Compendium of NP Optimization Problem, Web site: http://www.nada.kth.se/~viggo/wwwcompendium/node103.html

Díaz, B. D. (2007). Web site: http://neo.lcc.uma.es/radi-aeb/WebVRP/index.html

Fisher, M. L. & Jaikumar, R. (1981). A Generalized Assignment Heuristic for Vehicle Routing, *Networks*, Vol. 11, pp. 109--124.

Gendreau, M.; Hertz, A. & Laporte, G. (1994). A Tabu Search Heuristic for the Vehicle Routing Problem, *Management Science* ,Vol. 40, pp. 1276–1290.

Gendreau, M.; Laporte, G. & Potvin, J.-Y. (2002). Metaheuristics for the Capacitated VRP, In: *The Vehicle Routing Problem*, Toth P. & Vigo, D. (Ed), pp. 129–154, SIAM, Philadelphia,

Golden, B.L. & Wong, R.T. (1981). Capacitated Arc Routing Problems, *Networks*, Vol. 11, pp.305–315

Hasama, T.; Kokubugata H. & Kawashima H. (1998). A Heuristic Approach Based on the String Model to Solve Vehicle Routing Problem with Backhauls, *Preprint for 5th Annual World Congress on Intelligent Transport Systems*, No. 3025, Seoul, Korea, Oct. 1998

Hasama, T.; Kokubugata, H. & Kawashima H. (1999.) A Heuristic Approach Based on the String Model to Solve Vehicle Routing Problem with Various Conditions, *Preprint for World Congress on Intelligent Transport Systems*, No.3027, Toronto, Canada, Nov. 1999

Hertz, A.; Laporte, G. & Mittaz, M. (2000). A Tabu Search Heuristic for the Capacitated Arc Routing Problem, *Operations research*, Vol. 48, pp. 129–135

Johnson, D.S.; Aragon, C.R.; MacGeoch, L.A. & Schevon, C. (1989). Optimization by Simulated Annealing : An Experimental Evaluation, Part I, Graph Partitioning, *Operations research*, Vol. 37, pp. 865-892

Johnson, D.S.; Aragon, C.R.; MacGeoch, L.A. & Schevon, C. (1991). Optimization by Simulated Annealing : An Experimental Evaluation, Part II, Graph Colouring and Number Partitioning, *Operations research*, Vol. 39, pp. 378-406

Kokubugata, H.; Itoyama, H. & Kawashima, H. (1997). Vehicle Routing Methods for City Logistics Operations, *Preprint for 8th IFAC Symposium on Transportation Systems*, pp.727-732, Hania, Greece, June 1997

Kokubugata, H.; Hirashima, K. & Kawashima, H. (2006). A Practical Solution of Capacitated Arc Routing for City Logistics, *Proceeding of 11th IFAC Symposium on Control in Transportation Systems*, No.222, Delft, The Netherlands, Aug. 2006

Kokubugata, H.; Moriyama, A. & Kawashima, H. (2007). A Practical Solution Using Simulated Annealing for General Routing Problems with Nodes, Edges, and Arcs, *Lecture Notes in Computer Science*, Vol. 4638 (SLS2007), pp. 136-149, Springer, Berlin

Lacomme, P.; Prins, C. & Ramdane-Cherif, W. (2001). A Genetic Algorithm for the Capacitated Arc Routing Problem and Its Extensions, *Lecture Notes in Computer Science*, Vol. 2037, pp. 473–483, Springer, Berlin

Lin, S. & Kernighan, B. W. (1973). An Effective Heuristic Algorithm for the Traveling Salesman Problem, *Operations research*, Vol. 21, pp. 498-516.

Osman, I. H. (1993). Metastrategy Simulated Annealing and Tabu Search Algorithms for the Vehicle Routing Problem, *Annals of Operations Research*, Vol. 41, pp. 421-451

Prins, C. (2001). A Simple and Effective Evolutionary Algorithm for the Vehicle Routing Problem, *Research Report*, University of Technology of Troyes, France, *Computers & operations research*, 2004, Vol. 31, No. 12, pp. 1985-2002.

Prins, C. & Bouchenoua, S. (2004). A Memetic Algorithm Solving the VRP, the CARP and more General Routing Problems with Nodes, Edges and Arcs, In: *Recent Advances in Memetic Algorithms, Studies in Fuzziness and Soft Computing 166*, Hart W.; Kranogor N. & Smith J. (Eds.), pp. 65-85, Springer, Berlin

Solomon, M. (1987). Algorithms for the Vehicle Routing and Scheduling Problems with Time Window Constraints, *Operations Research*, Vol. 35, No. 2, pp. 254-265

Solomon, M., (2005). Web site: http://w.cba.neu.edu/~msolomon/home.htm

Taniguchi, E.; Thompson R.G.; Yamada T. & Van Duin R. (2001). *City Logistics: Network Modelling and Intelligent Transport Systems*, Pergamon, Oxford

Toth, P. & Vigo, D. (Eds.) (2002). *The Vehicle Routing Problem*, SIAM, Philadelphia

Van Breedam, A. (1996). An Analysis of the Effect of Local Improvement Operators in GA and SA for the Vehicle Routing Problem, *RUCA working paper 96/14*, University of Antwerp, Belgium

9

Theory and Applications of Simulated Annealing for Nonlinear Constrained Optimization[1]

Benjamin W. Wah[1], Yixin Chen[2] and Tao Wang[3]
[1]*Department of Electrical and Computer Engineering and the Coordinated Science Laboratory, University of Illinois,*
[2]*Department of Computer Science, Washington University,*
[3]*Synopsys, Inc.*
USA

1. Introduction

A general *mixed-integer nonlinear programming problem* (MINLP) is formulated as follows:

$$(P_m): \qquad \min_z \quad f(z), \qquad \text{subject to} \quad h(z) = 0 \text{ and } g(z) \le 0, \tag{1}$$

where $z = (x, y)^T \in Z$; $x \in \mathbb{R}^v$ and $y \in \mathbb{D}^w$ are, respectively, bounded continuous and discrete variables; $f(z)$ is a lower-bounded objective function; $g(z) = (g_1(z),\ldots, g_r(z))^T$ is a vector of r inequality constraint functions;[2] and $h(z)= (h_1(z),\ldots,h_m(z))^T$ is a vector of m equality constraint functions. Functions $f(z)$, $g(z)$, and $h(z)$ are general functions that can be discontinuous, non-differentiable, and not in closed form.

Without loss of generality, we present our results with respect to minimization problems, knowing that maximization problems can be converted to minimization ones by negating their objectives. Because there is no closed-form solution to P_m, we develop in this chapter efficient procedures for finding locally optimal and feasible solutions to P_m, demonstrate that our procedures can lead to better solutions than existing methods, and illustrate the procedures on two applications. The proofs that our procedures have well-behaved convergence properties can be found in the reference [27], We first define the following terms.

---

[1] Research supported by the National Science Foundation Grant IIS 03-12084 and a Department of Energy Early Career Principal Investigator Grant.

[2] Given two vectors V_1 and V_2 of the same dimension, $V_1 \ge V_2$ means that each element of V_1 is greater than or equal to the corresponding element of V_2; $V_1 > V_2$ means that at least one element of V_1 is greater than the corresponding element of V_2 and the other elements are greater than or equal to the corresponding elements of V_2.

Definition 1. A *mixed neighborhood* $\mathcal{N}_m(z)$ for $z = (x, y)^T$ in the mixed space $\mathbb{R}^v \times \mathbb{D}^w$ is:

$$\mathcal{N}_m(z) = \left\{(x', y)^T \mid x' \in \mathcal{N}_c(x)\right\} \cup \left\{(x, y')^T \mid y' \in \mathcal{N}_d(y)\right\}, \quad (2)$$

where $\mathcal{N}_c(x) = \{x' : \|x' - x\| \le \epsilon \text{ and } \epsilon \to 0\}$ is the *continuous neighborhood* of x, and the *discrete neighborhood* $\mathcal{N}_d(y)$ is a *finite* user-defined set of points $\{y' \in \mathbb{D}^w\}$ such that $y' \in \mathcal{N}_d(y) \Leftrightarrow y \in \mathcal{N}_d(y')$ [1]. Here, $\epsilon \to 0$ means that ϵ is arbitrarily close to 0.

Definition 2. Point z of P_m is a *feasible point* iff $h(z) = 0$ and $g(z) \le 0$.

Definition 3. Point z^* is a *constrained local minimum* (CLM_m) of P_m iff z^* is feasible, and $f(z^*) \le f(z)$ with respect to all feasible $z \in \mathcal{N}_m(z^*)$.

Definition 4. Point z^* is a *constrained global minimum* (CGM_m) of P_m iff z^* is feasible, and $f(z^*) \le f(z)$ for every feasible $z \in Z$. The set of all CGM_m of P_m is Z_{opt}.

Note that a discrete neighborhood is a user-defined concept because it does not have any generally accepted definition. Hence, it is possible for $z = (x, y)^T$ to be a CLM_m to a neighborhood $\mathcal{N}_d(y)$ but not to another neighborhood $\mathcal{N}_{d_1}(y)$. The choice, however, does not affect the validity of a search as long as one definition is consistently used throughout. Normally, one may choose $\mathcal{N}_d(y)$ to include discrete points closest to z, although a search will also be correct if the neighborhood includes "distant" points.

Finding a CLM_m of P_m is often challenging. First, $f(z)$, $g(z)$, and $h(z)$ may be non-convex and highly nonlinear, making it difficult to even find a feasible point or a feasible region. Moreover, it is not always useful to keep a search within a feasible region because there may be multiple disconnected feasible regions. To find high-quality solutions, a search may have to move from one feasible region to another. Second, $f(z)$, $g(z)$, and $h(z)$ may be discontinuous or may not be differentiable, rendering it impossible to apply existing theories based on gradients.

A popular method for solving P_m is the penalty method (Section 2.1). It transforms P_m into an unconstrained penalty function and finds suitable penalties in such a way that a global minimum of the penalty function corresponds to a CGM_m of P_m. Because it is computationally intractable to look for global minima when the penalty function is highly nonlinear, penalty methods are only effective for finding CGM_m in special cases.

This chapter is based on the theory of extended saddle points in mixed space [25, 29] (Section 2.2), which shows the one-to-one correspondence between a CLM_m of P_m and an *extended saddle point* (ESP) of the corresponding penalty function. The necessary and sufficient condition allows us to find a CLM_m of P_m by looking for an ESP of the corresponding penalty function.

One way to look for those ESPs is to minimize the penalty function, while gradually increasing its penalties until they are larger than some thresholds. The approach is not sufficient because it also generates stationary points of the penalty function that are not

CLM_m of P_m. To avoid those undesirable stationary points, it is possible to restart the search when such stationary points are reached, or to periodically decrease the penalties in order for the search to escape from such local traps. However, this simple greedy approach for updating penalties may not always work well across different problems.

Our goals in this chapter are to design efficient methods for finding ESPs of a penalty formulation of P_m and to illustrate them on two applications. We have made three contributions in this chapter.

First, we propose in Section 3.1 a constrained simulated annealing algorithm (CSA), an extension of conventional simulated annealing (SA) [18], for solving P_m. In addition to probabilistic descents in the problem-variable subspace as in SA, CSA does probabilistic ascents in the penalty subspace, using a method that controls descents and ascents in a unified fashion. Because CSA is sample-based, it is inefficient for solving large problems. To this end, we propose in Section 3.2 a constraint-partitioned simulated annealing algorithm (CPSA). By exploiting the locality of constraints in many constraint optimization problems, CPSA partitions P_m into multiple loosely coupled subproblems that are related by very few global constraints, solves each subproblem independently, and iteratively resolves the inconsistent global constraints.

Second, we show in Section 4 the asymptotic convergence of CSA and CPSA to a constrained global minimum with probability one in discrete constrained optimization problems, under a specific temperature schedule [27]. The property can be proved by modeling the search as a strongly ergodic Markov chain and by showing that CSA and CPSA minimize an implicit virtual energy at any constrained global minimum with probability one. The result is significant because it extends conventional SA, which guarantees asymptotic convergence in discrete unconstrained optimization, to that in discrete constrained optimization. It also establishes the condition under which optimal solutions can be found in constraint-partitioned nonlinear optimization problems.

Last, we evaluate CSA and CPSA in Section 5 by solving some benchmarks in continuous space and by demonstrating their effectiveness when compared to other dynamic penalty methods. We also apply CSA to solve two real-world applications, one on sensor-network placements and another on out-of-core compiler code generation.

2. Previous work on penalty methods

Direct and penalty methods are two general approaches for solving P_m. Since direct methods are only effective for solving some special cases of P_m, we focus on penalty methods in this chapter.

A penalty function of P_m is a summation of its objective and constraint functions weighted by penalties. Using penalty vectors $\alpha \in \mathbb{R}^m$ and $\beta \in \mathbb{R}^r$, the general penalty function for P_m is:

$$L_p\big((z,\alpha,\beta)^T\big) = f(z) + \alpha^T P(h(z)) + \beta^T Q(g(z)), \tag{3}$$

where P and Q are transformation functions. The goal of a penalty method is to find suitable $\alpha*$ and $\beta*$ in such a way that $z*$ that minimizes (3) corresponds to either a CLM_m or a CGM_m of P_m. Penalty methods belong to a general approach that can solve continuous, discrete, and mixed constrained optimization problems, with no continuity, differentiability, and convexity requirements.

When $P(g(z))$ and $Q(h(z))$ are general functions that can take positive and negative values, unique values of $\alpha*$ and $\beta*$ must be found in order for a local minimum $z*$ of (3) to correspond to a CLM_m or CGM_m of P_m. (The proof is not shown.) However, the approach of solving P_m by finding local minima of (3) does not always work for discrete or mixed problems because there may not exist any feasible penalties at $z*$. (This behavior is illustrated in Example 1 in Section 2.1.) It is also possible for the penalties to exist at $z*$ but (3) is not at a local minimum there. A special case exists in continuous problems when constraint functions are continuous, differentiable, and regular. For those problems, the Karush-Kuhn-Tucker (KKT) condition shows that unique penalties always exist at constrained local minima [21]. In general, existing penalty methods for solving P_m transform $g(z)$ and $h(z)$ in (3) into non-negative functions before finding its local or global minima. In this section, we review some existing penalty methods in the literature.

2.1 Penalty methods for constrained global optimization

Static penalty methods. A *static-penalty method* [21, 22] formulates P_m as the minimization of (3) when its transformed constraints have the following properties: a) $P(h(z)) \geq 0$ and $Q(g(z)) \geq 0$; and b) $P(h(z)) = 0$ iff $h(z) = 0$, and $Q(g(z)) = 0$ iff $g(z) \leq 0$. By finding suitable penalty vectors α and β, an example method looks for $z*$ by solving the following problem with constant $\rho > 0$:

$$(P_1): \qquad \min_z L_s\big((z,\alpha,\beta)^T\big) = \min_z \left[f(z) + \sum_{i=1}^{m} \alpha_i \, |h_i(z)|^\rho + \sum_{j=1}^{r} \beta_j \, \left(g_j(z)^+\right)^\rho \right], \qquad (4)$$

where $g_j(z)^+ = \max(0, g_j(z))$, and $g(z)^+ = (g_1(z)^+, \ldots, g_r(z)^+)^T$.

Given $z*$, an interesting property of P_1 is that $z*$ is a CGM_m of P_m iff there exist finite $\alpha* \geq 0$ and $\beta* \geq 0$ such that $z*$ is a global minimum of $L_s((z, \alpha**, \beta**)_T)$ for any $\alpha** > \alpha*$ and $\beta** > \beta*$. To show this result, note that α_i and β_j in P_1 must be greater than zero in order to penalize those transformed violated constraint functions $|h_i(z)|^\rho$ and $(g_j(z)^+)^\rho$, which are non-negative with a minimum of zero. As (4) is to be minimized with respect to z, increasing the penalty of a violated constraint to a large enough value will force the corresponding transformed constraint function to achieve the minimum of zero, and such penalties always exist if a feasible solution to P_m exists. At those points where all the constraints are satisfied, every term on the right of (4) except the first is zero, and a global minimum of (4) corresponds to a CGM_m of P_m.

Example 1. Consider the following simple discrete optimization problem:

$$\min_{\substack{y\in\{-3,-2,\\-1,0,1,2\}}} f(y) = \begin{cases} 0 & \text{if } y \geq 0 \\ y & \text{if } y = -1, -2 \\ -4 & \text{if } y = -3 \end{cases} \qquad \text{subject to } y = 0. \tag{5}$$

Obviously, $y^* = 0$. Assuming a penalty function $L_p((y,\ \alpha)^T) = f(y) + \alpha y$ and $\mathcal{N}_d(y) = \{y-1, y+1\}$, there is no single α^* that can make $L_p((y,\ \alpha^*)^T)$ a local minimum at $y^* = 0$ with respect to $y = \pm 1$. This is true because we arrive at an inconsistent α^* when we solve the following inequalities:

$$0 = L_p\big((0,\alpha^*)^T\big) \leq \begin{cases} L_p\big((-1,\alpha^*)^T\big) = f(-1) - \alpha^* = -1 - \alpha^* \\ L_p\big((1,\alpha^*)^T\big) = f(1) + \alpha^* = 0 + \alpha^* \end{cases} \Longrightarrow \begin{cases} \alpha^* \leq -1 & \text{when } y = -1 \\ \alpha^* \geq 0 & \text{when } y = 1. \end{cases}$$

On the other hand, by using $L_s((y,\ \alpha)^T) = f(y) + \alpha\ |y|$ and by setting $\alpha^* = \frac{4}{3}$, the CGM_d of (5) corresponds to the global minimum of $L_s((y,\ \alpha^{**})^T)$ for any $\alpha^{**} > \alpha^*$. ■

A variation of the static-penalty method proposed in [16] uses discrete penalty values and assigns a penalty value $\alpha_i(h_i(z))$ when $h_i(z)$ exceeds a discrete level ℓ_i (*resp.*, $\beta_j(g_j(z))$ when $g_j(z)^+$ exceeds a discrete level ℓ_j), where a higher level of constraint violation entails a larger penalty value. The penalty method then solves the following minimization problem:

$$(P_2): \quad \min_z L_s\big((z,\alpha,\beta)^T\big) = \min_z \left[f(z) + \sum_{i=1}^{m} \alpha_i(h_i(z))\, h_i^2(z) + \sum_{j=1}^{r} \beta_j(g_j(z))\big(g_j(z)^+\big)^2 \right]. \tag{6}$$

A limitation common to all static-penalty methods is that their penalties have to be found by trial and error. Each trial is computationally expensive because it involves finding a global minimum of a nonlinear function. To this end, many penalty methods resort to finding local minima of penalty functions. However, such an approach is heuristic because there is no formal property that relates a CLM_m of P_m to a local minimum of the corresponding penalty function. As illustrated earlier, it is possible that no feasible penalties exist in order to have a local minimum at a CLM_m in the penalty function. It is also possible for the penalties to exist at the CLM_m but the penalty function is not at a local minimum there.

Dynamic penalty methods. Instead of finding α^{**} and β^{**} by trial and error, a *dynamic-penalty method* [21, 22] increases the penalties in (4) gradually, finds the global minimum z^* of (4) with respect to z, and stops when z^* is a feasible solution to P_m. To show that z^* is a CGM_m when the algorithm stops, we know that the penalties need to be increased when z^* is a global minimum of (4) but not a feasible solution to P_m. The first time z^* is a feasible solution to P_m, the solution must also be a CGM_m. Hence, the method leads to the smallest

α** and β** that allow a CGM_m to be found. However, it has the same limitation as static-penalty methods because it requires computationally expensive algorithms for finding the global minima of nonlinear functions.

There are many variations of dynamic penalty methods. A well-known one is the *non-stationary method* (NS) [17] that solves a sequence of minimization problems with the following in iteration t:

$$(P_3): \quad \min_z L_t\big((z,\alpha,\beta)^T\big) \;=\; \min_z \left[f(z) + \sum_{i=1}^{m} \alpha_i(t)\ |h_i(z)|^\rho + \sum_{j=1}^{r} \beta_j(t)\big(g_j(z)^+\big)^\rho \right] \tag{7}$$

where $\alpha_i(t+1) = \alpha_i(t) + C \cdot |h_i(z(t))|, \quad \beta_j(t+1) = \beta_j(t) + C \cdot g_j(z(t))^+.$

Here, C and ρ are constant parameters, with a reasonable setting of $C = 0.01$ and $\rho = 2$. An advantage of the NS penalty method is that it requires only a few parameters to be tuned.

Another dynamic penalty method is the *adaptive penalty method* (AP) [5] that makes use of a feedback from the search process. AP solves the following minimization problem in iteration t:

$$(P_4): \quad \min_z L_t\big((z,\alpha,\beta)^T\big) = \min_z \left[f(z) + \sum_{i=1}^{m} \alpha_i(t)\ h_i(z)^2 + \sum_{j=1}^{r} \beta_j(t)\big(g_j(z)^+\big)^2 \right], \tag{8}$$

where $\alpha_i(t)$ is, respectively, increased, decreased, or left unchanged when the constraint $h_i(z) = 0$ is respectively, infeasible, feasible, or neither in the last ℓ iterations. That is,

$$\alpha_i(t+1) = \begin{cases} \frac{\alpha_i(t)}{\lambda_1} & \text{if } h_i(z(i)) = 0 \text{ is feasible in iterations } t-\ell+1,\ldots,t \\ \lambda_2 \cdot \alpha_i(t) & \text{if } h_i(z(i)) = 0 \text{ is infeasible in iterations } t-\ell+1,\ldots,t \\ \alpha_i(t) & \text{otherwise,} \end{cases} \tag{9}$$

where ℓ is a positive integer, $\lambda_1,\ \lambda_2 > 1$, and $\lambda_1 \neq \lambda_2$ in order to avoid cycles in updates. We use $\ell = 3$, $\lambda_1 = 1.5$, and $\lambda_2 = 1.25$ in our experiments. A similar rule applies to the updates of $\beta_j(t)$.

The *threshold penalty method* estimates and dynamically adjusts a near-feasible threshold $q_i(t)$ (*resp.*, $q'_j(t)$) for each constraint in iteration t. Each threshold indicates a reasonable amount of violation allowed for promising but infeasible points during the solution of the following problem:

$$(P_5): \quad \min_z L_t\big((z,\alpha,\beta)^T\big) = \min_z \left\{ f(z) + \alpha(t) \left[\sum_{i=1}^{m} \left(\frac{h_i(z)}{q_i(t)}\right)^2 + \sum_{j=1}^{r} \left(\frac{g_j(z)^+}{q'_j(t)}\right)^2 \right] \right\}. \tag{10}$$

There are two other variations of dynamic penalty methods that are not as popular: the death penalty method simply rejects all infeasible individuals [4]; and a penalty method that uses the number of violated constraints instead of the degree of violations in the penalty function [20].

Exact penalty methods. Besides the dynamic penalty methods reviewed above that require solving a series of unconstrained minimization problems under different penalty values, the *exact penalty methods* are another class of penalty methods that can yield an optimal solution by solving a single unconstrained optimization of the penalty function with appropriate penalty values. The most common form solves the following minimization problem in continuous space [35, 6]:

$$\min_x L_e\big((x,c)^T\big) = \min_x \left[f(x) + c\Big(\sum_{i=1}^{m} |h_i(x)| + \sum_{j=1}^{r} g_j(x)^+ \Big)\right]. \tag{11}$$

It has been shown that, for continuous and differentiable problems and when certain constraint qualification conditions are satisfied, there exists $c* > 0$ such that the $x*$ that minimizes (11) is also a global optimal solution to the original problem [35, 6]. In fact, c needs to be larger than the summation of all the Lagrange multipliers at $x*$, while the existence of the Lagrange multipliers requires the continuity and differentiability of the functions.

Besides (11), there are various other formulations of exact penalty methods [11, 12, 10, 3]. However, they are limited to continuous and differentiable functions and to global optimization. The theoretical results for these methods were developed by relating their penalties to their Lagrange multipliers, whose existence requires the continuity and differentiability of the constraint functions.

In our experiments, we only evaluate our proposed methods with respect to dynamic penalty methods P_3 and P_4 for the following reasons. It is impractical to implement P_1 because it requires choosing some suitable penalty values a priori. The control of progress in solving P_2 is difficult because it requires tuning many ($\ell \cdot (m+r)$) parameters that are hard to generalize. The method based on solving P_5 is also hard to generalize because it depends on choosing an appropriate sequence of violation thresholds. Reducing the thresholds quickly leads to large penalties and the search trapped at infeasible points, whereas reducing the thresholds slowly leads to slow convergence. We do not evaluate exact penalty methods because they were developed for problems with continuous and differentiable functions.

2.2 Necessary and sufficient conditions on constrained local minimization

We first describe in this section the theory of extended saddle points (ESPs) that shows the one-to-one correspondence between a CLM_m of P_m and an ESP of the penalty function. We then present the partitioning of the ESP condition into multiple necessary conditions and the formulation of the corresponding subproblems. Because the results have been published earlier [25, 29], we only summarize some high-level concepts without the precise formalism and their proofs.

Definition 5. For penalty vectors $\alpha \in \mathbb{R}^m$ and $\beta \in \mathbb{R}^r$, we define a *penalty function* of P_m as:

$$L_m\big((z,\alpha,\beta)^T\big) = f(z) + \alpha^T|h(z)| + \beta^T g(z)^+ = f(z) + \sum_{i=1}^{m} \alpha_i |h_i(z)| + \sum_{j=1}^{r} \beta_j g_j(z)^+. \tag{12}$$

Next, we informally define a constraint-qualification condition needed in the main theorem [25]. Consider a feasible point $z' = (x', y')^T$ and a neighboring point $z'' = (x' + \vec{p}, y')^T$ under an infinitely small perturbation along direction $\vec{p} \in X$ in the x subspace. When the *constraint-qualification condition* is satisfied at z', it means that there is no $\vec{p}$ such that the rates of change of all equality and active inequality constraints between z'' and z' are zero. To see why this is necessary, assume that $f(z)$ at z' decreases along $\vec{p}$ and that all equality and active inequality constraints at z' have zero rates of change between z'' and z'. In this case, it is not possible to find some finite penalty values for the constraints at z'' in such a way that leads to a local minimum of the penalty function at z' with respect to z''. Hence, if the above scenario were true for some $\vec{p}$ at z', then it is not possible to have a local minimum of the penalty function at z'. In short, constraint qualification at z' requires at least one equality or active inequality constraint to have a non-zero rate of change along each direction $\vec{p}$ at z' in the x subspace.

Theorem 1. Necessary and sufficient condition on CLM_m of P_m [25]. Assuming $z^* \in Z$ of P_m satisfies the constraint-qualification condition, then z^* is a CLM_m of P_m iff there exist some finite $\alpha^* \geq 0$ and $\beta^* \geq 0$ that satisfies the following extended saddle-point condition (ESPC):

$$L_m((z^*, \alpha, \beta)^T) \leq L_m((z^*, \alpha^{**}, \beta^{**})^T) \leq L_m((z, \alpha^{**}, \beta^{**})^T) \tag{13}$$

for any $\alpha^{**} > \alpha^*$ and $\beta^{**} > \beta^*$ and for all $z \in \mathcal{N}_m(z^*)$, $\alpha \in \mathbb{R}^m$, and $\beta \in \mathbb{R}^r$.

Note that (13) can be satisfied under rather loose conditions because it is true for a range of penalty values and not for unique values. For this reason, we call $(z^*, \alpha^{**}, \beta^{**})^T$ an *extended saddle point* (ESP) of (12). The theorem leads to an easy way for finding CLM_m. Since an ESP is a local minimum of (12) (but not the converse), z^* can be found by gradually increasing the penalties of those violated constraints in (12) and by repeatedly finding the local minima of (12) until a feasible solution to P_m is obtained. The search for local minima can be accomplished by any existing local-search algorithm for unconstrained optimization.

Example 1 (cont'd). In solving (5), if we use $L_m((y, \alpha)^T) = f(y) + \alpha|y|$ and choose $\alpha^* = 1$ we have an ESP at $y^* = 0$ for any $\alpha^{**} > \alpha^*$. This establishes a local minimum of $L_m((y, \alpha)^T)$ at $y^* = 0$ with respect to $\mathcal{N}_d(y) = \{y - 1, y + 1\}$. Note that the α^* that satisfies Theorem 1 is only required to establish a local minimum of $L_m((y, \alpha)^T)$ at $y^* = 0$ and is, therefore, smaller than the α^* $(= \frac{4}{3})$ required to establish a global minimum of $L_m((y, \alpha)^T)$ in the static-penalty method. ■

An important feature of the ESPC in Theorem 1 is that it can be partitioned in such a way that each subproblem implementing a partitioned condition can be solved by looking for any α^{**} and β^{**} that are larger than α^* and β^*.

Consider P_t, a version of P_m whose constraints can be partitioned into N subsets:

$$\begin{array}{llll} (P_t): & \min_z & f(z) & \\ & \text{subject to} & h^{(t)}(z(t)) = 0, \quad g^{(t)}(z(t)) \le 0 & \text{(local constraints)} \\ & \text{and} & H(z) = 0, \quad G(z) \le 0 & \text{(global constraints).} \end{array} \tag{14}$$

Each subset of constraints can be treated as a subproblem, where Subproblem t, $t = 1, \dots, N$, has local *state vector* $z(t) = (z_1(t), \dots, z_{u_t}(t))^T$ of u_t mixed variables, and $\cup_{t=1}^{N} z(t) = z$. Here, $z(t)$ includes all the variables that appear in any of the m_t local equality constraint functions $h^{(t)} = \left(h_1^{(t)}, \dots, h_{m_t}^{(t)}\right)^T$ and the r_t local inequality constraint functions $g^{(t)} = \left(g_1^{(t)}, \dots, g_{r_t}^{(t)}\right)^T$. Since the partitioning is by constraints, $z(1), \dots, z(N)$ may overlap with each other. Further, $z(g)$ includes all the variables that appear in any of the p global equality constraint functions $H = (H_1, \dots, H_p)^T$ and the q global inequality constraint functions $G = (G_1, \dots, G_q)^T$.

We first define $\mathcal{N}_m(z)$, the mixed neighborhood of z for P_t, and decompose the ESPC in (13) into a set of necessary conditions that collectively are sufficient. Each partitioned ESPC is then satisfied by finding an ESP of the corresponding subproblem, and any violated global constraints are resolved by finding some appropriate penalties.

Definition 6. $\mathcal{N}_{p_0}(z)$, the *mixed neighborhood* of z for P_t when partitioned by its constraints, is:

$$\mathcal{N}_{p_0}(z) = \bigcup_{t=1}^{N} \mathcal{N}_{p_1}^{(t)}(z) = \bigcup_{t=1}^{N} \left\{ z' \;\middle|\; z'(t) \in \mathcal{N}_{m_1}(z(t)) \text{ and } z_i' = z_i \; \forall z_i \notin z(t) \right\}, \tag{15}$$

where $\mathcal{N}_{m_1}(z(t))$ is the mixed neighborhood of $z(t)$ (see Definition 2).

Intuitively, $\mathcal{N}_{m_1}(z(t))$is separated into N neighborhoods, where the tth neighborhood only perturbs the variables in $z(t)$ while leaving those variables in $z \backslash z(t)$ unchanged.

Without showing the details, we can consider P_t as a MINLP and apply Theorem 1 to derive its ESPC. We then decompose the ESPC into N necessary conditions, one for each subproblem, and an overall necessary condition on the global constraints across the subproblems. We first define the penalty function for Subproblem t.

Definition 7. Let $\Phi((z,\gamma,\eta)^T) = \gamma^T|H(z)| + \eta^T G(z)^+$ be the sum of the transformed global constraint functions weighted by their penalties, where $\gamma = (\gamma_1, \dots, \gamma_p)^T \in \mathbb{R}^p$ and $\eta = (\eta_1, \dots, \eta_q)^T$are the penalty vectors for the global constraints. Then the penalty function for P_t in (14) and the corresponding penalty function in Subproblem t are defined as follows:

$$L_m((z,\alpha,\beta,\gamma,\eta)^T) = f(z) + \sum_{t=1}^{N} \left\{ \alpha(t)^T |h^{(t)}(z(t))| + \beta(t)^T \left(g^{(t)}(z(t))\right)^+ \right\} + \Phi((z,\gamma,\eta)^T), \tag{16}$$

$$\Gamma_m((z,\alpha(t),\beta(t),\gamma,\eta)^T) = f(z) + \alpha(t)^T|h^{(t)}(z(t))| + \beta(t)^T\left(g^{(t)}(z(t))\right)^+ + \Phi((z,\gamma,\eta)^T), \quad (17)$$

where $\alpha(t) = (\alpha_1(t),\ldots,\alpha_{m_t}(t))^T \in \mathbb{R}^{m_t}$ and $\beta(t) = (\beta_1(t),\ldots,\beta_{r_t}(t))^T \in \mathbb{R}^{r_t}$ are the penalty vectors for the local constraints in Subproblem t.

Theorem 2. *Partitioned necessary and sufficient ESPC on CLMm* of *Pt* [25]. Given $\mathcal{N}_{p_0}(z)$, the ESPC in (13) can be rewritten into $N + 1$ necessary conditions that, collectively, are sufficient:

$$\begin{aligned}\Gamma_m((z^*,\alpha(t),\beta(t),\gamma^{**},\eta^{**})^T) &\leq \Gamma_m((z^*,\alpha(t)^{**},\beta(t)^{**},\gamma^{**},\eta^{**})^T)\\ &\leq \Gamma_m((z,\alpha(t)^{**},\beta(t)^{**},\gamma^{**},\eta^{**})^T)\end{aligned} \quad (18)$$

$$L_m\left((z^*,\alpha^{**},\beta^{**},\gamma,\eta)^T\right) \leq L_m\left((z^*,\alpha^{**},\beta^{**},\gamma^{**},\eta^{**})^T\right) \quad (19)$$

for any $\alpha(t)^{**} > \alpha(t)^* \geq 0$, $\beta(t)^{**} > \beta(t)^* \geq 0$, $\gamma^{**} > \gamma^* \geq 0$, and $\eta^{**} > \eta^* \geq 0$, and for all $z \in \mathcal{N}_{p_1}^{(t)}(z^*)$, $\alpha(t) \in \mathbb{R}^{m_t}$, $\beta(t) \in \mathbb{R}^{r_t}$, $\gamma \in \mathbb{R}^p$, $\eta \in \mathbb{R}^q$, and $t = 1,\ldots,N$.

Theorem 2 shows that the original ESPC in Theorem 1 can be partitioned into N necessary conditions in (18) and an overall necessary condition in (19) on the global constraints across the subproblems. Because finding an ESP to each partitioned condition is equivalent to solving a MINLP, we can reformulate the ESP search of the tth condition as the solution of the following optimization problem:

$$\left(P_t^{(t)}\right): \quad \begin{aligned} &\min_{z(t)} \quad f(z) + \gamma^T|H(z)| + \eta^T G(z)^+ \\ &\text{subject to} \quad h^{(t)}(z(t)) = 0 \quad \text{and} \quad g^{(t)}(z(t)) \leq 0. \end{aligned} \quad (20)$$

The weighted sum of the global constraint functions in the objective of (20) is important because it leads to points that minimize the violations of the global constraints. When γ^T and η^T are large enough, solving $P_t^{(t)}$ will lead to points, if they exist, that satisfy the global constraints. Note that $P_t^{(t)}$ is very similar to the original problem and can be solved by the same solver to the original problem with some modifications on the objective function to be optimized.

In summary, we have shown in this section that the search for a CLM_m of P_m is equivalent to finding an ESP of the corresponding penalty function, and that this necessary and sufficient condition can be partitioned into multiple necessary conditions. The latter result allows the original problem to be decomposed by its constraints to multiple subproblems and to the reweighting of those violated global constraints defined by (19). The major benefit of this decomposition is that each subproblem involves only a fraction of the original constraints and is, therefore, a significant relaxation of the original problem with much lower complexity. The decomposition leads to a large reduction in the complexity of the original problem if the global constraints is small in quantity and can be resolved efficiently. We demonstrate in Section 5 that the number of global constraints in many benchmarks is indeed small when we exploit the locality of the constraints. In the next section, we describe our extensions to simulated annealing for finding ESPs.

3. Simulated annealing for constrained optimization

In this section, we present three algorithms for finding ESPs: the first two implementing the results in Theorems 1 and 2, and the third extending the penalty search algorithms in Section 2.1. All three methods are based on sampling the search space of a problem during their search and can be applied to solve continuous, discrete, and mixed-integer optimization problems. Without loss of generality, we only consider P_m with equality constraints, since an inequality constraint $g_j(z) \leq 0$ can be transformed into an equivalent equality constraint $g_j(z)^+ = 0$.

3.1 Constrained simulated annealing (CSA)

Figure 1 presents CSA, our algorithm for finding an ESP whose $(z^*, \alpha^{**})^T$ satisfies (13). In addition to probabilistic descents in the z subspace as in SA [18], with an acceptance probability governed by a temperature that is reduced by a properly chosen cooling schedule, CSA also does probabilistic ascents in the penalty subspace. The success of CSA lies in its strategy to search in the joint space, instead of applying SA to search in the subspace of the penalty function and updating the penalties in a separate phase of the algorithm. The latter approach would be taken in existing static and the dynamic penalty methods discussed in Section 2.1. CSA overcomes the limitations of existing penalty methods because it does not require a separate algorithm for choosing penalties. The rest of this section explains the steps of CSA [30, 28].

1. **procedure CSA**
2.   set starting point $\mathbf{z} \leftarrow (z, \alpha)^T$ and initialize $\alpha \leftarrow 0$;
3.   set starting temperature $T \leftarrow T_0$ and cooling rate $0 < \kappa < 1$;
4.   set $N_T \leftarrow$ number of trials per temperature;
5.   **while** stopping condition is not satisfied **do**
6.   **for** $k \leftarrow 1$ **to** N_T **do**
7.   generate trial point $\mathbf{z}' \in \mathcal{N}_m(\mathbf{z})$ using $G(\mathbf{z}, \mathbf{z}')$;
8.   **if** $\mathbf{z}'$ is accepted according to $A_T(\mathbf{z}, \mathbf{z}')$ **then** $\mathbf{z} \leftarrow \mathbf{z}'$
9.   **end_for**
10.   reduce temperature by $T \leftarrow \kappa\, T$;
11.   **end_while**
12. **end_procedure**

Figure 1. CSA: Constrained simulated annealing (see text for the initial values of the parameters). The differences between CSA and SA lie in their definitions of state $\mathbf{z}$, neighborhood $\mathcal{N}_m(\mathbf{z})$, generation probability $G(\mathbf{z}, \mathbf{z}')$ and acceptance probability $A_T(\mathbf{z}, \mathbf{z}')$.

Line 2 sets a starting point $\mathbf{z} \leftarrow (z, \alpha)^T$, where z can be either user-provided or randomly generated (such as using a fixed seed 123 in our experiments), and α is initialized to zero. Line 3 initializes control parameter *temperature* T to be so large that almost any trial point $\mathbf{z}'$ will be accepted. In our experiments on continuous problems, we initialize T by first randomly generating 100 points of x and their corresponding neighbors

$x' \in \mathcal{N}_c(x)$ in close proximity, where $|x'_i - x_i| \leq 0.001$, and then setting $T = \max_{x,x',i}\left\{|L_m((x',1)^T) - L_m((x,1)^T)|, |h_i(x)|\right\}$. Hence, we use a large initial T if the function is rugged ($|L_m((x',1)^T) - L_m((x,1)^T)|$ is large), or the function is not rugged but its constraint violation ($|h_i(x)|$) is large. We also initialize κ to 0.95 in our experiments.

Line 4 sets the number of iterations at each temperature. In our experiments, we choose $N_T \leftarrow \zeta(20n + m)$ where $\zeta \leftarrow 10(n + m)$, n is the number of variables, and m is the number of equality constraints. This setting is based on the heuristic rule in [9] using $n + m$ instead of n.

Line 5 stops CSA when the current **z** is not changed, *i.e.*, no other **z**' is accepted, in two successive temperature changes, or when the current T is small enough (*e.g.* $T < 10^{-6}$).

Line 7 generates a random point $\mathbf{z}' \in \mathcal{N}_m(\mathbf{z})$ from the current $\mathbf{z} \in \mathcal{S} = \mathcal{Z} \times \Lambda$, where $\Lambda = \mathbb{R}^m$ is the space of the penalty vector. In our implementation, $\mathcal{N}_m(\mathbf{z})$ consists of $(z', \alpha)_T$ and $(z, \alpha')_T$, where $z' \in \mathcal{N}_{m_1}(z)$ (see Definition 1), and $\alpha' \in \mathcal{N}_{m_2}(\alpha)$ is a point neighboring to α when $h(z) \neq 0$:

$$\mathcal{N}_m(\mathbf{z}) = \left\{(z', \alpha)^T \in \mathcal{S} \text{ where } z' \in \mathcal{N}_{m_1}(z)\right\} \cup \left\{(z, \alpha')^T \in \mathcal{S} \text{ where } \alpha' \in \mathcal{N}_{m_2}(\alpha)\right\} \tag{21}$$

$$\text{and } \mathcal{N}_{m_2}(\alpha) = \left\{\alpha' \in \Lambda \text{ where } (\alpha'_i < \alpha_i \text{ or } \alpha'_i > \alpha_i \text{ if } h_i(z) \neq 0) \text{ and } (\alpha'_i = \alpha_i \text{ if } h_i(z) = 0)\right\}. \tag{22}$$

According to this definition, α_i is not perturbed when $h_i(z) = 0$ is satisfied.

G(**z**, **z**'), the *generation probability* from **z** to $\mathbf{z}' \in \mathcal{N}_m(\mathbf{z})$, satisfies:

$$0 \geq G(\mathbf{z}, \mathbf{z}') \leq 1 \quad \text{and} \quad \sum_{\mathbf{z}' \in \mathcal{N}_m(\mathbf{z})} G(\mathbf{z}, \mathbf{z}') = 1. \tag{23}$$

Since the choice of $G(\mathbf{z}, \mathbf{z}')$ is arbitrary as long as it satisfies (23), we select **z**' in our experiments with uniform probability across all the points in $\mathcal{N}_m(\mathbf{z})$, independent of T:

$$G(\mathbf{z}, \mathbf{z}') = \frac{1}{|\mathcal{N}_m(\mathbf{z})|}. \tag{24}$$

As we perturb either z or α but not both simultaneously, (24) means that **z**' is generated either by choosing $z' \in \mathcal{N}_{m_1}(z)$ randomly or by generating α' uniformly in a predefined range.

Line 8 accepts **z**' with acceptance probability $A_T(\mathbf{z}, \mathbf{z}')$ that consists of two components, depending on whether z or α is changed in **z**':

$$A_T(\mathbf{z}, \mathbf{z}') = \begin{cases} \exp\left(-\frac{(L_m(\mathbf{z}') - L_m(\mathbf{z}))^+}{T}\right) & \text{if } \mathbf{z}' = (z', \alpha)^T \\ \exp\left(-\frac{(L_m(\mathbf{z}) - L_m(\mathbf{z}'))^+}{T}\right) & \text{if } \mathbf{z}' = (z, \alpha')^T. \end{cases} \tag{25}$$

The acceptance probability in (25) differs from the acceptance probability used in conventional SA, which only has the first case in (25) and whose goal is to look for a global minimum in the z subspace. Without the α subspace, only probabilistic descents in the z subspace are carried out.

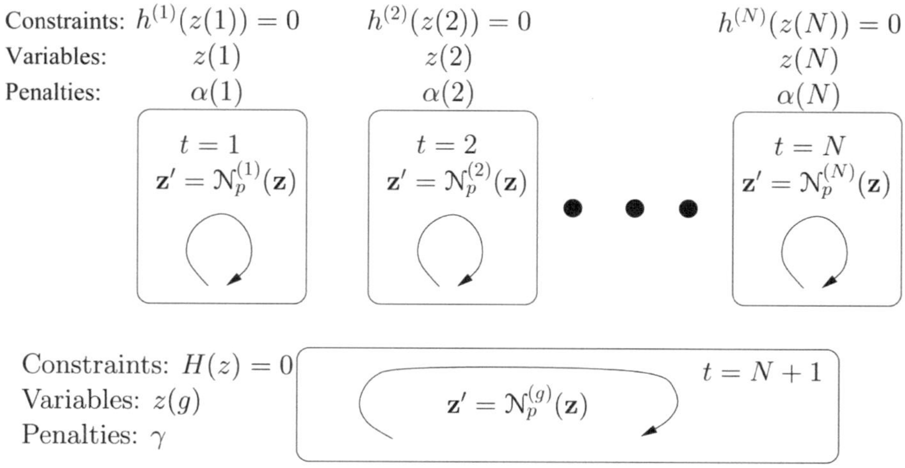

Figure 2. CPSA: Constraint-partitioned simulated annealing.

In contrast, our goal is to look for an ESP in the joint $Z \times \Lambda$ space, each existing at a local minimum in the z subspace and at a local maximum in the α subspace. To this end, CSA carries out *probabilistic descents* of $L_m\big((z,\alpha)^T\big)$ with respect to z for each fixed α. That is, when we generate a new z' under a fixed α, we accept it with probability one when $\delta_z = L_m\big((z',\alpha)^T\big) - L_m\big((z,\alpha)^T\big)$is negative; otherwise, we accept it with probability $e^{-\delta_z/T}$. This step has exactly the same effect as in conventional SA; that is, it performs descents with occasional ascents in the z subspace.

However, descents in the z subspace alone will lead to a local/global minimum of the penalty function without satisfying the corresponding constraints. In order to satisfy all the constraints, CSA also carries out *probabilistic ascents* of $L_m\big((z,\alpha)^T\big)$ with respect to α for each fixed z in order to increase the penalties of violated constraints and to force them into satisfaction. Hence, when we generate a new α' under a fixed z, we accept it with probability one when $\delta_\alpha = L_m\big((z,\alpha')^T\big) - L_m\big((z,\alpha)^T\big)$ is positive; otherwise, we accept it with probability $e^{-\delta_\alpha/T}$. This step is the same as that in conventional SA when performing ascents with occasional descents in the α subspace. Note that when a constraint is satisfied, the corresponding penalty will not be changed according to (22).

Finally, Line 10 reduces T by the following *cooling schedule* after looping N_T times at given T:

$$T \longleftarrow \kappa \cdot T \quad \text{where the cooling-rate constant } \kappa \leftarrow 0.95 \text{ (typically } 0.8 \leq \kappa \leq 0.99\text{).} \qquad (26)$$

At high T, (25) allows any trial point to be accepted with high probabilities, thereby allowing the search to traverse a large space and overcome infeasible regions. When T is reduced, the acceptance probability decreases, and at very low temperatures, the algorithm behaves like a local search.

3.2 Constraint-Partitioned Simulated Annealing (CPSA)

We present in this section CPSA, an extension of CSA that decomposes the search in CSA into multiple subproblems after partitioning the constraints into subsets. Recall that, according to Theorem 2, P_t in (14) can be partitioned into a sequence of N subproblems defined in (20) and an overall necessary condition defined in (19) on the global constraints across the subproblems, after choosing an appropriate mixed neighborhood. Instead of considering all the constraints together as in CSA, CPSA performs searches in multiple subproblems, each involving a small subset of the constraints. As in CSA, we only consider P_t with equality constraints.

Figure 2 illustrates the idea in CPSA. Unlike the original CSA that solves the problem as a whole, CPSA solves each subproblem independently. In Subproblem t, t = 1, ...,N, CSA is performed in the $(z(t),\ \alpha(t))^T$ subspace related to the local constraints $h^{(t)}(z(t))$ = 0. In addition, there is a global search that explores in the $(z(g),\gamma)^T$ subspace on the global constraints $H(z)$ = 0. This additional search is needed for resolving any violated global constraints.

1. **procedure CPSA**
2. set starting point $\mathbf{z} \leftarrow (z, \alpha, \gamma)^T$ and initialize $\alpha = \gamma \leftarrow 0$;
3. set starting temperature $T \leftarrow T^0$ and cooling rate $0 < \kappa < 1$;
4. set $N_T \leftarrow$ number of trials per temperature;
5. **while** stopping condition is not satisfied **do**
6. **for** $k \leftarrow 1$ **to** N_T **do**
7. set t to be a random integer between 1 and $N + 1$;
8. **if** $1 \leq t \leq N$ **then**
9. generate $\mathbf{z}' \in \mathcal{N}_p^{(t)}(\mathbf{z})$ using $G^{(t)}(\mathbf{z}, \mathbf{z}')$;
10. if $\mathbf{z}'$ is accepted according to $A_T(\mathbf{z}, \mathbf{z}')$ **then** $\mathbf{z} \leftarrow \mathbf{z}'$;
11. **else** /* $t = N + 1$ */
12. generate $\mathbf{z}' \in \mathcal{N}_p^{(g)}(\mathbf{z})$ using $G^{(g)}(\mathbf{z}, \mathbf{z}')$;
13. if $\mathbf{z}'$ is accepted according to $A_T(\mathbf{z}, \mathbf{z}')$ **then** $\mathbf{z} \leftarrow \mathbf{z}'$;
14. **end_if**
15. **end_for**
16. reduce temperature by $T \leftarrow \kappa\, T$;
17. **end_while**
18. **end_procedure**

Figure 3. The CPSA search procedure.

Figure 3 describes the CPSA procedure. The first six lines are similar to those in CSA.

To facilitate the convergence analysis of CPSA in a Markov-chain model, Lines 7-14 randomly pick a subproblem for evaluation, instead of deterministically enumerating the subproblems in a round-robin fashion, and stochastically accept a new probe using an acceptance probability governed by a decreasing temperature. This approach leads to a memoryless Markovian process in CPSA.

Line 7 randomly selects Subproblem i, $i = 1 \ldots, N+1$, with probability $P_s(t)$, where $P_s(t)$ can be arbitrarily chosen as long as:

$$\sum_{t=1}^{N+1} P_s(t) = 1 \text{ and } P_s(t) > 0. \tag{27}$$

When t is between 1 and N (Line 8), it represents a local exploration step in Subproblem t. In this case, Line 9 generates a trial point $\mathbf{z}' \in \mathcal{N}_p^{(t)}(\mathbf{z})$ from the current point $\mathbf{z} = (z, \alpha, \gamma)^T \in \mathcal{S}$ using a *generation probability* $G^{(t)}(\mathbf{z}, \mathbf{z}')$ that can be arbitrary as long as the following is satisfied:

$$0 \leq G^{(t)}(\mathbf{z}, \mathbf{z}') \leq 1 \quad \text{and} \quad \sum_{\mathbf{z}' \in \mathcal{N}_p^{(t)}(\mathbf{z})} G^{(t)}(\mathbf{z}, \mathbf{z}') = 1. \tag{28}$$

The point is generated by perturbing $z(t)$ and $\alpha(t)$ in their neighborhood $\mathcal{N}_p^{(t)}(\mathbf{z})$:

$$\mathcal{N}_p^{(t)}(\mathbf{z}) = \{(z', \alpha(t), \gamma) \in \mathcal{S} \mid z' \in \mathcal{N}_{p_1}^{(t)}(z)\} \cup \{(z, \alpha'(t), \gamma) \in \mathcal{S} \mid \alpha'(t) \in \mathcal{N}_{p_2}^{(t)}(\alpha(t))\} \tag{29}$$

$$\begin{aligned} \mathcal{N}_{p_2}^{(t)}(\alpha(t)) = \{&\alpha'(t) \in \Lambda^{(\alpha(t))} \text{ where } (\alpha_i'(t) < \alpha_i(t) \text{ or } \alpha_i'(t) > \alpha_i(t) \text{ if } h_i(z(t)) \neq 0) \\ &\text{and } (\alpha_i'(t) = \alpha_i(t) \text{ if } h_i(z(t)) = 0)\}, \end{aligned} \tag{30}$$

and $\mathcal{N}_{p_1}^{(t)}(z)$ is defined in (15) and $\Lambda^{(\alpha(t))} = \mathbb{R}^{m_t}$. This means that $\mathbf{z}' \in \mathcal{N}_p^{(t)}(\mathbf{z})$ only differs from $\mathbf{z}$ in $z(t)$ or $\alpha(t)$ and remains the same for the other variables. This is different from CSA that perturbs $\mathbf{z}$ in the overall variable space. As in CSA, α_i is not perturbed when $h_i(z(t)) = 0$ is satisfied. Last, Line 10 accepts $\mathbf{z}'$ with the Metropolis probability $A_T(\mathbf{z}, \mathbf{z}')$ similar to that in (25):

$$A_T(\mathbf{z}, \mathbf{z}') = \begin{cases} \exp\left(-\frac{(L_m(\mathbf{z}') - L_m(\mathbf{z}))^+}{T}\right) & \text{if } \mathbf{z}' = (z', \alpha, \gamma)^T \\ \exp\left(-\frac{(L_m(\mathbf{z}) - L_m(\mathbf{z}'))^+}{T}\right) & \text{if } \mathbf{z}' = (z, \alpha', \gamma)^T \text{ or } \mathbf{z}' = (z, \alpha, \gamma')^T. \end{cases} \tag{31}$$

When $t = N + 1$ (Line 11), it represents a global exploration step. In this case, Line 12 generates a random trial point $\mathbf{z}' \in \mathcal{N}_p^{(g)}(\mathbf{z})$ using a generation probability $G^{(g)}(\mathbf{z}, \mathbf{z}')$ that satisfies the condition similar to that in (28). Assuming $\mathcal{N}_{m_1}(z(g))$ to be the mixed neighborhood of $z(g)$ and $\Lambda^{(g)} = \mathbb{R}^p$, $\mathbf{z}'$ is obtained by perturbing $z(g)$ and γ in their neighborhood $\mathcal{N}_p^{(g)}(\mathbf{z})$::

$$\mathcal{N}_p^{(g)}(\mathbf{z}) = \{(z', \alpha, \gamma)^T \in \mathcal{S} \text{ where } z' \in \mathcal{N}_{p_1}^{(g)}(z)\} \cup \{(z, \alpha, \gamma')^T \in \mathcal{S} \text{ where } \gamma' \in \mathcal{N}_{p_2}^{(g)}(\gamma)\} \tag{32}$$

$$\mathcal{N}_{p_1}^{(g)}(z) = \{z' \text{ where } z'(g) \in \mathcal{N}_{m_1}(z(g)) \text{ and } z_i' = z_i \ \forall z_i \notin z(g)\} \tag{33}$$

$$\mathcal{N}_{p_2}^{(g)}(\gamma) \quad = \quad \{\gamma' \in \Lambda^{(g)} \text{ where } (\gamma_i' < \gamma_i \text{ or } \gamma_i' > \gamma_i \text{ if } H_i(z) \neq 0) \text{ and } (\gamma_i' = \gamma_i \text{ if } H_i(z) = 0)\}. \quad (34)$$

Again, $\mathbf{z}'$ is accepted with probability $A_T(\mathbf{z}, \mathbf{z}')$ in (31) (Line 13). Note that both $\mathcal{N}_p^{(t)}(\mathbf{z})$ (z) and $\mathcal{N}_p^{(g)}(\mathbf{z})$: ensure the ergodicity of the Markov chain, which is required for achieving asymptotic convergence.

When compared to CSA, CPSA reduces the search complexity through constraint partitioning. Since both CSA and CPSA need to converge to an equilibrium distribution of variables at a given temperature before the temperature is reduced, the total search time depends on the convergence time at each temperature. By partitioning the constraints into subsets, each subproblem only involves an exponentially smaller subspace with a small number of variables and penalties. Thus, each subproblem takes significantly less time to converge to an equilibrium state at a given temperature, and the total time for all the subproblems to converge is also significantly reduced. This reduction in complexity is experimentally validated in Section 5.

3.3 Greedy ESPC Search Method (GEM)

In this section, we present a dynamic penalty method based on a greedy search of an ESP. Instead of probabilistically accepting a probe as in CSA and CPSA, our greedy approach accepts the probe if it improves the value of the penalty function and rejects it otherwise.

One simple approach that does not work well is to gradually increase α^{**} until $\alpha^{**} > \alpha^*$, while minimizing the penalty function with respect to z using an existing local-search method. This simple iterative search does not always work well because the penalty function has many local minima that satisfy the second inequality in (13), but some of these local minima do not satisfy the first inequality in (13) even when $\alpha^{**} > \alpha^*$. Hence, the search may generate stationary points that are local minima of the penalty function but are not feasible solutions to the original problem.

To address this issue, Figure 4 shows a global search called the *Greedy ESPC Search Method* [32] (GEM). GEM uses the following penalty function:

$$L_g((z,\alpha)^T) = f(z) + \sum_{i=1}^{m} \alpha_i |h_i(z)| + \frac{1}{2}||h(z)||^2. \quad (35)$$

Lines 5-8 carries out Ng iterative descents in the z subspace. In each iteration, Line 6 generates a probe $z' \in \mathcal{N}_{m_1}(z)$ neighboring to z. As defined in (24) for CSA, we select z' with uniform probability across all the points in $\mathcal{N}_{m_1}(z)$. Line 7 then evaluates L_g $((z', \alpha)^T)$ and accepts z' only when it reduces the value of L_g. After the N_g descents, Line 9 updates the penalty vector α in order to bias the search towards resolving those violated constraints.

When α^{**} reaches its upper bound during a search but a local minimum of L_g does not correspond to a CLM_m of P_m, we can reduce α^{**} instead of restarting the search from a new starting point. The decrease will change the terrain of L_g and "lower" its barrier, thereby allowing a local search to continue in the same trajectory and move to another local minimum of L_g. In Line 10, we reduce the penalty value of a constraint when its maximum violation is not reduced for three consecutive iterations. To reduce the penalties, Line 11 multiplies each element in α by a random real number uniformly generated between 0.4 to 0.6. By repeatedly increasing α^{**} to its upper bound and by reducing it to some lower bound, a local search will be able to escape from local traps and visit multiple local minima of the penalty function. We leave the presentation of the parameters used in GEM and its experimental results to Section 5.

```
1.  procedure GEM
2.      set ϱ to be a positive real constant;
3.      set starting point z ← (z, α)^T and initialize α;
4.      repeat
5.          for k ← 1 to N_g /* N_g ← 20, a positive integer in our experiments */
6.              generate random trial point z' ∈ N_{m_1}(z);
7.              if (L_g((z, α)^T) > L_g((z', α)^T)) then z' ← z; end_if
8.          end_for
9.          update α ⟵ α + ϱ|h(z)|;
10.         if (condition to decrease α is satisfied) then
11.             reduce α in order to allow the search to escape from local traps;
12.         end_if
13.     until stopping conditions are satisfied;
14. end_procedure
```

Figure 4. Greedy ESPC search method (GEM).

4. Asymptotic convergence of CSA and CPSA

In this subsection, we show the asymptotic convergence of CSA and CPSA to a constrained global minimum in *discrete* constrained optimization problems. Without repeating the definitions in Section 1, we can similarly define a discrete nonlinear programming problem (P_d), a discrete neighborhood ($\mathcal{N}_d(y)$), a discrete constrained local minimum (CLM_d), a discrete constrained global minimum (CGM_d), and a penalty function in discrete space (L_d).

4.1 Asymptotic convergence of CSA

We first define the asymptotic convergence property. For a global minimization problem, let Ω be its search space, Ω_s be the set of all global minima, and $\omega(j) \in \Omega$, $j = 0, 1, \ldots,$ be a sequence of points generated by an iterative procedure ψ until some stopping conditions hold.

Definition 8. Procedure ψ is said to have *asymptotic convergence to a global minimum*, or simply *asymptotic convergence* [2], if ψ converges with probability one to an element in Ω_s; that is, $\lim_{j\to\infty} P(\omega(j) \in \Omega_s) = 1$, independent of $\omega(0)$, where $P(w)$ is the probability of event w.

In the following, we first state the result on the asymptotic convergence of CSA to a CGM_d of P_d with probability one when T approaches 0 and when T is reduced according to a specific cooling schedule. By modeling CSA by an inhomogeneous Markov chain, we show that the chain is strongly ergodic, that the chain minimizes an implicit virtual energy based on the framework of generalized SA (GSA) [24, 23], and that the virtual energy is at its minimum at any CGM_d. We state the main theorems without proofs [27] and illustrate the theorems by examples.

CSA can be modeled by an inhomogeneous Markov chain that consists of a sequence of homogeneous Markov chains of finite length, each at a specific temperature in a cooling schedule. Its *one-step transition probability matrix* is $P_T = [P_T(\mathbf{y}, \mathbf{y}')]$, where:

$$P_T(\mathbf{y},\mathbf{y}') = \begin{cases} G(\mathbf{y},\mathbf{y}')A_T(\mathbf{y},\mathbf{y}') & \text{if } \mathbf{y}' \in \mathcal{N}_d(\mathbf{y}) \\ 1 - \sum_{\mathbf{y}'' \in \mathcal{N}_d(\mathbf{y})} G(\mathbf{y},\mathbf{y}'')A_T(\mathbf{y},\mathbf{y}'') & \text{if } \mathbf{y}' = \mathbf{y} \\ 0 & \text{otherwise.} \end{cases} \tag{36}$$

Example 2. Consider the following simple discrete minimization problem:

$$\begin{aligned} \min_{y} \quad & f(y) = -y^2 \\ \text{subject to} \quad & h(y) = |(y-0.6)(y-1.0)| = 0, \end{aligned} \tag{37}$$

where $y \in \mathcal{Y} = \{0.5, 0.6, \ldots, 1.2\}$. The corresponding penalty function is:

$$L_d\big((y,\alpha)^T\big) = -y^2 + \alpha \cdot |(y-0.6)(y-1.0)|. \tag{38}$$

By choosing $\alpha \in \Lambda = \{2, 3, 4, 5, 6\}$, with the maximum penalty value α^{max} at 6, the state space is $\mathcal{S} = \{(y,\alpha)^T \in \mathcal{Y} \times \Lambda\}$ with $|\mathcal{S}| = 8 \cdot 5 = 40$ states. At $y = 0.6$ or $y = 1.0$ where the constraint is satisfied, we can choose $\alpha^* = 1$, and any $\alpha^{**} > \alpha^*$, including α^{max}, would satisfy (13) in Theorem 1.

In the Markov chain, we define $\mathcal{N}_d(\mathbf{y})$ as in (21), where $\mathcal{N}_{d_1}(y)$ and $\mathcal{N}_{d_2}(\alpha)$ are as follows:

$$\mathcal{N}_{d_1}(y) = \{y-0.1, y+0.1 \mid 0.6 \le y \le 1.1\} \cup \{y+0.1 \mid y = 0.5\} \cup \{y-0.1 \mid y = 1.2\}, \tag{39}$$

$$\begin{aligned} \mathcal{N}_{d_2}(\alpha) = \; & \{\alpha-1, \alpha+1 \mid 3 \le \alpha \le 5,\; y \ne 0.6 \text{ and } y \ne 1.0\} \cup \{\alpha - 1 \mid \alpha = 6, \\ & y \ne 0.6 \text{ and } y \ne 1.0\} \cup \{\alpha+1 \mid \alpha = 2,\; y \ne 0.6 \text{ and } y \ne 1.0\}. \end{aligned} \tag{40}$$

Figure 5 shows the state space S of the Markov chain. In this chain, an arrow from $\mathbf{y}$ to $\mathbf{y}' \in \mathcal{N}_d(\mathbf{y})$ (where $\mathbf{y}' = (y', \alpha)^T$ or $(y, \alpha')^T$) means that there is a one-step transition from $\mathbf{y}$ to $\mathbf{y}$ whose $P_T(\mathbf{y}, \mathbf{y}') > 0$. For $y = 0.6$ and $y = 1.0$, there is no transition among the points in the α dimension because the constraints are satisfied at those y values (according to (22)).

There are two ESPs in this Markov chain at $(0.6, 5)^T$ and $(0.6, 6)^T$, which correspond to the local minimum at $y = 0.6$, and two ESPs at $(1.0, 5)^T$ and $(1.0, 6)^T$, which correspond to the local minimum at $y = 1.0$. CSA is designed to locate one of the ESPs at $(0.6, 6)^T$ and $(1.0, 6)^T$. These correspond, respectively, to the CLM^d at $y^* = 0.6$ and $y^* = 1.0$. ■

Let $\mathbf{y}_{\text{opt}} = \{(y^*, \alpha^{\max})^T | \; y^* \in \mathcal{Y}_{\text{opt}}\}$, and N_L be the maximum of the minimum number of transitions required to reach $\mathbf{y}_{\text{opt}}$ from all $\mathbf{y} \in S$. By properly constructing $\mathcal{N}_d(\mathbf{y})$, we state without proof that P_T is irreducible and that N_L can always be found. This property is illustrated in Figure 5 in which any two nodes can always reach each other.

Let N_T, the number of trials per temperature, be N_L. The following theorem states the strong ergodicity of the Markov chain, where strong ergodicity means that state $\mathbf{y}$ of the Markov chain has a unique stationary probability $\pi_T(\mathbf{y})$. (The proof can be found in the reference [27].)

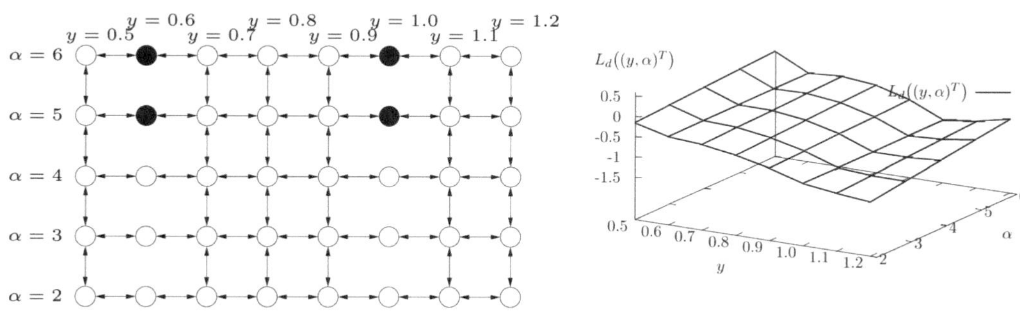

Figure 5. The Markov chain with the transition probabilities defined in (36) for the example problem in (37) and the corresponding penalty-function value at each state. The four ESPs are shaded in (a).

Theorem 3. The inhomogeneous Markov chain is *strongly ergodic* if the sequence of temperatures $\{T_k, \text{k} = 0, 1, 2, \ldots\}$ satisfies:

$$T_k \geq \frac{N_L \triangle_L}{log_e(k+1)}, \tag{41}$$

where $T_k > T_{k+1}$, $\lim_{k\to\infty} T_k = 0$, and $\triangle_L = 2 \max_{\mathbf{y}\in\mathcal{S}, \mathbf{y}'\in\mathcal{N}_d(\mathbf{y})} \left\{ |L_d(\mathbf{y}') - L_d(\mathbf{y})| \right\}$.

Example 2 (cont'd). In the Markov chain in Figure 5, $\Delta_L = 0.411$ and $N_L = 11$. Hence, the Markov chain is strongly ergodic if we use a cooling schedule $T_k \geq \frac{4.521}{log_e(k+1)}$. Note that the cooling schedule used in CSA (Line 10 of Figure 1) does not satisfy the condition.

Our Markov chain also fits into the framework of *generalized simulated annealing* (GSA) [24, 23] when we define an irreducible Markov kernel $P_T(\mathbf{y}, \mathbf{y}')$ and its associated *communication cost* $v(\mathbf{y}, \mathbf{y}')$, where $v\colon \mathcal{S} \times \mathcal{S} \to [0, +\infty]$ and $\mathbf{y}' \in \mathcal{N}_d(\mathbf{y})$:

$$v(\mathbf{y}, \mathbf{y}') = \begin{cases} (L_d(\mathbf{y}') - L_d(\mathbf{y}))^+ & \text{if } \mathbf{y}' = (y', \alpha)^T \\ (L_d(\mathbf{y}) - L_d(\mathbf{y}'))^+ & \text{if } \mathbf{y}' = (y, \alpha')^T. \end{cases} \tag{42}$$

Based on the communication costs over all directed edges, the *virtual energy* $W(\mathbf{y})$ (according to Definition 2.5 in [23, 24]) is the cost of the minimum-cost spanning tree rooted at $\mathbf{y}$:

$$W(\mathbf{y}) = \min_{g\in G(\mathbf{y})} V(g), \tag{43}$$

where $G(\mathbf{y})$ is the set of spanning trees rooted at $\mathbf{y}$, and $V(g)$ is the sum of the communication costs over all the edges of g.

The following quoted result shows the asymptotic convergence of GSA in minimizing $W(i)$:

Proposition 1 "(Proposition 2.6 in [14, 23, 24]). For every $T > 0$, the unique stationary distribution π_T of the Markov chain satisfies:

$$\pi_T(i) \longrightarrow \exp\left(-\frac{W(i) - W(E)}{T}\right) \quad \text{as} \quad T \longrightarrow 0, \tag{44}$$

where $W(i)$ is the virtual energy of i, and $W(E) = \min_{i \in \mathcal{S}} W(i)$."

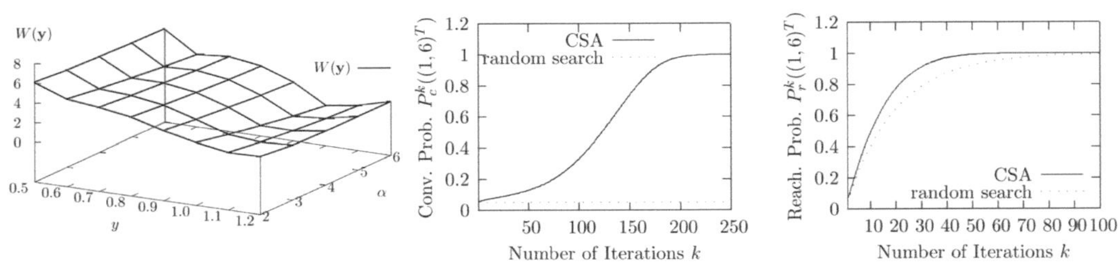

a) Virtual energy $W(\mathbf{y})$ b) Convergence prob. at $(1, 6)^T$ c) Reachability prob. at $(1, 6)^T$

Figure 6. Virtual energy of the Markov chain in Figure 5a and the convergence behavior of CSA and random search at $(1.0, 6)^T$.

In contrast to SA that strives to minimize a single unconstrained objective, CSA does not minimize $L_d((y, \alpha)^T)$. This property is illustrated in Figure 5b in which the ESPs are not at the global minimum of $L_d((y, \alpha)^T)$. Rather, CSA aims to implicitly minimize $W(\mathbf{y})$ according to GSA [24, 23]. That is, $y^* \in \mathcal{Y}_{\text{opt}}$ corresponds to $\mathbf{y}^* = (y^*, \alpha^{\max})^T$ with the minimum $W(\mathbf{y})$, and $W((y^*, \alpha^{\max})^T) < W((y, \alpha)^T)$ for all $y \neq y^*$ and $\alpha \in \Lambda$ and for all $y = y^*$ and $\alpha \neq \alpha^{\max}$. The following theorem shows that CSA asymptotically converges to $\mathbf{y}^*$ with probability one. (See the proof in the reference [27].)

Theorem 4. Given the inhomogeneous Markov chain modeling CSA with transition probability defined in (36) and the sequence of decreasing temperatures that satisfy (41), the Markov chain converges to a CGM_d with probability one as $k \rightarrow \infty$.

Example 2 (cont'd). We illustrate the virtual energy $W(\mathbf{y})$ of the Markov chain in Figure 5a and the convergence behavior of CSA and random search.

One approach to find $W(\mathbf{y})$ that works well for a small problem is to enumerate all possible spanning trees rooted at $\mathbf{y}$ and to find the one with the minimum cost. Another more efficient way adopted in this example is to compute $W(\mathbf{y})$ using (44). This can be done by first numerically computing the stationary probability $\pi_T(\mathbf{y})$ of the Markov chain at a given T using the one-step transition probability $P_T(\mathbf{y}, \mathbf{y}')$ in (36), where π_T evolves with iteration k as follows:

$$P_c^{k+1} = P_c^k \, P_T \qquad \text{for any given initial convergence probability vector } P_c^0, \tag{45}$$

until $||P_c^{k+1} - P_c^k|| \leq \varepsilon$. In this example, we set $\varepsilon = 10^{-16}$ as the stopping precision. Since $\pi_T = \lim_{k\to\infty} P_c^k$, independent of the initial vector P_c^0, we set $P_c^0(i) = \frac{1}{|\mathbb{S}|}$ for $i = 1, \cdots, |\mathbb{S}|$. Figure 6a shows $W((y, \alpha)^T)$ of Figure 5a. Clearly, $L_d((y, \alpha)^T) \neq W((y, \alpha)^T)$. For a given y, $W((y, \alpha)^T)$ is non-increasing as α increases. For example, $W((0.6, 3)^T) = 4.44 \geq W((0.6, 4)^T) = 4.03$, and $W((0.8, 2)^T) = 4.05 \geq W((0.8, 6)^T) = 3.14$. We also have $W((y, \alpha)^T)$ minimized at $y = 1.0$ when $\alpha = \alpha_{max} = 6$: $W((0.6, 6)^T) = 3.37 \geq W((0.8, 6)^T) = 3.14 \geq W((1.0, 6)^T) = 0.097$. Hence, $W((y, \alpha)^T)$ is minimized at $(y^*, \alpha_{max})^T = (1.0, 6)^T$, which is an ESP with the minimum objective value. In contrast, $L_d((y, \alpha)^T)$ is non-decreasing as α increases. In Figure 5b, the minimum value of $L_d((y, \alpha)^T)$ is at $(1.2, 2)^T$, which is not a feasible point.

To illustrate the convergence of CSA to $y^* = 1.0$, Figure 6b plots $P_c^k(\mathbf{y}^*)$ as a function of k, where $\mathbf{y}^* = (1.0, 6)^T$. In this example, we set $T_0 = 1.0$, $N_T = 5$, and $\kappa = 0.9$ (the cooling schedule in Figure 1). Obviously, as the cooling schedule is more aggressive than that in Theorem 3, one would not expect the search to converge to a CGM_d with probability one, as proved in Theorem 4. As T approaches zero, $W(\mathbf{y}^*)$ approaches zero, and $P_c^k(\mathbf{y}^*)$ monotonically increases and approaches one. Similar figures can be drawn to show that $P_c^k(\mathbf{y})$, $\mathbf{y} \neq \mathbf{y}^*$, decreases to zero as T is reduced. Therefore, CSA is more likely to find $\mathbf{y}^*$ as the search progresses. In contrast, for random search, $P_c^k(\mathbf{y}^*)$ is constant, independent of k.

Note that it is not possible to demonstrate asymptotic convergence using only a finite number of iterations. Our example, however, shows that the probability of finding a CGM_d improves over time. Hence, it becomes more likely to find a CGM_d when more time is spent to solve the problem.

Last, Figure 6c depicts the *reachability probability* $P_r^k(\mathbf{y}^*)$ of finding $\mathbf{y}^*$ in any of the first k iterations. Assuming all the iterations are independent, $P_r^k(\mathbf{y}^*)$ is defined as:

$$P_r^k(\mathbf{y}^*) = 1 - \prod_{i=0}^{k}\left(1 - P(\mathbf{y}^* \text{ found in the } i^{\text{th}} \text{ iteration})\right). \quad (46)$$

The figure shows that CSA has better reachability probabilities than random search over the 100 iterations evaluated, although the difference diminishes as the number of iterations is increased.

It is easy to show that CSA has *asymptotic reachability* [2] of $\mathbf{y}^*$; that is, $\lim_{k\to\infty} P_r^k(\mathbf{y}^*) = 1$. Asymptotic reachability is weaker than asymptotic convergence because it only requires the algorithm to hit a global minimum sometime during a search and can be guaranteed if the algorithm is ergodic. (Ergodicity means that any two points in the search space can be reached from each other with a non-zero probability.) Asymptotic reachability can be accomplished in any ergodic search by keeping track of the best solution found during the search. In contrast, asymptotic convergence requires the algorithm to converge to a global minimum with probability one. Consequently, the probability of a probe to hit the solution increases as the search progresses.

4.2 Asymptotic convergence of CPSA

By following a similar approach in the last section on proving the asymptotic convergence of CSA, we prove in this section the asymptotic convergence of CPSA to a CGM_d of P_d.

CPSA can be modeled by an inhomogeneous Markov chain that consists of a sequence of homogeneous Markov chains of finite length, each at a specific temperature in a given cooling schedule. The state space of the Markov chain can be described by state $\mathbf{y} = (y, \alpha, \gamma)^T$, where $y \in \mathcal{D}^w$, where $y \in \mathcal{D}^w$ is the vector of problem variables and α and γ are the penalty vectors.

According to the generation probability $G^{(t)}(\mathbf{y}, \mathbf{y}')$ and the acceptance probability $A^T(\mathbf{y}, \mathbf{y}')$, the *one-step transition probability matrix* of the Markov chain for CPSA is $P^T = [P^T(\mathbf{y}, \mathbf{y}')]$, where:

$$P_T(\mathbf{y},\mathbf{y}') = \begin{cases} P_s(t)G^{(t)}(\mathbf{y},\mathbf{y}')A_T(\mathbf{y},\mathbf{y}') & \text{if } \mathbf{y}' \in \mathcal{N}_p^{(t)}(\mathbf{y}),\ t = 1,\ldots,N \\ P_s(N+1)G^{(g)}(\mathbf{y},\mathbf{y}')A_T(\mathbf{y},\mathbf{y}') & \text{if } \mathbf{y}' \in \mathcal{N}_p^{(g)}(\mathbf{y}) \\ 1 - \sum_{t=1}^{N}\left[\sum_{\mathbf{y}''\in\mathcal{N}_p^{(t)}(\mathbf{y})} P_T(\mathbf{y},\mathbf{y}'')\right] - \sum_{\mathbf{y}''\in\mathcal{N}_p^{(g)}(\mathbf{y})} P_T(\mathbf{y},\mathbf{y}'') & \text{if } \mathbf{y}' = \mathbf{y} \\ 0 & \text{otherwise.} \end{cases} \quad (47)$$

Let $\mathbf{y}_{\text{opt}} = \left\{(y^*, \alpha^{\max}, \gamma^{\max})^T \mid y^* \in \mathcal{Y}_{\text{opt}}\right\}$, and N_L be the maximum of the minimum number of transitions required to reach $\mathbf{y}_{\text{opt}}$ from all $\mathbf{y} \in \mathcal{S}$. Given $\{T_k, k = 0, 1, 2, \ldots\}$ that satisfy (41) and N_T, the number of trials per temperature, be N_L, a similar theorem as in Theorem 3 can be proved [8]. This means that state $\mathbf{y}$ of the Markov chain has a unique stationary probability $\pi_T(\mathbf{y})$.

Note that Δ_L defined in Theorem 3 is the maximum difference between the penalty-function values of two neighboring states. Although this value depends on the user-defined neighborhood, it is usually smaller for CPSA than for CSA because CPSA has a partitioned neighborhood, and two neighboring states can differ by only a subset of the variables. In contrast, two states in CSA can differ by more variables and have larger variations in their penalty-function values. According to (41), a smaller Δ_L allows the temperature to be reduced faster in the convergence to a CGM_d.

Similar to CSA, (47) also fits into the framework of GSA if we define an irreducible Markov kernel $PT(\mathbf{y}, \mathbf{y}')$ and its associated communication cost $v(\mathbf{y}, \mathbf{y}')$, where v: $\mathcal{S} \times \mathcal{S} \to [0, +\infty]$:

$$v(\mathbf{y},\mathbf{y}') = \begin{cases} (L_d(\mathbf{y}') - L_d(\mathbf{y}))^+ & \text{if } \mathbf{y}' = (y', \alpha, \gamma)^T \\ (L_d(\mathbf{y}) - L_d(\mathbf{y}'))^+ & \text{if } \mathbf{y}' = (y, \alpha', \gamma)^T \text{ or } \mathbf{y}' = (y, \alpha, \gamma')^T. \end{cases} \quad (48)$$

In a way similar to that in CSA, we use the result that any process modeled by GSA minimizes an implicit virtual energy $W(\mathbf{y})$ and converges to the global minimum of $W(\mathbf{y})$ with probability one. The following theorem states the asymptotic convergence of CPSA to a CGM_d. The proof in the reference [27] shows that $W(\mathbf{y})$ is minimized at $(y^*, \alpha^{\max}, \gamma^{\max})^T$ for some $\alpha^{\max}$ and $\gamma^{\max}$.

Theorem 5. Given the inhomogeneous Markov chain modeling CPSA with transition probability defined in (47) and the sequence of decreasing temperatures that satisfy (41), the Markov chain converges to a CGM_d with probability one as $k \to \infty$.
Again, the cooling schedule of CPSA in Figure 3 is more aggressive than that in Theorem 5.

5. Experimental results on continuous constrained problems

In this section, we apply CSA and CPSA to solve some nonlinear continuous optimization benchmarks and compare their performance to that of other dynamic penalty methods. We further illustrate the application of the methods on two real-world applications.

5.1 Implementation details of CSA for solving dontinuous problems

In theory, any neighborhoods $\mathcal{N}_{c_1}(x)$ and $\mathcal{N}_{c_2}(\alpha)$ that satisfy (21) and (22) can be used. In practice, however, appropriate neighborhoods must be chosen in any efficient implementation.
In generating trial point $\mathbf{x}' = (x', \alpha)^T$ from $\mathbf{x} = (x, \alpha)^T$ where $x' \in \mathcal{N}_{c_1}(x)$, we choose x' to differ from x in the ith element, where i is uniformly distributed in $\{1, 2, \ldots, n\}$:

$$x' = x + \theta \otimes \mathbf{e_1} = x + (\theta_1 e_{1,1}, \theta_2 e_{1,2}, \ldots, \theta_n e_{1,n})^T \tag{49}$$

and $\otimes$ is the vector-product operator. Here, $\mathbf{e}_1$ is a vector whose i^{th} element is 1 and the other elements are 0, and θ is a vector whose i^{th} element θ_i is Cauchy distributed with density $f_d(x_i) = \frac{1}{\pi}\frac{\sigma_i}{\sigma_i^2 + x_i^2}$ and scale parameter σ_i. Other distributions of θ_i studied include uniform and Gaussian [30]. During the course of CSA, we dynamically update σ_i using the following modified 1-to-1 rate rule [9] in order to balance the ratio between accepted and rejected configurations:

$$\sigma_i \longleftarrow \begin{cases} \frac{\sigma_i[1+\beta_0(p_i - p_u)]}{1-p_u} & \text{if } p_i > p_u \\ \frac{\sigma_i}{[1+\beta_1(p_v - p_i)/p_v]} & \text{if } p_i < p_v \\ \text{unchanged} & \text{otherwise,} \end{cases} \tag{50}$$

where p_i is the fraction of x' accepted. If p_i is low, then too many trial points of $\mathbf{x}'$ are rejected, and σ_i is reduced; otherwise, the trial points of $\mathbf{x}'$ are too close to $\mathbf{x}$, and σ_i is increased. We set $\beta_0 = 7$, $\beta_1 = 2$, $p_u = 0.3$, and $p_v = 0.2$ after experimenting different combinations of parameters [30]. Note that it is possible to get somewhat better convergence results when problem-specific parameters are used, although the results will not be general in that case.
Similarly, in generating trial point $\mathbf{x}'' = (x, \alpha')^T$ from $\mathbf{x} = (x, \alpha)^T$ where $\alpha' \in \mathcal{N}_{c_2}(\alpha)$, we choose α' to differ from α in the jth element, where j is uniformly distributed in $\{1, 2, \ldots, m\}$:

$$\alpha' = \alpha + \nu \otimes \mathbf{e_2} = \alpha + (\nu_1 e_{2,1}, \nu_2 e_{2,2}, \ldots, \nu_m, e_{2,m})^T. \tag{51}$$

Here, the j_{th} element of $\mathbf{e}_2$ is 1 and the others are 0, and the ν_j is uniformly distributed in $[-\phi_j, \phi_j]$. We adjust ϕ_j according to the degree of constraint violations, where:

$$\phi = w \otimes h(x) = (w_1 h_1(x), w_2 h_2(x), \ldots, w_m h_m(x))^T. \tag{52}$$

When $h_i(x) = 0$ is satisfied, $\phi_i = 0$, and α_i does not need to be updated. Otherwise, we adjust ϕ_i by modifying w_i according to how fast $h_i(x)$ is changing:

$$w_i \longleftarrow \begin{cases} \eta_0 \; w_i & \text{if } h_i(x) > \tau_0 T \\ \eta_1 \; w_i & \text{if } h_i(x) < \tau_1 T \\ \text{unchanged} & \text{otherwise,} \end{cases} \tag{53}$$

where $\eta_0 = 1.25$, $\eta_1=0.95$, $\tau_0 = 1.0$, and $\tau_1 = 0.01$ were chosen experimentally. When $h_i(x)$ is reduced too quickly (*i.e.*, $h_i(x) < \tau_1 T$ is satisfied), $h_i(x)$ is over-weighted, leading to a possibly poor objective value or difficulty in satisfying other under-weighted constraints. Hence, we reduce α_i's neighborhood. In contrast, if $h_i(x)$ is reduced too slowly (*i.e.*, $h_i(x) > \tau_0 T$ is satisfied), we enlarge α_i's neighborhood in order to improve its chance of satisfaction. Note that w_i is adjusted using T as a referenc because constraint violations are expected to decrease when T decreases. Other distributions of ϕ_j studied include non-symmetric uniform and non-uniform [30].

Finally, we use the cooling schedule defined in Figure 1, which is more aggressive than that in (41). We accept the **x**′ or **x**″ generated according to the Metropolis probability defined in (25). Other probabilities studied include logistic, Hastings, and Tsallis [30]. We set the ratio of generating **x**′ and **x**″ from **x** to be $20n$ to m, which means that x is updated more frequently than α.

Example 3. Figure 7 illustrates the run-time behavior at four temperatures when CSA is applied to solve the following continuous constrained optimization problem:

$$\begin{aligned} \min_{x_1,\, x_2} \quad & f(x) = 10n + \sum_{i=1}^{2} \left(x_i^2 - 10\ \cos(2\pi x_i) \right) \quad \text{where } x = (x_1, x_2)^T \\ \text{subject to} \quad & |(x_i - 3.2)(x_i + 3.2)| = 0, \quad i = 1, 2. \end{aligned} \tag{54}$$

The objective function $f(x)$ is very rugged because it is made up of a two-dimensional Rastrigin function with 11^n (where $n = 2$) local minima. There are four constrained local minima at the four corners denoted by rectangles, and a constrained global minimum at (−3.2,−3.2).

Assuming a penalty function $L_c((x, \alpha)^T) = f(x) + \alpha_1 |(x_1-3.2)(x_1+3.2)| + \alpha_2 |(x_2-3.2)(x_2+3.2)|$ and that samples in x are drawn in double-precision floating-point space, CSA starts from $x = (0, 0)^T$ with initial temperature $T_0 = 20$ and a cooling rate $\kappa = 0.95$. At high temperatures (*e.g.* $T_0 = 20$), the probability of accepting a trial point is high; hence, the neighborhood size is large according to (50). Large jumps in the x subspace in Figure 7a are due to the use of the

Cauchy distribution for generating remote trial points, which increases the chance of getting out of infeasible local minima. Probabilistic ascents with respect to α also help push the search trajectory to feasible regions. As T is reduced, the acceptance probability of a trial point is reduced, leading to smaller neighborhoods. Finally, the search converges to the constrained global minimum at $x^*= (-3.2,-3.2)^T$. ■

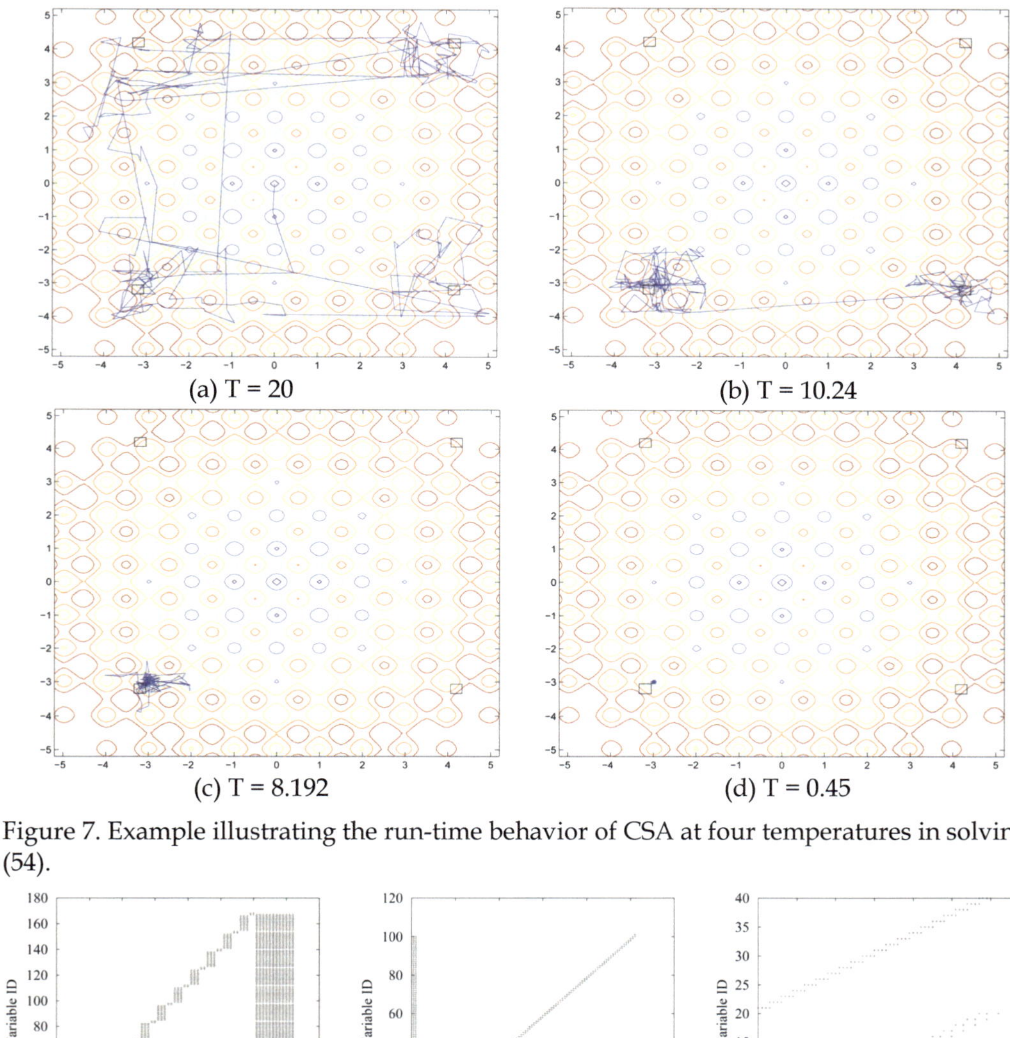

Figure 7. Example illustrating the run-time behavior of CSA at four temperatures in solving (54).

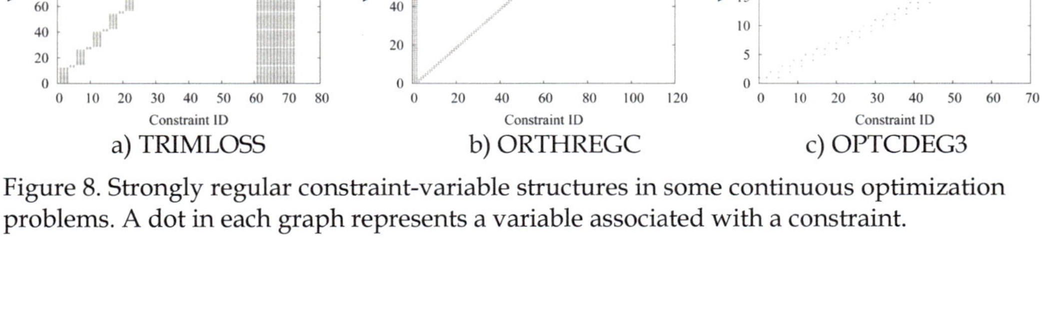

Figure 8. Strongly regular constraint-variable structures in some continuous optimization problems. A dot in each graph represents a variable associated with a constraint.

5.2 Implementation details of CPSA for solving continuous problems

We have observed that the constraints of many application benchmarks do not involve variables that are picked randomly from their variable sets. Invariably, many constraints in existing benchmarks are highly structured because they model spatial and temporal relationships that have strong locality, such as those in physical structures, optimal control, and staged processing.

Figure 8 illustrates this point by depicting the regular constraint structure of three benchmarks. It shows a dot where a constraint (with unique ID on the x axis) is related to a variable (with a unique ID on the y axis). When the order of the variables and that of the constraints are properly arranged, the figure shows a strongly regular constraint-variable structure.

In CPSA, we follow a previously proposed automated partitioning strategy [26] for analyzing the constraint structure and for determining how th constraints are to be partitioned. The focus of our previous work is to solve the partitioned subproblems using an existing solver SNOPT [15]. In contrast, our focus here is to demonstrate the improvement of CPSA over CSA and on their asymptotic convergence property.

Based on P_m with continuous variables and represented in AMPL [13], our partitioning strategy consists of two steps. In the first step, we enumerate all the indexing vectors in the AMPL model and select one that leads to the minimum R_{global}, which is the ratio of the number of global constraints to that of all constraints. We choose R_{global} as a heuristic metric for measuring the partitioning quality, since a small number of global constraints usually translates into faster resolution. In the second step, after fixing the index vector for partitioning the constraints, we decide on a suitable number of partitions. We have found a convex relationship between the number of partitions (N) and the complexity of solving P_m. When N is small, there are very few subproblems to be solved but each is expensive to evaluate; in contrast, when N is large, there are many subproblems to be solved although each is simple to evaluate. Hence, there is an optimal N that leads to the minimum time for solving P_m. To find this optimal N, we have developed an iterative algorithm that starts from a large N, that evaluates one subproblem under this partitioning (while assuming all the global constraints can be resolved in one iteration) in order to estimate the complexity of solving P_m, and that reduces N by half until the estimated complexity starts to increase. We leave the details of the algorithm to the reference [26].

Besides the partitioning strategy, CPSA uses the same mechanism and parameters described in Section 5.1 for generating trial points in the x, α, and γ subspaces.

5.3 Implementation details of GEM for solving continuous problems

The parameter in GEM were set based on the package developed by Zhe Wu and dated 08/13/2000 [32]. In generating a neighboring point of x for continuous problems, we use a Cauchy distribution with density $f_d(x_i) = \frac{1}{\pi}\frac{\sigma_i}{\sigma_i^2+x_i^2}$ for each variable x_i, $i = 1,\ldots, n$, where σ_i is a parameter controlling the Cauchy distribution. We initialize each σ_i to 0.1. For the last 50 probes that perturb x_i, if more than 40 probes lead to a decrease of L_m, we increase σ_i by a factor of 1.001; if less than two probes lead to a decrease of L_m, we decrease σ_i by a factor of 1.02. We increase the penalty σ_i for constraint h_i by $\alpha_i = \alpha_i + \varrho_i|h_i(x)|$, where ϱ_i is set to 0.0001 in our experiments. We consider a constraint to be feasible and stop increasing its penalty when its violation is less than 0.00001.

5.4 Evaluation results on continuous optimization benchmarks

Using the parameters of CSA and CPSA presented in the previous subsections and assuming that samples were drawn in double-precision floating-point space, we report in this section some experimental results on using CSA and CPSA to solve selected problems from CUTE [7], a constrained and unconstrained testing environment. We have selected those problems based on the criterion that at least the objective or one of the constraint functions is nonlinear. Many of those evaluated were from real applications, such as semiconductor analysis, chemical reactions, economic equilibrium, and production planning. Both the number of variables and the number of constraints in CUTE can be as large as several thousand.

Table 1 shows the CUTE benchmark problems studied and the performance of CPSA, CSA GEM in (35), P_3 in (7), and P_4 in (8). In our experiments, we have used the parameters of P_3 and P_4 presented in Section 2.2. For each solver and each instance, we tried 100 runs from random starting points and report the average solution found (Q_{avg}), the average CPU time per run of those successful runs (T_{avg}), the best solution found (Q_{best}), and the fraction of runs there were successful (P_{succ}). We show in shaded boxes the best Q_{avg} and Q_{best} among the five solvers when there are differences. We do not list the best solutions of P_3 and P_4 because they are always worse than those of CSA, CPSA, and GEM. Also, we do not report the results on those smaller CUTE instances with less than ten variables (BT*, AL*, HS*, MA*, NG*, TW*, WO*, ZE*, ZY*) [30] because these instances were easily solvable by all the solvers studied.

When compared to P_3, P_4, and GEM, CPSA and CSA found much better solutions on the average and the best solutions on most of the instances evaluated. In addition, CPSA and CSA have a higher success probability in finding a solution for all the instances studied.

The results also show the effectiveness of integrating constraint partitioning with CSA. CPSA is much faster than CSA in terms of T_{avg} for all the instances tested. The reduction in time can be more than an order of magnitude for large problems, such as ZAMB2-8 and READING6. CPSA can also achieve the same or better quality and success ratio than CSA for most of the instances tested. For example, for LAUNCH, CPSA achieves an average quality of 21.85, best quality of 9.01, and a success ratio of 100%, whereas CSA achieves, respectively, 26.94, 9.13, and 90%.

The nonlinear continuous optimization benchmarks evaluated in this section are meant to demonstrate the effectiveness of CSA and CPSA as dynamic penalty methods. We have studied these benchmarks because their formulations and solutions are readily available and because benchmarks on nonlinear discrete constrained optimization are scarce. These benchmarks, however, have continuous and differentiable functions and, therefore, can be solved much better by solvers that exploit such properties. In fact, the best solution of most of these problems can be found by a licensed version of SNOPT [15] (version 6.2) in less than one second of CPU time! In this respect, CSA and CPSA are not meant to compete with these solvers. Rather, CSA and CPSA are useful as constrained optimization methods for solving discrete, continuous, and mixed-integer problems whose constraint and objective functions are not necessarily continuous, differentiable, and in closed form. In these applications, penalty methods are invariably used as an effective solution approach. We illustrate in the following section the effectiveness of CSA for solving two real-world applications.

Problem	CPSA (with $\kappa = 0.8$ and 100 runs)				CSA (with $\kappa = 0.8$ and 100 runs)				GEM				P_3 Penalty Method			P_4 Penalty Method		
ID	Q_{avg}	Q_{best}	T_{avg}	P_{succ}	Q_{avg}	Q_{best}	T_{avg}	P_{succ}	Q_{avg}	Q_{best}	T_{avg}	P_{succ}	Q_{avg}	T_{avg}	P_{succ}	Q_{avg}	T_{avg}	P_{succ}
AVION2	$9.47 \cdot 10^7$	$9.47 \cdot 10^7$	7.93	100%	$9.47 \cdot 10^7$	$9.47 \cdot 10^7$	204.74	100%	$9.47 \cdot 10^7$	$9.47 \cdot 10^7$	3213.49	100%	$9.47 \cdot 10^7$	2798	100%	$9.47 \cdot 10^7$	2578	100%
BATCH	$2.14 \cdot 10^5$	$2.00 \cdot 10^5$	35.03	20%	-	-	-	-	$2.42 \cdot 10^5$	$1.94 \cdot 10^5$	13242.43	5%	–	–	–	–	–	–
CRESC4	29.23	1.78	3.48	100%	34.24	1.98	7.37	100%	82.84	2.17	31.82	100%	82.84	31.82	100%	82.84	31.82	100%
CSFI1	−38.87	-49.08	0.06	100%	−28.65	-49.08	1.24	100%	−17.34	-49.05	2.95	98%	−23.26	0.98	91%	−20.57	1.54	93%
DEMBO7	174.80	174.79	2.58	100%	174.80	174.80	65.86	83%	174.80	174.80	232.16	57%	174.81	198.23	42%	174.81	203.64	40%
DIPIGRI	680.63	680.63	0.17	100%	680.65	680.63	1.79	100%	680.64	680.63	11.18	100%	680.64	9.45	100%	680.64	14.38	100%
DNIEPER	$1.87 \cdot 10^4$	$1.87 \cdot 10^4$	80.36	25%	-	-	-	-	$1.87 \cdot 10^4$	$1.87 \cdot 10^4$	3071.67	3%	–	–	–	–	–	–
EXPFITA	1.20	0.06	8.15	100%	2.35	0.10	18.45	100%	1.24	1.12	60.18	100%	1.24	63.94	100%	1.26	76.18	100%
FLETCHER	14.65	11.65	0.07	100%	4227.11	11.65	0.7	100%	20.28	11.72	3.75	100%	23.97	4.76	100%	23.76	6.42	100%
GIGOMEZ2	1.95	1.95	0.02	50%	1.95	1.95	0.55	48%	1.95	1.95	9.67	50%	–	–	–	1.95	12.04	22%
HIMMELBI	−1734.83	-1735.39	195.28	100%	−1735.55	−1735.57	*5091.47	100%	–	–	–	–	–	–	–	–	–	–
HIMMELBJ	−1910.45	−1910.56	17.83	100%	−1909.98	-1910.33	*619.19	100%	−1909.39	-1910.05	3514.92	99%	−1904	2304.04	94%	−1908	1953.94	57%
HIMMELP2	−62.05	-62.05	0.02	100%	−62.05	-62.05	0.44	100%	−62.05	−62.05	0.95	97%	−62.05	0.95	89%	−62.05	0.95	19%
HIMMELP6	−59.01	-59.01	0.04	100%	−59.01	-59.01	0.62	100%	−59.01	−59.01	1.58	100%	−59.01	2.34	100%	−59.01	1.77	100%
HONG	22.53	22.53	0.06	100%	22.53	22.53	0.82	100%	22.57	22.57	8.68	100%	22.57	8.9	100%	22.57	10.3	100%
HUBFIT	0.017	$1.69 \cdot 10^{-2}$	0.02	100%	0.017	$1.69 \cdot 10^{-2}$	0.36	100%	0.017	$1.69 \cdot 10^{-2}$	14.73	100%	0.017	15.62	100%	0.017	16.07	100%
LAUNCH	21.85	9.01	12.33	100%	26.94	9.13	*495.89	90%	22.80	9.01	1205.03	87%	24.583	1403.40	40%	24.54	1543.04	34%
LIN	−0.02	-0.02	0.1	100%	−0.02	-0.02	1.21	100%	−0.019	−0.02	3.02	100%	−0.019	3.01	100%	−0.019	3.21	100%
LOADBAL	76.35	0.78	6.34	100%	100.71	33.53	*226.07	100%	13.40	2.66	2350.60	100%	13.45	2454.65	100%	14.54	1934.34	100%
LOOTSMA	1.41	1.41	0.04	100%	1.41	1.41	0.52	100%	1.41	1.41	1.56	100%	1.41	2.75	100%	1.41	2.43	100%
MESH	-10^5	-10^5	17.37	100%	-10^5	-10^5	*625.03	100%	-10^5	-10^5	14453.76	100%	-10^5	14560	100%	-10^5	12139	100%
MISTAKE	−1.00	-1.00	0.44	100%	−1.00	-1.00	11.18	100%	−1.00	−1.00	63.84	90%	−1.00	70.48	45%	−1.00	77.74	98%
MRIBASIS	30.11	21.52	31.27	100%	31.04	29.32	1031.34	100%	31.56	31.22	24345.34	100%	34.03	20434	90%	–	–	–
MWRIGHT	2564.35	1.53	0.04	100%	12029.65	1.53	0.6	100%	$1.3 \cdot 10^5$	35.83	9.83	100%	$1.4 \cdot 10^5$	11.84	100%	$2 \cdot 10^5$	10.34	100%
ODFITS	−2225.33	-2379.4	5.56	100%	−1442.48	-2379.4	6.95	100%	9393.45	2699.04	21.15	100%	9497.43	20.48	100%	10320.3	24.32	100%
OPTCNTRL	549.61	549.49	12.36	100%	549.61	549.49	103.34	100%	550.00	550.00	1376.45	100%	550.00	1487.73	100%	550.00	1432.54	100%
OPTPRLOC	−16.42	-16.42	6.23	100%	−16.42	-16.42	296.49	100%	−16.42	−16.42	1381.46	100%	−16.42	872.43	100%	−16.42	787.42	100%
PENTAGON	0.00	0.00	0.4	100%	0.00	0.00	6.92	100%	0.00	0.00	47.32	93%	0.00	49.38	75%	0.00	36.34	94%
POLAK5	50.00	50.00	0.03	100%	50.00	50.00	0.43	100%	50.00	50.00	1.68	100%	50.00	1.83	100%	50.00	1.98	100%
QC	−998.64	−1018.09	0.33	100%	−970.19	-1007.35	5.77	100%	−763.80	−956.14	29.56	100%	−743.65	30.56	100%	−743.22	23.49	100%
READING6	−58.45	−105.45	202.86	100%	−54.71	-97.3	3059.25	100%	−66.12	−94.72	26027*	100%	−66.33	29820*	100%	−68.12	30223*	100%
RK23	25906.32	13016.09	0.88	39%	29614.39	16928.29	7.45	13%	–	–	–	–	–	–	–	–	–	–
ROBOT	5.51	5.46	0.21	100%	5.47	5.46	4.86	100%	5.46	5.46	38.85	100%	5.46	40.66	100%	5.46	38.95	100%
S316-322	334.13	334.13	0.01	100%	334.13	334.13	0.25	100%	334.30	334.30	1.20	100%	334.30	1.24	100%	334.30	1.50	100%
SINROSNB	0.00	0.00	0.02	100%	0.00	0.00	0.4	100%	–	–	–	–	–	–	–	–	–	–
SNAKE	0.00	0.00	0.02	100%	79.12	0.00	0.38	100%	267.08	0.00	2.45	100%	268.54	2.56	100%	269.18	2.48	100%
SPIRAL	360.21	0.00	0.05	100%	360.86	0.00	0.88	100%	505.70	0.00	2.70	100%	512.56	2.72	100%	505.80	2.67	100%
STANCMIN	4.29	4.25	0.03	100%	4.25	4.25	0.63	100%	4.25	4.25	2.53	100%	4.25	2.57	100%	4.25	2.54	100%
SVANBERG	15.73	15.73	0.78	100%	15.73	15.73	16.2	100%	–	–	–	–	–	–	–	–	–	–
SYNTHES1	2.76	0.76	0.13	100%	2.33	0.76	2.2	100%	2.61	0.76	18.93	100%	2.98	19.23	100%	2.86	13.43	100%
SYNTHES2	−0.56	-0.56	0.77	100%	−0.56	-0.56	17.63	100%	−0.55	-0.55	95.36	100%	−0.55	92.98	100%	−0.55	92.21	100%
SYNTHES3	15.08	15.08	4.85	100%	15.09	15.08	48.54	100%	15.08	15.08	336.45	100%	15.08	458.92	100%	15.08	492.3	100%
TENBARS4	1586.97	1586.97	11.54	77%	2566.82	509.5	15.55	9%	–	–	–	–	–	–	–	–	–	–
ZAMB2-8	−0.13	-0.15	364.06	100%	1.35	-0.15	6247.57	83%	–	–	–	–	–	–	–	–	–	–

* Only ten runs were made for these problems due to the extensive CPU time required for each run.

Table 1. Experimental results comparing CPSA, CSA, GEM, P_3, and P_4 in solving selected nonlinear continuous problems from CUTE. Each instance was solved by a solver 100 times from random starting points. The best Q_{avg} (*resp.* Q_{best}) among the five solvers are shown in shaded boxes. '−'means that no feasible solution was found in a time limit of 36,000 sec. All runs were done on an AMD Athlon MP2800 PC with RH Linux AS4.

5.5 Applications of CSA on two real-world applications

Sensor-network placement optimization. The application involves finding a suitable placement of sensors in a wireless sensor network (WSN) [31, 33]. Given N sensors, the problem is to find their locations that minimize the false alarm rate, while maintaining a minimum detection probability for every point in a 2-D region A [34]:

$$\begin{array}{ll} \min & P_F \\ \text{subject to} & P_D(x,y) \geq \beta, \quad \forall (x,y) \in A, \end{array} \tag{55}$$

where $P_D(x, y)$ denotes the detection probability of location (x, y), and P_F denotes the false alarm rate over all locations in A. To compute P_D and P_F, we need to first compute the local detection probability P_{D_i} and the local false alarm rate P_{F_i} for each sensor i, $i = 1,\dots,N$, as follows:

$$P_{F_i} = \int_{b_i}^{\infty} \frac{1}{\sqrt{2\pi\sigma}} \exp\left(-\frac{z^2}{2\sigma^2}\right) dz, \tag{56}$$

$$P_{D_i}(x,y) = \int_{b_i}^{\infty} \frac{1}{\sqrt{2\pi\sigma}} \exp\left(-\frac{z-\sqrt{\frac{e}{d((x,y),(x_i,y_i))^a}}}{2\sigma^2}\right) dz. \tag{57}$$

The probabilistic model is based on a Gaussian noise assumption [34], where b_i, σ, a, and e are constants, and (x_i, y_i) is the coordinates of the ith sensor. After all the local decisions have been sent to a fusion center, the center will find that an event happens at (x, y) if a majority of the sensors have reported so. Therefore, we have the following equations:

$$P_D(x,y) = \sum_{|S_1|>|S_0|} \prod_{i \in S_0} (1 - P_{D_i}(x,y)) \prod_{j \in S_1} P_{D_j}(x,y), \tag{58}$$

$$P_F = \sum_{|S_1|>|S_0|} \prod_{i \in S_0} (1 - P_{F_i}) \prod_{j \in S_1} P_{F_j}, \tag{59}$$

where S_0 and S_1 denote the set of nodes that, respectively, detect or do not detect an event. The functions in the above formulation are very expensive to evaluate. In fact, the cost for computing $P_D(x, y)$ is $\Theta(2_n)$, since we need to consider all combinations of S_0 and S_1. The cost is so expensive that it is impossible to directly compute $P_D(x, y)$ or its derivatives. Thus, the problem has no closed form and without gradient information. Instead, a Monte-Carlo simulation is typically used to estimate $P_D(x, y)$ within reasonable time [34]. Previous work in WSN have solved this problem using some greedy heuristic methods that are ad-hoc and suboptimal [34].

We have applied CSA to solve (55) and have found it to yield much better solutions than existing greedy heuristics [34]. In our approach, we find the minimum number of sensors by a binary search that solves (55) using multiple runs of CSA. For example, in a 20 ×20 grid,

CSA can find a sensor placement with only 16 sensors to meet the given thresholds of $P_D \geq$ 95% and $P_F \leq 5\%$, while a previous heuristic method [34] needs 22 sensors. In a 40×40 grid, CSA can find a sensor placement with only 28 sensors to meet the same constraints, while the existing heuristic method [34] needs 43 sensors.

Synthesis of out-of-core algorithms. A recent application uses CSA to optimize the out-of-core code generation for a special class of imperfectly nested loops encoding tensor contractions that arise in quantum chemistry computation [19]. In this task, the code needs to execute some large, imperfectly nested loops. These loops operate on arrays that are too large to fit in the physical memory. Therefore, the problem is to find the optimal tiling of the loops and the placement of disk I/O statements.

Given the abstract code, the loop ranges, and the memory limit of the computer, the out-of-core code-generation algorithm first enumerates all the feasible placements of disk read/write statements for each array. To find the best combination of placements of all arrays, a discrete constrained nonlinear optimization problem is formulated and provided as input to CSA.

The variables of the problem include tile sizes and the placement variables. The constraints include the input-array constraints, which specify that the read statement for an input array can only be placed for execution before the statement where it is consumed. They also include the input-output-array constraints, which specify that the write statement for an output array can only be placed after the statement where it is produced. Lastly, there are a number of other intermediate-array constraints.

Experimental measurements on sequential and parallel versions of the generated code show that the solutions generated by CSA consistently outperform previous sampling approach and heuristic equal-tile-size approach. When compared to previous approaches, CSA can reduce the disk I/O cost by a factor of up to four [19].

6. Conclusions

We have reported in this chapter constrained simulated annealing (CSA) and constraint-partitione simulated annealing (CPSA), two dynamic-penalty methods for finding constrained global minima of discrete constrained optimization problems. Based on the theory of extended saddle points (ESPs), our methods look for the local minima of a penalty function when the penalties are larger than some thresholds and when the constraints are satisfied. To reach an ESP, our methods perform probabilistic ascents in the penalty subspace, in addition to probabilistic descents in the problem-variable subspace as in conventional simulated annealing (SA). Because both methods are based on sampling the search space of a problem during their search, they can be applied to solve continuous, discrete, and mixed-integer optimization problems without continuity and differentiability.

Based on the decomposition of the ESP condition into multiple necessary conditions [25], we have shown that many benchmarks with highly structured and localized constraint functions can be decomposed into loosely coupled subproblems that are related by a small number of global constraints. By exploiting constraint partitioning, we have demonstrated that CPSA can significantly reduce the complexity of CSA.

We have shown the asymptotic convergence of CSA and CPSA to a constrained global minimum with probability one. The result is theoretically important because it extends SA, which guarantees asymptotic convergence in discrete unconstrained optimization, to that in

discrete constrained optimization. Moreover, it establishes a condition under which optimal solutions can be found in constraint-partitioned nonlinear optimization problems.
Lastly, we illustrate the effectiveness of CSA and CPSA for solving some nonlinear benchmarks and two real-world applications. CSA and CPSA are particularly effective when the constraint and objective functions and their gradients are too expensive to be evaluated or are not in closed form.

7. References

E. Aarts and J. Korst. *Simulated Annealing and Boltzmann Machines*. J. Wiley and Sons, 1989.

S. Anily and A Federgruen. Simulated annealing methods with general acceptance probabilities. *Journal of Appl. Prob.*, 24:657–667, 1987.

A. Auslender, R. Cominetti, and M. Maddou. Asymptotic analysis for penalty and barrier methods in convex and linear programming. *Mathematics of Operations Research*, 22:43–62, 1997.

T. Back, F. Hoffmeister, and H.-P. Schwefel. A survey of evolution strategies. In *Proc. of the 4th Int'l Conf. on Genetic Algorithms*, pages 2–9, 1991.

J. C. Bean and A. B. Hadj-Alouane. A dual genetic algorithm for bounded integer programs. In *Tech. Rep. TR 92-53, Dept. of Industrial and Operations Engineering, The Univ. of Michigan*, 1992.

D. P. Bertsekas and A. E. Koksal. Enhanced optimality conditions and exact penalty functions. *Proc. of Allerton Conf.*, 2000.

I. Bongartz, A. R. Conn, N. Gould, and P. L. Toint. CUTE: Constrained and unconstrained testing environment. *ACM Trans. on Mathematical Software*, 21(1):123–160, 1995.

Y. X. Chen. *Solving Nonlinear Constrained Optimization Problems through Constraint Partitioning*. Ph.D. Thesis, Dept. of Computer Science, Univ. of Illinois, Urbana, IL, September 2005.

A. Corana, M. Marchesi, C. Martini, and S. Ridella. Minimizing multimodal functions of continuous variables with the simulated annealing algorithm. *ACM Trans. on Mathematical Software*, 13(3):262–280, 1987.

J. P. Evans, F. J. Gould, and J. W. Tolle. Exact penalty functions in nonlinear programming. *Mathematical Programming*, 4:72–97, 1973.

R. Fletcher. A class of methods for nonlinear programming with termination and convergence properties. In J. Abadie, editor, *Integer and Nonlinear Programming*. North-Holland, Amsterdam, 1970.

R. Fletcher. An exact penalty function for nonlinear programming with inequalities. *Tech. Rep. 478, Atomic Energy Research Establishment, Harwell*, 1972.

R. Fourer, D. M. Gay, and B. W. Kernighan. *AMPL: A Modeling Language for Mathematical Programming*. Brooks Cole Pub. Co., 2002.

M. I. Freidlin and A. D. Wentzell. *Random perturbations of dynamical systems*. Springer, 1984.

P. E. Gill, W. Murray, and M. Saunders. SNOPT: An SQP algorithm for large-scale constrained optimization. *SIAM J. on Optimization*, 12:979–1006, 2002.

A. Homaifar, S. H-Y. Lai, and X. Qi. Constrained optimization via genetic algorithms. *Simulation*, 62(4):242–254, 1994.

J. Joines and C. Houck. On the use of non-stationary penalty functions to solve nonlinear constrained optimization problems with gas. In *Proc. of the First IEEE Int'l Conf. on Evolutionary Computation*, pages 579–584, 1994.

S. Kirkpatrick, C. D. Gelatt, Jr., and M. P. Vecchi. Optimization by simulated annealing. *Science*, 220(4598):671–680, May 1983.

S. Krishnan, S. Krishnamoorthy, G. Baumgartner, C. C. Lam, J. Ramanujam, P. Sadayappan, and V. Choppella. Efficient synthesis of out-of-core algorithms using a nonlinear optimization solver. Technical report, Dept. of Computer and Information Science, Ohio State University, Columbus, OH, 2004.

A. Kuri. A universal eclectric genetic algorithm for constrained optimization. In *Proc. 6th European Congress on Intelligent Techniques and Soft Computing*, pages 518–522, 1998.

D. G. Luenberger. *Linear and Nonlinear Programming*. Addison-Wesley, Reading, MA, 1984.

R. L. Rardin. *Optimization in Operations Research*. Prentice Hall, 1998.

A. Trouve. Rough large deviation estimates for the optimal convergence speed exponent of generalized simulated annealing algorithms. Technical report, LMENS-94-8, Ecole Normale Superieure, France, 1994.

A. Trouve. Cycle decomposition and simulated annealing. *SIAM Journal on Control and Optimization*, 34(3):966–986, 1996.

B. Wah and Y. X. Chen. Constraint partitioning in penalty formulations for solving temporal planning problems. *Artificial Intelligence*, 170(3):187–231, 2006.

B. W.Wah and Y. X. Chen. Solving large-scale nonlinear programming problems by constraint partitioning. In *Proc. Principles and Practice of Constraint Programming, LCNS-3709*, pages 697–711. Springer-Verlag, October 2005.

B. W. Wah, Y. X. Chen, and T. Wang. Simulated annealing with asymptotic convergence for nonlinear constrained optimization. *J. of Global Optimization*, 39:1–37, 2007.

B. W. Wah and T. Wang. Simulated annealing with asymptotic convergence for nonlinear constrained global optimization. In *Proc. Principles and Practice of Constraint Programming*, pages 461–475. Springer-Verlag, October 1999.

B. W. Wah and Z. Wu. The theory of discrete Lagrange multipliers for nonlinear discrete optimization. In *Proc. Principles and Practice of Constraint Programming*, pages 28–42. Springer- Verlag, October 1999.

T. Wang. *Global Optimization for Constrained Nonlinear Programming*. Ph.D. Thesis, Dept. of Computer Science, Univ. of Illinois, Urbana, IL, December 2000.

X. Wang, G. Xing, Y. Zhang, C. Lu, R. Pless, , and C. Gill. Integrated coverage and connectivity configuration in wireless sensor networks. In *Proc. First ACM Conf. on Embedded Networked Sensor Systems*, pages 28–39, 2003.

Z. Wu. *The Theory and Applications of Nonlinear Constrained Optimization using Lagrange Multipliers*. Ph.D. Thesis, Dept. of Computer Science, Univ. of Illinois, Urbana, IL, May 2001.

G. Xing, C. Lu, R. Pless, , and Q. Huang. On greedy geographic routing algorithms in sensing-covered networks. In *Proc. ACM Int'l Symp. on Mobile Ad Hoc Networking and Computing*, pages 31–42, 2004.

G. Xing, C. Lu, R. Pless, and J. A. O'Sullivan. Co-Grid: An efficient coverage maintenance protocol for distributed sensor networks. In *Proc. Int'l Symp. on Information Processing in Sensor Networks*, pages 414–423, 2004.

W. I. Zangwill. Nonlinear programming via penalty functions. *Management Science*, 13:344–358, 1967.

10

Annealing Stochastic Approximation Monte Carlo for Global Optimization

Faming Liang
Department of Statistics Texas A&M University
USA

1. Introduction

During the past several decades, simulated annealing (Kirkpatrick *et al.*, 1983) and the genetic algorithm (Holland, 1975; Goldberg, 1989) have been applied successfully by many authors to highly complex optimization problems in different fields of sciences and engineering. In spite of their successes, both algorithms suffer from some difficulties in convergence to the global optima.

Suppose that we are interested in minimizing the function $U(x)$ over a given space X. Throughout this article, $U(x)$ is called the energy function in terms of physics. Simulated annealing works by simulating a sequence of distributions defined as

$$f_k(x) = \frac{1}{Z_k} \exp\{-U(x)/\tau_k\}, \quad x \in \mathcal{X}, \quad k = 1, 2, \ldots,$$

where τ_k is called the temperature. The temperatures form a decreasing ladder $\tau_1 > \ldots > \tau_k > \ldots$ with τ_1 being reasonably large such that the Metropolis-Hastings (MH) moves (Metropolis *et al.*, 1953; Hastings, 1970) have a high acceptance rate at this level and $\lim_{k\to\infty} \tau_k = 0$. It has been shown by Geman and Geman (1984) that the global minima of U(x) can be reached by simulated annealing with probability 1 if the temperature decreases at a logarithmic rate. In practice, this cooling schedule is too slow; that is, CPU times can be too long to be affordable in challenging problems. Most frequently, people use a linearly or geometrically decreasing cooling schedule, which can no longer guarantee the global minima to be reached.

The genetic algorithm solves the minimization problem by mimicking the natural evolutionary process. A population of candidate solutions (also known as individuals), generated at random, are tested and evaluated for their energy values; the best of them are then bred through mutation and crossover operations; the process repeated over many generations, until an individual of satisfactory performance is found. The mutation operation is modeled by random perturbations of the individuals. The crossover operation is modeled by random perturbations of the couples formed by two individuals selected according to some procedure, e.g., a roulette wheel selection or a random selection. Through the crossover operation, the solution information distributed across the population can be effectively used in the minimization process. Schmitt (2001) showed that under certain conditions, the genetic algorithm can converge asymptotically to the global minima at a logarithmic rate in analogy to simulated annealing.

Quite recently, the stochastic approximation Monte Carlo (SAMC) algorithm (Liang *et al.*, 2007) has been proposed in the literature as a dynamic importance sampling technique. A remarkable feature of SAMC is that it possesses the self-adjusting mechanism and is thus not trapped by local energy minima. In this article, we consider applications of SAMC in optimization. Two modified versions of SAMC, annealing SAMC (Liang, 2007; Zhu *et al.*, 2007) and annealing evolutionary SAMC (Liang, 2008), are discussed. Both algorithms have inherited self-adjusting ability from the SAMC algorithm. The annealing SAMC algorithm works in the same spirit as the simulated annealing algorithm but with the sample space instead of temperature shrinking with iterations. The annealing evolutionary SAMC algorithm represents a further improvement of annealing SAMC by incorporating some crossover operators originally used by the genetic algorithm into its search process. Under mild conditions, both annealing SAMC and annealing evolutionary SAMC can converge weakly toward a neighboring set of global minima in the space of energy. The new algorithms are tested on two optimization problems with comparisons with simulated annealing and the genetic algorithm. The numerical results favor to the new algorithms.
The remainder of this article is organized as follows. In Section 2, w describe the ASAMC and AESAMC algorithms and study their convergence. In Section 3, we illustrate the new algorithms with two function minimization problems, one has a rugged energy landscape and the other is a complex least square estimation problem encountered in economic research. In Section 4, we conclude the paper with a brief discussion.

2. Annealing stochastic approximation Monte Carlo algorithms

2.1 Stochastic approximation Monte Carlo

Before describing the annealing SAMC algorithms, we first give a brief description of SAMC. In our description, some of the conditions have been slightly modified from those given in Liang *et al.* (2007) to make the algorithm more suitable for solving optimization problems. Suppose that we are working with the following Boltzmann distribution,

$$f(x) = \frac{1}{Z} \exp\{-U(x)/\tau\}, \quad x \in \mathcal{X}, \tag{1}$$

where Z is the normalizing constant, τ is the temperature, and $\mathcal{X}$ is the sample space. For the reason of mathematical simplicity, we assume that $\mathcal{X}$ is compact. This assumption is reasonable, because for optimization problems we are usually only interested in the optimizers instead of samples drawn from the whole sample space and we have often some rough ideas where the optimizers are. Furthermore, we suppose that the sample space has been partitioned according to the energy function into m disjoint subregions denoted by $E_1 = \{x : U(x) \le u_1\}$, $E_2 = \{x : u_1 < U(x) \le u_2\}$, ..., $E_{m-1} = \{x : u_{m-2} < U(x) \le u_{m-1}\}$, and $E_m = \{x : U(x) > u_{m-1}\}$, where $u_1, \ldots, u_{m-1}$ are real numbers specified by the user. Let $\psi(x)$ be a non-negative function defined on the sample space with $0 < \int_{\mathcal{X}} \psi(x)dx < \infty$, and $g_i = \int_{E_i} \psi(x)dx$. In practice, we often set $\psi(x) = \exp\{-U(x)/\tau\}$.
SAMC seeks to draw samples from each of the subregions with a pre-specified frequency. If this goal can be achieved, then the local-trap problem can be avoided successfully. Let $x^{(t+1)}$

denote a sample drawn from a MH kernel $K_{\theta^{(t)}}(x^{(t)}, \cdot)$ with the proposal distribution $q(x^{(t)}, \cdot)$ and the stationary distribution

$$f_{\theta^{(t)}}(x) \propto \sum_{i=1}^{m} \frac{\psi(x)}{e^{\theta_i^{(t)}}} I(x \in E_i), \tag{2}$$

where $\theta^{(t)} = (\theta_1^{(t)}, \ldots, \theta_m^{(t)})$ is an m-vector in a space Θ.

Let $\pi = (\pi_1, \ldots, \pi_m)$ be an m-vector with $0 < \pi_i < 1$ and $\sum_{i=1}^{m} \pi_i = 1$, which defines a desired sampling frequency for the subregions. Henceforth, π will be called the desired sampling distribution. Define $H(\theta^{(t)}, x^{(t+1)}) = (e^{(t+1)} - \pi)$, where $e^{(t+1)} = (e_1^{(t+1)}, \ldots, e_m^{(t+1)})$ and $e_i^{(t+1)} = 1$ if $x^{(t+1)} \in E_i$ and 0 otherwise. Let $\{\gamma_t\}$ be a positive non-decreasing sequence satisfying the conditions,

$$(i) \sum_{t=0}^{\infty} \gamma_t = \infty, \qquad (ii) \sum_{t=0}^{\infty} \gamma_t^{\delta} < \infty, \tag{3}$$

for some $\delta \in (1, 2)$. In this article, we set

$$\gamma_t = \left(\frac{t_0}{\max(t_0, t)} \right)^{\eta} \tag{4}$$

for some specified values of $t_0 > 1$ and $\eta \in (\frac{1}{2}, 1]$. A large value of t_0 will allow the sampler to reach all subregions very quickly even for a large system. Let $J(x)$ denote the index of the subregion the sample x belongs to. With above notations, one iteration of SAMC can be described as follows.

<u>*SAMC algorithm:*</u>

i. Generate $x^{(t+1)} \sim K_{\theta^{(t)}}(x^{(t)}, \cdot)$ with a single Metropolis-Hastings simulation step:

   (*i.1*) Generate y according to the proposal distribution $q(x^{(t)}, y)$.

   (*i.2*) Calculate the ratio

$$r = e^{(\theta_{J(x^{(t)})}^{(t)} - \theta_{J(y)}^{(t)})} \frac{\psi(y)}{\psi(x^{(t)})} \frac{q(y, x^{(t)})}{q(x^{(t)}, y)}.$$

   (i.3) Accept the proposal with probability $\min(1, r)$. If it is accepted, set $x^{(t+1)} = y$; otherwise, set $x^{(t+1)} = x^{(t)}$.

ii. Set $\theta^{*} = \theta^{(t)} + \gamma_t H(\theta^{(t)}, x^{(t+1)})$, where γ_t is called the gain factor.

iii. If $\theta^{*} \in \Theta$, set $\theta^{(t+1)} = \theta^{*}$; otherwise, set $\theta^{(t+1)} = \theta^{*} + c^{*}$, where $c^{*} = (c^{*}, \ldots, c^{*})$ and c^{*} is chosen such that $\theta^{*} + c^{*} \in \Theta$.

A remarkable feature of ASAMC is its self-adjusting mechanism. If a proposal is rejected, the weight of the subregion that the current sample belongs to will be adjusted to a larger value, and thus the proposal of jumping out from the current subregion will less likely be rejected in the next iteration. This mechanism warrants that the algorithm will not be trapped by local minima. This is very important for the systems with multiple local energy minima.

The parameter space Θ is set to $[-B_\Theta, B_\Theta]^m$ with B_Θ being a huge number e.g., 10^{100}, which, as a practical matter, is equivalent to setting $B = \mathbb{R}^m$. In theory, this is also fine. As implied by Theorem 5.4 of Andrieu *et al.* (2005), the varying truncation of θ^*can only occur a finite number of times, and thus $\{\theta^{(t)}\}$ can be kept in a compact space during simulations. Note that $f_{\theta^{(t)}}(x)$ is invariant with respect to a location transformation of $\theta^{(t)}$—that is, adding to or subtracting a constant vector from $\theta^{(t)}$ will not change $f_{\theta^{(t)}}(x)$.

The proposal distribution $q(x, y)$ used in the MH moves satisfies the minorisation condition, i.e.,

$$\sup_{\theta\in\Theta}\sup_{x,y\in\mathcal{X}}\frac{f_{\theta^{(t)}}(y)}{q(x,y)} < \infty. \tag{5}$$

The minorisation condition is a natural condition in study of MCMC theory (Mengersen and Tweedie, 1996). In practice, this kind of proposals can be easily designed for both discrete and continuous problems. Since both Θ and $\mathcal{X}$ are compact, a sufficient design for the minorisation condition is to choose $q(x, y) > 0$ for all $x, y \in \mathcal{X}$. For example, for a continuous problem, $q(x, y)$ can be chosen as a random walk Gaussian proposal $y \sim N(x, \sigma^2)$ with σ^2 being calibrated to have a desired acceptance rate. Issues on implementation of the algorithm, such as how to partition the sample space, how to choose the gain factor sequence, and how to set the number of iterations, have been discussed at length in Liang *et al.* (2007).

SAMC falls into the category of stochastic approximation algorithms (Benveniste et al.,1990; Andrieu et al., 2005). The convergence of this algorithm can be extended from a theorem presented in Liang *et al.* (2007). Under mild conditions, we have

$$\theta_i^{(t)} \to \begin{cases} C + \log\left(\int_{E_i}\psi(x)dx\right) - \log(\pi_i + \pi_0), & \text{if } E_i \neq \emptyset, \\ -\infty. & \text{if } E_i = \emptyset, \end{cases} \tag{6}$$

as $t \to \infty$, where C is an arbitrary constant, $\pi_0 = \sum_{j\in\{i:E_i=0\}} \pi_j/(m-m_0)$, and $m_0 = \#\{i : E_i = ;\}$ is the number of empty subregions. A subregion E_i is called empty if $\int_{E_i}\psi(x)dx = 0$. In SAMC, the sample space partition can be made blindly by simply specifying some values of $u_1, \ldots, u_{m-1}$. This may lead to some empty subregions. The constant C can be determined by imposing a constraint on $\theta^{(t)}$, say, $\sum_{i=1}^m e^{\theta_i^{(t)}}$ is equal to a known number.

Let $\hat{\pi}_i^{(t)} = P(x^{(t)} \in E_i)$ be the probability of sampling from the subregion E_i at iteration t. Equation (6) implies that as $t \to \infty$, $\hat{\pi}_i^{(t)}$ will converge to $\pi_i + \pi_0$ if $E_i \neq 0$ and 0 otherwise. With an appropriate specification of $\boldsymbol{\pi}$, sampling can be biased to the low energy subregions to increase the chance of finding the global energy minima.

The subject of stochastic approximation was founded by Robbins and Monro (1951). After five decades of continual development, it has developed into an important area in systems control and optimization. Many of the neural network training algorithms, such as the simultaneous perturbation stochastic approximation algorithm (Spall, 1992), the Widrow Hoff algorithm (also known as the "least mean square" algorithm) (Haykin, 1999, pp.128-135), the Alopex algorithm (Harth & Tzanakou, 1974) and self-organizing maps (Kohonen, 1990), can be regarded as special instances of stochastic approximation. Refer to Bharath & Borkar (1999) for more discussions on this issue. Recently, stochastic approximation has been used with Markov chain Monte Carlo for solving maximum likelihood estimation problems (Gu & Kong, 1998; Delyon *et al.*, 1999). The critical difference between SAMC and other stochastic approximation algorithms is at sample space partitioning. Sample space partitioning improves the performance of stochastic approximation in optimization. It forces each non-empty subregion to be visited with a fixed frequency, and thus increases the chance to locate the global energy minimizer.

2.2 Annealing stochastic approximation Monte Carlo

Like conventional Markov chain Monte Carlo algorithms, SAMC is able to find the global energy minima if the run is long enough. However, due to the broadness of the sample space, the process may be slow even when sampling has been biased to low energy subregions. To accelerate the search process, we shrink the sample space over iterations. As argued below, this modification preserves the theoretical property of SAMC when a global proposal distribution is used.

Suppose that the subregions $E_1, \ldots, E_m$ have been arranged in ascending order by energy; that is, if $i < j$, then $U(x) < U(y)$ for any $x \in E_i$ and $y \in E_j$. Let $\varpi(u)$ denote the index of the subregion that a sample x with energy u belongs to. For example, if $x \in E_j$, then $\varpi(U(x)) = j$. Let $\mathcal{X}^{(t)}$ denote the sample space at iteration t. Annealing SAMC initiates its search in the entire sample space $\mathcal{X}_0 = \bigcup_{i=1}^{m} E_i$, and then iteratively searches in the set

$$\mathcal{X}_t = \bigcup_{i=1}^{\varpi(U_{\min}^{(t)}+\aleph)} E_i, \quad t = 1, 2, \ldots, \tag{7}$$

where $U_{\min}^{(t)}$ is the best energy value obtained until iteration t, and $\aleph > 0$ is a user specified parameter which determines the broadness of the sample space at each iteration. Since the sample space shrinks iteration by iteration, the algorithm is called annealing SAMC. In summary, the ASAMC algorithm consists of the following steps:

ASAMC algorithm:

a) (Initialization) Partition the sample space $\mathcal{X}$ into m disjoint subregions $E_1, \ldots, E_m$ according to the objective function $U(x)$; specify a desired sampling distribution π; initialize $x^{(0)}$ by a sample randomly drawn from the sample space $\mathcal{X}$, $\theta^{(0)} = (\theta_1^{(0)}, \ldots, \theta_m^{(0)}) = (0, 0, \ldots, 0)$, $\aleph$, and $\mathcal{X}_0 = \bigcup_{i=1}^{m} E_i$; and set the iteration number $t = 0$. Let Θ be a compact subset in R^m, $\theta^{(0)} = (\theta_1^{(0)}, \ldots, \theta_m^{(0)}) = (0, 0, \ldots, 0)$, and $\theta^{(0)} \in \Theta$.

b) (Sampling) Update the current sample $x^{(t)}$ by a single or few MH moves which admit the following distribution as the invariant distribution,

$$f_{\theta^{(t)}}(x) \propto \sum_{i=1}^{\varpi(U_{\min}^{(t)}+\aleph)} \frac{\psi(x)}{e^{\theta_i^{(t)}}} I(x \in E_i), \tag{8}$$

where $I(x \in E_i)$ is the indicator function, $\theta^{(t)} i$ is a working weight associated with the subregion E_i, $\psi(x) = \exp\{-U(x)/\tau\}$ is an unnormalized Boltzmann density, and τ is a user-specified parameter. Denote the new sample by $x^{(t+1)}$.

c) (Working weight updating) Update the working weight $\theta^{(t)}$ as follows:

$$\theta_i^* = \theta_i^{(t)} + \gamma_{t+1}\left[I(x^{(t+1)} \in E_i) - \pi_i\right], \quad i = 1, \ldots, \varpi(U_{\min}^{(t)} + \aleph),$$

where γ_t is called the gain factor. If $\theta^* \in \Theta$, set $\theta^{(t+1)} = \theta^*$; otherwise, set $\theta^{(t+1)} = \theta^* + \boldsymbol{c}^*$, where $\boldsymbol{c}^* = (c^*, \ldots, c^*)$ and c^* is chosen such that $\theta^* + \boldsymbol{c}^* \in \Theta$

d) (Termination Checking) Check the termination condition, e.g., a fixed number of iterations or an optimal solution set have been reached. Otherwise, set $t \leftarrow t + 1$ and go to step (b).

It has been shown in Liang (2007) that if the gain factor sequence satisfie (3) and the proposal distribution satisfies the minorisation condition (5), ASAMC can converge weakly toward a neighboring set of the global minima of $U(x)$ in the space of energy. More precisely, the sample $x^{(t)}$ converges in distribution to a random variable with the density function

$$f_\theta(x) \propto \sum_{i=1}^{\varpi(u_{\min}+\aleph)} \frac{\pi_i' \psi(x)}{\int_{E_i} \psi(x)dx} I(x \in E_i), \tag{9}$$

where u_{min} is the global minimum value of $U(x)$, $\pi_i' = \pi_i + (1 - \sum_{j \in \{k: E_k \neq 0, k=1,\ldots,\varpi(u_{min}+\aleph)\}} \pi_i)/m_0$, m_0 is the cardinality of the set $\{k : Ek \neq 0, k = 1, \ldots, \varpi(u_{min} + \aleph)\}$, and 0 denotes an empty set. The subregion E_i is called empty if $\int_{E_i} \psi(x)dx = 0$. An inappropriate specification of u_i's may result in some empty subregions. ASAMC allows for the existence of empty subregions in simulations.

2.3 Annealing evolutionary stochastic approximation Monte Carlo

Like the genetic algorithm, AESAMC also works on a population of samples. Let $x = (x_1, \ldots, x_n)$ denote the population, where n is the population size, and $x_i = (x_{i1}, \ldots, x_{id})$ is a d-dimensional vector called an individual or chromosome in terms of genetic algorithms. Thus, the minimum of $U(x)$ can be obtained by minimizing the function $U(x) = \sum_{i=1}^{n} U(x_i)$. An unnormalized Boltzmann density can be defined for the population as follows,

$$\psi(\boldsymbol{x}) = \exp\{-\boldsymbol{U}(\boldsymbol{x})/\tau\}, \quad \boldsymbol{x} \in \mathcal{X}^n, \tag{10}$$

where $\mathcal{X}_n = \mathcal{X} \times \cdots \times \mathcal{X}$ is a product sample space. The sample space can be partitioned according to the function $U(x)$ into m subregions: $\mathbb{E}_1 = \{x : U(x) \leq u_1\}$, $\mathbb{E}_2 = \{x : u_1 < U(x) \leq u_2\}$, . . ., $\mathbb{E}_{m-1} = \{x : u_{m-2} < U(x) \leq u_{m-1}\}$, and $\mathbb{E}_m = \{x : U(x) > u_{m-1}\}$, where $u_1, \ldots, u_{m-1}$ are $m-1$ known real numbers. As in ASAMC, we suppose that the subregions have been arranged in ascending order by the function $U(x)$. We note that here the sample space is not necessarily partitioned according to the function $U(x)$, for example, $\lambda(x) = \min\{U(x_1), \ldots, U(x_n)\}$ is also a good choice. The population can then evolve under the framework of ASAMC with an appropriate specification of the proposal distribution for the MH moves. At iteration t, the MH moves admit the following distribution as the invariant distribution,

$$\boldsymbol{f}_{\theta^{(t)}}(\boldsymbol{x}) \propto \sum_{i=1}^{\varpi(\boldsymbol{U}_{\min}^{(t)}+\aleph)} \frac{\boldsymbol{\psi}(\boldsymbol{x})}{e^{\theta_i^{(t)}}} I(\boldsymbol{x} \in \mathbb{E}_i), \quad \boldsymbol{x} \in \mathcal{X}_t^n, \tag{11}$$

where $U_{\min}^{(t)}$ denotes the best value of $U(x)$ obtained by iteration t. As discussed before, $\{\theta^{(t)}\}$ can be kept in a compact space in simulations.

Since, in AESAMC, the state of the MH chain has been augmented to a population, the crossover operators used in the genetic algorithm can be employed to accelerate the evolution of the population. However, to satisfy the Markov chain reversibility condition, these operators need to be modified appropriately. As demonstrated by Liang and Wong (2000, 2001), Goswami and Liu (2007), and Jasra *et al.* (2007), incorporating genetic type moves into Markov chain Monte Carlo can often improve the mixing rate of the simulation. Note that the crossover operators used in these work may not be suitable for AESAMC, because asymptotic independence between individuals is required to be remained in the operations. Whilst this is not required in AESAMC. The sample space partition makes the individuals dependent on each other, although $\psi(x)$ is defined as a product of the functions $\psi(x_i)$, $i = 1, \ldots, n$. The crossover operators used in AESAMC can be described as follows.

K-Point Crossover This proposal is the same as that used in Liang and Wong (2001). To make the article self-contained, it is briefly described as follows. Two chromosomes, say x_i and x_j with $i < j$, are selected from the current population x according to some selection procedure as parental chromosomes and two offspring chromosomes x'_i and x'_j are generated as follows: sample K integer crossover points without replacement from the set $\{1, \ldots, d-1\}$; sort these points in ascending order; and construct offspring chromosomes by swapping the genes of the parental chromosomes between each odd and the next even crossover points (d is set as an additional crossover point when K is odd). The new population can then be formed as $x' = (x_1, \ldots, x_{i-1}, x'_i, x_{i+1}, \ldots, x_{j-1}, x'_j, x_{j+1}, \ldots, x_n)$. In this article, 1 and 2-point crossover operators are applied equally when the K point crossover operator is selected in simulations. An extreme case of the K-point crossover is the uniform crossover, in which each element of x'_i (i.e., genotype) is randomly chosen from the two corresponding elements of the parental chromosomes and the corresponding element of x'_j is assigned to the element not chosen by x_{0i}.

Throughout this article, the parental chromosomes for the K-point crossover operator are selected as follows. The first parental chromosome is selected from the current population according to the distribution

$$w_1(x) = \frac{\exp\{-U(x)/\tau_s\}}{\sum_{k=1}^{n}\exp\{-U(x_k)/\tau_s\}}, \quad x \in \{x_1, \ldots, x_n\}, \tag{12}$$

where τ_s is the selection temperature. In this article, we set $\tau_s = \tau / 10$. Let x_i denote the first parental chromosome. The second parental chromosome is then selected from the subpopulation $\boldsymbol{x} \setminus \{x_i\}$ according to the distribution

$$w_2(x|x_i) = \frac{\exp\{-U(x)/\tau_s\}}{\sum_{k\neq i}\exp\{-U(x_k)/\tau_s\}}, \quad x \in \{x_1, \ldots, x_{i-1}, x_{i+1}, \ldots, x_n\}. \tag{13}$$

For a given pair of chromosomes (x_i, x_j), the selection probability is $P_s(x_i, x_j \mid \boldsymbol{x}) = w_1(x_i)w_2(x_j \mid x_i) + w_1(x_j)w_2(x_i \mid x_j)$.
To have the distribution (11) invariant with respect to the crossove operation, the acceptance of the new population x' should be moderated by the MH rule; that is, accepting $x'$with probability

$$\min\left\{1, [\boldsymbol{f}_{\theta^{(t)}}(\boldsymbol{x}')T(\boldsymbol{x}' \to \boldsymbol{x})]/[\boldsymbol{f}_{\theta^{(t)}}(\boldsymbol{x})T(\boldsymbol{x} \to \boldsymbol{x}')]\right\}, \tag{14}$$

where the transition probability ratio is

$$T(\boldsymbol{x}' \to \boldsymbol{x})/T(\boldsymbol{x} \to \boldsymbol{x}') = P_s(x_i', x_j'|\boldsymbol{x}')/P_s(x_i, x_j|\boldsymbol{x}).$$

Snooker Crossover This operator proceeds as follows:

a) Randomly select one chromosome, say x_i, from the current population $\boldsymbol{x}$.
b) Select the other chromosome, say, x_j, from the subpopulation $\boldsymbol{x} \setminus \{x_i\}$ according to the distribution $w_2(x \mid x_i)$ as defined in (13).
c) Let $e = (x_j - x_i)/\|x_j - x_i\|$, and let $x'_i = x_i + re$, where r is a random variable drawn for a normal distribution $N(0, \sigma_c^2)$ with the standard deviation σ_c being calibrated such that the operation has a reasonable overall acceptance probability.
d) Construct a new population $\boldsymbol{x}'$ by replacing x_i with the offspring x'_i, and accept the new population with probability $\min\{1, \boldsymbol{f}_{\theta^{(t)}}(x')/\boldsymbol{f}_{\theta^{(t)}}(x)\}$. For this operator, the transition probability ratio is 1; that is, $T(x \to x') = T(x' \to x)$.

We note that this operator is a little different from the the snooker sampler described in Gilks *et al.* (1994) and the snooker crossover operator described in Liang and Wong (2001) where x_i is required to be independent of other individuals and the operation is required to leave the marginal distribution of x_i invariant. These requirements are waived here because AESAMC allows for the dependence among the individuals.
Linear Crossover This operator has the same procedure with the snooker crossover operator except that step (c) is changed as follows.

(c) Set $x'_i = x_i + rx_j$, where $r \sim$ Unif $[-1, 1]$.

This operator is designed for exploration of the triangular region between x_i and x_j and that between x_i and $-x_j$.

Mutation In addition to the crossover operators, AESAMC also needs some mutation operators. Since the population size can be large, we here assume that the population is updated in the style of the Gibbs sampler, individual by individual, or component by component by viewing the population as a long vector. Furthermore, we assume that the mutation operator satisfies the minorisation condition

$$\sup_{\theta \in \Theta} \sup_{x \in \mathcal{X}} \frac{\boldsymbol{f}_\theta(x'_i, \boldsymbol{x}_{[-i]})}{q(x_i \to x'_i | \boldsymbol{x}_{[-i]})} < \infty, \quad \forall\, i = 1, \ldots, n, \tag{15}$$

where $\boldsymbol{x}_{[-i]} = (x_1, \ldots, x_{i-1}, x_{i+1}, \ldots, x_n)$ and $q(x_i \to x'_i \,|\, \boldsymbol{x}_{[-i]})$ denotes the proposal distribution use for updating x_i. Note that the condition (15) can be further relaxed for AESAMC, requiring the inequality holds for any components of x_i. Since both $\mathcal{X}$ and Θ are compact, it is easy to verify that the mutation operators described below satisfy the minorisation condition.

Two types of mutation operators, MH-Gibbs mutation and point mutations, are used in this article. The MH-Gibbs mutation, also called the "Metropolis-within-Gibbs" sampler (Müller, 1991) or the hybrid MCMC sampler (Robert & Casella, 2004, pp.393), proceeds as follows. For $i = 1, \ldots, n$, given the population $\boldsymbol{x}^{(t+1,i-1)} = (x_1^{(t+1)}, \ldots, x_{i-1}^{(t+1)}, x_i^{(t)}, \ldots, x_n^{(t)})$:

a) Generate a random direction vector e from a uniform distribution on the surface of a unit d-dimensional hypersphere.

b) Generate a random number $r \sim N(0, \sigma_m^2)$ and set $x'_i = x_i^{(t)} + re$, where σ_m is calibrated such that the operator has a reasonable overall acceptance rate.

c) Construct a new population by replacing $x_i^{(t)}$ with x'_i, accept the new population according to the MH rule as in the snooker crossover, and denote the new population by $\boldsymbol{x}^{(t+1,i)}$.

For the reason of mathematical simplicity, we keep the working weights $(\theta_1^{(t)}, \ldots, \theta_m^{(t)})$ unchanged in the cycle of the MH-Gibbs mutation. If the vector e used in step (b) is a (0,1)-binary vector with the positions of nonzero elements being selected randomly, the above operator is called the point mutation operator. If the total number of nonzero elements in e is K, then the operator is called the K-point mutation operator. In this article, 1 and 2-point mutation operators are applied equally when the K-point mutation operator is selected in simulations. Let σ_p denote the step size of the K-point mutation; that is, the operator can be expressed as $x'_{ij} = x_{ij}^{(t)} + r_j e_j$ for $j = 1, \ldots, d$, where r_j is a random number drawn from the normal $N(0, \sigma_p^2)$ and σ_p is called the step size of the operator.

AESAMC Algorithm Let $\rho_1, \ldots, \rho_5$, $0 < \rho_i < 1$ and $\sum_{i=1}^{5} \rho_i = 1$, denote the respective probabilities for the MH-Gibbs mutation, K-point mutation, K point crossover, snooker crossover, and linear crossover operators to work at each iteration. In this article, we set $\rho_1 = \rho_2 = 0.05$ and $\rho_3 = \rho_4 = \rho_5 = 0.3$. The AESAMC algorithm can be summarized as follows.

AESAMC algorithm:

a) (Initialization) Partition the sample space $\mathcal{X}_n$ into m disjoint subregions $\mathbb{E}_1, \ldots, \mathbb{E}_m$; choose the threshold value $\aleph$ and the working probabilities $\rho_1, \ldots, \rho_5$; initialize a population $\boldsymbol{x}^{(0)}$ at random; and set $\theta^{(0)} = (\theta_1^{(0)}, \ldots, \theta_m^{(0)}) = (0, 0, \ldots, 0)$, $\mathcal{X}_0^n = \bigcup_{i=1}^m \mathbb{E}_i$, $\boldsymbol{U}_{\min}^{(0)} = \boldsymbol{U}(\boldsymbol{x}^{(0)})$ and $t = 0$.
b) (Sampling) Update the current population $\boldsymbol{x}^{(t)}$ using the MH-Gibbs mutation, K-point mutation, K-point crossover, snooker crossover, and linear crossover operators according to the respective working probabilities.
c) (Working weight updating) Update the working weight $\theta^{(t)}$ by setting

$$\theta_i^* = \theta_i^{(t)} + \gamma_{t+1} H_i(\theta^{(t)}, \boldsymbol{x}^{(t+1)}), \quad i = 1, \ldots, \varpi(\boldsymbol{U}_{\min}^{(t)} + \aleph),$$

where $H_i(\theta^{(t)}, \boldsymbol{x}^{(t+1)}) = I(\boldsymbol{x}^{(t+1)} \in \mathbb{E}_i) - \pi_i$ for the crossover operators, and $H_i(\theta^{(t)}, \boldsymbol{x}^{(t+1)}) = \sum_{j=1}^{n} I(\boldsymbol{x}^{(t+1,j)} \in \mathbb{E}_i)/n - \pi_i$ for the mutation operators. If $\theta^* \in \Theta$, set $\theta^{(t+1)} = \theta^*$; otherwise, set $\theta^{(t+1)} = \theta^* + \boldsymbol{c}^*$, where $\boldsymbol{c}^* = (c^*, \ldots, c^*)$ and c^* is chosen such that $\theta^* + \boldsymbol{c}^* \in \Theta$.
d) (Termination Checking) Check the termination condition, e.g., a fixed number of iterations or an optimal solution set have been reached. Otherwise, set $t \rightarrow t + 1$ and go to step (b).

It has been shown in Liang (2008) that if the mutation operator satisfies the minorisation conditio (5) and the gain factor sequence satisfies (3), AESAMC also converges weakly toward a neighboring set of global minima of $\boldsymbol{U}(\boldsymbol{x})$ in the space of energy.

2.4 Practical issues

Liang *et al.* (2007) discussed practical issues on implementation of SAMC Some rules developed there, e.g., those on sample space partitioning and convergence diagnostic, are still applicable to ASAMC and AESAMC. Briefly speaking, the sample space should be partitioned such that the MH moves within the same subregion have a reasonable acceptance rate. In this article, the sample space is partitioned such that each subregion has an equal energy bandwidth Δu, i.e., $u_{i+1} - u_i \equiv \Delta u$ for all $i = 1, \ldots, m - 1$. To ensure that the moves within the same subregion have a reasonable acceptance rate, it is set $\Delta u = 0.2\tau$. The convergence can be diagnosed by examining the difference of the patterns of the working weights obtained in multiple runs. In the below, we discuss three more issues related to ASAMC and AESAMC.

- On the choice of π. Liang *et al.* (2007) suggest to set π biased to the low energy regions if one aims at minimization. However, this is different for ASAMC and AESAMC, as it includes an extra parameter, namely, $\aleph$, to control its search space at each iteration. In our experience, a uniform setting is often better than a low-energy biasing setting in terms of efficiency of the two algorithms, especially when $\aleph$ is small. Under the uniform setting, the system has more chances to visit higher energy regions, and thus has more chances to transit between disconnected regions. In this chapter, we set π to be uniform over all subregions, i.e., $\pi_1 = \ldots = \pi_m = 1/m$, in all computations.
- On the choice of $\aleph$, T_0 and N, where N denotes the total number of iterations. Since $\aleph$ determines the size of the neighboring set toward which ASAMC and AESAMC

converge, $\aleph$ should be chosen carefully for better efficiency of the algorithms. If $\aleph$ is too small, it may take a long time for the algorithms to locate the global minima. In this case, the sample space may contain a lot of separated regions, and most of the proposed transitions will be rejected if the proposal distribution is not spread enough. If $\aleph$ is too large, it may also take a long time for the algorithms to locate the global energy minimum due to the broadness of the sample space. In principle, the value of $\aleph$ should be chosen according to the roughness of the energy function. The rougher the energy function is, the larger value of $\aleph$ one should choose. A large value of $\aleph$ should associate with a large value of T_0, as a larger value of T_0 means faster transitions over the entire sample space. In practice, the values of $\aleph$, T_0 and N can be determined through a trial and error process based on the diagnosis for the convergence of the algorithms. If they fail to converge, the parameters should be tuned to larger values. Finally, we point out that due to the population effect, AESAMC can often work with a smaller value of $\aleph$ than ASAMC.

- On the choice of population size for AESAMC. The genetic algorithm often works with a large population, because the crossover operation is the key to its efficiency. In AESAMC, the crossover operator has been modified to serve as a proposal for the MH moves, and it is no longer as critical as to the genetic algorithm. In AESAMC, the population size is usually set to a moderate number, ranging from 5 to 50. As known by many people, the crossover operation favors to high dimensional problems.

3. Numerical examples

3.1 A multiple local minima problem

To illustrate ASAMC, we consider minimizing the following function on $[-1.1, 1.1]^2$:

$$U(\boldsymbol{x}) = -\left(x_1 \sin(20x_2)+x_2 \sin(20x_1)\right)^2 \cosh\left(\sin(10x_1)x_1\right)-\left(x_1 \cos(10x_2)-x_2 \sin(10x_1)\right)^2 \cosh\left(\cos(20x_2)x_2\right),$$

whose global minimum is -8.12465 attained at $(x_1, x_2) = (-1.0445,-1.0084)$ and $(1.0445,-1.0084)$ This example is identical to Example 6.1 of Liang (2005). Figure 1 shows that $U(\boldsymbol{x})$ has a multitude of local energy minima separated by high-energy barriers.

Since the dimension of the problem is low, AESAMC was not applied to this example. In applyin ASAMC to this example, we partitioned the sample space into 41 subregions with an equal energy bandwidth: $E_1 = \{\boldsymbol{x} \in \mathcal{X} : U(\boldsymbol{x}) \le -8.0\}$, $E_2 = \{(\boldsymbol{x}) \in \mathcal{X} : -8.0 < U(\boldsymbol{x}) \le -7.8\}, \ldots,$ and $E_{41} = \{(\boldsymbol{x}) \in \mathcal{X} : -0.2 < U(\boldsymbol{x}) \le 0\}$, set $\psi(\boldsymbol{x}) = \exp(-U(\boldsymbol{x})/0.1)$, $t_0 = 100$, and $\aleph = 6$, and choose the proposal distribution as $N_2(\boldsymbol{x}, 0.3_2 I_2)$, where I_d denotes an identity matrix of size d by d. The algorithm was run for 50000 iterations, and 500 samples were collected at equally spaced time intervals.

For comparison, SAMC and SA were also applied to this example. SAMC was run for 50000 iterations with the same setting as ASAMC (the parameter $\aleph$ does not exist in SAMC), and 500 samples were collected at equally spaced time intervals. For SA, we tried the linear and geometric cooling schedules.

a) Linear. The temperature decreases linearly, i.e.,

$$T_k = T_{k-1} - \varrho_l,\ k = 1, \ldots, K,$$

where $\varrho_l = (T_1 - T_K)/(K - 1)$.

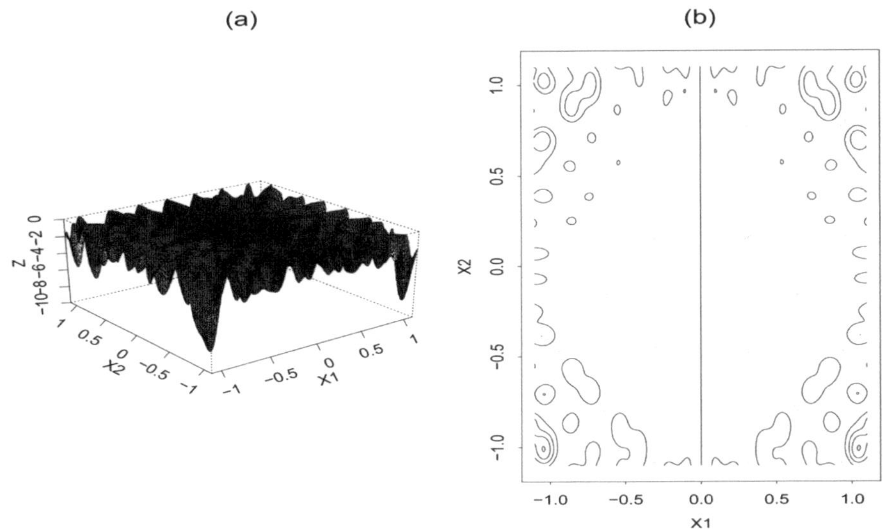

Figure 1. Grid (a) and contour (b) representations of the function $U(\boldsymbol{x})$ on $[-1.1, 1.1]^2$. This figure characterizes multiple local minima problems.

b) Geometric. The temperature decreases geometrically with a constant rate, i.e.,

$$T_k = \varrho_e T_{k-1},\ k = 1, \ldots, K,$$

where $\varrho_e = \exp\{(\log T_K - \log T_1)/(T-1)\}$.

In all simulations, we set the total number of temperature levels $K = 500$, and set the number of iterations performed at each temperature level to $N_k = N/K$, where N is the total numbers of iterations of a run. For this example, we set $T_1 = 10$, $T_{500} = 0.01$ and $N = 50000$ for both cooling schedules. The resulting values of ϱ_l and ϱ_e are 0.02 and 0.986, respectively. The proposal distribution used at level k is $N(\boldsymbol{x}_t, 0.1^2 T_k I_2)$. In each run, 500 samples were collected at equally spaced time intervals.

Figure 2 shows the evolving paths of the samples collected in the above runs. It is remarkable that ASAMC is ergodic as shown by Figure 2(a). Even though the sample space has been restricted to four isolated regions (four corners) by the choice of $\aleph$, successful transitions between different regions can still be made due to the use of the global proposal distribution. This also explains why a widely spread proposal distribution is preferred in ASAMC. Comparing to the sample path of SAMC, we can see that in ASAMC, sampling is more focused on the low energy regions. Hence, ASAMC is potentially more efficient than SAMC in optimization.

Figures 2(c) and 2(d) show that at high temperatures, SA results in a random walk in the sample space; and that at low temperatures, SA tends to get trapped in a local minimum. Note that the linear cooling schedule contains more high temperature levels than the geometric cooling schedule. The sample paths of SA are significantly different from those of SAMC and ASAMC. The central part of the sample space (Figure 1(b)) has a big area, which is about half of the total area of the sample space, but it is seldom visited by ASAMC and SAMC. However, this part is visited by SA frequently with both linear and geometric cooling schedules. The reason is that SA tends to have a random walk in the sample space at high temperatures, whereas ASAMC (so is SAMC) tends to have a random walk in the space of subregions, if each subregion is regarded as a single point. This implies that potentially ASAMC can overcome any barriers on the energy landscape and locate global energy minima quickly. Figure 2 shows that during the above runs SAMC and ASAMC have located the global energy minima many times, whilst SA has only located them a few times.

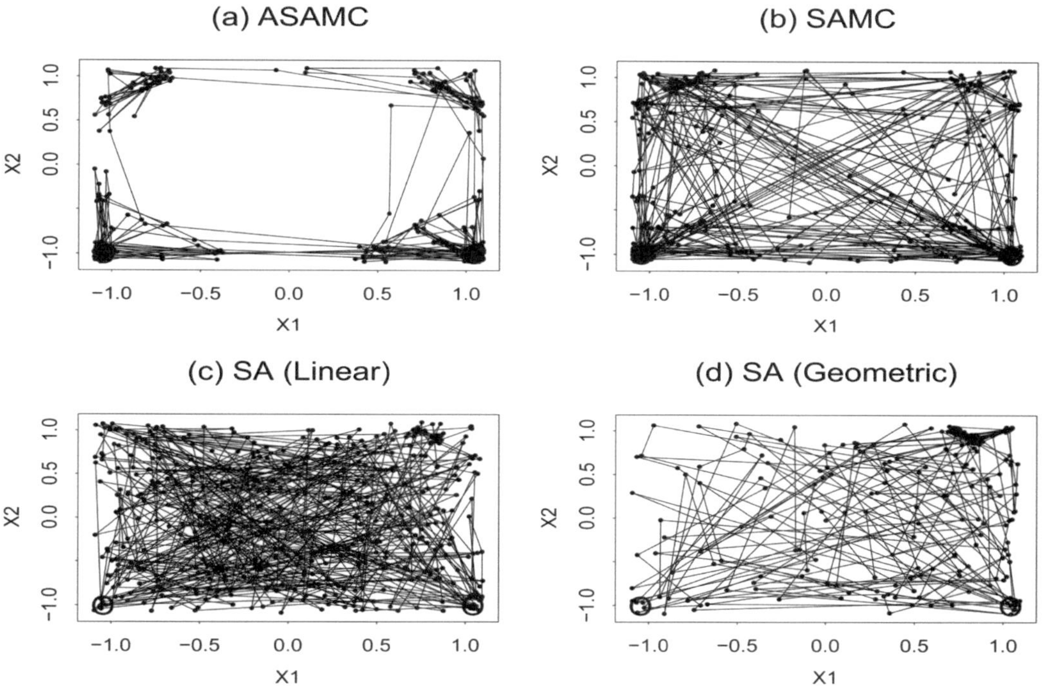

Figure 2. Sample paths of the ASAMC, SAMC and SA samples. The circles in the plots show the locations of the two global energy minima. (a) Sample path of ASAMC. (b) Sample path of SAMC. (c) Sample path of SA with the linear cooling schedule. (d) Sample path of SA with the geometric cooling schedule. This figure characterizes the performance of ASAMC for multiple local minima problems: it is capable of transiting between different local minimum regions.

To compare efficiency of ASAMC, SAMC and SA in global optimization, we conducted the following experiment. Each algorithm was run 1000 times independently. Each run consisted of 20000 iterations. ASAMC and SAMC were run under the same setting as used above except that the proposal distribution was changed to $N_2(\boldsymbol{x}, 0.1^2 I_2)$. This change would force them to move more locally and thus to have more chances to locate the global energy minima. The proposal distribution used in SA has already been fine enough, and was not changed in this experiment. The numerical results are summarized in Table 1. The comparison shows that both ASAMC and SAMC are superior to SA for this example. Note that in all runs of the three algorithms, the total numbers of iterations were the same, and they cost about the same CPU times because the CPU time cost by each iteration is dominated by the part used for energy evaluation. This is especially true for more complicated problems, e.g., the neural network training problems studied in Liang (2007).

Algorithm	Mean	SD($\times 10^{-3}$)	Minimum	Maximum	Proportion
ASAMC	-8.12320	0.047	-8.12465	-8.11278	968
SAMC	-8.12308	0.059	-8.12465	-8.10191	944
SA-1	-8.10326	1.264	-8.12465	-7.77922	572
SA-2	-8.08168	3.102	-8.12466	-7.33146	609

Table 1: Comparison of the SAMC, ASAMC, and SA algorithms for the multiple local minima example. Notations: let z_i denote the minimum energy value obtained in the ith run for $i = 1, \ldots, 1000$, "Mean" is the average of z_i, "SD" is the standard deviation of "Mean", "Minimum"$= \min_{i=1}^{1000} z_i$, "Maximum"$= \max_{i=1}^{1000} z_i$, and "Proportion"$= \#\{i : z_i \leq -8.12\}$. The cooling schedules used in SA-1 and SA-2 are linear and geometric, respectively.

3.2 Rational-expectations model

To illustrate the performance of AESAMC, we consider the following example, which is specified by the system of equations,

$$
\begin{aligned}
y_{1t} &= g_{1t}(\boldsymbol{\alpha}, \boldsymbol{\beta}, \boldsymbol{\gamma}) + \epsilon_{1t}, \\
y_{2t} &= g_{2t}(\boldsymbol{\alpha}, \boldsymbol{\beta}, \boldsymbol{\gamma}) + \epsilon_{2t}, \\
x_{t1} &= \gamma_1 x_{t-1,1} + u_{t1}, \\
x_{t2} &= \gamma_2 x_{t-1,2} + u_{t2}, \\
x_{t3} &= \gamma_3 x_{t-1,3} + u_{t3},
\end{aligned}
\tag{16}
$$

where $\alpha = (\alpha_{11}, \alpha_{12}, \alpha_{13}, \alpha_{21}, \alpha_{22}, \alpha_{23})$, $\beta = (\beta_{11}, \beta_{12}, \beta_{21}, \beta_{22})$, $\gamma = (\gamma_1, \gamma_2, \gamma_3)$, $\Lambda = [1 - \beta_{12}\beta_{21}(1 - \beta_{11})(1 - \beta_{22})]^{-1}$, and

$$
\begin{aligned}
g_{1t}(\boldsymbol{\alpha}, \boldsymbol{\beta}, \boldsymbol{\gamma}) &= \alpha_{11} x_{t1} + \alpha_{12} x_{t2} + \alpha_{13} x_{t3} + \beta_{11} E_{t-1} y_{t1} + \beta_{12} E_{t-1} y_{t2}, \\
g_{2t}(\boldsymbol{\alpha}, \boldsymbol{\beta}, \boldsymbol{\gamma}) &= \alpha_{21} x_{t1} + \alpha_{22} x_{t2} + \alpha_{23} x_{t3} + \beta_{21} E_{t-1} y_{t1} + \beta_{22} E_{t-1} y_{t2}, \\
E_{t-1} y_{t1} &= \frac{\Lambda}{1 - \beta_{11}} \{\alpha_{11}\gamma_1 x_{t-1,1} + \alpha_{12}\gamma_2 x_{t-1,2} + \alpha_{13}\gamma_3 x_{t-1,3} \\
&\quad + \beta_{12}(1 - \beta_{22})^{-1} [\alpha_{21}\gamma_1 x_{t-1,1} + \alpha_{22}\gamma_2 x_{t-1,2} + \alpha_{23}\gamma_3 x_{t-1,3}]\}, \\
E_{t-1} y_{t2} &= \frac{\Lambda}{1 - \beta_{11}} \{\alpha_{21}\gamma_1 x_{t-1,1} + \alpha_{22}\gamma_2 x_{t-1,2} + \alpha_{23}\gamma_3 x_{t-1,3} \\
&\quad + \beta_{21}(1 - \beta_{11})^{-1} [\alpha_{11}\gamma_1 x_{t-1,1} + \alpha_{12}\gamma_2 x_{t-1,2} + \alpha_{23}\gamma_3 x_{t-1,3}]\}.
\end{aligned}
$$

The parameters (α,β,γ) can be estimated by minimizing the function

$$U(\boldsymbol{\alpha},\boldsymbol{\beta},\boldsymbol{\gamma},x_{01},x_{02},x_{03}) = \sum_{t=1}^{T}(y_{1t} - g_{1t}(\boldsymbol{\alpha},\boldsymbol{\beta},\boldsymbol{\gamma}))^2 + \sum_{t=1}^{T}(y_{2t} - g_{2t}(\boldsymbol{\alpha},\boldsymbol{\beta},\boldsymbol{\gamma}))^2 + \sum_{i=1}^{3}\sum_{t=1}^{T}(x_{ti} - \gamma_i x_{t-1,i})^2, \tag{17}$$

on the space: $|\alpha_{ij}| \le 10$, $|\beta_{ij}| \le 10$, $|\gamma_i| \le 1$ and $|x_{0i}| \le 10$.

This example is constructed by Dorsey & Mayer (1995) based on the rational-expectations model encountered in economic research (Hoffman & Schmidt, 1981). Following Dorsey & Mayer (1995), we use a dataset consisting of 40 observations simulated under the specifications: $\alpha_{ij} = 1$ and $\beta_{ij} = 0.2$ for all i and j, $\gamma_1 = 0.1$, $\gamma_2 = 0.2$, $\gamma_3 = 0.8$, $\epsilon_{t1} \sim N(0, 25_2)$, $\epsilon_{t2} \sim N(0, 1)$, $u_{t1} \sim N(0, 36_2)$, $U_{u2} \sim N(0, 4_2)$, and $u_{t3} \sim N(0, 9_2)$. Dorsey and Mayer (1995) assessed the computational difficulty of this problem by running the Marquardt-Levenberg gradient algorithm from 50 different randomly chosen points in the search space. In 49 out of 50 runs, the Marquardt-Levenberg algorithm failed to converge because of either singularities or floating-point overflow, and on the one run that did converge was discovered to be suboptimal.

AESAMC was first applied to this example with the following specifications: the temperature $\tau = 100$, the population size $n = 25$, the mutation step sizes $\sigma_m = \sigma_p = 1.5$, the snooker crossover step size $\sigma_c = 1$, the threshold value $\aleph = 5000$, the gain factor scale $T_0 = 20000$, and total number of iterations $N = 5 \times 10^6$. To examine the performance of AESAMC in a long run, we set N to a large number. The algorithm was run 20 times. On average, each run requires 1.85×10^7 function evaluations and about 180s CUP time on a 2.8GHZ computer. The results are summarized in Table 2 and Figure 3. To assess the robustness of AESAMC to the choices of $\aleph$ and T_0, the algorithm was also run 20 times with $\aleph = 15000$ and $T_0 = 50000$ (keeping the values of other parameters unchanged). As discussed earlier, a large value of $\aleph$ should associate with a large value of T_0. The results suggest that the performance of AESAMC is quite robust to the choice of $\aleph$ and T_0.

For comparison, ASAMC, SA and the genetic algorithm were also applied to this example. ASAMC and SA employed the mutation operators used by AESAMC as their local samplers. For ASAMC, we tried two different settings of ($\aleph$, T_0): (10000, 20000) and (20000, 50000). Under each setting, ASAMC was run 20 times, and each run consists of 1.85×10^7 iterations. For SA, we tried three different choices of the highest temperature: 500, 1000, and 2000. For each choice, SA was also run 20 times. Each run consists of 100 stages, each stage consists of 1.85×10^5 iterations, and the temperature ladder decreases at a rate of 0.95.

The genetic algorithm has many variants, each covering different applications and aspects. The variant we adopted here is the so-called real-coded genetic algorithm (RGA), which is described in Ali *et al.* (2005). RGA includes three free parameters, namely, the population size, the number of individuals to be updated at each generation, and the number of generations. RGA has been tested by Ali *et al.* (2005) on a variety of continuous global optimization problems. The results indicate that it is effective and comparable or favorable to other stochastic optimization algorithms, such as controlled random search (Price, 1983;

Ali and Storey, 1994) and differential evolution (Storn & Price, 1997). For this example, we tried three different settings of population size: 50, 100 and 200. The number of individuals to be updated at each generation was set to one-fifth of the population size, and the number of generations was chosen such that the total number of function evaluations in each run is about 1.85×10^7. Under each setting, RGA was also run 20 times. The results are summarized in Table 2 and Figure 3.

Table 2 shows that the averages of the best function values produced by AESAMC are lower than those produced by other algorithms, although the runs are so long. Figure 3 plots the average progression curves of the best function values produced by these algorithms. RGA performs less well than SA and ASAMC for this example. This implies that this example does not favor to the crossover operations. Even so, AESAMC still significantly outperforms other algorithms. The average of the best function values produced by ASAMC with 1.85×10^7 function evaluations is about the same as that produced by AESAMC with about 6×10^6 function evaluations. This translates to a 3- fold improvement. The results produced by SA and RGA are not comparable to that produced by AESAMC at all. In our experience, high dimensional optimizations usually favor to the crossover operations.

Algorithm	Setting	Minimum	Maximum	Average	SD	Cost
AESAMC	$\aleph = 5000,\ T_0 = 20000$	62694	62984	62815	19	1.85×10^7
	$\aleph = 15000,\ T_0 = 50000$	62694	63078	62813	29	1.85×10^7
ASAMC	$\aleph = 10000,\ T_0 = 20000$	62694	63893	62864	71	1.85×10^7
	$\aleph = 20000,\ T_0 = 50000$	62694	63370	62940	64	1.85×10^7
SA	$\tau_{high} = 500$	62699	63956	63412	84	1.85×10^7
	$\tau_{high} = 1000$	62695	64242	63543	84	1.85×10^7
	$\tau_{high} = 2000$	62700	64779	63501	118	1.85×10^7
RGA	$n = 50$	64585	66703	65140	122	1.9×10^7
	$n = 100$	64579	65299	64822	65	1.9×10^7
	$n = 200$	64579	65288	64861	63	1.9×10^7

Table 2. Comparison of AESAMC, ASAMC, SA and RGA for minimization of the function (17). Let u_i denote the best function value produced in the i-th run. The numbers in the columns of Minimum, Maximum, Average, and SD are calculated, respectively, as follows: $\min_{1 \le i \le 30} u_i$, $\max_{1 \le l \le 30} u_i$, $\sum_{i=1}^{30} u_i/30$, and the standard deviation of the average. Cost: the number of function evaluations in each run.

4. Discussion

In this article, we have described the ASAMC and AESAMC algorithms. A remarkable feature of the two algorithms is that they are not trapped by local energy minima. Under mild conditions they can converge weakly toward a neighboring set of the global minima in the space of energy. The algorithms were tested on two examples. The numerical results indicate that ASAMC and AESAMC can significantly outperform their competitors, including SAMC, simulating annealing and genetic algorithms, in terms of quality of the solutions obtained with the same CPU time.

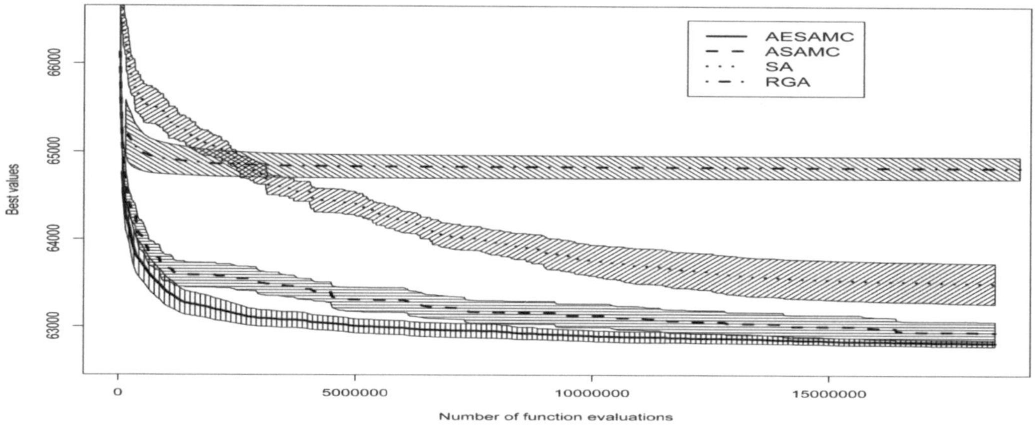

Figure 3: Average progression curves of the best function values (over 20 runs) and their 95% confidence regions (shaded area) produced by AESAMC ($\aleph = 5000$, $T_0 = 20000$), ASAMC ($\aleph = 10000$, $T_0 = 20000$), SA ($\tau_{high} = 10$) and RGA ($n = 100$) for minimizing the function (17).

In this paper, both ASAMC and AESAMC are described for continuous optimization problems only. Extension to discrete optimization problems is straightforward. For discrete optimization problems, the mutation and crossover operators required by AESAMC can be designed as in Liang & Wong (2000) and Goswami & Liu (2006). The K-point crossover operator described in this paper can also be used for discrete problems.

Although ASAMC and AESAMC are proposed as optimization techniques, they can also be used as importance sampling techniques by keeping the sample space unshrinked through iterations. AESAMC has provided a general framework on how to incorporate crossover operations into dynamically weighted MCMC simulations, e.g., dynamic weighting (Wong & Liang, 1997; Liang, 2002) and population Monte Carlo (Cappé *et al.*, 2004). This framework is potentially more useful than the conventional MCMC framework provided by evolutionary Monte Carlo (Liang & Wong, 2000, 2001). Under the conventional MCMC framework, the crossover operation has often a low acceptance rate. The MH rule will typically reject an unbalanced pair of offspring samples for which one has a high density value and other low. In AESAMC, this difficulty has been much alleviated due to the self-adjusting ability of the algorithm.

In this article, the parameter $\aleph$ is set to a constant. If we associate it with iterations by letting $\aleph(t)$ be a monotonically decreasing function of t with the limit 0, then ASAMC and AESAMC will converge in distribution toward the set of global energy minima. An interesting problem is to find the decreasing rate of $\aleph(t)$ under which ASAMC and AESAMC can converge faster to the global energy minima.

5. Acknowledgments

The author's research was partially supported by grants from the National Science Foundation (DMS-0607755) and the National Cancer Institute (CA104620).

6. References

Ali, M.M., Khompatraporn, C. and Zabinsky, Z.B. (2005). A numerical evaluation of several stochastic algorithms on selected continuous global optimization test problems. *Journal of Global Optimization*, 31(4), 635 672.

Ali, M.M. and Storey, C. (1994). Modified controlled random search algorithms. *International Journal of Computer Mathematics*, 53(3), 229-235.

Andrieu, C., Moulines, É., and Priouret, P. (2005). Stability of Stochastic Approximation Under Verifiable Conditions. *SIAM J. Control and Optimization*, 44(1), 283-312.

Benveniste, A., Métivier, M., and Priouret, P. (1990). *Adaptive Algorithms and Stochastic Approximations*, Springer-Verlag, New York.

Bharath, B. and Borkar, V.S. (1999). Stochastic approximation algorithms: overview and recent trends. *Sadhana* 24 (4&5), 425-452.

Cappé, O., Guillin, A., Marin, J.M. and Robert, C.P. (2004). Population Monte Carlo. *Journal of Computational and Graphical Statistics*, 13(4), 907 929.

Delyon, B., Lavielle, M. and Moulines, E. (1999). Convergence of a stochastic approximation version of the EM algorithm. *Annals of Statistics* 27(1), 94-128.

Dorsey, R.E. and Mayer, W.J. (1995). Genetic algorithms for estimation problems with multiple optima, non-differentiability, and other irregular features. *Journal of Business and Economic Statistics*, 13(1), 53-66.

Geman, S. and Geman, D. (1984). Stochastic relaxation, Gibbs distribution and the Bayesian restoration of images. *IEEE Transactions on Pattern Analysis and Machine Intelligence* 6(6), 721-741.

Gilks, W.R., Roberts, G.O. and George, E.I. (1994). Adaptive direction sampling. *The Statistician*, 43(1), 179-189.

Goldberg, D.E. (1989). Genetic Algorithms in Search, Optimization, & Machine learning, Addison Wesley.

Goswami, G.R. and Liu, J.S. (2007). Evolutionary Monte Carlo methods for clustering. *Journal of Computational and Graphical Statistics*, 16(4), 855-876.

Gu, M.G. and Kong, F.H. (1998). A stochastic approximation algorithm with Markov chain Monte Carlo method for incomplete data estimation problems. *Proceedings of the National Academy of Sciences USA*, 95(13), 7270-7274.

Harth, E. and Tzanakou, E. (1974). Alopex: A stochastic method for determining visual receptive fields. *Vision Res.* 14(12), 1475-1482.

Hastings, W.K. (1970). Monte Carlo Sampling Methods Using Markov Chains and Their Applications. *Biometrika*, 57(1), 97-109.

Haykin, S. (1999). *Neural Networks: A Comprehensive Foundation* (2nd edition). Prentice Hall, New York.

Hoffman, D.L. and Schmidt, P. (1981). Testing the restrictions implied by the rational expectations hypothesis. *Journal of Econometrics*, 15(2), 265-287.

Holland, J.H. (1975). *Adaptation in Natural and Artificial Systems*. Ann Arbor, University of Michigan Press.

Jasra, A., Stephens, D.A. and Holmes, C.C. (2007). On population-based simulation for static inference. *Statistics and Computing*, 17(3), 263-279.

Kirkpatrick, S., Gelatt, C.D., and Vecchi, M.P. (1983). Optimization by simulated annealing. *Science*, 220(4598), 671-680.

Kohonen, T. (1990). The self-organizing map. *Proceedings of the Institute of Electrical and Electronics Engineers*, 78(9), 1464-1480.

Liang, F. (2002). Dynamically weighted importance sampling in Monte Carlo Computation, *Journal of the American Statistical Association*, 97(459), 807-821.

Liang, F. (2005). Generalized Wang-Landau algorithm for Monte Carlo Computation. *Journal of the American Statistical Association*, 100(472), 1311-1327.

Liang, F. (2007). Annealing Stochastic Approximation Monte Carlo for Neural Network Training. *Machine Learning*, 68(3), 201-233.

Liang, F. (2008). Annealing evolutionary stochastoc approximation Monte Carlo for global optimization. Technical Report, Texas A&M University.

Liang, F., Liu, C., and Carroll, R.J. (2007). Stochastic Approximation in Monte Carlo Computation. *Journal of the American Statistical Association*, 102(477), 305-320.

Liang, F. and Wong. W.H. (2000). Evolutionary Monte Carlo sampling: applications to *Cp* model sampling and change-point problem. *Statistica Sinica*, 10(2), 317-342.

Liang, F. and Wong. W.H. (2001). Real parameter evolutionary sampling with applications in Bayesian Mixture Models, *Journal of the American Statistical Association*, 96(454), 653-666.

Mengersen, K.L. and Tweedie, R.L. (1996). Rates of convergence of the Hastings and Metropolis algorithms. *The Annals of Statistics*, 24(1), 101-121.

Metropolis, N., Rosenbluth, A.W., Rosenbluth, M.N., Teller, A.H., and Teller, E. (1953). Equation of state calculations by fast computing machines. *Journal of Chemical Physics*, 21(6), 1087- 1091.

M¨uller, P. (1991). A generic approach to posterior integration and Gibbs sampling. Technical report, Purdue University, West Lafayette, Indiana.

Price, W.L. (1983). Global optimization by controlled random search. *Journal of Optimization Theory and Applications*, 40(3), 333-348.

Robbins, H. and Monro, S. (1951). A stochastic approximation method. *Annals of Mathematical Statistics* 22(3), 400-407.

Robert, C.P. and Casella, G. (2004). *Monte Carlo Statistical Methods* (2nd edition). Springer, New York.

Schmitt, L.M. (2001). Theory of genetic algorithms. *Theoretical Computer Science*, 259(1), 1-61.

Spall, J.C. (1992). Multivariate stochastic approximation using a simultaneous perturbation gradient approximation. *IEEE Transactions on Automatic Control*, 37(3), 332-341.

Storn, R. and Price, K. (1997). Differential evolution: A simple and efficient heuristic for global optimization over continuous spaces. *Journal of Global Optimization*, 11(4), 341-359.

Wong, W.H. and Liang, F. (1997). Dynamic weighting in Monte Carlo and optimization, *Proc. Natl. Acad. Sci. USA*, 94(26) , 14220-14224.

Zhu, H.T., Liang, F., Gu, M. and Peterson, B. (2007). Stochastic approximation algorithms for estimation of spatial mixed models. In *Handbook of Computing and Statistics with Applications*, Vol.1, S.Y. Lee (Ed.), pp.399-421, Elsevier, Amsterdam.

11

Application of Simulated Annealing on the Study of Multiphase Systems

Maurice G. Politis[1], Michael E. Kainourgiakis[2], Eustathios S. Kikkinides[1] and Athanasios K. Stubos[2]
[1] *University of Western Macedonia, Department of Engineering and Management of Energy Resources, Bakola & Sialvera Str., 50100, Kozani*
[2] *National Center for Scientific Research Demokritos, 15310 Ag. Paraskevi Attikis, Athens, Greece*

1. Introduction

"πάντα δὲ δοκιμάζετε, τὸ καλὸν κατέχετε, ἀπὸ παντὸς εἴδους πονηροῦ ἀπέχεσθε."
"Try everything, keep the good, stay away from all form of evil."
(St. Paul, 1 Thessalonians 5:21-22)

The study of multiphase systems is of great importance in various fields of technological and environmental interest such as oil recovery, gas separations by adsorption, study of hazardous waste repositories and catalysis (Mohanty, 2003). In the past decade there has been considerable interest in numerical simulation studies (Baldwin et al., 1996; Torquato, 2005; Kumar et al. 2008) where an accurate representation of the complex multiphase matrix at the pore scale enables detailed studies of equilibrium and dynamic processes in these structures. Understanding the relationship between multiphase distribution at the microscale and transport properties is a general problem in applications involving multiphase systems (Kosek et al., 2005; Bruck et al., 2007). However, the direct correlation of experimental transport data to the underlying microscopic multiphase distribution is often found to be a very complicated procedure mainly because the multiphase configuration structure itself is highly complex and inadequately known. Hence, there is a strong need for a direct quantitative description of the pore-solid structure and the single or multi phase fluid distribution within this structure that should provide the basis for a reliable determination of the respective macroscopic transport properties. Such a methodology could contribute significantly to the efficient design of improved porous materials and multiphase flow processes.

Simulated Annealing has become a paradigm methodology in many areas of non-linear multiparameter global optimization. It represents a powerful and algorithmically simple solution to some of the most demanding computational task. One could summarize the method in one sentence: try all that matter, keep the best and stay away from local traps. The scope of this chapter is to demonstrate the effectiveness of SA for the realistic three-dimensional (3D) representation of the complex landscapes of multiphase systems thus enabling the simulation of disordered microstructures as they are experimentally observed in real materials.

Disordered materials, such as glasses, liquids and random heterogeneous materials, (Torquato, 2002) have a structure that is stochastic in nature. Their microstructure defines a random field, fully characterized by n-moments of the phase-function or simplified phenomenological expressions that contain semi-empirical parameters that implicitly depend on these moments. In this context are defined the effective properties of the system that can be expressed as ensemble averages (expectations) of the moment generating probability functions. It is then natural to approximate such properties by ergodic averages through Monte Carlo simulation. The derivation of the mathematical expressions for the ensemble averages is the subject of homogenisation theory and gives the necessary formal justification for the definition of effective properties such as conductivity, permeability, elastic moduli and wetting factors.

The SA methodology will be illustrated in two applications:

1. To solve an inverse problem for a two-phase, solid-void medium, namely the 3D microstructure reconstruction from statistical descriptors based on two-dimensional (2D) cross-sections of real-world materials.
2. To determine the fluid spatial distribution in a multiphase system (pore-solid-fluid).

An inverse, ill-posed problem implies that there are many realizations of a porous medium that share the same objective function and there is no unique solution. When solving the reconstruction problem, the minimization of the objective function (system 'energy') has no physical significance and only serves as an ad hoc optimization variable. Thus, even intermediate, far from optimal, solutions represent a physically valid microstructure. This should be distinguished conceptually from finding the global minimum for the fluid distribution case that entails only the optimal solution as the one corresponding to a situation matching reality. Examples of the latter are common in many areas of Physical Chemistry where Statistical Thermodynamics formulations provide the theoretical basis for Monte Carlo simulations.

To determine the fluid spatial distribution in the three-phase system it is also necessary to decouple the effect of the solid-void interface, which is structure depended and thus requires geometrical analysis, from the effect fluid-solid and fluid-fluid interface which depend on thermodynamic and physicochemical concepts and require the application of microscopic analysis in the form of simple or complex thermodynamic rules (Kainourgiakis et al., 2002).

2. Optimization problem

The multiphase distribution problem can be formulated as an optimization problem, seeking to minimize the difference between the statistical properties of the generated structure and the imposed ones. Simulated annealing (SA) was originally formulated as an optimization algorithm by Kirkpatrick and coworkers (Kirkpatrick et al., 1983). They used the Metropolis algorithm to solve combinatorial problems establishing an analogy between the annealing process in solids, the behavior of systems with many degrees of freedom in thermal equilibrium at a finite temperature and the optimization problem of finding the global minimum of a multi-parameter objective function.

A randomly generated perturbation of the current system configuration is applied so that a trial configuration is obtained. Let E_c and E_t denote the energy level of the current and trial configurations, respectively. If $E_c \geq E_t$, then a lower energy level has been reached, the trial configuration is unconditionally accepted and becomes the current configuration. On the other hand, if $E_c < E_t$ then the trial configuration is accepted with a probability given by $P(\Delta E) = e^{(-\Delta E/k_B T)}$ where $\Delta E = E_t - E_c$, k_B is the Boltzmann constant and T is the temperature (or an arbitrary analog of it, used only to symbolically represent the degree of randomness in the spatial distribution of the system phases). This step prevents the system from being trapped in a local lowest-energy state. After a sufficient number of iterations, the system approaches equilibrium, where the free energy reaches its minimum value. By gradually decreasing T and repeating the simulation process (using every time as initial configuration the one found as equilibrium state for the previous T value), new lower energy levels become achievable. The process is considered complete when despite the change in T the number of accepted changes in different configurations becomes lower than a pre-specified value.

The two applications that will be presented can be seen in from a very different perspective. The reconstruction of random media is an intriguing inverse problem that must be interpreted in the appropriate physical context whereas the fluid-phase distribution is a purely numerical exercise in finding the global minimum.

In trying to address the non-uniqueness problem we have proposed (Politis et al., 2008) a novel methodology that uses a simple process-based structure, matching only limited structural information with the target material, to initialize the simulated annealing and thus reduce the search-space, constraining the solution path. The stochastic / process-based hybrid method starts with a random sphere pack obtained using the ballistic deposition algorithm as the process-based step and then uses SA to minimize the least-squares error functional of the correlation functions (Kainourgiakis et al., 1999; Kainourgiakis et al., 2005).

3. Reconstruction of random media

The reconstruction of realizations of random media is of interest although it is possible to directly obtain, at least for some materials, high resolution (~200nm/pixel) 3D microtomography images (Spanne et al 2001; Tomutsa & Radmilovic 2003). The use of limited information from low-order correlations can offer a valuable theoretical probe to the very nature of the complex structure (Sheehan & Torquato, 2001; Torquato, 2005). Exploring all physically realizable correlation functions enables the investigation of effective properties in ad hoc reconstructed materials that suit the experimenter.

There are several techniques to statistically generate the 3D structures but broadly fall in three categories:

1. *Gaussian Random Fields*: Based on thresholding a Gaussian random field, was the first to be introduced by P. M. Adler and co-workers (Adler et al., 1990; Adler, 1992; Thovert et al., 2001). The reconstruction is based on and limited to the porosity and 2-point correlation function of the sample, measured by image analysis. The method is

computationally very efficient but can not use additional spatial correlation functions or extended to non-Gaussian statistics.

2. *Simulated Annealing optimization*: These methods attempt to reconstruct the phase function from theoretically any number of stochastic functions that describe the sample geometry (Rintoul & Torquato, 1997; Yeong & Torquato 1998a; Yeong & Torquato 1998b; Torquato, 2002). Computationally they can be demanding if higher order statistical moments are used (e.g. chord length, lineal path or 3-point correlation).
3. *Maximum entropy methods*: They are derived from Bayesian statistics methods first applied for inverse problems is signal processing. Microstructures are assumed to be samples from a governing probability distribution function (PDF) which is computed from the limited available statistical descriptors (correlation functions) using maximum entropy theory (Sankaran & Zabaras, 2006).

An alternative method to obtain the microstructure is to simulate the physical (thermo-mechanical) process that they result from, in effect recreating the material synthesis history. This is an extremely complex and computationally very expensive process but still viable in small domains (Bakke & Oren, 1997; Bryant & Blunt, 2004).

Effective reconstruction of random two-phase heterogeneous media can be realized from statistical descriptors, namely n-point correlation functions, obtained from digitized images of a material. The n-point correlation function is a measure of the probability of finding n-points (in a specified geometrical arrangement) all lying in the region of space occupied by one constituent of a two-phase material. For example the one-point correlation function is the probability that any point lies in a specific phase (either pore or solid phase). Thus if we define the phase function of a porous material as follows (Berryman, 1985; Torquato, 2002):

$$Z(\mathbf{x}) = \begin{cases} 1, \text{ if } \mathbf{x} \text{ is in phase 1 (pore)} \\ 0, \text{ if } \mathbf{x} \text{ is in phase 2 (solid)} \end{cases} \tag{1}$$

If the medium is statistically homogeneous, then the probability functions are translationally invariant in space and depend only on the spatial separation between the points. Then it follows that the 1-point correlation function is by definition equal to the porosity:

$$\varepsilon = S_1(\mathbf{u}) = \langle Z(\mathbf{x}) \rangle \tag{2}$$

The angular brackets denote an ensemble average. Accordingly, the 2-point correlation function is the probability that two points at a specified distance can be found both in the same phase of the material:

$$S_2(\mathbf{u}) = \langle Z(\mathbf{x}) \rangle \langle Z(\mathbf{x}+\mathbf{u}) \rangle \tag{3}$$

In general,

$$S_n(\mathbf{x}_1, \ldots, \mathbf{x}_n) = \left\langle \prod_{i=1}^{n} Z(\mathbf{x}_i) \right\rangle \tag{4}$$

An additional simplification can be made if the medium is statistically isotropic. For an isotropic medium, $S_2(u)$ becomes one-dimensional as it is only a function of $u = |\mathbf{u}|$. It is often preferable to work with the 2-point auto-correlation function $R_z(\mathbf{u})$ which is a normalized version of $S_2(u)$:

$$R_Z(\mathbf{u}) = \frac{\langle (Z(\mathbf{x}) - \varepsilon) \cdot (Z(\mathbf{x} + \mathbf{u}) - \varepsilon) \rangle}{\varepsilon - \varepsilon^2} \tag{5}$$

Note that if we reverse the phase function in order to calculate the n-point correlation functions for the solid phase we observe that $R_z(u)$ remains exactly the same; simply change Z to 1-Z, and ε to 1-ε everywhere in eq. (5). For a statistically homogenous and spatially ergodic medium, the spatial average is equivalent to the ensemble average and thus we can define and compute the average quantities of the medium.

Based on the work of Debye (Debye et al., 1957), the 2-point correlation function can be related to the interface area per unit volume of the material. The specific internal surface area per unit volume (S_v) can be determined from the slope of $R_z(\mathbf{u})$ at u=0 using eq. (6), adjusted for a digitized 3D medium (Jiao et al., 2007):

$$S_v = -6\varepsilon(1-\varepsilon)\frac{dR}{du}\Big|_{u=0} \tag{6}$$

S_v can also be directly calculated from the reconstructed binary realization by counting the pixels at the void-solid interface.

A reconstruction of a porous medium in three dimensions should reproduce the same statistical correlation properties as those obtained from the two-dimensional image and defined by the n-moments of the phase function. In this work we only match the trivial one-point correlation function, the porosity ε, and the two-point auto-correlation function which contain information about the phase size, orientation and surface area. Other important descriptors that can be used are the lineal path function, the chord length function and the three-point correlation function (Torquato & Lee, 1990; Torquato, 2002). Reconstructing a material using limited microstructural information is an inverse, ill-posed problem, i.e. there are many realizations of a porous medium that share same the porosity and two-point correlation function. The choice to use only two functions can thus sometimes be inadequate to reproduce the material microstructure. Matching higher order correlation functions should also be considered (Kainourgiakis et al., 2000) but it is computationally much more expensive for the realization of sufficiently large 3D domains.

3.1 SA and process-based hybrid reconstruction of porous media

In the typical SA method we start from a completely random initial distribution of the phase function in space. In the proposed hybrid method we start with an initial configuration

provided by the output of a process-based method such as the described ballistic deposition of equal spheres. The porosity of the initial structure must be equal with that of the original structure (usually the source image).
The next step is to define the Energy, E, of our system. In this case E is the sum of squared differences between experimental correlation functions obtained from the SEM micrographs, and those calculated from the 3D generated structure.

$$E = \sum_i \sum_j \left[S_i(u_j) - S_i^{\exp}(u_j) \right]^2 \tag{7}$$

index i corresponds to the degree of the correlation function, and index j, corresponds to the digitized distance u. If only the two-point correlation function interests us, then $i = 2$ and the first summation is dropped out from eq. (7). Note that in the above algorithm, the one-point correlation function (porosity) is always identical to the experimental by construction. The SA algorithm for the reconstruction problem has as follows:

1. Create a candidate 3D image using random packing of spheres with a volume fraction equal to the target microstructure. Adjust the porosity, if necessary, using Grain Consolidation to match that of the target medium. Calculate the initial energy E_c.
2. A new trial state is obtained by interchanging (swapping) two arbitrarily selected pixels of different phases. This way the initial porosity of the structure is always preserved. Accordingly the energy of the trial state E_t is determined through eq. (7).
3. If $E_c \geq E_t$, the trial configuration is unconditionally accepted, and becomes the current configuration. On the other hand, if $E_c < E_t$ then the trial configuration is accepted with a probability $P(\Delta E) = e^{-\Delta E/k_B T}$.
4. Steps 2, 3 are repeated at the same temperature T.
5. Decrease temperature by a very slow rate and repeat steps 2-4.
6. The process terminates when the successful exchanges become less than a specified number per iteration.

The process is terminated when the number of accepted changes in different configurations becomes lower than a pre-specified value. The most time-consuming step in the SA method is the determination of E through the repeated calculation of the correlation function(s) at each pixel interchange. Nevertheless, this calculation can be improved considerably be observing that once $S_2(\mathbf{u})$ of the initial structure is calculated there is no need to fully sample all intermediate (trial) structures since any change in the correlation function(s) will be only due to the change along the x-, y- and z- direction that cross each altered pixel (two pixels at each swapping). This change in S_2 can be simply evaluated by invoking the sampling procedure only along those rows, columns and heights crossing the altered pixels, adjusting appropriately the initially stored $S_2(\mathbf{u})$.

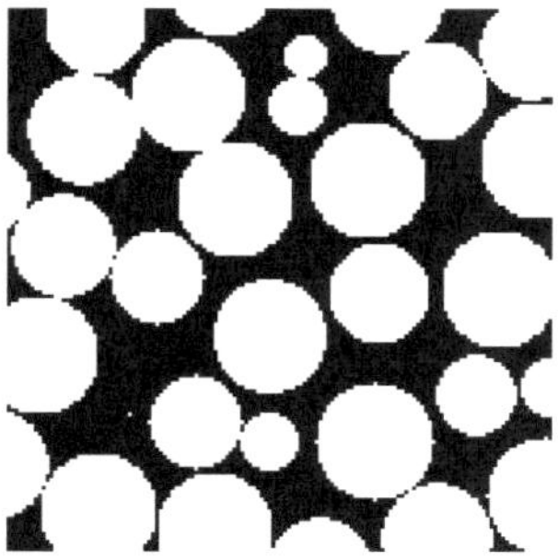

(a) Starting from a random sphere pack (ε=0.4)

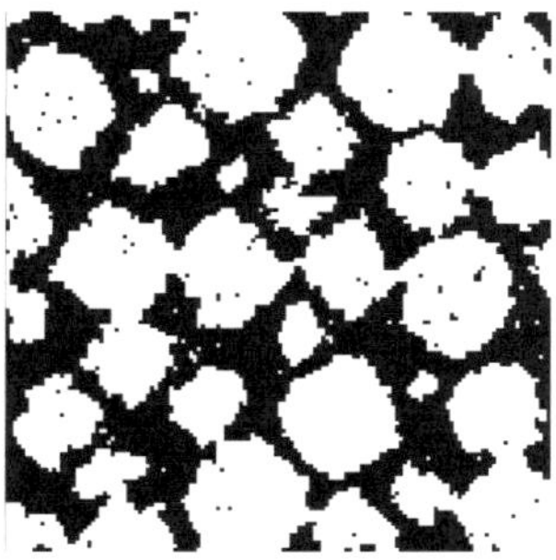

(b) Structure at step 25

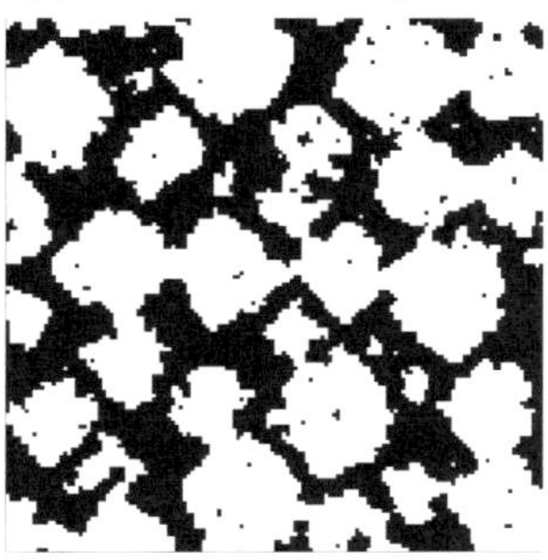

(c) Structure at step 70

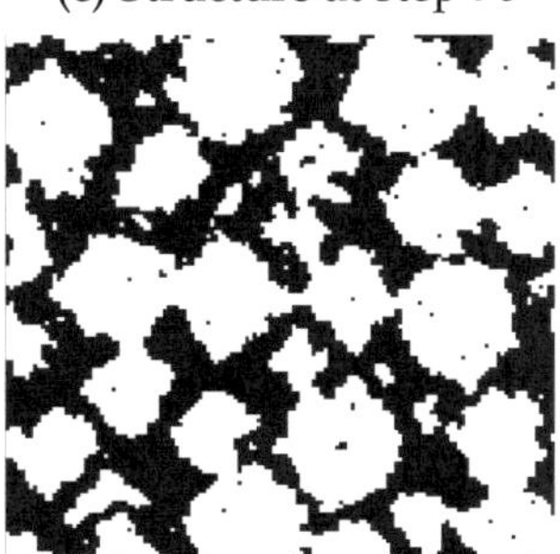

(d) Final structure (step 112)

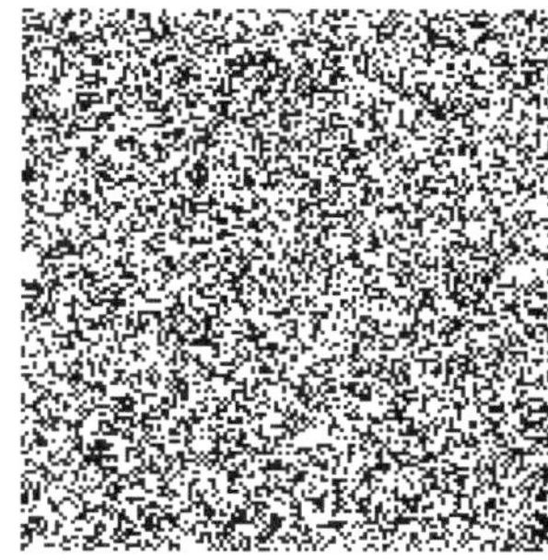

(e) Starting from a random material (ε=0.4)

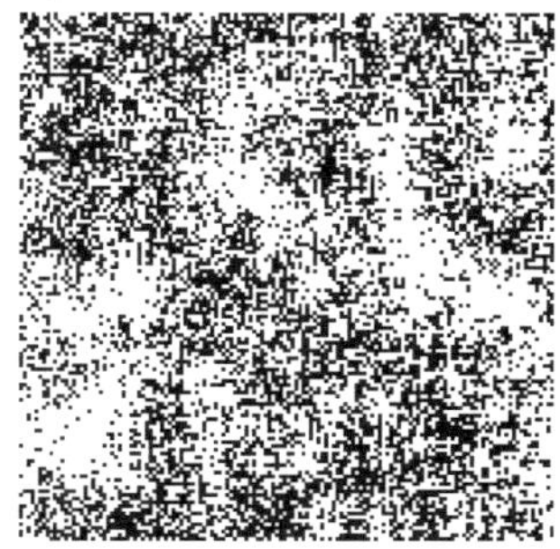

(f) Structure at step 83

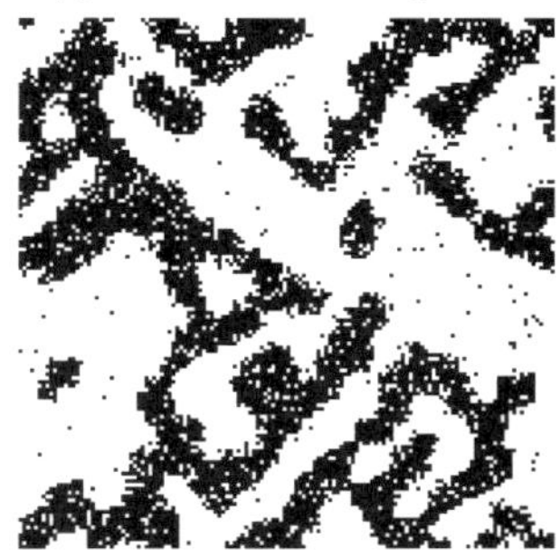

(g) Structure at step 110

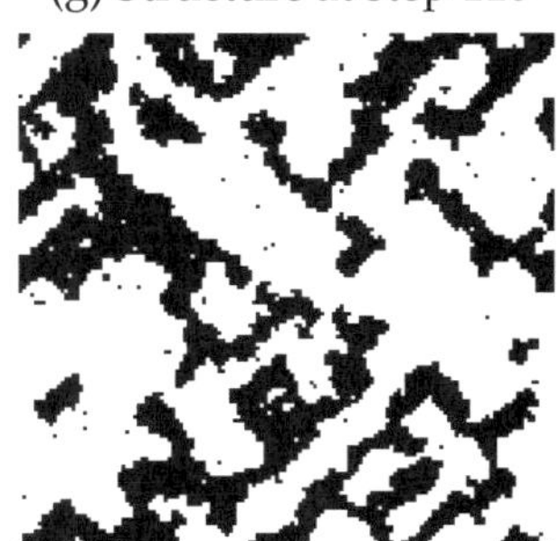

(h) Final structure (step 245)

Figure 1. Progress of the evolving microstructure at specific SA instances. The material shown is the sintered SiC case ($\varepsilon = 0.4$). Image size is 140×140 pixels. (solid is shown white)

An important parameter in the SA algorithm is the initial temperature T_0, particularly if the original structure is not truly random but has some noticeable degree of correlation as it is the case of starting with a random sphere pack as input. If T_0 is too low then the algorithm is quite immobile, not many swaps are accepted and the initial structure is quite close to the final structure. On the other hand, if T_0 is not too low, the algorithm becomes quite mobile, swaps are accepted more easily and the initial structure is not close to the final structure.

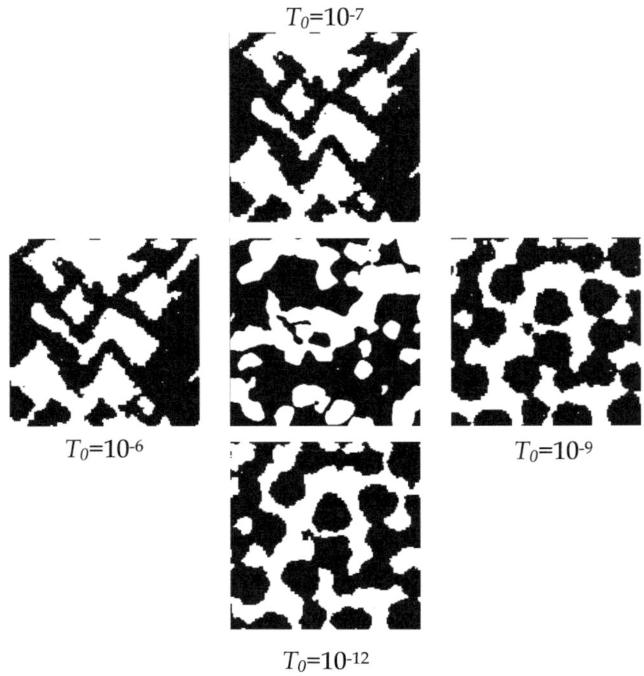

Figure 2. The effect of initial SA temperature, the target structure is in the middle, porosity is ~42% and solid-space is shown black.

4. Determination of the spatial fluid distribution

To determine the multi-phase fluid distribution in porous material, the porous structure is represented by a set of cubic voxels of length ℓ. Each voxel is labeled by an integer that corresponds to its phase. The solid phase is labeled as 0 while the fluid phases as $1,2,3,\cdots,n$. The saturation of the phase *i*, denoted as S_i, is the volume fraction of the pore space occupied by the phase *i*. The distribution of the *n* fluid phases in the pore space is determined assuming that the total interfacial free energy, G_s, is minimal. The function G_s can be evaluated by:

$$G_s = \sum_{i=0}^{n-1} \sum_{j>i}^{n} A_{ij} \sigma_{ij} \tag{8}$$

where A_{ij} is the elementary *ij* interfacial area and σ_{ij} the interfacial free energy per unit area of *ij* interface. The interfacial free energies obey Young's equation and consequently the following set of $\frac{n(n-1)}{2}$ equations is satisfied (van Kats & Egberts, 1998):

$$\sigma_{0i} = \sigma_{0j} + \sigma_{ij} \cos\theta_{ij} \tag{9}$$

where θ_{ij} is the contact angle that the ij interface forms with the solid surface, $i \neq 0$, $j \neq 0$ and $i < j$. The determination of the spatial distribution of fluid phases that corresponds to the minimum G_s is achieved by exploring all possible configurations. In practice this is impossible since the number of configurations is extremely high and consequently, the optimal one must be determined by importance-sampling procedures. When only two fluid phases are present, the simplest and rather inefficient heuristic technique that can be used is the following: A specified number of voxels, in random positions of the pore space, are marked as sites occupied by phase 1 while the rest are marked as belonging to phase 2. The number of sites occupied by each fluid phase corresponds to a desired fraction of pore space occupied by that phase (saturation). Then two randomly selected sites occupied by different fluid phases exchange their positions. This change results in a variation of G_s by an amount ΔG_s. To minimize G_s, one can accept every phase exchange trial with $\Delta G_s \leq 0$ and reject those where $\Delta G_s > 0$. However, due to the complicated G_s landscape with respect to the spatial distribution of the fluid phases, local minima are present and when the system reaches one of them no escape is possible (Knight et al., 1990).

The SA algorithm is used for the minimization of the multidimensional functions as originally adapted for a similar problem by Knight et al. (1990). Now, the new configuration that is generated by the phase exchange of random voxels is accepted with a probability given by:

$$p = \min\left(1, e^{-\Delta G_s / G_{ref}}\right) \tag{10}$$

where G_{ref} is an analog of the $k_B T$ parameter in the Metropolis algorithm and k_B, T are the Boltzmann constant and the ambient temperature respectively. After a sufficient number of iterations (usually ten-times the number of the pixels occupied by the fluid phases) and for a specific G_{ref} value, the system approaches the equilibrium state. By gradually decreasing G_{ref}, according to a specified "cooling schedule" and repeating the simulation process, using every time as initial configuration the one found as equilibrium state for the previous G_{ref} value, new lower energy levels of G_s become achievable. The process is considered complete when despite the change in G_{ref}, the number of accepted changes in different configurations becomes lower than a pre-specified value (typically when the ratio of the number of acceptable moves to the total number of trials becomes lower than 10^{-5}).

The above technique can be generalized for n fluid phases distributed in the pore space. Each voxel of the pore space is randomly characterized by an integer, $1,2,\ldots,n$, that corresponds to one of the existing fluid phases. The number of voxels that are occupied by

each phase satisfies a predefined saturation of the specific phase, S_i. Then, two voxels belonging to fluid phases are randomly selected, their phases are exchanged and the swap is accepted with probability according to eq. (10). This procedure is termed procedure (A).
To employ a more efficient minimization strategy, termed procedure B, n voxels occupied by different fluid phases are randomly selected at each minimization step. Then, $n(n-1)/2$ voxel-phase interchanges are performed. For the case of three fluid phases, the trial swaps are 1-2, 1-3 and 2-3. Each trial swap is accompanied by a variation of G_s by $\Delta G_{s,ij}$, where $i<j$. If at least one $\Delta G_{s,ij}<0$, the trial swap with the minimum $\Delta G_{s,ij}$ is accepted. In the opposite case, where every $\Delta G_{s,ij}>0$, the swap ij is accepted with probability p_{ij} defined as:

$$p_{ij}=\frac{e^{-\Delta G_{s,ij}/G_{ref}}}{n(n-1)/2} \tag{11}$$

Note that since $e^{-\Delta G_{s,ij}/G_{ref}}$ then $\sum_{i=1}^{n-1}\sum_{j>i}^{n} p_{ij}\le 1$ and therefore the system remains unchanged with probability $q=1-\sum_{i=1}^{n-1}\sum_{j>i}^{n} p_{ij}$. After a sufficient number of iterations, G_{ref} is gradually decreased and the system approaches the lowest energy configuration. It must be noticed that for $n=2$ the acceptance rule described by eq. (10) is recovered.
The simple case of a single pore with square cross section containing three fluid phases is selected to start with. The size of the pore is $50\times 50\times 100$ and the saturation of each phase is equal to $1/3$. The corresponding interfacial free energies in arbitrary energy units per unit area (square voxel length) are $\sigma_{01}=3000$, $\sigma_{02}=2500$, $\sigma_{03}=1200$, $\sigma_{12}=500$, $\sigma_{13}=1800$, $\sigma_{23}=1200$ and consequently $\theta_{12}=\theta_{13}=\theta_{23}=0$. Thus, the labels $1,2,3$ correspond to the non-wetting, intermediate wetting and wetting phases respectively. The "cooling schedule", the initial choice of G_{ref} and the minimization strategy are determined with the help of this simple pore geometry. The results obtained are used for the determination of the phase distribution in more complicated porous domains. The "cooling schedule" applied is:

$$G_{ref}=f^{N}G_{ref,0} \tag{12}$$

where f is a tunable parameter obeying $0<f<1$, N is the number of iterations for a given G_{ref} and $G_{ref,0}$ is the initial choice of G_{ref}. A "cooling schedule" of this form is used by Knight et al. (1990) and has the advantage that during the annealing process the variation of G_{ref} decreases, allowing for better resolution as the system approaches the optimal configuration. The value of the parameter f plays a dominant role in the simulation. Small f values decrease G_{ref} quickly resulting in fast simulations, however the risk of local minima trapping is high in that case. Contrarily, when f approaches unity the simulation becomes lengthy in time but the system escapes more efficiently from metastable configurations. Figure 3 illustrates the distribution of the fluid phases obtained for different f values. It is observed that for $f < 0.999$ the simulation produces final configurations where, although some clusters are present, the phases are rather randomly mixed. As f increases, physically sound configurations appear. The wetting phase (blue) is located in contact with the solid walls, the non wetting phase (red) forms a cylinder-like cluster at the center of the pore while the intermediate wetting phase (green) fills the space between the wetting and the non-wetting ones. In Fig. 4 the minimum total interfacial energy, $G_{s,min}$, is plotted against f. It is noteworthy that the total interfacial energy values are considerably close to each other, compared with their absolute values, although the distribution of the fluid phases in Fig. 3 is undoubtedly different. This indicates that the minimization procedure must be handled with care. In the present work, in order to achieve as accurately as possible the configuration with minimum interfacial energy, $f = 0.999$ is used.

At the beginning of the simulation, another important issue that must be considered is the initial choice of G_{ref}. The value of $G_{ref,0}$ must be large enough, approximately 30-times the highest σ_{ij} value, in order to ensure that the system is initially in a "molten" state and not trapped in a local minimum. When $G_{ref,0}$ is not large enough the system cannot approach the optimal distribution.

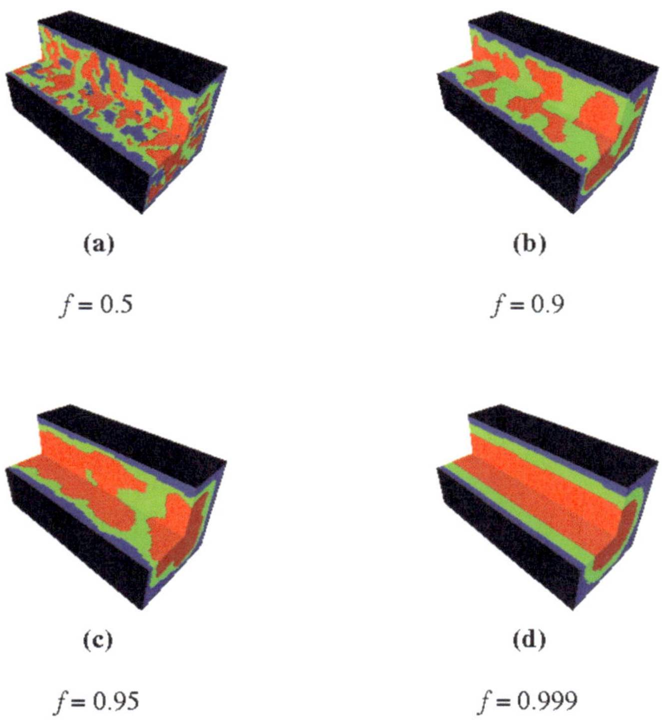

Figure 3. Phase distribution in a rectangular pore for different f values when three fluid phases are present. Blue color: wetting phase, green color: intermediate wetting phase, red color: non wetting phase. The saturation of each phase is $1/3$.

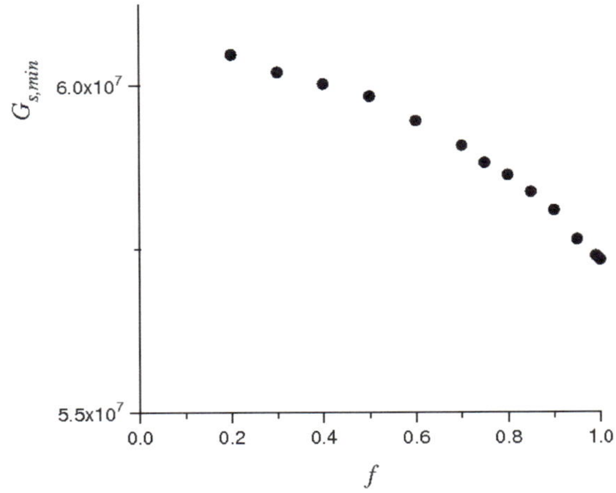

Figure 4. Minimum interfacial energy vsf for rectangular pore containing three fluid phases. The saturation of each phase is $1/3$ and the initial choice of G_{ref} is 10^5.

Figure 5. Phase distribution in a random sphere packing when three fluid phases are present. Blue color: wetting phase, green color: intermediate wetting phase, red color: non wetting phase. The saturation of each phase is $1/3$.

5. Evaluation of the SA method for the reconstruction problem

To demonstrate the proposed method (Politis et al., 2008) we have chosen to calculate the air permeability of a sintered silicon carbide (SiC) ceramic characterized in-house and the Ni-YSZ anode cermet of a solid oxide fuel cell (SOFC) found in the literature (Lee et al, 2004). The backscatter electron SEM micrographs of both materials were digitized using standard image processing techniques (Ioannidis et al., 1996). Both materials are consolidated, produced using a fine powder substrate that is sintered at an elevated temperature. In total we have generated two realizations for each material: one using the hybrid method and starting from the porosity-matching random sphere pack and one by using the SA algorithm with a random initial structure.

5.1 Constructing the microstructure

The reconstructed material domains are three-dimensionally periodic with a simulation volume of 140³ pixels and a porosity of ~40%. The mean pore size though differs by almost an order of magnitude: 10.2 μm for SiC and 0.9 μm for Ni-YSZ. In Fig. 6, we plot the two-point auto-correlation function for the test-target materials, as obtained from the digitized SEM images. The corresponding two-point correlation function of the reconstructed structure it is not shown as it is an exact match. This is expected because it is the only optimization target for the SA algorithm. If more additional correlation functions are added then the match becomes non-trivial. We can noticed that for SiC the $R_z(u)$ drops practically to zero after ~16 μm, meaning that there is no correlation after this length. Similarly, for Ni-YSZ, there is no correlation after ~4 μm. The domains used in the computations are equal to 140^3 pixels for both structures, resulting in spatial dimensions of 200 μm³ for SiC and 21.5 μm3 for Ni-YSZ.

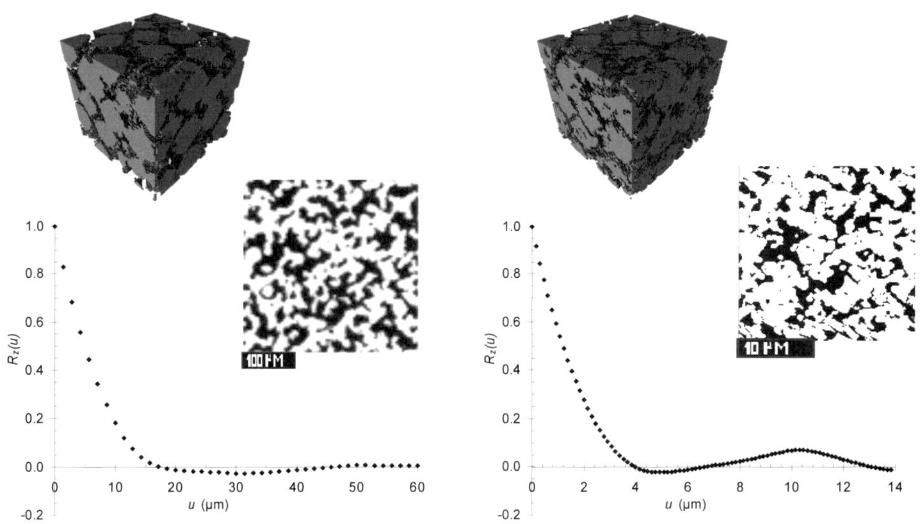

(a) SiC (100μm scale-bar) (b) Ni-YSZ cermet (10μm scale-bar)

Figure 6. Binarized SEM image, 2-point autocorrelation function and 3D hybrid reconstruction realization with a volume of 100³ pixels that represent 142.8 μm³ for the SiC and 15.4 μm³ for the Ni-YSZ (pore space is transparent for clarity). The Ni-YSZ porosity is 0.40 with an image size of 154×154 pixels (pixel length ~0.154 μm). The SiC porosity is 0.40 with an image size of 235×235 (pixel length ~1.428 μm).

5.2 Absolute permeability calculations

The absolute permeability of the porous material gives a measure of the resistance of the porous medium in the viscous incompressible fluid flow through its pore space. In a representative macroscopic element of homogeneous and isotropic porous material the superficial velocity, $\langle v_s \rangle$, of a viscous fluid is described by Darcy's law

$$\langle v_s \rangle = -\frac{k}{\eta} \cdot \overline{\nabla p} \tag{13}$$

where $\overline{\nabla p}$ is a prescribed pressure gradient, k is the permeability coefficient, which depends on the spatial distribution of solid and void phase and η is the fluid viscosity.

The calculation of the permeability coefficient k, requires the determination of the flow field at the microscale at creeping flow conditions, described by the Stokes equation coupled with the continuity equation:

$$\eta \nabla^2 \mathbf{v} = \nabla p \tag{14a}$$

$$\nabla \cdot \mathbf{v} = 0 \tag{14b}$$

where $\mathbf{v}$ and p are the local fluid velocity vector and the pressure, respectively. The boundary conditions are no-slip of the fluid at the solid-void interface and periodicity.

The numerical method employed in this work is a finite difference scheme, used previously in similar studies (Quiblier, 1984; Adler et al., 1990; Coelho, 1997; Liang et al., 2000). A staggered marker-and-cell mesh is used, with the pressure defined at the centre of the cell, and the velocity components defined along the corresponding surface boundaries of the rectangular cell. A successive overrelaxation method is used to solve for the microscopic velocity field. To cope with the numerical instabilities caused by the continuity equation, an artificial compressibility technique has been employed (Roache, 1982). In this fashion, the steady state problem is replaced by an unsteady one, which converges to the incompressible steady state solution at sufficiently long time. Convergence was achieved when the calculated flow rate values fluctuated less than 1% across the various cross-sections of the medium (Kikkinides & Burganos, 1999).

The results for the permeability of two different porous materials, using air as the flowing fluid, are summarized in Table 1.

	Air Permeability (m²)		
	Experiment	Simulation	
		Hybrid method	SA only
Ni-YSZ cermet	6.0×10^{-15}	5.67×10^{-15}	4.00×10^{-15}
Sintered SiC	9.4×10^{-13}	1.07×10^{-12}	8.12×10^{-13}

Table 1: Numerically calculated and experimentally measured permeability values for the Ni-YSZ cermet and sintered SiC.

It is evident that the permeability results obtained from the hybrid reconstruction method in excellent agreement for Ni-YSZ (within 5%) and very close for SiC (within 13%). The permeability of the SiC that resulted using the SA alone, overestimates the experimental value as much as the hybrid method underestimates it. For Ni-YSZ the error is much more pronounced (~33%) when using SA alone. The hybrid algorithm requires less than half the processing steps of the purely SA approach (see Fig. 1) resulting in a significant speed-up of the computations.

6. Evaluation of the SA method for the multiphase distribution problem

The assessment of the validity of the generated multiphase distributions in a pore structure is achieved by the measurement of the relative permeability of the porous material when two or more fluids are present. A significant simplification in the calculation of this property is to consider that only one fluid is flowing each time, the rest of the fluid(s) being immobile and simply treated as additional "solid" phase in the pore structure. In such a case one can still use the methodology outlined above for the determination of the absolute permeability treating the immobile fluid(s) as an expansion of the solid phase. This procedure can be performed sequentially for each fluid in order to get the relative permeability for each fluid in the multiphase configuration (Kainourgiakis et al. 2003; Galani et al, 2007).

6.1 Relative permeability calculations

The effective permeability for fluid i, $k_{e,i}$, which depends on the spatial distribution of solid and fluid phases, is calculated again through Darcy's law:

$$\langle v_{s,i} \rangle = -\frac{k_{e,i}}{\eta_i} \cdot \overline{\nabla p} \tag{15}$$

Where $\langle v_{s,i} \rangle$ is the superficial velocity of a viscous fluid in a sample of the homogeneous and isotropic porous medium and η_i is the fluid viscosity. Then the relative permeability for fluid i, $k_{R,i}$, is defined by dividing the effective permeability, $k_{e,i}$, with the absolute permeability, k, measured in the absence of other fluids:

$$k_{R,i} = \frac{k_{e,i}}{k} \tag{16}$$

It is evident that $k_{R,i}$ is a non-dimensional parameter.

Galani et al (2007) calculate the relative permeabilities of two and three phase fluid distributions for mono-dispersed random sphere packs when only one fluid phase is moving with low flow rate while the other fluid phase(s) are immobile and considered as an "expansion" of the solid phase. The results for the case of a two-phase fluid system of a wetting and non-wetting fluid are given in Fig. 7 and 8.

Fig. 7 presents relative permeability as a function of the effective saturation of the wetting phase (phase 2), $S_{e,2} = (S_2 - S_{im,2})/(1 - S_{im,2})$, where $S_{im,2}$ is the residual or immobile saturation of phase 2 when the non-wetting phase (phase 1) is stagnant while the wetting phase (phase 2) is flowing. Residual saturation is the amount of a fluid (e.g. oil) that remains in a porous material after the displacement of this fluid from another immiscible fluid (e.g. water) which penetrates the porous medium. The remaining fluid is stagnant and may form scattered clusters instead of a continuous phase. Fig. 7 also presents the corresponding experimental results that were obtained by Stubos (1990) for steel particle beads of porosity 0.4, as well as semi-empirical correlations from Levec (1986). In the present work, the residual saturation value, $S_{im,2}$, is set equal to 0.25, just as it was measured by Stubos (1990).

In all cases the computed relative permeability curves in very good agreement with the experiments in the whole spectrum of the effective saturation of the wetting phase, $S_{e,2}$.

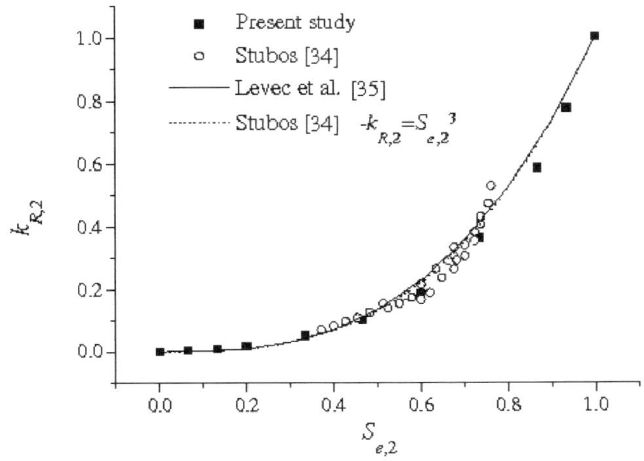

Fig. 7. Relative permeability of the wetting phase vs. the effective saturation of that phase, $S_{e,2}$, for the random packing of non-overlapping spheres of porosity 0.41.

Fig. 8 presents relative permeability as a function of the effective saturation of the non-wetting phase (phase 1), $S_{e,1} = (S_1 - S_{im,1})/(1 - S_{im,1})$, when the wetting phase (phase 2) is

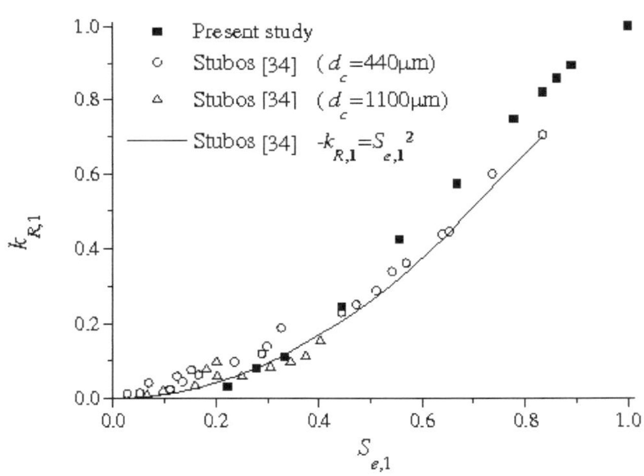

Fig. 8. Relative permeability of the non-wetting phase vs. the effective saturation of that phase, $S_{e,1}$, for the random packing of non-overlapping spheres of porosity 0.41.

stagnant while the non-wetting phase is flowing. The corresponding relative permeability experimental data that are used for comparison purpose have been obtained for low flow rates of the non-wetting phase. Fig. 8 also presents the corresponding experimental results that have been obtained by Stubos (1990) for steel particle beads of porosity 0.4, for two different values of equivalent diameters, d_c and also those of the correlated function $k_{R,1} = S^2_{e,1}$. In the present work, the residual saturation value, $S_{im,1}$, was set equal to 0.12, as it was measured by Stubos (1990). The observed differences between the results of the present work and the corresponding experimental ones are again relatively small and can be explained by potential deviations between the calculated and the experimental fluid-phase distribution.

7. Summary

The SA method was applied to the study of multiphase, disordered systems. Determining the phase distribution in the microstructure is of fundamental importance in making a connection with their effective properties that ultimately provides a tool to design optimized and tailor-made materials. SA was shown to provide a flexible and simple to implement methodology. Two conceptually distinct problem classes were used to illustrate the method: 1) an inverse problem, the 3D microstructure reconstruction from statistical descriptors (correlation functions) extracted from standard microscopic imaging methods (e.g. SEM/TEM) and 2) finding the global optimum corresponding to the minimum energy configuration in a multiphase system (pore-solid-fluid).

In solving the reconstruction problem there are many realizations of a porous medium that satisfy the minimization of the objective function that constitutes a functional of statistical descriptors with no physical significance per se. We have proposed a novel, hybrid methodology using a defined initial structure that attempts to incorporate the natural synthesis history of the material and thus address the non-uniqueness of solution issues in the inverse problem. The method was implemented with a random sphere pack obtained using ballistic deposition as the process-based step and then matched the porosity and pair correlation function of the material with SA.

For the multiphase system, tracing the minimum of the total free interfacial energy with SA is directly equivalent with the thermodynamic distribution of the fluid phases in the pore space. The optimum configuration for a given degree of phase partitioning is derived assuming that in equilibrium the total interfacial free energy reaches a global minimum value.

The procedure has been validated by the determination of the absolute and relative permeability in the multiphase system. The agreement of the results with pertinent literature data reinforces the validity of the proposed techniques.

8. References

Adler, P.M., Jacquin, C.G. & Quiblier, J.A. (1990), "Flow in simulated porous media", *International Journal of Multiphase Flow*, vol. 16, no. 4, pp. 691-712.

Adler, P.M. 1992, *Porous Media: Geometry and Transports*, . Butterworth-Heinemann, Boston, 1992

Bakke, S. & Øren, P.-. (1997), "3-D pore-scale modelling of sandstones and flow simulations in the pore networks", *SPE Journal*, vol. 2, no. 2, pp. 136-149.

Baldwin, C.A., Sederman, A.J., Mantle, M.D., Alexander, P. & Gladden, L.F. 1996, "Determination and characterization of the structure of a pore space from 3D volume images", *Journal of Colloid and Interface Science*, vol. 181, no. 1, pp. 79-92.

Berryman, J.G. (1985), "Measurement of spatial correlation functions using image processing techniques", *Journal of Applied Physics*, vol. 57, no. 7, pp. 2374-2384.

Bruck, H.A., Gilat, R., Aboudi, J. & Gershon, A.L. (2007), "A new approach for optimizing the mechanical behavior of porous microstructures for porous materials by design", *Modelling and Simulation in Materials Science and Engineering*, vol. 15, no. 6, pp. 653-674.

Bryant, S. & Blunt, M. (1992), "Prediction of relative permeability in simple porous media", *Physical Review A*, vol. 46, no. 4, pp. 2004-2011.

Coelho, D., Thovert, J.-. & Adler, P.M. (1997), "Geometrical and transport properties of random packings of spheres and aspherical particles", *Physical Review E, vol. 55*, no. 2, pp. 1959-1978.

Debye, P., Anderson Jr., H.R. & Brumberger, H. (1957), "Scattering by an inhomogeneous solid. II. the correlation function and its application", *Journal of Applied Physics*, vol. 28, no. 6, pp. 679-683.

Galani, A.N., Kainourgiakis, M.E., Papadimitriou, N.I., Papaioannou, A.T. & Stubos, A.K. (2007), "Investigation of transport phenomena in porous structures containing three fluid phases", *Colloids and Surfaces A: Physicochemical and Engineering Aspects*, vol. 300, no. 1-2 SPEC. ISS., pp. 169-179.

Jiao, Y., Stillinger, F.H. & Torquato, S. (2007), "Modeling heterogeneous materials via two-point correlation functions: Basic principles", *Physical Review E* - Statistical, Nonlinear, and Soft Matter Physics, vol. 76, no. 3.

Ioannidis, M.A., Kwiecien, M.J. & Chatzis, I. (1996), "Statistical analysis of the porous microstructure as a method for estimating reservoir permeability", *Journal of Petroleum Science and Engineering*, vol. 16, no. 4, pp. 251-261.

Kainourgiakis, M.E., Kikkinides, E.S., Galani, A., Charalambopoulou, G.C. & Stubos, A.K. (2005), "Digitally reconstructed porous media: Transport and sorption properties", *Transport in Porous Media*, vol. 58, no. 1-2, pp. 43-62.

Kainourgiakis, M.E., Kikkinides, E.S., Charalambopoulou, G.C. & Stubos, A.K. (2003), "Simulated annealing as a method for the determination of the spatial distribution of a condensable adsorbate in mesoporous materials", *Langmuir*, vol. 19, no. 8, pp. 3333-3337.

Kainourgiakis, M.E., Kikkinides, E.S. & Stubos, A.K. (2002), "Diffusion and flow in porous domains constructed using process-based and stochastic techniques", *Journal of Porous Materials*, vol. 9, no. 2, pp. 141-154.

Kainourgiakis, M.E., Kikkinides, E.S., Steriotis, T.A., Stubos, A.K., Tzevelekos, K.P. & Kanellopoulos, N.K. (2000), "Structural and transport properties of alumina porous membranes from process-based and statistical reconstruction techniques", *Journal of Colloid and Interface Science*, vol. 231, no. 1, pp. 158-167.

Kainourgiakis, M.E., Kikkinides, E.S., Stubos, A.K. & Kanellopoulos, N.K. (1999), "Simulation of self-diffusion of point-like and finite-size tracers in stochastically reconstructed Vycor porous glasses", *Journal of Chemical Physics*, vol. 111, no. 6, pp. 2735-2743.

Kikkinides, E.S. & Burganos, V.N. (1999), "*Structural and flow properties of binary media generated by fractional Brownian motion models*", Physical Review E, vol. 59, no. 6, pp. 7185-7194.

Kirkpatrick, S., Gelatt Jr., C.D. & Vecchi, M.P. (1983), "Optimization by simulated annealing", *Science*, vol. 220, no. 4598, pp. 671-680.

Kosek, J., Stepanek, F. & Marek, M. (2005), "Modeling of transport and transformation processes in porous and multiphase bodies", *Advances in Chemical Engineering*, vol 30, pp. 137-203.

Knight, R., Chapman, A. & Knoll, M. (1990), "Numerical modeling of microscopic fluid distribution in porous media", *Journal of Applied Physics*, vol. 68, no. 3, pp. 994-1001.

Kumar, N.C., Matouš, K. & Geubelle, P.H. (2008), "Reconstruction of periodic unit cells of multimodal random particulate composites using genetic algorithms", *Computational Materials Science*, vol. 42, no. 2, pp. 352-367.

Liang, Z., Ioannidis, M.A. & Chatzis, I. 2000, "Permeability and electrical conductivity of porous media from 3D stochastic replicas of the microstructure", *Chemical Engineering Science*, vol. 55, no. 22, pp. 5247-5262.

Lee, D.-., Lee, J.-., Kim, J., Lee, H.-. & Song, H.S. (2004), "Tuning of the microstructure and electrical properties of SOFC anode via compaction pressure control during forming", *Solid State Ionics*, vol. 166, no. 1-2, pp. 13-17.

Levec, J., Saez, A.E. & Carbonell, R.G. (1986), "Hydrodynamics of trickling flow in packed beds. Part II: experimental observations.", *AIChE Journal*, vol. 32, no. 3, pp. 369-380.

Mohanty, K.K. 2003, "The near-term energy challenge", *AIChE Journal*, vol. 49, no. 10, pp. 2454-2460.

Quiblier, J.A. (1984), "New three-dimensional modeling technique for studying porous media", *Journal of Colloid and Interface Science*, vol. 98, no. 1, pp. 84-102.

Politis, M.G., Kikkinides, E.S., Kainourgiakis, M.E. & Stubos, A.K. (2008), "A hybrid process-based and stochastic reconstruction method of porous media", *Microporous and Mesoporous Materials*, vol. 110, no. 1, pp. 92-99.

Rintoul, M.D. & Torquato, S. (1997), "Reconstruction of the structure of dispersions", *Journal of Colloid and Interface Science*, vol. 186, no. 2, pp. 467-476.

Roache, J. (1982), *Computational Fluid Dynamics*, Hermosa Publishing, Albuquerque.

Sankaran, S. & Zabaras, N. (2006), "A maximum entropy approach for property prediction of random microstructures", *Acta Materialia* vol. 54, pp. 2265–2276.

Sheehan, N. & Torquato, S. (2001), "Generating microstructures with specified correlation functions", *Journal of Applied Physics*, vol. 89, no. 1, pp. 53-60.

Spanne, P., Thovert, J.F., Jacquin, C.J., Lindquist, W.B., Jones, K.W. & Adler, P.M. (1994), "Synchrotron computed microtomography of porous media: Topology and transports", *Physical Review Letters*, vol. 73, no. 14, pp. 2001-2004.

Stubos, A. (1990) *Modeling and Applications of Transport Phenomena in Porous Media*, von Karman Institute for Fluid Dynamics, Lecture Series 1990-01.

Thovert, J.-., Yousefian, F., Spanne, P., Jacquin, C.G. & Adler, P.M. (2001), "Grain reconstruction of porous media: Application to a low-porosity Fontainebleau sandstone", *Physical Review E*, vol. 63, no. 6 I.

Tomutsa, L., Silin, D.B. & Radmilovic, V. (2007), "Analysis of chalk petrophysical properties by means of submicron-scale pore imagIng and modeling", *SPE Reservoir Evaluation and Engineering*, vol. 10, no. 3, pp. 285-293.

Torquato, S. (2005), *Microstructure Optimization*, in Handbook of Materials Modeling, Edited by Sidney Yip, Springer-Verlag, New York

Torquato, S. (2002), *Random Heterogeneous Materials: Microstructure and Macroscopic Properties*, Springer-Verlag, New York.

Torquato, S. & Lee, S.B. (1990), "Computer simulations of nearest-neighbor distribution function and related quantities for hard-sphere systems", *Physica A*, vol. 167, pp. 361-383.

Van Kats, F.M. & Egberts, P.J.P. (1998), "Spreading dynamics modeled by lattice-Boltzmann techniques", *Journal of Colloid and Interface Science*, vol. 205, no. 1, pp. 166-177.

Yeong, C.L.Y. & Torquato, S. (1998a), "Reconstructing random media", *Physical Review E*, vol. 57, no. 1, pp. 495-506.

Yeong, C.L.Y. & Torquato, S. (1998b), "Reconstructing random media. II. Three-dimensional media from two-dimensional cuts", *Physical Review E*, vol. 58, no. 1, pp. 224-233.

12

Simulated Annealing for Mixture Distribution Analysis and its Applications to Reliability Testing

Cher Ming Tan and Nagarajan Raghavan
Nanyang Technological University, Singapore
National University of Singapore

1. Introduction

1.1 Objective

Reliability is a very important field of study in today's era of technology. It is essential to quantitatively estimate the reliability of a product or device before it is mass produced and sold in the market through accelerated life tests. In reliability testing and data analysis, global optimization of the log-likelihood function plays a key role. An effective technique for this optimization is *Simulated Annealing (SA)*.
The objective of this chapter is to illustrate the applicability of *SA* to reliability data analysis. In particular, this optimization technique is very useful for *mixture distribution analysis* which will be described in detail later. The flow of the chapter goes as follows. A brief introduction to reliability statistics will be provided, intended to provide a basic outlook into this fascinating field to readers who are new to it. The role of SA in reliability statistics will be made clear through the developed log-likelihood function which needs to be optimized. This is followed by an insight into the need for mixture distribution analysis in reliability testing and assessment. The origin and methodology underlying the SA algorithm is then described in detail. The application of SA to mixture distribution analysis is presented and two practical examples of this application are provided from the microelectronics industry where electronic device reliability for gate oxide breakdown and electromigration phenomenon is assessed. Towards the end, techniques proposed in the literature to improve the efficiency of search for SA is presented and a concluding section directs the reader on the path to pursue further research investigations in simulated annealing.

1.2 Scope

The most fundamental form of the SA algorithm is employed in the reliability analysis presented in this chapter. Although more efficient designs of the SA algorithm have been made, they are not utilized in this work. The application case studies illustrate the application of SA for reliability analysis only in the field of microelectronics. The approach presented in this paper is nevertheless applicable to all practical reliability studies.

2. Introduction to reliability testing

2.1 Need for reliability

In today's competitive world and the age of globalization, it has become very essential for the manufacturing industry to keep up to the rapidly rising demands and expectations of the customers. To stay upbeat in the industry and capture large market shares, companies have been marketing aggressively through various strategies one of which is the value-add to their products. Cost competition will always be a lose-lose strategy. Reliability of a product is a good value-add to a product, and this is even more so for high-end electronic products that have revolutionized the world that we live in today. Good reliability brings good reputation and near zero field return during warranty period of the product.

Prior to implementing techniques to improve reliability of a manufactured product, it is essential to characterize and quantify reliability in a statistically credible manner so that improvement efforts can be evaluated. Reliability in itself is a large and wide field of research that encompasses statistical distributions to model failure characteristics and physics of failure to understand the nature of a failure mechanism and its associated failure mode.

The statistics of reliability modeling has been well investigated in the past few decades and therefore the statistical techniques for reliability quantification are established. However, the successful application of these models to practical usage has not been very fruitful. The problem lies in the inappropriate usage of these theories by practicing reliability engineers in the field as the assumptions behind some of the theories are not well understood by engineers in the industry and the lack of familiarity with the methodology to account for the presence of multiple failure mechanisms in a given reliability test data.

2.2 Accelerated life testing

As product reliability is being enhanced, the time taken to obtain the product failure time gets excessively longer, and a common practice therefore is to evaluate product reliability using ***accelerated life testing*** **(ALT)**. It is a technique whereby a product is stressed to failure at a much higher stress condition than the normal field operating condition experienced by it. The high stress condition serves to accelerate the failure mechanism so that failures can be observed sooner and adequate time-to-failure (TTF) data for the product can be collected for reliability analysis. Reliability analysis is most useful when it is obtained at the earliest stages of product development so as to facilitate improvements targeted at prolonging the lifetime of a product before it is mass produced and marketed to the customers. ALT is therefore gaining more relevance today as time-to-market gets shorter and shorter.

It is crucial that the high stress in ALT should only accelerate the failure mechanism observed in the field use condition and that it should not give rise to new unseen failure mechanisms which are not typically found at use stress levels. Otherwise, estimation and extrapolation of the product lifetime to the field conditions will not reflect field failures appropriately and this will defeat the very purpose of performing an ALT. On the other hand, there are many potential pitfalls to ALT as outlined by Meeker *et al.* (1998) and Suhir (2002), one of which is the occurrence of multiple failure mechanisms due to the high stress applied during the ALT.

To uncover the different failure modes and mechanisms underlying a product failure, it is necessary to perform a failure analysis (FA) on the failed products. Such an analysis requires precise sample preparation and accurate examination using various FA instrumentation tools and these observations do provide useful information on the physical nature of the localized failure site and the necessary corrective action to be taken to prolong or avoid these failures in the field. However, performing failure analysis for all the reliability test failures is practically impossible, and a way to classify and categorize failed products into different failure mechanisms based on statistical means is necessary so that only a few representative failed products in each category will need to be analyzed. In this chapter, we will present this method using the Simulated Annealing.

2.3 Statistical analysis of failure data

Having discussed the relevance of reliability and ALT in quality and reliability improvement strategies, we shall now get acquainted with the fundamental probabilistic and statistical definitions underlying reliability. We shall then show where ***Simulated Annealing (SA)*** comes into the picture of reliability data analysis. Please note that the terms *"device"*, *"system"* and *"product"* all refer to the same entity and they may be used interchangeably in this work.

2.3.1 Reliability Fundamentals

Reliability is defined as the probability that a product will perform its intended function over a time period t given that it is being used under stated operating conditions (Ebeling, 2005). It is a continuous function of time t and is denoted by $R(t)$. Mathematically, reliability can be expressed as in (1) where T is a continuous random variable representing the time to failure of the product with $T \geq 0$. For a given value of t, $R(t)$ is the probability that the time to failure is greater than or equal to t. Note that $\forall t \geq 0, 0 \leq R(t) \leq 1$; $R(0) = 1$ and $\lim_{t \to \infty} R(t) = 0$.

$$R(t) = \Pr\{T \geq t\} \tag{1}$$

The complementary function of R(t) is the failure probability or ***cumulative density function*** (CDF) which is denoted by F(t) and is written as:

$$F(t) = 1 - R(t) = \Pr\{T < t\} \tag{2}$$

The time derivative of the CDF gives the probability density function (PDF) of the distribution, denoted by f(t). The failure rate, $\lambda(t)$, represents the instantaneous rate of failures in a sample. It is an alternative way of describing a failure distribution. It is expressed as in (3). When $\lambda(t)$ is an increasing, decreasing or constant function of time, they are characterized by increasing failure rate (IFR), decreasing failure rate (DFR) or constant failure rate (CFR) respectively (Ebeling, 2005). A typical characteristic of the failure rate of any product is represented by the ***bathtub curve*** in Fig 1 (US Army, 2005) which shows the life pattern of the failure rate of the product from the instant of manufacturing and initial field use up to the later stages of the aging (wear-out) phenomenon. DFR relates to the infant mortality initial period of a system's operation; CFR is the period of useful system operation with the lowest failure rate and IFR accounts for the aging mechanism in the product due to gradual wear-out which is characteristic of its intrinsic failure. It is always desirable to ship out a product after its DFR regime so as to minimize field returns (this is done using a screening mechanism known as ***burn-in***) and prolong the CFR regime as long as possible such that the product's useful desired lifetime does not include the wear-out IFR region where increasing number of failures are expected to be seen.

$$\lambda(t) = \frac{dF(t)/dt}{R(t)} = \frac{f(t)}{R(t)} \tag{3}$$

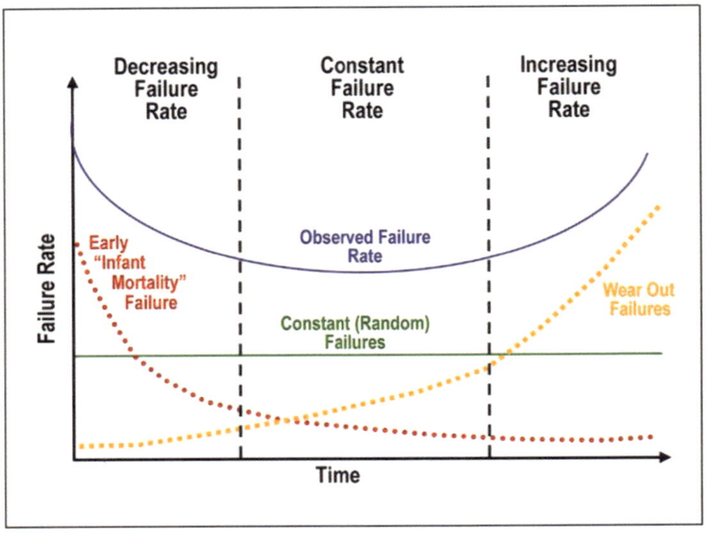

Fig. 1. Bathtub curve representing the failure rate regimes of a typical system (*US Army*, 2005).

The mean time to failure (***MTTF***) of a product is an important reliability metric and is given by (4). It represents the area under the reliability function spanning the whole range of the time continuum starting at t = 0.

$$MTTF = \int_0^\infty R(t)\,dt \tag{4}$$

There are various statistical distributions that are used to model the statistics of failure time of products. Examples are the exponential, weibull, normal, lognormal and gamma distributions, to name a few. The most widely applicable distribution amongst these for microelectronic devices are the Weibull and Lognormal distributions. The parameters of these distributions can be tuned so as to fit any set of failure data be it decreasing, increasing or a constant failure rate in the bathtub curve.
These statistical distributions are associated with different degradation behaviors of a product. For example, Weibull distribution is typically used to characterize catastrophic failures while the Lognormal distribution is used to represent gradual rates of degradation (Tobias *et al.*, 1995). We shall be considering the Weibull and Lognormal distributions in our case studies later on in this chapter and it is therefore useful to know the form that their

reliability functions take as shown below in (5) and (6). In (5), β is the shape parameter and η is the scale parameter which is also called the ***characteristic life*** of the product. The ranges $\beta < 1$, $\beta = 1$ and $\beta > 1$ represent the early failure, constant failure and wear-out failure regions of the bathtub curve respectively. The lognormal reliability function in (6) is also characterized by two parameters viz. the shape parameter (σ) and the median time to failure (t_{50}). The function $\Phi(z)$ is the standardized normal CDF.

$$R_{weibull}(t) = e^{-\left(\frac{t}{\eta}\right)^{\beta}} \tag{5}$$

$$R_{\log normal}(t) = 1 - \Phi\left(\frac{1}{\sigma} \cdot \ln \frac{t}{t_{50}}\right) \tag{6}$$

2.3.2 Failure data analysis

As mentioned earlier, to expedite the process of reliability testing and obtain useful information on the system (device) reliability prior to mass production, it is necessary to perform ALT. Having performed the ALT, there is a standardized set of rules to follow in collecting, transforming, fitting and analyzing the obtained failure data.

Having collected the failure data (t_i), the empirical CDF values, $F(t_i)$ are calculated as in (7) where n is the total number of product sample under test (i.e. sample size of ALT test) and i is the failure order number when the Time to Failure (TTF) values (t_i) and their order numbers are listed in ascending order. This approach to compute the empirical $F(t_i)$ values is known as the ***median rank method*** (O'Connor, 2002). Note that the expression in (7) is valid only for the case where all the devices are tested until failure is observed. In some cases however, we might terminate an ALT prior to all the devices failing in which case the test is said to be ***censored***. The test could be censored after a certain number of failures are observed (***failure terminated test***) or after a pre-determined fixed test time duration (***time-terminated test***). In the case of censored data, the index i is slightly modified to account for the effect of censoring. The details of these changes due to censoring are not critical here and readers interested in gaining more in-depth knowledge on this subject could refer to (O'Connor, 2002) for the complete details.

$$\hat{F}(t_i) = \frac{i - 0.3}{n + 0.4} \tag{7}$$

The empirical CDF values obtained are plotted on a graph paper that is unique to different statistical distributions and it is necessary to find the best fitting distribution parameters to fit this set of data accurately. One of the approaches to fit the data is to maximize the so called ***Likelihood function*** (***LKL***) which is given by the expression in (8) where t_f refers to the time-to-failure (TTF) data of the failed samples and t_c represents the censored data corresponding to those devices whose failure was not observed (Jiang *et al.*, 1992). Note that there could be various reasons for observing censor data such as unprecedented withdrawal of the test device during the test for other purposes, failure of the device due to some other failure mechanism which is not of interest in the analysis etc… In (8), n is the total number of devices under test while r is the number of actual failures observed during the test ($r \le n$); the symbol ψ represents the set of distribution parameters which is $\{\beta, \eta\}$ for a Weibull distribution and $\{t_{50}, \sigma\}$ for a Lognormal distribution and $f(t)$ and $R(t)$ are the PDF and reliability functions respectively.

$$LKL(t;\psi) = \frac{n!}{(n-r)!} \cdot \prod f(t_f|\psi) \cdot \prod R(t_c|\psi) \tag{8}$$

Typically, instead of maximizing the likelihood (LKL) function, it is conventional to perform a monotonic transformation of *LKL* by taking its natural logarithm and maximizing ln(LKL), which is called the ***Log-Likelihood function***, denoted here by *LLKL*. The expression for LLKL is given by (9) and the best fitting distribution parameter set, ψ, that fits the median rank CDF data in (7) is determined by optimizing the LLKL function.

$$LLKL(t;\psi) = \ln\left(\frac{n!}{(n-r)!}\right) + \sum \ln\left(f(t_f|\psi)\right) + \sum \ln\left(R(t_c|\psi)\right) \tag{9}$$

This *LLKL* function is the focus of our attention from now on since it is this function we will be optimizing to obtain the best fit to the ALT test data.

Fig 2 illustrates the median rank data plotted on a Lognormal distribution plot for a set of ALT data. The straight line fit shown is obtained by maximizing the *LLKL* function for the Lognormal distribution using the expression given in (9).

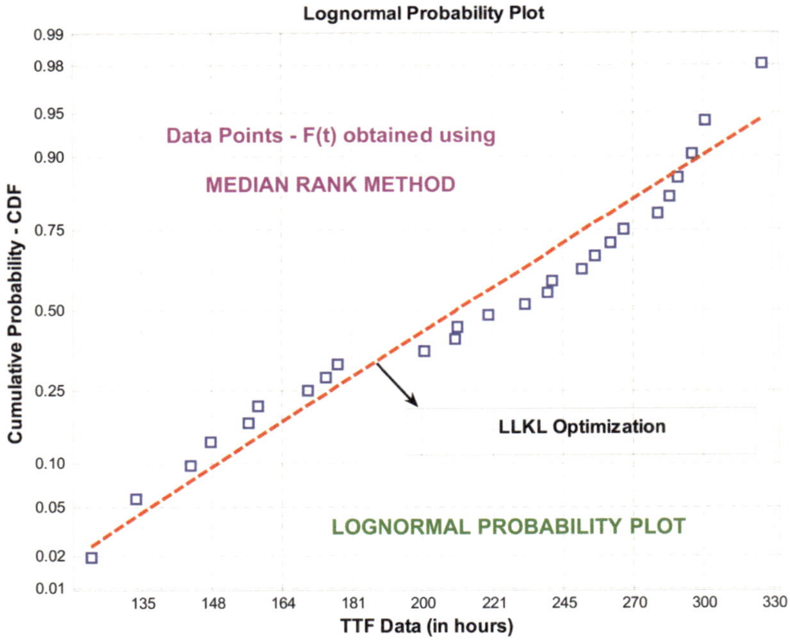

Fig. 2. Illustrating the Median Rank CDF data plotted on a Lognormal probability plot.

2.3.3 Optimization techniques for likelihood function

The *LLKL* function described in (9) is a multi-dimensional function of the statistical distribution parameters (ψ) that *f(t)* and *R(t)* are associated with depending on the distribution used. When the median rank CDF data needs to be fitted by suitable distribution parameters, various techniques could be used to do so. One of the approaches would be to plot the $F(t_i)$ points on the distribution probability plot graph paper and fit the points approximately by a straight line. The other approach would be to perform a least-square line of best fit regression analysis to determine the correlation coefficient and the slope and intercept of the fitting line which would in turn provide the values for ψ.

Other approaches include the Newton-Raphson method, Brent's method, Downhill Simplex method, Conjugate Gradient methods, Quasi-Newton methods etc... that are described in sufficient detail in (Press *et al.*, 2002). Some of these methods might only work under special cases where the gradients of the function to be maximized are defined at all points. In other words, they could be *gradient sensitive*. A few other methods above might work but might not be easy to code and implement. The most important fact regarding the above methods are that they are all *local optimization* algorithms and therefore, if we make use of these methods to find the global optimum, we would most likely end up getting a local optimum depending on the initial guess for the distribution parameters at the beginning of the algorithm execution. Since these methods are highly sensitive to the initial guess and are capable only of local optimization, it is necessary to look out for other techniques which are capable of finding the global optimum and are relatively insensitive to the user's initial guess.

One of the most useful, easy to implement and robust techniques for global optimization of the *LLKL* function is ***Simulated Annealing*** (SA) (Brooks *et al.*, 1995). It is useful for *LLKL* functions here because SA is capable of efficiently finding the *global optimum* of any *n-dimensional* function. As mentioned earlier, since *LLKL* functions are typically multi-dimensional, SA would be an easy approach to use to optimize them.

In optimization literatures, the function to be optimized is usually referred to as the ***objective function*** (Press *et al.*, 2002). We will follow the same convention here and call our *LLKL* function as the *objective function*. The equation to be solved for obtaining the best fit distribution parameters to the ALT test data is now expressed as in (10) where φ_1, φ_2, φ_3, ..., φ_k etc... are the statistical distribution parameter elements belonging to the set ψ. In short, $\psi = \{\varphi_1, \varphi_2, \varphi_3, \ldots, \varphi_k\}$. The log-likelihood function is being maximized with respect to each of the distribution parameters to obtain the optimal solution.

$$\frac{\partial LLKL(\psi)}{\partial \varphi_1} = \frac{\partial LLKL(\psi)}{\partial \varphi_2} = \frac{\partial LLKL(\psi)}{\partial \varphi_3} = \ldots = \frac{\partial LLKL(\psi)}{\partial \varphi_k} = 0 \tag{10}$$

Remember we mentioned earlier that a simple straight line fit to the median rank data on the probability plot paper would be sufficient to approximately determine the value of the distribution parameters. This method would however work only in the case where the failure data collected consists of a single distribution. In many cases, if there are more than one failure mechanisms in a device, then each failure mechanism would have its own statistical distribution with a uniquely defined set of parameters and hence, the overall failure data plotted would contain more than one distribution which cannot be represented by a single straight line. Such distributions which comprise of a mixture of more than one distribution are called ***mixture distributions*** (Titterington *et al.,* 1985). In the case of parameter estimation for a mixture distribution, simulated annealing is all the more useful since it helps determine the optimal set of parameters for any mixture distribution given its ability to perform global optimization for any n-dimensional system.

In summary, this section has provided a brief overview on the fundamentals of reliability statistics. The statistical theory on reliability data analysis was introduced and the relevance of simulated annealing in this context was highlighted. It should now be clear that our purpose is to make use of SA to globally maximize the n-dimensional log-likelihood function which will in turn help determine the optimal values of the distribution parameters that fit a given set of failure test data. In the next section, we shall treat mixture distribution in greater detail and show the stochastic process associated with it and the final form of the log-likelihood (*LLKL*) function for a mixture distribution that we will be maximizing.

3. Mixture distribution analysis

3.1 What are mixture distributions?

Any product or device in the field could fail due to various reasons. It is rare to find a device which fails due to only a single cause. In some cases, the presence of a failure mechanism triggers other failure mechanisms to evolve and as a result, the final device failure could be caused by the interaction and combined effects of these multiple failure mechanisms.

Every failure mechanism has its own statistical distribution that is dictated by the inherent physics of failure and the rate of degradation of the device is governed by the kinetic processes embedded in the failure physics. When there are more than one failure mechanisms, there are more than one statistical distributions present in the failure data. Therefore, the overall distribution describing the data is a ***mixture distribution***. Fig 3 shows the mixture distribution PDF plot consisting of two component distributions corresponding to two different failure mechanisms.

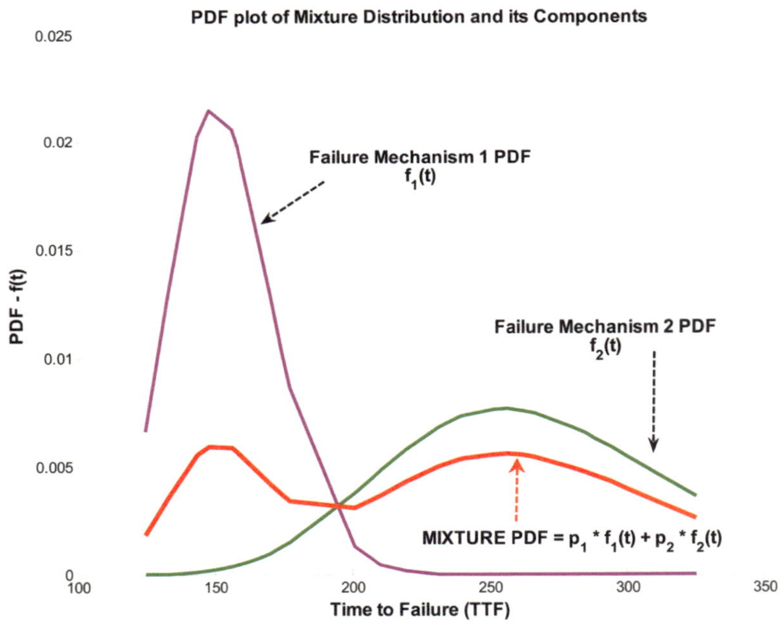

Fig. 3. PDF plot illustrating the effect of multiple failure mechanisms on the mixture distribution PDF.

Such mixture distributions are very commonly observed in ALT test data due to the high stress employed in the test. In the field of microelectronics, for example, package failures could occur due to solder electromigration at the bond pads or due to corrosion effects as a result of exposure to moisture. Similarly, the gate oxide layer in a MOS transistor could fail due to manufacturing induced voids and defects causing extrinsic failures, or percolation / leakage path evolution connecting the metal gate to the Si substrate due to intrinsic failures that evolve as a consequence of aging and wear-out phenomenon. Another popular observation includes the void nucleation and growth in the aluminium or copper interconnect metal lines that connect the transistor devices in an integrated circuit. While some voids evolve in the narrow high current density vertical vias connecting different levels of metallization, others evolve in the main interconnect line itself. One of the later sections clearly describes case studies that show the presence of mixture distributions in electronic device reliability.

3.2 Assumptions

In the mixture distribution analysis technique to be presented in this section, there are a few critical assumptions to be taken note of. One of the key assumptions is that the different failure mechanisms in the tested device are *independent* of each other and hence they do not influence the degradation or failure rate of each other. This assumption helps us in making use of the *principle of superposition* to model the overall mixture PDF. The other assumption we make is that the components of the mixture distribution belong to the same type of statistical distribution (e.g. Weibull, Lognormal etc…) and they are different only in the values of the distribution parameters that they take. Although this assumption is not necessary, it helps simplify the theory presented. Also, we assume that the number of distribution components in a given set of data is known apriori. There are various methods in the statistical literature that help estimate the number of distribution components in a given set of failure test data (Akaike, 1974; Bucar *et al.*, 2004). However, they are beyond the scope of our study here.

3.3 Mixture distribution theory

Let us now take a closer look at the statistics underlying the mixture distribution theory (Titterington *et al.*, 1985). For a device / system with *n* failure mechanisms each with its own failure distribution, the probability density function of the mixture distribution, $f_{MIX}(t)$, is given by (11) where $\{p_1, p_2, p_3, \ldots, p_n\}$ refer to the mixing weight or proportion of each component distribution in the overall mixture and $f_k(t)$ refers to the PDF of the kth component failure distribution; $k \in [1, n]$.

$$f_{MIX}(t) = p_1 \cdot f_1(t) + p_2 \cdot f_2(t) + \ldots + p_k \cdot f_k(t) + \ldots + p_n \cdot f_n(t) = \sum_{k=1}^{n} p_k \cdot f_k(t) \quad (11)$$

Based on this expression, the mixture CDF is given by (12) where $F_{MIX}(t)$ refers to the overall mixture distribution CDF and $F_k(t)$ corresponds to the CDF of each individual component distribution. The expression in (12) is obtained by a simple integration of (11) respect to time, *t*.

$$F_{MIX}(t) = \int_0^t f_{MIX}(t)dt = \sum_{k=1}^{n}\left[p_k \cdot \int_0^t f_k(t)dt \right] = \sum_{k=1}^{n} p_k \cdot F_k(t) \tag{12}$$

A similar expression to that in (12) may be written for the mixture distribution reliability function, $R_{MIX}(t) = 1 - F_{MIX}(t)$. Based on the above expressions, the log-likelihood function (*LLKL*) for a mixture distribution may be expressed as in (13), where $\psi = \{\varphi_1^{(1)}, \varphi_2^{(1)}, \varphi_1^{(2)}, \varphi_2^{(2)}, \ldots, \varphi_1^{(n)}, \varphi_2^{(n)}\}$ represents all the parameters of the n-component mixture distribution. The superscript (n) in the above notation refers to the index of each component distribution and ***n'*** and ***r'*** are the number of failure and censor data.

$$\begin{aligned} LLKL(t;\psi) &= \ln\left(\frac{n'!}{(n'-r')!}\right) + \sum\nolimits_f \ln\left[f_{MIX}(t_f|\psi)\right] + \sum\nolimits_c \ln\left[R_{MIX}(t_c|\psi)\right] \\ &= \ln\left(\frac{n'!}{(n'-r')!}\right) + \sum\nolimits_f \ln\left[\sum_{k=1}^{n} p_k \cdot f_k(t_f|\psi)\right] + \sum\nolimits_c \ln\left[\sum_{k=1}^{n} p_k \cdot R_k(t_c|\psi)\right] \end{aligned} \tag{13}$$

For example, in the case of a *Weibull n-component* mixture distribution, $\psi = \{\beta_1, \eta_1, p_1, \beta_2, \eta_2, p_2, \ldots, \beta_n, \eta_n, p_n\}$ where β, η and p refer to the shape parameter, scale parameter and mixing weight of each component of the mixture distribution. Since every failure results from one of the n-component distributions, the sum of all the mixing weights must add up to 1 as shown in (14). A higher mixing weight for a particular component implies that the failure mechanism corresponding to it is more dominating than other existing secondary failure mechanisms.

$$\sum_{k=1}^{n} p_k = 1 \tag{14}$$

Having developed the expression for *LLKL*, the optimal set of parameters in the set, ψ, are obtained by global maximization of the multi-dimensional *LLKL* function for which, as mentioned earlier, SA is one of the best techniques to use. The number of dimensions or independent variables in the *LLKL* function may be determined using (15) where n is the number of component distributions, r is the number of distribution parameters for each component distribution and m is the overall dimension of the objective function (*LLKL*) to be optimized. In (15), (r + 1) represents the number of distribution parameters accounting for the mixing weight p in addition to the standard parameters of the statistical distribution function.

$$m = n \cdot (r+1) - 1 \tag{15}$$

In this section, a concise description of the mixture distribution theory has been provided. The usefulness and relevance of mixture distributions in device reliability analysis is highlighted. The log-likelihood function for the case of mixture distributions is developed and this well-defined objective function will next need to be optimized using the SA method.

The next section describes the SA methodology and its algorithm in sufficient detail along with an insight into the interesting origin of this method. This will then be followed by two case studies on applying SA to reliability analysis of two critical microelectronic device failure mechanisms viz. gate oxide failures and electromigration phenomenon.

4. Application of simulated annealing

The methodology of Simulated Annealing can be traced back to the thermodynamic and kinetic processes of cooling, annealing and crystallization of materials such as metals and some liquids (Brooks *et al.*, 1995). When the initial temperature of a material is high, the atoms in it have a high diffusivity such that they can hop around to various lattice positions with different energies. When the temperature is reduced slowly or under conditions of slow cooling or gradual annealing, the atoms have sufficient time to diffuse and find lattice points of subsequently lower energies. Even if an atom happened to settle down at an intermediate local energy metastable equilibrium, the slow cooling and high initial temperature of the material system ensure that the atom overcomes the kinetic activation barrier to jump from the local energy equilibrium well and enter into the well that could possibly contain the global energy minimum. Note that any material would always want to globally minimize its Gibbs free energy and reach the most stable equilibrium state if sufficient time is provided for such a phenomenon to occur. Eventually, as this process of slow cooling is continued and as we let the material system equilibrate at each of the stepwise reductions in the ambient temperature, the atoms are most probable to have entered the energy well containing the global minimum and finally attain the global minimum energy level at sufficiently low temperatures. These low temperatures at later stages of the cooling (annealing) schedule are required in order to ensure that an atom which has entered the global energy minimum well does not jump out of it again.

In contrast, if the rate of cooling was rapid (also called *quenching*), then the atoms are most likely to settle down at local minimal energy metastable equilibrium states, which could result in the formation of polycrystalline or amorphous structures as opposed to crystalline structures that would result during a slow cooling process. Therefore, in order to reliably attain a global minimum energy state, two things are necessary – (A) High initial temperature (T_0) and (B) Slow rate of cooling.

Fig 4 (a) – (c) clearly illustrates the various transitions of atomic energies that could take place at a high initial temperature of T_0, lower intermediate temperature, T_K and final temperature of T_∞ under slow cooling rate conditions. Fig 5 shows the case of rapid cooling that results in a metastable local equilibrium. These figures supplement the explanation above and hopefully give a clear and simple illustration of the physics of annealing.

Based on the kinetics of annealing described above, the above concept has been adopted in optimization literatures as *simulated annealing*. The energy of the atom is analogous to the value of the objective function to be optimized. The position and movement of the atom is analogous to the parameter settings and shifts in its values as the optimization is carried out. The concept of temperature is adopted as it is using the Boltzmann criterion here and we could call the temperature as the "*mathematical temperature*" of the optimization system.

Having understood the origin of simulated annealing as an optimization procedure and its analogy to the physical cooling phenomenon, we shall now get acquainted with some of the common terminologies that we will be using in this section and then proceed on to explain the annealing algorithm in an easy to understand fashion.

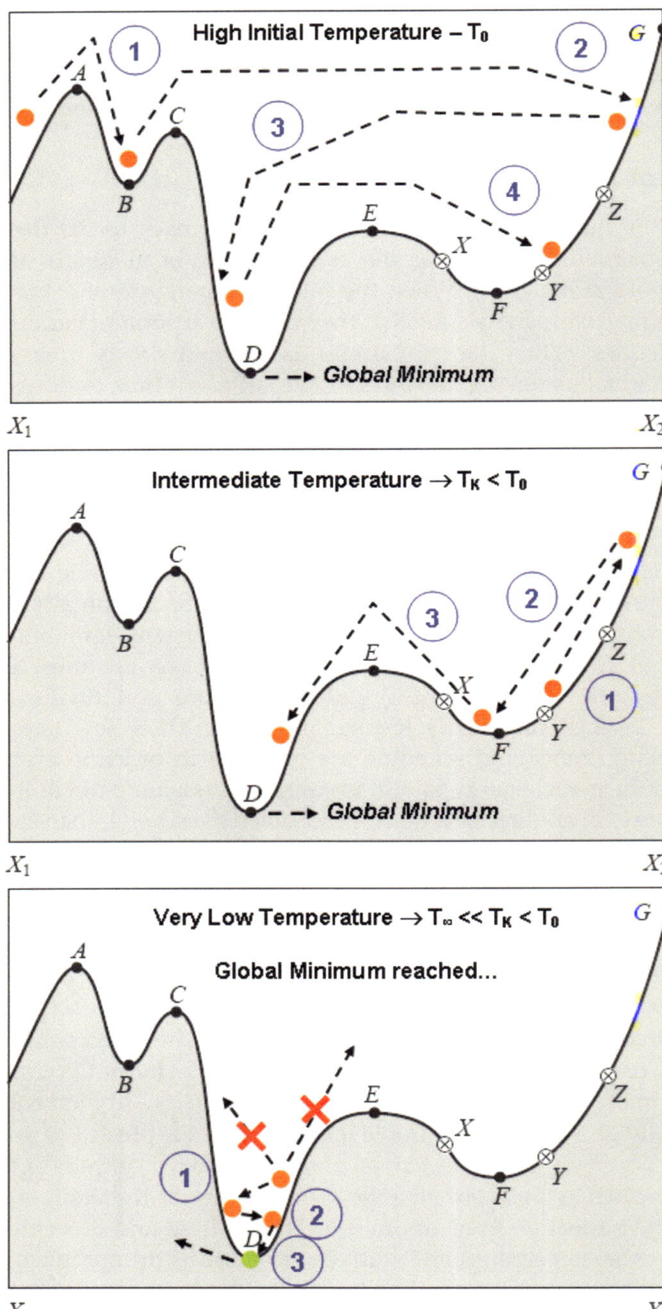

Fig. 4. (a) – (c): Illustrating the energy transitions of an atom in a material which undergoes slow cooling from a high initial temperature of T_0. Note that the basic sketch of the figure has been adopted from (Press *et al.*, 2002). The numbers in circles represent the successful energy transitions from one state to the other.

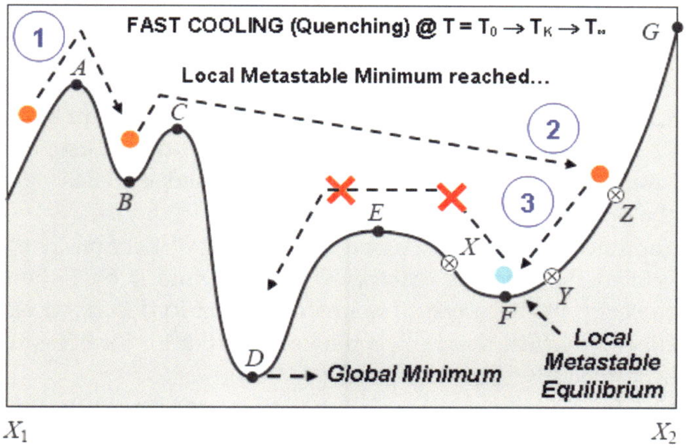

Fig. 5. Illustrating the energy transitions of an atom in a material which is subjected to rapid cooling that prevents it from entering the global energy minimum well. The atom finally attains a local metastable equilibrium state. Note: The basic sketch of the figure has been adopted from (Press *et al.*, 2002). The numbers in circles represent successful energy transitions from one state to the other.

4.2 Terminologies

Different authors use different terminologies to refer to the same parameter in the field of simulated annealing. Therefore, it is necessary to familiarize ourselves with the terms that we will be using in our approach to designing the SA algorithm. Let us now look at some of these terminologies:

- **Temperature Reduction Coefficient (λ)** – Since the accuracy of reaching the global minimum in SA depends on the *rate of cooling*, it is necessary to define rate of cooling as an input parameter of the SA algorithm.

$$T_K = \lambda^K \cdot T_0 \ ; \ K \in Z_0^+ \ ; \ 0 < \lambda < 1 \tag{16}$$

- **Initial Temperature (T_0)** – As mentioned earlier, we define the so-called "mathematical temperature" of a system analogous to the physical temperature in a kinetic process. The initial temperature for optimizing an objective function (such as the *LLKL* in our case) has to be kept high and it could be set to the approximate range of variation of the objective function which can be determined by a random space search of the objective function value for different input parameter combinations. Note that a precise value for T_0 is not required. We only need to specify a reasonable value for it that would ensure a successful SA algorithm run and a good start for this would be to set T_0 to the range of the objective function. We have been advocating that a high value of T_0 is essential for the SA to attain the global optimum value. It should be realized however that setting too high a value for T_0 makes the SA inefficient as it takes a longer time to reach the global optimum in this case. Very high values of T_0 make SA less preferred as it implies slower processing speed, larger memory requirements and increased computational load, all of which are undesirable. There is no hard and fast rule for setting the T_0 value. However, good judgment should be exercised when a user sets a value for it.

- **Markov Chain Iteration Number (N)** - This refers to the number of random space searches for the objective function at every temperature value. For every temperature the SA algorithm performs N random space searches in order to approach towards the global minimum. This sequence of N searches in the space spanned by the parameters is considered a *Markov Chain*. The value of N is to be set by the user and it should be set such that a quasi-static equilibrium state is reached at each temperature before transiting to the next lower temperature.
- **Objective Function (E_J)** - As discussed at the end of Section 2, the function to be optimized is called the *objective function* and we denote it by E_J here where E is the equivalent of energy in the physical annealing scenario described earlier and J is the index of the function which means E_J is the value of E after J successful state transitions from the initial value of $E = E_0$ at time t = 0.
- All the objective functions that we would be optimizing are to find the *global minimum* although SA could be easily tuned to find the global maximum too. This is because it is easier to interpret SA for global minimization given its analogy to Gibb's energy minimization of the atoms in a material. Therefore, if any of the functions (such as *LLKL* in our case) need to be maximized, then we can tune the objective function so that it is to be minimized. As an example, instead of maximizing the log-likelihood function (**LLKL**), we could equivalently minimize its negated function (**-LLKL**) since the maximum of a function is the same as the minimum of its negative
- **Boltzmann Theorem of Statistical Physics** - The probability that a system is in some state with energy E is given by (17) where k_b is the Boltzmann's constant and Z(T) is normalization function (Brooks *et al.*, 1995).

$$\Pr(Energy = E) = \frac{1}{Z(T)} \cdot \exp\left(-\frac{k}{k_b T}\right) \tag{17}$$

- **Metropolis Acceptance Criterion (MAC)** - In the physical process of annealing, Boltzmann's theory suggests that an atom could temporarily move from a lower energy state to a higher energy state at times in order to jump out a local minimum energy well in search of the well containing a global minima, although the probability of such jumps to higher energies is quite low. Applying this analogy to our mathematical optimization system, the probability that the system transits from a lower objective function value (E_J) to a higher objective function value (E_{J+1}); $E_{J+1} > E_J$ is given by (18) where $\Delta = (E_{J+1} - E_J)$. Since the accuracy of reaching the global minimum in SA depends on the *rate of cooling*, it is necessary to define rate of cooling as an input parameter of the SA algorithm.

$$\begin{aligned} &\Pr\left(E_J \to E_{J+1} \middle| E_{J+1} > E_J\right) = \exp\left(-\frac{E_{J+1} - E_J}{T}\right) \\ &\Pr\left(E_J \to E_{J+1} \middle| E_{J+1} < E_J\right) = 1 \end{aligned} \tag{18}$$

The Metropolis Acceptance Criterion (MAC) suggests that a state transition from a lower value (EJ) to a higher value (EJ+1) will successfully occur if and only if the probability of such a transition as given by (18) is more than the random number U generated from a uniform distribution with end limits 0 and 1. In short:

$$\left(E_J \rightarrow E_{J+1} \middle| E_{J+1} > E_J\right) \Leftrightarrow \exp\left(-\frac{E_{J+1}-E_J}{T}\right) \geq U(0,1) \tag{19}$$

With all the terminologies involved in the SA algorithm listed out and interpreted we know that the three main input parameters for executing SA are λ, T_0 and N. Having familiarized with these notations and their meaning, we can now dive straight into the stepwise procedure to be adhered to in implementing the actual SA algorithm.

4.3 Annealing algorithm

The stepwise execution of the annealing algorithm is as follows:

1. For every input parameter, φ_r, of the objective function, $E(\varphi_1, \varphi_2, \varphi_3, \ldots, \varphi_r)$, define the range of values $[\varphi_r^{MIN}, \varphi_r^{MAX}]$ that each of these parameters can take. This range could be guessed by the user's intuition or it could be set as wide as possible based on the realistic limits the parameters could take. For example, the obvious lower and upper limits for the mixing weight in the log-likelihood function has to be 0 and 1 respectively since it is a proportional quantity. If the user has some prior knowledge of the parameters of the objective function, then a narrower range can be defined for the parameters and this would help reduce the size of the parameter space to be spanned for locating the optimum and could help to reach the global minimum faster. Therefore, a narrow range for the parameters would be very useful in improving the efficiency of the SA algorithm.
2. Determine the initial value of temperature, T_0, by performing a random space search over the parameter subspace and finding the range of the objective function values obtained. Set this range to the value of T_0 as indicated in (20).

$$T_0 \equiv \left|E_{MAX} - E_{MIN}\right| \tag{20}$$

3. Set the values for the parameters λ and N. Typical values for λ range from 0.75 to 0.95 while for N, which is the number of markov state transitions for every temperature, values ranging from 1000 to 5000 can be set as a good rule of thumb.
4. At the initial temperature of $T = T_0$, start with an initial guess of the objective function E_0 by using some randomly generated combination of values for the input parameter based on the range defined for them.
5. Compare this value of E_0 with another randomly generated objective function value, E_1 and do the following:

IF $E_1 < E_0$
$\rightarrow$ Transit from State $E_0 \rightarrow E_1$.

ELSE-IF $(E_1 > E_0)$ and ***MAC*** criterion is satisfied
$\rightarrow$ Transit from State $E_0 \rightarrow E_1$.

ELSE
$\rightarrow$ Remain in State E_0
$\rightarrow$ Repeat the above steps for a different value of E_1.

END

6. The above pseudo code is iteratively followed N times for the initial temperature, T_0. If a transition takes place from $E_J \rightarrow E_{J+1}$ based on the above criteria, we call the transition a *successful transition*. Else, if some iteration does not lead to any transition to a different objective function value, then we refer to it as an *unsuccessful transition*. For the given temperature, T_0, the *fraction of successful state transitions* or what we call ***success ratio***, Ω is recorded.
7. Based on the annealing schedule defined by the temperature reduction coefficient in (16), transit to the new lower temperature of $T_1 = \lambda \bullet T_0$ and follow steps (5) and (6) iteratively N times.
8. This temperature reduction takes place sequentially and as steps (5) and (6) are executed for K successive cycles of temperature transitions, the objective function enters the global minima well and slowly approaches the global minimum point.
9. During the initial high temperature conditions, the Boltzmann probability is expected to be high and therefore, the MAC criterion is likely to be accepted most of the time thus resulting in a high value for the success ratio, Ω. However, as temperatures are reduced, MAC criterion is rarely satisfied and further transitions to lower objective function values also becomes less likely thus causing the Ω value to decrease. Eventually, after a large number of temperature cycles, we would reach a stage when the Ω value could be as low as 0.0001 which means that 1 in every 10000 transitions is successful. Such low values of Ω clearly indicate that the objective function has approached very close to the global minimum. In such a case, further algorithm execution is no longer necessary and the SA routine can be stopped. Therefore, the Ω parameter helps us define a stopping criterion that dictates the end of the SA routine code. Typically, we set values of $\Omega = 0.0001$ (1×10^{-4}) or 0.00001 (1×10^{-5}).

```
START

Initial Definition – {N, λ, T0}

Define Ω = 1, K = 0, J = 0.

Random space search → EJ.

WHILE (Ω > 0.0001)

    TK = λ^K • T0;

        FOR (x = 1:N)

            Random space search → EJ+1.

            IF EJ+1 < EJ
                → Transit from State EJ → EJ+1.

            ELSE-IF (EJ+1 > EJ) and MAC criterion is satisfied
                → Transit from State EJ → EJ+1.

            ELSE
                → Remain in State EJ
                → Repeat the above steps for a different value of EJ+1.

            END

        END

END

K = K + 1;

STOP
```

The SA algorithm execution explained above may be summarized in the form of a simple pseudo code as shown. The readers should by now have realized that the SA algorithm is a very easy to understand and simple to implement technique, yet so powerful in its ability to perform multi-dimensional global optimization. Note that for our case of mixture distribution analysis, the objective function, E, above would be replaced by the log-likelihood function (*LLKL*) defined earlier in (13).

4.4 Benefits and drawbacks of simulated annealing

Simulated annealing is a very powerful technique since it enables optimization of any n-dimensional objective function. It is one of the very few methods that can reliably find the global minimum or maximum value as desired. It is easy to comprehend and can be implemented using a simple C program code without any complexities. Another advantage of this approach is the gradient insensitivity since it does not optimize the function by taking its derivative unlike other methods such as the Newton-Raphson for example. Therefore, SA would be able to work for functions which have singularities and also non-analytical functions which might not have a closed form.

There are however, a few drawbacks in using the SA method. It is highly dependent on the initial temperature, T_0. For very large values of T_0, the algorithm might take too long to converge. Compared to other optimization techniques, it is more computationally intensive and relatively slow. The computational time scales exponentially with the dimensions of the objective function to be solved. We have been mentioning that the SA method converges to the global minimum as the success ratio, $\boldsymbol{\Omega}$, attains a very low value such as 0.0001. It should be noted that $\Omega \neq 0$ implies that there is still a possibility of a lower value existing in the global minima well which could not be found by the random searches performed. Therefore, although the SA method helps approach the global minima, it may not necessarily reach the exact optimum point.

These drawbacks necessitate the use of other local optimization algorithms in conjunction with the SA method so that the exact global minimum may be located (Tan *et al.*, 2007a). Also, in order to get around the problem of long execution times of SA, approaches to localize the search of the parameter subspace during the later executions when the global well might have been found could be investigated. A combined global - local search method would help make SA more efficient than its simplest version implemented above. These techniques to improve the SA algorithm will be briefly touched upon in Section 6. In the next section, we show the application of the SA algorithm to two real case studies on the reliability analysis of electronic device failure mechanisms viz. gate oxide breakdown and electromigration.

5. Case study – microelectronic device reliability

The very first attempts to apply *Simulated Annealing* for reliability analysis in microelectronic devices was taken up by Tan *et al.*, (2007a, 2008). This section brings out the application of SA into microelectronics reliability.

5.1 Gate oxide breakdown in MOSFETs

5.1.1 Physics of gate oxide breakdown

The progress in the electronics industry has been accelerating exponentially after the advancement of semiconductor technology and materials. In order to achieve higher computational capability and more compact portable devices, transistor dimensions are being downscaled rigorously from a 2 µm technology a decade ago to a 45 nm technology today in accordance to Moore's Law (ITRS, 2007). Downscaling of devices involves the proportionate shrinking of all the dimensions of the device in accordance to the constant field scaling rule (Taur *et al.*, 1998) including the gate oxide which is a thin insulating layer between the polysilicon gate and the silicon substrate in a conventional transistor as shown in Fig 6.

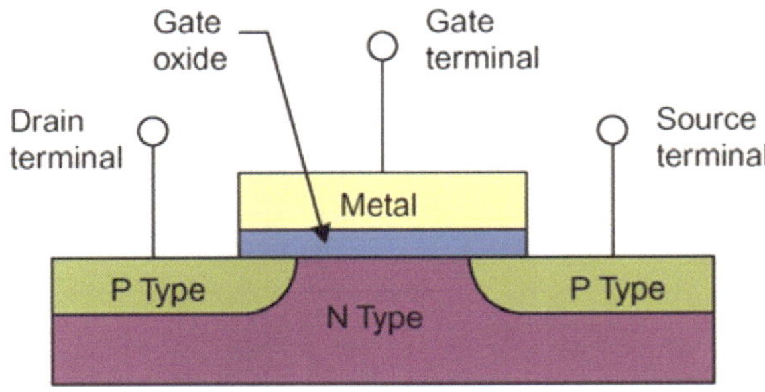

Fig. 6. Schematic of a MOS transistor showing the gate oxide layer sandwiched between the polysilicon gate and the Si substrate.

Although downscaling of device dimensions has helped realize faster and smaller electronic gadgets, we have reached the limit of downscaling where the gate oxide thickness is as low as 3 - 5 Å which is just one or two monolayers of the insulating material. Such thin oxides result in high leakage currents from the gate (G) to the substrate / body (B) due to percolation paths being formed that connect the two terminals. Moreover, during deposition of gate oxide using processes such as atomic layer deposition, some defects may be introduced in the oxide as a result of imprecise manufacturing or non-optimized processing. While these induced defects cause *extrinsic failures* of the device, the gradual formation of a percolation path in a perfect gate oxide layer could cause *intrinsic failures*. These intrinsic and extrinsic failure mechanisms consist of different distribution parameters although both of them belong to the Weibull distribution since gate oxide breakdown is catastrophic in nature. Therefore, based on physical considerations and previous failure analysis investigations, gate oxide breakdown can be characterized by a ***bimodal mixture distribution*** (Degraeve *et al.*, 1998). We shall make use of our SA approach to maximize the *LLKL* function for a two-component two-parameter Weibull mixture distribution.
The details of the test performed and the data collected are presented next. This will be followed by the results showing the application of SA to gate oxide failure data and final conclusions on the reliability of the tested gate oxide will be provided.

5.1.2 Accelerated life testing

A total of 51 MOS capacitor devices were subjected to an accelerated test at a high electric field stress of 10.4 MV/cm (Tan *et al.*, 2007a). The test was terminated at 207.5 s and 44 failures were observed. The remaining 7 devices either did not fail or were removed from the test prior to failure for other reasons. These 7 devices are considered as "censored". Based on the conducted test, the TTF data is obtained as shown in Table 1. The censored times of 4 devices removed from the test prior to failure are 0.15, 2.5, 19.03 and 120.21s. Three other devices remained operating at the test termination time of 207.5 s.

Table 1
TDDB failure data for the accelerated test at E-field stress of 10.4 MV/cm

5.847×10^{-10}	5.543×10^{-9}	2.999×10^{-8}	5.138×10^{-8}
4.628×10^{-7}	5.631×10^{-7}	5.301×10^{-5}	8.097×10^{-5}
2.246×10^{-4}	8.172×10^{-4}	2.09×10^{-3}	0.112
0.142	3.217	6.515	8.599
19.205	21.347	72.218	131.85
145.08	145.98	146.67	154.37
157.17	159.13	159.75	164.04
168.56	169.78	171.77	172.89
173.75	174.30	176.38	180.43
182.26	186.43	186.44	186.69
186.69	187.29	206.07	207.5

Table 1. Gate oxide breakdown failure data obtained from the accelerated life test (Tan *et al.*, 2007a).

5.1.3 Simulated annealing applied…

For a bimodal Weibull distribution, the mixture PDF, $f_{MIX}(t)$ may be expressed as in (21) where β and η are the shape and scale parameters and p is the mixing weight or proportion of each component distribution. The *LLKL* function is expressed as in (22). Note that there are 5 independent parameters to be determined in this function. They are η_1, η_2, β_1, β_2 and p_1. The mixing weight of the second component distribution, p_2 is dependent on p_1 since $p_1 + p_2 = 1$. Therefore, the SA optimization routine in this case comprises of five dimensions. Instead of maximizing the ***LLKL*** function, we shall be minimizing the negated ***–LLKL*** function using the standard SA algorithm as prescribed in the previous section.

$$f_{MIX}(t) = p_1 \cdot f_1(t;\beta_1,\eta_1) + (1 - p_1) \cdot f_2(t;\beta_2,\eta_2) \quad (21)$$

$$LLKL(\eta_1,\beta_1,\eta_2,\beta_2,p_1,(1-p_1)) =$$
$$\ln\left(\frac{n'!}{(n'-r')!}\right) + \sum_f \ln\left[\sum_{k=1}^{2} p_k \cdot f_k(t_f|\beta_k,\eta_k)\right] + \sum_c \ln\left[\sum_{k=1}^{2} p_k \cdot R_k(t_c|\beta_k,\eta_k)\right] \; ; \; \sum_{k=1}^{2} p_k = 1 \quad (22)$$

Table 2 shows the range of values that are set for each of the 5 parameter in the *LLKL* function. As discussed earlier, the range for the mixing weight is set to its default lower and upper limits of 0 and 1 respectively. A good precise range can be defined for these distribution parameters based on the user's understanding of the failure data and its spread. The SA routine is now executed as usual and the results of the algorithm are shown in Table 3 which gives the optimal values of the distribution parameters and also indicates the total number of attempted transitions in reaching the global minimum as a guide. Notice that it has taken 82,446 space search attempts to reach the optimum point from the initial random guess. Fig 7 shows the decrease in the *success ratio* (**Ω**) as the temperature is reduced. The number of temperature cycles $T_0 \rightarrow T_\infty$ needed was 58.

Range of Values for Distribution Parameters		
Parameter	Minimum	Maximum
η_1	0.001	100
β_1	0.01	2
η_2	130	250
β_2	6	12
p_1	0	1

Table 2. Range of values defined for the input parameters of the log-likelihood objective function in the SA algorithm.

Optimum values of the Distribution Parameters	
Parameter	Optimum Value
η_1	3.128
β_1	0.155
η_2	182.49
β_2	11.19
p_1	0.52
# transition attempts	82446

Table 3. Optimal values of the distribution parameters after the SA algorithm execution.

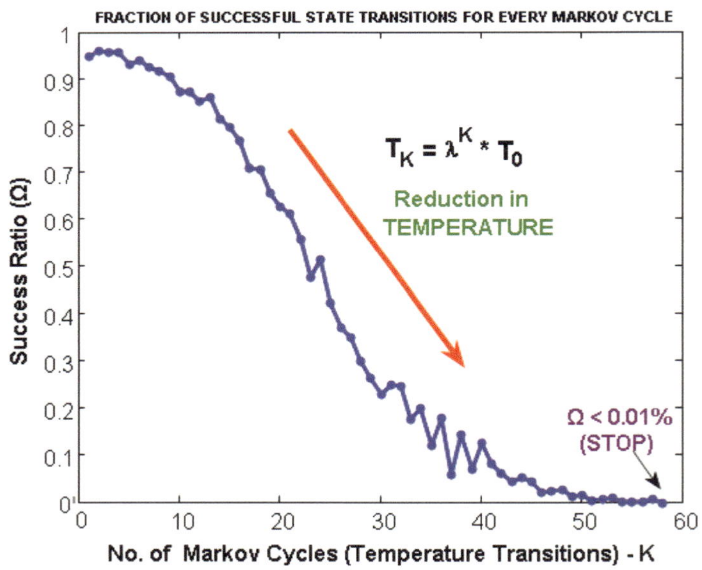

Fig 7. Drop in success ratio as the temperature is reduced and the global minimum is approached. The SA routine is stopped when $\Omega < 0.01\%$.

The trend of the log-likelihood function convergence during the SA algorithm execution for every successful Markov transition was traced out and this convergence trend is clearly evident in Fig 8. Note from the abscissa of this figure that the total number of successful Markov transitions was around 43,000 out of the 82,446 attempts.

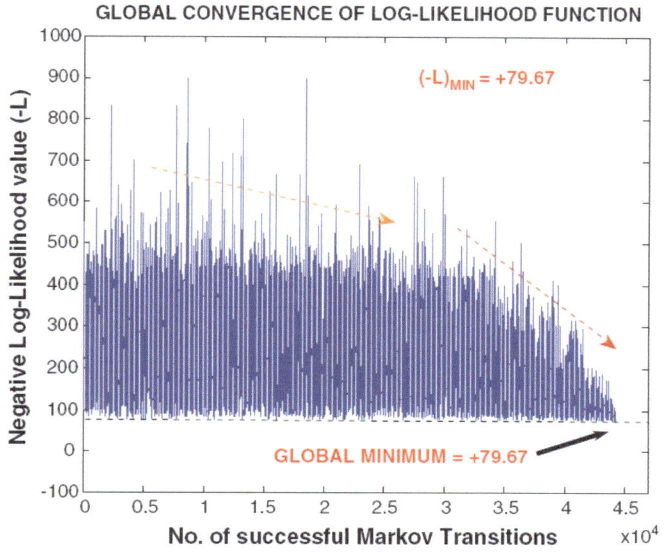

Fig 8. Convergence of the negative log-likelihood function (-LLKL) to the global minimum (Tan *et al.*, 2007a).

5.1.4 Reliability analysis results

5.2.1 Electromigration physics

Another key reliability concern in the microelectronics industry is the *electromigration* (EM) phenomenon in which the momentum exchange between the high speed electrons and the atoms in an Al or Cu metallization results in the movement of the atoms along with the electrons from the cathode (-) to the anode (+) thereby leading to void formation at the cathode ends causing high resistance and possibly open circuit and at the same time hillock formation at the anode terminal due to accumulation of metal atoms that could cause a short circuit if the hillock happens to protrude into the neighboring metal line. This *electron wind force* induced atomic migration is known as ***electromigration*** (Tan *et al.*, 2007b). Since the process of void nucleation and void growth is gradual, the statistical nature of EM is well represented by the *Lognormal distribution* (Tobias *et al.*, 1995, Tan *et al.*, 2007c).

Physical evidence reveals that there are potentially two regions in the interconnect structure where high current densities could cause voids to nucleate. These are at the inter-line via and the interconnect line itself. The voids tend to nucleate earlier in the via because of its lower cross-section and hence higher current density. The void formation in each of these two locations implies that each failure site has its own Lognormal distribution. Therefore, the overall statistics describing the EM phenomenon would involve a ***bimodal lognormal***

distribution (Raghavan *et al.*, 2007; Tan *et al.*, 2007d). Fig 10 shows a simple schematic of the interconnect test structure where voids are formed.

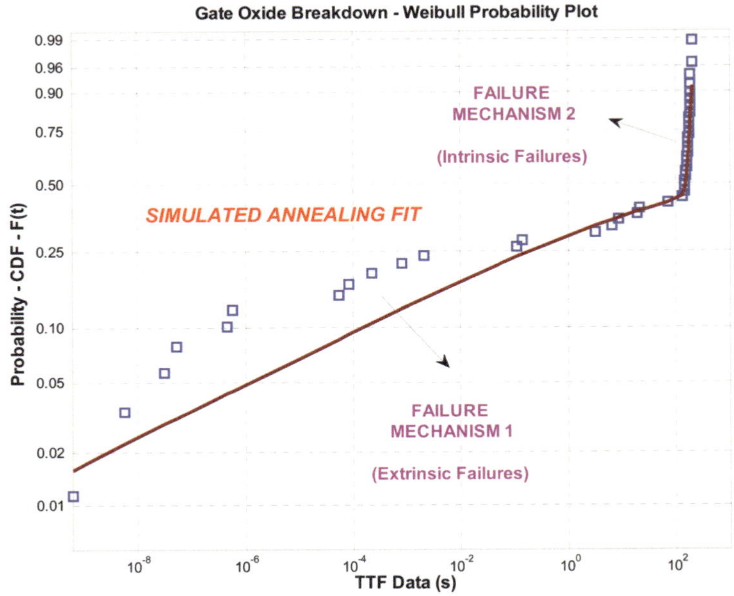

Fig 9. Cumulative Weibull probability plot of the gate oxide breakdown data showing a good fit (Tan *et al.*, 2007a).

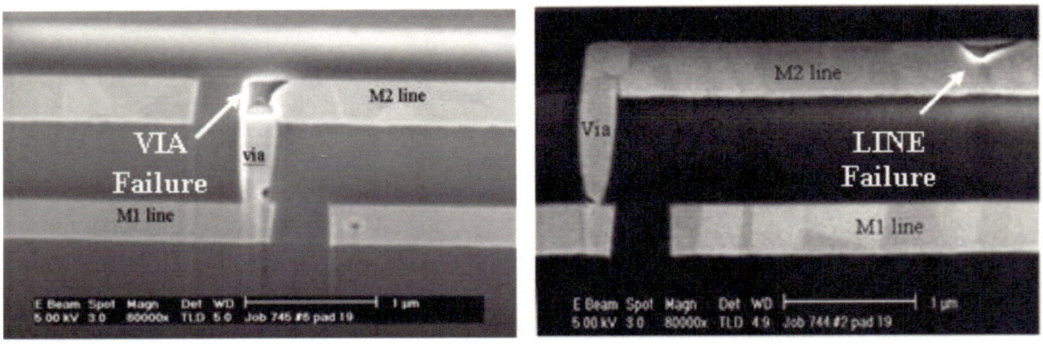

Fig 10. Void nucleation sites at the via and line during the EM phenomenon corresponding to a bimodal failure distribution (Tan et al., 2005).

5.2.2 Accelerated life testing

Experimental EM test data was obtained by performing accelerated package-level EM tests on aluminium via-line test structures with a current density stress that is ten times the nominal value and a stress temperature of 175ºC. The total number of failure data obtained was 26 and there were 6 censored data in this time-terminated test, indicated with an asterisk (*) in Table 4.

*100.21**	124.86	133.22	143.98
148.20	156.44	158.63	*165.19**
170.26	174.54	177.48	201.00
209.80	210.65	219.97	231.78
239.46	*240.74**	241.14	251.53
256.37	261.91	266.68	280.18
284.93	288.54	294.34	299.66
325.31	*330**	*330**	*330**

Table 4. Accelerated EM test data on an Al via-line test structure (Raghavan *et al.*, 2007).

5.2.3 Simulated annealing applied...

For a bimodal Lognormal distribution, the mixture PDF, $f_{MIX}(t)$ is given by(23) where t_{50}, σ and X_0 are the median life, shape parameter and incubation times of the failure process respectively and p is the mixing weight or proportion of each component distribution. The *LLKL* function is expressed as in (24). Notice that in addition to the standard two parameters t_{50} and σ in a Lognormal distribution, we have introduced a third parameter called ***incubation time*** (X_0) (Tan *et al.*, 2008). This third parameter refers to the time before which no void nucleation occurs in the EM phenomenon. In statistical literature, X_0 is referred to as the ***failure-free time***. The effect of X_0 on the PDF of a lognormal distribution is shown in (25). This is called a 3-parameter Lognormal distribution. Each failure mechanism (void and line failure) is expected to have its own failure-free time (X_0).

$$f_{MIX}(t) = p_1 \cdot f_1(t;t_{50(1)},\sigma_1,X_{0(1)}) + (1-p_1)\cdot f_2(t;t_{50(2)},\sigma_2,X_{0(2)}) \tag{23}$$

$$\begin{aligned} LLKL(t_{50(1)},\sigma_1,X_{0(1)},t_{50(2)},\sigma_2,X_{0(2)},p_2,(1-p_2)) &= \ln\left(\frac{n'!}{(n'-r')!}\right) \\ &+ \sum_f \ln\left[\sum_{k=1}^{2} p_k \cdot f_k\left(t_f \middle| t_{50(k)},\sigma_k,X_{0(k)}\right)\right] + \sum_c \ln\left[\sum_{k=1}^{2} p_k \cdot R_k\left(t_c t_{50(k)},\sigma_k,X_{0(k)}\right)\right] \end{aligned} \tag{24}$$

$$f(t;t_{50},\sigma,X_0) = \frac{1}{(t-X_0)\cdot\sqrt{2\pi}\cdot\sigma}\exp\left[-\frac{\ln^2\left(\frac{t-X_0}{t_{50}-X_0}\right)}{2\sigma^2}\right] \;;\; t > X_0 \tag{25}$$

$$f(t;t_{50},\sigma,X_0) = 0 \;;\; t < X_0$$

For the *LLKL* function in (24), there are 7 independent parameters whose optimal combination needs to be found. They are $t_{50(1)}$, σ_1, $X_{0(1)}$, $t_{50(2)}$, σ_2, $X_{0(2)}$and p_1. The mixing weight of the second component distribution, p_2 is dependent on p_1 since $p_1 + p_2 = 1$. Since the SA routine here is 7-dimensional as opposed to the 5-dimensional case when we investigated the gate oxide failures, the SA algorithm is expected to take longer time and more transition attempts would be required to find the global optimum of *LLKL*. As usual, instead of maximizing the ***LLKL*** function, we shall be minimizing the negated ***–LLKL*** function.

Table 5 shows the range of values that are set for each of the 7 parameters in the *LLKL* function. The SA algorithm is executed based on the parameter space defined in Table 5 and the critical values of the parameters that optimize *LLKL* are found. The results are depicted in Table 6. Notice that it has taken 620,000 space search attempts to reach the optimum point from the initial random guess. Out of these, 314,000 attempts resulted in successful state transitions. Fig 11 shows the decrease in the *success ratio* (**Ω**) as the temperature is reduced. The number of temperature cycles $T_0 \rightarrow T_\infty$ needed was 178.

Range of Values for Distribution Parameters		
Parameter	*Minimum*	*Maximum*
$t_{50(1)}$	125	325
σ_1	0.01	0.40
$X_{0\,(1)}$	0	120
$t_{50(2)}$	125	325
σ_2	0.01	0.40
$X_{0\,(2)}$	0	300
p_1	0	1

Table 5. Range of values defined for the input parameters of the log-likelihood objective function in the SA algorithm.

Optimum values of the Distribution Parameters	
Parameter	*Optimum Value*
$t_{50(1)}$	156.94
σ_1	0.397
$X_{0\,(1)}$	99.52
$t_{50(2)}$	259.81
σ_2	0.238
$X_{0\,(2)}$	127.74
p_1	0.375
# transition attempts	620,000
# successful transitions	314,000

Table 6. Optimal values of the distribution parameters after the SA algorithm execution.

The trend of the log-likelihood function convergence during the SA algorithm execution for every successful Markov transition was traced out and this convergence trend is as shown in Fig 12 which indicates the number of successful state transitions is 314,000.

5.2.4 Reliability analysis results

Based on the optimal values of the parameters obtained in Table 6, the cumulative probability plot of the failure data and the fitting line were represented on a Lognormal plot as shown in Fig 13. As seen in the plot, a very good fit of the data has been obtained and this is clearly indicative that the SA algorithm has approached the global minimum.

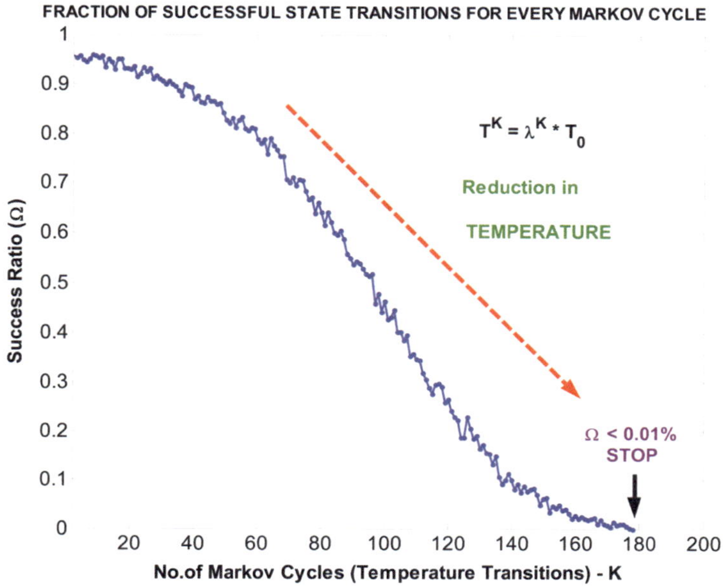

Fig. 11. Drop in success ratio as the temperature is reduced and the global minimum is approached. The SA routine is stopped when Ω < 0.01%.

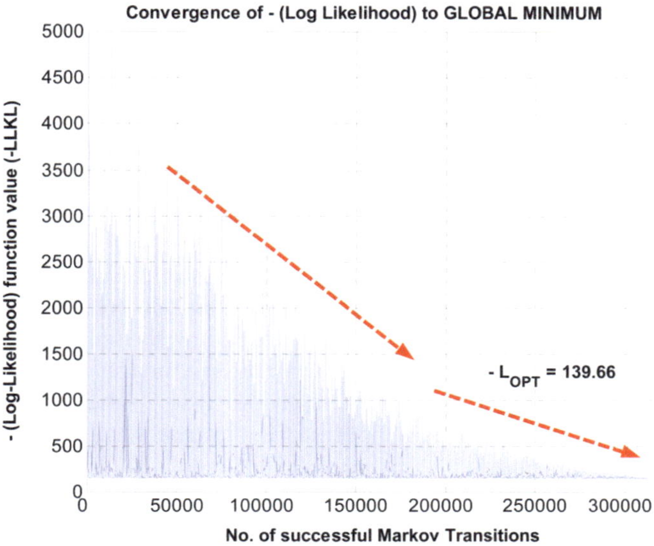

Fig 12. Convergence of negative log-likelihood function (-LLKL) to the global minimum for the bimodal lognormal distribution.

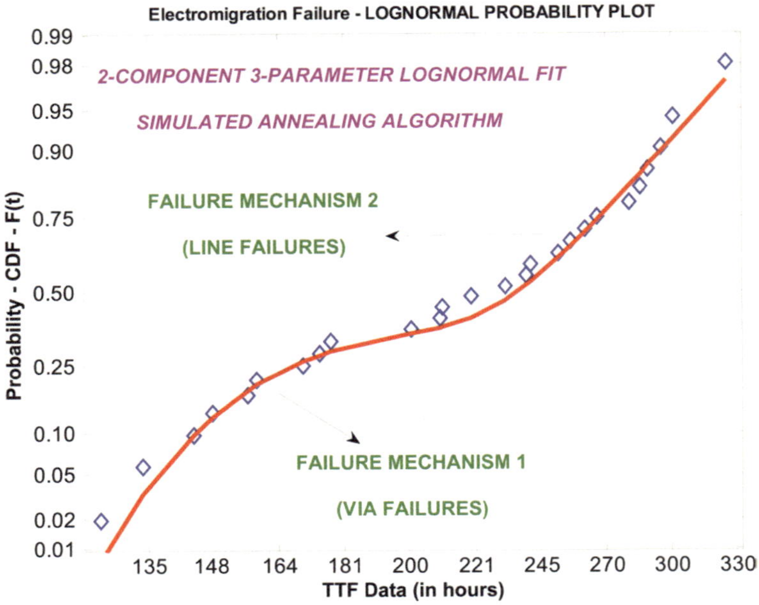

Fig 13. Cumulative bimodal Lognormal probability plot for the electromigration ALT test data showing a good fit (Tan *et al.*, 2007d).

The two case studies presented above have clearly illustrated the application of *simulated annealing* in reliability analysis. The reader should now be convinced that SA is indeed a very powerful optimization tool which comes in handy for log-likelihood optimization in mixture distribution analysis. Statistical literatures in the past have indicated that the conventional Newton-Raphson and similar techniques could be used to locally optimize *LLKL* only if all the components of the mixture distribution belong to the same type of statistical distribution (e.g. Lognormal, Weibull etc…) (Jiang *et al.*, 1992). They suggest that if different components of the mixture belong to different classes of statistical distributions, then optimization is a very difficult task. This difficulty is however overcome with ease when SA is used. Irrespective of the classes of distributions in the mixture, SA can reliably locate the global optimum value.

As discussed in Section 4.4, there has been a lot of research focusing on techniques to improve the efficiency of the SA algorithm. The algorithm that we have made use of is the simplest version of its kind. Although it is *effective* in finding the solution, it is not as *efficient* as we would want it to be. Most of the SA simulations for the case studies above took around 5 - 15 minutes using a *Pentium II* microprocessor, which is quite a long time considering practical situations where optimization might have to be performed very frequently.

We shall now briefly sketch out the recent efforts that have been undertaken towards improving the efficiency of *simulated annealing*.

6. Techniques to improve algorithm efficiency

Since SA takes a long time to approach the global optimum value especially for objective functions with many dimensions (parameters), some researchers have proposed the use of ***hybrid approach*** (Brooks *et al.*, 1995) whereby the SA is used only to enter the global well containing the optimum point. Once, the SA helps the objective function to enter into the global well, we switch over to conventional local optimization methods such as Simplex search, Newton-Raphson etc… which are highly efficient in exactly locating the local optimum. This approach would obviously work because the local optimum in a global well in fact corresponds to the global optimum. The usefulness of this approach is that it reduces the computational time and also helps locate the exact optimum point unlike SA which is capable of only *approaching* the optimal point in most cases. However, the problem of using this *hybrid approach* lies in determining the number of temperature shift downs after which the SA execution must be halted such that it has already entered the global well. This is a difficult question to answer.

However, successful attempts of using this approach have been carried out in the past (Brooks *et al.*, 1995). We investigated the suitability of this approach to our analysis on gate oxide breakdown (Tan *et al.*, 2007a) in the previous section. We halted the SA routine after a sufficiently long time and then used the *Expectation – Maximization* (E&M) algorithm (Jiang *et al.*, 1992) which uses the Newton-Raphson method to locate the local optimum of the log-likelihood function. Using this approach, we found that the fitting of the data improved considerably and a very accurate fit was obtained as shown below in Fig 14 in contrast to the fitting using SA alone in Fig 9. This is a clear indicator that a ***hybrid approach*** would be very useful to improve the efficiency as well as to locate the optimal point precisely.

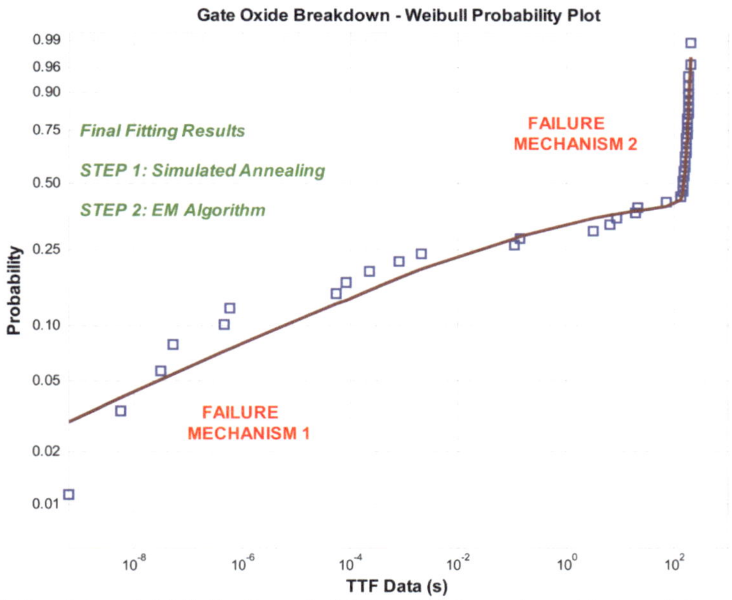

Fig 14. Cumulative bimodal Weibull probability plot for gate oxide breakdown failure data using the HYBRID SA approach (Tan *et al.*, 2007a) The fit to the data has improved considerably after the hybrid approach was implemented.

7. Conclusion

In spite of the robustness of the SA algorithm, there are still many improvements needed in order to improve its efficiency. This could be done using novel hybrid approaches as mentioned in Section 6 or using better localized space search techniques.
This chapter only gives a taste of the most basic form of *Simulated Annealing*. Other advanced implementations of SA have been successfully demonstrated in the recent past. This includes use of efficient algorithms to localize the space search around the global well and combining SA with other optimization approaches such as Genetic Algorithms and Neural Networks. For a comprehensive outlook into the novel forms of SA, interested readers may refer to (Goffe *et al.*, 1994; Yao., 1995; Bolte *et al.*, 1999; Suman *et al.*, 2006) for additional information. These sources will serve as a useful resource for heading towards further research in this field.
We have developed an in-house stand-alone reliability software called **MiDiAn** *Soft* ™ which has been developed to apply SA to reliability analysis and the results presented in Section 5 were based on the developed software package.
This chapter provides a good insight into the application of simulated annealing for mixture distribution analysis in the field of reliability engineering. We started of by talking about the need and importance of reliability in the manufacturing sector. The fundamentals of reliability statistics were introduced in Section 2 and the need for an accelerated life test was highlighted. The section on reliability math led us through to the log-likelihood function which needed to be globally optimized. We then established the link of simulated annealing in the context of reliability analysis and suggested the use of SA as a potential tool for global maximization of log-likelihood. The concept of mixture distribution was brought up in Section 3 and the log-likelihood expression was suitably modified to account for the presence of multiple failure mechanisms (multiple component failure distributions). A comprehensive yet simplified outlook into the simulated annealing algorithm was presented in Section 4 and this included a useful discussion on how the idea of annealing was borrowed from the thermodynamics inherent in the annealing process of materials. Having dealt with the theory of SA, we investigated two practical case studies in Section 5 from the field of microelectronic devices to clearly illustrate the application of SA to reliability analysis. Finally, a brief description of the approaches to modify SA so as to make it more efficient was presented.
We hope this chapter helped the reader realize and understand the robustness of the Simulated Annealing (SA) technique and its potential widespread applications in the field of reliability engineering. This chapter has been written with the intention to inspire reliability engineers to make best use of the Simulated Annealing approach.

8. Acknowledgements

The first author would like to acknowledge the opportunity provided by the School of Electrical and Electronics Engineering (EEE), ***Nanyang Technological University*** (NTU), Singapore for his reliability research. The second author would like to thank the ***Singapore-MIT Alliance*** (SMA) and ***National University of Singapore*** (NUS) for their encouragement and support.

9. References

Akaike, H., "A New Look at the Statistical Model Identification", *IEEE Transactions on Automatic Control*, AC-19, Vol. 6, pp.716-723, (1974).

Bolte, A. and Thonemann, U.W., "Optimizing simulated annealing schedules with genetic programming", *European Journal of Operational Research*, Vol. 92, Issue 2, pp.402-416, (1996).

Brooks, S.P. and Morgan, B.J.T., "Optimization using Simulated Annealing", *The Statistician*, Vol. 44, No. 2, pp.241-257, (1995).

Bucar, T., Nagode, M. and Fajdiga, M., "Reliability approximation using finite Weibull mixture distributions", *Reliability Engineering & System Safety*, Vol. 84, No. 3, pp.241-251, (2004).

Degraeve, R., Ogier, J.L., Bellens, R., Roussel, P.J., Groeseneken, G. and Maes, H.E., "A New Model for the field dependence of Intrinsic and Extrinsic Time-Dependent Dielectric Breakdown", *IEEE Transactions on Electron Devices*, Vol. 45, No. 2, pp.472-481, (1998).

Ebeling, C.E., "An Introduction to Reliability and Maintainability Engineering", *Waveland Press*, (2005).

International Technology Roadmap for Semiconductors, Executive Summary, www.itrs.net, (2007).

Goffe, W.L., Ferrier, G.D. and Rogers, J., "Global optimization of statistical functions with simulated annealing", *Journal of Econometrics*, Vol. 60, pp.65-99, (1994).

Jiang, S. and Kececioglu, D., "Maximum likelihood estimates, from censored data, for mixed-Weibull distributions", *IEEE Transactions on Reliability*, Vol. 41, Issue 2, pp.248-255, (1992).

Meeker, W.Q. and Escobar, L.A., "Pitfalls of Accelerated Testing", *IEEE Transactions on Reliability*, Vol. 47, No. 2, pp.114-118, (1998).

O'Connor, P, "Practical Reliability Engineering", *John Wiley & Sons*, (2002).

Press, W.H., Teukolsky, S.A., Vetterling, W.T. and Flannery, B.P., "Numerical Recipes in C – The Art of Scientific Computing", Chapter 10, *Cambridge University Press*, (2002).

Raghavan, N. and Tan, C.M., "Statistical Analysis of Multi-Censored Electromigration Data using the EM Algorithm", *14th IEEE International Symposium on the Physical and Failure Analysis of Integrated Circuits*, Bangalore, India, pp.257-262, (2007).

Suhir, E., "Accelerated life testing (ALT) in microelectronics and photonics : its role, attributes, challenges, pitfalls and interaction with qualification tests", *Proceedings of the SPIE – The International Society for Optical Engineering*, Vol. 4703, pp.162-183, (2002).

Suman, B. and Kumar, P., "A survey of Simulated Annealing as a tool for single and multiobjective optimization", *Journal of the Operational Research Society*, Vol. 57, pp.1143-1160, (2006).

Tan, C.M., Anand, V.A., Zhang, G., Krishnamoorthy, A. and Mhaisalkar, S., "New Analysis Technique for time to failure data in copper electromigration", *JEDEX Conference*, San Jose, (2005).

Tan, C.M. and Raghavan, N., "An approach to Statistical Analysis of Gate Oxide breakdown mechanisms", *Microelectronics Reliability*, Vol. 47, pp.1336-1342, (2007a).

Tan, C.M. and Roy, A., " Electromigration in ULSI Interconnects", *Materials Science & Engineering* R, Vol. 58, No. 1-2, pp. 1-75, (2007b)

Tan, C.M., Raghavan. N. and Roy, A., "Application of Gamma Distribution in Electromigration for Submicron Interconnects", *Journal of Applied Physics*, Vol. 102, 103703, (2007c)

Tan, C.M. and Raghavan, N., "Unveiling the Electromigration Physics of ULSI Interconnects through Statistics", *Semiconductor Science & Technology*, Vol.22, pp.941-946, (2007d)

Tan, C.M. and Raghavan, N., "A bimodal 3-parameter Lognormal Mixture Distribution for Electromigration Failures", *Thin Solid Films*, Accepted, In Press (2008).

Taur, Y. and Ning, T.H., "Fundamentals of Modern VLSI Devices", *World Scientific*, (1998).

Titterington, D.M., Smith, A.F.M. and Makov, U.E., "Statistical Analysis of Finite Mixture Distributions", *John Wiley & Sons*, (1985).

Tobias, P.A. and Trindade, D.C., "Applied Reliability", Second Edition, *CRC Press*, (1995). US Army Document, (2005).

Yao, X., " A new simulated annealing algorithm" *International Journal of Computer Mathematics*, Vol. 56, Issue 3 & 4, pp.161-168, (1995).

13

Reticle Floorplanning and Simulated Wafer Dicing for Multiple-project Wafers by Simulated Annealing

Rung-Bin Lin, Meng-Chiou Wu and Shih-Cheng Tsai
Computer Science and Engineering, Yuan Ze University
Taiwan

1. Introduction

As semiconductor process technology relentlessly advances into deeper submicron feature sizes following the Moore's Law, the cost of mask tooling is growing inexorably, up to 1, 1.5, and 3 million dollars for 90nm, 65nm, and 32nm process technology, respectively (LaPedus, 2006). Basically, the majority of smaller fabless integrated circuit (IC) design houses can hardly afford to have one mask set per design just for prototyping or low-volume production. In this circumstance, multiple project wafer (MPW) fabrication (or called shuttle run), long being used as a low-cost mechanism by the academics or industries (Pina, 2001; Morse, 2003) for prototyping their innovative designs, has become an indispensable chip fabrication vehicle. By way of an MPW program, the mask cost can be amortized among various designs placed in the same reticle (i.e., the same mask). Despite of assuming a lower mask cost per design, MPW requires each design to share more wafer fabrication cost. To minimize MPW wafer fabrication cost, the chips participating in a shuttle run should be properly placed in a reticle. This gives rise to the reticle floorplanning problem. Moreover, the wafers must be properly sawn to maximize the dicing yield. This gives rise to the simulated wafer dicing problem.

In this chapter, we propose several approaches based on simulated annealing (SA) to solving reticle floorplanning and simulated wafer dicing problems. Since SA's introduction (Kirkpatrick et al., 1983), it has played an important role in electronic design automation (Wong et al., 1988) such as circuit partitioning, placement, routing, etc. Many commercial physical design tools of this sort often employ SA as the last resort to optimize a design. The reasons for using SA are due to its ease of handling hard-to-be-satisfied constraints by transforming them into part of the objective function and a higher probability of finding a global optimum solution enabled by the capability of escaping local optima in practical implementations. Besides, an objective function for SA can be non-analytic or even does not have a closed-form expression so that it can only be evaluated using a non-calculus approach. Our simulated wafer dicing problem, though not having any hard-to-be-satisfied constraints, has a non-analytic objective function which makes SA quite suitable for solving this problem. Our reticle floorplanning problem has an even more difficult objective function which is the number of wafers required to be fabricated for a shuttle run and can only be evaluated using simulated wafer dicing. Despite of being able to handle non-analytic objective function, SA should not employ a hard-to-be-evaluated objective function because it would take too much time just to calculate the objective function for each new solution generated in the search process. To cope with this difficulty, we need to find a simple objective function that can best correspond to the original one, i.e., transforming the original objective function into a simpler one. Therefore, rather than solving a complicate simulated wafer dicing problem, we devise a much simpler objective function for our reticle floorplanning problem. Although we can not guarantee an exact correspondence between optimal solutions in the original problem and the one with a simpler objective function, such a transformation generally enables us to find a sufficiently good solution in a short time. Another key factor to successful applications of SA is about solution encoding. If a solution encoding could theoretically make SA reach every solution in the solution space, such solution encoding is certainly the best. However, if a solution encoding can not make this happen, the subspace defined by such solution encoding should include at least one global optimum. Unfortunately, we normally do not have such kind of insight. The two solution encodings used for our reticle floorplanning are no exception. However, both of them have their own edges. One enables SA to find a solution with a minimum number of wafers fabricated, whereas the other enables SA to find a solution with a smaller reticle area and with the number of required wafers very close to that of the former. The experimental results show that our approach when compared to the previous work (Kahng et al., 2005) not only achieves a double-digit saving in the number of wafers fabricated per shuttle run, but also produces a reticle floorplan with considerably smaller reticle area. This means a lot of saving in mask tooling and wafer fabrication costs.

Although minimizing the number of wafers fabricated in a shuttle run is often a good objective for reticle floorplanning, a minimum wafer use does not necessarily mean a minimum-cost wafer fabrication (not including mask tooling cost), not to mention a minimum-cost shuttle production (including mask tooling cost). Reticle floorplanning for cost minimization is a multiple objective optimization problem where the mask tooling and wafer fabrication costs are two conflicting goals (Bonn, 2001). Minimizing mask tooling cost favors a smaller reticle size (the smaller the reticle, the less the mask tooling cost, as shown in Figure 1), but this would pack chips closely within a reticle and hence create excessive sawing conflicts. As a consequence, more wafers must be fabricated. On the other hand, an attempt to align chips in a reticle to reduce sawing conflicts often requires a larger reticle and hence increases the mask tooling cost. Our reticle floorplanning method has a coefficient in the SA's objective function that can be explored to find a solution balancing these two objectives. We have employed our reticle floorplanning and simulated wafer dicing methods to perform a reticle design space exploration for finding a minimum-cost solution (Lin et al., 2007). In this article, we will not discuss this issue any further. Our presentation will focus on using SA for solving reticle floorplanning and simulated wafer dicing problems with an objective of minimizing the number of wafers fabricated. A lot of the material presented here can also be found in our previous work (Lin et al., 2007; Wu & Lin, 2007; Wu et al., 2008). For ease of presentation, we will use chip, project, and design interchangeably in this article.

The rest of this chapter is organized as follows. In Section 2, we elaborate on simulated wafer dicing and reticle floorplanning problems and their related work. In Sections 3 and 4, we present our SA implementations for these two problems, respectively. In Section 5, we draw a conclusion for our work.

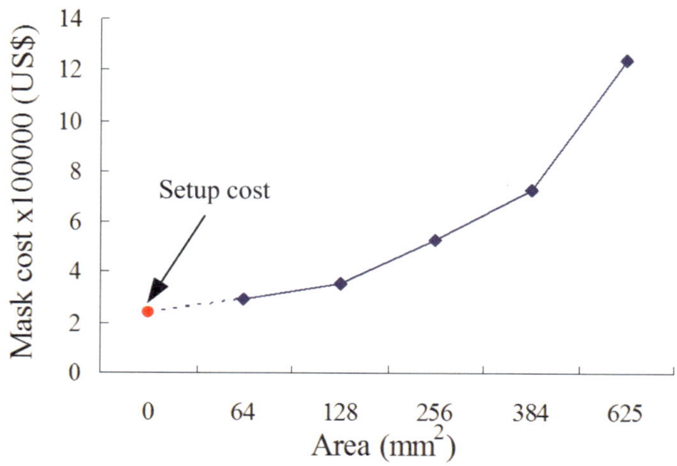

Fig. 1. Mask set cost for various field sizes for a 90nm technology node assuming that a chip has 8 very critical layers, 8 critical layers, and 12 non-critical layers (Pramanik et al., 2003)

2. Problem definition and related work

2.1 Problem definition

Here, we will give a problem definition of simulated wafer dicing and reticle floorplanning problems, respectively. Before doing this, we briefly describe how an MPW wafer is fabricated. Figure 2 shows a simplified wafer lithography apparatus. A reticle is placed between a condensing and a projection lens. The patterns in the reticle are exposed to the light so that a copy of these patterns can be transferred to the wafer during exposure. We call the region that has the patterns formed per exposure a *field*. The above process is repetitively executed to form an array of fields on a wafer. Normally, there is a 4X or 5X reduction in dimensions for the patterns printed on the wafer, i.e., the field dimensions are 1/4 or 1/5 of the reticle dimensions.

Prior to wafer fabrication, we need to know the number of wafers that must be fabricated. If a reticle contains multiple copies of the layout design for only one chip, these copies are normally arranged into an *m*-by-*n* matrix so that the number of wafers that must be fabricated can be easily determined. However, this cannot be done easily for MPWs because the chips in a reticle cannot usually be arranged into an *m*-by-*n* matrix, as shown on the left of Figure 3. In this situation, wafer sawing done to obtain dice for a chip may destroy many dice for other chips. This complicates the calculation for the number of wafers that must be fabricated. Therefore, simulated wafer dicing must be performed to determine the number of required wafers. In simulated wafer dicing, wafer sawing is tentatively performed on an MPW to determine which dice will be obtained. Normally, a sawing line must run across from one side of a wafer to the other side of the wafer, without stopping at the middle of the wafer. This requirement is called *the side-to-side dicing constraint*. To yield a good die, sawing should be performed at each of the four borders of a die with no other sawing line running across it. The example in Figure 3 shows that we can employ sawing lines v1, v2, v3, h1, h2, and h3 to obtain three good bare dice respectively for chips 4, 5, and 8, but this also destroys the dice for chips 6, 7, and 10. Although the dice for chips 1, 2, 3, and 9 are not destroyed, they are discarded due to a difficulty packaging them. The sawing lines made for a reticle (field) form a *reticle dicing plan*. All of the reticle dicing plans used for sawing a wafer form a wafer dicing plan (Kahng et al., 2004). Because of the side-to-side dicing constraint, all of the fields on the same row (column) will have the same horizontal (vertical) dicing plan. The problem is how to choose a set of reticle dicing plans to maximize dicing yield per wafer and thus minimize the number of wafers fabricated for a shuttle run. Figure 4(a) shows a wafer dicing plan that yields six dice per wafer respectively for the four chips 1, 2, 3, and 4 contained in a reticle. Given that the required production volumes are 24, 48, 24, and 48 dice for chips 1, 2, 3, and 4, respectively, the number of wafers needed is eight. However, the number of wafers is reduced to six if the wafer dicing plan in Figure 4(b) is used. The simulated wafer dicing problem is formally defined below.

Simulated Wafer Dicing Problem (SWDP): *Given a reticle floorplan of N chips and the required production volume V_p for chip p, p=1..N, determine the wafer dicing plan for each of the Q wafers under the side-to-side dicing constraint such that the number B_p of good bare dice is greater than or equal to V_p and Q is minimized.*

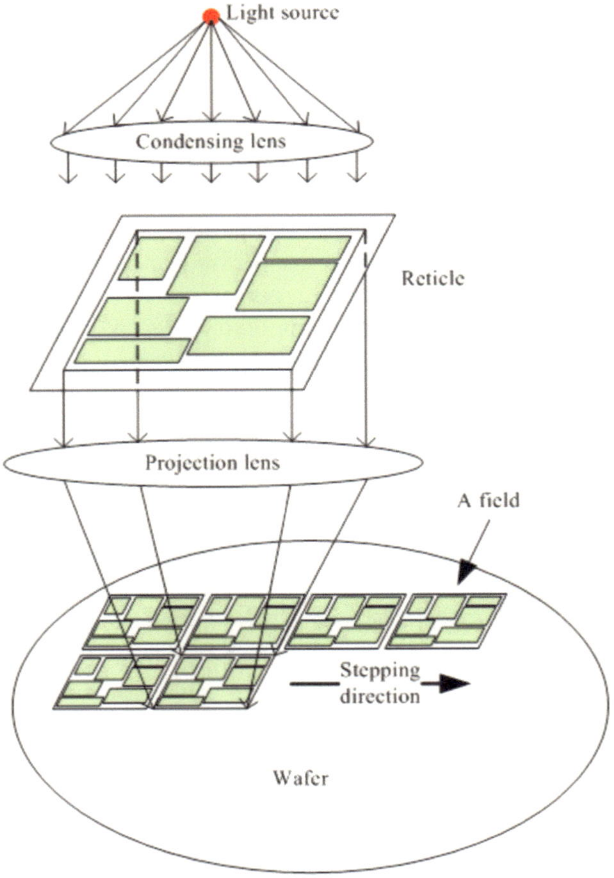

Fig. 2. Wafer lithography

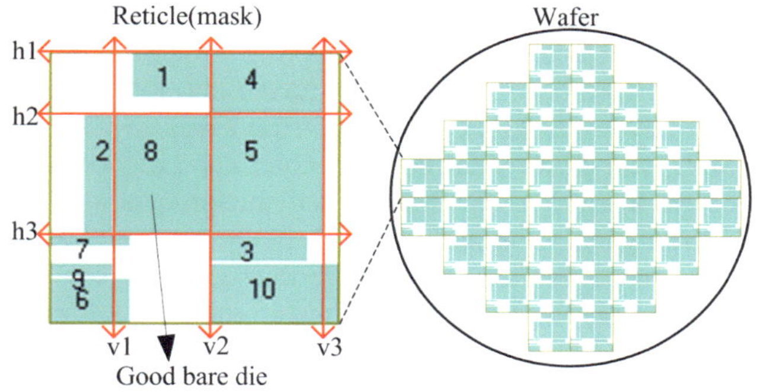

Fig. 3. A multi-project wafer

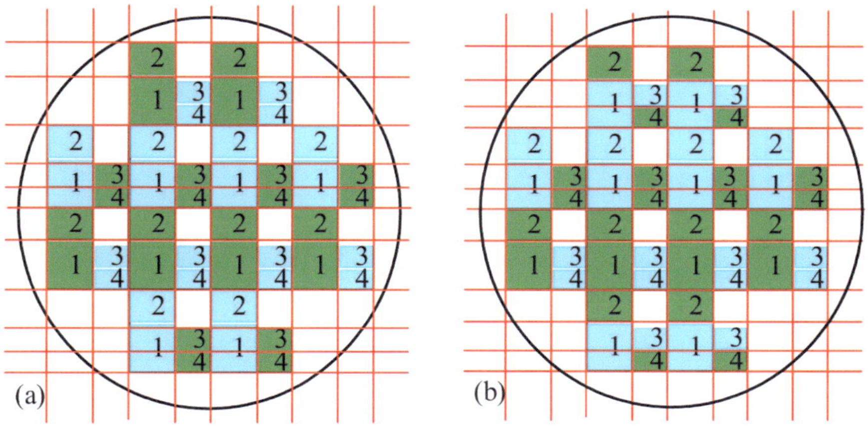

Fig. 4. Two wafer dicing plans (good dice in darker color (green))

Reticle floorplanning determines the positions of the chips in a reticle and thus has a profound effect on dicing yield. Figure 5 shows another reticle floorplan along with a dicing plan for the same chips given in Figure 4. This reticle floorplan has a smaller size, but the dicing plan yields only 2, 6, 4, and 4 dice per wafer for the four chips, respectively. For the same required production volumes as above, 12 wafers need to be fabricated. As one can see, reticle floorplanning has a great influence on the number of required wafers. Our reticle floorplanning problem is formally defined below.

Reticle Floorplanning Problem (RFP): *Given a set of N chips and their required production volumes Vp, p=1..N, determine the coordinates of the chips such that the number of wafers used to attain the required production volumes of these chips is minimized on the condition that no chips overlap and all the chips are inside the reticle whose dimensions are not larger than the maximally permissible values.*

2.2 Related work for SWDP

In the past, a few simulated wafer dicing methods have been proposed (Xu et al., 2004; Kahng et al., 2004; Chen & Mak, 2006). These methods, distinguished by the ways of satisfying required production volumes, are classified into two groups. The first group, as suggested in (Xu et al., 2004), uses a reticle conflict graph G_r to describe the dicing conflicts among all the chips in a reticle. Figure 6 shows a G_r for the reticle floorplan on the left of Figure 3. This graph is created as follows. A chip in a reticle floorplan is modeled as a vertex. A conflict edge between any two chips (vertices) is created if they can not be both good bare dice at the same time. Thus, dicing out the chips in a reticle is equivalent to coloring a conflict graph. The chips with the same color can be good bare dice at the same time and are said to form a color set. Each color set can serve as a reticle dicing plan that consists of the dicing lines used to obtain all the chips in the color set. We call this sort of wafer sawing *coloring dicing*. Given that a reticle conflict graph is c-colorable, i.e., having c color sets, the number of wafers required for the chips in color set S_j is then

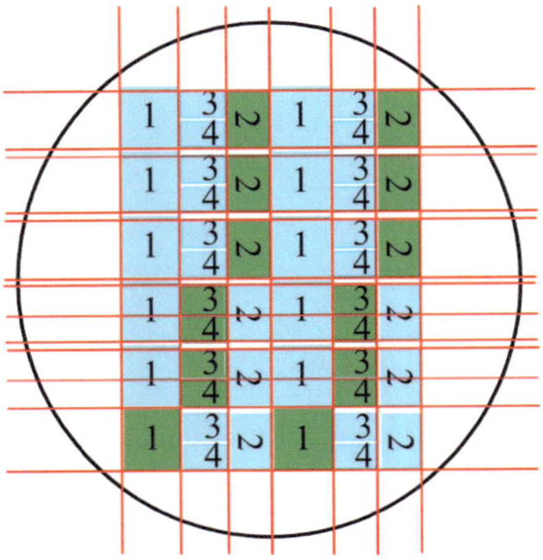

Fig. 5. Yet another reticle floorplan along with a wafer dicing plan

$$Q_{S_j} = \left\lceil \max_{p \in S_j} \frac{V_p}{u} \right\rceil, \tag{1}$$

where u is the number of fields printed on a wafer. The number of wafers required for all of the chips is

$$Q = \sum_{j=1,\ldots,c} Q_{S_j} . \tag{2}$$

For example, we can use color set {4, 5, 6, 7} to obtain 40 good dice from a wafer for chips 4, 5, 6, and 7. Similarly, we can use color set {1, 2, 10} to obtain good dice for chips 1, 2, and 10 and color set {3, 8, 9} to obtain good dice for chips 3, 8, and 9. We need three wafers to attain the required production volume of 40 dice for each project (chip) and six wafers for a required volume ranging from 41 to 80 dice. If wafer dicing is performed in this way, the number of wafers required is at least equal to c regardless of the required production volumes. In general, a minimum color solution does not mean a minimum number of wafers fabricated if the projects do not have the same required production volumes. Wu and Lin (2007) suggest that this sort of SWDP should take into account the production volumes and also allow a chip to be in more than one color set. We can easily prove that the SWDP formulated in this way is an NP-hard problem. Although we can also use SA to solve this problem, it can be solved more effectively using mathematical programming approaches. One can refer to the work (Wu & Lin, 2007) for the details. Especially, the integer linear programming models presented in (Wu & Lin, 2007) are very effective for solving an SWDP with large production volumes. We will not discuss this sort of methods any further.

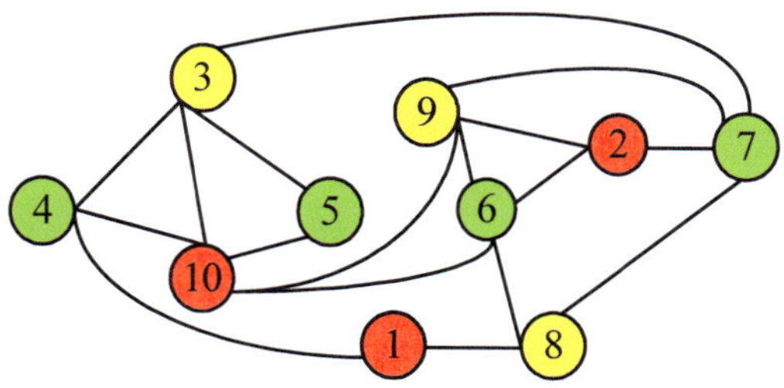

Fig. 6. A reticle conflict graph

The second kind of simulated wafer dicing (Kahng et al., 2004) attempts to saw out some good dice from a wafer for all the chips participating in a shuttle run. Suppose the number of good dice produced from sawing a wafer is $B_p > 0$ for each chip p, the dicing yield of a wafer is

$$z_1 = \min_{p=1..N} \frac{B_p}{V_p}. \tag{3}$$

Then, the number of required wafers is

$$Q = \lceil 1/z_1 \rceil. \tag{4}$$

For example, employing such a definition for performing dicing, we could obtain 7, 6, 6, 9, 7, 6, 6, 6, 6, and 6 good bare dice from a wafer for the chips shown in Figure 7, respectively. With a required production volume of 40 dice for each chip, we have dicing yield z_1=0.15 and the number of required wafers Q=7. Such a problem formulation implies that all wafers will have the same dicing plan, but the fields on the same wafer may not have the same dicing plan. To saw out dice for some chips, this approach may adversely destroy many dice for other chips on the same wafer. Since it deals with only a wafer, we call this approach *1-wafer yield dicing*. It can be extended to sawing k wafers at the same time. We call it k-wafer yield dicing. For k-wafer yield dicing, we have the following relation:

$$z_k \geq k z_1. \tag{5}$$

Then, the total number of wafers used is

$$Q = k\lceil 1/z_k \rceil. \tag{6}$$

Based on the concept of wafer yield dicing, Kahng et al. (2004) propose a non-linear programming (NLP) model, three ILP models, and one heuristic to maximize wafer dicing yield for square wafers. All these methods use two conflict graphs derived from a reticle floorplan to find out a wafer dicing plan. A vertical (horizontal) reticle conflict graph R_v (R_h)

can be created in a manner similar to a reticle conflict graph, only considering the dicing conflicts created by the vertical (horizontal) dicing lines among the chips in a reticle. An independent set in a R_v (R_h) defines a set of vertical (horizontal) dicing lines that can be used simultaneously to saw out all the chips in the independent set without destroying each other. Thus, to saw out as many chips as possible, a maximal independent set should be employed.

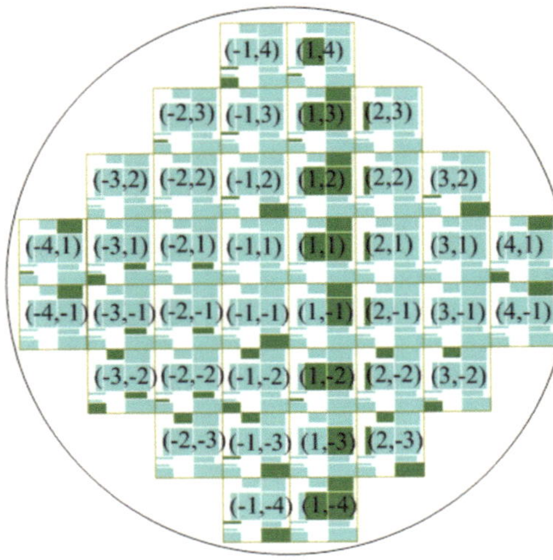

Fig. 7. Wafer dicing yield (good dice in darker color (green))

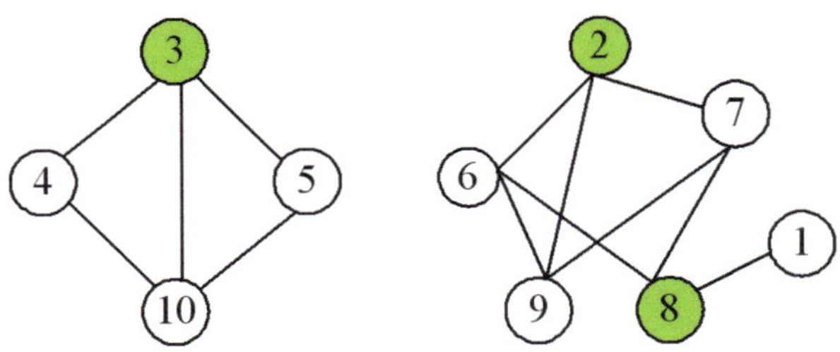

Fig. 8. A vertical reticle conflict graph

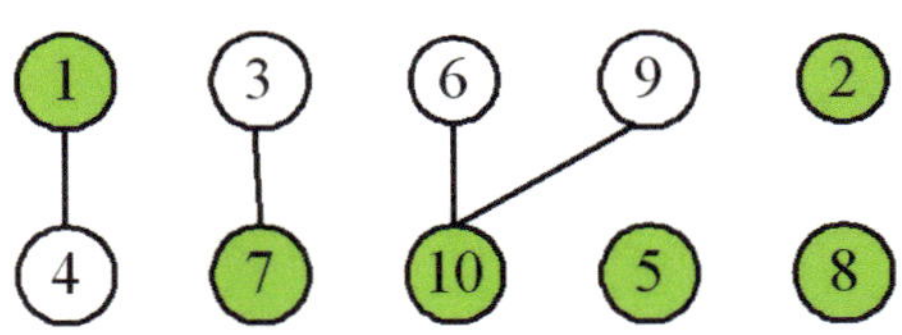

Fig. 9. A horizontal reticle conflict graph

A reticle dicing plan can be obtained by intersecting a maximal independent set in R_v with a maximal independent set in R_h. Those chips belonging to the intersection will be good bare dice if the reticle dicing plan defined by the chips in the intersection is used. For example, given the vertical reticle conflict graph in Figure 8 and horizontal reticle conflict graph in Figure 9, the intersection of maximal vertical independent set {2,3,8} with maximal horizontal independent set {1,2,5,7,8,10} is {2,8}. Thus, chips 2 and 8 can be good bare dice at the same time. It is worth noting that the intersection {2,8} is not a maximal independent set in the reticle conflict graph in Figure 6. Because of this, a simulated wafer dicing method using maximal independent sets in R_v and R_h may fail to produce a good wafer dicing plan. It is likely that an intersection is empty. For example, the intersection of maximal vertical independent set {1,3,9} with maximal horizontal independent set {2,4,5,7,8,10} is empty.

Apparently, wafer yield dicing is quite different from coloring dicing. Wafer yield dicing requires that at least one good bare die be produced from the wafers sawn. This may generate a large number of different reticle dicing plans on a wafer. On the contrary, coloring dicing normally generate the same reticle dicing plan for all the fields in a wafer and produces the dice only for the chips in a color set. The consequence of this difference is that wafer yield dicing can result in a smaller number of wafers fabricated for low-volume production. For high-volume production, both approaches perform equally well, but wafer-yield dicing is more time consuming. In this article, we will present a wafer yield dicing method based on SA using maximal independent sets derived from vertical and horizontal conflict graphs.

2.3 Related work for RFP

In the past, many reticle floorplanning methods have been proposed. These methods can generally be classified into the following groups.

- *Slicing tree packing*

Chen and Lynn (2003) perform reticle floorplanning using slicing trees (Wong & Liu, 1986) for reticle area minimization. Xu et al. (2003) employ slicing trees to perform reticle area minimization while taking die-to-die inspection into consideration. Xu et al. (2004; 2005) further consider metal density optimization (Tian et al., 2001) to improve wafer planarization. These methods consider only reticle area minimization.

- *Shelf-packing*

Kahng et al. (2004) propose a shelf-packing heuristic that places chips in several shelves. A so-obtained solution is improved by simulated annealing interlacing with a dicing heuristic to maximize dicing yield while minimizing reticle area. Several mathematical programming models for determining wafer dicing lines are also presented there. However, this work considers only square wafers.

- *Grid floorplan*

Andersson et al. (2003) propose to pack chips into a two-dimensional array of grids, each of which holds at most one chip such that chips can be aligned in horizontal and vertical directions. Kahng and Reda (2004) propose a branch-and-bound algorithm to find a grid floorplan with the largest dicing yield. This work considers only square wafers. Chen and Mak (2006) propose a method to solve a reticle floorplanning problem for chips using a different number of metal layers. Ching and Young (2006) define a special type of grid, called modified alpha-restricted grid, to reduce the size of the solution space for grid floorplan.

- *Hierarchal quadrisection floorplanning*

Kahng et al. (2005) further propose a hierarchal quadrisection reticle floorplanning method based on simulated annealing which directly minimizes the upper bound on the number of required wafers. A shot-map optimization method is exploited to define the fields printed on a wafer. We will elaborate on this approach later since one of our reticle floorplanning methods is closely related to it.

Besides the aforementioned works, Wu and Lin (2005) propose a non-linear programming model for solving a reticle floorplanning problem with flexible chip dimensions. Wu et al. (2006) also propose a method based on B*-tree (Chang et al., 2000) for solving multiple reticles floorplanning problem.

3. Simulated wafer dicing by simulated annealing

Our simulated annealing implementation for SWDP has its root from an efficient heuristic called Iterative Augment and Search Algorithm (IASA) presented by Kahng et al. (2004). IASA first assigns a vertical (horizontal) reticle dicing plan for each of the first c_v columns of fields (the first c_h rows of fields), where c_v (c_h) is the minimum number of colors used to color a vertical (horizontal) reticle conflict graph. These vertical (horizontal) reticle dicing plans are derived from a minimum coloring of a vertical (horizontal) reticle conflict graph. Vertical (horizontal) dicing plans, i.e., maximal vertical (horizontal) independent sets that maximize wafer dicing yield are then one-by-one respectively assigned to the remaining columns (rows) until all the columns (rows) have their own dicing plans. Before assigning a vertical (horizontal) dicing plan to one of the remaining columns (rows), the dicing plans of the already assigned columns (rows) each are replaced by a dicing plan that can attain the largest yield. This step is repeated until dicing yield can not be further improved. IASA can find a wafer dicing plan very fast, but it tends to be greedy. In the next subsection, we will elaborate on our SA method for solving this problem.

3.1 Simulated annealing implementation

Here, we will introduce a k-wafer yield dicing method based on SA. This method is called HVMIS-SA-Z. Our method has its root from IASA. It also employs maximal vertical and horizontal independent sets. A typical SA is responsible for choosing a viable k-wafer dicing plan. Figure 10 gives the pseudo code for HVMIS-SA-Z. The objective function directly maximizes k-wafer dicing yield z_k. Our neighbourhood function generates a new solution by randomly replacing the dicing plan of a column (row) with a new dicing plan selected from the set of maximal vertical (horizontal) independent sets. The column (row) being replaced with a new dicing plan could be any column (row) on any of the k wafers. It takes some trick to update k-wafer dicing yield for a new solution. We need only to recalculate the number of good bare dice produced from the column (row) selected for being replaced with a new dicing plan. Solution encoding for SWDP is trivial, i.e., a column (row) is simply assigned a maximal vertical (horizontal) independent set. This solution encoding can represent each of the solutions in the solution space of the k-wafer yield dicing problem. The neighborhood function also makes our SA with a non-zero probability of reaching every solution in the solution space. SA terminates if no better dicing plan is found for a number of consecutive inner *while* loops.

The reason for exploring k-wafer yield dicing is that $\lceil 1/z_1 \rceil$ can be a very poor estimator (upper bound) for the number of required wafers as it can be observed from the work done by Wu & Lin (2007). We have two ways of performing k-wafer yield dicing. First, we can use HVMIS-SA-Z to find a smallest k so that $z_k \geq 1$. The problem is that we would need to repeat running HVMIS-SA-Z for all possible k's values. This is very time consuming if the required production volumes are large. Second, we use HVMIS-SA-Z to compute $\lceil k/z_k \rceil$ for k from one up to a certain value (10, for example). We then select a k's value that has the smallest $y = \lceil k/z_k \rceil$. We repeatedly run HVMIS-SA-Z to obtain z_y and a new y with $y = \lceil k/z_k \rceil$ until a smallest y that makes $z_y \geq 1$ can be attained. In this manner, HVMIS-SA-Z can find a better solution more efficiently for a problem with large production volumes. The reason why this works effectively is because $\lceil k/z_k \rceil$ rather than $\lceil 1/z_k \rceil$ is a good bound on the number of wafers used. The data in the column denoted by HVMIS-SA-Z in Table 2 are obtained using such an approach.

```
void HVMIS-SA-Z(k, FR, PV) {
//FR: a given reticle floorplan for a shuttle run.
//PV: required production volumes for all the chips in a shuttle run
//k: number of wafers sawn simultaneously
double zk, zkn, best_zk; // k-wafer dicing yield
set MHIS, MVIS; // sets of maximal horizontal and vertical independent set, respectively
k_wafer_dicing_plan best_dp, current_dp, next_dp;
double T; // temperature
double alpha=0.95;
int frozen( ), equilibrium( );

MHIS=find_maximal_horizontal_indepedent_set(FR);
MVIS=find_maximal_vertical_indepedent_set(FR);
current_dp=find_initial_dicing_plan(k, MHIS, MVIS);
zk=calculate_k_wafer_dicing_yield(current_dp, PV);
best_dp=current_dp;
T=determine_initial_temperature(k,MHIS, MVIS);
while(not frozen( )){
    while(not equilibrium( )){
        next_dp=generate_next_wafer_dicing_plan(current_dp, MHIS, MVIS);
        zkn= calculate_k_wafer_dicing_yield(next_dp, PV);
        if(zkn>zk){
          current_dp=next_dp;
          zk=zkn;
          if(zkn>best_zk){
           best_zk=zkn;
           best_dp=next_dp;}}
        else if( random( ) < e^((zkn-zk)/T) ){
              current_dp=next_dp;
               zk=zkn; }
    }
    T=alpha*T;
}
return(best_dp, best_zk);
}
```

Fig. 10. Simulated annealing implementation for SWDP

3.2 Experimental results for simulated wafer dicing

Here, we perform some experiments with two wafer dicing approaches: IASA and HVMIS-SA-Z. We first investigate which dicing method could attain the largest 1-wafer dicing yield. We then make a comparison between IASA (Kahng et al., 2004) and *k*-wafer yield dicing. All experiments are executed on a 2.8 GHz Pentium 4 CPU with 512Mb memory. We use MILP-VOCO proposed in Wu et al. (2008) to obtain the reticle floorplans for all the test cases. Our study is made on 200mm (8 inches) and 300mm (12 inches) wafers.

In the first experiment, we use the three floorplans shown in Figure 11. Floorplan (b) taken from Kahng et al. (2004) is 3-colorable. Floorplan (a) is a quick re-floorplanning of (b). It is also 3-colorable. Floorplan (c) is also a re-floorplanning of (b) and is 2-colorable. These floorplans are obtained based on satisfying the same production volume of the chips. Table 1 gives a comparison of the two dicing methods for 1-wafer yield dicing. The time taken for IASA is within a second. The time taken for HVMIS-SA-Z is within five minutes. Overall, HVMIS-SA-Z is better. The difference in dicing yield obtained by these two methods for a test case can be up to 20%. Note that the volume requirement R_2 is specially designed such that the two conflicting chips 3 and 10 have larger production volumes. R_3 is randomly made to simulate the production volume requirements prescribed independently by different customers. Inspecting the data in Table 1 further, we notice that floorplan (c) does better than (b) for required volume set R_1. Floorplan (c) is as good as floorplan (b) for required volume set R_2. However, floorplan (b) does better than floorplan (c) for the required volume set R_3 despite the fact that floorplan (c) is 2-colorable and floorplan (b) is 3-colorable. This indicates that not only the number of colors of a reticle conflict graph (i.e., reticle floorplan) but also the required production volumes determine the number of wafers used. Therefore, a reticle floorplan should be made in accordance with the required production volumes. This observation helps us develop a good reticle floorplanning method.

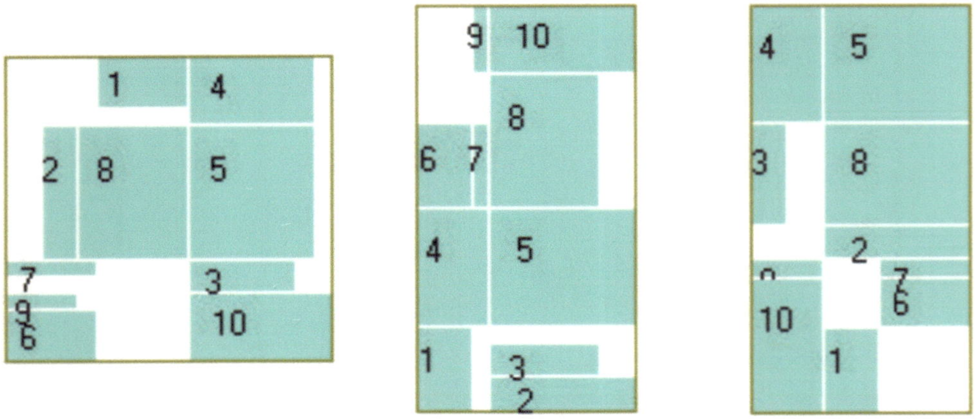

(a) (W, H)=(18, 18) $|MHIS| = 8, |MVIS| = 15$

(b) (W, H)=(12, 24) $|MHIS| = 4, |MVIS| = 4$

(c) (W, H)=(12, 24) $|MHIS| = 2, |MVIS| = 4$

Fig. 11. Different floorplans of the same test case (*W*: reticle width; *H*: reticle height)

Required volumes	Floorplan	200mm wafer		300mm wafer	
		IASA (Kahng et al., 2004)	HVMIS-SA-Z	IASA (Kahng et al., 2004)	HVMIS-SA-Z
R_1=(40,40,40,40,40,40,40,40,40,40)	(a)	0.35	0.38	0.80	0.93
	(b)	0.63	0.68	1.43	1.55
	(c)	0.70	0.78	1.65	1.75
R_2=(40,40,80,40,40,40,40,40,40,120)	(a)	0.19	0.23	0.52	0.60
	(b)	0.35	0.42	0.86	0.93
	(c)	0.38	0.40	0.79	0.91
R_3=(170,60,30,60,100,70,110,140,100,210)	(a)	0.13	0.15	0.31	0.36
	(b)	0.20	0.23	0.48	0.51
	(c)	0.17	0.20	0.44	0.45

Table 1. 1-wafer dicing yield for the three floorplans given in Figure 11

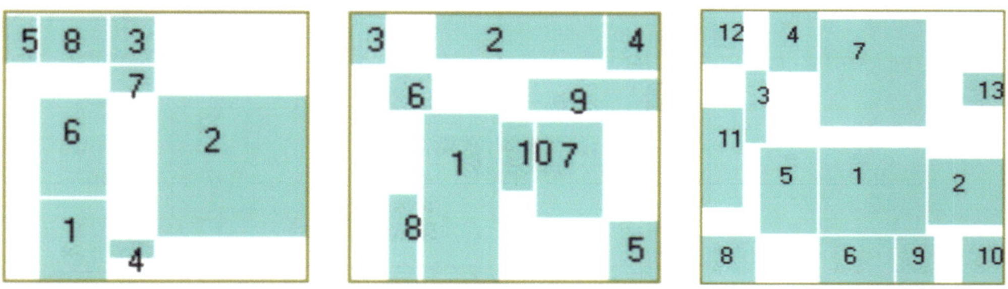

I4: (W, H)= (13.1,13.1)
Required volumes:
60, 60, 200, 200, 400, 400, 600, 600

I5: (W, H)= (10,10)
Required volumes:
100, 200, 300, 200, 200, 200, 200, 200, 80, 60

I6: (W, H)= (18,19.9)
Required volumes:
60, 100, 120, 120, 160, 160, 200, 200, 200, 200, 200, 200, 200

Fig. 12. Floorplans for the three industry test cases

Table 2 shows the number of wafers used (columns denoted by #*wf*) and the times taken by wafer yield dicing methods for the three industrial test cases shown in Figure 12 and the test case in Figure 11(c) with the required volume set R_1. The three industrial test cases are obtained from Global UniChip. To see how these methods scale with the production volumes, we scale the required volumes by a factor of 5, 10, 100, and 1000. HVMIS-SA-Z attains better results for larger production volumes. Compared to IASA (Kahng et al., 2004), HVMIS-SA-Z could achieve up to 50% wafer reduction for some cases. It achieves on average 18% and 37% fewer wafers for low and high volume productions, respectively. The data for IASA are obtained using 1-wafer yield dicing. The time spent for obtaining each datum for IASA is that for finding out 1-wafer dicing yield z_1 defined in (3).
Figure 13 shows a wafer dicing plan for one of the two wafers obtained by HVMIS-SA-Z for I4. As one can see, several different reticle dicing plans have been created to generate some dice for each of the chips in the reticle.

Floorplan	Required volumes	IASA (Kahng et al., 2004) #wf	t(sec.)	HVMIS-SA-Z #wf	t(sec.)
Figure 11(c) with required volume set R_1	1X	1	0	1	8
	5X	4	0	2	19
	10X	7	0	4	44
	100X	61	0	39	121
	1000X	607	0	385	500
I4	1X	2	0	2	20
	5X	8	0	8	67
	10X	16	0	16	89
	100X	160	0	160	161
	1000X	1596	0	1596	1101
I5	1X	2	1	2	41
	5X	10	1	6	122
	10X	19	1	11	216
	100X	189	1	110	1398
	1000X	1887	1	1095	1301
I6	1X	6	0	4	62
	5X	28	0	16	105
	10X	56	0	31	148
	100X	556	0	297	1028
	1000X	5556	0	2959	1102
Average reduction	1X	0%		18%	
	5X	0%		36%	
	10X	0%		37%	
	100X	0%		37%	
	1000X	0%		37%	

Table 2. Simulated wafer dicing for various production volumes

4. Reticle floorplanning by simulated annealing

In this section we first review two solution encodings used in our SA for RFP. We then describe a simple objective function for approximating the most accurate objective function used for RFP. One may recall that the most accurate objective function for RFP is the number of required wafers, which can only be obtained using a simulated wafer dicing method. The simulated wafer dicing method IASA described in Section 3 is originally used for such a purpose. Finally, we will describe how SA is implemented to solve RFP.

4.1 Solution encoding

We use B*-tree (Chang et al., 2000) as one of our solution encodings. B*-tree was originally designed for finding a minimum-area floorplan for an ASIC design. A B*-tree corresponds to a reticle floorplan. A node in a B*-tree represents a chip in a reticle. The chip corresponding to the root is placed at the bottom-left corner of a reticle. The chip corresponding to the left child j is abutted to the right of the chip corresponding to the parent node i with $x_j = x_i + w_i$. The chip corresponding to the right child is placed immediately above the chip corresponding to the parent with the same x coordinate. Recursively traversing a whole tree using depth-first search from the root, we can convert a tree representation into a reticle floorplan. Once this is done, chips are normally pushed to the left and then to the bottom to form a compact floorplan. Figure 14 shows a B*-tree and its corresponding floorplan (without doing pushing). B*-tree can not represent non-compact floorplans in the solution space defined for RFP. This might have an impact on finding a solution that incurs the minimum use of wafers. However, its capability of obtaining a compact floorplan is important for mask tooling cost minimization as shown in Figure 1.

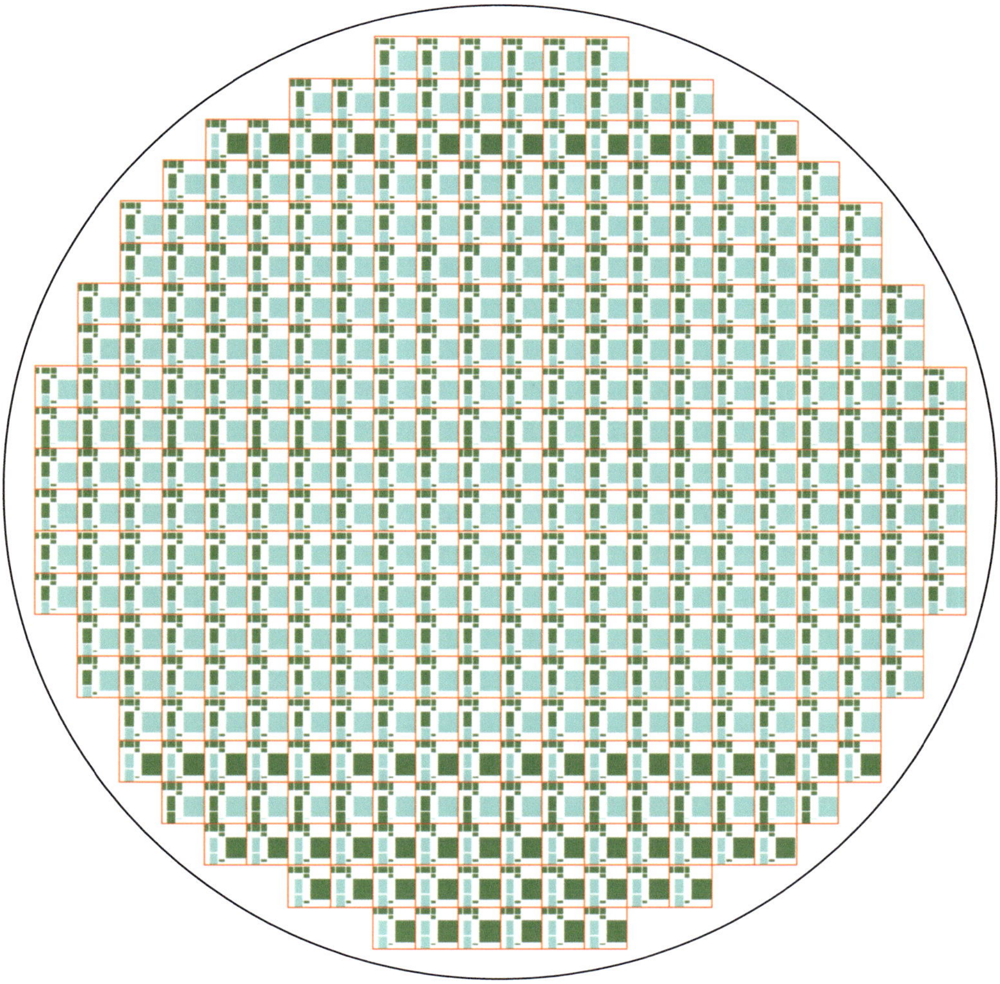

Fig. 13. A wafer dicing plan obtained by HVMIS-SA-Z for I4 with 1X volume (good dice in darker color (green))

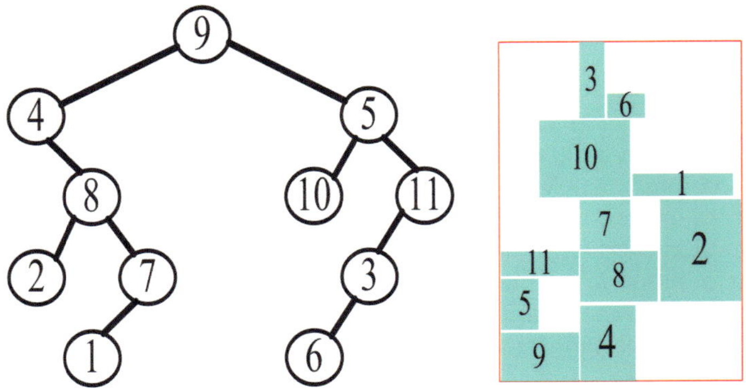

Fig. 14. A B*-tree and its corresponding floorplan

We also employ a solution encoding called hierarchical quadrisection (Kahng et al., 2005) in our work. Hierarchal quadrisection (HQ) recursively divides a reticle into four regions, each of which holds at most one chip. It partitions the chips into 2^l disjoint subsets, where l is the number of levels in a hierarchy. As an example shown in Figure 15, the reticle is divided into 16 regions (i.e., l=2), each of which contains at most one chip. The four disjoint subsets are {2,3}, {4,8}, {1,6} and {5,7}. The chips in the same subset can be sawn out simultaneously. This representation was originally used in Kahng et al. (2005) to facilitate to compute an upper on the number of required wafers. This bound is then used as the objective function for a reticle floorplanning method based on SA. An SA implementation based on HQ outperforms the shelf-packing heuristic (Kahng et al., 2004) and the grid-floorplan-based branch-and-bound algorithm (Kahng & Reda, 2004) proposed by the same research group. As one can see, HQ can not represent compact floorplans. This is in contrast to B*-tree. Compactly packed floorplans obtained from B*-tree will incur a number of dicing conflicts. However, this drawback is compensated by having a smaller reticle size so that more fields will be printed on a wafer. On the contrary, non-compact floorplans obtained from HQ will create fewer conflicts but generally have lager reticle size.

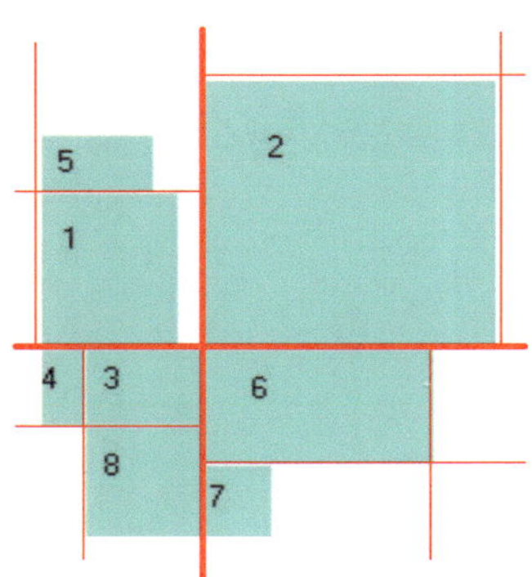

Fig. 15. A hierarchical quadrisection floorplanning

4.2 Objective function

The objective function for RFP is the number of wafers fabricated if the underlying reticle floorplan is employed for a shuttle run. However, the exact number of required wafers can only be obtained using simulated wafer dicing, which is too time consuming for an SA implementation. As one may recall, HQ can facilitate to construct a reticle floorplanning objective function which calculates an upper bound on the number of required wafers. Unfortunately, given a reticle floorplan the so-obtained bound is constantly far from the minimum number of required wafers. Other more accurate bounds are presented in Wu et al. (2008). However, the solution quality obtained using this sort of objective functions is not comparable to that obtained using our objective function. Our objective function is based on a simple observation that two chips should be placed at the positions where no dicing conflict between them can be created if their required production volumes are large. We call these two chips compatible. This concept is called volume-driven compatibility optimization or VOCO for short. The objective function based on VOCO is as follows:

$$Max \quad F = \delta \sum_{p=1}^{N-1} \left(\sum_{q=p+1}^{N} E_{pq}(V_p + V_q) \right) - (1-\delta)\beta WH \,, \tag{7}$$

where $\beta = (N-1)\sum_{p=1}^{N} V_p / (W_{\max} + H_{\max})$ is a normalizing factor; H (H_{max}) and W (W_{max}) are the (maximum allowable) reticle height and width, respectively. V_p and V_q are the required production volumes for chips p and q respectively; $E_{pq} = 1$ if chips p and q are compatible, otherwise, it is zero. δ is a weighing factor for compatibility and reticle dimensions. If $\delta = 0$, the objective function minimizes only reticle dimensions. If $\delta = 1$, the objective function maximizes compatibility for given reticle dimensions. As one can see, reticle area is part of the objective function. This objective function can be evaluated easily for a given floorplan. We need only to calculate E_{pq}, which is much simpler than doing simulated wafer dicing. We hope that this objective function will correspond well to the number of required wafers. That is to say, given any two floorplans a and b, we would like to have $Q_a < Q_b$ if $F_a > F_b$, where Q_a and Q_b are the number of wafers required for floorplans a and b and F_a and F_b are the objective function's values for floorplans a and b, respectively. Unfortunately, the number of required wafers is related to reticle area and compatibility, which are two conflicting goals of optimization. The degree of such a relation varies significantly from one problem instance to another so that no single value of δ can render a good correspondence between the objective function's value and the number of required wafers. In this work, a number of δs values between zero and one will be tried for obtaining the best solution.

4.3 Simulated annealing implementation

Using the aforementioned two solution encodings along with the objective function, we devise two simulated annealing implementations for RFP. Figure 16 shows the pseudo code of our implementation. If the solution encoding is B*-tree, we call this implementation BT-VOCO. To generate a new solution for BT-VOCO, we need only to move around a node in the tree, exchange two nodes, rotate a node, move a sub-tree to another place, etc. Although the neighbourhood function can flexibly derive one B*-tree from another, one should remember that only compact floorplans can be obtained. On the other hand, if the solution encoding is HQ, we call this implementation HQ-VOCO. To generate a new solution we need only to move around a node, exchange two nodes, or rotate a node within the regions defined by HQ. SA terminates if no better reticle floorplan is found for a number of consecutive inner *while* loops. As one can see, we make δ as one of the arguments of VOCO_RFP so that a number of δ's values between zero and one can be tried.

```
void VOCO_RFP(SC, PV, δ, H_max, W_max, solution_encoding) {
//SC: a set of chips participating in a shuttle run
//PV: required production volumes for all the chips in a shuttle run
//δ: a weighing factor for objective function
//H_max (W_max): maximum allowable reticle height (width)
//solution encoding: B*-tree or HQ
double c_current, c_next, c_best; // objective function's values for current, next, best solutions
floorplan current_fp, next_fp, best_fp;
double T; // temperature
double alpha=0.95;
int frozen( ), equilibrium( );

current_fp=find_initial_floorplan(SC, H_max, W_max, solution_encoding);
c_current=eveluate_objective_function(current_fp, PV, δ);
best_fp=current_fp;
T=determine_initial_temperature(SC, H_max, W_max, solution_encoding, PV, δ)
while(not frozen( )){
    while(not equilibrium( )){
        next_fp=generate_next_floorplan(current_fp, H_max, W_max, solution_encoding);
        c_next= eveluate_objective_function(next_fp, PV, δ);
        if(c_next>c_current){
          current_fp=next_fp;
          c_current=c_next;
          if(c_next>c_best){
           c_best=c_next;
           best_fp=next_fp;}}
        else if( random( ) < e^((c_next-c_current)/T) ){
             current_fp=next_fp;
             c_current=c_next; }
    }
    T=alpha*T;
}
return (best_fp);
}
```

Fig. 16. Simulated annealing implementation for RFP

4.4 Experimental results for reticle floorplanning

In this subsection we perform some experiments to evaluate the proposed floorplanning methods. The floorplanning methods investigated include BT, BT-VOCO, HQ-RCV, and HQ-VOCO. BT is a special case of BT-VOCO with $\delta = 0$ that simply minimizes the reticle area (Chang et al., 2000). HQ-RCV is the original method proposed by Kahng et al. (2005) where an upper bound on the number of required wafers is used as the reticle floorplanning objective function. To determine the number of wafers needed to meet the production volumes, we employ HVMIS-SA-Z for low-volume dicing and ILP models using the maximal independent sets in a reticle conflict graph as done in Kahng et al. (2005) for high-volume dicing. CPLEX 9.0 from ILOG (Hentnryck, 2000) is used to obtain a best feasible solution for the ILP models. The test cases are given in Table 3. Cases I1~I6 are obtained from Global Unichip. The number of chips per test case is from 3 to 40. Since we are experimenting with 300mm wafers, the 1X volume requirement is often too small to make a difference in the number of wafers used. We scale the volume requirements by a factor of 4 and 10. Such scaling can evaluate the viability of the proposed methods for solving the problems with higher production volumes.

Case	Chip dimensions (*w*, *h*) (mm)	W_{max} x H_{max} (mm)	Required volumes
I1	(9.5, 9.5), (2, 2), (2.5, 2.5)	20x20	60, 200, 200
I2	(4, 5.5), (4, 3.78), (3, 3), (3, 2.2)	20x20	80, 150, 80, 80
I3	(7, 2.5), (5, 2), (5, 3), (3, 2), (2, 2)	20x20	120, 120, 120, 120,120
I4	(4, 3), (6.5, 7), (2, 2.5), (2, 1), (1.5, 2.5), (5, 3), (2, 1.5), (3, 2.5)	15x15	60, 60, 200, 200, 400, 400, 600, 600
I5	(2.5, 6.25), (1.8, 5.5), (2, 1.25), (2.2, 1.75), (1.7,2.25), (1.5, 1.55), (2.3, 3.75), (1, 3.25),(1.3, 4.25), (2.7, 1.1)	20x20	100, 200, 300, 200, 200, 200, 200, 200, 80, 60
I6	(6.5, 6.5), (4.5, 5), (5.5, 1.5), (4.5, 3), (6.5, 3.5), (4.5, 3.5), (6.5, 8), (3.3,3.5), (2.5, 3.5), (3.5, 2.5), (7.5, 2.5), (4, 2.5), (2.5, 2.5)	20x20	60, 100, 120, 120, 160, 160, 200, 200, 200, 200, 200, 200, 200
I7	Combining all chips from I1 to I4	20x20	Inherited from original test case
I8	Combining all chips from I2 to I5	20x20	Inherited from original test case
I9	Replicating the chips in I5 4 times	20x20	Randomly generated and ranging from 40 to 350
Ind2	The test case Ind2 from Kahng et al. (2005)	20x20	Randomly generated and ranging from 25 to 67

Table 3. Test cases

Our experiments were run on a 2.4 GHz AMD K8 CPU with 2GB memory. We performed 5 BT-VOCO runs and HQ-VOCO runs for each of δ values, 0.1, 0.2, 0.3, ..., 0.9, 1.0. There were 50 BT-VOCO and HQ-VOCO runs for each test case, respectively. For a fair comparison, there were also 50 BT runs for each test case. There were 20 HQ-RCV runs for each test case using a run time approximately equal to that of 50 BT-VOCO runs. Table 4 gives the minimum number of wafers (columns denoted by *#wf*) and the corresponding reticle size (columns denoted by *ave area*). Since there can be more than one floorplan that achieves the minimum wafers, the corresponding reticle size is an average value. A row denoted by *Norm* gives the normalized number of wafers (reticle area) with respect to the number of wafers (reticle area) achieved by HQ-RCV (Kahng et al., 2005). Figure 17 presents the spread of the number of wafers attained using each method. Clearly, BT which simply minimizes reticle area using B*-tree works poorly with respect to the number of wafers used. HQ-

Volume	Case	BT (Chang et al., 2000)		BT- VOCO		HQ-RCV (Kahng et al. 2005)		HQ-VOCO	
		#wf	ave area	#wf	ave area	#wf	ave area	#wf	ave area
	I1	1	114	1	136	1	139	1	138
	I2	1	58	1	67	1	69	1	65
1X	I3	1	53	1	67	1	124	1	94
	I4	3	95	2	115	2	192	2	135
	I5	2	62	2	106	2	146	2	115
	I6	4	249	3	266	4	303	3	296
	I7	7	305	4	333	6	371	4	352
	I8	7	267	5	337	9	383	5	310
	I9	10	244	7	288	10	352	6	308
	Ind2	2	189	2	242	2	344	2	264
	Total	38	1635	28	1956	38	2423	27	2077
	Norm	1	0.67	0.74	0.81	1	1	0.71	0.86
	I1	4	114	3	138	3	138	3	138
	I2	1	58	1	67	1	65	1	65
4X	I3	1	53	1	66	2	111	1	87
	I4	10	96	5	109	6	132	5	115
	I5	4	61	4	72	4	79.2	3	67
	I6	13	250	9	252	12	284	10	287
	I7	24	305	16	333	23	360	15	340
	I8	28	266	19	345	22	310	17	339
	I9	29	244	21	266	27	354	22	281
	Ind2	4	189	3	220	4	245	3	229
	Total	118	1636	82	1867	104	2079	80	1948
	Norm	1.13	0.79	0.79	0.90	1	1	0.77	0.94
	I1	9	114	6	138	6	138	6	138
	I2	3	58	2	65	3	68	3	65
10X	I3	2	53	2	53	4	98	2	92
	I4	22	95	12	105	14	127	12	110
	I5	9	61	7	65	9	86	8	72
	I6	31	250	22	252	26	271	23	287
	I7	57	305	38	314	53	351	37	340
	I8	64	268	47	333	52	309	43	308
	I9	63	244	50	266	57	298	52	306
	Ind2	9	189	8	214	8	223	7	225
	Total	269	1636	194	1804	232	1969	193	1944
	Norm	1.16	0.83	0.84	0.92	1	1	0.83	0.99

Table 4. Minimum number of wafers and the average reticle area (mm^2)

VOCO (BT-VOCO) is 17%~29% (16%~26%) better than HQ-RCV. HQ-VOCO is about 1%~3% better than BT-VOCO. As one can see, BT-VOCO and HQ-VOCO were most viable approaches for minimizing the number of wafers. It is also interesting to see that the improvement percentage achieved by BT-VOCO and HQ-VOCO decreases as the volume requirement increases. The reason is that the objective function used by HQ-RCV is dictated by the chromatic number used to color a reticle conflict graph. However, minimum chromatic coloring does not necessarily imply a minimum use of wafers for low-volume production. This leads to a larger denominator for normalization and thus smaller normalized values for BT-VOCO (HQ-VOCO) with low-volume production. As for reticle area, BT-VOCO is 8%~19% smaller than HQ-RCV, 4%~7% smaller than HQ-VOCO, but 9%~14% larger than BT.

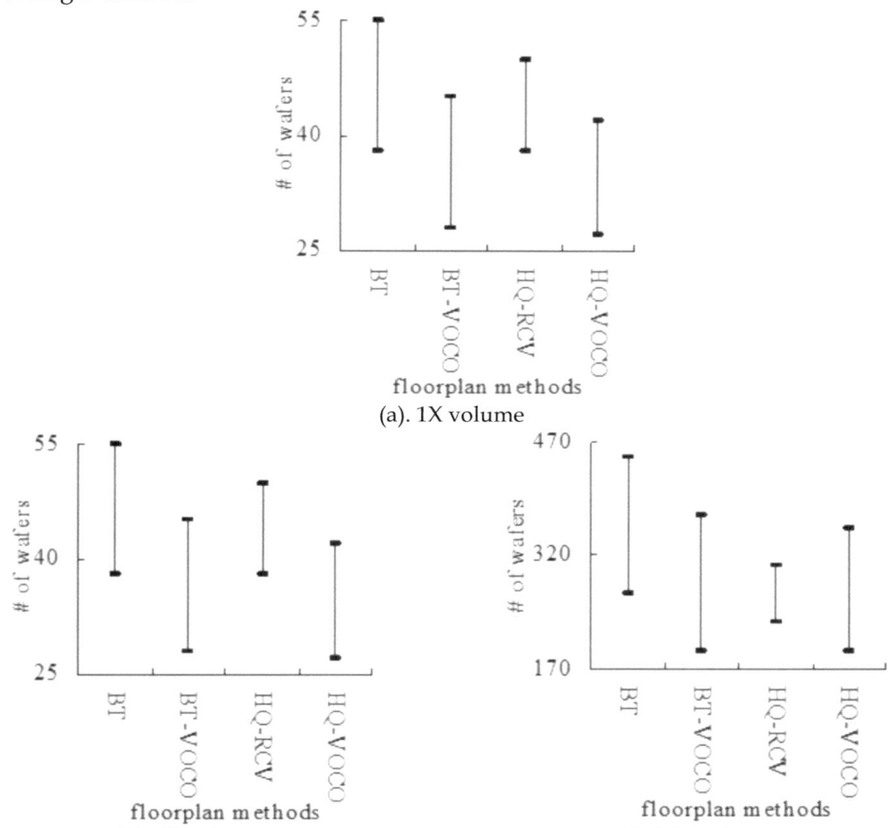

(a). 1X volume

(b). 4X volume

(c). 10X volume

Fig. 17. Spread of the number of wafers

The total run time for obtaining the above results is given in Table 5. Note that HQ-VOCO is almost two times faster than BT-VOCO. The run time is specially set to make HQ-RCV and BT-VOCO use about the same amount of time. Figure 18 shows the best floorplans obtained using each of the methods for I9.

5. Conclusions and future work

In this chapter we have demonstrated how simulated annealing is used to solve two NP-hard problems: simulated wafer dicing and reticle floorplanning problems for MPW. For simulated wafer dicing, we suggest that HVMIS-SA-Z be employed to find the wafer dicing plans, especially for low-volume production. As for reticle floorplanning, BT-VOCO and

HQ-VOCO should be used, depending on production volumes, mask tooling cost (relating to reticle area), and wafer fabrication cost (relating to the number of wafers fabricated). Because MPW production cost is a sum of mask tooling and wafer fabrication costs, we suggest that one should employ BT-VOCO and/or HQ-VOCO to perform a reticle design space exploration for obtaining a minimum-cost reticle floorplan, rather than a minimum-wafer-use reticle floorplan. As part of future work, it is interesting to find a solution encoding that can express compact versus non-compact floorplans.

Case	BT	BT-VOCO	HQ-RCV	HQ-VOCO
I1	4	4	45	3
I2	5	8	60	3
I3	7	12	76	6
I4	21	38	163	19
I5	28	62	203	26
I6	49	127	276	54
I7	112	388	606	274
I8	201	884	988	535
I9	484	2615	1837	1326
Ind2	47	135	240	58
Total	958	4273	4494	2304

Table 5. Total run time (sec.)

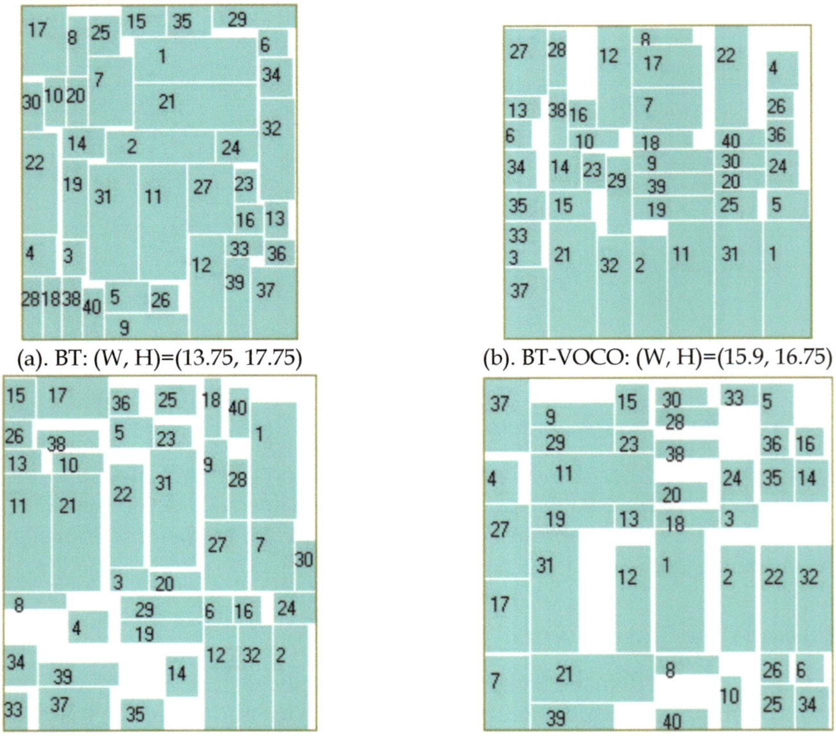

(a). BT: (W, H)=(13.75, 17.75)

(b). BT-VOCO: (W, H)=(15.9, 16.75)

(c). HQ-RCV: (W, H)=(16.05, 18.55)

(d). HQ-VOCO: (W,H)=(17.4, 17.6)

Fig. 18. Best reticle floorplans respectively obtained by each of the RFP methods for I9

6. References

Andersson, M.; Gudmundsson, J. & Levcopoulos, C. (2005). Chips on wafer, *Computational Geometry - Theory and Applications*, 30(2), 95-111

Bonn, J.; Sisler, S. & Tivnan, P. (2001). Balancing mask and lithography cost, *Proceedings of Advanced Semiconductor Manufacturing Conf.*, pp. 25-27

Chang, Y. C.; Chang, Y. W.; Wu, G. M. & Wu, S. W. (2000). B*-trees: a new representation for non-slicing floorplans, *Proceedings of ACM/IEEE Design Automation Conference*, pp. 458-463

Chen, C. C. & Mak, W. K. (2006). A multi-technology-process reticle floorplanner and wafer dicing planner for multi-project wafers, *Proceedings of Asia and South Pacific Design Automation Conference*, pp. 777-782

Chen, S. & Lynn, E. C. (2003). Effective placement of chips on a shuttle mask, *Proceedings of SPIE*. Vol. 5130, pp. 681-688

Ching, R. L. S. & Young, E. F. Y. (2006). Shuttle mask floorplanning with modified alpha-restricted grid, *Proceedings of ACM Great Lakes Symposium on VLSI*, pp. 85-90

Global UniChip, http://www.globalunichip.com

Hentnryck, P. V. (2000). *ILOG OPL Programming Language Reference Manual*, Massachusetts Institute of Technology

Kahng, A. B.; Mandoiu, I. I.; Wang, Q.; Xu, X. & Zelikovsky, A. (2004). Multi-project reticle floorplanning and wafer dicing, *Proceedings of International Symposium on Physical Design*, pp.70-77

Kahng, A. B. & Reda, S. (2004). Reticle floorplanning with guaranteed yield for multi-project wafers, *Proceedings of International Conference on Computer Design*, pp. 106-110

Kahng, A. B.; Mandoiu, I. I.; Xu, X. & Zelikovsky, A. (2005). Yield-driven multi-project reticle design and wafer dicing, *Proceedings of 25th Annual BACUS Symposium on Photomask Technology*, pp. 1247-1257

Kirkpatrick, S.; Gelatt, C. D. & Vecchi, Jr. M. P. (1983). Optimization by simulated annealing, *Science*, Vol. 220, No. 4598, May 13, pp. 671-680

LaPedus, M. (2006). Mask prices flatten but tool costs soar, *EE TIMES*, March 15

Lin, R. B.; Wu, M. C. & Tsai, S. C. (2007). Reticle design for minimizing multiproject wafer production cost, *IEEE Transactions on Automation Science and Engineering*, Vol. 4, No. 4, pp. 589-595

Morse, R. D. (2003). Multiproject wafers: not just for million-dollar mask sets, *Proceedings of SPIE*, Vol. 5043, pp. 100-113

Pina, C. A. (2001). MOSIS: IC prototyping and low volume production service, *Proceedings of Intl. Conf. on Microelectronic Systems Education*, pp. 4-5

Pramanik, D.; Kamberian, H.; Progler, C.; Sanie, M. & Pinto, D. (2003). Cost effective strategies for ASIC masks, *Proceedings of SPIE*, Vol. 5043, pp. 142-152

Tian, R.; Wong, D. F. & Boone, R. (2001). Model-based dummy feature placement for oxide chemical–mechanical polishing manufacturability, *IEEE Trans. Computer-Aided Design*, Vol. 20, No. 7. pp. 902–910

Wong, D. F. & Liu, C. L. (1986). A new algorithm for floorplan design, *Proceedings of ACM/IEEE* Design *Automation Conference*, pp. 101–107

Wong, D. F.; Leong, H. W. & Liu, C. L. (1988). *Simulated Annealing for VLSI Design*, Kluwer Academic Publishers

Wu, M. C. & Lin, R. B. (2005). Reticle floorplanning of flexible chips for multi-project wafers, *Proceedings of IEEE/ACM Great Lake Symposium on VLSI*, pp. 494-497

Wu, M. C.; Tsai, S. C. & Lin, R. B. (2006). Floorplanning multiple reticles for multi-project wafers, *Proceedings of International Symposium on VLSI Design, Automation, and Test*, pp. 143-146

Wu, M. C. & Lin, R. B. (2008). Finding dicing plans for multiple project wafers fabricated with shuttle mask, *Journal of Circuits, Systems, and Computers*, Vol. 17, No. 1, pp. 15-31

Wu, M. C.; Lin, R. B. & Tsai, S. C. (2008). Chip placement in a reticle for multiple project wafer fabrication, *ACM Transactions on Design Automation of Electronic Systems*, Vol. 13, No. 1

Xu, G.; Tian, R.; Wong, D. F., & Reich, A. J. (2003). Shuttle mask floorplanning, *Proceedings of SPIE*, Vol. 5256, pp. 185-194

Xu, G.; Tian, R.; Pan, D. Z. & Wong, D. F. (2004). A multi-objective floorplanner for shuttle mask optimization, *Proceedings of SPIE*, Vol. 5567, pp. 340-350

Xu, G.; Tian, R.; Pan, D. Z. & Wong, D. F. (2005). CMP aware shuttle mask floorplanning, *Proceedings of Asia and South Pacific Design Automation Conference*, pp. 1111-1114

14

Structural Optimization Using Simulated Annealing

Fazil O. Sonmez
Department of Mechanical Engineering
Bogazici University
Turkey

1. Introduction

The increasing demand from the industry for lightweight, high-performance and low-cost structures drives the considerable current research going on in the field of structural optimization. In the early stages, structural optimization was restricted to sizing optimization. Now, there are broadly three problem areas that the researchers and engineers face. One is shape optimization, which involves finding the best profile for a structure under various constraints imposed by the requirements of the design. The objective may be to minimize weight or maximize mechanical performance. The other is topology optimization, which involves finding the best configuration or layout for a structure. The last one is composites optimization. Better performance may be obtained by optimizing the material system itself such as fibre orientations, filler or fibre volume fraction, ply thickness, stacking sequence.

Locating globally optimum structural designs is a difficult problem, requiring sophisticated optimization procedures. In typical structural optimization problems, there may be many locally optimal configurations. For that reason, a downhill-proceeding algorithm, in which a monotonically decreasing value of objective function is iteratively created, may get stuck into a locally optimal point other than the globally optimal solution. Therefore, researchers adopted global search algorithms like simulated annealing in their studies of structural optimization.

This chapter gives a review of the current research on these fields. The objective functions, constraints, design variables and search algorithms adopted in these studies will be discussed. Then, this chapter will focus on the applications of simulated annealing to structural optimization.

2. Shape optimization

In shape optimization, contours of a structure are modified to achieve savings in weight and improvements in structural performance. Fig. 1 depicts a typical shape optimization problem. This is an eccentrically loaded plate restrained at one end and loaded at the other. The shape of the boundary excluding the portion on which boundary conditions are applied is optimized for minimum weight.

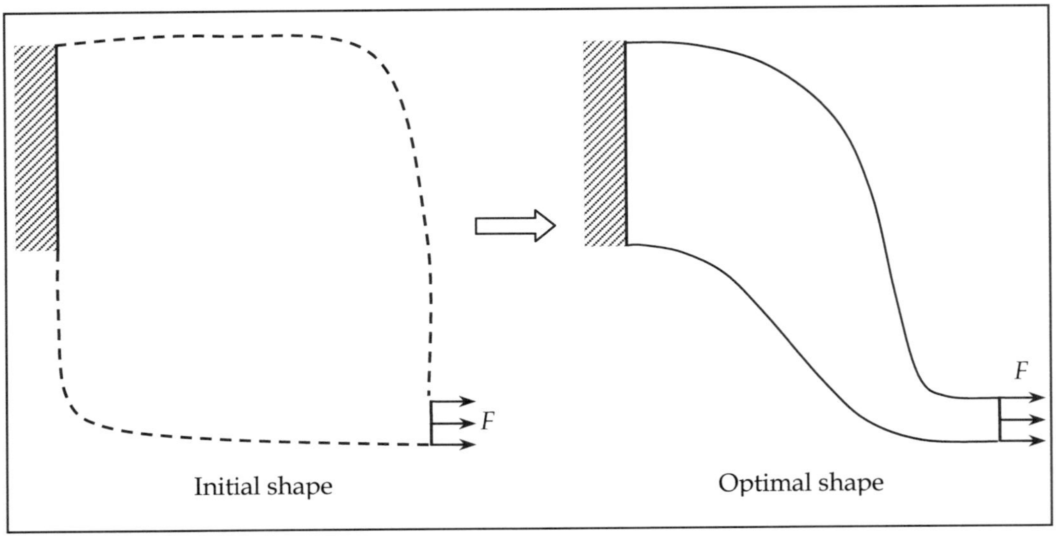

Fig. 1. An illustration of a shape optimization problem.

Applications in this field include optimum shape designs of 2D structures like eccentrically loaded plates as depicted in Fig. 1, fillets, cams, torque arms, pin joints, brackets, (see Fig. 2. *a*, *b*, *c*, *d*, *e*), hooks, holes in plates, rings, chain links, plates containing cracks, saw blades etc, beams, tubes, shell structures, components in contact, thermal fins, axisymmetric structures, 3D structures like engine bearing cap, turbine blades (see Fig. 2. *f*), engine mount bracket, (see Fig. 2. *g*) and slider bearings (see Fig. 2. *h*).

In any optimization process, there should be an objective function according to which effectiveness of a design can be evaluated. In shape optimization, either the most efficient use of material or the best performance is sought. The goal may be to minimize weight of a structure or to increase mechanical performance, e.g. to minimize stress concentration, peak contact stress, compliance etc.; or maximize static strength, fracture strength, buckling strength, fatigue life etc.

In order for a designer to optimize a structure, he/she should be allowed to change some of its properties affecting the objective function. As for a shape optimization problem, some parts of the boundary should be allowed to vary. Boundaries of structures may be defined using spline curves passing through a number of key points. Coordinates of these points thus become design variables. By changing the positions of the key points during an optimization process, a new shape can be obtained (Fig. 3). The advantage of using spline curves is that the shape of a structure can be defined using just a few design variables and a smooth boundary is obtained. Some parameterized equations can also be used for boundary curve; the parameters then control the size, shape, and aspect ratio of the boundary. Alternatively, simply dimensions of individual parts of the structures, radius of a hole, length of an edge etc., can be taken as design variables; but the number of configurations that can be generated may be too limited for efficient optimization. Also, by removing or restoring materials within the elements of a finite element model, the shape of a structure may be changed. In that case, presence of material becomes a design variable. In this approach, a structural model is first divided into small finite element blocks and then these blocks are removed or restored to obtain a new shape (Fig. 4). One difficulty with this method is that removing and restoring an element may violate model connectivity.

Whenever a new configuration is generated its connectivity should be checked. Another difficulty is the roughness of the resulting boundaries. If smooth boundaries are desired, small elements should be used, which may result in long computational times.

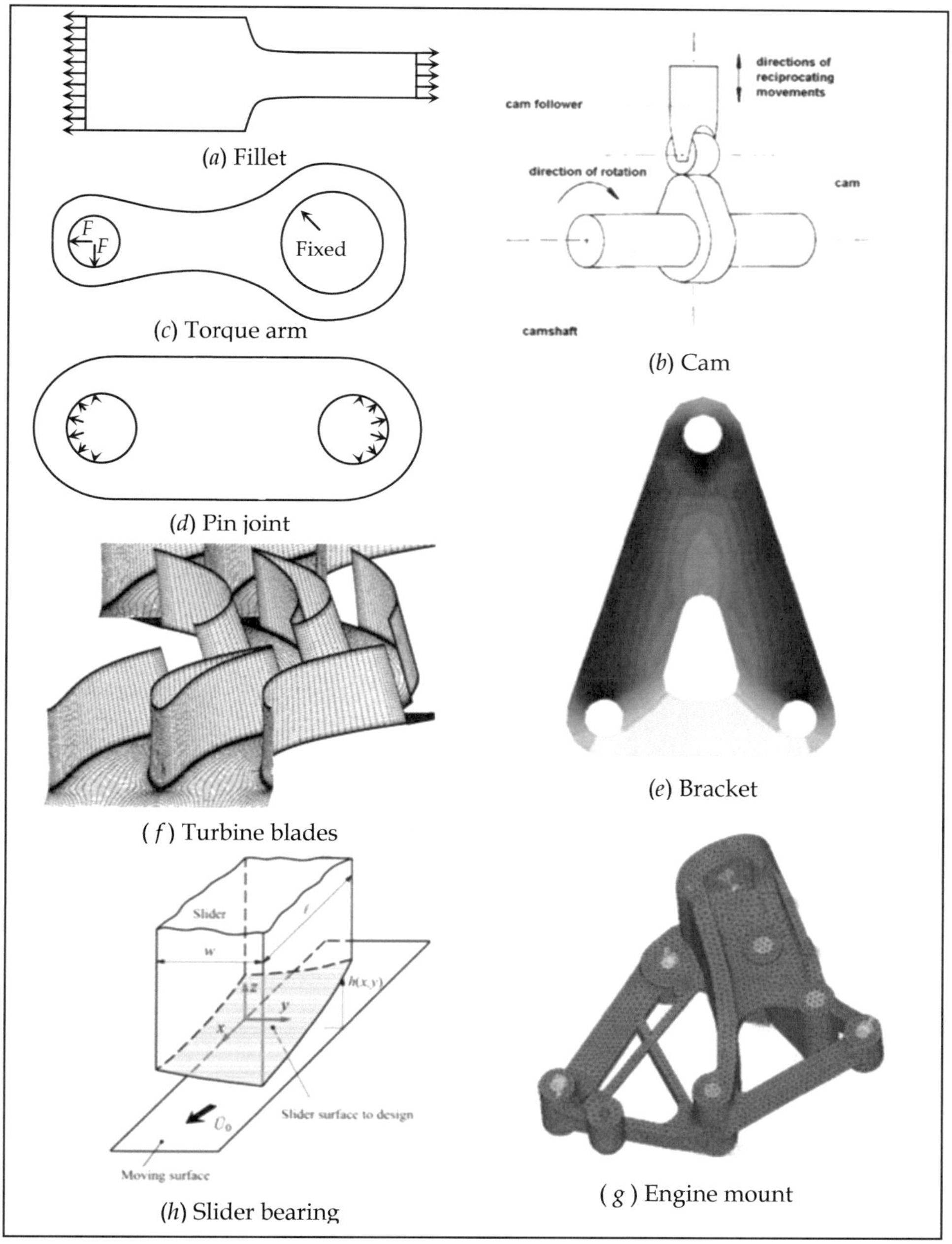

Fig. 2. Shape optimization problems: (*a*) fillet, (*b*) cam (Lampinen, 2003), (*c*) torque arm, (*d*) pin joint, (*e*) bracket (Kim et al., 2003), (*f*) turbine blades (Jung et al.,2005), (*g*) engine mount bracket (Shen & Yoon, 2003), (*h*) slider bearing (Chang & Cheng, 2005).

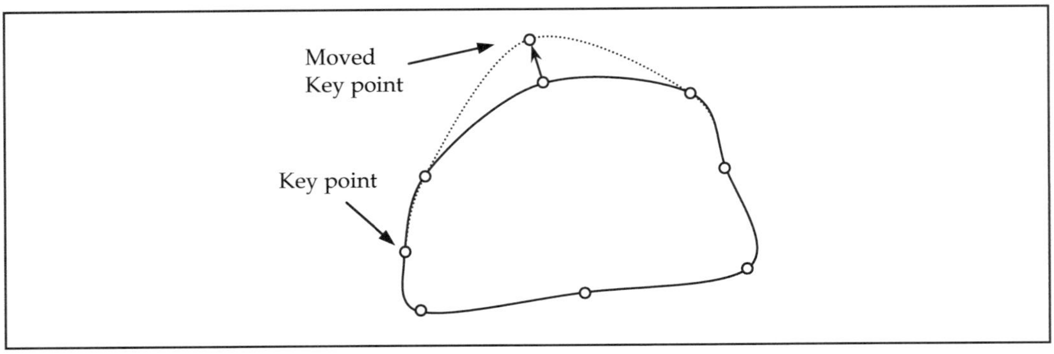

Fig. 3. Modifying the shape of the boundary defined by spline curves by changing the position of a key point.

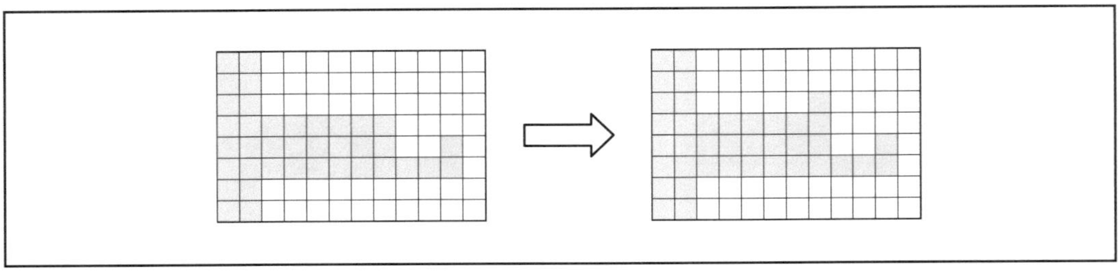

Fig. 4. Obtaining a new shape by removing or restoring material in a grid.

During a shape optimization process, geometry of the structure may undergo substantial changes, such that it can no longer be considered as a viable structure, e.g. geometric model may become infeasible, e.g. some parts of the structure may lose their connection to the supports, this means that the structure may no longer remain in one piece, stresses may exceed the allowable stress, fatigue life may become shorter than the desired life, natural frequency may be lower than a certain limit, displacements may be too large, finite element mesh may become too distorted, the area or volume may become too large, manufacturing may become too difficult etc. In these cases, behavioural constraints should be imposed.

2.1 Precision of an optimum design

One of the requirements for a search of the best possible design is the precise definition of the optimized system. How well the optimized system is defined by the design variables is a measure of precision. Some of the parameters that define the system are allowed to be changed during an optimization process. The number of these parameters and the range of values that they may take determine the degree at which the system can be tailored to the best performance. By increasing the number of design variables and range of their values, one may obtain a better definition and also a better optimum design. If the system is complex, complete definition of it may require large numbers of design variables. If all of them are used as optimization variables, that means if the optimized system is precisely defined, long computational times are needed, and also likelihood of locating the globally optimum design may become very low. If the definition of the system is based on a limited number of design variables, that means if the definition allows for only a limited number of distinct configurations, the resulting optimum configuration can not reflect the best possible design. Although using the most precise definition of the system during optimization is desirable, this is usually not practicable; but if a less precise definition is used, one should be aware of its impact on how well the final design represents the best possible design.

In a shape optimization problem, by using a larger number of variables one may better describe the boundary and obtain a better optimum design. Consider the weight minimization problem depicted in Fig. 1. This problem was solved by Sonmez (2007) first by using five moving key points to describe the boundary, then seven and nine key points. Fig. 5 shows the optimal shapes with their finite element meshes. The lateral areas of the optimum shapes defined by five, seven, and nine key points were found to be 37.100, 36.313, and 35.903 cm^2, respectively. Consequently, with a larger number of key points, one can obtain a better definition of shape and also find an optimum configuration with a lower cost.

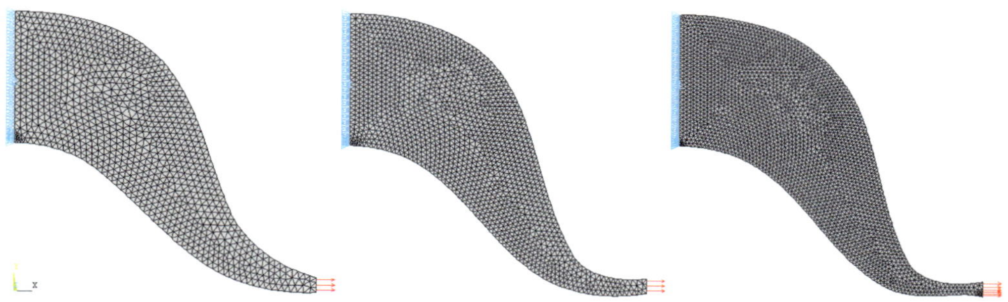

(*a*) (*b*) (*c*)

Fig. 5. Optimal shapes for an eccentrically loaded plate using (*a*) five, (*b*) seven, (c) nine key points (Sonmez, 2007).

2.2 Accuracy of an optimum design

Another concern in shape optimization is the accuracy, i.e. how well the resulting optimum shape reflects the best possible shape. As one of the sources detracting from the accuracy, search algorithm may get stuck into one of the local optimums that fail to approximate the global optimum. One may not ensure that the resulting configuration is globally optimal; but one may use reliable search algorithms such as simulated annealing. Another source of low accuracy is due to errors in calculating the cost of a configuration. In many structural optimization problems, maximum stress value is used either in calculating the cost function or in checking constraint violations. Designers usually carry out a finite element (FE) analysis to calculate the stress state in the structure, but they tend to choose a rough FE mesh to alleviate the computational burden. However, this may lead to erroneous values of stress, and the resulting design may not even be similar to the globally optimum design. The significance of accuracy in FE calculations is better seen in Fig. 6, which shows the optimum shape obtained when a rough mesh is used. Although the error in stress level is only 5%, the discrepancy in shape is quite large. Imprecise definition of shape also leads to optimal shapes not similar to the best possible shape as shown in Fig. 5.

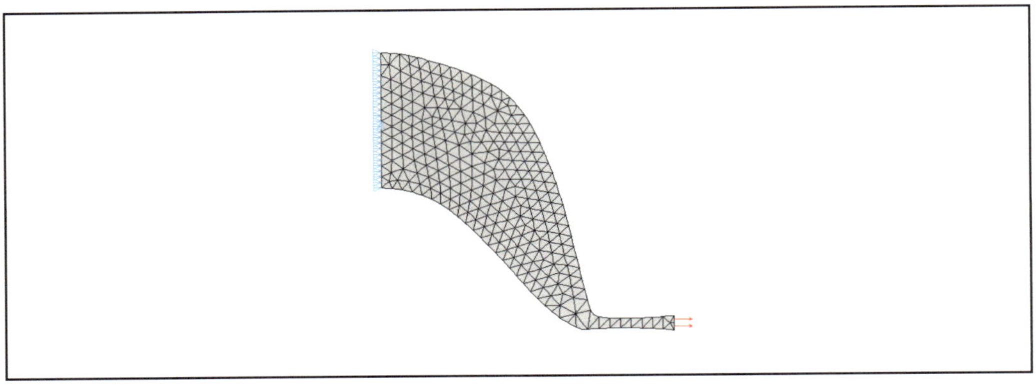

Fig. 6. Inaccurate optimal shape obtained with a rough mesh (Sonmez, 2007).

2.3 Application of simulated annealing to shape optimization

In shape optimization problems, typically there exist quite a number of locally optimum designs, which may be far worse than the globally optimum design according to the chosen criterion of effectiveness. For that reason, a downhill proceeding algorithm, in which a monotonically decreasing value of objective function is iteratively created, may get stuck into a locally minimum point other than the globally minimum one. Its success depends on the choice of initial design, i.e. on designer's intuition; therefore it may not reflect the best possible design. An optimization procedure based on a local-search algorithm can only be successful if the objective is to improve the current design or only a small segment of the boundary is allowed to move, or only a small number of dimensional parameters are used to define its shape. Another disadvantage is that if the starting point is outside the feasible region, the algorithm may converge to a local minimum within the infeasible domain. The advantage of using local search algorithms, on the other hand, is their computational efficiency. Just a small number of iterations are needed to obtain an improved design.

One of the optimization methods that have been used to obtain optimal structural designs is evolutionary structural optimization. The approach is to gradually remove inefficient materials until the shape of the structure evolves into an optimum. Although this method is not a global search algorithm, because of its simplicity and effectiveness, it has been applied to many structural optimization problems (Qing et al., 2001; Das et al., 2005; Cervera & Trevelyan, 2005; Li et al., 2005). This method is also suitable for topology optimization, where not only outer boundary but also geometry of inner regions is allowed to change. There are also similar algorithms which can effectively be used to find improved designs such as biological growth methods (Tekkaya & Guneri, 1996; Wessel et al., 2004) and metamorphic development methods (Liu, et al., 2005).

In order to find the absolute minimum of an objective function without being sensitive to the starting position, a global optimization method has to be employed in structural optimization problems. Stochastic optimization techniques are quite suitable in this respect. Among their advantages, they are not sensitive to starting point, they can search a large solution space, and they can escape local optimum points because they allow occasional uphill moves. The genetic algorithm (GA) and simulated annealing (SA) algorithm are two of the most popular stochastic optimization techniques.

Many researchers applied genetic algorithms to shape optimization problems (Sandgren & Jensen, 1992; Kita & Tanie, 1997; Annicchiarico & Cerrolaza, 2001; Woon et al., 2003; Garcia & Gonzales, 2004; Zhang et al., 2005). These algorithms are based on the concepts of genetics and Darwinian survival of the fittest. The idea is to start the search process with a set of designs, called population. The search procedure is a simulation of the evolution process. The genetic algorithm transforms one population into a succeeding population using operators of reproduction, recombination, and mutation. Convergence to the global minimum depends on the proper choice of the design parameters, rules of the reproduction and mutation.

Kirkpatrick et al. (1983) first proposed simulated annealing (SA) as a powerful stochastic search technique. SA is superior to other optimization algorithms in that it is generally more reliable in finding the global optimum, i.e. the probability of locating the global optimum is high even with large numbers of design variables. Another advantage of SA is that it does not require derivatives of objective function or constraint functions, being a zero order algorithm like GA. The main drawback, on the other hand, is the requirement of quite a number of iterations for convergence; but with the today's ever increasing computational power, this is becoming less and less problem.

Application of simulated annealing to shape optimization of the structures is quite rare. Anagnostou et al. (1992) used SA to design a thermal fin with a minimum use of material. Sonmez (2007) used SA to obtain optimal designs for two-dimensional structures with minimum weight. Sonmez (2007) employed an improved variant of SA called direct search simulated annealing (DSA), proposed by Ali et al. (2002). DSA differs from SA basically in two aspects. Firstly, DSA keeps a set of current configurations rather than just one current configuration. Secondly, it always retains the best configuration. In a way, this property imparts a sort of memory to the optimization process. If a newly generated configuration is accepted, it just replaces the worst configuration.

Shape optimization is a constrained optimization; but SA is only applicable to unconstrained optimization problems. By integrating a penalty function for constraint violations into the objective function, the constrained optimization problem can be transformed into an unconstrained problem, for which the algorithm is suitable. Consider the volume minimization problem for a 2D structure having constant thickness. A combined objective function may be constructed as

$$f = \frac{A}{A_{ini}} + c \left\langle \frac{\sigma_{\max}}{\sigma_{allow}} - 1 \right\rangle^2 \tag{1}$$

Here, the bracketed term is defined as

$$\left\langle \frac{\sigma_{\max}}{\sigma_{allow}} - 1 \right\rangle = \begin{cases} 0 & \text{for } \sigma_{\max} \le \sigma_{allow} \\ \left(\sigma_{\max}/\sigma_{allow}\right) - 1 & \text{for } \sigma_{\max} > \sigma_{allow} \end{cases} \tag{2}$$

where A_{ini} is the lateral area of the initial configuration; c is a weighing coefficient. Any excursion into the infeasible region ($\sigma_{\max} > \sigma_{allow}$) results in an increase in the objective function.

2.3.1 Optimal shape design of a Pin-Joint

Consider a pin-joint depicted in Fig. 2.*d*. The problem is to find the minimum-weight pin-joint that will not fail under static loading. The magnitude of the load is taken to be 200 MPa at the centre of the contact zone decreasing to zero towards the end. Radius of the circular holes is 1 cm, and the distance between their centres is 13 cm. During the optimization process, the entire outer boundary is allowed to vary. Because of symmetry, only one quarter of the component is considered for analysis as shown in Fig. 7. The slope of the spline curve is set to 90° at the top, 0° at the bottom in order to ensure symmetry. The key points at these locations are movable; but one is restricted to move in the horizontal direction, the other in the vertical direction. The allowable stress of the material is taken as 300 MPa.

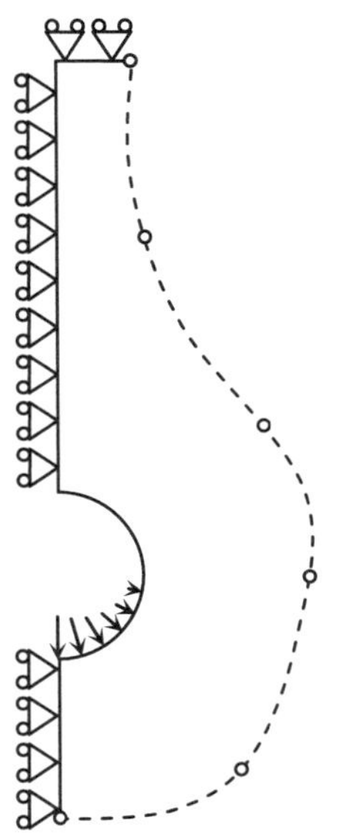

Fig. 7. Domain of analysis for the pin-joint and the boundary conditions (Sonmez, 2007).

Fig. 8 shows the optimal shapes obtained using four, six, eight, and ten moving key points. The lateral areas of them were 13.757, 12.603, 11.948, and 11.895 cm^2, respectively. This means that with a more precise definition of the boundary, a better optimal shape is obtained. The resulting optimum shape is somewhat surprising. This does not look like any of the commonly used pin-joints. A curved indent appears at the side of the hole. This shows that the optimal shapes obtained through an optimization algorithm may not conform to the intuition of the designer. One may conjecture that the curved indent tends to reduce the stress concentration effect of the curvature of the hole.

In the physical annealing process, mobility of atoms is high at high temperatures, which decreases as the temperature is lowered. In order to search the global optimum within a large domain, this aspect of the physical annealing process should be incorporated to the simulated annealing optimization procedure. This is achieved for the problem discussed above, by allowing large changes in the positions of the key points during the initial phases of optimization, where the temperature parameter is high, and gradually restricting their movements in later stages. In this way, not only near neighbourhood of the initially chosen design is searched, but also quite different designs are tried.

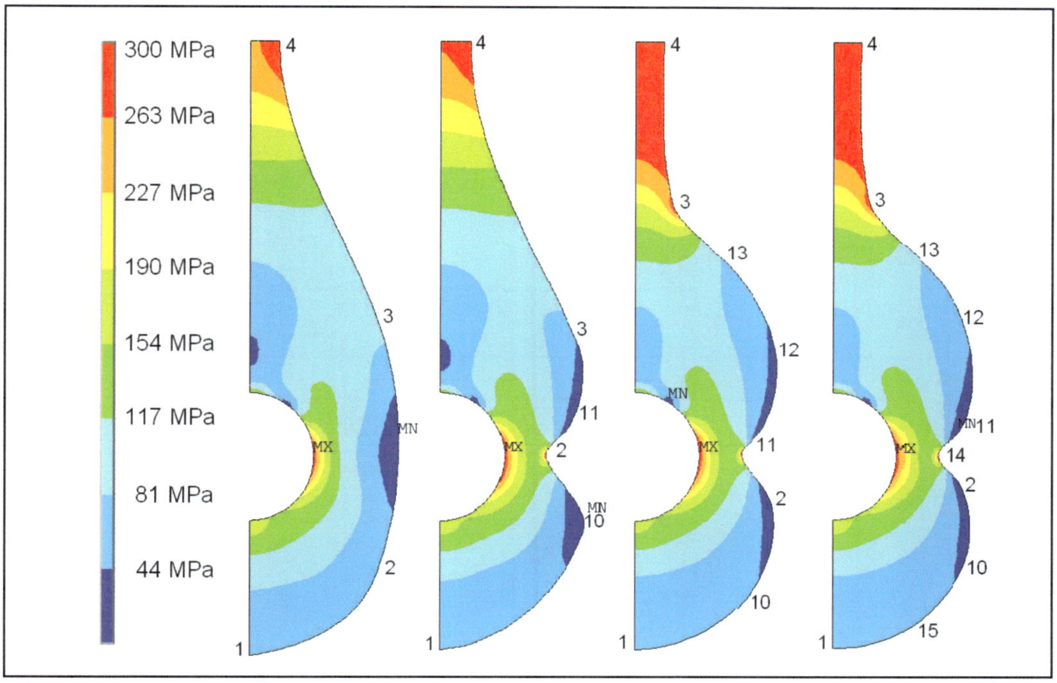

Fig. 8. The optimal shapes found using four, six, eight, and ten key points (Sonmez, 2007).

2.3.2 Optimal shape design of a torque arm

Another problem is the optimal design of a torque arm as depicted in Fig. 9. The radii of the circular holes on the left and the right are 6 mm and 3 mm, respectively. The border of the circular hole on the left is restrained from movement, while the other is loaded as shown. The entire boundary is allowed to move during optimization except that the holes are fixed. Because the structure is symmetric with respect to the axis passing through the centres of the holes, only the coordinates of the key points on one of its sides are design variables, and the two key points on it are constrained to move along this axis. As shown in the figure, the search domain, *S*, within which the key points can only move, is defined by a rectangle of dimension 75 mm × 22 mm. The allowable stress of the material is taken as 600 MPa. Figure 10 shows the optimal shape obtained using 10 moving key points, which has a lateral area of 7.1753 cm^2. A hump appears close to the larger hole.

2.3.3 Feasibility of global search using a local search algorithm

Computational burden of global search algorithms is known to be considerable, while local search algorithms converge at most in a few hundred iterations. One may wonder whether local search algorithms are better alternatives to global search, which may be achieved by repeated runs each time starting from a different initial configuration.

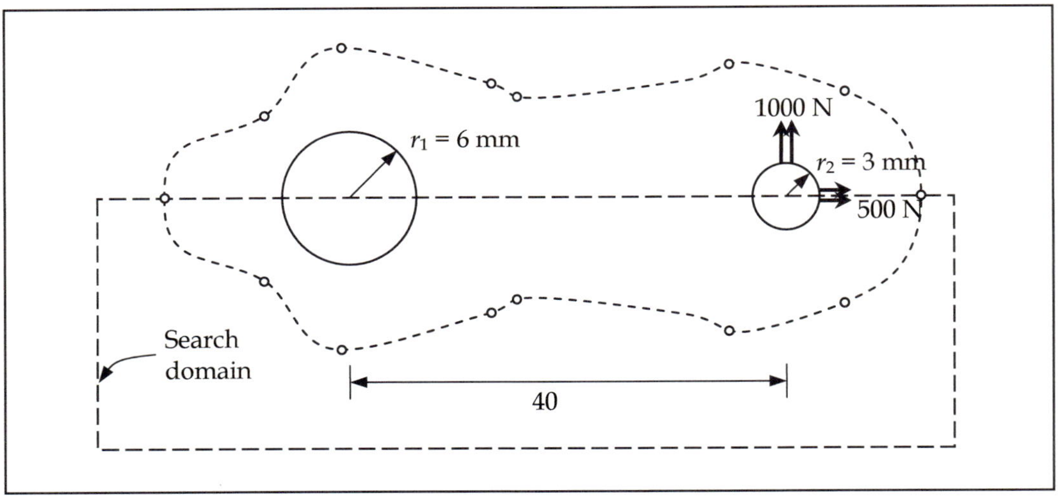

Fig. 9. Optimum design problem for a torque arm (Sonmez, 2007).

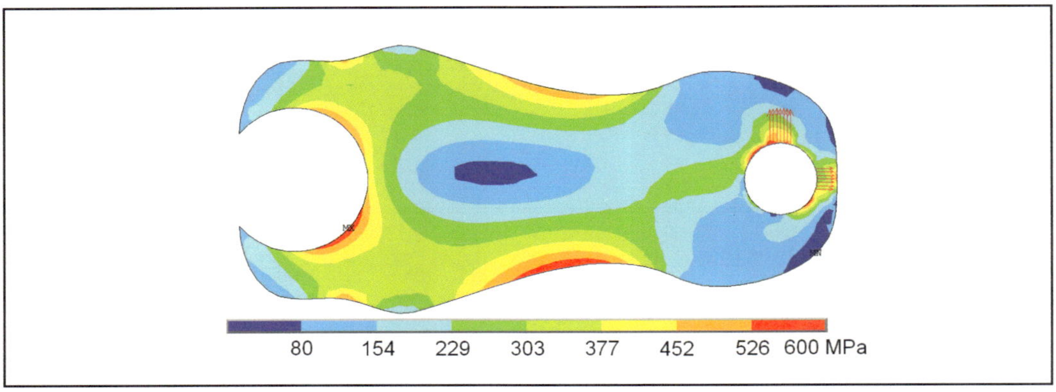

Fig. 10. The optimal shape found using 10 key points. (Sonmez, 2007)

Although first or second order algorithms are more efficient, they are not suitable for global search in shape optimization. Because, it is very likely that connectivity of the structure is lost during iterations. In that case, the objective function cannot be calculated since a finite element analysis of an unrestrained structure cannot be carried out; only a large penalty value can be assigned. Accordingly, derivative of the objective function cannot be calculated. For this reason, first and second order local search algorithms may only be employed to improve a current design since connectivity is not expected to be lost if the search is restricted to near neighbourhood of the initial design. Therefore, we are left with zero order methods, which only require calculation of objective function values corresponding to a given set of optimization variables not their derivatives. Among them, Nelder-Mead method was chosen and employed repeatedly starting from arbitrarily generated initial shapes. Figure 11 shows the lateral areas of the generated optimum shapes. Every one of them had a larger area than the one obtained by the global search algorithm. The optimization process was repeated 350 times, which required more than 200 thousand

FE analyses of the structure. Therefore, global search through a local search algorithm is also not computationally efficient; the reason for this is obvious if one examines the shape in Figure 12, which suggests that there are infinitely different ways a local optimum shape can show itself. Figure 13 shows the best shape found by Nelder-Mead algorithm. This has a lateral area of 7.5040 cm², which is about 4% larger than the best area found by the global search algorithm, DSA. This implies that starting with arbitrary shapes it is very unlikely for a local search algorithm to locate the globally optimum shape. Also, precision and accuracy cannot be checked. Accordingly, we may conclude that local search algorithms are not suitable for global search in shape optimization problems.

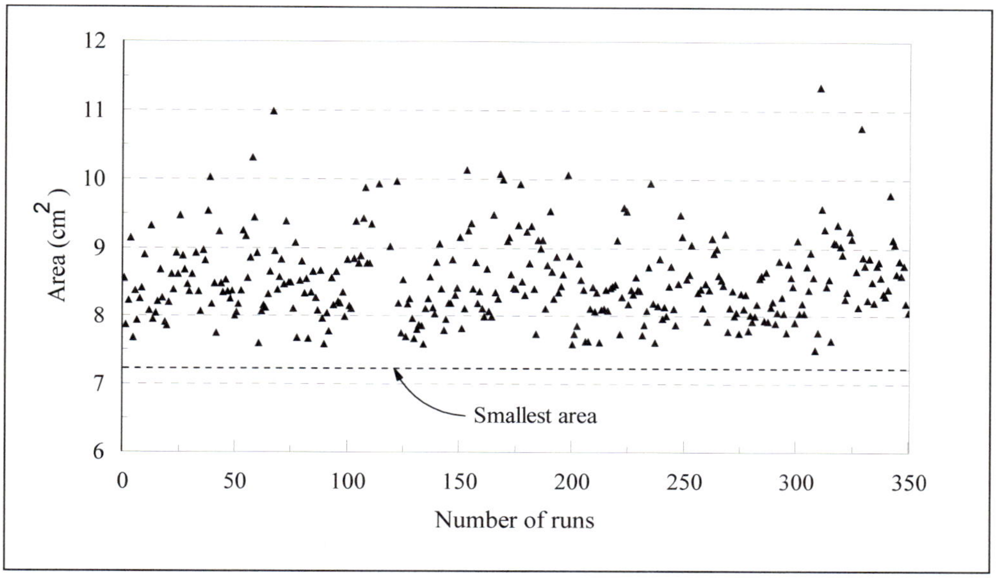

Fig. 11. Lateral areas of the optimum shapes generated through repeated runs using Nelder-Mead algorithm each starting with randomly generated initial shapes (Sonmez, 2007).

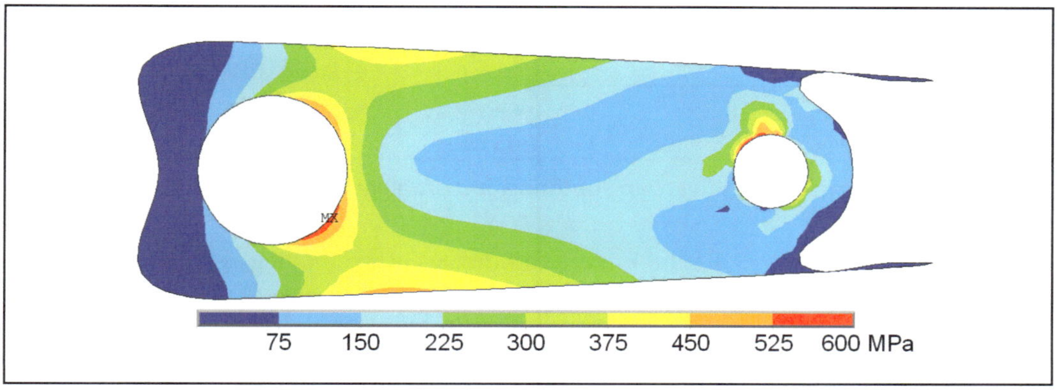

Fig. 12. A typical shape found by a local search algorithm (Nelder-Mead), which is trapped into a local minimum with a high objective function value (Sonmez, 2007).

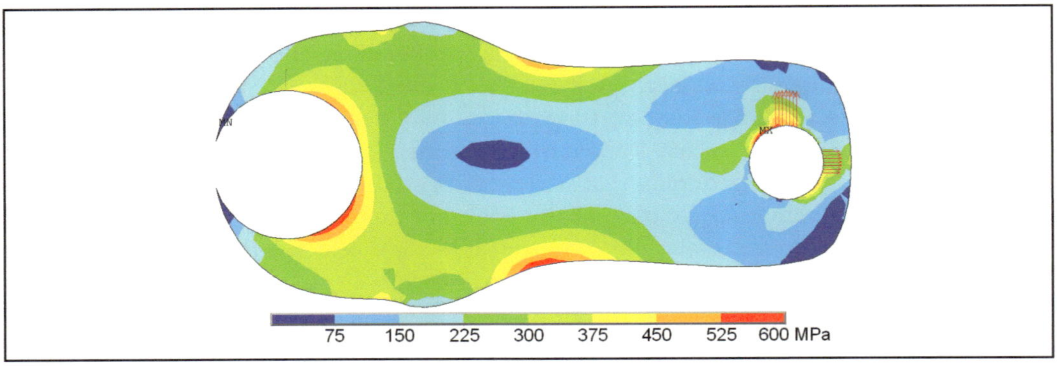

Fig. 13. The best shape found by a local search algorithm (Nelder-Mead) (Sonmez, 2007).

2.3.4 Optimal shape design of a shoulder fillet

Consider an optimal shape design problem of minimizing stress concentration in a shouldered shaft subject to axial loading as depicted in Fig. 14. The geometric features having determining effect on stress concentration factor are the ratios of D/d and $\ell/(D-d)$ and most importantly the shape of the fillet. ℓ is the length of the transition region. The objective is to minimize the peak equivalent stress induced in the structure. The objective function can then be expressed in the following form:

$$f = \frac{(\sigma_q)_{\max}}{\sigma_{allow}} \tag{3}$$

where $(\sigma_q)_{\max}$ is the maximum equivalent stress developed in the structure, σ_{allow} is the allowable stress.

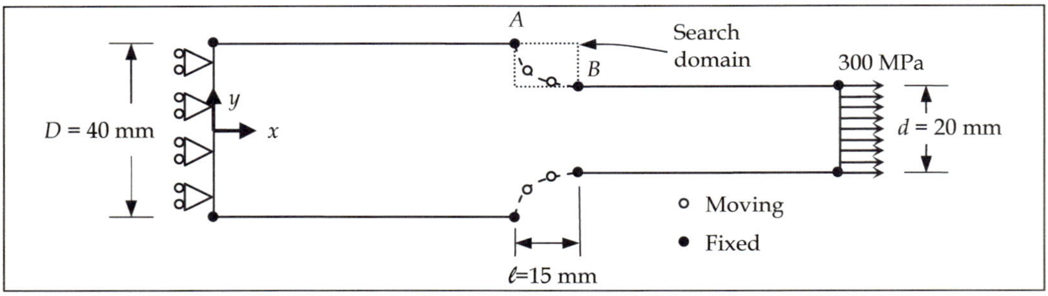

Fig. 14. Representation of a fillet shape optimization problem for a shouldered plate (Sonmez, 2008).

The optimization variables are the x and y coordinates of the moving key points. There are some restrictions on the movements of the key points, i.e. constraints on optimization variables. First of all, the key points are allowed to move only within a search region, S, defined by the designer. Although search of a globally optimum design without restricting the movements of the key points is possible, computational time becomes unnecessarily much longer. Search domain should not be too restrictive, but should exclude the regions that are definitely expected to be away from the optimal boundary.

The main drawback of SA algorithm is its high computational burden. Use of this algorithm can only be feasible for shape design optimization applications, if some ways of increasing its efficiency can be found without compromising from its reliability in locating globally optimal designs. This example shows one of the computationally efficient ways of finding the best possible design. This is achieved through successively obtaining more and more precise optimal shapes and a judicious way of determining the bounds of the search domain.

If optimal shapes are obtained using a low number of moving key points, definition of the boundary will be imprecise, but the globally optimal shape can reliably be obtained to a high degree of accuracy. However, imprecisely defined optimal shape even if it is globally optimum for the chosen design variables may not represent the best possible shape. When the number of the key points is increased, the boundary can be defined more precisely, but whether the globally optimal design has been accurately obtained or not becomes questionable. This is because the likelihood of getting stuck into a local optimum will be high with a large number of optimization variables even if a global search algorithm is used. However, if some regions of the search domain that are expected to be away from the globally optimal point are excluded, reliability of the search algorithm can be increased. Restricting the search domain for a more precisely defined shape design problem by considering the optimal shape obtained using a lower number of key points, one may obtain a higher reliability. By successively generating more and more precise optimal shapes and each time restricting the search domain, one may locate the best possible shape as shown in the following shape design problem.

For the shape design optimization problem of a shouldered shaft, first, the fillet was defined by two moving key points and its shape was optimized using DSA algorithm. Fig. 15 shows the optimal shape of the fillet and the stress distribution within the plate. The maximum equivalent stress is 346.25 MPa. "B" indicates the position of the fixed key point at the right end of the transition region shown in Fig. 14, while "1" and "2" point to the optimal positions of the moving key points.

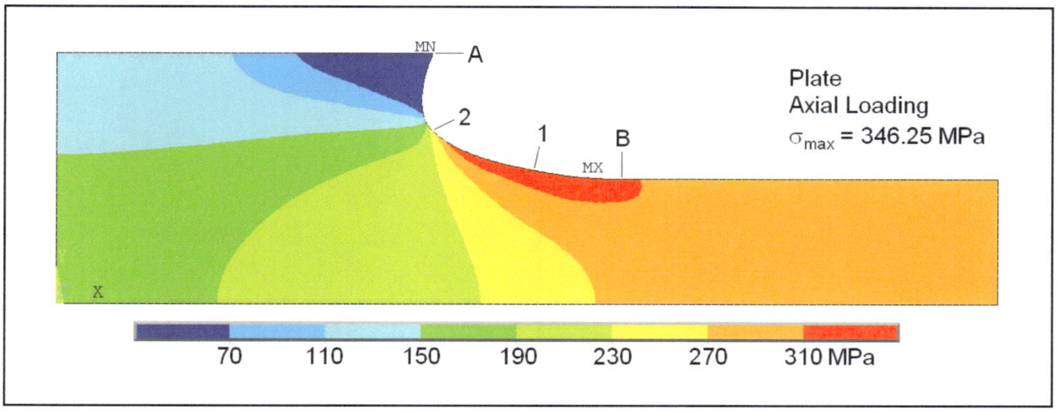

Fig. 15. Stress distribution within the optimal shaped plate with a shoulder fillet defined by two key points (Sonmez, 2008).

The optimal shape obtained by two moving key points implies that the search region shown in Fig. 14 is unnecessarily large. Movements of the key points towards the region around the upper right corner certainly result in worse designs. Inclusion of this region within the search domain leads to generation of many unnecessary configurations, and thus high computational cost. For this reason, the search domain shown in Fig. 16 was adopted in optimizing the fillet defined by three key points. However, the optimum fillet shape obtained with two key points was not used as an initial configuration in the new optimization process. Again, initial coordinates of the moving key points were randomly generated within the search domain. The resulting optimal shaped plate and the stress state are shown in Fig. 17. The maximum equivalent stress turned out to be 344.68 MPa. Because three key points provided a more precise definition of shape, allowing generation of shapes not possible for two key points, a better shape with a lower stress concentration was obtained.

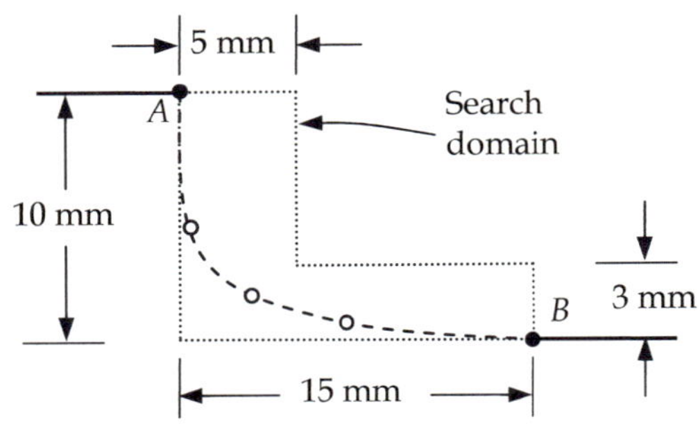

Fig. 16. Search domain used for three moving key points (Sonmez, 2008).

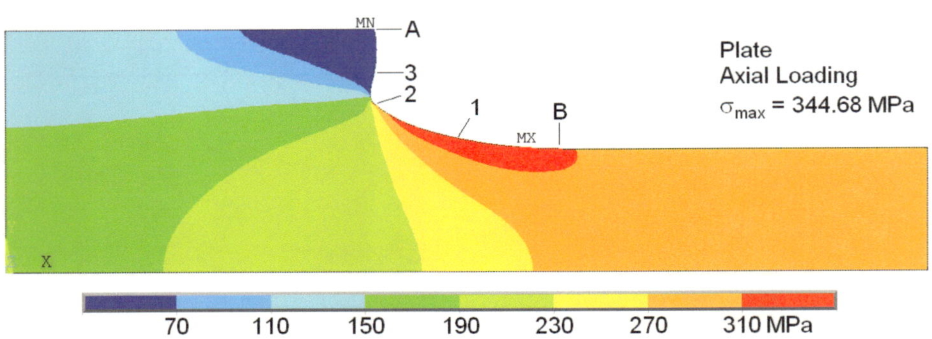

Fig. 17. Stress distribution within the optimal shaped plate with a shoulder fillet defined by three key points (Sonmez, 2008).

Next, the fillet shape defined by four key points was optimized. This time, a separate search domain was used for each key point (Fig. 18). This eliminates generation of very irregular shapes, but allows generation of every possible near optimum shape. Fig. 19 shows the optimal shape and the stress state in the plate. The maximum stress is 343.87 MPa. Unlike the previous shapes, a protrusion develops at the upper portion of the fillet. Because the algorithm tries to minimize the maximum stress and this is a lower stressed region, one may assume that the algorithm places the 3. and 4. key points to provide a better curvature in the highly stressed lower portion of the fillet rather than to minimize stresses in the upper portion. Accordingly, in these three trials, although the shapes of the upper portion are quite different, the lower portions are quite similar as seen in Figures 15, 17, and 19.

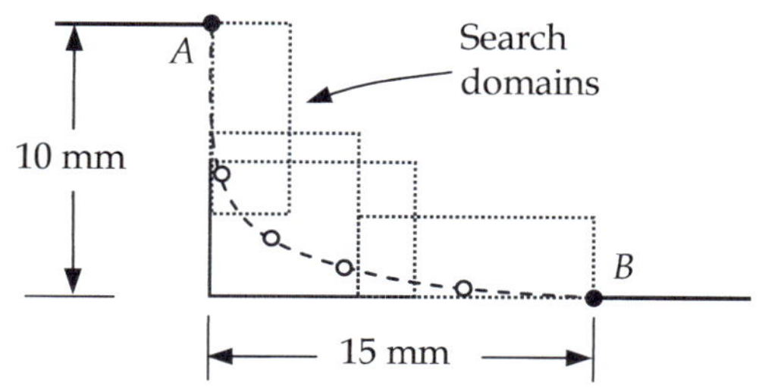

Fig. 18. Separate search domains for four moving key points (Sonmez, 2008).

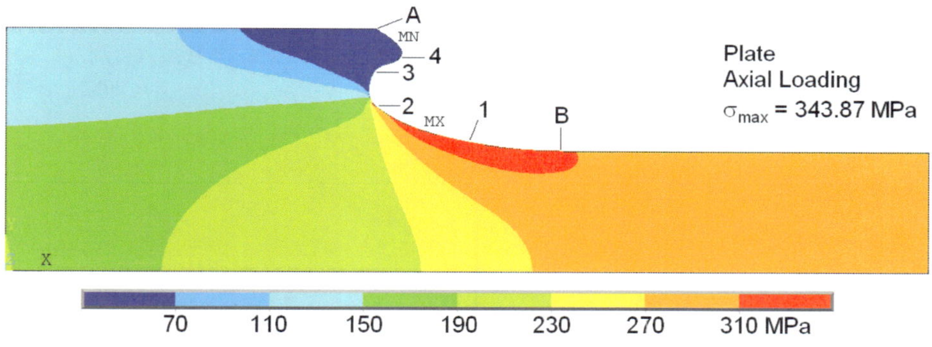

Fig. 19. Stress distribution within the optimal shaped plate with a shoulder fillet defined by four key points (Sonmez, 2008).

The fillet shape was then defined more precisely by six key points. Because such a high number of key points may lead to generation of very irregular shapes which are difficult to analyze by FEM, a small and separate search domain was defined for each key point (Fig. 20). In order to decide on the location and size of the search domains, the optimal fillet shape defined by four key points was used. However, initial positions of the key points were again arbitrarily chosen by the algorithm within the search domains. If a key point in the best current configuration gets close to its border during the optimization process, its search domain was expanded. Fig. 21 shows the optimal shape and the stress distribution in the plate. The maximum equivalent stress is 340.82 MPa.
Finally, the number of key points was increased to eight, and the fillet shape was optimized. This time, the maximum equivalent stress developed in the plate was 339.70 MPa. One may still find a better shape by further increasing the number of moving key points; however the small gain thus achieved does not justify the increased computational effort. In order to

validate the assumption that a protrusion was formed in the lower stressed region to provide the optimal curvature in the highly stresses region, this protrusion was removed and a FE analysis of the remaining plate was carried out. As seen in Fig. 22, the same stress state was obtained.

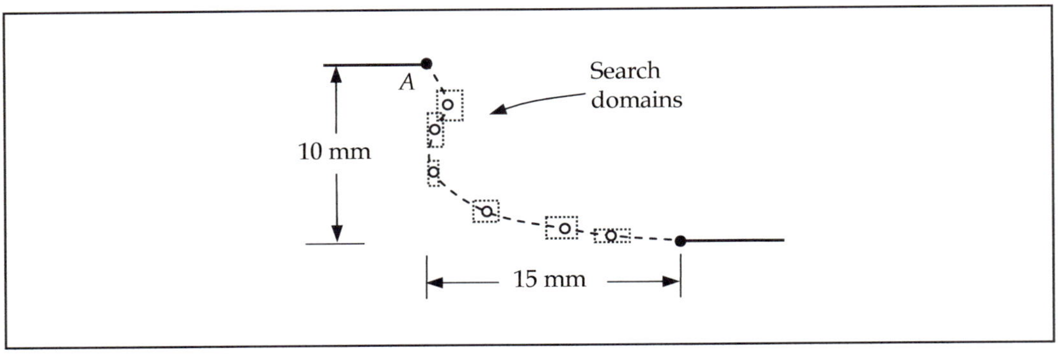

Fig. 20. Separate search domains for 6 moving key points (Sonmez, 2008).

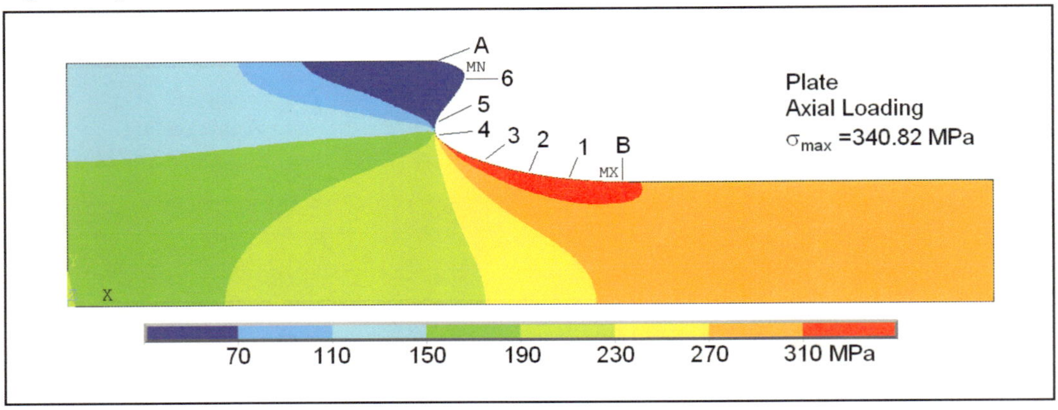

Fig. 21. Stress distribution within the optimal shaped plate with a shoulder fillet defined by six key points (Sonmez, 2008).

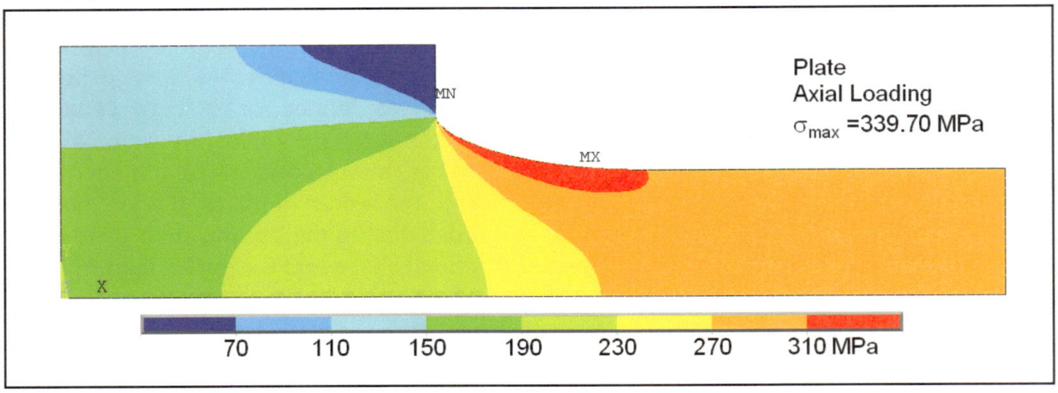

Fig. 22. Stress distribution within the optimal shaped plate with a shoulder fillet defined by eight key points. The protruding portion was removed (Sonmez, 2008).

Assuming that increasing the number of key points further does not lead to appreciable improvement in the objective function, one may consider the plate with the protrusion removed as the optimal shape. In that case, the stress concentration factor, K_q, calculated for the optimum shape is equal to 1.132. Considering that D/d ratio of the plate, which is 2.0, is quite large, one may not obtain such low values with circular fillet profiles except for very large fillets. The stress concentration factor for a circular fillet having the same transition length is about 20% higher.

3. Topology optimization

The objective in topology optimization is to find the best structural layout for a given loading as depicted in Fig. 23. In other words, the number, size, and (/or) shape of components and the way they are connected are optimized. Topology optimization may include shape optimization of individual components, which increases the difficulty of the problem.

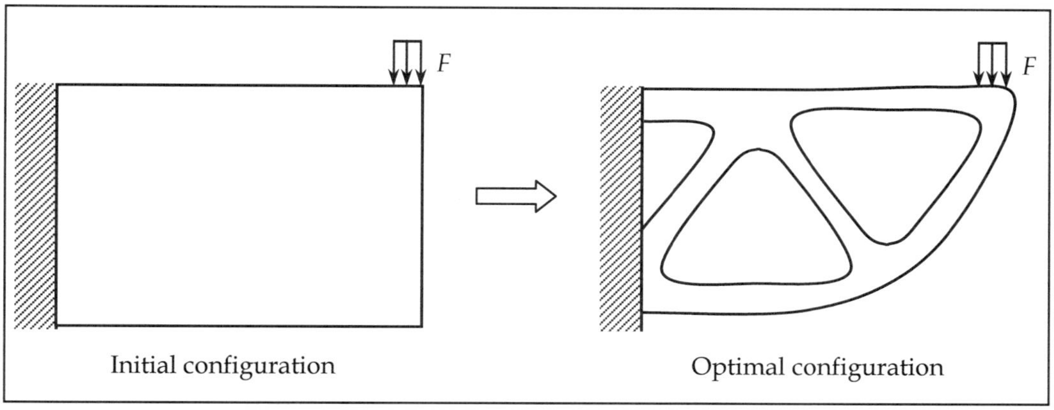

Fig. 23. An illustration of a topology optimization problem.

The criteria of effectiveness according to which a configuration generated during an optimization process for the topology of the structure is evaluated are the same as that of a shape optimization problem. The objective is either minimizing weight or maximizing mechanical performance. The design variables may be existence or absence of material at a certain element as shown in Fig. 4, connectivity matrix of individual components, size of the individual parts etc. A number of researchers applied simulated annealing to topology-optimization problems. (Dhingra & Bennage, 1995; Topping et al., 1996; Shim & Manoochehri, 1997; Liu et al., 1997; Bureerat & Kunakote, 2006; Lamberti & Pappalettere, 2007). Their results show the promise of SA to solve topology optimization problems.

3.1 Application of simulated annealing to topology optimization

3.1.1 Optimal topology design of a torque arm

Consider the optimal topology design problem of a torque arm solved by Shim & Manoochehri (1997) for the loading and radii of holes indicated in Fig. 9. The objective was to minimize the volume of the structure. The design variables were the existence or absence of material in the finite elements (Fig. 4). The maximum stress was constrained not to exceed the allowable stress. Another constraint was the maintenance of model connectivity such that removing or adding material should not result in a disconnected structure. Fig. 24 shows the initially chosen design and the finite element mesh and Fig. 25 shows the optimal topologies. They achieved about 90% reduction in volume and obtained quite different optimal topologies for different magnitudes of allowable stress. This shows that rules of thumb for optimal designs are not tenable. Small changes in material, boundary conditions, or geometry may greatly change optimal configurations.

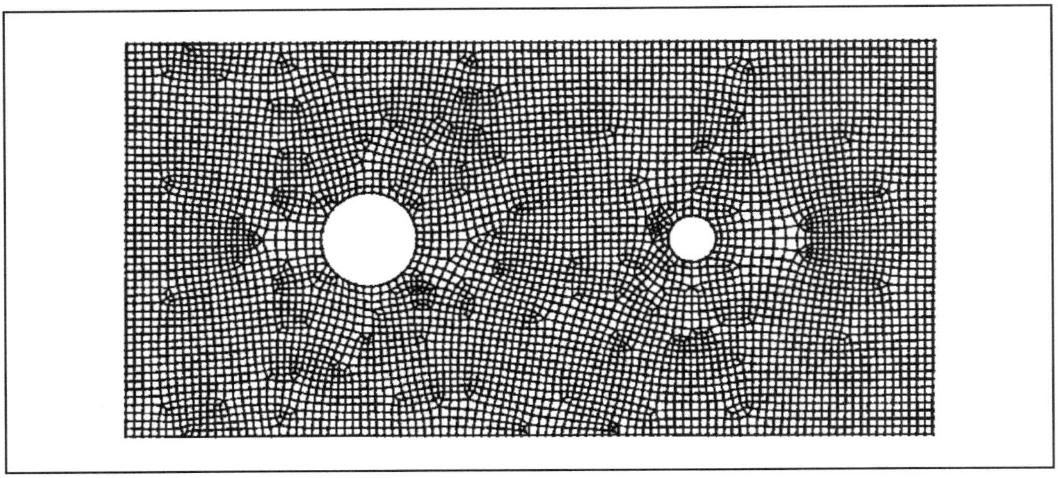

Fig. 24. The initial design and finite element mesh for torque arm (Shim & Manoochehri, 1997).

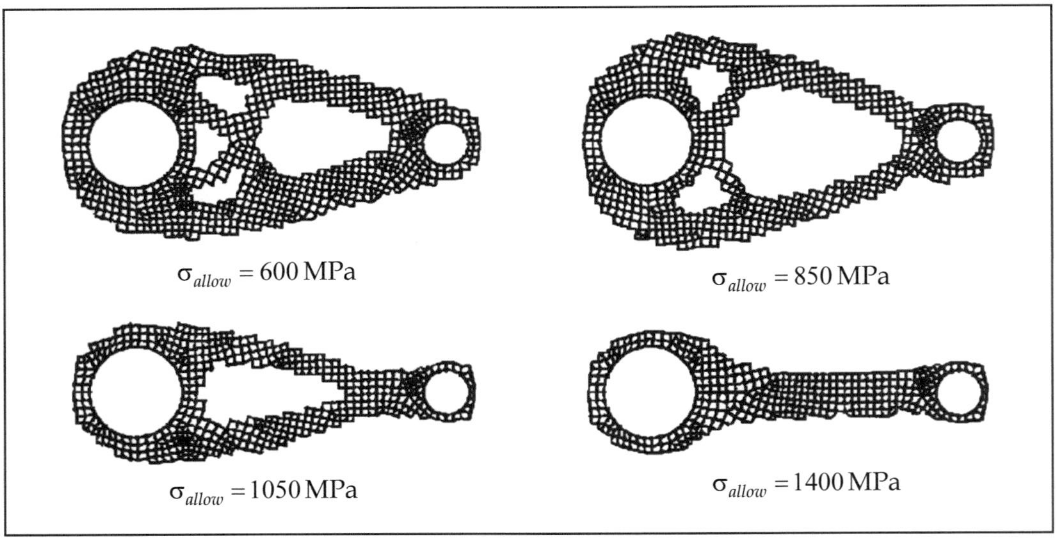

Fig. 25. The optimal topology designs for torque arm (Shim & Manoochehri, 1997).

3.1.2 Optimal topology design of an MBB beam

Bureerat & Kunakote (2006) considered a multi - objective optimization problem of minimizing both compliance and mass of an MBB beam depicted in Fig. 26. They also used a material removal technique (Fig. 4) to generate different configurations. Connectivity of the structure was also chosen as a constraint. Fig. 26 shows the optimal topology of the beam obtained using SA algorithm. They also tried other global search algorithms like genetic algorithms (GA) and population-based incremental learning (PBIL) algorithm, and found the performance of SA to be better.

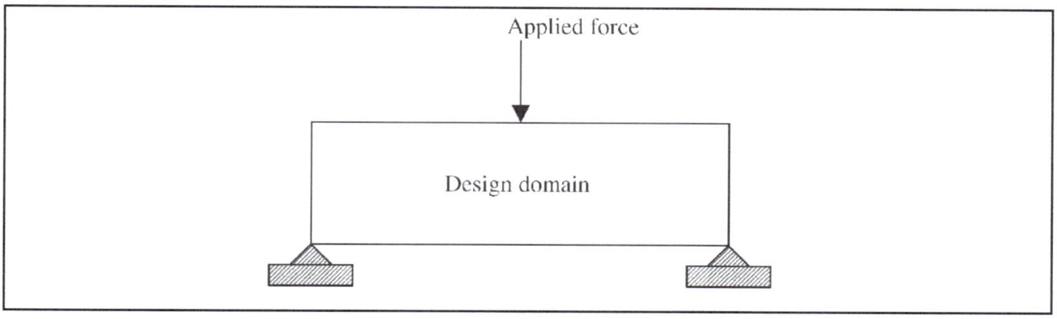

Fig. 26. Initial design of an MBB beam (Bureerat & Kunakote, 2006).

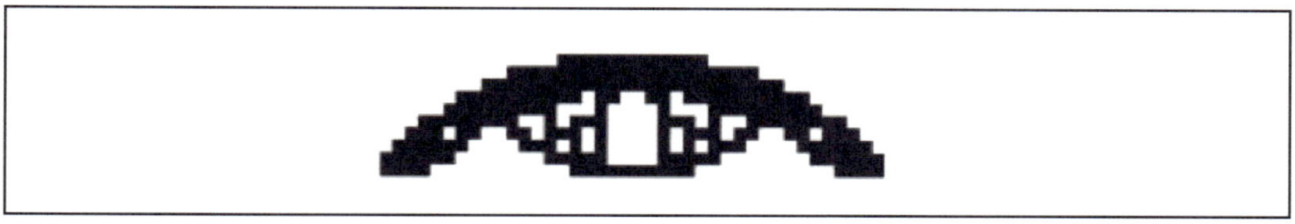

Fig. 27. Optimal topology of the MBB beam (Bureerat & Kunakote, 2006).

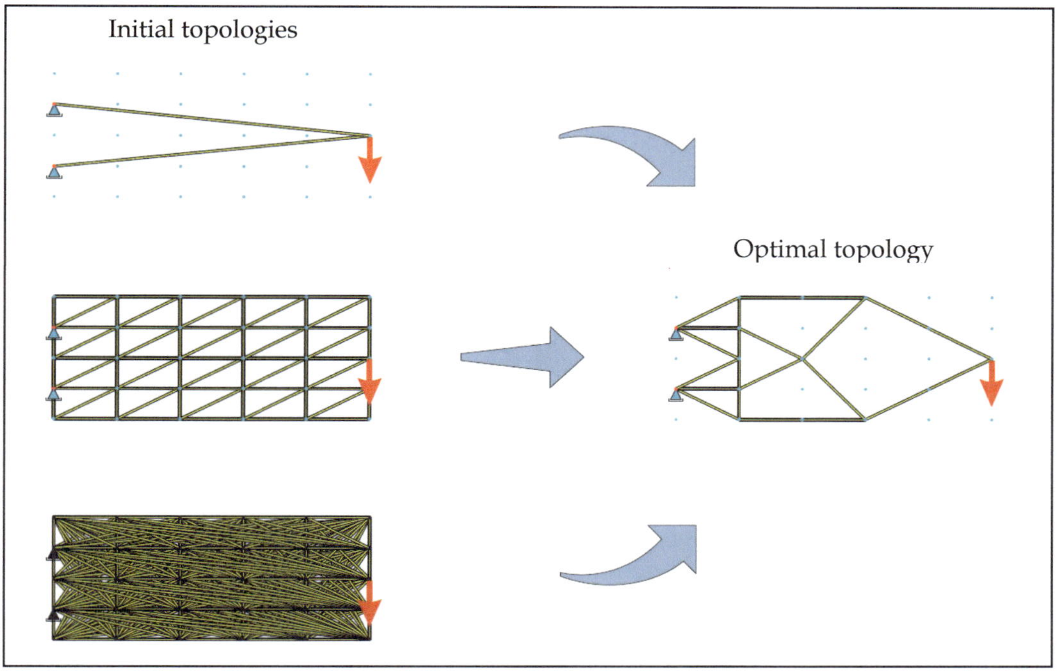

Fig. 28. Various initial designs and the optimal design (Baumann & Kost, 2005).

3.1.3 Optimal topology design of a truss structure

A number of researchers considered topology optimization of discrete structures like trusses. Baumann & Kost (2005) used three stochastic global search algorithms, SA, GA, and random cost, to find the optimal truss topology having the minimum weight. Starting with different initial configurations (Fig. 28), they employed these algorithms each time with a different random sequence and compared relative performance of these algorithms. SA turned out to be the most reliable of the three. SA located the optimal solution in 24 runs out of 25. Its success also did not depend on the initially chosen design.

4. Composites optimization

Composite materials are widely used in the industry because of their superior mechanical, thermal, and chemical properties, e.g. high stiffness-to-weight and strength-to-weight ratios, corrosive resistance, low thermal expansion, vibration damping. As a further advantage, composite materials offer a great flexibility in design, allowing change of the material system in many ways. Configurations of a laminate, i.e. fibre orientation, ply thickness, stacking sequence, type and volume fraction of reinforcement can be tailored to make a better use of material or attain a desired property, e.g. strength, elastic modulus, thermal and electrical conductivity, thermal expansion coefficient. One may thus significantly decrease the weight of a structure by optimizing the design of the composite material itself, or increase its performance using the same amount of material without changing the shape or topology of the structure.

Because of large numbers of design variables, the traditional approach of designing by trial and error, which heavily relies on designer's experience and intuition, promises little success. For that reason, optimization of composite materials drew the attention of many researchers. In these studies, various types of composite structures were considered for optimization: laminated composite plates or shells, hybrid laminates composed of layers with different materials, stiffened plates or shells, pressure vessels, pipes, stiffened cylinders, leaf springs, wrenches, beams, bolted joints, etc.

The purpose of composites optimization is to find the best design for a composite materials system according to a chosen criterion under various constraints imposed by the requirements of the design. The optimum design provides either the most efficient and effective use of material or the best performance. The goal may be to minimize thickness, weight, cost, fatigue damage, displacements, dynamic response, stress concentration, or the difference between current and target values of material properties like elastic modulus, thermal conductivity, and density. In this type of optimizations, the problem is to find the design resulting in the minimum value of an undesired feature of the structure. On the other hand, the objective may be to maximize a desired property of the structure, i.e. the static strength of a composite laminate for a given thickness, strength-to-weight ratio, buckling strength, stiffness, energy absorption capacity, stiffness-to-weight ratio, etc. Besides, one may face with multi - objective optimization problems where cost and weight, weight and deflection, or weight and strain energy may be minimized; buckling strength, static strength together with stiffness may be maximized, etc.

In order to optimize a composite structure, some of its features affecting the objective function are allowed to be changed; i.e. there should be some design variables, which may be fibre orientation angle, layer thickness, material of the layers, geometric parameters, fibre volume fraction, types of matrix and fibre materials, type of reinforcement, parameters related to spacing, configuration, and geometry of stiffeners, etc.

Although composite materials offer great flexibility in product design with a large number of design variables, this feature also leads to an immense number of locally optimum designs. Locating globally optimum designs for composite structures is a difficult problem requiring sophisticated optimization procedures. Locating the globally optimal material design with a local search algorithm is almost a hopeless enterprise. For this reason, many researchers preferred global search algorithms like genetic algorithms (Soremekun et al., 2001; Todoroki & Tetsuya, 2004; Kang & Kim, 2005), simulated annealing algorithm (Soares et al., 1995; Jayatheertha et al., 1996; Sciuva et al., 2003; Correia et al., 2003; Erdal & Sonmez, 2005; Moita et al., 2006; Akbulut & Sonmez, 2008), improving hit-and run (Savic et al., 2001).

4.1 Application of simulated annealing to composite optimization

4.1.1 Optimal design of a composite laminate for minimum thickness

In this problem, the structure to be optimized is a symmetric 2-D multilayered structure reinforced by continuous fibres subject to in-plane normal and shear loading as shown in Fig. 29. Accordingly, no bending and twisting moments are considered in the analysis of its mechanical behaviour. The laminate consists of plies having the same thickness. The objective is to find the optimum design of the laminate to attain the minimum possible laminate thickness with the condition that it does not fail. The Tsai-Wu criterion of static failure together with the maximum stress criterion is employed to check static failure. The number of distinct fibre orientation angles, m, is given. The orientation angles, θ_k, and how many plies, n_k, are oriented along each angle are to be determined in the design process. Accordingly, the number of design variables is $2m$. The laminate thickness can be expressed as

$$t = 2t_o \sum_{k=1}^{m} n_k \tag{4}$$

where t_o is the thickness of an individual ply and n_k is the number of plies with fibre angle

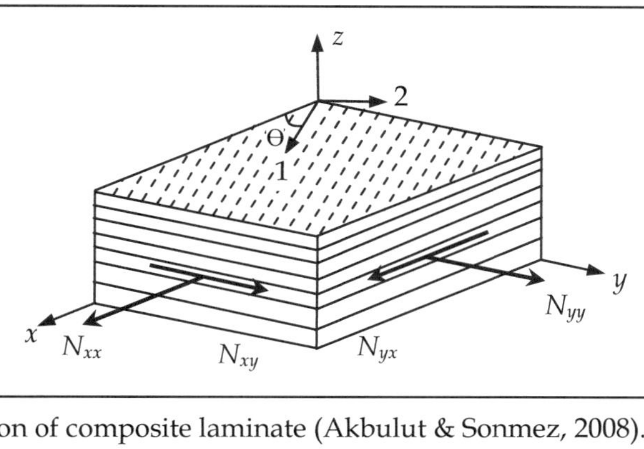

Fig. 29. An illustration of composite laminate (Akbulut & Sonmez, 2008).

θ_k. The factor '2' appears because of the symmetry condition for the laminate with respect to its middle plane. Because the plies are made of the same material, minimizing thickness leads to the same optimum configuration as the minimization of weight. The orientation angles take discrete values; they are chosen from a given set of angles. According to the manufacturing precision, the interval between the consecutive angles may be 15°, 10°, 5°, 1°, 0.5° or even smaller.

Table 1 shows the optimal laminate designs for various biaxial loading cases obtained using two distinct fibre angles. For the loading case N_{xx} = 10, N_{yy} = 5, N_{xy} = 0 MPa·m, the optimal lay-up is $[37_{27}/-37_{27}]_s$, which means 27 plies out of 54 are oriented with 37° and others with -37°. When N_{xx} is increased to 20 MPa·m, strangely the thickness of the optimal laminate becomes smaller. This counter intuitive result can be explained by considering the differences in the stress states. When N_{xx} is increased to 20 MPa·m and the laminate design is changed to $[31_{23}/-31_{23}]_s$, ε_{xx} increases from 0.323×10^{-2} to 0.729×10^{-2}, ε_{yy}, on the other hand, turns from tension to (8.39×10^{-5}) compression (-0.237×10^{-2}) due to Poisson's effect. The stress transverse to the fibres then decreases from 18.49 MPa to 15.85 MPa, while the other principal stresses (shear stress and normal stress along the fibre direction) increase. Because, the transverse tensile stresses are critical, a thinner laminate could carry a larger load. When N_{xx} is increased to 40 MPa·m, the same trend continues. However, when it is increased to 80 or 120 MPa·m, a thicker laminate is required.

Loading: $N_{xx}/N_{yy}/N_{xy}$ (MPa.m)	**Optimum lay-up sequences**	**Half laminate thickness**	**Safety factor for Tsai-Wu**	**Safety factor for max. stress**
10 / 5 / 0	$[37_{27}/-37_{27}]_s$	54	1.0068	1.0277
20 / 5 / 0	$[31_{23}/-31_{23}]_s$	46	1.0208	1.1985
40 / 5 / 0	$[26_{20}/-26_{20}]_s$	40	1.0190	1.5381
80 / 5 / 0	$[21_{25}/-19_{28}]_s$	53	1.0113	1.2213
120 / 5 / 0	$[17_{35}/-17_{35}]_s$	70	1.0030	1.0950

Table 1. The optimum lay-ups obtained using two distinct fibre angles for various biaxial loading cases (Akbulut & Sonmez, 2008).

5. Conclusions

In typical structural optimization problems, there are quite numerous local optimum designs. Use of a local search algorithm even with multiple starts is not a viable approach. For this reason, one needs to apply a global search algorithm like simulated annealing. Some researchers compared performances of a number of global search algorithms and found SA to be better. Its reliability, that means the probability of locating globally optimum design, was found to be the highest of all. The main disadvantage of SA is computational inefficiency. For this reason, one needs to find some ways of increasing its efficiency like judiciously choosing search domain or using SA together with local search algorithms.

Many of the optimal structural designs found by the researchers are counter to the intuition of designers. Even an experienced designer may not guess the optimal shape in many cases. Besides some changes in material, geometry or boundary conditions were observed to lead to quite discrepant optimal structural designs. This means that simple rules of thumb for optimal designs are not justifiable.

A global optimization scheme should search a large domain in order to find the globally optimal design. If only near neighbourhood of the initial design is searched, one may regard the resulting optimal design only as an improvement over the current one not as the globally optimum one. Searching a large domain can be achieved by allowing large changes in the current configurations to obtain a new configuration. As in the physical annealing process, where the mobility of the atoms decrease during cool down, the extent of changes should be reduced in later stages of optimization.

By defining the structural configuration more precisely by using a large number of design variables, one may obtain a better optimal design. Although increased precision poses difficulties for the algorithm to locate the globally optimal design accurately, one may find ways of overcoming this difficulty.

6. References

Akbulut, M. & Sonmez, F.O. (2008). Optimum design of composite laminates for minimum thickness, *Computers & Structures*, to appear.

Ali, M.M., Torn, A. & Viitanen, S. (2002). A direct search variant of the simulated annealing algorithm for optimization involving continuous variables. *Computers & Operations Research*, Vol. 29, pp. 87-102.

Anagnostou G., Ronquit, E.M. & Patera, A.T. (1992). A computational procedure for part design, *Comp. Meth. in Appl. Mech. and Eng.*, Vol .97, pp.33-48.

Annicchiarico, W. & Cerrolaza, M. (2001). Structural shape optimization 3D finite -element models based on genetic algorithms and geometric modeling, *Finite Elements in Analysis and Design*, Vol. 37, pp. 403-415.

Baumann, B. & Kost, B. (2005). Structure assembling by stochastic topology optimization, *Computers & Structures*, Vol. 83, No. 25-26, pp. 2175-2184.

Bureerat, S. & Kunakote, T. (2006). Topological design of structures using population - based optimization methods, *Inverse Problems in Science and Engineering*, Vol. 14, No. 6, pp. 589–607.

Cerrolaza, M., Annicchiarico, W. & Martinez, M. (2000). Optimization of 2D boundary element models using β- splines and genetic algorithms, *Engineering Analysis with Boundary Elements*, Vol. 24, pp. 427-440.

Cervera, E. & Trevelyan, J. (2005). Evolutionary structural optimization based on boundary representation of NURBS. Part1: 2D algorithms, *Computers and Structures*, Vol. 83, pp. 1902-1916.

Chang, M.-H. & Cheng, C.-H. (2005). Optimal design of slider shape for satisfying load demands under specified operation conditions, *Tribology International*, Vol. 38, pp. 757-768.

Correia, V.M.F., Soares, C.M.M. & Soares, C.A.M. (2003). Buckling optimization of composite laminated adaptive structures, *Composite Structures*, Vol.62, pp. 315-321.

Das, R., Jones, R. & Xie Y.M. (2005). Design of structures for optimal static strength using ESO, *Engineering Failure Analysis*, Vol. 12, pp. 61-80.

Dhingra A.K. & Bennage, W.A. (1995). Topological optimization of truss structures using simulated annealing, *Engineering Optimization*, Vol. 24, No. 4, pp. 239-259.

Erdal O. & Sonmez, F.O. (2005). Optimum design of composite laminates for maximum buckling load capacity using simulated annealing, *Composite Structures*, Vol. 71, pp. 45-52.

Garcia, M.J. & Gonzales, C.A. (2004). Shape optimisation of continuum structures via evolution strategies and fixed grid finite element analysis, *Struct. Multidisc. Optim.*, Vol. 26, pp. 92-98.

Jayatheertha, C., Webber, J.P.H. & Morton, S.K. (1996). Application of artificial neural networks for the optimum design of a laminated plate, *Computers & Structures*, Vol. 59, No. 5, pp. 831-845.

Jung, A.; Kammerer, S.; Paffrath, M. & Wever, U. (2005). 3D shape optimization of turbine blades, *ZAMM · Z. Angew. Math. Mech.*, Vol. 85, No. 12, pp. 878 – 895.

Kang J.H. & Kim, C.G. (2005). Minimum-weight design of compressively loaded composite plates and stiffened panels for post buckling strength by genetic algorithm, *Composite Structures*, Vol. 69, pp. 239-246.

Kim, N.H., Choi, K.K. & Botkin, M.E. (2003). Numerical method for shape optimization using meshfree method, *Struct. Multidisc. Optim.*, Vol. 24, pp. 418-429.

Kirkpatrick, S., Gelatt, C.D. & Vecchi, M.P. (1983). Optimization by simulated annealing, *Science*, Vol. 220, pp. 671-680.

Kita, E. & Tanie, H. (1997). Shape optimization of continuum structures by genetic algorithm and boundary element method, *Engineering Analysis with Boundary Elements*, Vol. 19, pp. 129-136.

Lamberti, L. & Pappalettere, C. (2007). Weight optimization of skeletal structures with multi-point simulated annealing, *Computer Modeling in Engineering & Sciences*, Vol. 18, No. 3, pp. 183-221.

Lampinen, J. (2003). Cam shape optimization by genetic algorithm, *Computer-Aided Design*, Vol. 35, pp. 727-737.

Li, W.L., Li, Q., Steven, G.P. & Xie, Y.M. (2005). An evolutionary shape optimization for elastic contact problems subject to multiple load cases, *Comp. Meth. in Appl. Mech. and Eng.*, Vol. 194, pp. 3394-3415.

Liu, J.-S, Parks, G.T. & Clarkson, P.J. (2005). Topology / shape optimization of axisymmetric continuum structures - a metamorphic development approach, *Struct. Multidisc. Optim.*, Vol. 29, pp. 73-83.

Liu, X., Begg, D. W. & Matravers, D. R. (1997). Optimal topology/actuator placement design of structures using SA, *Journal of Aerospace Engineering*, Vol. 10, No. 3, pp. 119-125.

Moita, J.M.S., Correia, V.M.F. & Martins, P.G. (2006). Optimal design in vibration control of adaptive structures using a simulated annealing algorithm, *Composite Structures*; Vol. 75, pp. 79-87.

Qing, L., Steven, G.P. Querin, O.M. & Xie, Y.M. (2001). Stress Based Optimization of Torsional Shafts Using and Evolutionary Procedure, *International Journal of Solids and Structures*, Vol. 38, pp. 5661-5677.

Sandgren, E., & Jensen, E. (1992). Automotive Structural Design Employing a Genetic Optimization Algorithm, *AIAA Journal*, Vol. 30, pp. 920772-920776.

Savic, V., Tuttle, M.E. & Zabinsky, Z.B. (2001). Optimization of composite I-sections using fiber angles as design variables, *Composite Structures*, Vol. 53, pp. 265-277.

Sciuva, M.D., Gherlone, M. & Lomario, D. (2003). Multiconstrained optimization of laminated and sandwich plates using evolutionary algorithms and higher-order plate theories, *Composite Structures*, Vol. 59, pp. 149-154.

Shen, J. & Yoon D. (2003) .A new scheme for efficient and direct shape optimization of complex structures represented by polygonal meshes, *Int. J. Numer. Meth. Engng*, Vol. 58, pp. 2201-2223.

Shim, P.Y. & Manoochehri, S. (1997). Generating optimal configurations in structural design using simulated annealing, *Int. J. Numer. Meth. Engng*, Vol. 40, pp. 1053-1069.

Siegwart, R. (2001). Name of paper. *Name of Journal in Italics*, Vol., No., (month and year of the edition) page numbers (first-last), ISSN

Soares, C.M.M., Correia, V.F., Mateus, H. & Herskovits, J. (1995). A discrete model for the optimal design of thin composite plate - shell type structures using a two - level approach, *Composite Structures*, Vol. 30, pp. 147-157.

Sonmez, F.O. (2007). Shape optimization of 2D structures using simulated annealing, *Comp. Meth. in Appl. Mech. and Eng.*, Vol. 196, pp. 3279-3299.

Sonmez, F.O. (2008). Optimal shape design of shoulder fillets for flat and round bars under various loadings, *In review*.

Soremekun, G., Gurdal, Z., Haftka, R.T. & Watson, L.T. (2001). Composite laminate design optimization by genetic algorithm with generalized elitist selection. *Computers & Structures*, Vol. 79, pp. 131-143.

Tekkaya, A.E. & Guneri, A. (1996). Shape optimization with the biological growth method: A parametric study, *Engineering Computations*, Vol. 13(8), pp. 4-18.

Todoroki A. & Tetsuya, I. (2004). Design of experiments for stacking sequence optimizations with genetic algorithm using response surface approximation, *Composite Structures*, Vol. 64, pp. 349-357.

Topping, B.H.V., Khan, A.I. & Leite, J.P.D. (1996). Topological design of truss structures using simulated annealing, *Structural Engineering Review*, Vol. 8, pp. 301-314.

Wessel, C., Cisilino, A. & Sensale, B. (2004). Structural shape optimisation using boundary elements and the biological growth method. *Struct. Multidisc. Optim.*, Vol. 28, pp. 221-227.

Woon, S.Y., Querin, O.M. & Steven, G.P. (2001). Structural application of a shape optimization method based on a genetic algorithm, *Struct. Multidisc. Optim.*, Vol. 22, pp. 57-64.

Woon, S.Y., Tong, L., Querin, O.M. & Steven, G.P. (2003). Knowledge-based algorithms in fixed-grid GA shape optimization, *Int. J. Numer. Meth. Engng*, Vol. 58, pp. 643-660.

Zhang, Z.Q., Zhou, J.X., Zhou, N., Wang, X.M. & Zhang, L. (2005). Shape optimization using kernel particle method and an enriched genetic algorithm, *Comp. Meth. in Appl. Mech. and Eng.*, Vol. 194, pp. 4048-4070.

15

Optimization of Reinforced Concrete Structures by Simulated Annealing

F. González-Vidosa, V. Yepes, J. Alcalá, M. Carrera, C. Perea and I. Payá-Zaforteza
School of Civil Engineering, Universidad Politécnica Valencia, Spain

1. Introduction

Early attempts of optimised structural designs go back to the 1600s, when Leonardo da Vinci and Galileo conducted tests of models and full-scale structures [1]. A 1994`s review of structural optimization can be found in the study by Cohn and Dinovitzer [2], who pointed out that there was a gap between theoretical studies and the practical application in practice. They also noted the short number of studies that concentrated on concrete structures. A review of structural concrete optimization can be found in the 1998`s study by Sarma and Adeli [3]. The methods of structural optimization may be classified into two broad groups: exact methods and heuristic methods. The exact methods are the traditional approach. They are based on the calculation of optimal solutions following iterative techniques of linear programming [4,5]. The second main group comprises the heuristic methods, whose recent development is linked to the evolution of artificial intelligence procedures. This group includes a broad number of search algorithms [6-9], such as genetic algorithms, simulated annealing, threshold accepting, tabu search, ant colonies, etc. These methods have been successful in areas different to structural engineering [10]. They consist of simple algorithms, but require a great computational effort, since they include a large number of iterations in which the objective function is evaluated and the structural restrictions are checked.

Among the first studies of heuristic optimization applied to structures, the contributions of Jenkins [11] and of Rajeev and Krishnamoorthy [12] in the early 1990s are to be mentioned. Both authors applied genetic algorithms to the optimization of the weight of steel structures. As regards RC structures, early applications in 1997 include the work of Coello et al [13], who applied genetic algorithms to the economic optimization of RC beams. Recently, there has been a number of RC applications [14-16], which optimize RC beams and building frames by genetic algorithms. Also recently, our research group has applied simulated annealing and threshold acceptance to the optimization of walls, frame bridges and building frames [17-20]. However, despite advances on structural concrete optimization, present design-office practice of concrete structures is much conditioned by the experience of structural engineers. Most procedures are based on the adoption of cross-section dimensions and material grades based on sanctioned common practice. Once the structure is defined, it follows the analysis of stress resultants and the computation of passive and active reinforcement that satisfy the limit states prescribed by concrete codes. Should the dimensions or material grades be insufficient, the structure is redefined on a trial and error basis. Such process leads to safe designs, but the economy of the concrete structures is, therefore, very much linked to the experience of the structural designer.

The structures object of this work are walls, portal frames and box frames which are usually built of RC in road construction and RC frames widely used in building construction. RC earth retaining walls are generally designed with a thickness at the base of 1/10 of the height of the wall and a footing width of 0.50-0.70 the height of the wall. Box and portal frames are used with spans between 3.00 and 20.00 m for solving the intersection of transverse hydraulic or traffic courses with the main upper road. Box frames are preferred when there is a low bearing strength terrain or when there is a risk of scour due to flooding. The depth of the top and bottom slab is typically designed between 1/10 to 1/15 of the horizontal free span; and the depth of the walls is typically designed between 1/12 of the vertical free span and the depth of the slabs. Building frames have typical horizontal beams of 5.00 to 10.00 m of horizontal span that sustain the vertical loads of the floors and transfer them to vertical columns of height between 3.00 to 5.00 m. Moderate horizontal loads are usually included in the design, but high levels of horizontal loading are transferred to adjacent shear walls. The structures here analyzed are calculated to sustain the loads prescribed by the codes and have to satisfy all the limit states required as an RC structure. The method followed in this work has consisted first in the development of evaluation computer modules where dimensions, materials and steel reinforcement have been taken as design variables. These modules compute the cost of a solution and check all the relevant structural limit states. Simulated annealing is then used to search the solution space.

2. Simulated annealing optimization procedure

2.1 Problem definition

The structural concrete design problem that is put forward in the present study consists of an economic optimization. It deals with the minimization of the objective function F of expression (1), satisfying also the structural constraints of expressions (2).

$$F(x_1, x_2, \ldots x_n) = \sum_{i=1,r} p_i * m_i(x_1, x_2, \ldots, x_n) \tag{1}$$

$$g_j(x_1, x_2, \ldots\ldots x_n) \leq 0 \tag{2}$$

Note that the objective function in expression (1) is the sum of unit prices multiplied by the measurements of the construction units (concrete, steel, formwork, etc). And that the constraints in expression (2) are all the service and ultimate limit states that the structure must satisfy. Unit prices considered are given in Table 1 and 2.

2.2 Simulated annealing procedure

The search method used in this study is the simulated annealing (SA henceforth), that was originally proposed by Kirkpatrick et al. [21] for the design of electronic circuits. The SA algorithm is based on the analogy of crystal formation from masses melted at high temperature and let cool slowly. At high temperatures, configurations of greater energy

Unit	Cost (€)
kg of steel (B-500S)	0.58
m^2 of lower slab formwork	18.03
m^2 of wall formwork	18.63
m^2 of upper slab formwork	30.65
m^3 of scaffolding	6.01
m^3 of lower slab concrete (labour)	5.41
m^3 of wall concrete (labour)	9.02
m^3 of upper slab concrete (labour)	7.21
m^3 of concrete pump rent	6.01
m^3 of concrete HA-25	48.24
m^3 of concrete HA-30	49.38
m^3 of concrete HA-35	53.90
m^3 of concrete HA-40	59.00
m^3 of concrete HA-45	63.80
m^3 of concrete HA-50	68.61
m^3 of earth removal	3.01
m^3 of earth fill-in	4.81

Table 1. Basic prices of the cost function for the road structures.

Unit	Cost (€)
kg of steel (B-500S)	1.30
m^2 of beams formwork	25.05
m^2 of columns formwork	22.75
m^2 of beams scaffolding	38.89
m^3 of concrete HA-25	78.40
m^3 of concrete HA-30	82.79
m^3 of concrete HA-35	98.47
m^3 of concrete HA-40	105.93
m^3 of concrete HA-45	112.13
m^3 of concrete HA-50	118.60

Table 2. Basic prices of the cost function for the building frames.

than previous ones may randomly form, but, as the mass cools, the probability of higher energy configurations forming decreases. The process is governed by Boltzmann expression $exp(-\Delta E/T)$, where ΔE is the increment of energy of the new configuration and T is the temperature. The present algorithm starts with a feasible solution randomly generated and a high initial temperature. The present SA algorithm then modifies the initial working solution by a small random move of the values of the variables. The new current solution is evaluated in terms of cost. Lower cost solutions are accepted and greater cost solutions are only accepted when a 0 to 1 random number is smaller than the expression $exp(-\Delta E/T)$, where ΔE is the cost increment and T is the current temperature. The current solution is then checked against structural constraints and it is adopted as the new working solution when it is feasible, i.e. when it satisfies the structural constraints. On the other hand, the current solution is discarded when it does not satisfy the structural constraints. The procedure is repeated many times, which give way to a trajectory of feasible solutions that start in the initial solution and ends up in the converged solution result. The initial temperature is decreased geometrically ($T=kT$) by means of a coefficient of cooling k. A number of iterations called Markov chains is allowed at each step of temperature. The algorithm stops when the temperature is a small percentage of the initial temperature (typically 1% and 1-2 chains without improvements). The SA method is capable of surpassing local optima at high-medium temperatures and gradually converges as the temperature reduces to zero. The SA method requires calibration of the initial temperature, the length of the Markov chains and the cooling coefficient. Adopted values for the four examples of this study will be given below. The initial temperature was adjusted following the method proposed by Medina [22], which consists in choosing an initial value and checking whether the percentage of acceptances of higher energy solutions is between 10-30 percent. If the percentage is greater than 30%, the initial temperature is halved; and if it is smaller than 10%, the initial temperature is doubled. Computer runs were performed 9 times so as to obtain minimum, mean and standard deviation of the random results. Note that the algorithm is random in the initial solution and in the moves from one solution to the next in the trajectory and, hence, results are basically random. This random nature makes necessary to run several times the algorithm so as to obtain a statistical population of results.

3. Application to earth retaining walls

The problem defined in section 2.1 is firstly applied to earth retaining RC cantilever walls used in road construction. This type of structure has already being studied by the authors in Ref. 17, which gives a detailed account of the analysis and optimization of this type of walls, while the present section gives an outline and two additional examples. Fig.1 shows the 22 design variables presently considered for the modelling of the walls. They include 4 geometrical variables (the thickness of the stem and 3 dimensions for the footing), 4 concrete and steel grades (stem and footing) and 14 variables for the definition of steel reinforcement, which includes both areas of reinforcement and bar lengths. Variables are continuous except for material grades which are discrete. The modelling of the reinforcement in concrete structures is very important. It has to be detailed enough to cover the variation of structural stress resultants, but not to complex in order to maintain a certain degree of simplicity and practicability. Note that the present arrangement includes three vertical bars for the main tension reinforcement in the kerb (A_1 to A_3 in Fig. 1), tension top and bottom reinforcement bars in the footing (A_9 and A_8) and stirrups in the footing and the bottom part of the kerb (A_{11} and A_7). The remaining bars are basically minimum amounts of reinforcement for shrinkage and thermal effects. Apart from the design variables, a total of 17 parameters are considered for the complete definition of the problem. The most relevant parameters are the total height of the wall H (stem plus footing, see Fig.1), the top slope of the fill and the acting top uniform distributed load, the internal friction angle of the fill φ, the permissible ground stress and the partial coefficients of safety. Structural constraints considered followed a standard analysis by Calavera [23], which includes checks against sliding, overturning, ground stresses and service-ultimate limit states of flexure and shear of different cross-sections of the wall and the footing. No vertical inclination of the earth pressure was considered. Additionally, a constraint of deflection at the top of 1/150 of the height of the stem was also considered.

The simulated annealing algorithm was programmed in Visual Basic 6.3 with an Excel input/output interface. Typical runs were 21 minutes in a Pentium IV of 2.41 GHz. The calibration of the SA recommended Markov chains of 1000 iterations and a cooling coefficient of 0.80. As regards the type of moves, the most efficient move found consisted of random variation of 14 of the 22 design variables. Fig. 2 shows a typical cost evolution by the SA algorithm. Table 3 gives the details of parameters for the two walls analysed of 5.20 and 9.20 m of total height (H in Fig.1). Table 4 details the design results of the SA analysis for the two walls. The total cost of the walls is 505.06 and 1536.47 euros/m. Results indicate that the inclusion of a limit on deflections of 1/150 of the height of the stem is crucial, since otherwise the slenderness of the stem goes up to 1/24 and deflections are as high as 1/40 of the height of the stem. Should the top deflection be limited to 1/150, the slenderness goes down to 1/11.4 and 1/9.4, which is quite similar to the standard 1/10 adopted in practice by many practitioners.

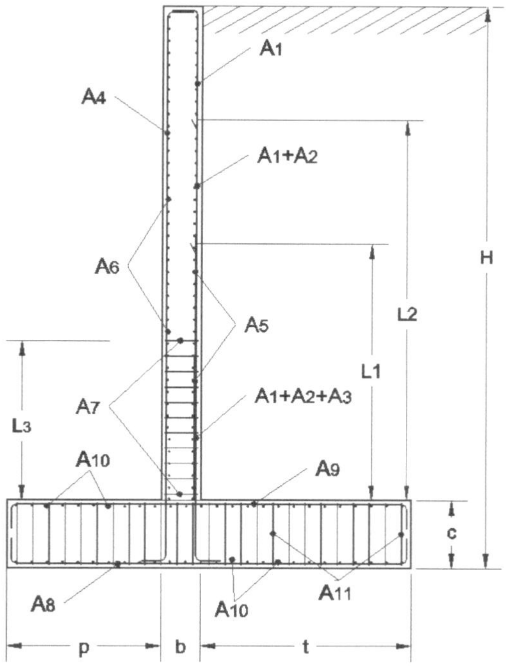

Figure 1. Variables of earth retaining walls for case study 1.

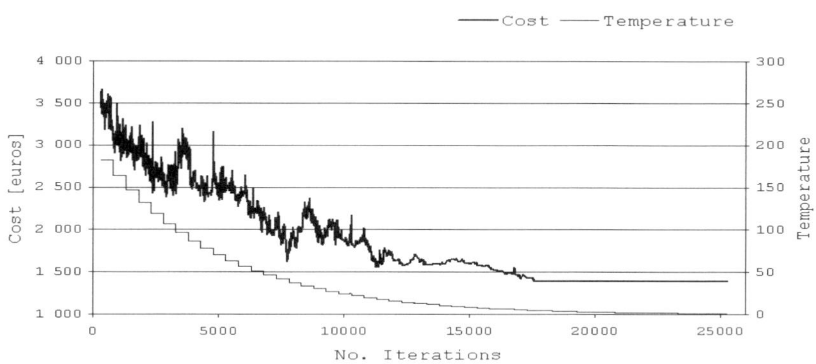

Figure 2. Typical cost evolution of SA algorithm.

Top slope of the fill	0
Uniform distributed load on top surface	10 kN/m^2
Specific weight of the fill	20 kN/m^3
Internal friction angle of the fill	30°
Inclination of the earth pressure	0°
Ground friction coefficient	0.577
Permissible ground stress	0.3 MPa
Overturning safety coefficient	1.8
Sliding safety coefficient	1.5
Execution type of control	Normal
ULS safety coefficient of concrete	1.50
ULS safety coefficient of steel	1.15
Max.displacement of the kerb/height of kerb	150
EHE ambient type	IIa

Table 3. Parameters of the reported walls (total height 5.20 and 9.20 m)

Variable	H = 5.2 m	H = 9.2 m
b	0.43 m	0.91 m
p	0.30 m	0.67 m
t	1.34 m	2.10 m
c	0.30 m	1.07 m
fck,ste	35 MPa	40 MPa
fck,foo	25 MPa	25 MPa
fyk,ste	500 MPa	500 MPa
fyk,foo	500 MPa	500 MPa
A1	9.26 cm^2	22.35 cm^2
A2	3.04 cm^2	2.89 cm^2
A3	4.49 cm^2	10.97 cm^2
A4	1.95 cm^2	2.72 cm^2
A5	4.65 cm^2	9.82 cm^2
A6	9.21 cm^2	19.42 cm^2
A7	0.00 cm^2	0.00 cm^2
A8	8.52 cm^2	18.94 cm^2
A9	12.05 cm^2	19.44 cm^2
A10	6.06 cm^2	12.75 cm^2
A11	0.00 cm^2	0.00 cm^2
L1	0.97 m	2.80 m
L2	0.54 m	0.98 m
L3	0.00 m	0.00 m

Table 4. Summary of best walls (total height 5.20 and 9.20 m)

4. Application to road portal frames

The second example studied relates to portal RC frames used in road construction [24]. Fig. 3 shows the 28 variables considered in this analysis. Variables include 5 geometrical values:

the depth of the walls, the depth of the top slab and the depth of the footing, plus 2 dimensions for the size of the base of the footing; 3 different grades of concrete for the 3 types of elements; and 20 types of reinforcement bars following a standard setup. The reinforcement setup includes 2 variables for the basic negative bending moments, A_1 and A_8, plus a corner additional bar of area A_7. The positive bending moment in the top slab and the wall is covered by bars A_2 and A_9. And positive and bending moments in the footing are covered by bars A_{15} and A_{16}. Additionally several other bars cover shear in the different parts of the frame. All variables are discrete in this analysis. The total number of parameters is 16, the most important of which are the horizontal free span, the vertical free span, the earth cover, the permissible bearing stress and the partial coefficients of safety. Structural constraints considered followed standard provisions for Spanish design of this type of structure [25,26], that include checks of the service and ultimate limit states of flexure and shear for the stress envelopes due to the traffic loads and the earth fill. Traffic loads considered are a uniform distributed load of 4 kN/m^2 and a heavy vehicle of 600 kN. Stress resultants and reactions were calculated by an external finite element program using a 2-D mesh with 30 bars and 31 sections (out of plane bending moments had to be assumed as a practical one fifth proportion of in plane bending moments). Deflections were limited to 1/250 of the free span for the quasi-permanent combination. Fatigue of concrete and steel was not considered since this ultimate limit state is rarely checked in road structures.

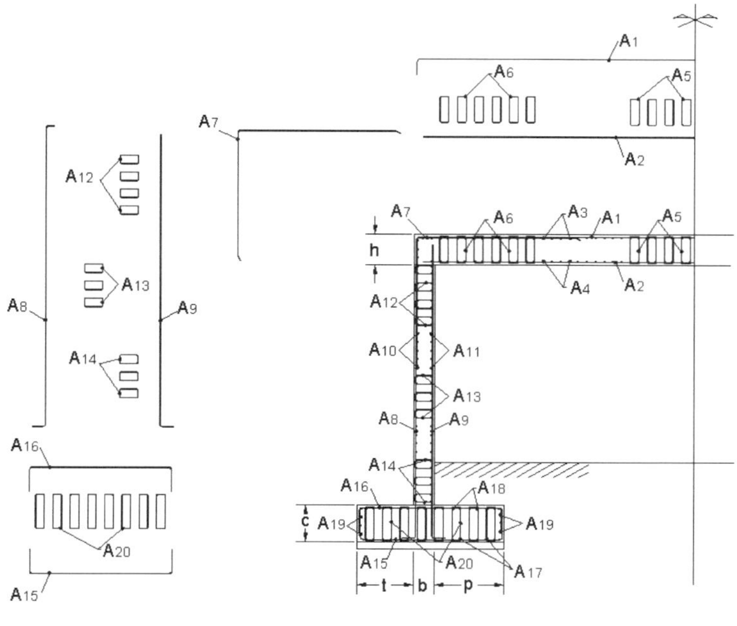

Figure 3. Variables for the RC portal frame.

The SA algorithm was programmed in Visual Basic 6.3. Typical runs were 10.76 hours in an AMD Athlon processor of 1.49 GHz. In this case, the calibration recommended Markov chains of 375 iterations and a cooling coefficient of 0.70, the total amount of iterations being about 7500. The most efficient move found consisted of random variation of 4 of the 28 variables of the problem. Table 5 details the main results of the SA analysis for two portal frames of 10.00 and 15.00 m of horizontal free span, 6.00 m of vertical free span and 0.10 m of asphalt cover (additional parameters are 0.25 MPa permissible bearing stress, specific weight of the fill of 20 kN/m^3, 30 degrees internal friction angle of the fill and partial safety coefficients of 1.60 for loading and 1.50-1.15 for concrete-steel as materials). The depth of the top slab is only 0.375 m for the 10.00 m span, which means a very slender span/depth ratio of 26.67. The cost of this solution is 2619 euros/m. This best solution was then checked by hand calculations against fatigue of structural concrete. The loading considered was a 468 kN heavy vehicle prescribed for fatigue by the Spanish loading code for bridges [25]. It was found that the solution did not comply with Eurocode 2 limitations for fatigue [27]. Hence, it was concluded that this rarely checked ULS should be included in future works of optimization dealing with road structures.

Variables	L=10.00 m	L=15.00 m
Slab depth	0.375 m	0.450 m
Wall thickness	0.400 m	0.475 m
Footiing depth	0.400 m	0.400 m
Footing toe	0.950 m	0.650 m
Footing heel	0.750 m	1.650 m
Footing conc.	HA-25	HA-30
Wall concrete	HA-25	HA-25
Slab concrete	HA-25	HA-25
A_1	15ø12/m	15ø12/m
A_2	10ø20/m	10ø25/m
A_6	12.06 cm^2/m	12.56 cm^2/m
A_7	15ø12/m	12ø20/m
A_8	8ø16/m	10ø16/m
A_9	12ø8/m	6ø16/m
A_{15}	10ø16/m	12ø12/m
A_{16}	12ø10/m	12ø8/m
A_{20}	9.05 cm^2/m	11.30 cm^2/m

Table 5. Summary of best portal frames.

5. Application to road box RC frames

The third example studied relates to box RC frames used in road construction. A detailed account of the modelling of frames and the SA-TA proposed algorithms can be found in the study by Perea et al [18]. The present section gives an outline of the analysis and optimization procedures and an additional example. Fig. 5 shows the 44 variables considered in this analysis for the modelling of the frames. Variables include 2 geometrical values: the depth of the walls and slabs; 2 different grades of concrete for the 2 types of elements; and 40 types of reinforcement bars and bar lengths following a standard setup.

The reinforcement setup includes 3 variables for the basic negative bending moments, A_{14}, A_8 and A_1, plus two corner additional bars of area A_6 and A_{12}. The positive bending moment in the top slab, the bottom slab and the wall is covered by pairs of bars A_2-A_3, A_{13}-A_{15} and A_7-A_9. Additionally several other bars cover shear in the different parts of the frame. All variables are again discrete in this analysis. The most important parameters are the horizontal free span, the vertical free span, the earth cover, the ballast coefficient of the bearing and the partial coefficients of safety. Structural restrictions considered followed standard provisions similar to those of portal frames. However, this time the ULS of fatigue was included following the conclusions from the previous section. Stress resultants and reactions were calculated by an external finite element program using a 2-D mesh with 40 bars and 40 sections.

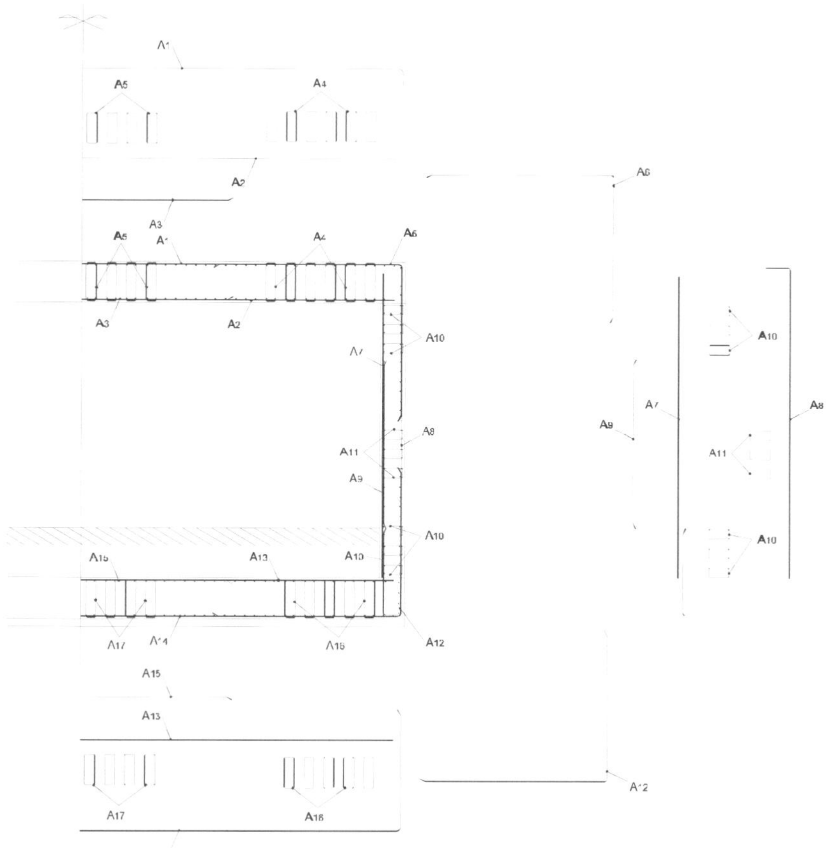

Figure 5. Variables for the RC box frame.

The SA algorithm was programmed this time in Compaq Visual Fortran Professional 6.6.0. Typical runs reduced to 20 seconds in a Pentium IV of 2.4 GHz. In this case, the calibration recommended Markov chains of 500 iterations and a cooling coefficient of 0.90. The most efficient move found was random variation of 9 variables of the 44 of the problem. Fig. 6 details the main results of the SA analysis for a box frame of 13.00 m of horizontal free span, 6.17 m of vertical free span and 1.50 m of earth cover (additional parameters are 10 MN/m^3

ballast coefficient, specific weight of the fill of 20 kN/m³, 30 degrees internal friction angle of the fill and partial safety coefficients of 1.50 for loading and 1.50-1.15 for concrete-steel as materials). The cost of this solution is 4478 euros/m. The depth of the slabs is 0.65 m of C30 (30 MPa of characteristic strength), which represents a slender span/depth ratio of 20. And the depth of the wall is 0.50 m in C45, which represents a vertical span/depth ratio of 12.34. The overall ratio of reinforcement in the top slab is 160 kg/m³. It may, hence, be concluded that results of the optimization search tend to slender and highly reinforced structural box frames. As regards deflections and fatigue limit states, their inclusion has shown to be crucial. Neglecting both limit states leads to a 7.9% more economical solution, but obviously unsafe. It is important to note that fatigue checks are usually considered in railways designs but, on the other hand, they are commonly neglected in road structures design and, as it has been shown, this may lead to unsafe designs.

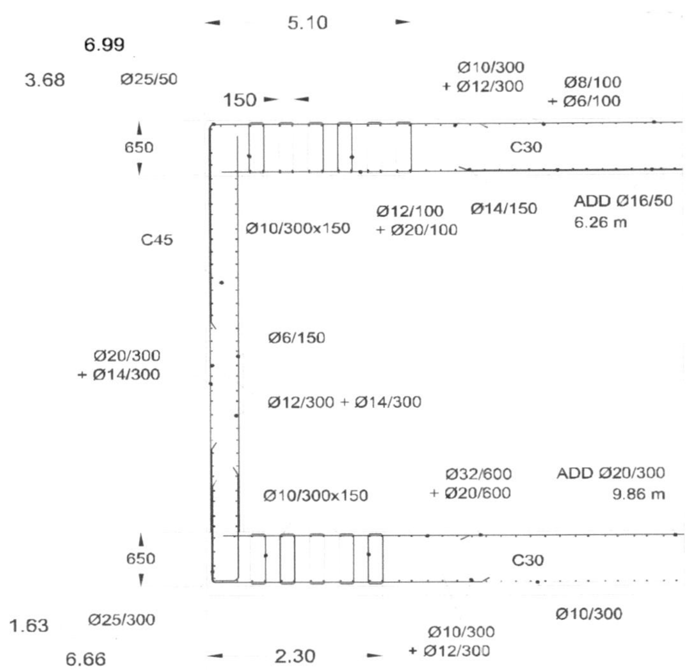

Figure 6. Optimized design of RC box frame.

6. Application to RC building frames

The last example studied relates to RC frames commonly used in building construction. A detailed account of the modelling of frames and the SA proposed algorithms is done in the study by Payá et al [19]. The present section gives an outline of the analysis and optimization procedures and an additional example. The RC frame studied here is the symmetrical frame of 2 bays and 5 floors shown in Fig. 7. This example has 95 variables, including 5 material types of concrete, 30 cross-section dimensions and 60 passive reinforcement bars following a standard setup in columns and beams. Fig. 8 shows a typical longitudinal reinforcement setup of the beams of the structure. It includes a basic top and bottom bars and positive and negative extra reinforcements of a standard length. Variables for beam stirrups include 3 zones of left, central and right positions of transverse reinforcement. Longitudinal reinforcement of columns includes 330 possible values and it varies from a minimum of 4ø12 to a maximum of 34ø25 whereas transverse reinforcement of columns includes 21 possible values. The most important parameters are the horizontal spans of the bays, the vertical height of the columns, the vertical and horizontal loads considered and the partial coefficients of safety. Structural restrictions considered followed standard provisions for Spanish design of this type of structure [26,28], that include checks of the service and ultimate limit states of flexure, shear and instability for the stress envelopes due to the vertical loads and the horizontal wind loads. Vertical loads amount to a total uniform distributed load of 35 kN/m (7.00 kN/m^2 of self weight plus life load and 5.00 m of spacing between parallel frames). As regards wind loads, they amount to a total uniform distributed load of 4.5 kN/m. Stress resultants and reactions were calculated by an internal matrix method program using a 2-D mesh. Deflections were limited to 1/250 of the horizontal span for the total load and to 1/400 for the active deflection; which is the part of the deflection measured after construction of the elements that can be damaged due to vertical displacements.

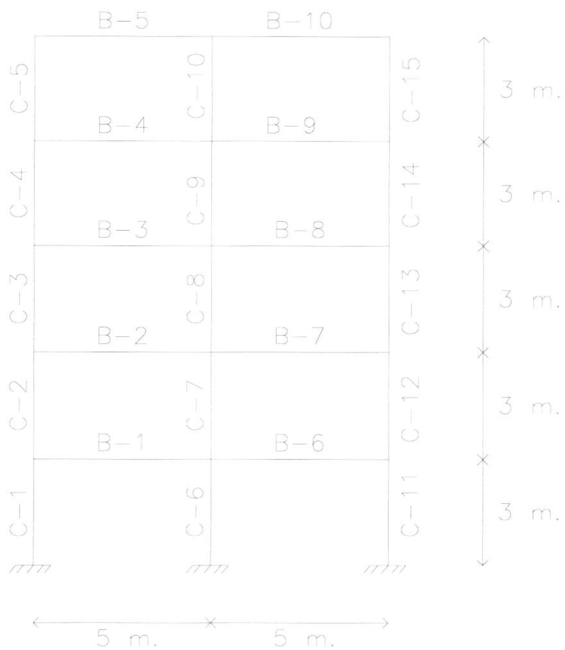

Figure 7. Typical RC building frame of 2 bays and 5 floors.

The SA algorithm was programmed in Compaq Visual Fortran Professional 6.6.0. Typical runs took a time of 97 minutes in a Pentium IV of 3.2 GHz. In this case, the calibration recommended Markov chains of 105000 iterations, a cooling coefficient of 0.80 and two

Markov chains without improvement as stop criterion. The most efficient move found was random variation of 3 or up to 3 variables of the 95 of the problem. Tables 3, 4 and 5 detail the main results of the best SA analysis for the building frame of Fig. 7. The cost of this solution is 4458.08 euros. Concrete is HA-45 in the whole structure. The restrictions that guided the design were the ultimate limit states of flexure and shear in beams and instability in columns, and the service limit state of deflections in beams.

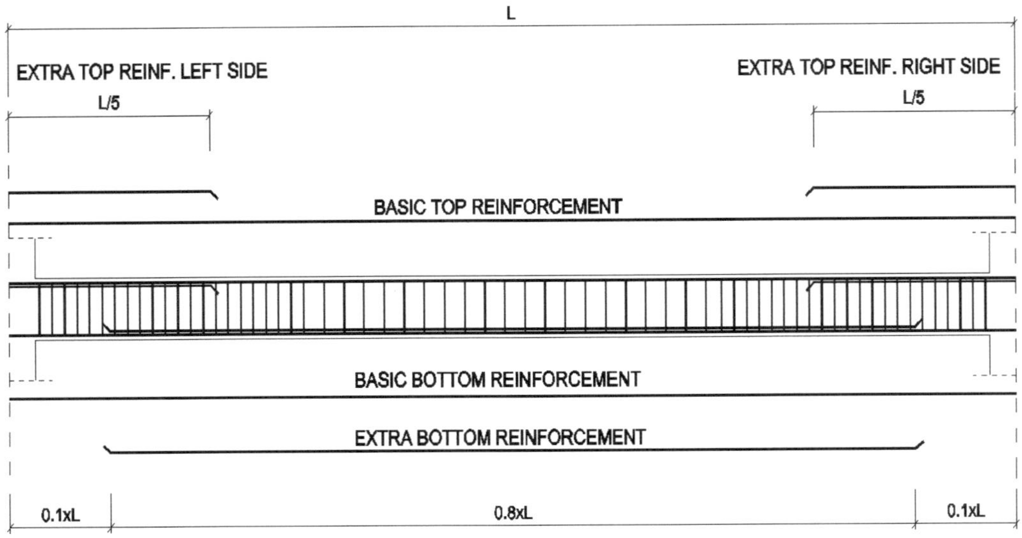

Figure 8. Typical longitudinal reinforcement bars of the beams of RC building frames.

Beam	Dimensions (cm)		Top reinforcement		
	Depth	Width	Base	Extra Left	Extra Right
B-1	0.48	0.20	2ø20	-	1ø25
B-2	0.50	0.20	2ø16	1ø10	2ø20
B-3	0.50	0.20	2ø10	1ø20	2ø25
B-4	0.51	0.21	2ø10	2ø12	3ø16
B-5	0.54	0.22	2ø10	1ø16	2ø25

Table 3. Beam results of the SA: dimensions and top reinforcement

Beam	Bottom reinf.		Shear reinforcement		
	Base	Extra	Left	Span	Right
B-1	3ø12	2ø10	Ø8/25	Ø8/30	Ø6/10
B-2	3ø12	2ø10	Ø8/25	Ø8/30	Ø8/20
B-3	2ø12	1ø20	Ø6/15	Ø6/15	Ø10/30
B-4	4ø10	1ø16	Ø6/15	Ø8/30	Ø8/20
B-5	4ø10	2ø10	Ø8/30	Ø8/30	Ø6/15

Table 4. Beam results of the SA: bottom and shear reinforcement

Column	Dimensions (cm)		Longitudinal Reinforcement			Ties
	a	b	Corners	Side a	Side b	
C-1	0.25	0.25	4ø12	-	-	Ø6/15
C-2	0.25	0.25	4ø16	-	-	Ø6/15
C-3	0.25	0.25	4ø12	2ø12	-	Ø6/15
C-4	0.25	0.25	4ø12	-	2ø12	Ø6/15
C-5	0.25	0.25	4ø16	-	-	Ø6/15
C-6	0.25	0.45	4ø12	-	2ø12	Ø6/15
C-7	0.25	0.40	4ø12	-	-	Ø6/15
C-8	0.25	0.40	4ø12	-	-	Ø6/15
C-9	0.25	0.35	4ø12	-	-	Ø6/15
C-10	0.25	0.30	4ø12	-	-	Ø6/15

Table 5. Column results of the SA for Column results of the SA (columns "b" side is parallel to beams axis).

6. Conclusions

As regards the SA procedure, it has proved an efficient search algorithm for the 4 case studies of walls, portal and box frames used in road construction and building frames. The study of earth retaining walls optimization shows that the inclusion of a limit of 1/150 on the deflection of the top of the walls is needed. Otherwise, results of the SA optimization are excessively deformable. Results of the optimization of portal road frames indicated the need of including the rarely checked ULS of fatigue in the list of structural restrictions for the optimization of road structures. The study of road box frames shows the importance of the inclusion of the SLS of deflections and the ULS of fatigue. The SA optimization of the 13 m free horizontal span box frame results in a slender and highly reinforced top slab. Results of the optimization of the building frame indicate that instability in columns and flexure, shear and deflections in beams are the main restrictions that condition its design.

7. References

Grierson D.E., Practical optimization of structural steel frameworks, in *Advances in Design Optimization*, Ed. H. Adeli, Taylor & Francis, 1994.

Cohn M.Z. and Dinovitzer A.S., Application of structural optimization. *ASCE Journal of Structural Engineering*, 120(2): pp.617-649, 1994.

Sarma K.C. and Adeli H., Cost optimization of concrete structures, *ASCE Journal of Structural Engineering*, 124(5), pp.570-578, 1998.

Hernández S. and Fontan A., *Practical Applications of Design Optimization,* WIT Press: Southampton, 2002.

Fletcher R., *Practical Methods of Optimization,* Wiley: Chichester, 2001.

Jones M.T., *Artificial Intelligence Application Programming,* Charles River Media: Hingham (Massachussets), 2003.

Holland J.H., *Adaptation in natural and artificial systems,* University of Michigan Press: Ann Arbor, 1975.

Goldberg D.E., *Genetic algorithms in search, optimization and machine learning,* Addison-Wesley, 1989.

Glover F. and Laguna M., *Tabu Search,* Kluwer Academic Publishers: Boston, 1997.

Yepes V. and Medina J.R., Economic heuristic optimization for the heterogeneous fleet VRPHESTW. *ASCE Journal of Transportation Engineering,* 132(4), 303-311, 2006.

Jenkins W.M., Plane frame optimum design environment based on genetic algorithm, *ASCE Journal of Structural Engineering,* 118(11), pp. 3103-3112, 1992.

Rajeev S. and Krisnamoorthy C.S., Discrete optimization of structures using genetic algorithms, *ASCE Journal of Structural Engineering,* 118(5), pp. 1233-1250, 1992

Coello C.A., Christiansen A.D. and Santos F., A simple genetic algorithm for the design of reinforced concrete beams, *Engineering with Computers,* 13, pp. 185-196, 1997.

Leps M. and Sejnoha M., New approach to optimization of reinforced concrete beams, *Computers and Structures,* 81, pp. 1957-1966, 2003.

Lee C. and Ahn J., Flexural design reinforced concrete frames by genetic algorithm, *ASCE Journal of Structural Engineering,* 129(6), pp. 762-774, 2003.

Camp C.V., Pezeshk S. and Hansson H., Flexural design reinforced concrete frames using a genetic algorithm, *ASCE Journal of Structural Engineering,* 129(1), pp. 105-115, 2003.

Yepes V, Alcala J, Perea C and Gonzalez-Vidosa F., A parametric study of earth-retaining walls by simulated annealing, *Engineering Structures,* 30(3): 821-830, 2008.

Perea C, Alcala J, Yepes V, Gonzalez-Vidosa F, Hospitaler A. Design of reinforced concrete bridge frames by heuristic optimization. *Advances in Engineering Software,* 39(8):676-688, 2008.

Paya I., Yepes V., Gonzalez-Vidosa F. and Hospitaler A. Multiobjective Optimization of Concrete Frames by Simulated Annealing. Accepted for publication in *Computer-Aided Civil and Infrastructure Engineering.*

Gonzalez-Vidosa F., Yepes V., Alcala J., Carrera M. and Perea C. Simulated annealing optimization of walls, portal and box reinforced concrete road structures. In *Proceedings of the Ninth International Conference on Computer Aided Optimum Design in Engineering,* Skiathos (Greece), May 2005, 175-186.

Kirkpatrick S., Gelatt C.D. and Vecchi M.P., Optimization by simulated annealing, *Science,* 220(4598), pp. 671-680, 1983.

Medina J.R., Estimation of incident and reflected waves using simulated annealing, *ASCE Journal of Waterway, Port, Coastal and Ocean Engineering,* 127(4), pp. 213-221, 2001.

Calavera, J., *Muros de contención y muros de sótano,* 3rd ed, INTEMAC: Madrid, 2001.

Carrera M., Alcalá J., Yepes V and González-Vidosa F., Heuristic optimization of reinforced concrete road portal frames (in Spanish), *Hormigón y Acero,* No.236, pp.85-95, 2005.

M. Fomento, *IAP-98. Code about the actions to be considered for the design of road bridges (in Spanish),* M. Fomento, Madrid, 1998.

M. Fomento, *EHE. Code of Structural Concrete (in Spanish),* M. Fomento, Madrid, 1998.

CEN, *Eurocode 2. Design of Concrete Structures. Part 2: Concrete Bridges,* CEN: Brussells, 1996.

M. Fomento, *NBE AE-88. Code about the actions to be considered in buildings (in Spanish),* M. Fomento, Madrid, 1988.

16

Best Practices for Simulated Annealing in Multiprocessor Task Distribution Problems

Heikki Orsila, Erno Salminen and Timo D. Hämäläinen
Department of Computer Systems
Tampere University of Technology
P.O. Box 553, 33101 Tampere,
Finland

1. Introduction

Simulated Annealing (SA) is a widely used meta-algorithm for complex optimization problems. This chapter presents methods to distribute executable tasks onto a set of processors. This process is called *task mapping*. The most common goal is to decrease execution time via parallel computation. However, the presented mapping methods are not limited to optimizing application execution time because the cost function is arbitrary. The cost function is also called an objective function in many works. A smaller cost function value means a better solution. It may consider multiple metrics, such as execution time, communication time, memory, energy consumption and silicon area constraints. Especially in embedded systems, these other metrics are often as important as execution time.

A multiprocessor system requires exploration to find an optimized architecture as well as the proper task distribution for the application. Resulting very large design space must be pruned systematically with fast algorithms, since the exploration of the whole design space is not feasible. Iterative algorithms evaluate a number of application mappings for each architecture, and the best architecture and mapping is selected in the process.

The optimization process is shown in Figure 1(a). The application, the HW platform and an initial solution are fed to a mapping component. The mapping component generates a new solution that is passed to a simulation component. The simulation component determines relevant metrics of the solution. The metrics are passed to a cost function which will evaluate the badness (*cost*) of the solution. The cost value is passed back to the mapping component. The mapping component will finally terminate the optimization process and output a final solution.

The system that is optimized is shown in Figure 1(b). The system consists of the application and the HW platform. The application consists of tasks which are mapped to processing elements (PEs). The PEs are interconnected with a communication network.

The chapter has two focuses:

- optimize the cost function and
- minimize the time needed for simulated annealing.

First, the task distribution problem is an NP problem which implies that a heuristic algorithm is needed. The focus is on reaching as good as possible mapping. Unfortunately the true optimum value is unknown for most applications, and therefore the relative goodness of the solution to the true optimum is unknown. Experiments rely on convergence rates and extensive simulations to reduce this uncertainty. This chapter focuses on single-objective rather than multi-objective optimization.

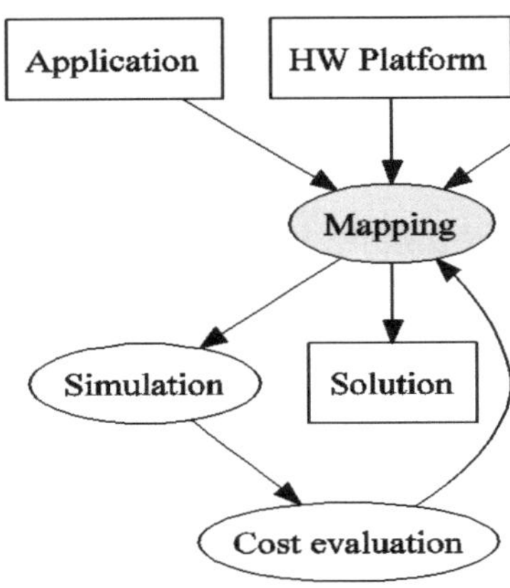

Figure 1(a). Optimization process. Boxes indicate data. Ellipses indicate operations. This chapter focuses on the mapping part.

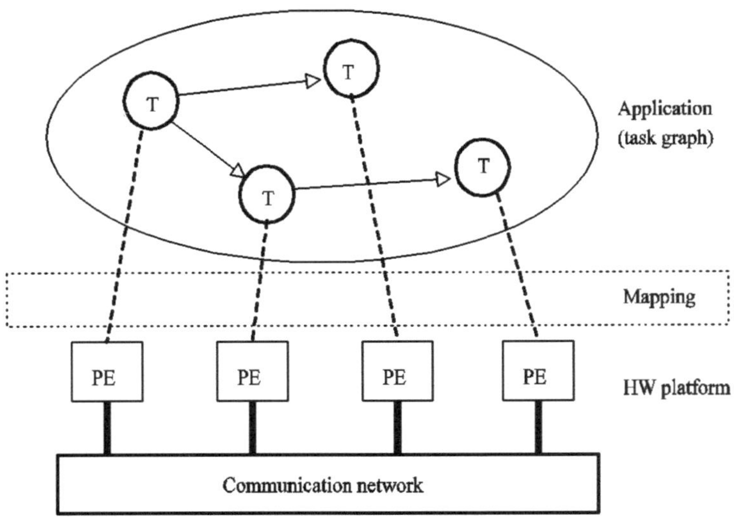

Figure 1(b). The system that is optimized. The system consists of the application and the HW platform. PE is processing element.

Second, the focus is minimizing the optimization time. A valid solution must be found in a reasonable time which depends on the application and the target multiprocessor platform.
This chapter is structured as follows. We first introduce the problem of mapping a set of tasks onto a multiprocessor system. Then, we present a generic SA algorithm and give detailed analysis how the major functions may be implemented. That is followed by an overview of reported case studies, including our own. Last we discuss the findings and present the most important open research problems.

2. Task mapping problem

The application in Figure 1(b) is divided into tasks. Tasks are defined as smallest components in the application that can be relocated to any or some PEs in the HW platform. A mapping algorithm will find a location for each task on some PE. The application model is irrelevant for the general mapping problem as long as the application model has mappable tasks. Mapping can be done on run-time or design-time. There are several types of application models that are used in literature: directed acyclic task graphs (Kwok & Ahmad, 1999), Kahn Process Networks (Wikipedia, 2008b) and others.

The mapping affects several properties of the system. Affected hardware properties are processor utilization, communication network utilization and power. Affected software and/or hardware properties are execution time, memory usage, and application and hardware context switches.

2.1 Application model

Tasks can be dependent on each other. Task *A* depends on task *B* if task *A* needs data or control from task *B*. Otherwise tasks are independent. There are application models with dependent and independent tasks. Models with independent tasks are easier to map because there is zero communication between tasks. This enables the problem to be solved in separate sub-problems. However, independent tasks may affect each other if they compete for shared resources, such as a PE or a communication network. Scheduling properties of the application model may complicate evaluating a mapping algorithm.

2.2 Hardware platform model

The HW platform in Figure 1(b) can be heterogeneous which means that it executes different tasks with different characteristics. These characteristics include speed and power, for example. This does not complicate the mapping problem, but affects the simulation part in Figure 1(a). The mapping problem is the same regardless of the simulation accuracy, but the mapping solution is affected. This enables both fast and slow simulation models to be used with varying accuracy. Inaccurate models are usually based on estimation techniques. Accurate models are based on hardware simulation or native execution of the system that is being optimized. Accurate models are usually much slower than inaccurate models and they may not be available at the early phase of the system design.

Depending on the application model, all PEs can not necessarily execute all tasks. Restricting mappability of tasks makes the optimization problem easier and enables shortcut heuristics to be used in optimization. The previous definition for tasks excludes application components that can not be relocated, and therefore each task has at least *2* PEs where it can be executed.

2.3 Limiting the scope of problems

We assume that communicating between two processors is much more expensive than communicating within a single processor. To generalize this idea, it is practically happening inside single processor computer systems because registers can be *100* times as fast as physical memory, and cache memory is *10* times as fast as physical memory. Multiprocessor systems could spend thousands of cycles to pass a message from one processor to other.

This trend is constantly changing as multicore and non-asymmetric computer architectures are becoming more common.
We also assume that distributed applications are not embarrassingly parallel (Wikipedia, 2008a).
Without previous two assumptions the optimization algorithms can be trivially replaced with on-demand best-effort distributed job queues.
This paper only considers the single-objective optimization case. Single-objective optimization finds the minimum for a given objective function. Multi-objective optimization tries to minimize several functions, and the result is a set of trade-offs, or so called *Pareto-optimal* solutions. Each trade-off solution minimizes some of the objective functions, but not all. Having a systematic method for selecting a single solution from the trade-off set reduces the problem into a single-objective optimization task.

2.4 Random mapping algorithm

Random mapping algorithm is a simple *Monte Carlo* algorithm that randomizes processor assignment of each task at every iteration. The Monte Carlo process converges very slowly as it does not have negative feedback for moves into worse mappings. Random mapping algorithm is important because it sets the reference for minimum efficiency of any mapping algorithm. Any mapping algorithm should be able to do better than random mapping. Simulated Annealing algorithm produces a "Monte Carlo -like" effect at very high temperatures as almost all worsening moves are accepted.

3. Simulated annealing

Simulated Annealing is a probabilistic non-greedy algorithm (Kirkpatrick et al., 1983) that explores the search space of a problem by annealing from a high to a low temperature. Probabilistic behavior means that SA can find solutions of different goodness between independent runs. Non-greedy means that SA may accept a move into a worse state, and this allows escaping local minima. The algorithm always accepts a move into a better state. Move to a worse state is accepted with a changing probability. This probability decreases along with the temperature, and thus the algorithm starts as a non-greedy algorithm and gradually becomes more and more greedy.
This chapter focuses only on using SA for mapping. The challenge is to find efficient optimization parameters for SA. (Braun et al., 2001) is a comparison of different mapping algorithms, such as *Tabu Search, Genetic Algorithms, Load Balancing* algorithms and others.
Figure 2 shows an example of SA optimization process. Optimization begins from a high temperature where the accepted cost changes chaotically. As the temperature decreases the accepted cost changes less chaotically and the algorithm becomes greedier.
Figure 3 shows the general form of Simulated Annealing algorithm pseudo-code. Table 1 shows symbols, functions and various parameters for the pseudo-code. The algorithm starts with an initial solution S_0 (state). SA iterates through solutions until a termination condition is reached. At each temperature level, SA moves one or several tasks to different PEs and evaluates the cost of the new mapping solution. Then SA either accepts or rejects the new solution. If the new solution is accepted, it is used as a basis for the next iteration. Otherwise, the new solution is thrown away.

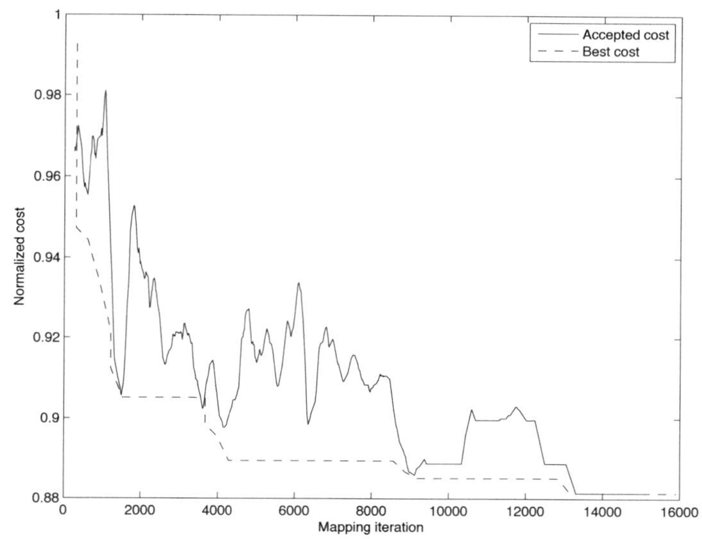

Figure 2. Cost per iteration plotted for Simulated Annealing when mapping a *100* task application to a *4* processor system. The cost is normalized so that initial cost $C_0 = 1.0$. The plot is average filtered with a *256* sample window to hide the chaotic nature of the random process. This is also the reason why accepted cost does not always seem to touch the best cost line.

```
SIMULATED_ANNEALING(S_0)
S ← S_0
C ← COST(S_0)
S_best ← S
C_best ← C
R ← 0
for i ← 0 to ∞
   do T ← TEMP(i)
      S_new ← MOVE(S, T)
      C_new ← COST(S_new)
      ΔC ← C_new − C
      if ΔC < 0 or ACCEPT(ΔC, T)
        then if C_new < C_best
               then S_best ← S_new
                    C_best ← C_new
             S ← S_new
             C ← C_new
             R ← 0
        else  R ← R + 1
      if TERMINATE(i, R) = True
        then break
return S_best
```

Figure 3. Pseudo-code of the Simulated Annealing algorithm. See Table 1 for explanation of symbols.

Symbol	Value range	Definition	A	B	C
$Accept(\Delta C, T)$	{**False**, **True**}	Return accept (**True**) or reject (**False**) for a worsening move		B B	
$C = Cost()$	$C > 0$	Accepted cost (to be minimized)		B	
C_0	$C_0 > 0$	Initial cost			C
C_{new}	$C_{new} > 0$	Cost of the next state			C
$\Delta C = C_{new} - C$	$\mathbb{R}$	Change of cost due to move			C
i	$i > 0$	Mapping iteration			C
L	$L > 0$	# Iterations per temperature level		B	
M	$M > 1$	Number of processors	A		
N	$N > 1$	Number of tasks	A		
q	$0 < q < 1$	Geometric temperature scaling factor		B	
R	$R \geq 0$	Number of consecutive rejected moves		B	
S	mapping space	Accepted state			C
S_0	mapping space	Initial state		B	
S_{new}	mapping space	Next state			C
$Move(S, T)$	mapping space	Returns the next state		B	
$T = Temp(i)$	$T > 0$	Return temperature T at iteration i		B	
T_0	$T_0 > 0$	Initial temperature		B	
T_f	$0 < T_f < T_0$	Final temperature		B	
T_N	$T_N > 0$	Number of temperature levels		B	
$Terminate(i, R)$	{**False**, **True**}	Return terminate (**True**) or continue (**False**)		B	
$x = random()$	$0 \leq x < 1$	Return a random value			C
α	$\alpha > 0$	The number of neighbors for each state: $\alpha = M(N-1)$	A		

Table 1. Simulated Annealing parameters and symbols. Column A indicates parameters related to the size of the mapping/optimization problem. Column B indicates parameters of the SA algorithm. Column C indicates an internal variable of the SA.

The general algorithm needs a number of functions to be complete. Most common methods are presented in following sections. Implementation effort for most methods is low, and trying different combinations requires little effort. Therefore many alternatives should be tried. Most of the effort goes to implementing the *Cost()* function and finding proper optimization parameters. The cost function is the simulation and cost evalution part in Figure 1(a). In some cases the Move heuristics can be difficult to implement.

3.1 Cost function: Cost(S)

Cost(S) evaluates the cost for any given state *S* of the optimization space. Here, each point in the optimization space defines one mapping for the application. *Cost()* can be a function of any variables. Without loss of generality, this chapter is only concerned about minimizing execution time of the application. Other factors such as power and real-time properties can be included. For example, $Cost(S) = t^{w_1} A^{w_2} P^{w_3}$, where t is the execution time of the application, A is the silicon area and P is the power, and w_1, w_2 and w_3 are user-defined coefficients.

3.2 Annealing schedule: Temp(i) function

Temp(i) determines the temperature as a function of the iteration number *i*. Initial temperature $T_0 = Temp(0)$. The final temperature T_f is determined implicitly by *Temp()* and *Terminate()* functions. *Temp()* function may also contain internal state, and have access to other annealing metrics, such as cost. In those cases *Temp()* is not a pure function. For example, remembering cost history can be used for intelligent annealing schedules.

In geometric temperature schedules the temperature is multiplied by a factor $0 < q < 1$ between each temperature level. It is the most common approach. T_N is the number of temperature levels. Define *L* to be the number of iterations on each temperature level.

There are *3* common schedules that are defined in following paragraphs.

Geometric Temperature Schedule

$$Temp(i) = T_0 q^{\left\lfloor \frac{i}{L} \right\rfloor} \tag{1}$$

$\left\lfloor \frac{i}{L} \right\rfloor$ means rounding down the fraction. The number of mapping iterations is LT_N.

Fractional Temperature Schedule

$$Temp(i) = \frac{T_0}{i+1} \tag{2}$$

The number of mapping iterations is T_N. It is inadvisable to use a fractional schedule because it distributes the number of iterations mostly to lower temperatures. Doubling the total number of iterations only halves the final temperature. Therefore, covering a wide relative temperature range $\frac{T_0}{T_f} >> 1$ is expensive. The geometric schedule avoids this problem. For this reason the geometric temperature schedule is the most common choice.

Koch Temperature Schedule

$$Temp(i) = \begin{cases} \dfrac{Temp(i-1)}{1+\delta \dfrac{Temp(i-1)}{\sigma_{i-L,i}}} & \text{if } \operatorname{mod}(i,L) = 0 \\ Temp(i-1) & \text{if } \operatorname{mod}(i,L) \neq 0 \\ T_0 & \text{if } i = 0 \end{cases} \tag{3}$$

where

$$\sigma_{i-L,i} = stddev\{Cost(S_k) \mid i - L \le k < i\} \tag{4}$$

Koch temperature schedule (Koch, 1995; Ravindran, 2007) decreases temperature with respect to cost standard deviation on each temperature level. Deviation is calculated from the *L* latest iterations. Higher standard deviation, i.e. more chaotic the annealing, leads to lower temperature decrease between each level. The number of mapping iterations depends on the problem.

3.3 Acceptance function: Accept (ΔC,T)

$Accept(\Delta C,T)$ returns **True** if a worsening move should be accepted, otherwise **False**. An improving move ($\Delta C < 0$) is always accepted by the SA algorithm, but this is not a part of Accept() behavior (although there are some implementations that explicitly do it).

ΔC has an arbitrary range and unit that depends on system parameters and the selected cost function. Since $\frac{\Delta C}{T}$ is a relevant measure in acceptance functions, the temperature range needs to be adjusted to the ΔC range, or vice versa. Following paragraphs define *4* different acceptance functions.

3.3.1 Inverse exponential form

$$Accept(\Delta C,T) = \mathbf{True} \Leftrightarrow random() < \frac{1}{1+\exp(\frac{\Delta C}{T})} \tag{5}$$

It is important to notice that when $\Delta C = 0$, the transition happens at *50%* probability. This makes SA rather likely to shift between equally good solutions and thus find new points in space where a move to a better state is possible. Accepting a worsening move always has a probability less than *50%*. Despite this, SA is rather liberal in doing random walks even at low temperatures. Small increases in cost are allowed even at low temperatures, but significant increases in cost are only accepted at high temperatures.

Note that some implementations write the right part of (5) as $random() > \frac{1}{1+\exp(\frac{-\Delta C}{T})}$, which is probabilistically equivalent.

3.3.2 Normalized inverse exponential form

$$Accept(\Delta C,T) = \mathbf{True} \Leftrightarrow random() < \frac{1}{1+\exp(\frac{\Delta C}{C_0 T})} \tag{6}$$

This case has all the properties of the inverse exponential form, but the cost value difference is normalized. The idea is that selecting the temperature range $[T_f, T_0]$ is easier when it is independent of the cost function and the temperature always lies inside the same range $0 < T \leq 1$. Specifically, changing the hardware platform should not make temperature range selection harder. Normalization keeps acceptance probabilities in a relevant range even if the cost function changes. Figure 4 shows specific probability curves for $\Delta C_r = \frac{\Delta C}{C_0}$ that is used inside the *exp()* function.

3.3.3 Exponential form

$$Accept(\Delta C,T) = \mathbf{True} \Leftrightarrow random() < \exp(\frac{-\Delta C}{T}) \tag{7}$$

Exponential form is similar to the inverse exponential form, but $\Delta C = 0$ transition happens always whereas the inverse exponential form accepts the same move with *50%* probability. See the reasoning in inverse exponential case.

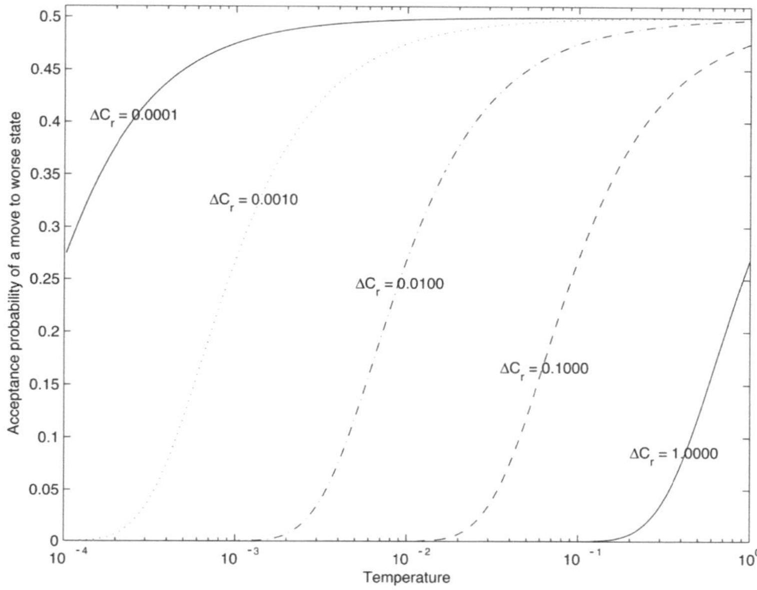

Figure 4. Acceptance probability curves for the normalized inverse exponential function (6) with $\mathbf{q = 0.95}$. The curve represents constant values of $\mathbf{\Delta C_r = \frac{\Delta C}{C_0}}$. Probability of moving to a worse state decreases when the temperature decreases. Moves to slightly worse state have higher probability than those with large degradation.

3.3.4 Normalized exponential form

$$Accept(\Delta C, T) = \textbf{True} \Leftrightarrow random() < \exp(\frac{-\Delta C}{C_0 T}) \tag{8}$$

This case has all the properties of the exponential form, but in addition it is implied that temperature lies in range $0 < T \leq 1$. This is reasoned in the normalized inverse exponential case.

3.4 On effective temperature range

Annealing starts with a high acceptance rate p_0 for bad moves and it decreases to a very low acceptance rate p_f. It is important to control the acceptance probability. If inverse exponential function (5) is solved with respect to T for a given probability p, we get:

$$T = \frac{\Delta C}{\ln(\frac{1}{p} - 1)} \tag{9}$$

Assuming minimum expected cost change $\Delta C_{\min}$ and maximum expected cost change $\Delta C_{\max}$, we get the proper temperature range

$$T_f = \frac{\Delta C_{\min}}{\ln(\frac{1}{p_f} - 1)} < T < \frac{\Delta C_{\max}}{\ln(\frac{1}{p_0} - 1)} = T_0 \tag{10}$$

Initial acceptance probability p_0 should be set close to *0.5*, i.e. the maximum acceptance rate for inverse exponential function, but not too close to save optimization iterations. For example, $p_0 = 0.45$ is sufficiently close to *0.5*, but saves *58* temperature levels of iterations compared to $p_0 = 0.49$, assuming $q = 0.95$. When $\Delta C = 0$ the acceptance probability is always *50%*.

Final acceptance probability p_f can be set large enough so that a worsening move happens n times in the final temperature level, where n is a parameter set by the designer. If there are L iterations per temperature level, we set $p_f = n / L$. If we set $n = 0.1$, the final temperature level is almost entirely greedy, and a worsening move happens with *10%* probability on the temperature level for a given $\Delta C_{\min}$. The temperature range becomes

$$T_f = \frac{\Delta C_{\min}}{\ln(\frac{L}{n} - 1)} < T < \frac{\Delta C_{\max}}{\ln(\frac{1}{p_0} - 1)} = T_0 \tag{11}$$

The derivation of (10) and (11) for normalized inverse exponential, exponential and normalized exponential functions is similar.

3.5 Methods to determine the initial temperature

The initial temperature T_0 was not defined in annealing schedule functions in Section 3.2. As was explained in Section 3.3, the initial temperature is highly coupled with the acceptance function. Following paragraphs present common methods for computing the initial temperature. Note that final temperature is usually determined implicitly by the *Terminate()* function.

3.5.1 Heating

The initial temperature is grown large enough so that the algorithm accepts worsening moves with some given probability p_0. This requires simulating a sufficient number of moves in the optimization space. Either moves are simulated in the neighborhood of a single point, or moves are simulated from several, possibly random, points. The average increase in cost ΔC_{avg} is computed for worsening moves. Given an acceptance function, T_0 is computed such that $Accept(\Delta C_{avg}, T_0) = p_0$. The solution is trivial for all presented acceptance functions. An example of heating is given in Section 4.2.

3.5.2 Application and hardware platform analysis

Application and hardware platform analysis can be used to determine the initial temperature. Rapid methods in this category do not use simulation to initialize parameters, while slow but more accurate methods use simulation. An example, see (10), (11) and Section 4.3.

3.5.3 Manual tuning

Parameters can be set by manually testing different parameters. This option is discouraged for an automated optimization system where the problem varies significantly.

3.5.4 Cost change normalization

In this method the temperature scale is made independent of the cost function values. This is either accomplished by (6) or setting $T_0 = C_0$ for (5). By using (6) it is easier to use other initial temperature estimation methods.

3.6 Move function and heuristics: Move(S, T)

Move(S, T) function returns a new state based on the application specific heuristics and the current state S and temperature T. Move heuristics vary significantly. The simple ones are purely random. The complex ones analyze the structure of the application and the hardware, and inspect system load.

It should be noted that given a current state value, randomizing a new state value should exclude the current value, i.e. current PE of the moved task in this case, for randomization process. For example, in two-processor system, there is a *50%* probability of selecting the same CPU again, which means that half of the iterations are wasted. Many papers do not specify this aspect for random heuristics.

Common choices and ideas for move heuristics from literature are presented in following sections.

3.6.1 Single: move task to another processor

Choose a random task and move it to a random processor.

3.6.2 Multiple: move several tasks to other processors

Instead of choosing only a single task to move to another processor, several tasks can be moved at once. The moved tasks are either mapped to the same processor, or different processors. If these tasks are chosen at random and each of their destinations are chosen at random, this approach is less likely to find an improving move than just moving a single task. This is a consequence of combinatorics as improving moves are a minority group in all possible moves.

If a good heuristics is applied for moving multiple tasks, it is possible to climb up from a steep local minimum. A heuristics that only moves a single task is less likely to climb up from a steep local minimum.

3.6.3 Swap: swap processes between processors

Choose two different random processors, choose a random process on both processors, and swap the processes between processors.

3.7 Heuristic move functions

A heuristic move uses more information than just knowing the mapping space structure. Some application or hardware specific knowledge is used to move or swap tasks more efficiently.

3.7.1 ECP: Enhanced critical path

Enhanced Critical Path method (Wild et al., 2003) is a heuristic move for directed acyclic task graphs. ECP favors swapping and moving processes that are on the *critical path* of the graph, or near the critical path. Critical path is the path with the largest sum of computation and communication costs in the graph.

3.7.2 Variable grain move

A variable grain move is a single task move that starts by favoring large execution time tasks statistically. Thus, tasks with large execution time are moved more likely than tasks with small execution time. The probability distribution is then gradually flattened towards equal probability for each task. At low temperatures each task is moved with the same probability.

3.7.3 Topological move

Assume tasks A and B, where A sends a message to B with a high probability after A has been activated. If B is the only task that gets a message from A with a high probability then it can be benefitial to favor moving them to the same processor.

This heuristics could be implemented into Single task move by favoring processors of adjacent tasks. The probability distribution for processor selection should be carefully balanced to prevent mapping all tasks to the same processor, thus preventing speedup of a multiprocessor system. If a task sends messages to more than one task with a high probability, this heuristics is at least dubious and needs experimental verification.

3.7.4 Load balancing move

This heuristics makes heavily loaded processors less likely to get new tasks, and make slightly loaded processes more likely to get new tasks. Each processor's load can be determined by a test vector simulation, by counting the number of tasks on each processor, or by using more sophisticated load calculations. Each task can be attributed a constant load based on test vector simulations, and then each processor's load becomes the sum of loads of its tasks.

3.7.5 Component move

A task graph may consist from application or system level components each having multiple tasks. Separate components are defined by the designer. Instead of mapping single tasks, all tasks related to a single component could be mapped. This could be a coarse-grain starting point for finer-grain mapping.

3.8 Other move heuristics

3.8.1 Hybrid approach

A hybrid algorithm might use all of the above move functions. For example, combine weighted task selection with weighted target PE selection (Sec 3.7.2 + 3.7.3). The move function can be selected by random on each iteration, or different move function can be used in different optimization phases.

3.8.2 Compositional approach

SA can be combined with other algorithms. The move function may use another optimization algorithm to make more intelligent moves. For example, the single move heuristics might be adapted to give more weight to the best target processor determined by actually simulating each target.

3.8.3 Optimal subset mapping move

The move function can optimize a subset of the task graph. Each move will by itself determine a locally optimal mapping for some small subset of tasks. The number of mapping combinations for a subset of N_{sub} tasks and M processors is $M^{N_{sub}}$ for the brute-force approach. The number of brute-combinations for a single subset should only be a tiny fraction of total number of mappings that are evaluated, that is, a large number of subsets should be optimized. A brute-force based approach may yield rapid convergence but the final result is somewhat worse than with traditional SA (Orsila et al., 2007). It is suitable for initial coarse-grain optimization.

3.8.4 Move processors from router to router

In a Network-on-Chip (NoC) system, processors can be moved from router to router to optimize communication between system components.

3.8.5 Task scheduling move

Scheduling of tasks can be done simultaneously with mapping them. Scheduling means determining the priorities of tasks on each processor separately. Priorities for tasks is determined by a permutation of all tasks. Task A has higher priority than task B if it is located before task B in the permutation. A permutation can be altered by swapping two random tasks in the Move function. The order of tasks is only relevant for tasks on the same processor. As an optimization for the move heuristics, most permutations need not be considered.

3.9 Termination function: Terminate(*i*, R)

Terminate(i, R) returns **True** when the optimization loop should be terminated. R is the number of consecutive rejected moves, $i_{\max}$ is a user-defined maximum number of iterations, and $R_{\max}$ is a user-defined maximum number of consecutive rejects. *Terminate()* function often uses the T emp() function for determining the current temperature T.
Following paragraphs present examples and analysis of commonly used termination functions from literature:

3.9.1 Maximum number of iterations

Annealing is stopped after i_{max} iterations:

$$Terminate(i, R) = \textbf{True} \Leftrightarrow i \geq i_{\max} \tag{12}$$

This approach is discouraged because annealing success is dependent on actual temperatures, rather than iterations. Final temperature and annealing schedule parameters can be selected to restrict the maximum number of iterations.

3.9.2 Temperature threshold

Annealing is stopped at a specific temperature T_f :

$$Terminate(i, R) = \textbf{True} \Leftrightarrow Temp(i) < T_f \tag{13}$$

This approach is discouraged in favor of coupled temperature and rejection threshold because there can be easy greedy moves left.

3.9.3 Cost threshold
Annealing is stopped when a target cost is achieved:

$$Terminate(i, R) = \textbf{True} \Leftrightarrow Cost(S) < Cost_{target} \tag{14}$$

For example, if the cost function measures real-time latency, annealing is stopped when a solution that satisfies real-time requirements is found. This heuristics should not be used alone because if the target cost is not achieved, the algorithm loops forever.

3.9.4 Rejection threshold
Annealing is stopped when $R \geq R_{\max}$:

$$Terminate(i, R) = \textbf{True} \Leftrightarrow R \geq R_{\max} \tag{15}$$

This approach is discouraged because there is a risk of premature termination.

3.9.5 Uncoupled temperature and rejection threshold
Annealing is stopped at a low enough temperature or if no improvement has occured for a while:

$$Terminate(i, R) = \textbf{True} \Leftrightarrow Temp(i) < T_f \vee R \geq R_{\max} \tag{16}$$

This approach is discouraged because there is a risk of premature termination.

3.9.6 Coupled temperature and rejection threshold
Annealing is stopped at a low enough temperature only when no improvement has occured for a while:

$$Terminate(i, R) = \textbf{True} \Leftrightarrow Temp(i) < T_f \wedge R \geq R_{\max} \tag{17}$$

This approach has the benefit of going through the whole temperature scale, and continue optimization after that if there are acceptable moves. This will probably drive the solution into a local minimum.

3.9.7 Hybrid condition
Any logical combination of conditions 3.9.1 - 3.9.6 is a valid termination condition.

4. Case studies

This section summarizes 5 relevant works on the use of SA for task mapping. Task mapping problems are not identical but comparable in terms of SA parameterization. Selected SA parameterizations are presented to give insight into possible solutions. Table 2 shows move heuristics and acceptance functions, and Table 3 shows annealing schedules for the same cases. These cases are presented in detail in following sections.

Implementation	Move Function	Acceptance Function
Braun (Sec 4.1)	Single	Normalized Inverse Exponential
Coroyer (Sec 4.2)	Single, Task Scheduling	Exponential
Orsila (Sec 4.3)	Single	Normalized Inverse Exponential
Ravindran (Sec 4.4)	Single	Exponential
Wild (Sec 4.5)	Single, ECP	N/A

Table 2. Simulated Annealing move heuristics and acceptance functions

Implementation	Annealing Schedule	T_0	End condition	L
Braun (Sec 4.1)	Geometric, $q = 0.90$	C_0	$T_f = 10^{-200}$	1
Coroyer (Sec 4.2)	Geometric, Fractional	Heuristic	Heuristic	α
Orsila (Sec 4.3)	Geometric, $q = 0.95$	Heuristic	Heuristic	α
Ravindran (Sec 4.4)	Koch	$T_0 = 1$	N/A	N/A
Wild (Sec 4.5)	Geometric, $q = N/A$	N/A	Heuristic	N/A

Table 3. Simulated Annealing schedules. See Table 1 for symbols.

Single move (Sec 3.6.1) and the Geometric annealing scheduling (1) are the most common choices. They should be tested in every new experiment. All the cases use a single move so it is not covered in each case. Other choices are explicitly documented.

4.1 Braun case

(Braun et al., 2001) uses an inverse exponential form (5) as an acceptance function. However, the method uses it to actually implement a normalized inverse exponential form (6) by setting $T_0 = C_0$.

A geometric temperature schedule (1) with $q = 0.90$ and $L = 1$ is used.

The termination condition is an uncoupled temperature and rejection threshold (16). Optimization is terminated when $T_f = 10^{-200}$ or when $R_{max} = 200$ consecutive solutions are identical. The choice for L and T_f values are not explained. If the HW platform or the number of tasks were changed, then trivially the number of iterations should be adjusted as well.

The initial mapping used was a random mapping of tasks.

The paper compares SA to ten other heuristics for independent task mapping problem. SA got position *8/11*, where *1/11* is the best position received by a genetic algorithm. We believe SA was used improperly in this comparison. Based on (11), we think T_f was set too low, and L should be much larger than *1*.

4.2 Coroyer case

(Coroyer & Liu, 1991) do both single and task scheduling (Sec 3.8.5) moves.

The acceptance function is exponential (7) accompanied with a heating process that puts acceptance probabilities to a relevant range. Initial temperature is set high enough so that $p_0 = 0.95$ of new mappings are accepted. If ΔC_{avg} is the average increase in cost for generating new solutions, the initial temperature is set to $T_0 = \frac{-\Delta C_{avg}}{\ln p_0}$. This approach depends on the exponential acceptance function, but it can easily be adopted for other acceptance functions. The average increase is determined by simulating a sufficient number of moves. See Section 3.5.1.

Both fractional (2) and geometric (1) temperature schedules are used with various parameters. The number of mapping iterations per temperature level is $L = \alpha = N(M-1)$.
The termination condition is an uncoupled temperature and rejection threshold (16). Optimization is terminated when $T_f \leq 10^{-2}$ or when $R_{max} = 5\alpha$ consecutive solutions are identical. Also, a given temperature threshold (13) is used.
The initial mapping used was a random mapping of tasks.
They show that SA gives better results than priority-based heuristics for task mapping and scheduling, but SA is also much slower.
Systematic methods are not used to tune parameters.

4.3 Orsila case

This case presents methods to derive SA parameters systematically from the problem parameters (Orsila et al., 2006).

The annealing schedule is geometric with $q = 0.95$. The number of iterations per temperature level is $L = \alpha = N(M-1)$.

The initial and final temperature range $[T_f, T_0] \subset (0,1]$ is defined with

$$T_0 = \frac{kt_{max}}{t_{min\,sum}} \tag{18}$$

$$T_f = \frac{t_{min}}{kt_{max\,sum}} \tag{19}$$

where t_{max} and t_{min} are the maximum and minimum execution time for any task (when it is activated) on any processor, $t_{min\,sum}$ is the sum of execution times for all tasks on the fastest processor in the system, $t_{max\,sum}$ is the sum of execution times for all tasks on the slowest processor in the system, and $k \geq 1$ is a coefficient.
The temperature range is tied to a slightly modified version of (6). The factor 0.5 is the only difference.

$$Accept(\Delta C, T) = \mathbf{True} \Leftrightarrow random() < \frac{1}{1 + \exp(\frac{\Delta C}{0.5 C_0 T})} \tag{20}$$

The rationale is choosing an initial temperature where the longest single task will have a fair transition probability of being moved from one processor to another, and the same should hold true for the shortest single task with respect to final temperature.
Coefficient k has an approximate relation to p_f. Substituting $\frac{\Delta C_{min}}{0.5 C_0}$ in place of ΔC_{min} to make (10) compatible with (20) gives

$$T_f = \frac{\Delta C_{min}}{0.5 C_0 \ln(\frac{1}{p_f} - 1)} < T \tag{21}$$

Now, $\frac{\Delta C_{\min}}{0.5C_0}$ is approximated with $\frac{t_{\min}}{t_{\max sum}}$ from (19)

$$T_f \sim \frac{t_{\min}}{t_{\max sum} \ln(\frac{1}{p_f} - 1)} < T \tag{22}$$

Now comparing (19) and (22) we get the relation

$$k \sim \ln(\frac{1}{p_f} - 1) \tag{23}$$

Solving (23) with respect to p_f gives us

$$p_f \sim \frac{1}{e^k + 1} \tag{24}$$

For $k = 1$ the probability p_f to accept a worsening move on the final temperature level given a cost change of order $t_{\min}$ is approximately 27%. For $k = 2$, probability is 12%. As k increases p_f decreases exponentially. Suitable values for k are in range [1, 9] unless L is very large (hundreds of thousands or even millions of iterations). The temperature range implied by $k = 1$ is shown in Figure 5. The temperature range is calculated with (18) and (19). (Orsila et al., 2007) uses $k = 2$ and reaches are a local minimum more likely in the end, but it is more expensive than $k = 1$.

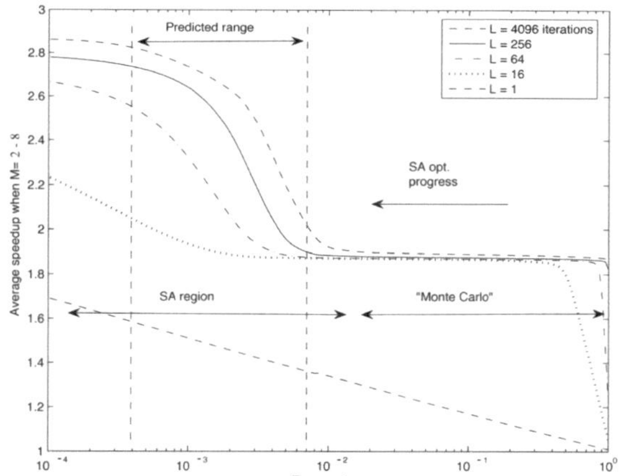

Figure 5. Averaged speedup with respect to temperature for *300* node graphs with different *L* values. The temperature given with (18)(19) *k = 1* is labeled „predicted range". Notice that temperature and the number of iterations increase in different directions. The number of mapping iterations increases as the temperature decreases.

The end condition is the coupled temperature and rejection threshold (17) with $R_{\max} = \alpha$.

4.4 Ravindran case

(Ravindran, 2007) uses an exponential acceptance function (7).

A Koch temperature schedule (3) was used with parameters, including initial and final temperature, set manually. Termination condition is the temperature threshold (13). Systematic methods are not used to tune parameters. However, the Koch temperature schedule is mitigating factor since it affects the number of temperature levels and iterations based on the problem.

4.5 Wild case

(Wild et al., 2003) use a geometric annealing schedule (1) with unknown parameters. The termination condition is the uncoupled temperature and rejection threshold (16). They show that an ECP move heuristics (Sec 3.7.1) is significantly better than the single move with directed acyclic graphs. Systematic methods are not used to tune parameters.

5. Analysis and discussion

Following sections analyze the effect of iterations per temperature level, saving the number of iterations, give best practices for SA, and finally, SA is compared to two greedy algorithms and random mapping.

5.1 Iterations per temperature level

Figure 6 shows speedup of a $N = 300$ task directed acyclic graph with respect to iterations per temperature level L. Speedup is defined as $\frac{t_1}{t}$, where t is the execution time of the optimized solution on multiprocessor system and t_1 is the execution time on a single processor system.

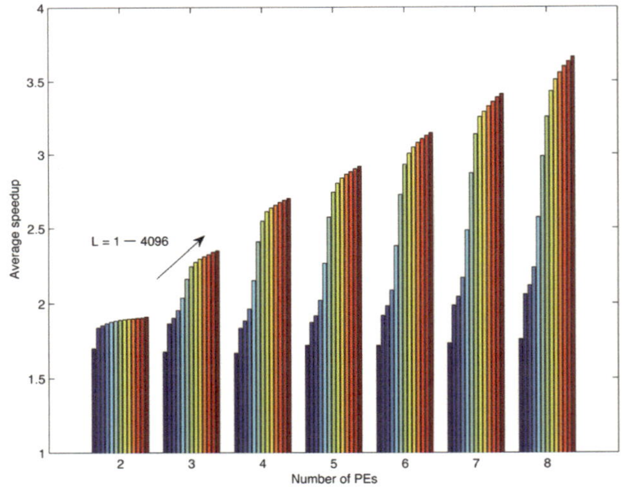

Figure 6. Averaged speedups for 300 node graphs with M=*2-8* processing elements and different L values (L = *1, 2, 4, ..., 4096*) for each processing element set.

Figure 7 shows the speedup and the number of iterations for each L. These figures show that having $L \geq \alpha = N(M-1) = [300,600,900,\ldots,2100]$ for the number of processors $M = [2,3,\ldots,8]$ does not yield a significant improvement in performance but optimization time is increased heavily. Parameter $L = 1$ performs very poorly (Orsila et al., 2006).

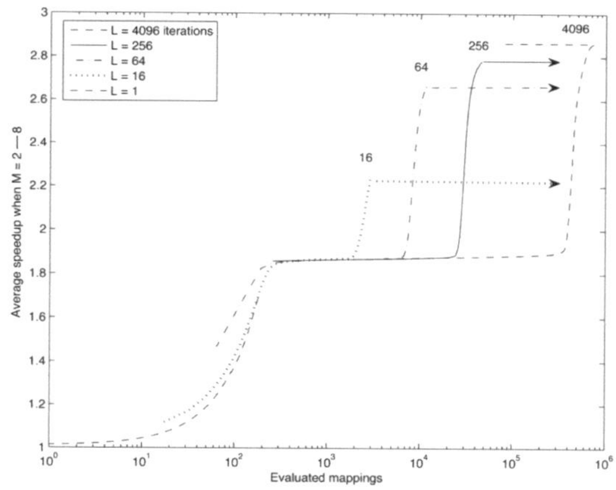

Figure 7. Averaged speedup with respect to mapping evaluations for 300 node graphs with different L values.

5.2 Saving optimization effort

Choosing initial temperature T_0 and final temperature T_f is crucial for saving optimization iterations. With too high an initial temperature the optimization process is practically Monte Carlo which means it converges very slowly, and thus, initial iterations are practically wasted because bad moves are accepted with too high a probability. This effect is visible in Figure 5 at high temperatures, i.e. $T > 10^{-2}$. Also, too low a probability reduces the annealing to greedy optimization. Greedy optimization becomes useless after a short time because it can not espace local minima. Therefore the final temperature must be set as high as possible without sacrificing the greedy part in optimization. This is the rationale for (Orsila et al., 2006) in Section 4.3.

5.3 Simulated annealing best practices

Based on our experiments, we have identified few rules of thumb for using SA to task mapping.

1. Choose the number of iterations per temperature level $L \geq \alpha = N(M-1)$, where N is the number of tasks and M is the number of PEs. Thus, α is the number of neighbouring mapping solutions because each of the N tasks could be relocated into at most $M-1$ alternatives.
2. Use geometric temperature schedule with $0.90 \leq q \leq 0.98$. This is the most common choice.
3. Device a systematic method for choosing the initial and final temperatures. As an example, see (10).
4. Use coupled temperature and rejection threshold as the end condition (Section 3.9.6) with $R_{max} = L$ (the number of iterations per temperature level)
5. If in doubt, use the single task move (Sec 3.6.1). This is the most common choice. Other move heuristics can be very useful depending on the system. For example, ECP heuristics (Sec 3.7.1) is efficient for directed acyclic task graphs.
6. Use normalized inverse exponential function (6) as the acceptance function. This implies that temperature is always in range *(0, 1]*. This also means that convergence of

separate annealing problems can be compared with each other, and thus, effective annealing temperatures become more apparent through experiments.

7. Optimize the same problem many times. On each optimization run start with the best known solution so far. As simulated annealing is a probabilistic algorithm it can happen that the algorithm drives itself to a bad region in the optimization space. Running the algorithm several times reduces this risk.
8. If in doubt of any of the parameters, find them experimentally
9. Record the iteration number when the best solution was reached. If the termination iteration number is much higher than the best solution iteration, maybe the annealing can be made more efficient without sacrificing reliability.

5.4 Comparing SA to greedy algorithms

Figure 8 compares SA to two greedy algorithms and Random Mapping (Orsila et al., 2007). A *300* task application is distributed onto *8* processors to optimize execution time. Group Migration (GM) is a deterministic greedy algorithm that converges slowly. GM needs many iterations to achieve any speedup, but once that occurs, the speedup increases very rapidly. Optimal Subset Mapping (OSM) is a stochastic greedy algorithm that converges very rapidly. It reaches almost the maximum speedup level with very limited number of iterations. SA convergence speed is between GM and OSM but in the end it reaches a better solution. Random mapping saturates quickly and further iterations are unable to provide any speedup. Note that SA follows the random mapping line initially as it resembles a Monte Carlo process at high temperatures. Random mapping is the base reference for any mapping algorithm since any intelligent algorithm should do better than just random.

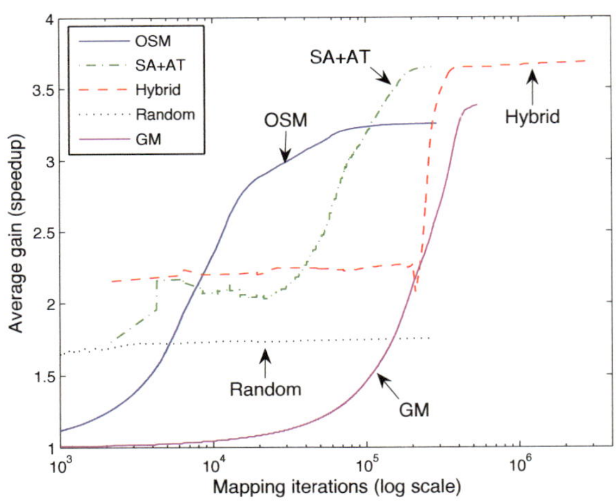

Figure 8. SA convergence speed compared to GM, OSM and Random Mapping algorithms for mapping *300* tasks to *8* processors. SA+AT is a Simulated Annealing algorithm presented in Section 4.3. GM and OSM are greedy heuristics.

SA yields *8%* better result than GM, *12%* better than OSM, and *107%* better than random mapping. SA is better than the greedy algorithms because it can espace local minima. However, when measuring the best speedup divided with the number of iterations needed to achieve the best result for each algorithm the relative order is different. We normalize the results so that random mapping gets value *1.00*. SA gets *2.58*, OSM *6.11* and GM *1.21*. That is, OSM is *2.4* times as efficient as SA is in terms of speedup divided by iterations. SA is *2.1* times as efficient as GM. Thus, we note that greedy local search methods can converge much faster than SA.

6. Open research challenges

This section identifies some open research challenges related to using SA for task mapping. The challenges are in order of importance.

What is the optimal annealing schedule for task mapping given a hardware, application model and a trade-off between solution quality and speed? The hardware and application model determine all possible cost changes in the system, and this is tied to probabilistic SA transitions. Not all temperatures are equally useful, so iterations can be saved by not annealing on irrelevant temperatures. For example, it is not benefitial to use lots of iterations at high temperatures because the process is essentially a Monte Carlo process which converges very slowly.

What are the best move heuristics for each type of application and hardware model? For example, ECP (Sec 3.7.1) is useful for application models that have the concept of critical path.

What is the optimal transition probability for $\Delta C = 0$? The probability is *0.5* in (5) and *1.0* in (7), but it can be selected arbitrarily. This probability determines the tendency at which SA travels equally good solutions in the neighborhood. Is there advantage to using either (5) or (7) due to this factor?

Can SA be made faster or better by first doing coarse-grain optimization on the application level and then continue with finer-grain optimization? Current optimization strategies are concerned with sequential small changes rather than employ a top-level strategy.

What are the relevant test cases for comparing SA to other algorithms, or other SA implementations? (Barr et al., 1995) have laid out good rules for comparing heuristics.

Excluding optimization programs, is there a problem where running SA as the main loop of the program would be benefitial? Each *Cost()* call would go one or several steps further in the program. In other words, is SA a feasible for run-time optimization rather than being used as an offline optimizer? Even small problems can take significant amount of iterations to get parameters correctly. The application must also tolerate slowdowns.

7. Conclusions

This chapter presents an overview of using SA for mapping application tasks to multiprocessor system. We analyze the different function variants needed in SA. Many choices are suboptimal with respect to iteration count or discouraged due to poor optimization results. We find that SA is a well performing algorithm if used properly, but in practice it is too often used badly. Hence, we present best practices for some of those and review the most relevant open research challenges.

For best practices we recommend following. Iterations per temperature level should depend on the problem size. Systematic methods should be used for the temperature range. Normalized inverse exponential function should be used.

For open research challenges we prioritize following. Find an optimal annealing schedule, move function and transition probabilities for each type of common task mapping problems. For example, it is possible to do critical path analysis for some task mapping problems.

8. References

Barr, R. S.; Golden, B. L & Kelly, J. P. & Resende, M. G. C. & Stewart, W. R. (1995). Designing and Reporting on Computational Experiments with heuristic Methods, Springer Journal of Heuristics, Vol. 1, No. 1, pp. 9-32, 1995.

Braun, T. D.; Siegel, H. J. & Beck, N. (2001). A Comparison of Eleven Static Heuristics for Mapping a Class of Independent Tasks onto Heterogeneous Distributed Systems, IEEE Journal of Parallel and Distributed Computing, Vol. 61, pp. 810-837, 2001.

Cerny, V. (1985). Thermodynamical Approach to the Traveling Salesman Problem: An Efficient Simulation Algorithm, Journal of Opt. Theory Appl., Vol. 45, No. 1, pp. 41-51, 1985.

Coffman, E. G. Jr. & Graham, R. L. (1971). Optimal Scheduling for Two-Processor Systems, Springer Acta Informatica, Vol. 1, No. 3, pp. 200-213, September, 1971.

Coroyer, C. & Liu, Z. (1991). Effectiveness of Heuristics and Simulated Annealing for the Scheduling of Concurrent Tasks - An Empirical Comparison, Rapport de recherch´ de l'INRIA - Sophia Antipolis, No. 1379, 1991.

Kirkpatrick, S.; Gelatt, C. D. Jr. & Vecchi, M. P. (1983). Optimization by simulated annealing, Science, Vol. 200, No. 4598, pp. 671-680, 1983.

Koch, P. (1995). Strategies for Realistic and Efficient Static Scheduling of Data Independent Algorithms onto Multiple Digital Signal Processors. Technical report, The DSP Research Group, Institute for Electronic Systems, Aalborg University, Aalborg, Denmark, December 1995.

Kwok, Y.-K. & Ahmad, I. (1999). Static scheduling algorithms for allocating directed task graphs to multiprocessors, ACM Comput. Surv., Vol. 31, No. 4, pp. 406-471, 1999.

Orsila, H.; Kangas, T. & Salminen, E. & Hämäläinen, T. D. (2006). Parameterizing Simulated Annealing for Distributing Task Graphs on Multiprocessor SoCs, International Symposium on System-on-Chip 2006, Tampere, Finland, November, pp. 1-4, 2006.

Orsila, H.; Salminen, E. & Hännikäinen, M. & Hämäläinen, T. D. (2007). Optimal Subset Mapping And Convergence Evaluation of Mapping Algorithms for Distributing Task Graphs on Multiprocessor SoC, International Symposium on System-on-Chip 2007, Tampere, Finland, November, pp. 1-6, 2007.

Ravindran, K. (2007). Task Allocation and Scheduling of Concurrent Applications to Multiprocessor Systems, PhD Thesis, UCB/EECS-2007-149, [online] http://www.eecs.berkeley.edu/Pubs/TechRpts/2007/EECS-2007-149.html, 2007.

Wikipedia. (2008). Embarrassingly Parallel, [online] http://en.wikipedia.org /wiki/Embarrassingly_parallel

Wikipedia. (2008). Kahn Process Network, [online] http://en.wikipedia.org /wiki/Kahn_Process_Network

Wild, T.; Brunnbauer, W. & Foag, J. & Pazos, N. (2003). Mapping and scheduling for architecture exploration of networking SoCs, Proc. 16th Int. Conference on VLSI Design, pp. 376-381, 2003.

17

Simulated Annealing of Two Electron Density Solution Systems

Mario de Oliveira Neto[2], Ronaldo Luiz Alonso[1], Fabio Lima Leite[2], Osvaldo N. Oliveira Jr[2], Igor Polikarpov[2] and Yvonne Primerano Mascarenhas[2]
[1] *University of São Paulo, Institute of Mathematical Sciences and Computing, São Paulo*
[2] *University of São Paulo, Institute of Physics of São Carlos, São Carlos, São Paulo*
[1,2] *Brazil*

1. Introduction

Resolving the structure of a macromolecule such as a protein or synthetic polymer is important to predict its properties, especially in the case of proteins whose structure determines their function in a living cell. With crystallography and nuclear magnetic resonance (NMR) techniques, the protein structure may be solved at a high atomic resolution. However, these high resolution methods apply only in rather specific conditions, for low molecular weight proteins in NMR and when a crystal may be formed in crystallography. In order to obtain structural information for systems that do not satisfy the requirements above, one has to resort to methods such as X-ray and neutron small angle scattering (SAS), in which macromolecules in solution can yield only low-resolution information (from 1–100 nm), but are applicable to a broader range of conditions and particle sizes (Feigin and Svergun (1987)).
In this chapter we shall concentrate on small angle X-ray scattering (SAXS), and elaborate on the theory and possible applications for proteins and conjugated polymers. In order to obtain low resolution models of such complex systems, several assumptions must be made. For instance, the system needs to be monodisperse, diluted and with particles possessing an electron density that is considerably different from the density of the medium. Of particular relevance will be the use of global optimization techniques, such as simulated annealing, for proteins. The aim is to find the structure of a monodisperse diluted system of protein solution from one-dimensional SAXS data (Glatter and Kratky (1982)). The Chapter is organized as follows: In Section 2 the main principles of X-ray scattering are introduced, including scattering of X-ray by free electrons and a pair of electrons, in addition to scattering of X-ray by atoms and a group of *n* atoms. Section 3 deals with analysis of SAXS curves, whereas the method of simulated annealing is discussed in Section 4. In Section 5 the results of simulated annealing in two electron densities systems are discussed. Concluding remarks close the chapter in Section 6.

2. Principles of small angle X-ray scattering

2.1 Scattering of X-ray by free electrons

The use of X-rays in structural characterization of materials explores essentially their interaction with matter through the electrons of atoms and molecules. The electrons are sensitive to the sinusoidal *electric and magnetic fields* of the impinging X-rays, which for a monochromatic electromagnetic wave may be represented by periodic functions of the type:

$$\vec{E} = \vec{E}_0 \cos 2\pi\omega t$$
$$\vec{H} = \vec{H}_0 \cos 2\pi\omega t \tag{1}$$

where $\vec{E}_0$ and $\vec{E}$ are the incident and scattered electric fields, respectively, $\vec{H}_0$ and $\vec{H}$ are the incident and scattered magnetic fields, respectively, and ω is the radiation frequency.
The direction of X-ray propagation can be given by the *Poynting vector*: $\vec{P} = (c/4\pi)\vec{E} \times \vec{H}$.
Let us consider an electron located at the origin of a system of coordinates xyz shown in figure 1, on which a parallel beam of polarized and monochromatic X-rays impinges. Under the electric field of the incident wave the electron suffers a force:

$$\vec{F} = e\vec{E}_0 \cos 2\pi\omega t \tag{2}$$

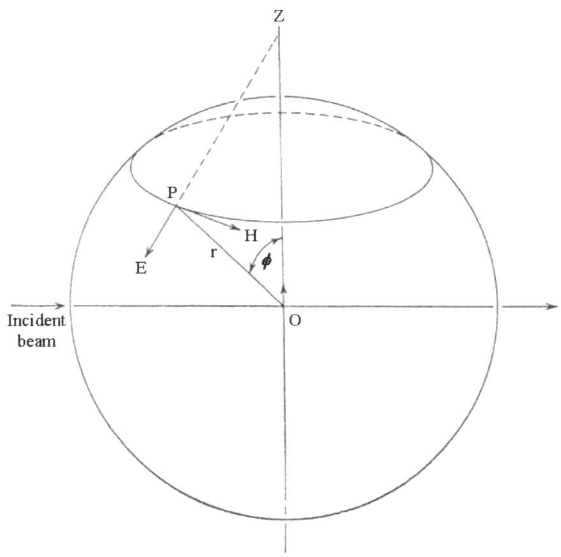

Figure 1. Schematic view of the X-ray scattering by free electrons. An electron is located at the origin O on which a parallel beam of polarized, monochromatic X-rays is incident.

The electron is then accelerated according to:

$$\vec{a} = \frac{\vec{F}}{m} = \frac{e\vec{E}_0}{m} \cos 2\pi\omega t \tag{3}$$

The electron thus accelerated becomes a spherical source of electromagnetic waves of the same frequency of the incident radiation (elastic scattering). So, an electron will oscillate around its average position under this electric field. The electron scattering was analyzed by J. J. Thomson, who derived the field at P in figure 1:

$$E = \frac{ea \sin \phi}{4\pi R \varepsilon_0 c^2} \quad (4)$$

Substituting equation 3 in equation 4:

$$E = \frac{e^2 E_0}{m} \cos 2\pi wt \frac{\sin \phi}{4\pi R \varepsilon_0 c^2} \quad (5)$$

where ϕ is the angle between the scattered beam direction and the electric field of the incident wave, ε_0 is the vacuum permittivity, R is the distance between the electron and the observation point, c is the speed of light, m is the electron mass and e is the electron charge. The expression $\frac{e^2}{4\pi\varepsilon_0 c^2 m}$ has the dimension of length, being the scattering length in the classical electromagnetism, referred to as electron radius ($2.82.10^{-15} m$). To simplify the notation the amplitude of the scattered wave by a free electron will henceforth be designated as A_e.

$$A_e = \frac{e^2}{4\pi\varepsilon_0 c^2 m} \quad (6)$$

For a non-polarized incident beam, the electric field may be decomposed into two mutually perpendicular components. Figure 2 depicts a parallel, non-polarized beam propagating in the Ox direction, impinging on an electron located at O. To determine the scattered electric field in the direction OP, the incident field can be decomposed in two components: a parallel one to the plane OXP, $\mathbf{E}_{//}$, and a perpendicular component, $\mathbf{E}_{\perp}$.

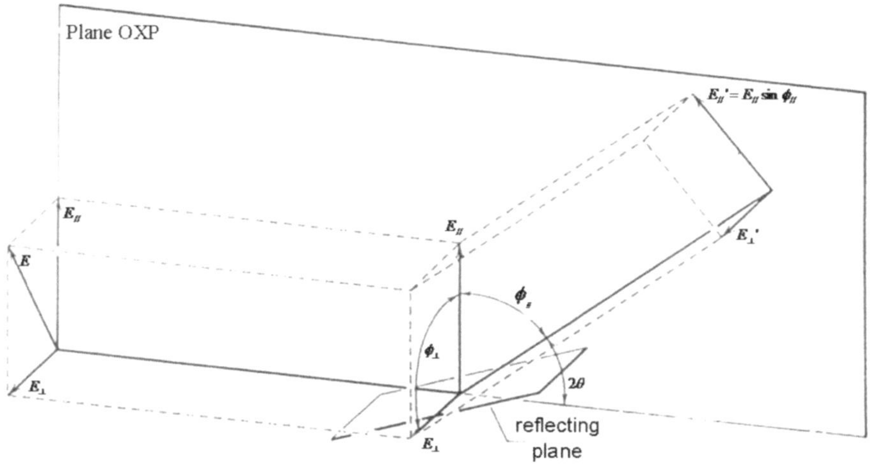

Figure 2. Schematic view of an electron located at the origin O on which a parallel, monochromatic and non-polarized X-ray beam is incident in the Ox direction. The incident field has a component parallel to the plane OXP, $E_{//}$, and another perpendicular to this plane, $E_{\perp}$.

Under the action of those fields the electron acquires acceleration with parallel and perpendicular components given by $a_{\perp} = eE_{\perp} / m$ and $a_{//} = eE_{//} / m$. Using these expressions in equation 5, one obtains the electric field of the scattered wave:

$$E_{\perp}' = \frac{e^2 E_{\perp}}{4\pi\varepsilon_0 R c^2 m} = \frac{A_e E_{\perp}}{R}$$
$$E_{//}' = \frac{e^2 E_{//} \cos 2\theta}{4\pi\varepsilon_0 R c^2 m} = \frac{A_e E_{//} \cos 2\theta}{R} \tag{7}$$

The intensity I_o of the incident beam can also be decomposed into a perpendicular and a parallel component, proportional to $E_{\perp}^2$ and $E_{//}^2$, respectively:

$$E_{//}^2 = E_{\perp}^2 \propto \frac{I_0}{2} \tag{8}$$

The total intensity scattered at point P is:

$$I(2\theta) = [E_{//}'^2 + E_{\perp}'^2]$$
$$I(2\theta) = \frac{I_0}{R^2}\left(\frac{e^2}{4\pi\varepsilon_0 c^2 m}\right)^2 \frac{(1+\cos^2 2\theta)}{2} \tag{9}$$
$$I(2\theta) = \left(\frac{I_0}{R^2}\right)(A_e)^2 \frac{(1+\cos^2 2\theta)}{2}$$

Since I_0 and R can be taken as constant during the measurement, the scattered intensity of the electron is:

$$I_e(R, 2\theta) = A_e^2 \frac{(1+\cos^2 2\theta)}{2} \tag{10}$$

From equation 9 and 6 we infer that only the electrons contribute to the scattered intensity, which decreases with the square of the particle mass. Therefore, even though the nuclei also suffer the action of the impinging electric field, the effect is negligible because of the heavy mass of a nucleus (mass of the proton = 1837 times the mass of the electron). The term $(1 + \cos^2 2\theta)/2$ is the polarization factor, and indicates that the scattered wave is partially polarized even for a non-polarized incident beam. In SAXS experiments, the maximum scattering angle is usually around 5 degrees and $(1 + \cos^2 2\theta)/2$ is practically 1.

2.2 Scattering of X-ray by a pair of electrons, interference

To introduce the interference concept, we consider two electrons in a particle spaced by a distance r, immersed in a parallel monochromatic X-rays beam, as illustrated in figure 3a. The scattered waves will be coherent. Incoherent scattering may also occur but it can be neglected at small angles.

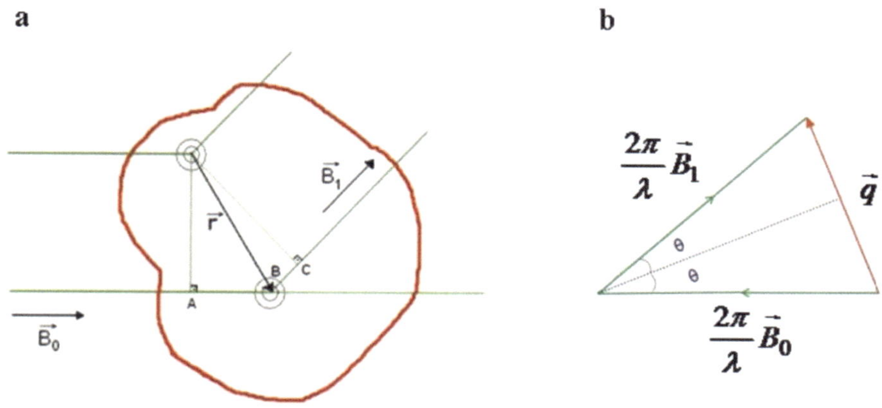

Figure 3. Schematic view for X-ray scattering by a pair of electrons. **a.** An electron is at the origin and the other is at a distance $\vec{r}$. There is a difference (AB + BC) in the optical paths between the two scattered beams, leading to a phase difference. **b.** Geometric relationships among the vectors $\vec{B}_1$, $\vec{B}_0$, and $\vec{q}$.

The phase difference due to the distinct optical paths for the electrons at the origin and at a distance $\vec{r}$ is

$$\Delta\varphi = \frac{2\pi\Delta l}{\lambda} \tag{11}$$

Since the difference in optical path $\Delta l = \mathrm{A}B + BC$, the phase difference is

$$\Delta\varphi = \frac{2\pi(\mathrm{A}B + BC)}{\lambda} \tag{12}$$

The directions of the incident and scattered beams are given by $\vec{B}_0$ and $\vec{B}_1$ unit vectors respectively.

$$AB = \vec{r}\cdot\vec{B}_0 \text{ and } BC = -\vec{r}\cdot\vec{B}_1 \tag{13}$$

The phase difference is:

$$\Delta\varphi = \frac{-2\pi\vec{r}(\vec{B}_1 - \vec{B}_0)}{\lambda} \tag{14}$$

Where:

$$\vec{q} = \frac{2\pi(\vec{B}_1 - \vec{B}_0)}{\lambda} \tag{15}$$

Then:

$$\Delta\varphi = -\vec{r}\cdot\vec{q} = -rq\cos 2\theta \qquad (16)$$

where 2θ is the angle between $\vec{r}$ and $\vec{q}$.

Only the product of the components $\vec{r}\cdot\vec{q}$ is relevant to $\Delta\varphi$. It might now be possible to obtain the resulting amplitude by summing up all secondary waves, considering the scattering phase factor $e^{i\Delta\varphi}$ among them. Due to the enormous number of electrons in a macromolecule, it is convenient to introduce the electron density $\rho(\vec{r})$. The scattering amplitude will be then given by:

$$A(\vec{q}) = \int \rho(\vec{r}) A_e e^{i\Delta\varphi} \qquad (17)$$

Substituting Equation 16 into 17

$$A(\vec{q}) = \int A_e \rho(\vec{r}) e^{-i\vec{r}\cdot\vec{q}} dV \qquad (18)$$

Figure 3b displays the geometric relationships among the vectors $\frac{2\pi\vec{B}_1}{\lambda}$, $\frac{2\pi\vec{B}_0}{\lambda}$, and $\vec{q}$. It can be seen easily that $\vec{q}$ is perpendicular to the bisector of the angle between $\frac{2\pi\vec{B}_1}{\lambda}$ and $\frac{2\pi\vec{B}_0}{\lambda}$, with a module equal to:

$$q = \frac{4\pi\sin\theta}{\lambda} \qquad (19)$$

2.3 Reciprocity law

Any scattering process is characterized by a reciprocity law that gives an inverse relationship between particle size and scattering angle. Let us consider in figure 4 the case of two spheres with constant electron density $\rho(\vec{r})$ and radius R_1 and R_2 under the same X-ray beam; *dI* is the scattered intensity for an element of volume dV for two different points from each sphere. There is a difference in optical path to the two spheres. If 2θ is zero, so is *q*, and $\Delta\varphi$ for all the volume elements is null. The same path difference of one λ occurs at a higher angle for the smaller sphere. The scattering curves for the two spheres clearly reveal a reciprocity relationship between the real and the scattering spaces, referred to as reciprocal space.

2.4 The phase problem

The scattering intensity $I(\vec{q})$ is the measurable quantity, proportional to the square of *A(q)*:

$$I(\vec{q}) \propto A(\vec{q})\cdot A(\vec{q})^* \qquad (20)$$

where $A(\vec{q})^*$ it is the complex conjugate of $A(\vec{q})$.

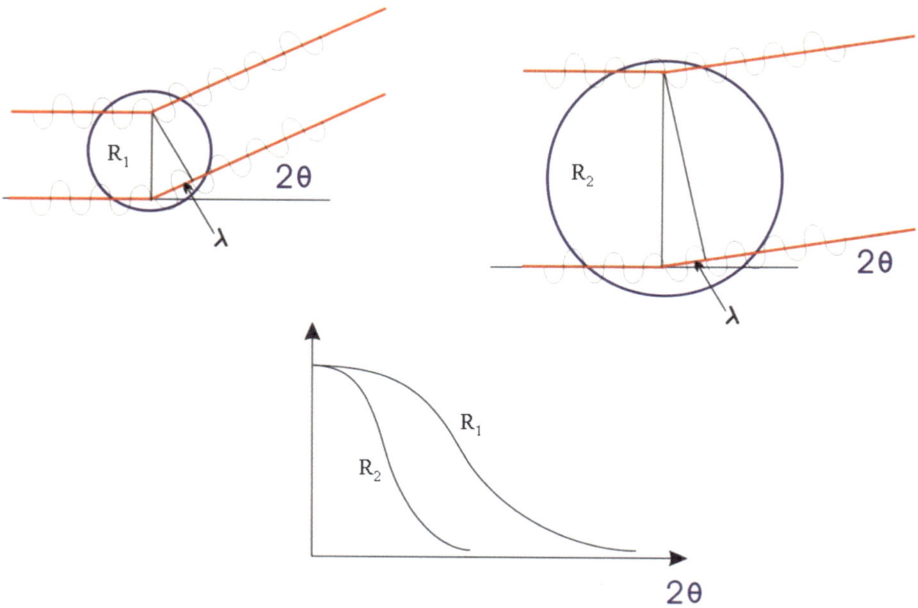

Figure 4. **Reciprocity law.** Two spheres with constant electron density $\rho(\vec{r})$ and radius R_1 and R_2 under the same X-ray beam.

According to the properties of Fourier transforms, the inverse transform of $A(\vec{q})$, equation 18, allows for the calculation of $\rho(\vec{r})$, which is a real, positive quantity. However, to obtain $\rho(\vec{r})$ the phase and module of the wave vector $A(\vec{q})$ are required:

$$A(\vec{q}) = |A(\vec{q})| e^{i\phi} \tag{21}$$

The intensity will be then:

$$I(\vec{q}) \propto \left(A(\vec{q}) \right)^2 = |A(\vec{q})|^2 e^{i\phi} e^{-i\phi} = |A(\vec{q})|^2 \tag{22}$$

Hence, as from the measurement only $I(\vec{q})$ is obtained the knowledge of the phase being lost.

2.5 Scattering of X-rays by atoms

Equation 18 can be calculated for any atom, provided that $\rho(\vec{r})$ is known, which is usually obtained with quantum methods assuming spherical symmetry. For $\vec{q}$ = 0 the integral in equation 18 gives the total number of electrons of a neutral atom, *i.e.*, its atomic number Z. As $\vec{q}$ grows, the phase differences lead to a progressive decrease in $A(\vec{q})$. Curves of the type shown in figure 5 are obtained for carbon and oxygen.

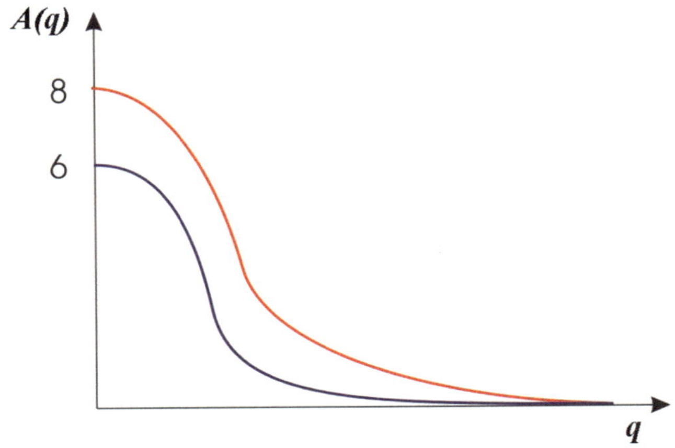

Figure 5. Schematic representation of the atomic scattering factor for carbon (blue line) and oxygen (red line).

The atomic scattering factor is defined as the ratio between the scattered amplitude for the atom and the scattered amplitude for one electron.

$$f(\vec{q}) = \frac{A(\vec{q})_{atom}}{A_e} \tag{23}$$

2.6 Scattering by a group of n atoms

With the atomic scattering factors, equation 18 can be rewritten considering the position vector $\vec{r}_j$ of each atom, and making a sum over all the n atoms, each one with a scattering factor f_j:

$$A(\vec{q}) = \sum_{j=1}^{n} f_j e^{-i\vec{q}\cdot\vec{r}_j} \tag{24}$$

The scattered intensity of the particle can be obtained if the atomic coordinates of the atoms are known. For n atoms with scattering factors $f_j(\vec{q}) = f_j$ and coordinates $\vec{r}_j$ for the center of each particle:

$$I(\vec{q}) = \sum_{j=1}^{n}\sum_{k=1}^{n} f_j f_k e^{-i\vec{q}\cdot\vec{r}_{jk}} \tag{25}$$

2.7 Inverse Fourier transform of the intensity

Because of the Phase Problem, it is not possible to invert $A(\vec{q})$ directly to obtain $\rho(\vec{r})$. Patterson (1935) proposed a method for calculating the Fourier transform taking as coefficients the intensities of scattered beams, obtained from the square of the amplitude in equation 18:

$$I(\vec{q}) = \int\int dV_1 dV_2 \rho(\vec{r}_1)\rho(\vec{r}_2)e^{-i\vec{q}(\vec{r}_1-\vec{r}_2)} \quad (26)$$

Integration of equation (26) may be performed in two steps: first integrating over all the pairs of points of equal distance in the particle and then integrating on all relative distances in the particle. These steps are summarized as follows:

1st step: Mathematically it corresponds to calculating the auto-correlation function $\tilde{\rho}(\vec{r})$, making $\vec{r} = \vec{r}_2 - \vec{r}_1$ constant.

$$\tilde{\rho}(\vec{r}) = \rho(\vec{r}_1)\rho(\vec{r}_2)dV \quad (27)$$

This function, known as Patterson function, is defined on a new space *C(r)* (correlation space) in which each $\vec{r}$ corresponds to a distance $(\vec{r}_2 - \vec{r}_1)$ taken over the whole scattered object and whose value is the average of the products between electron densities in points $\vec{r}_1$ and $\vec{r}_2$.

2nd step: It consists in integrating the remaining function in the space *C(r)* to obtain $I(\vec{q})$:

$$I(\vec{q}) = \int dV \tilde{\rho}^2(\vec{r})e^{-i\vec{q}\cdot\vec{r}} \quad (28)$$

This integral depends only on the relative distances between the elements in the volume and on the product of the corresponding electron densities.

For a concentrated system, the scattering intensity is $I_*(\vec{q}) = I(\vec{q}).S(\vec{q})$, where $I(\vec{q})$ is the form factor, and should be related to intra-particles distances, while $S(\vec{q})$ is the structure factor, associated with inter-particles correlations. For diluted systems, $S(\vec{q})$ can be taken as 1, and only the form factor contributes to the scattering curve (Craievich (2005)). In this chapter we will discuss only diluted systems.

According to equation 28, the distribution of the scattered intensities in reciprocal space is a function of electron density distribution in the scattering particle through its auto-correlation function. It can be obtained directly from the scattered intensities by calculating the inverse Fourier transform:

$$\tilde{\rho}^2(\vec{r}) = (\tfrac{1}{2\pi})^3 \int I(\vec{q})dV^* e^{-i\vec{q}\cdot\vec{r}} \quad (29)$$

where dV^* is the volume element of the reciprocal space.

An important property of the auto-correlation function is the existence of an inversion center, because $\rho(\vec{r}_1)\rho(\vec{r}_2)$ is equal $\rho(\vec{r}_2)\rho(\vec{r}_1)$, resulting in the same value for $\vec{r}$ as for -$\vec{r}$, regardless of whether the scattering particle has an inversion center. Furthermore, there is a reciprocity relationship between equations 28 and 29, because their values just depend on the product $\vec{q}\cdot\vec{r}$. Therefore, an increase in $\vec{r}$ leads to a smaller $\vec{q}$.

2.8 Isotropic and diluted systems

A consequence of the reciprocity relationships between the direct and reciprocal spaces is that large particles will lead to smaller intervals for 2θ in which scattering is observed. For analyzing SAXS curves we need to adopt simplifying restrictions:

(a) The system is statistically isotropic either due to the particle scattering form, or to its spatial distribution and even random movement in the medium.
(b) There is no long range order among the particles, i.e., they should be sufficiently apart.
With restriction (a), $\tilde{\rho}^2(\vec{r})$ is centro-symmetric depending only on the module of $\vec{r}$. This may not be true in the real space, and we can substitute the phase factor $e^{-i\vec{q}\cdot\vec{r}}$ by its average value taken around $\vec{r}$, that is, applying Debye's formula:

$$\left\langle e^{-i\vec{q}\cdot\vec{r}} \right\rangle = \frac{\sin qr}{qr} \tag{30}$$

This allows us to rewrite equations 25 and 29:

$$I(q) = \sum_{i=1}^{n}\sum_{j=1}^{n} f_i f_j \frac{\sin qr_{ij}}{qr_{ij}} \tag{31}$$

$$I(q) = \int dV \tilde{\rho}^2(r) \frac{\sin qr}{qr} \tag{32}$$

Again, the expression of reciprocity between r and q is apparent in Debye's formula. If the product qr is kept constant, an increase in r causes a decrease in q.
Because sin qr is a periodic function, the denominator qr is a dampening factor, generating smaller maxima. The first zero should happen for $qr = 2\pi$. We can thus verify, recalling that $q = (4\pi \sin\theta)/\lambda$, that $\theta \approx 2.5^\circ$ for r = 50 Å and λ = 1.54 Å. Therefore, the useful interval for measuring the scattering curve is approximately from 0 to 2.5º.
The consequence of the second restriction is that at large r the electron densities become independent, and might be replaced by the average $\langle\rho\rangle$. The auto-correlation function must tend towards a constant value $V\langle\rho\rangle^2$, while at the origin $\tilde{\rho}^2(0)$ takes the value $V\overline{\rho^2}$ (the maximum, of course). So, in space *C(r)* relevant structural information will be only in the area such that ρ is significantly different from its final constant value. For that reason the auto-correlation function is redefined to $\eta = \rho - \langle\rho\rangle$, expressing in fact only the fluctuations of electron density responsible for scattering:

$$\tilde{\eta}^2(r) = (\rho(r) - \langle\rho\rangle)^2 = V\gamma(r) \tag{33}$$

With a convenient change of notation, the correlation function $\gamma(r)$ is introduced, which is associated with the average of the density fluctuations for two electrons separated by r, where $r = |r_1 - r_2|$.

$$\gamma(r) = \langle \eta(r_1)\eta(r_2) \rangle \tag{34}$$

The fluctuations in electron density, relative to the medium that contains the scattering centers, can be negative or positive. For instance, pores in a material lead to a negative η

fluctuation. However $\gamma(r)$ will be positive as it is given (cf. eq. 33) by $\tilde{\eta}^2(r)$, with $\gamma(0)=\overline{\eta^2}$ and $\gamma \to 0$ for large r. Adding $\gamma(r)$ in eq. 32, with integration limits from 0 to ∞ and changing the integration parameter to dr, the intensity is:

$$I(q)=V\int_0^\infty 4\pi r^2 dr\gamma(r)\frac{\sin qr}{qr} \tag{35}$$

For $q = 0$

$$I(0)=V\int_0^\infty 4\pi r^2 dr\gamma(r) \tag{36}$$

$\gamma(r)$ is found from the inverse Fourier transform of eq. 35:

$$V\gamma(r)=\frac{1}{2\pi^2}\int_0^\infty q^2 dqI(q)\frac{\sin qr}{qr} \tag{37}$$

For $r = 0$

$$V\gamma(0)=\frac{1}{2\pi^2}\int_0^\infty q^2 dqI(q)=V\overline{\eta^2} \tag{38}$$

It is not possible to measure $I(0)$ in equation 36 because it coincides with the incident beam direction. However, it can be obtained by extrapolation of the curve I(q), thus allowing at least an estimate of the number of electrons in the volume of the particle.
From equation 38 the integral of the intensity in the reciprocal space is constant. Even if a given particle has its form altered, but remaining as a whole intact, the integral is constant, equal to $V\overline{\eta^2}$, though the diffraction pattern or scattering may be changed. This constant is the so-called "invariant", given by:

$$Q=\int_0^\infty q^2 dqI(q) \tag{39}$$

The restricting condition of isotropic systems allows one to obtain averages that are treated as scalar quantities in the distribution of the autocorrelation function in the $C(r)$ space.

2.9 Redefinition of correlation function

Because the square electron density difference is always positive and constant, it is convenient to separate $\gamma(r)$, defined in equation 33, in the form

$$\gamma(r)=(\Delta\rho)^2\gamma_0(r) \tag{40}$$

Where $\gamma_0(r)$ is a new correlation function, just for the geometry of the particle, with $\gamma_0(0)=1$ and $\gamma_0(r\geq D_{\max})=0$ (where $D_{\max}$ is the maximum intra-particle distance). $\gamma_0(r)$ is called "characteristic function" and has a more intuitive meaning.
Thus, it is convenient to rewrite equations 35, 36, 37, 38 and 39:

$$I(q) = V(\Delta\rho)^2 \int_0^D 4\pi r^2 dr \gamma_0(r) \frac{\sin qr}{qr} \quad (41)$$

$$I(0) = V(\Delta\rho)^2 \int_0^D 4\pi r^2 dr \gamma_0(r) \approx (\Delta\rho)^2 V^2 \quad (42)$$

$$V\gamma_0(r) = \frac{1}{2\pi^2(\Delta\rho)^2} \int_0^\infty q^2 dq I(q) \frac{\sin qr}{qr} \quad (43)$$

$$V\gamma_0(0) = \frac{1}{2\pi^2(\Delta\rho)^2} \int_0^\infty q^2 dq I(q) \quad (44)$$

$$Q = \int_0^\infty q^2 dq I(q) = V 2\pi^2 (\Delta\rho)^2 \quad (45)$$

2.10 Isotropic, diluted and monodisperse systems

Let us assume that the system of interest is a diluted solution of identical particles (monodisperse) with constant electron density ρ, embedded in a medium of constant ρ_0 *(solvent)*. Thus only $\Delta\rho = (\rho - p_0)$ is relevant for scattering. The condition of diluted system guarantees that each particle makes independent contributions to the scattering intensity, so that only one single particle needs to be considered.

A more complete data analysis for the determination of the particle's geometry can still be made through the calculation, starting from the experimental data, of the pair distribution function *p(r)*, where $p(r) = 4\pi r^2 \gamma_0(r)$. Thus, equation 41 can be rewritten as

$$I(q) = V(\Delta\rho)^2 \int_0^D p(r) dr \frac{\sin qr}{qr} \quad (46)$$

Therefore, *p(r)* can be obtained from the inverse Fourier transform of *I(q)*. The *p(r)* function is zero for the maximum particle dimension D_{max}. It should be reminded that we assumed restrictive conditions such that "the solution needs to be monodisperse and sufficiently diluted to avoid inter-particle effects". It is also worth noting that a good contrast in electron density is needed between the solute and the solvent. The distance distribution function *p(r)* contains the same information as the scattering intensity *I(q)*, but the real space representation is more intuitive. Furthermore, information about particle shape can often be deduced by straightforward visual inspection of *p(r)*. Spherical particles have a Gaussian p(r) with maximum at $D_{max}/2$. Departures from a Gaussian curve are indicative of more anisotropic particles in solution.

3. Analysis of SAXS curves

To analyze the SAXS curve it is convenient to distinguish three regions related to different distances in real space. With this procedure, it is possible to calculate the radius of gyration, the relation *I(0)/Q* and the surface/volume ratio.

3.1 Small *q* in SAXS curves, determination of the radius of gyration

Assuming the ideal case of non-interacting, dilute spherical particles and isotropic solutions, A. Guinier showed for $q \rightarrow 0$ that the intensity curve can be described by an exponential function:

$$I(q) = I(0)e^{\frac{-q^2 R_g^{\ 2}}{3}} \tag{47}$$

Where R_g is the radius of gyration corresponding to the quadratic average distance from the electron to the center of gravity of the electron density, analogously to the radius of inertia in mechanics. Similar approximations, not shown here, can be considered for rod-like and flat particles. For ideal monodisperse systems, the Guinier plot $\ln I(q) \times q^2$ should be a straight line whose intercept gives *I (0)* and the slope yields the radius of gyration R_g. One should, however, always bear in mind that the Guinier approximation is valid for very small angles only, namely in the range $q < 1.3/R_g$, and fitting a straight line beyond this range is unphysical. It is also possible to obtain R_g as the normalized second moment of the pair distribution function *p(r)* of the particle (Svergun & Koch (2003)).

3.2 Central slope of the SAXS curve, determination of the volume

Dividing equation 42 by 45, the term corresponding to the absolute intensity is canceled out and:

$$\frac{I(0)}{Q} = \frac{V}{2\pi^2} \tag{48}$$

Because the data normally appear in arbitrary units, *I*(0) and Q are given in a relative scale. Hence, $I(0)/Q$ is also valid in an arbitrary scale. To obtain V the data are extrapolated to $I(0)$ using the Guinier plot.

3.3 Final slope of the SAXS curve, determination of the surface/volume ration

An analysis of the slope in the final region of the SAXS curve should contain information on finer aspects of the particle's structure, expressed by the behavior of $\gamma_0(r)$ at smaller r_s. Porod showed that a relationship exists between this part of the curve and the fourth power of *q* given by:

$$I(q) \rightarrow (\Delta\rho)^2 V \frac{8\pi}{q^4} = (\Delta\rho)^2 \frac{2\pi}{q^4} S \tag{49}$$

The asymptotic value for the curve *I(q) x* q^4 is expected to be proportional to the total surface of the particle:

$$\frac{S}{V} = \frac{\pi}{Q} \lim_{q \to \infty} q^4 I(q) \tag{50}$$

The data at large angles are assumed to follow a linear plot in $q^4 I(q)$ against q^4 coordinates. Nevertheless, if there are heterogeneities in electron densities in the scattering particles a relation of the form $q^4 I(q) \approx Bq^4 I(q) + A$ may appear. By subtracting the constant *B* (Porod constant) from *I (q),* the scattering corresponds to that of a homogeneous body.

In summary, three characteristic parameters of the particle are obtained, viz. radius of gyration, volume and surface, which can be used to design a possible low resolution model for the scattering particle.

4. Simulated annealing

The first paper suggesting the use of simulated annealing for minimization of a function with no obvious physical correspondence was the Kirkpatrick procedure for minimizing printed circuit board line crosses (Kirkpatrick *et al.,* (1983)). This paper constructs a non physical function based on crossing circuits and chooses a random line to uncross, as the equivalent of a physical atom. The situation in this case is quite different from the true simulated annealing, because the function used has no physical correspondence, but the ideas work in the same way. The simulated annealing algorithm in this case may be described by the following macro procedure (Svergun (1999)):

Start from a random configuration X_0 at a high temperature T_0. In this case T_0 may be a function of X_0.

Select an atom at random, randomly change its phase (configuration X'), and compute $\Delta = f(X') - f(X)$.

If $\Delta < 0$, move to X'

Else if $\exp(-\Delta / T) < random$

move to X', else continue on X.

Hold T constant for 100 N reconfigurations or 10 N successful reconfigurations, whichever comes first, then cool the system ($T' = 0.9T$)

Continue cooling until no improvement in $f(X)$ is observed.

As the temperature decreases, these modifications become less random and sharper because the system is freezing. Note that only one dummy atom is changed per move so that only a single summand in equation must be updated to calculate the partial amplitudes. This summand is the most time consuming operation. It is exactly this acceleration that makes it possible to use simulated annealing, because it causes the evaluation of f(x) to be N times faster.

4.1 *Ab initio* reconstruction based on simulated annealing

The reconstruction of a three-dimensional model of an object from its one-dimensional scattering pattern is not easy. In addition, its uniqueness is not guaranteed, as different models may yield the same SAS curve with nearly the same accuracy (Vladimir *et al.,* (2003)). To simplify the description of the low-resolution models that can legitimately be obtained, data interpretation is often performed in terms of homogeneous bodies (the influence of internal inhomogeneities for single component particles can largely be eliminated by subtracting the Porod constant). In the past, shape modeling was done by trial-and-error using Debye's formula, computing scattering patterns from different shapes and comparing them with the experimental data. The models were either three-parameter geometrical bodies like prisms, triaxial ellipsoids, elliptical or hollow circular cylinders, etc, or shapes built from assemblies of regularly packed spheres (beads). The first *ab initio* shape determination method was proposed by Stuhrmann (1970). The particle shape was represented by an angular envelope function $r = F(\omega)$ describing the particle boundary in spherical coordinates (r, ω). The use of the angular envelope function was, however, limited to relatively simple shapes (in particular, without holes inside the particle).

A more comprehensive description is achieved with the bead methods (Chacon *et al.*, (1998), Svergun (1999)). Such an approach uses the tremendous power of modern computers, and is based on the same idea used in the past for the trial and error with Debye's formula. Initially a spherical region with diameter $D_{\max}$ is filled with N subunits (spheres) with hexagonal packing. Each of these subunits belongs either to the particle (index=1) or to the solvent (index=0). The geometric form composed by these subunits can be viewed as a vector with N components, and each of the components is either a zero or one. This model is known as the dummy atom model (DAM). The idea is to randomly modify this model by a Monte-Carlo procedure for obtaining a chain, i.e., a geometric configuration, for which the simulated scattering curve fits the experimental data. This approach was implemented on Dammin program, which works as follows: A model of a *K*-phase particle $K \geq 1$ is generated and its scattering is calculated. The next step is to define a spherical shape enclosing the particle. This corresponds to the step cited above, in which a sphere with diameter $D_{\max}$ is defined and filled up with N dummy spheres ($N \approx (R/r_0)^3$, where R is sphere radius and r_0 is the dummy atom radius.

Each dummy atom is assigned an index X_j indicating the phase to which it belongs (X_j ranges from 0 (solvent) to K). Given the fixed atomic positions, the shape and structure of the dummy atom model are completely described by a phase assignment vector X (configuration).

The dummy atoms of the k-th phase are assumed to have contrast $\Delta\rho_k$, and the scattering intensity from the Dummy Atom Model (DAM) is:

$$I(q) = \left\langle \left[\sum_{k=1}^{K} \Delta\rho_k A_k(q) \right] \right\rangle_{\Omega} \qquad (51)$$

where $A_k(q)$ is the scattering amplitude from the volume occupied by the k_{th} phase. The scattering amplitude in the formula above can be given in terms of spherical harmonic functions $Y_{lm}(\Omega)$ as:

$$A_k(q) = \sum_{l=0}^{\infty} \sum_{m=-1}^{1} A_{lm}^{(k)}(q) Y_{lm}(\Omega) \qquad (52)$$

The terms $A_{lm}^{(k)}(s)$ are obtained by mathematical manipulation, i.e., rearrangement of terms, given by:

$$A_{lm}^{(k)}(q) = i^l \sqrt{2/\pi} f(q) \sum_{j=1}^{N_k} j_1(qr_j) Y_{lm}^{*}(\omega_j) \qquad (53)$$

The intensity is (Stuhrmann (1970b)):

$$I(q) = 2\pi^2 \sum_{l=0}^{\infty} \sum_{m=-1}^{1} \left[\sum_{k=1}^{K} [\Delta\rho_k A_{lm}^{(k)}(q)]^2 + 2 \sum_{n>k} \Delta\rho_k A_{lm}^{(k)}(q) \Delta\rho_n [A_{lm}^{(n)}(q)]^{*} \right] \qquad (54)$$

where the sum runs over the dummy atoms of the k_{th} phase, r_j, v_j are their polar coordinates, $j_l(x)$ is the spherical Bessel function, and $f(q)$ is the scattering from a single atom (form factor).

The looseness criterion is applied to a set of $M \geq 1$ experimental curves $I_{\exp}^{(i)}(q), i = 1,..., M$, and the procedure in the Dammin program tries to minimize the discrepancy:

$$\chi^2 = \frac{1}{M}\sum_{i=1}^{M}\sum_{j=1}^{N(i)}[(I_{\exp}^{(i)}(q_j) - I^{(i)}(q_j)) / \sigma(q_j)]^2 \tag{55}$$

In the formula above, $N(i)$ is the number of points of the i-th curve and $\sigma(s)$ denotes the experimental errors. For an adequate description of a structure the number of dummy atoms must, however, be as large as the number of true atoms ($N \approx 10^3$). On the other hand, if the resolution is low, the uniqueness of such a model cannot be meaningfully discussed.
The program assumes an hexagonal packing $N_c = 12$, except for the border atoms. The connectivity is defined by an exponential form $C(N_e) = 1 - P(N_e) = 1 - [e^{-0.5N_e} - e^{-0.5N_c}]$, where $C(12) = 1$ for ideal connectivity, and smaller values for $N_e < 12$ are assumed to emphasize loosely connected dummy atoms. The compactness of a given configuration X can be computed as an average connectivity of all nonsolvent atoms $\langle C(N_e)\rangle$. Then, a configuration is characterized by the average looseness $P(X) = 1 - \langle C(N_e)\rangle$. The final step is to define a function to be minimized and to run the simulated annealing procedure. In this way, the Dammin program adds a penalty term *P(X)* and the function to be minimized becomes:

$$f(X) = \chi^2 + \alpha P(X) \tag{56}$$

where $\alpha > 0$, is the weight of the looseness penalty. The purpose of the penalty term is to guarantee the compactness of the resulting form.

5. Results of simulated annealing in two electron density solution systems

For the application of the simulated annealing the studied system must be monodisperse, diluted and with basically two electron densities. ($\langle\rho\rangle$- ρ_0), were $\langle\rho\rangle$ is the average electron density of particles in solution and ρ_0 is the solvent electron density. The models were generated by the simulated annealing procedure implemented with the Dammin program (Svergun (1999)). Other programs such as Gasbor (Svergun *et al.*, (2001)) may be used to evaluate models by simulated annealing. To exemplify the usefulness of the simulated annealing application, some *ab initio* three-dimensional models of proteins in solution generated from SAXS data were chosen, according to Figueira *et al.*, (2007). Determination of the molecular shapes and oligomeric forms of the thyroid hormone nuclear receptor (TR) by SAXS can be shown as an example. Thyroid hormone (TH) plays important roles in cell differentiation, growth, and metabolism and is a major regulator of mitochondrial activity. In its physiologically most relevant form of triiodothyronine (T3), TH exerts most of its effects by binding to thyroid hormone receptors (TRs), which are members of the nuclear receptor (NR) family of transcription factors. Crystallographic structures of separate DNA and ligand binding domains (DBD and LBD) of TR have yielded significant insights into TR action but up to now no crystallographic structures of the complete TR structure or even of the construct containing both DBD and LBD were resolved. Low-resolution X-ray structures of the isoform β of the TR DBD-LBD were reconstructed form SAXS data measured in solution. SAXS data (figure 6), the overall parameters (table) and simulated annealing modeling (figure 7) reveal significant changes in the oligomeric state of the receptor, suggesting that apo TRs form tetramers in solution which dissociate into dimers upon hormone binding.

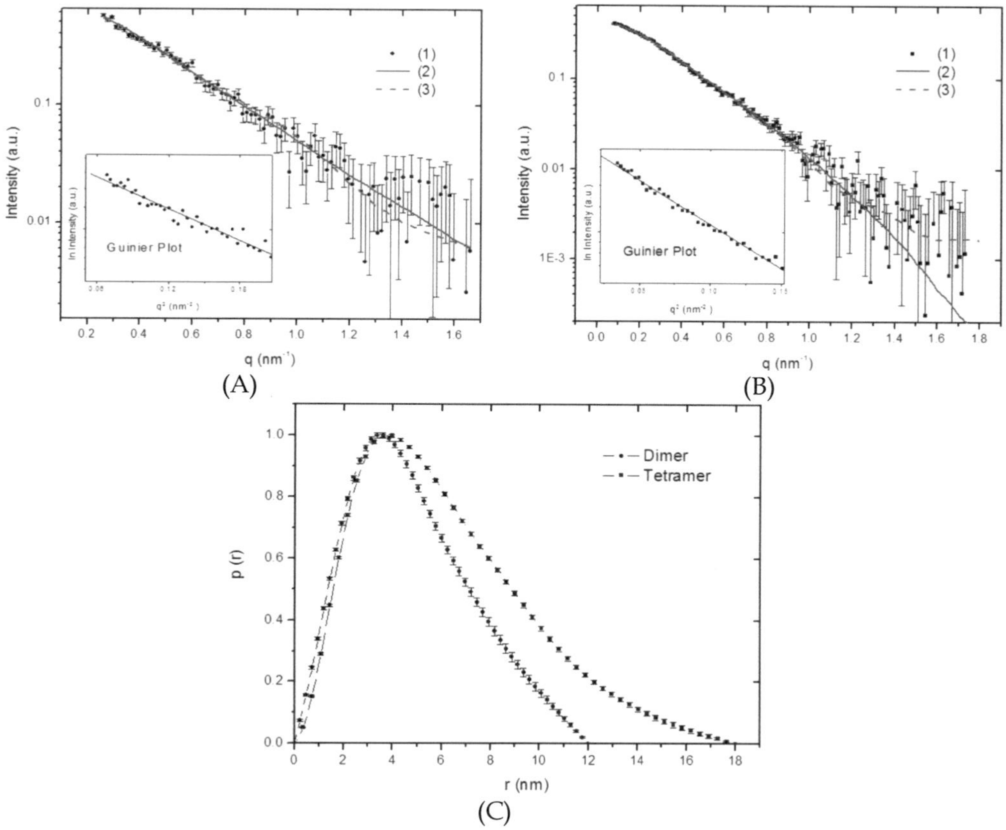

Figure 6. Experimental scattering curves for hTRβ1 DBD-LBD construct in solution, which were fitted with the low and high-resolution models, and the distance distribution functions: (A) dimer and (B) tetramer. Log I vs q focusing on the fitting of the experimental curve at high q values with an inset containing the corresponding Guinier plots (log I vs q^2): (1) experimental curve, (2) scattering intensity from the DAMs [Dammim], and (3) scattering intensity from the high resolution models. (C) Distance distribution functions of hTRβ1 DBD-LBD dimers (•) and tetramers (■) are given.

This methodology was also applied to other nuclear receptors and protein systems (Fischer *et al.*, (2003), Garcia *et al.* (2006), Grimm *et al.* (2006), Calgaro *et al.* (2007), Nascimento *et al.* (2007), Mario Oliveira Neto *et al.* (2008)), in an addition to polymers in solutions (Leite *et al.* (2007)). For the latter, the initial part of the curve, probably due to larger particles, had to be disregarded, thus considering the polymer system as approximately monodisperse. Figure 8 shows molecular models for the particle shape of poly(o-ethoxyaniline) at distinct pHs, obtained through an *ab initio* procedure based on simulated annealing using the dummy atom model (DAM). A less-packed, coiled structure is observed for pH 3, while at pH 10 blobs are formed.

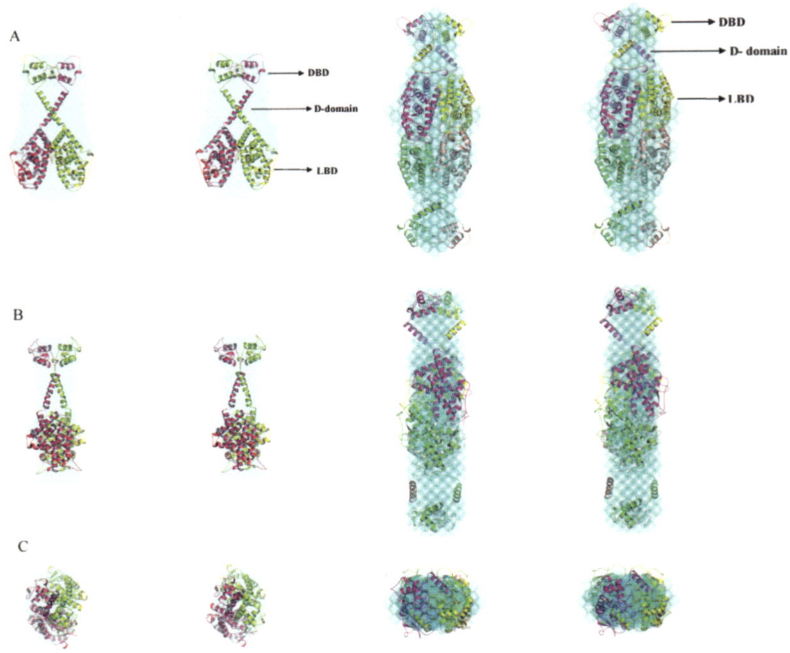

Figure 7. Steroviews showing the superposition of DAM and crystallographic structures for TRβ DBD-LBD dimer (left) and hTRβ DBD-LBD tetramer (right). Panels A-C display three orthogonal views. *Ab initio* simulations were performed using protocols implemented in Dammin.

Parameters/ sample	hTRβ1 DBD-LBD dimer			hTRβ1 DBD-LBD tetramer		
	exp[a]	mod[b]	DAM[c]	exp[a]	mod[b]	DAM[c]
D_{max} (nm)	12.00 ± 1.00	12.80	12.10	18.00 ± 1.00	18.61	17.84
R_g (nm)	3.79 ± 0.50	3.82	3.66	4.97 ± 0.50	4.96	4.84
Discrepancy χ	-	0.9	0.9	-	1.2	1.1
Resolution (nm)	3.8	-	3.8	3.5	-	3.5

[a] Calculated from the experimental data.
[b] Parameters of the dimer and tetramer models.
[c] Parameters of the dummy atom models averaged over 20 models.

Table 1. structural parameters derived from SAXS data

6. Conclusion

Many structural studies have been performed with a combination of SAXS and simulated annealing to reconstruct three dimensional models. Simulated annealing is suitable for the study of monodisperse, diluted and two-electron densities systems. In this chapter we showed how the simulated annealing procedure can be used to minimize the discrepancy between two functions: the simulated intensity and the experimental one-dimensional SAXS curve. The goal was to find the most probable form for a protein molecule in a monodisperse dilute solution. In the past, this simulated intensity was obtained using

Debye's formula, in time-consuming trial-and-error procedures. Today, with the power of modern computers, it can be applied quite straightforwardly generating low resolution models of proteins in an efficient way. The main advantage of solution scattering is its ability to probe the structure of native particles in nearly physiological conditions and to analyze structural changes in response to variations in external parameters. Then, the oligomerization state of proteins and large conformational changes may be monitored. Moreover, the approach can be extended to conjugated polymers in solution, as described in this Chapter.

(a) (b) (c)

Figure 8. Average DAM for POEA in pH (a) 10.0, (b) 5.0 and (c) pH 3.0 (HCl) (adapted from Leite *et al.* (2007)).

7. Acknowledgments

This work was supported by FAPESP, CNPq, IMMP/MCT and Capes (Brazil).

8. References

Calgaro, M. R.; Oliveira Neto, M.; Figueira, A. C. M.; Santos, M. A. M.; Portugal, R. V.; Guzzi, C. A.; Saidemberg, D. M.; Bleicher, L.; Vernal, J.; Fernandez, P.; Terenzi, H.; Palma, M. S. & Polikarpov, I. (2007). Orphan nuclear receptor NGFI-B forms dimers with nonclassical interface. *Protein Sci.* Vol. 16, pp. 1762-1772.

Chacon, P.; Moran, F.; Diaz, J. F.; Pantos, E. & Andreu, J. M. (1998). Low-resolution structures of proteins in solution retrieved from X-ray scattering with a genetic algorithm. *Biophys J*, Vol. 74, pp. 2760-75.

Craievich, A. F. (2005). Small-Angle X-ray Scattering by Nanostructured Materials . In: *Handbook of Sol-Gel Science and Technology*. A. Sakka; R. Almeida. (Ed.), pp. 161-189, Kluwer Academic Publishers, ISBN 978-1402079696, Norwell.

Feigin, L. A. & Svergun, D. I. (1987). *Structure Analysis by Small-Angle X-Ray and Neutron Scattering*, Plenum Press, ISBN 978-0306426292, New York.

Figueira, A. C. M.; Oliveira Neto, M. O.; Bernardes, A.; Dias, S. M. G.; Craievich, A. F.; Baxter, J. D.; Webb, P. & Polikarpov, I. (2007). Low resolution structures of thyroid hormone receptor dimers and tetramers in solution. *Biochemistry*, Vol. 46, pp. 1273-1283.

Fischer, H.; Dias, S. M. G.; Santos, M.A.; Alves, A.C.; Zanchin, N; Craievich, A. F.; Apriletti, J. W.; Baxter, J. D.; Webb, P.; Neves, F.A.; Ribeiro, R.C. & Polikarpov, I. (2003). Low Resolution Structures of the Retinoid X Receptor DNA-binding and Ligand-binding Domains Revealed by Synchrotron X-ray Solution Scattering. *J. Bio. Chem.* Vol. 278, pp. 16030-16038.

Garcia, W.; de Araújo, A. P. U.; Oliveira Neto, M.; Ballestero, M. R. M.; Polikarpov, I.; Tanaka, M.; Tanaka, T. & Garratt, R. C. (2006). Dissection of a Human Septin: Definition and Characterization of Distinct Domains within Human SEPT4. *Biochemistry*; Vol. 45, pp. 13918-13931.

Glatter, O. & Kratky, O. (1982). *Small Angle X-ray Scattering*, Academic Press, ISBN 978-0122862809, London.

Grimm, E. D.; Portugal, R. V.; Oliveira Neto, M.; Martins, N. H.; Polikarpov, I.; Zaha, A. & Ferreira, H. B. (2006). Structural Analysis of an Echinococcus granulosus Actin-Fragmenting Protein by Small-Angle X-Ray Scattering Studies and Molecular Modeling. *Biophys. J.* Vol. 90, pp. 3216-3223.

Kirkpatrick, S.; Gelatt Jr., C. D. & Vecchi, M. P. (1983). Optimization by Simulated Annealing. *Science,* Vol. 220, pp. 671 - 680.

Leite, F. L.; Oliveira Neto, M.; Paterno, L. G.; Ballestero, M. R. M.; Polikarpov, I.; Mascarenhas, Y. P.; Herrmann, P. S. P.; Mattoso, L. H. C. & Oliveira Jr., O. N. (2007). Nanoscale conformational ordering in polyanilines investigated by SAXS and AFM. *J. Colloid Interface Sci.* Vol. 316, pp. 376–387.

Matozo, H. C.; Santos, M. A. M.; Oliveira Neto, M.; Bleicher, L.; Lima, L. M. T. R.; Iuliano, R.; Fusco, A. & Polikarpov, I. (2007). Low-resolution structure and fluorescence anisotropy analysis Of protein tyrosine phosphatase η catalytic. *Biophys. J.* Vol. 92, pp. 4424–4432.

Nascimento, A. S.; Dias, S. M. G.; Nunes, F. M.; Aparício, R.; Ambrosio, A. L. B.; Bleicher, L.; Figueira, A. C. M.; Santos, M. A. M.; Oliveira Neto, M.; Fischer, H.; Togashi, M.; Craievich, A. F., Garratt, R. C.; Baxter, J. D.; Webb, P. & Polikarpov, I. (2006). *Structural Rearrangements in the Thyroid Hormone Receptor Hinge Domain and Their Putative Role in the Receptor Function. J. Mol. Biol.* Vol. 360, pp. 586-98.

Nascimento, A. S.; Catalano-Dupuy, DL.; Bernardes, A.; Oliveira Neto, M.; Santos, M. A. M.; Ceccarelli, E. A. & Polikarpov, I. (2007). Crystal structures of Leptospira interrogans FAD-containing ferredoxin-NADP+ reductase and its complex with NADP+BMC. *Structural Biology*; Vol. 7, pp. 69-81.

Oliveira Neto, M.;Ferreira Júnior, J. R.; Fischer, H.; Nascimento, A. S.; Craievich, A. F.; Colau, D.; Dumoutier, L.; Renauld, J.-C. & Polikarpov, I. (2008). Interleukin-22 forms dimers which are recognized by two interleukin-22R1 receptor chains. *Biophys. J.*, Vol. 94, pp. 1754–1765.

Patterson, A. L. (1935). A direct method for the determination of the components of interatomic distances in crystals. *Z. Kristallogr. A* Vol. 90, pp. 517-542.

Stuhrmann, H. B. (1970). Ein neues Verfahren zur Bestimmung der Oberfla chenform und der inneren Struktur von gelosten globularen Proteinen. *Zeitschr. Physik. Chem. Neue Folge,* Vol. 72, pp. 177–198.

Stuhrmann, H. B. 1970b. Interpretation of small-angle scattering of dilute solutions and gases. A representation of the structures related to a one-particle scattering functions. *Acta Crystallogr.*, Vol. A26, pp. 297–306.

Svergun, D. I. (1999). Restoring low resolution structure of biological macromolecules from solution scattering using simulated annealing. *Biophys J,* Vol. 76, pp. 2879-86.

Svergun, D.I.; Petoukhov, M.V. & Koch, M.H.J. (2001). Determination of domain structure of proteins from X-ray solution scattering. *Biophys. J.* Vol. 80, pp. 2946-2953.

Svergun, D.I. & Koch M.H.J. (2003). Small-angle scattering studies of biological macromolecules in solution. Rep. Prog. Phys. Vol. 66, pp. 1735–1782.

Volkov, V. V. & Svergun, D. I. (2003). Uniqueness of *ab initio* shape determination in small-angle scattering. *J. Appl. Cryst.* Vol. 36, pp. 860-864.

18

Improving the Neighborhood Selection Strategy in Simulated Annealing using the Optimal Stopping Problem

Saed Alizamir, Steffen Rebennack and Panos M. Pardalos
University of Florida
Center of Applied Optimization
USA

1. Introduction

Simulated Annealing is one the most well known local search methods. In practice, it is often used to solve discrete optimization problems; especially very tough problems, [54, 37, 34, 3, 2, 41]. Global optimization is computationally extremely challenging and for large instances, exact methods reach their limitations quickly. Hence, in practice, often local optimization methods are used. Simulated annealing provides a powerful tool for escaping local optima by allowing moves to lower quality solutions with a pre-specified probability. Another big plus of Simulated Annealing is its ease of implementation.

At each iteration of Simulated Annealing, the objective function value of the current solution and a new generated solution are compared. Improving moves are always accepted while only a fraction of non-improving moves are performed with the aim to escape local optimal solutions. The probability of accepting a non-improving move depends on the non-increasing parameter of temperature. This technique comes from annealing in metallurgy. In this process, a metal is heated and slowly cooled off, in order to increase the size of its crystals while reducing the number of defects. The heating dissolves out atoms from their initial positions which can be seen as a local minimum with respect to energy level. Such atoms can then freely move around. Slowly cooling off has the effect that the free atoms can end up in positions with lower energy level than the initial positions. The crucial factor is to choose the cooling procedure appropriately, as cooling off to fast may not enable atoms to find better energy levels and cooling off to slowly is very time consuming.

Simulated Annealing was introduced by Kirkpatrick et al. [33] in 1983 and independently by Černý [13] in 1985. It is an adaptation of a special Mont Carlo method generating sample states of a thermodynamic system which was introduced by Metropolis et al. in 1953, [38]. In 1986, Lundy and Mees were able to proof that under some technical assumptions Simulated Annealing converges with probability 1 to the global optimum, [36].

In this work we equip the simulated annealing algorithm with K neigh- borhood strategies and apply the Optimal Stopping Problem to determine the optimal time for changing the temperature. This study is organized as follows. In Section 2, we give an introduction to meta-heuristics in general and show the connection to Simulated Annealing. The concept of negative dynamic programing is introduced in Section 3. This provides the mathematical background for the modified Simulated Annealing algorithm provided in Section 4 using the optimal stopping problem. We illustrate this new method on the Traveling Salesman Problem in Section 5. We close with some conclusions in Section 6.

2. Metaheuristics and simulated annealing

Metaheuristic methods perform a more or less systematic search over the solution space by simultaneously employing processes to improve the solution quality as well as strategies to escape local optima. Metaheuristics got a lot of attention in the scientific community over the last decades. The significant advantages of metaheuristics over other solution methods have made them the favorable practical solution method for solving complex combinatorial optimization problems, [24].

Although these methods cannot guarantee optimality of their solutions, they have shown a credible performance in solving real world problems compared to exact methods. Moreover, metaheuristics can improve their performances in some circumstances when they are equipped with mechanisms borrowed fro the exact methods, *e.g.* bounding, [44, 9].

There is a wide range of metaheuristic methods, each one using its own ap- proach [8, 22, 7]. However, all of these methods can be classified into a few groups based on their structures. One of the most basic heuristics which plays a critical role in almost all metaheuristic methods is called *local search*. Local search starts from an initial solution and tries to improve its quality by a sequence of moves toward a local optimum [32]. Many metaheuristics are based on local search techniques; among them are for instance Simulated Annealing (SA), Variable Neighborhood Search (VNS) [39, 28], Tabu Search (TS) [23, 25], Greedy Randomized Adaptiv Search Procedures (GRASP) [19, 20], Genetic Algorithm (GA) [30, 26], Differential Evolution (DE) [43, 21] and Ant Colony Optimization (ACO) [17].

In general, all metaheuristics can be broken down into the following three main components [1]:

- **Initial Solution:** The quality of the initial solution affects the performance of the metaheuristics. To diminish this dependency, some methods start their search from multiple initial solutions.
- **Neighborhood Selection:** The way in which a metaheuristic moves from one solution to its neighbor is another critical component in all meta heuristics. In the early applications and theoretical developments of search methods in metaheuristics, the impact of the neighborhood selection has been underestimated. Instead, the neighbor selection has been limited to some factors such as ease of implementation, evaluation speed, usage of other researchers and empirical studies, [5]. In fact, mataheuristics often use the same neighborhood selection strategy during the course of thei search. Using different neighborhood selection strategies in a systematic way can significantly improve their efficiency and effectiveness. Especially selecting the neighborhood in multiple ways can be a powerful tool in preventing the method from being trapped in local optima. To the best knowledge of the authors, the only metaheuristic focusing on different neighborhood structures is VNS, see [24, 29].
- **Optimization Strategy:** Optimization strategy is the policy deciding about the acceptance or rejection of a new solution. This is the most diverse aspect of metaheuristics and it varies from a simple procedure to a complex and sophisticated algorithm.

2.1 Neighborhood selection analysis

There are several factors to consider when defining a neighborhood structure. The following are characterizations of a proper neighborhood structure, [1]:

- **Effectiveness:** the power of the neighborhood structure in covering th whole feasible space.
- **Efficiency:** the efficiency of a neighborhood structure which is the quality of its performance in covering the feasible region depends on several (contradictory) factors:
  - **Speed:** the number of moves needed to reach any arbitrary point in the feasible region.
  - **Computational Effort:** the computations needed for each movement.
  - **Size (Number of Neighbors):** the size of a neighborhood struc- ture is defined as the number of solutions which are accessible in an immediate move from the current solution. A larger number is usu- ally an advantage as any arbitrary solution can be reached in less number of moves.
  - **Information Volume:** the amount of information transformed. This information may be used to perform better moves through the feasible space. For instance, there are gradients, Hessian matrix, eigenvalues and convexity information for the continuous space and taboo list, function characteristics and lower & upper bounds for the discrete space.

2.2 Simulated annealing

Here, we describe SA in a mathematical manner. We do not go into full details but brief all the concepts we need in the later sections. For further mathematical analysis including the convergence rate and analysis, please refer, for instance, to the book by Otten and Ginneken [40] or the book by Salamon et al. [49].

Suppose Ω is the set of all feasible solutions and $f : \Omega \rightarrow \mathbb{R}$ is the objectiv function defined over the solution space. The purpose is to solve the (nonconvex) optimization problem

$$\max f(\omega) \tag{1}$$

$$\text{s.t. } \omega \in \Omega \tag{2}$$

That is, we want to find the global maximum ω^* in the solution space Ω. The global maximum ω^* has the property that for every $\omega \in \Omega$ we have $f(\omega) \leq f(\omega^*)$.
Let us define $N(\omega)$ as the neighborhood function for any $\omega \in \Omega$ and consider Algorithm 2.1 for a generic SA. GSA starts from an initial solution $\omega_0 2 \Omega$. At each *iteration*, GSA chooses the next solution among the neighbors of the current one, stage 5. The thermodynamic behavior of the system is modeled through the *Metropolis function* such that the probability of accepting the new solution ω' is defined as

$$\begin{cases} \exp\left(\frac{f(\omega')-f(\omega)}{t_p}\right), & \text{if } f(\omega') - f(\omega) < 0 \\ 1, & \text{otherwise} \end{cases}$$

in which t_p is the temperature parameter defined in the *iteration* loop p such that $\lim_{p\rightarrow\infty} t_p = 0$, stages 4 to 11 of Algorithm 2.1. For each temperature t_p, this process is repeated M_p times, stage 4. After these M_p iterations are performed, the current temperature t_p is decreased, stage 12. One of the easiest cooling procedures is a geometric sequence

$$t_p = \gamma^p \cdot t_0 \quad , \qquad 0 < \gamma < 1$$

in which the temperature at each *step* is γ times the temperature of the previ ous step. GSA repeats these steps until some stopping criteria is met, stage 3, and returns its current solution ω. Recognize that this might not be the best solution found and hence, one could modify the generic algorithm to store in addition to the current solution also the best solution. We brief on possible stopping criteria in Section 2.2.1.

Algorithm 2.1 Generic Simulated Annealing (GSA)

Input: initial feasible solution ω_0, initial temperature t_0, number of iterations M_p for each p, neighborhood structure $N(\omega)$, overall stopping criteria and temperature decreasing rule

Output: feasible solution ω

```
1: initialize step counter: p = 0
2: set current solution ω to initial solution ω0: ω = ω0
3: while the stopping criteria are not met do
4:    for Mp iterations do
5:       compute a solution belonging to the neighborhood of the current solu-
         tion: ω' ∈ N(ω).
6:       if f(ω') − f(ω) ≥ 0 then
7:          ω ← ω'
8:       else
9:          ω ← ω' with probability exp((f(ω') − f(ω))/tp)
10:      end if
11:   end for
12:   decrease temperature tp
13:   p ← p + 1
14: end while
15: return feasible solution ω.
```

As already mentioned, the cooling procedure is a key element in the search mechanism of SA. If the cooling procedure is slow enough, then the system can reach its steady state at each temperature t_p. This steady state follows th Boltzmann machine which can be defined as the probability of system being in state ω with the objective function value of $f(\omega)$ at temperature t_p [35]. The probability of the system being in state ω at temperature t_p is then given by

$$\frac{\exp\left(-f(\omega)/t_p\right)}{\sum_{\omega' \in \Omega} \exp\left(-f(\omega')/t_p\right)} \quad .$$

2.2.1 Implementation issues of simulated annealing

In general, the implementation of simulated annealing can be analyzed from two different points of views [18]:

1. The generic choices, being the same among all problems.
2. The problem-specific choices, changing from one problem to another.

The generic options for the implementation of SA can be stated as

- **Generation Probability Function:** determines the probability of choosing each of the current solution's neighbors. It is often set as a unifor function. However, sometimes other distributions are preferable, based on smarter mechanisms.
- **Acceptance Probability:** the probability of accepting a solution wit a lower quality.
- **Cooling Schedule:** the rate in which the temperature decreases may heavily affect the performance of SA. In fact the convergence of the algo- rithm is proven when the temperature decreases with a logarithmic rate [42]. A low cooling rate may increase the running time of the algorithm while a high cooling rate may cause being trapped in a local optimum.
- **Stopping Rule:** the stopping criteria of the algorithm. It can be defined in many different ways. For instance, a simple stopping rule can be an upper limit on the number of iterations or an upper limit on the number of decreases in the temperature. The following two rules are among the most common stopping rules [42]:
  - If the best value found for the objective function so far does not increases by at least ε_1% after performing p_1 number of temperature decreases, the algorithm stops.
  - If the number of accepted moves in p_2 temperature decreases is less than ε_2%, then the algorithm stops.

The problem-specific choices should be chosen carefully based on the nature of each problem. They are:

- **Objective Function and Solution Space:** their structure is very im- portant in implementing the simulated annealing method. While the soft constraints can be added to the objective function with a penalty function, the hard constraints should be considered in defining the feasible region [52].
- **Neighborhood Selection Strategy:** the way in which the algorithm travels through the feasible space. This is the main focus of this study.

More about implementation issues of SA can be found in the book [34, Chapter 5]. For a discussion of the advantages and pitfalls of SA refer, for instance, to [31].

3. Negative dynamic programming

A *stochastic process*

$$X = \{X_t, t \in T\}$$

is a collection of random variables. That is, X_t is a random variable for each t belonging to index set T. Here, t refers to time and X_t is the state of the process at time t, [48, Chapter 1.9]. Consider a stochastic process that is observed at the beginning of a discrete time period to be in a particular state X_0. After observation of the state, an action must be chosen. Based only on the state at that time and the action chosen, an expected reward is earned and the probability distribution for the next state is determined. We call the set of all possible actions to be chosen at each state the *action space*, [47, Chapter 3].

Now consider a stochastic process in which the state space is defined as a countable subset of non-negative integer numbers and with the action space of A. In addition, assume that if we are in state i and the action a is taken, then the cost of

$$C(i,a) \geq 0 \tag{3}$$

is imposed to the system. As this problem is equivalent to a system with non positive reward function $R(i, a) = -C(i, a)$, we call this problem *Negative Dynamic Programming*. For a comprehensive introduction to Negative Dynamic Programming, see [53].
A policy is defined as a procedure introducing the action to be chosen as function of the state of the process. For each policy π, we define the expected profit function as

$$V_\pi(i) = \mathbb{E}_\pi\left[\sum_{n=0}^{\infty} C(X_n, a_n) \mid X_0 = i\right] \qquad \forall i \geq 0 \quad . \tag{4}$$

Equation (4) is derived from dynamic programming techniques [6] and indicates that the expected profit, if we start in state i and choose our action based on policy π, is equal to the expected value of the summation of all rewards (costs) obtained in each single state.
Since $C(i,a) \geq 0$, V_π may become infinite. If

$$V(i) = \inf_\pi V_\pi(i) < \infty \quad ,$$

then π^* is the optimal policy if

$$V_{\pi^*}(i) = V(i)$$

for each $i \geq 0$. If $V(i)$ is infinite then all policies are optimal with infinite expected profit. For those instances where there is at least one state i with the property $V(i) < \infty$, the following two theorems can be stated.
Theorem 1 ([47]). *The optimality equation for an infinite horizon can be defined as*

$$V(i) = \min_a \left[C(i,a) + \sum_j P_{ij}(a) V(j)\right]$$

for each $i \geq 0$.
Theorem 2 ([47]). *Let f be a stationary policy defined by*

$$C(i, f(i)) + \sum_j P_{ij}(f(i)) V(j) = \min_a \left[C(i,a) + \sum_j P_{ij}(a) V(j)\right] \qquad \forall i \geq 0 \quad , \tag{5}$$

then, for each $i \geq 0$, we have $V_f(i) = V(i)$. In other words, f is an optimal stationary policy.
In fact, this theorem indicates that if the policy f at each state choose that action minimizing the expected cost of the system if it starts from that particular state and continues to infinity, then this policy is optimal. For more references on the application of dynamic programming in stochastic processes and more advanced topics, see [45, 50].

3.1 Optimal stopping problem

The *Optimal Stopping Problem* is a classic problem in Negative Dynamic Programming and has been widely studied, [47, 16]. It has a broad range of applications in different areas including statistics and finance. For advanced topics and applications, see [15]. The reader is

referred to [51, 14, 11, 12, 55] for different settings of the problem. We use its solution approach to develop a new method in neighborhood search for Simulated Annealing.
The Optimal Stopping Problem can be stated as follows. Given is a syste with non-negative integer states. Suppose, in each state the decision maker has the opportunity to either stop in the current state i and gain the corresponding reward of $R(i)$, or pay a cost of $C(i)$ and continue the process for one more step. If she decides to continue, she will be in state j in the next iteration with probability P_{ij}. All values of $R(i)$ and $C(i)$ are non-negative. Let us define action 1 as the stop decision and state 2 as the continue decision. Theoretically, we can decide to continue at each state and never stop. Therefore, for technical reasons, we define state ∞ to represent the stop state. From these definitions, the following transition probabilities are immediate

$$P_{i,\infty}(1) = 1, \quad P_{i,\infty}(2) = 0, \quad P_{i,j}(1) = 0, \quad P_{i,j}(2) = P_{ij}, \quad P_{\infty,\infty}(a) = 1 \quad , \tag{6}$$

for all states i, j and all actions $a \in \{1, 2\}$. Moreover, the cost function is given by

$$C(\infty, a) = 0, \quad C(i, 1) = -R(i), \quad C(i, 2) = C(i) \quad , \tag{7}$$

for all states i.
As we have seen in equation (3), Negative Dynamic Programming require non-negative cost. In fact, the rewards $R(i)$ can be considered as negative costs, $C(i, 1) = -R(i) \le 0$. Hence, the Optimal Stopping Problem cannot be embedded in the Negative Dynamic Programming framework in its current form. Thus, we need a method to transform it to a Negative Dynamic Programming problem. To do so, we make the following two assumptions

$$\inf_i C(i) > 0 \quad \text{and} \tag{8}$$

$$\sup_i R(i) < \infty \quad . \tag{9}$$

Equation (8) means that the cost of continuing the process is strictly positive. That is, it is bounded from below by a positive value $\varepsilon > 0$. Similarly, equation (9) ensures that the reward in each state is bounded from above.
Using assumptions (8) and (9), we set

$$R = \sup_i R(i)$$

and re-define the Optimal Stopping Problem in the following way. Everything stays the same with the only difference that the reward earned in state i is $R(i)-R$, when deciding to stop. Equivalently, the cost of $R-R(i) \ge 0$ is paid. Similar to equation (4), we define V_π as the expected cost for each policy π. It can be shown that for such a policy we have

$$\overline{V}_\pi(i) = V_\pi(i) + R \qquad \forall i \ge 0 \quad .$$

The proof is straightforward and can be found, for instance, in [47, Chapter 3]. As a consequence, any optimal policy for the Optimal Stopping Problem is optimal for the re-defined version, and vice versa.

A *Markovian stochastic process* [48, 45] is a stochastic process in which the state of the system in the future given the past and present states, is independent of the past states and depends only on the present state.
Since the re-defined problem is a Markovian decision process with non-negative costs, it can be considered as a Negative Dynamic Programming problem and can be treated using the above cited theorems. Theorem 1 implies

$$\overline{V}(i) = \min\left[R - R(i), C(i) + \sum_j P_{ij}\overline{V}(j)\right] \qquad i \geq 0 \quad .$$

As $V(i) = \overline{V}(i) - R$, we have

$$V(i) = \min\left[-R(i), C(i) + \sum_j P_{ij}V(j)\right] \quad .$$

Hence, the optimal policy is the same in both problems. Now, let $V_0(i) = -R(i)$ and define $V_n(i)$ as the minimum expected cost if the decision maker starts in state i and has at most n decision opportunities before stopping. Then, for $n > 0$ we have

$$V_n(i) = \min\left[-R(i), C(i) + \sum_j P_{ij}V_{n-1}(j)\right] \qquad i \geq 0 \quad .$$

Since adding one more decision opportunity will increase the chance to gain more, the following inequality holds

$$V_n(i) \geq V_{n+1}(i) \geq V(i) \quad .$$

Finally, we can conclude that

$$\lim_{n\to\infty} V_n(i) = V(i) \quad . \tag{10}$$

Equation (10) is called *Stability condition*. A system satisfying this condition is called *stable*. It can be shown that the two assumptions (8) and (9) result in stability, [47, Chapter 3].
Let us define set B as

$$\begin{aligned} B &= \left\{ i : -R(i) \leq C(i) - \sum_{j=0}^{\infty} P_{ij}R(j) \right\} \\ &= \left\{ i : R(i) \geq \sum_{j=0}^{\infty} P_{ij}R(j) - C(i) \right\} \quad . \end{aligned}$$

Set B is in fact the set of all states where stopping is at least as good as continuing for exactly one more step and then stopping. The policy which stops at the first time when the system enters a state i belonging to set B is called *One-Stage Look-Ahead policy*.

Next, we see that if set B is a closed set over the state space, *i.e.*, when the system enters a state in B then the probability leaving B is 0, then the One-Stage Look-Ahead policy is optimal, assuming the stability assumptions.

Theorem 3 ([47]). *If a process is stable and* $P_{ij} = 0$ *for* $i \in B$ *and* $j \notin B$, *then the optimal policy stops at state i, if and only if i 2 B. In other words, the One-Stage Look-Ahead policy is optimal.*

Note that the assumption we have made for set B is in fact equivalent to the closeness of this set over the state space.

4. Simulated annealing with optimal stopping time

The use of multiple neighborhood structures has not received too much attentio in the literature of SA. In fact, the only paper in which SA is implemented using several neighborhood structure is by Bouffard and Ferland, [10]. In that paper, SA annealing is integrated with VNS to solve the resource-constrained scheduling problem. Three nested neighborhood structures have been employed along with a separately designed one. Their numerical studies confirms the advantage of multiple neighborhood selection strategies in SA. However, their algorithm is different than ours in the way in which the number of iteration at each temperature is determined and how the change in neighborhood structure is proposed. We are using Optimal Stopping Problem while their algorithm is based on Variable Neighborhood Search Method.

In this section, we introduce a novel variation of SA using the Optimal Stopping Problem for solving the combinatorial optimization problem P. Without loss of generality, we can assume P to be a maximization problem in the form stated in equations (1) and (2). The main difference of the new algorithm with the generic SA is the usage of K different neighborhood structures. These structures can be defined based on any heuristic approach and are mostly problem-specific. We have to decide which of the K structures to use at each step. In fact, in each step we have to solve a decision problem with K different alternatives. After choosing the neighborhood structure in the current temperature t_p, in each iteration, we are encountered with a two-alternative decision problem, either to continue or to stop. When we decide to stop, we may either switch to another neighborhood structure, if there is a profitable one, or decrease the temperature and repeat the process. These decisions are made using stochastic dynamic programming with a small amount of computational effort. Next to the K neighborhood structures, compared to the generic Simulated Annealing, the parameter of M_p iterations is determined by an optimal stopping decision.

Assume that the objective function f can take n different values. In the case that it is continuous, we can divide the range of changes in the value of the objective function into n smaller intervals; each of them is represented by their mid-point. Such a range can be obtained by lower and upper bounds on the value of the objective function f. As we have a maximization problem, any feasible solution determines a lower bound. To obtain an upper bound, we may use different kinds of relaxation such as LP relaxation or Lagrangian Relaxation.

The *state* of the system is defined as the best value of the objective function found so far. For instance, if the best found value for the objective function happens to be in an interval with mid-point r, we assert that the system is in state r. The justification for this definition is provided later in this section when we associate the state of the system with SA. Also, we define $P_{ij}^{(k)}$ as the transition probability which is the probability of going from state i to state

j if the neighborhood structure k is employed. We explain how these transition probabilities can be obtained in Section 4.1. Since each neighborhood structure incurs a different amount of computational time, we define $C^{(k)}$ as the cost of using the neighborhood structure k for one iteration. In general, this cost can also be state-dependent to represent the bigger effort needed as the value of objective function improves. But in our case, we keep it constant for each neighborhood structure.

As is Section 3.1, we define ∞ as the stop state, 1 as the stopping decision and 2 as the continuing decision. Let us define now the cost and transition probabilities obtained in formulae (6) and (7) for our case. Obviously, we have

$$C(i, 2) = C^{(k)} .$$

The cost of the system when stopping at a solution with the objective function value of i is equal to the negation of the highest value of the objective functio that we have found so far. Assume we stop at a solution with the objectiv function of i with a current temperature of t_p after doing M_p iterations. If O_m represents the value of the objective function at iteration m, then we have

$$C(i, 1) = -\max\{O_1, O_2, O_3, \ldots, O_{M_p}, M_p = i\} .$$

This means, if we found a solution with the objective function value of $j > i$ a iteration m, then our system has the *recall property*, that is, it remembers this solution as the best solution found until a solution with a better value of the objective function is found or the system stops. In the case of stop, if j is still the best solution found, then it is reflected as the state of the system. Hence, we get the following transition probabilities

$$P_{ij}^{(k)} = \begin{cases} g^{(k)}(i,j), & \text{if } j > i \\ \sum_{j \le i} g^{(k)}(i,j), & \text{if } j = i \\ 0, & \text{if } j < i \end{cases} .$$

where $g^{(k)}(i, j)$ is the probability of moving from a solution with the objective value in range i to a solution with the objective value in range j using the kth neighborhood structure; regardless of any other decision. It is easy to see that the above probabilities sum up to 1.

Similar to Section 3.1, where we transformed the Optimal Stopping Proble to a Negative Dynamic Programming problem, we define a second problem with non-negative costs and the same optimal policy as the original problem. This enables us to use the Optimal Stopping Problem principles to find the optimal policy for the original problem. Now, redefine the cost of each state as

$$C(i,1) = U - \max\{O_1, O_2, O_3, \ldots, O_{M_p}\} \quad , \tag{11}$$

where U is a known upper bound for the value of the objective function. By definition (11), it is obvious that $C(i, 1) \geq 0$.

Comparing this problem with the Optimal Stopping Problem defined in the Section 3.1, bears in mind that the optimal policy for this problem has the following structure. If the highest value of the objective function found so far is greater than or equal to a threshold value i_k^*, then stop and otherwise continue Hence, the stopping criterion is defined as

$$\max\{O_1, O_2, O_3, \ldots, O_{M_p}\} \geq i_k^* \quad .$$

Next, let us find the optimal value of i_k^*. Define set B as

$$B = \{i : i \geq i_k^*\} \quad .$$

It is clear that B is a closed set; *i.e.*, if the system enters a state belonging to B, then the probability that the next states of the system are not in B is equal to 0. The reasoning can be as follows. If we reach a value of the objective function which is in B, then it remains the highest value so far or it improves, but it is not possible that the best found value of the objective function declines. Hence, we can summarize this in the following formula

$$\left.\begin{array}{lll} i \in B & \rightarrow & i \geq i_k^* \\ j \notin B & \rightarrow & j < i_k^* \end{array}\right\} \longrightarrow j < i \longrightarrow P_{ij}^{(k)} = 0 \quad .$$

Regarding this new definition of our transition probabilities which implies the closeness of B, it follows that all the assumption of Theorem 3 are satisfied and the One-Stage Look-Ahead policy is optimal.

Now, let us restate set B as

$$\begin{aligned} B &= \left\{ i : i \geq i \sum_{j \leq i} g^{(k)}(i,j) + \sum_{j>i} j g^{(k)}(i,j) - C(k) \right\} \\ &= \left\{ i : C_{(k)} \geq i \sum_{j \leq i} g^{(k)}(i,j) - i + \sum_{j>i} j g^{(k)}(i,j) \right\} \\ &= \left\{ i : C_{(k)} \geq \sum_{j>i} (j-i) g^{(k)}(i,j) \right\} \\ &= \{i : i \geq i^*\} \end{aligned}$$

So at each temperature t_p, while implementing the kth neighborhood structure, in iteration 0, it is enough to find the value of i_k^* and continue until reaching a value of the objective function which is greater than or equal to i_k^*. Then, we stop and investigate whether proceeding with a new neighborhood structure, or reducing the temperature, is more beneficial. This decision can be made by comparing the updated values of i_k^* for each neighborhood structure with the cost of its implementation. In other words, after the system stops with respect to the current neighborhood structure, all the values of i_k^* are updated. These values are in fact the expected value of objective function when implementing this neighborhood structure. It is up to the decision maker to decide if it is worthy to continue with a new neighborhood structure knowing the value of i_k^* and $C^{(k)}$.

The only missing step in the chain of our proposed algorithm is which neighborhood structure has to be chosen after decreasing the temperature; *i.e.*, which neighborhood structure is the best to start with in the new temperature. Of course, that neighborhood structure is desirable maximizing the expected value of the objective function. For example, consider the two neighborhood structures k and k'. By definition, i_k^* is the expected profit before stopping in the case of using k, and $i_{k'}^*$ is the expected profit before stopping in the case of using k'. So at each temperature, we compute the values of i_k^* before starting. Afterwards, we implement the neighborhood structure having the highest value of i_k^*.

4.1 How to obtain the transition probabilities

As mentioned in Section 4, to find the transition probabilities $P_{ij}^{(k)}$ we need the values of $g^{(k)}(i, j)$. They are defined as the probability of moving from range I to range j using the neighborhood structure k regardless to whether we accept or reject the new solution. To obtain these values, we have to find out how the neighborhood structure affects the change in the value of objective function in general. As a neighborhood structure changes more components of the current solution, the range of changes in the value of objective function for the resulted solution increases. Roughly speaking, a more complicated neighborhood structure may cover a wide range of the feasible region and has the potential of moving far away in a few number of iterations while a simple neighborhood structure needs far more iterations to move from one part of feasible region to another. Thus, the probability of a specific change in the value of objective function plays a critical role in finding the transition probabilities.

Define $\gamma_d^{(k)}$ as the probability of a change equal to d in the objective function f using neighborhood structure k. Then the transition probabilities $P_{ij}^{(k)}$ can be computed by considering the difference between i and j compared to the value of d. For an illustration, see Section 5 where it has been applied to the traveling salesman problem.

The only missing part in this procedure is that $\gamma_d^{(k)}$ actually represents the probability of change and does not provide any information about the directio of this change. In fact, this depends strongly on the value of the objective function in the current solution. For instance, if the value of the objective function in the current solution is in range i, then the bigger the value of i, the higher is the possibility that the change will happen in the negative direction. This implies that, in addition to $\gamma_d^{(k)}$, we need a quantitative measure to evaluate the direction of change. To do so, we use the lower bound L and upper bound U of the objective function and define the *improvement index* as

$$\alpha_i = \frac{i - L}{U - L} \quad .$$

The closer the value of α is to 0, the higher is the possibility of moving in the positive direction. So, if i is the current value of the objective function then

$$(1 - \alpha_i)\gamma_d^{(k)}$$

is the probability of moving to $i + d$ in the next iteration and

$$\alpha_i \gamma_d^{(k)}$$

is the probability of moving to $i - d$ in the next iteration. Finally, $\gamma_d^{(k)}$ can be defined based on the problem information. The way to do so depends heavily on the nature of the problem under study. We illustrate this procedure in Section 5 for the traveling salesman problem.

4.2 Summary of the algorithm

Please consider Algorithm 4.1. Algorithm SAOST is similar to Algorithm 2.1, but having k different neighborhood structures instead of one. These neighborhood structure are defined beforehand based on any heuristic approach. In stage 3 of Algorithm 4.1, the cost of using each neighborhood structure for one iteration $C^{(k)}$ are computed, regarding to the computational burden imposed by each neighborhood structure and all other impacting factors. After that, in stage 5, the initial values for the transition probabilities are computed; *i.e.*, the values for $\gamma_d^{(k)}$ with respect to each neighborhood structure are found and used to determine $P_{ij}^{(k)}$. In case we do not have enough information to compute these probabilities, we can start with a uniform distribution and update the values as the algorithm proceeds. In the outer while loop, stage 5, the the optimal value of i_k^* for each neighborhood structure is computed in stage 6. This allows us to find the neighborhood structure

$$k^* = \operatorname{argmax} \{ i_k, k = 1, 2, \ldots, K \}$$

having the highest value. The inner while loop, stages 8 to 15, is basically the same as stages 4 to 11 of Algorithm 2.1 but replacing parameter M_p by the dynamically updated criteria

$$f(\omega) < i_{k^*}^* .$$

After leaving the inner while loop, update the lower bounds and, if applicable also update the upper bounds; stage 16. Using the new lower and upper bound, the current value of the objective function and the change probabilities $\gamma_d^{(k)}$, the transition probability matrix is determined in stage 17. Afterwards, one can decided to continue in the current temperature with a new neighborhood structure or to decrease the temperature according to a predefined cooling scheme.

4.3 Advantages and disadvantages

Despite the variety of heuristic algorithms, there are some measures that enable us to evaluate each method and decide about its properness for a specifi problem. Following Glover and Kochenberger, a good metaheuristic must have the followings properties [24, Chapter 6]:

1. **Simplicity:** A good meta-heuristic algorithm should be based on some simple principles which are applicable in all cases.
2. **Precision:** Different steps of a meta-heuristic should be defined mathematically in an exact way and ambiguous terms should be avoided.
3. **Coherence:** All steps of a meta-heuristic for any specific problem have to follow the main principles of that heuristic.
4. **Efficiency:** A good meta-heuristic should have the ability of finding an optimal or near-optimal solution for a large group of real world problems.
5. **Effectiveness:** A good meta-heuristic should find its final solution in a reasonable amount of computational time.
6. **Robustness:** The performance of a meta-heuristic need to be verified on a large variety of problems. A good meta-heuristic is the one which is consistent with a wide range of problems.

7. **User friendliness:** A meta-heuristic algorithm need to be easy to un- derstand and more importantly, easy to implement.
8. **Innovation:** It is expected for a new meta-heuristic to have some kind on innovation in its principles and applications.

Algorithm 4.1 Simulated Annealing with Optimal Stopping Time (SAOST)

Input: initial feasible solution ω_0, initial temperature t_0, lower bound L and upper bound U for the objective function f, k neighborhood structures N_k, overall stopping criteria and temperature decreasing rule

Output: feasible solution ω

initialize *step* counter: $p = 0$
set current solution ω to initial solution ω_0: $\omega = \omega_0$
compute the cost of using each neighborhood structure: $C^{(k)}$
compute the initial values for the transition probability matrix: $P_{ij}^{(k)}$

while the stopping criteria are not met **do**
    find the value of i_k^* for each neighborhood structure
    choose the neighborhood structure k^* having the highest value

    while $f(\omega) < i_{k^*}^*$ **do**
        compute a solution belonging to neighborhood structure k^* of the current solution: $\omega' \in N_{k^*}(\omega)$
        if $f(\omega') - f(\omega) \geq 0$ **then**
            $\omega \leftarrow \omega'$
        else
            $\omega \leftarrow \omega'$ with probability $\exp\left(\frac{f(\omega') - f(\omega)}{t_p}\right)$
        end if
    end while

    update the lower and upper bounds
    construct the transition probability matrix for each neighborhood structure: $P_{ij}^{(k)}$
    if decided to decrease temperature **then**
        decrease temperature t_p
        $p \leftarrow p + 1$
    end if
end while

return feasible solution ω.

The following advantages can be stated for our proposed method:

- Its ability to use the past information of the problem in making future decisions (tuning the search strategies)

- Less computational effort at each temperature because the best number of iteration in known
- Less algorithm parameters
- The ability to cover a wide range of the feasible space via appropriate selection of neighborhood structures
- Its flexibility in employing different neighborhood structure
- Considering different computational time for each neighborhood structure using the cost parameter

5. TSP as an illustrative example

In this section, we apply the proposed algorithm to the traveling salesman problem (TSP) just like the first application of SA by Černý [13]. The purpose is to illustrate the new algorithm. Hence, we only consider two basic neighborhood structures and do not discuss how to derive bounds or initial solutions. For a detailed discussion of the TSP, refer to [27, 4]. Different neighborhood structures are discussed in detail in [46]. From now on, we assume that the TSP has n nodes and the graph is complete.

In the first neighborhood structure, two adjacent nodes are randomly selected in the current solution and their positions are swapped. This is shown in Figure 1. The chain of nodes illustrate the order in which the nodes are visited in a tour starting from node 1 and returning after the nth node to node 1 again. As shown, two edges need to be removed and two new edges have to be created.

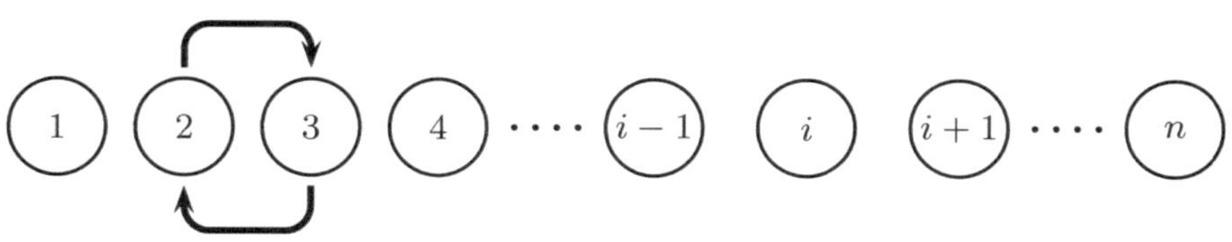

Figure 1. The edges (1, 2) and (3, 4) should be substituted with the edges (1, 3) and (2, 4) in the new solution.

This neighborhood structure has the following characterizations:

- For every arbitrary solution, exactly n neighbor solutions exist for $n \geq 5$. These solutions are obtained by exchanging the position of every two consecutive nodes in the current solution.
- The *speed* of a neighborhood structure is defined as the number of moves needed to go from a solution to any other arbitrary solution. This number is $O(n^2)$ for this neighborhood structure. Considering a sequence of n distinct numbers and a desired order, the first number may need $n - 1$ moves to reach its appropriate position. This is $n-2$ for the second number and so on for others. This clearly gives us $O(n^2)$ number of moves. The only difference in this case with a TSP tour is that in a TSP tour, since we have loop and elements can move in both directions, we may need fewer number of moves to seat every node. But this at most may give us half of what we get above for the sequence of numbers which keeps the complexity still $O(n^2)$.
- The computational effort needed for each move is four units, as two edges need be removed and two new edges have to be created.

The second neighborhood structure used in our numerical analysis is defined by exchanging the position of every two arbitrary nodes. This neighborhood structure is shown in Figure 2.

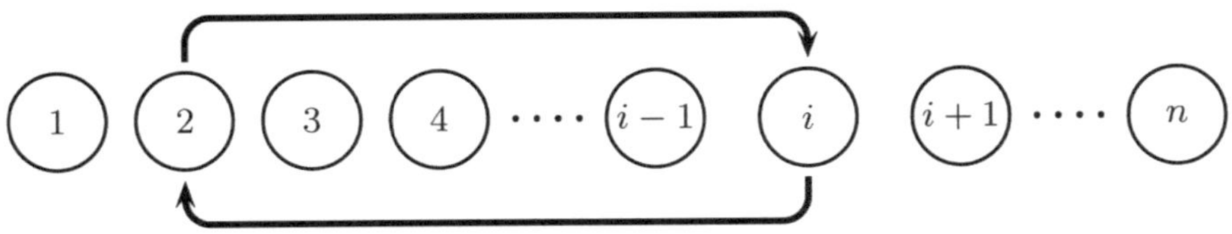

Figure 2. The edges between (1, 2), (2, 3), $(i-1, i)$ and $(i, i+1)$ should be substituted with the edges $(1, i)$, $(i, 3)$, $(i-1, 2)$ and $(2, i+1)$ in the new solution.

The following characterizations can be stated for this neighborhood structure:

- There exist $\binom{n}{2} = \frac{n(n-1)}{2}$ neighbors for each solution. These solutions are obtained by exchanging the position of every two arbitrary nodes.
- The speed of this neighborhood structure is $O(n)$: Note that in this case, the number of moves needed to go from a solution to any arbitrary solution in the worst case would be $O(n)$. This is as in the worst case, each node needs at most one move to be seated in its appropriate position.
- The computational effort is eight units. As it is clear from Figure 2, four existing edges need to be substituted with four new edges.

Next, we define the transition probabilities $P_{ij}^{(k)}$ of going from state i to state j using neighborhood structure k. To find the values of $\gamma_d^{(k)}$, the probability of an objective function change of d using neighborhood structure k, 1000 random moves are generated for each neighborhood structure k. For example, for the first neighborhood structure two edges are randomly picked and substituted with two other edges. The difference between the summation of the first two and the second two edges is recorded as the value of d for this experiment. Note that all of this process is performed regardless to feasibility. Recognize that we have not produced any feasible or infeasible solution. The purpose is to get a measure of how much the value of the objective function on average changes if a random move is implemented. For the second neighborhood structure, a similar process is performed but by exchanging four edges instead of two. Finally the values of d for each neighborhood structure are sorted in a frequency histogram and a discrete probability distribution is obtained. These probability distributions are in fact the values of $\gamma_d^{(k)}$.

The remaining parts of the procedure are based on the algorithm itself. Problem-specific are only the definition of the neighborhood structures and the computation of the transition probabilities, next to the usual variables of SA as initial solution, stopping criteria or cooling scheme.

6. Conclusion

We developed a new SA-based algorithm for solving combinatorial optimization problems by modifying its search process. This algorithm takes advantage of multiple neighborhood structures at the same time to reduce the chance of being trapped in the local optima. Unlike the Variable Neighborhood Search method which selects the neighborhood structure in a deterministic way, the idea behind this new method is based on a well-known problem in Stochastic Processes called Optimal Stopping Problem. At each iteration, the proposed algorithm chooses that neighborhood structure which has a higher expected improvement in the objective function. The generality of this method allows us to adapt and apply it to a wide range of complex problems with combinatorial nature.

7. References

An Analysis Framework for Metaheuristics: A Mathematical Approach. York 14 Conference, Bath, England, 2005.

Simulated Annealing Algorithm for Daily Nursing Care Scheduling Problem. Proceedings of the 3rd Annual IEEE Conference on Automation Science and Engineering, 2007. Scottsdale, AZ, USA.

Emile Aarts, Jan Korst, and Wil Michiels. *Simulated Annealing*, chapter 7. Springer, 2005. Search Methodologies: Introductory Tutorials in Optimization and Decision Support Techniques.

David L. Applegate, Robert E. Bixby, Vasek Chvatal, andWilliam J. Cook, editors. *The Traveling Salesman Problem: A Computational Study*. Princeton Series in Applied Mathematics. Princeton University Press, 2007.

J. W. Barnes, N. Colletti, and D. Neuway. Using group theory and tran- sition matrices to study a class of metaheuristic neighborhoods. *Europea Journal of Operational Research*, 138:531–544, 2002.

Dimitri P. Bertsekas. *Dynamic Programming and Optimal Control*, vol- ume 2. Athena Scientific, 3rd edition, 2007.

L. Bianchi, M. Dorigo, L. Gambardella, and W. Gutjahr. Metaheuristics in stochastic combinatorial optimization: a survey. Technical report, IDSIA, Dalle Molle Institute for Artificial Intelligence, 2006.

Christian Blum and Andrea Roli. Metaheuristics in combinatorial optimization: Overview and conceptual comparison. *ACM Comput. Surv.*, 35(3):268–308, 2003.

A. Bolte and U. W. Thonemann. Optimizing simulated annealing schedules with genetic programming. *European Journal of Operational Research*, 92:402–416, 1996.

V. Bouffard and J. A. Ferland. Improving simulated annealing with variable neighborhood search to solve the resource-constrained scheduling problem. *J Sched*, 10:375–386, 2007.

W. M. Byoce. Stopping rules for selling bonds. *Bell J. Econ. Manage Sci.*, 1:27–53, 1970.

W. M. Byoce. On a simple optimal stopping problem. *Discrete Math.*, 5:297–312, 1973.

V. Černý. Thermodynamical Approach to the Traveling Salesman Problem An Efficient Simulation Algorithm. *Journal of Optimization Theory and applications*, 45(1):41–51, 1985.

R. W. Chen and F. K. Hwang. On the values of an (m,p) urn. *Congr. Numer*, 1:75–84, 1984.

Yuan Shih Chow, Herbert Robbins, and David Siegmund. *Great expecta tions: The theory of optimal stopping*. Houghton Mifflin, 1971.

Morris H. DeGroot. *Optimal Statistical Decisions*. Wiley Classics Library Wiley-Interscience, 2004.

M. Dorigo. *Optimization, Learning and Natural Algorithms*. PhD thesis, Politecnico di Milano, Italy, 1992.

R. W. Eglese. Simulated annealing: a tool for operational research. *Euro- pean Journal of Operational Research*, 46:271–281, 1990.

T.A. Feo and M.G.C. Resende. A probabilistic heuristic for a computationally difficult set covering problem. *Operations Research Letters*, 8:67–71, 1989.

T.A. Feo and M.G.C. Resende. Greedy randomized adaptive search procedures. *J. of Global Optimization*, 6:109–133, 1995.

V. Feoktistov. Differential Evolution - In Search of Solutions, volume 5 o Optimization And Its Applications. Springer, 2006.

Michel Gendreau and Jean-Yves Potvin. Metaheuristics in combinatorial optimization. *Annals of Operations Research*, 140(1):189–213, 2005.

F. Glover. Future paths for Integer Programming and Links to Artificia Intelligence. *Computers and Operations Research*, 13(5):533–549, 1986.

F. Glover and G. A. Kochenberger, editors. *Handbook of Metaheuristics*. Kluwer Academic Publishers, New York, 2003.

F. Glover and M. Laguna. *Tabu Search*. Kluwer Academic Publishers, 1997.

D.E Goldberg. Genetic algorithms in search, optimization and machine learning. Addison-Wesley, 1989.

Gregory Gutin and Abraham P. Punnen, editors. *The Traveling Salesman Problem and Its Variations*. Combinatorial Optimization. Springer, 2007.

P. Hansen and N. Mladenovi´c. An introduction to variable neighborhood search. In S. Voss, S. Martello, I. H. Osman, and C. Roucairol, editors, *Meta-heuristics, Advances and trends in local search paradigms for optimization*, pages 433–458. Kluwer Academic Publishers, 1998.

P. Hansen and N. Mladenović. Variable neighborhood search: Principle and applications. *European Journal of Operational Research*, 130:449–467, 2001.

J. H. Holland. Adaptation in Natural and Artificial Systems: An Introductory Analysis with Applications to Biology, Control, and Artificial Intelligence. Ann Arbor, MI: University of Michigan Press, 1975.

A. L. Ingber. Simulated annealing: Practice versus theory. *J Mathl. Comput. Modelling*, 18(11):29–57, 1993.

D.S. Johnson, C.H. Papadimitriou, and M. Yannakakis. How easy is local search? *Journal of Computer and System Sciences*, 17:79–100, 1988.

S. Kirkpatrick, C. D. Gelatt Jr., and M. P. Vecchi. Optimization by Simulated Annealing. *Science*, 220(4598):671–680, 1983.

P. J. M. Laarhoven and E. H. L. Aarts, editors. *Simulated annealing: theory and applications*. Kluwer Academic Publishers, Norwell, MA, USA, 1987.

F. T. Lin, C. Y. Cao, and C. C. Hsu. Applying the genetic approach to simulated annealing in solving some np-hard problems. *IEEE Transactions on Systems, Man. and Cybernetics*, 23(6):1752–1767, 1993.

M. Lundy and A. Mees. Convergence of an annealing algorithm. *Mathematical Programming*, 34:11–124, 1986.

Thelma D. Mavridou and Panos M. Pardalos. Simulated annealing and genetic algorithms for the facility layout problem: A survey. *Computational optimization and Applications*, 7:111–126, 1997.

Nicholas Metropolis, AriannaW. Rosenbluth, Marshall N. Rosenbluth, Augusta H. Teller, and Edward Teller. Equation of State Calculations by Fast Computing Machines. *The Journal of Chemical Physics*, 21(6):1087–1092, 1953.

N. Mladenović. A variable neighborhood algorithm - a new metaheuristic for combinatorial optimization. In *Abstracts of papers presented at Optimization Days, Montréal*, page 112. 1995.

R. H. J. M. Otten and L. P. P. P. van Ginneken. *The Annealing Algorithm*. Kluwer Academic Publishers, 1989.

D. T. Pham and D. Karaboga. Intelligent Optimisation Techniques: Genetic Algorithms, Tabu Search, Simulated Annealing and Neural Networks. Springer, 2000.

M. Pirlot. General local search methods. *European Journal of Operational Research*, 92:493–511, 1996.

Kenneth V. Price. Genetic annealing. *Dr. Dobb's Journal*, 220:127–132, 1994.

Jakob Puchinger and G"unther R. Raidl. *Combining Metaheuristics and Exact Algorithms in Combinatorial Optimization: A Survey and Classification*, pages 41–53. Springer, 2005. Artificial Intelligence and Knowledge Engineering Applications: A Bioinspired Approach.

Martin L. Puterman. *Markov Decision Processes: Discrete Stochastic Dynamic Programming*. Wiley Series in Probability and Statistics. Wiley- Interscience, 2005.

Gerhard Reinelt. *The Traveling Salesman: Computational Solutions for TSP Applications*. Lecture Notes in Computer Science. Springer, 1991.

Sheldon M. Ross. *Introduction to Stochastic Dynamic Programming*. Probability and Mathematical Statistics. Academic Press, 1995.

Sheldon M. Ross. *Stochastic Processes*. Wiley Series in Probability and Mathematical Statistics. Johnson Wiley & Sons, Inc., 2nd edition, 1996.

Peter Salamon, Paolo Sibani, and Richard Frost. *Facts, Conjectures, and Improvements for Simulated Annealing*. SIAM Monographs on Mathematical Modeling and Computation, 2002.

Linn I. Sennott. *Stochastic Dynamic Programming and the Control of Queueing Systems*. Wiley Series in Probability and Statistics. Wiley- Interscience, 1998.

L. A. Shepp. Explicit solutions to some problems of optimal stopping. *Annals of Mathematical Statistics*, 40:993–1010, 1969.

J. M. Stern. simulated annealing with a temperature dependent penalty function. *ORSA Journal on Computing*, 4:311–319, 1992.

Ralph E. Strauch. Negative dynamic programming. *Annals of Mathematical Statistics*, 37(4):871–890, 1966.

B. Suman and P. Kumar. A survey of simulated annealing as a tool for single and multiobjective optimization. *Journal of the Operational Research Society*, 57:1143–1160, 2006.

David D. Yao and Shaohui Zheng. Sequential inspection under capacity constraints. *Operations Research*, 47(3):410–421, 1999.

19

A Comparison of Simulated Annealing, Elliptic and Genetic Algorithms for Finding Irregularly Shaped Spatial Clusters

Luiz Duczmal, André L. F. Cançado, Ricardo H. C. Takahashi and Lupércio F. Bessegato
Universidade Federal de Minas Gerais
Brazil

1. Introduction

Methods for the detection and evaluation of the statistical significance of spatial clusters are important geographic tools in epidemiology, disease surveillance and crime analysis. Their fundamental role in the elucidation of the etiology of diseases (Lawson, 1999; Heffernan et al., 2004; Andrade et al., 2004), the availability of reliable alarms for the detection of intentional and non-intentional infectious diseases outbreaks (Duczmal and Buckeridge, 2005, 2006a; Kulldorff et al., 2005, 2006) and the analysis of spatial patterns of criminal activities (Ceccato, 2005) are current topics of intense research. The spatial scan statistic (Kulldorff, 1997) and the program SatScan (Kulldorff, 1999) are now widely used by health services to detect disease clusters with circular geometric shape. Contrasting to the naïve statistic of the relative count of cases, the scan statistic is less prone to the random variations of cases in small populations. Although the circular scan approach sweeps completely the configuration space of circularly shaped clusters, in many situations we would like to recognize spatial clusters in a much more general geometric setting. Kulldorff et al. (2006) extended the SatScan approach to detect elliptic shaped clusters. It is important to note that for both circular and elliptic scans there is a need to impose size limits for the clusters; this requisite is even more demanding for the other irregularly shaped cluster detectors.
Other methods, also using the scan statistic, were proposed recently to detect connected clusters of irregular shape (Duczmal et al., 2004, 2006b, 2007, Iyengar, 2004, Tango & Takahashi, 2005, Assunção et al., 2006, Neill et al., 2005). Patil & Tallie (2004) used the relative incidence cases count for the objective function. Conley et al. (2005) proposed a genetic algorithm to explore a configuration space of multiple agglomerations of ellipses; Sahajpal et al. (2004) also used a genetic algorithm to find clusters shaped as intersections of circles of different sizes and centers.
Two kinds of maps could be employed. The point data set approach assigns one point in the map for each case and for each non-case individual. This approach is interested in finding, among all the allowed geometric shape candidates defined within a specific strategy, the one that encloses the highest ratio of cases vs. non-cases, thus defining the most likely cluster. The second approach assumes that a map is divided into M regions, with total population N and C total cases. Defining the zone z as any set of connected regions, the

objective is finding, among all the possible zones, which one maximizes a certain statistic, thus defining it as the most likely cluster. Although the first approach has higher precision of population distribution at small scales, the second approach is more appropriate when detailed addresses are not available. The genetic algorithms proposed by Conley et al. (2005) and Sahajpal et al. (2004), and also Iyengar (2004) used the point data set methodology.

The ideas discussed in this text derived from the previous work on the simulated annealing scan (Duczmal et al., 2004, 2006b), the elliptic scan (Kulldorff et al. 2006) and the genetic algorithm scan (Duczmal et al. 2007). The simulated annealing scan finds a sub-optimal solution trying to analyze only the most promising connected subsets of regions of the map, thus discarding most configurations that seem to have a low value for the scan likelihood ratio statistic. The initial explorations start from many and widely separated points in the configuration space, and concentrates the search more thoroughly around the configurations that show some increase in the scan statistic (the objective function). Thus we expect that the probability of overlooking a very high valued solution is small, and that this probability diminishes as the search goes on. Although the simulated annealing approach has high flexibility, the algorithm may be very computer intensive in certain instances, and the computational effort may not be predictable a priori for some maps. For example, the Belo Horizonte City homicide map analyzed in Duczmal et al. (2004) presented a very sharply delineated irregular cluster that was relatively easy to detect, with the relative risk inside the cluster much higher than the adjacent regions. This should be compared with the inconspicuous irregular breast cancer cluster in the US Northeast map studied in Duczmal et al. (2006b), which required more computer time to be detected, also using the simulated annealing approach. Although statistically significant, that last cluster was more difficult to detect due to the fact that the relative risk inside the cluster was just slightly above the remainder of the map. Besides, the intrinsic variance of the value of the scan likelihood ratio statistic for the sub-optimal solutions found at different runs of the program with the same input may be high, due to the high flexibility of the cluster instances that are admissible in this methodology. This flexibility leads to a very high dimension of the admissible cluster set to be searched, which in turn leads the simulated annealing algorithm to find sub-optimal solutions that can be quite different in different runs. These issues are addressed in this paper. We describe and evaluate a new approach for a novel genetic algorithm using a map divided into M regions, employing Kulldorff´s spatial scan statistic.

There is another important problem, common to all irregularly shaped cluster detectors: the scan statistic tries to find the most likely cluster over the collection of all connected zones, irrespectively of shape. Due to the unlimited geometric freedom of cluster shapes, this could lead to low power of cluster detection (Duczmal et al., 2006b). This happens because the best value of the objective function is likely to be associated with "tree shaped" clusters that merely link the highest likelihood ratio cells of the map, without contributing to the appearance of geographically meaningful solutions that delineate correctly the location of the true clusters. The first version of the simulated annealing method (Duczmal et al., 2004) controlled in part the amount of freedom of shape through a very simple device, limiting the maximum number of regions that should constitute the cluster. Without limiting appropriately the size of the cluster, there was an obvious tendency for the simulated annealing algorithm to produce much larger cluster solutions than the real ones. Tango & Takahashi (2005) pointed out this weakness, when comparing the simulated annealing scan with their flexible shape scan, which makes the complete enumeration of all sets within a circle that includes the *k-1* nearest neighbors. Nevertheless, the size limit feature mentioned above was not explored in their numerical comparisons, thus impairing the comparative performance analysis of the algorithms. In Duczmal et al. (2006b) a significant improvement in shape control was developed, through the concept of geometric "non-compactness", which was used as a penalty function for the very irregularly shaped clusters, generalizing an idea that was used for the special case of ellipses (Kulldorff et al., 2006). Finally, the method proposed by Conley et al. (2005) employed a tactic to "clean-up" the best configuration found in order to simplify geometrically the cluster. It is not clear, though, how these simplifications impact the quality of the cluster shape, or how this could improve the precision of the geographic delineation of the cluster.

Our goal is to describe cluster detectors that incorporate the desirable features discussed above. They use the spatial scan statistic in a map divided into a finite number of regions, offering a strategy to control the irregularity of cluster shape. The algorithms provide a geometric representation of the cluster that makes easier for a practitioner to soundly interpret the geographic meaning for the cluster found, and attains good solutions with less intrinsic variance, with good power of detection, in less computer time. In section 2, we review Kulldorff's spatial scan statistic, the simulated annealing scan, the elliptic scan and the non-compactness penalty function. The genetic algorithm is discussed in section 3. The power evaluations and numerical tests are described in section 4. We present an application for breast cancer clusters in Brazil in section 5. We conclude with the final remarks in section 6.

2. Scan statistics and the non-compactness penalty function

Given a map divided into M regions, with total population N and C total cases, let the zone Z be any set of connected regions. Under the null hypothesis (there are no clusters in the map), the number of cases in each region follows a Poisson distribution. Define $L(Z)$ as the likelihood under the alternative hypothesis that there is a cluster in the zone Z, and L_0 the likelihood under the null-hypothesis. The zone Z with the maximum likelihood is defined as *the most likely cluster*. If μ_Z is the expected number of cases inside the zone Z under the null hypothesis, c_Z is the number of cases inside Z, $I(Z) = c_Z / \mu_Z$ is the relative incidence inside Z, $O(Z) = (C - c_Z)/(C - \mu_Z)$ is the relative incidence outside Z, it can be shown that

$$LR(Z) = L(Z) / L_0 = I(Z)^{c_Z} O(Z)^{C - c_Z}$$

when $I(Z) > 1$, and 1 otherwise. The zone that constitutes the most likely cluster maximizes the likelihood ratio $LR(Z)$ (Kulldorff, 1997). $LLR(Z) = \log(LR(Z))$ is used instead of $LR(Z)$.

2.1 The simulated annealing scan statistic

It is useful to treat the centroids of every cell in the map as vertices of a graph whose edges link cells with a common boundary. For the simulated annealing (SA) spatial scan statistic, the collection of connected irregularly shaped zones consists of all those zones for which the corresponding subgraphs are connected. This collection is very large, and it is impractical to calculate the likelihood for all of them. Instead we shall try to visit only the most promising zones, as follows (see Duczmal & Assunção (2004) for details). The zones z and w are neighbors when only one of the two sets $w - z$ or $z - w$ consists of a single cell. Starting from some zone z(0), the algorithm chooses some neighbor z(1) among all the neighbors of z(0). In the next step, another neighbor z(2) is chosen among the neighbors of z(1), and so on. Thus, at each step we build a new zone adding or excluding one cell from the zone in the previous step. It is only required that there is a maximum size for the number of cells in each zone (usually half of the total number of cells). Instead of always choosing the highest LR neighbor at every step, the SA algorithm evaluates if there has been little or no LR improvement during the latest steps; in that case, the algorithm opts for choosing a random neighbor. This is done while trying to avoid getting stuck at LR local maxima.

We restart the search many times, each time using each individual cell of the map as the initial zone. Thus, the effect of this strategy is to keep the program openly exploring the most promising zones in the configuration space and abandoning the directions that seems uninteresting. The best solution found by the program is called a quasi-optimal solution and, for our purposes, it is a compromise due to computer time restraints for the identification of the geographical location of the clusters.

Duczmal, Kulldorff and Huang (2006) developed a geometric penalty for irregularly shaped clusters. Many algorithms frequently end up with a solution that is nothing more than the collection of the highest incidence cells in the map, linked together forming a "tree-shaped" cluster spread through the map; the associated subgraph resembles a tree, except possibly for some few additional edges. This kind of cluster does not add new information with regard to its special geographical significance in the map. One easy way to avoid that problem is simply to set a smaller upper bound to the maximum number of cells within a zone. This approach is only effective when cluster size is rather small (i.e., for detecting those clusters occupying roughly up to 10% of the cells of the map). For larger upper bounds in size, the increased geometric freedom favors the occurrence of very irregularly shaped tree-like clusters, thus impacting the power of detection. Another way to deal with this problem is to have some shape control for the zones that are being analyzed, penalizing the zones in the map that are highly irregularly shaped. For this purpose the geometric compactness of a zone is defined as the area of z divided by the circle with the perimeter of the convex hull of z. Compactness is dependent on the shape of the object, but not on its size. Compactness also penalizes a shape that has small area compared to the area of its convex hull. A user defined exponent a is attached to the penalty to control its strength; larger values of a increases the effect of the penalty, allowing the presence of more compact clusters. Similarly, lower a values allows more freedom of shape. The idea of using a penalty function for spatial cluster detection, based on the irregularity of its shape, was first used for ellipses in Kulldorff et al. (2006), although a different formula was employed.

We will penalize the zones in the map that are highly irregularly shaped. Given a planar geometric object z , define $A(z)$ as the area of z and $H(z)$ as the perimeter of the convex hull of z . Define the *compactness* of z as $\mathrm{K(z)} = 4\pi \mathrm{A(z)/H(z)}^2$. Compactness penalizes a shape that has small area compared to the area of its convex hull (Duczmal et al., 2006b). The strength of the compactness measure, employed here as a penalty factor, may be varied through a parameter $a \geq 0$, using the formula $K(z)^a$, instead of $K(z)$. The expression $LR(z)^{K(z)^a}$ is employed in this general setting as the corrected likelihood test function replacing $LR(z)$. The penalty function works just because the compactness correction penalizes very strongly those clusters which are even more irregularly shaped than the legitimate ones that we are looking for.

2.2 The elliptic scan statistic

Kulldorff et al. (2006) presented an elliptic version of the spatial scan statistic, generalizing the circular shape of the scanning window. It uses an elliptic scanning window of variable location, shape (eccentricity), angle and size, with and without an eccentricity penalty. An ellipse is defined by the x and y coordinates of its centroid, and its size, shape, and angle of the inclination of its longest axis. The shape is defined as the ratio of the length and width of the ellipse. For a given map, we define a finite collection of ellipses E as follows. For computational reasons, the shapes s in E are restricted to 1, 2, 4, 8 and 20. A finite set of angles is chosen such that we have an overlapping of about 70% for neighboring ellipses with the same shape, size and centroid. The ellipses' centroids are set identical to the cells' centroids in the map. We choose a finite number of ellipses whose sizes define uniquely all the possible zones z formed by the cells in that map whose centroids lie within some ellipse of the subset. The collection E is thus formed by grouping together all these subsets, for each cell's centroid, shape, and angle. We further define E(s) as the subset of E that includes all the shapes listed above in this section up to and including s. The choice of the collection E and its associated collection of zones is done beforehand and only once for a given map. The spatial scan statistic is thus applied to the collection of zones defined by E. The cluster likelihood was adjusted with a penalty function, the eccentricity penalty function

$$4s/(s+1)^2$$

so that the adjusted log likelihood is

$$LLR * [4s/(s+1)^2]^a$$

and s is the cluster shape defined as the length of the longest axis divided by the length ofthe shortest axis of the ellipse. The tuning parameter a is similar to the parameter used in the simulated annealing scan.

3. The genetic algorithm approach

We approach the problem of finding the most likely cluster by a Genetic Algorithm specifically designed for dealing with this problem structure. Genetic Algorithms (GA' s) constitute a family of optimization algorithms that are devoted to find extreme points (minima or maxima) of functions of rather general classes.

3.1 The general structure of the genetic algorithm

A GA is defined as any algorithm that is essentially structured as:

- A set of N current candidate-solution points is maintained at each step of the algorithm (instead of a single current candidate-solution that is kept in most of optimization algorithms), and from the iteration to the next one the whole set is updated. This set is called the algorithm *population* (by analogy with a biological species population, which evolves according to natural selection laws), and each candidate-solution point in the population is called an *individual*.
- In an iteration, the algorithm applies the following *genetic operations* to the individuals in the population:
    - Some individuals (a subset of the population, randomly chosen) receive some random perturbations; this operation is called *mutation* (in analogy with the biological mutation);

- Some individuals (another random subset of the population) are randomly paired, and each pair of individuals (*parent individuals*) is combined, in such a way that a new set of individuals (*child individuals*, or *offspring*) is generated as a combination of the features of the initial ones. This is called *crossover* (in analogy with the biological crossover);
- After mutation and crossover, a new population is chosen, via a procedure that selects N individuals from ones that result from the mutation, from the crossover, and also from the former population. This procedure has some stochastic component, but necessarily attributes a greater chance of being chosen to the individuals with better objective function. This procedure is called the selection (by analogy with the natural selection of biological species), and results in the new population that will be subjected to the same operations, in the next iteration.

- Other operations can be applied, in addition to these basic genetic operations, including: the *elitism* operation (a deterministic choice of the best individuals in a population to be included in the next population); a *niche* operation (a decrement of the probability of an individual being chosen if it belongs to a region that is already covered by many individuals); several kinds of *local search*; and so forth.

Notice that the mutation introduces a kind of random walk motion to the individuals: an individual that were mutated iteration after iteration would follow a Markovian process. The crossover promotes a further exploitation of a region that is already being sampled by the two parent individuals. The selection introduces some direction to the search, eliminating the intermediate outcomes that don't present good features, keeping the ones that are promising. The search in new regions (mainly performed via mutation) and in regions already sampled (mainly performed via crossover) is guided by selection.

This rather general structure leads to optimization algorithms that are suitable for the optimization of a large class of functions. No assumption of differentiability, convexity, continuity, or unimodality, is needed. Also, the function can be defined in continuous spaces, or can be of combinatorial nature, or even of hybrid nature. The only implicit assumption is that the function should have some "global trend" that can be devised from samples taken from a region of the optimization variable space. If such a "global trend" exists, the GA is expected to catch it, leading to reasonable estimates of the function optima without need for an "exhaustive search".

There is a large number of different Genetic Algorithms already known and the number of possible ones is supposed to be very large, since each genetic operation can be structured in a large number of different ways, and the GA can be formed by any combination of operators. However, it is known that some GA's are much better than other ones, under the viewpoint of both reliability of solution and computational cost for finding it (Takahashi et al., 2003). In particular, for problems of combinatorial nature, it has been established that algorithms employing specific crossover and mutation operators can be much more efficient than general-purpose GA's (Carrano et al., 2006). This is due to the fact that a "blind" crossover or mutation that would be performed by a general-purpose operator would have a large probability of generating an unfeasible individual, since most of combinations of variables are usually unfeasible. Specific operators are tailored in order to preserve feasibility, giving rise only to feasible individuals, by incorporating the specific rules that define the valid combinations of variables in the specific problem under consideration. The GA that is presented here has been developed with specific operators that consider the structure of the cluster identification problem.

3.2 The offspring generation

We shall now discuss the genetic algorithm developed here for cluster detection and inference. The core of the algorithm is the routine that builds the offspring resultant from the crossing of two given parents. Each parent and each offspring is thus a set of connected regions in the map, or zone. We should associate a node to each region in the map. Two nodes are connected by an edge if the corresponding regions are neighbors in the map. In this manner, the whole map is associated to a non-directed graph, consisting of nodes connected by edges. Given the non-disjoint parents A and B, let $C = A \cap B$, and $D \subseteq C$ a randomly chosen maximal connected set. We shall now assign a *level*, that is, a natural number to each of the nodes of the parent A. All the nodes in D are marked as level zero. Define the *neighbors of the set U in the set V* as the nodes in V that are neighbors of some node belonging to U. Pick up randomly one neighbor x_1 of $A_0 = D$, $x_1 \in A - A_0$, and assign the level 1 to it. Then pick up randomly one neighbor x_2 of $A_1 = D \cup \{ x_1 \}$, $x_2 \in A - A_1$, and assign the level 2 to it. At the step n, pick up randomly one neighbor x_n of $A_{n-1} = D \cup \{x_{1,\dots,} x_{n-1} \}$, $x_n \in A - A_{n-1}$, and assign the level n to it. In this fashion, choose the nodes, , $x_1,\dots, x_m$ for all the m nodes of the set $A - D$ and assign levels to them. These m nodes, plus the virtual root node r , along with all the oriented edges (x_j, x_k) , where x_k was chosen as the neighbor of x_j in the step k ($j < k$) , and the oriented edges (r, x_k) , where x_k is a neighbor of D, forms an oriented tree T_A , with the following property:

Lemma 1: For each node $x_i \in A - D$ there is a path from the root node r to x_i, consisting only of nodes from the set $\{x_{1,\dots,} x_{i-1} \}$.

Proof: Follow the oriented path contained in the tree T_A from r to x_i.

Note that the task of assigning levels to the nodes is not uniquely defined.

Repeat the construction above for the parent B and build the corresponding oriented tree T_B, but at this time using negative values -1,-2,-3,... for the levels, instead of 1,2,3,... (see the example in Figure 1). If $A - D$ and $B - D$ are non-disjoint, the nodes $y \in C - D$ are assigned with levels from both trees T_A and T_B (refer to Figure 1 again).

We now construct the *offspring of the parents A and B* as follows. Let $m_A \geq 2$ and $m_B \geq 1$ be respectively the number of elements of the sets $A - D$ and $B - D$, and suppose, without loss of generality, that $m_A \geq m_B$. The offspring is formed by the $m_B + (m_A - m_B - 1) = m_A - 1$ ordered sets of nodes corresponding to the sequences of levels (remembering that the level zero corresponds to the nodes of the set D):

$$m_A - 1,\dots,1,0,-1$$

$$m_A - 2,\dots,1,0,-1,-2$$

$$\vdots$$

$$m_A - m_B,\dots,1,0,-1,-2,\dots,-m_B$$

$$m_A - m_B - 1,\dots,1,0,-1,-2,\dots,-m_B$$

$$\vdots$$

$$2,1,0,-1,-2,\dots,-m_B$$

$$1,0,-1,-2,\dots,-m_B$$

If some sequence has two levels corresponding to the same node (it can happen only for the nodes in the set $C - D$), then count this node only once. Every set in the offspring has no more than $m_A + m_D$ nodes, where m_D is the number of nodes in D.

Lemma 2: All the sets in the offspring of the parents A and B are connected.
Proof: Apply lemma 1 to each node of each set in the offspring to check that there is a path from that node to the set D.
Figure 1A shows an example with two possible level assignments and their respective trees. The root node is formed by two regions. In the example of Figure 1B the set C is non-connected and consequently the node e has double level assignment. The successive construction of the ordered sets in the offspring requires a minimum of computational effort: from one set to the next, we need only to add and/or remove a region, simplifying the computation of the total population and cases for each set. Those totals are used to compute the spatial scan statistic. Besides, there is no need to check that each set is connected, because of lemma 2 (this checking alone accounted for 25% of the total computation time). Even more important is the fact that the offspring is evenly distributed along an imaginary "segment" across the configuration space, with the parents at the segment's tips, making easier for the program to stay next to a good solution, which could be investigated further by the next offspring generation.

3.3 The population evolution

The organization of the genetic algorithm is standard. We start with an initial population of M sets, or seeds, to be stored in the *current generation list*. Each seed is built through an aggregation process: starting from each map cell at a time, adjoin the neighbor cell that maximizes the likelihood ratio of the aggregate of cells adjoined so far, or exclude an existing one (provided that it does not disconnect the cluster), if the gain in likelihood ratio is greater; continue until a maximum number of cells is reached, or it is not possible to increase the likelihood of the current aggregate. In this fashion, the initial population consists of M (not necessarily distinct) zones, in such a way that each one of the M cells of the map becomes included in at least one zone.
We sort the current generation list in decreasing order by the LLR (modified as $\log(LR(z)^{K(z)^a})$ in section 2), and pick up randomly pairs of parent candidates. If the conditions for offspring generation are fulfilled, the offspring is constructed and stored in an *offspring list*. This list is sorted in decreasing LLR order. The top 10% parents are maintained in the M-sized *new generation list*, and the remaining 90% posts of the list are filled with the top offspring population. At this step, *mutation* is introduced. We simply remove and add one random region at a small fraction of the new generation list (checking for connectedness). Numerical experiments show that the effect of mutation is relatively small (less than 0.1 in LLR gain for mutation rate up to 5%), and we adopt here 1% as the standard mutation rate. After that, the current generation list is updated with the LLRordered new generation list. The process is repeated for G generations.
We make at most tc_{MAX} tentative crossings in order to produce wsc_{MAX} well succeeded crossings (i.e., when $A \cap B \neq \phi$) at each generation. The graph of Figure 2 shows the results of numerical experiments. Each curve consists of the average of 5,000 runs of the algorithm, varying wsc_{MAX} and G such that $wsc_{TOTAL} = wsc_{MAX} * G$, the total number of well-succeeded crossings, remains equal to 4,000. Smaller wsc_{MAX} values cause more frequent sorting of the offspring, and also make the program to remove low LLR configurations faster. As a consequence, high LLR offspring is quickly produced in the first generations, at the expense

of the depletion of the potentially useful population with lower LLR configurations. That depletion impacts the increase of the LLR on the later generations, because it is more difficult now to find parents pairs that generate increasingly better offspring. Conversely, greater wsc_{MAX} values causes less frequent sorting of the offspring, lowering the LLR increase a bit in the first generations, but maintains a varied pool that produces interesting offspring, impacting less the LLR tax in the later generations. So, given the total number of well-succeeded crossings that we are willing to simulate, wsc_{TOTAL}, we need to specify the optimal values of wsc_{MAX} and G that produce the best average LLR increase. From the result of this experiment, we are tempted to adopt the following strategy: allow smaller values of wsc_{MAX} for the first generations and then increase wsc_{MAX} for the last generations. That will produce poor results, because once we remove the low LLR configurations early in the process, there will not be much room for improvement by increasing wsc_{MAX} later, when the pool is relatively depleted. Therefore, a fixed value of wsc_{MAX} is used.

4. Power and performance evaluation

In this section we build the alternative cluster model for the execution of the power evaluations. We use the same benchmark dataset with real data population for the 245 counties Northeastern US map in Figure 4, with 11 simulated irregularly shaped clusters, that has been used in Duczmal et al. (2006b). Clusters A-E are mildly irregularly shaped, in contrast to the very irregular clusters F-K. For each simulated data under these 11 artificial alternative hypotheses, 600 cases are distributed randomly according to a Poisson model using a single cluster; we set a relative risk equal to one for every cell outside the real cluster, and greater than one and identical in each cell within the cluster. The relative risks were defined such that if the exact location of the real cluster was known in advance, the power to detect it should be 0.999 (Kulldorff et al., 2003). Table 1 displays the power results for the elliptic, GA and SA scan statistics. For the GA and SA scans, for each upper limit of the detected cluster size, with (a=1) and without (a=0) noncompactness penalty correction, 100,000 runs were done under null hypothesis, plus 10,000 runs for each entry in the table, under the alternative hypothesis. The upper limit sizes allowed were 8, 12, 20 and 30 regions, indicated in brackets in Table 1. An equal number of simulations was done for the elliptic scan, for the E(1) (circular), E(2), E(4), E(8) and E(20) sets of ellipses, without using the eccentricity penalty correction (a=0).

The power values for the statistics analyzed here are very similar. For the SA and GA scans, the higher power values occur generally when the maximum size allowed matches the true size of the simulated cluster. For the elliptic scan, the maximum power was attained when the eccentricity of the ellipses matched better the elongation of the clusters.

The power performance was good, and approximately the same on both scan statistics for clusters A-E. The performance of the GA was somewhat better compared to the SA algorithm for the remaining clusters F-K, although the power was reduced on both algorithms for those highly irregular clusters. The GA performed generally slightly better for the highly irregular clusters I-K. For the clusters G (size 26) and H (size 29) the GA performance was better when the maximum size was set to 20 and 30, and worse when the maximum size was set to 8 and 12. For the clusters F and H, the GA performed generally slightly better using the full compactness correction (a=1) and worse otherwise (a=0).

cluster	size	E(1)	E(2)	E(4)	E(8)	E(20)	penalty	GA (SA) [8]	GA (SA) [12]	GA (SA) [20]	GA (SA) [30]
A	13	0.85	0.88	0.89	0.89	0.88	a=0	.84 (.87)	.84 (.86)	.79 (.79)	.68 (.66)
							a=1	.85 (.86)	.85 (.86)	.84 (.84)	.80 (.79)
B	16	0.79	0.83	0.84	0.82	0.80	a=0	.81 (.83)	.82 (.84)	.80 (.81)	.74 (.74)
							a=1	.81 (.78)	.84 (.84)	.86 (.86)	.84 (.83)
C	7	0.88	0.89	0.90	0.90	0.90	a=0	.87 (.87)	.86 (.84)	.82 (.77)	.72 (.65)
							a=1	.80 (.79)	.78 (.79)	.74 (.74)	.68 (.65)
D	15	0.86	0.89	0.90	0.90	0.88	a=0	.88 (.89)	.89 (.90)	.87 (.88)	.81 (.81)
							a=1	.86 (.85)	.89 (.89)	.90 (.90)	.87 (.87)
E	21	0.81	0.85	0.86	0.85	0.83	a=0	.83 (.82)	.86 (.85)	.87 (.87)	.84 (.84)
							a=1	.77 (.72)	.82 (.81)	.86 (.86)	.87 (.85)
F	23	0.70	0.72	0.75	0.75	0.73	a=0	.54 (.58)	.58 (.61)	.57 (.59)	.50 (.51)
							a=1	.45 (.44)	.46 (.45)	.48 (.46)	.44 (.44)
G	26	0.46	0.52	0.56	0.59	0.61	a=0	.58 (.61)	.62 (.63)	.66 (.62)	.68 (.59)
							a=1	.50 (.49)	.53 (.52)	.55 (.52)	.55 (.50)
H	29	0.66	0.69	0.71	0.72	0.71	a=0	.66 (.69)	.67 (.70)	.70 (.69)	.69 (.67)
							a=1	.64 (.62)	.66 (.67)	.67 (.67)	.64 (.64)
I	23	0.77	0.83	0.83	0.82	0.81	a=0	.66 (.65)	.71 (.67)	.74 (.69)	.71 (.67)
							a=1	.62 (.59)	.64 (.64)	.68 (.66)	.70 (.65)
J	55	0.68	0.71	0.72	0.72	0.70	a=0	.58 (.60)	.64 (.66)	.69 (.69)	.72 (.70)
							a=1	.56 (.54)	.62 (.63)	.68 (.67)	.68 (.67)
K	78	0.80	0.84	0.82	0.81	0.78	a=0	.53 (.51)	.61 (.60)	.69 (.68)	.75 (.72)
							a=1	.47 (.43)	.56 (.55)	.67 (.66)	.72 (.71)

Table 1: Power comparison between the elliptic scan (E), the genetic algorithm (GA), and the simulated annealing algorithm (SA), in parenthesis. For the last two methods, the noncompactness penalty correction parameter a was set to 1 (full correction) or 0 (no correction). The numbers in brackets indicate the maximum allowed size for the most likely cluster found.

The optimal power of the circular (E(1)) scan was above 0.83 for clusters A–E, I, and K, and below 0.75 for the remaining data with clusters F, G, H, and J. The performance was very poor on simulated data with cluster G, and the optimal power achieved was only 0.61, using the maximum shape parameter 20. Similar comments apply for clusters F, H, and J, with optimal power about 0.70 and maximum shape parameters 4 and 8. Better power was not achieved when we increased the maximum elliptic shape to 20 for these data. When clusters are shaped as twisted long strings, the elliptic scan tended to detect only straight pieces within them: this phenomenon was observed in clusters F, G, H, and J, resulting in diminished power. Otherwise, when a cluster fits well within some ellipse of the set, best power results were attained, as observed for the remaining clusters. The elliptic scan obtained somewhat better results for clusters A, C, F, I and K, which are easily matched by ellipses, and worse for the "non-elliptical" clusters E, G and J.
Numerical experiments show that the GA scan is approximately ten times faster, compared to the SA scan presented in Duczmal et al. (2004). For the GA, the typical running time for the cluster detection and the 999 Monte Carlo replications in the 72 regions São Paulo State map of section 5 and the 245 regions Northeast US were respectively 5 and 15 minutes with a Pentium 4 desktop PC. Using exactly the same input for 5,000 runs for both the GA and SA scans, calibrated to achieve the same LLR average solution values in the Northeast US map under null hypothesis, we have verified that the GA sub-optimal solutions have about five times less LLR variance compared to the SA scan approach.

5. An application for breast cancer clusters

The genetic algorithm is applied for the study of clusters of high incidence of breast cancer in São Paulo State, Brazil. The population at risk is 8,822,617, formed by the female population over 30-years old, adjusted for age applying indirect standardization with 4 distinct 10 years age groups: 30-39, 40-49, 50-59, and 60+. In the 4 years period 2000-2003, a total of 14,831 cases were observed. The São Paulo State map was divided into 72 regions. The breast cancer data was obtained from Brazil´s Ministry of Health DATASUS homepage (www.datasus.gov.br) and de Souza (2005). Figure 3A shows the relative incidence of cases for each region, where the darker shades indicate higher incidence of cases. The other three maps (Figures 3B-D) show respectively the clusters that were found using values 1.0, 0.5 and 0.0 for the parameter *a*, which controls the degree of geometric shape penalization. Using 999 Monte Carlo replications of the null hypothesis, it was verified that all the clusters are statistically significant (p-values 0.001). The maximum size allowed was 18 regions for all the clusters. Notice that when a = 1.0 the cluster is approximately round, but with a hole, corresponding to a relatively low count region that was automatically deleted. As the value of the parameter *a* decreases we observe the appearance of more irregularly shaped clusters. As more irregularly shaped cluster candidates are allowed, due to the lower values of the parameter *a*, the LLR values for the most likely cluster increase, as can be seen in Table 2. The case incidence is about the same in all the clusters, by Table 2. It is a matter of the practitioner's experience to decide which of those clusters is the most appropriate in order to delineate the "true" cluster. The cluster in Figure 3B should be compared with the primary circular cluster that was found by SatScan (the rightmost circle in Figure 3D). It is also interesting to compare the cluster in Figure 3D with the primary and secondary circular clusters that were found by the circular SatScan algorithm (see the circles in Figure 3D).

Figure	*A*	Size	Cases	Population	Incidence	LLR	p-value
3B	1.0	16	3,324	394,294	0.00843	298.9	0.001
3C	0.5	16	3,078	361,373	0.00852	343.8	0.001
3D	0.0	18	2,924	346,024	0.00845	449.6	0.001

Table 2. The three clusters of Figure 3B-D.

6. Conclusions

We described and evaluated a novel elitist genetic algorithm for the detection of spatial clusters, which uses the spatial scan statistic in maps divided into finite numbers of regions. The offspring generation is very inexpensive. Children zones are automatically connected, accounting for the higher speed of the genetic algorithm. Although random mutations are computationally expensive, due to the necessity of checking the connectivity of zones, they are executed relatively few times. Selection for the next generation is straightforward. All these factors contribute to a fast convergence of the solution. The variance between different test runs is small. The exploration of the configuration space was done without a priori restrictions to the shapes of the clusters, employing a quantitative strategy to control its geometric irregularity. The elliptic scan is well suited for those clusters that fit well within some ellipse. The circular, elliptic, and SA scans have similar power in general. The elliptic scan method is computationally faster and is well suited for mildly irregular-shaped cluster

detection, but the non-compactness corrected SA and GA scans detects clusters with every possible shape, including the highly irregular ones. The choice of the statistic depends on the initial assumptions about the degree of shape irregularity to allow, and also on the availability of computer time.
The power of detection of the GA scan is similar to the simulated annealing algorithm for mildly irregular clusters and is slightly superior for the very irregular ones. The GA scan admits more flexibility in cluster shape than the elliptic and the circular scans, and its power of detection is only slightly inferior compared to these scans. The genetic algorithm is more computer-intensive when compared to the elliptic and the circular scans, but is faster than the simulated annealing scan. The use of penalty functions for the irregularity of cluster's shape enhances the flexibility of the algorithm and gives to the practitioner more insight of the geographic cluster delineation. We believe that our study encourages further investigations for the use of genetic algorithms for epidemiological studies and syndromic surveillance.

7. Acnowledgements

This work was partially supported by CNPq and CAPES.

8. References

Andrade LSS, Silva SA, Martelli CMT, Oliveira RM, Morais Neto OL, Siqueira Júnior JB, Melo LK, Di Fábio JL, 2004. Population-based surveillance of pediatric pneumonia: use of spatial analysis in an urban area of Central Brazil. Cadernos de Saúde Pública, 20(2), 411-421.

Assunçao R, Costa M, Tavares A, Ferreira S, 2006. Fast detection of arbitrarily shaped disease clusters. Statistics in Medicine 25;1-723-742.

Carrano, E.G., Soares, L.A.E, Takahashi, R.H.C, Saldanha, R.R., and Neto, O.M., 2006. Electric Distribution Network Multiobjective Design using a Problem-Specific Genetic Algorithm, *IEEE Transactions on Power Delivery*, 21, 995–1005.

Ceccato V, 2005 Homicide in São Paulo, Brazil: Assessing a spatial-temporal and weather variations. Journal of Enviromental Psychology, 25, 307-321

Conley J, Gahegan M, Macgill J, 2005. A genetic approach to detecting clusters in point-data sets. Geographical Analysis, 37, 286-314.

Duczmal L, Assunção R, 2004. A simulated annealing strategy for the detection of arbitrarily shaped spatial clusters, Comp. Stat. & Data Anal., 45, 269-286.

Duczmal L, Buckeridge DL., 2005. Using modified Spatial Scan Statistic to Improve Detection of Disease Outbreak When Exposure Occurs in Workplace - Virginia, 2004. *Morbidity and Mortality Weekly Report*, Vol.54 Suppl.187.

Duczmal L, Buckeridge DL, 2006a. A Workflow Spatial Scan Statistic. Stat. Med., 25; 743-754.

Duczmal L, Kulldorff M, Huang L., 2006b. Evaluation of spatial scan statistics for irregularly shaped clusters. J. Comput. Graph. Stat. 15:2;1-15.

Duczmal, L., Cançado, A.L.F., Takahashi, R.H.C., and Bessegato, L.F., 2007, A Genetic Algorithm for Irregularly Shaped Spatial Scan Statistics, *Computational Statistics and Data Analysis* 52, 43– 52.

Heffernan R, Mostashari F, Das D, Karpati A, Kulldorff M, Weiss D, 2004. Syndromic surveillance in public health practice, New York City. Emerging Infectious Diseases, 10:858

Iyengar, VS, 2004. Space-time Clusters with flexible shapes. IBM Research Report RC23398 (W0408-068) August 13, 2004.

Kulldorff M, Nagarwalla N, 1995. Spatial disease clusters: detection and inference. *Statistics in Medicine,* 14, 779-810.

Kulldorff M, 1997. A Spatial Scan Statistic, *Comm. Statist. Theory Meth.,* 26(6), 1481-1496.

Kulldorff M, 1999. Spatial scan statistics: Models, calculations and applications. In *Scan Statistics and Applications,* Glaz and Balakrishnan (eds.). Boston: Birkhauser, 303-322.

Kulldorff M, Tango T, Park PJ., 2003. Power comparisons for disease clustering sets, *Comp. Stat. & Data Anal.,* 42, 665-684.

Kulldorff M, Mostashari F, Duczmal L, Yih K, Kleinman K, Platt R., 2007, Multivariate Scan Statistics for Disease Surveillance. *Stat. Med.* (to appear).

Kulldorff M, Huang L, Pickle L, Duczmal L, 2006. An Elliptic Spatial Scan Statistic. *Stat. Med.* (to appear).

Lawson A., Biggeri A., Böhning D. *Disease mapping and risk assessment for public health.* New York, John Wiley and Sons, 1999.

Neill DB, Moore AW, Cooper GF, 2006. A Bayesian Spatial Scan Statistic. *Adv. Neural Inf.Proc.Sys. 18(in press)*

Patil GP, Taillie C, 2004. Upper level set scan statistic for detecting arbitrarily shaped hotspots. *Envir. Ecol. Stat.,* 11, 183-197.

Sahajpal R., Ramaraju G. V., Bhatt V., 2004 Applying niching genetic algorithms for multiple cluster discovery in spatial analysis. *Int. Conf. Intelligent Sensing and Information Processing.*

de Souza Jr. GL, 2005. Underreporting of Breast Cancer: A Study of Spatial Clusters in São Paulo State, Brazil. *M.Sc. Dissertation, Statistics Dept., Univ. Fed. Minas Gerais, Brazil.*

Takahashi RHC, Vasconcelos JA, Ramirez JA, Krahenbuhl L, 2003. A multiobjective methodology for evaluating genetic operators. *IEEE Transactions on Magnetics,* 39(3), 1321-1324.

Tango T, Takahashi K., 2005. A flexibly shaped spatial scan statistic for detecting clusters. *Int. J. Health Geogr.,* 4:11.

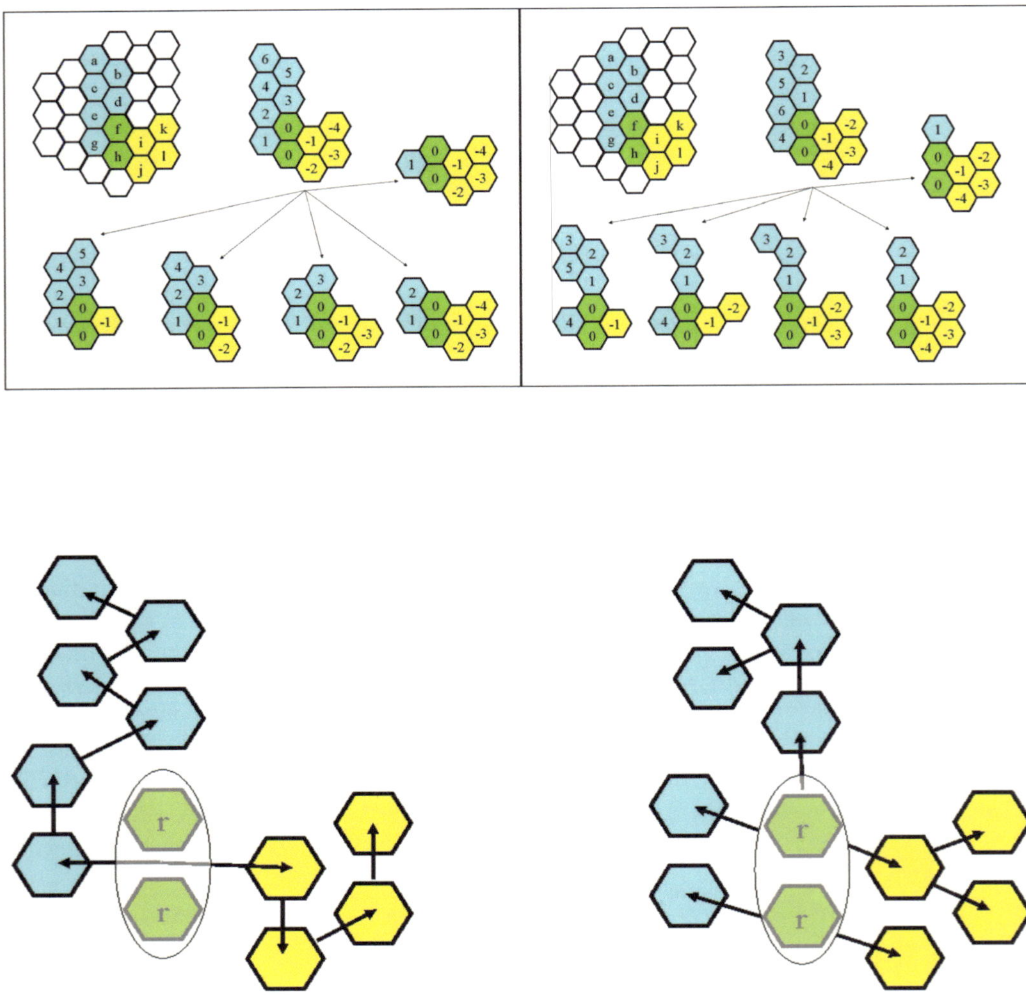

Figure 1A. The parents A ={a,b,c,e,f,g,h} and B ={f,h,i,j,k,l} have a common part C ={f,g}. Two possible level assignments are shown with their respective sets of trees. The level assignment to the left produces more regularly shaped offspring clusters, compared to the level assignment to the right of the figure.

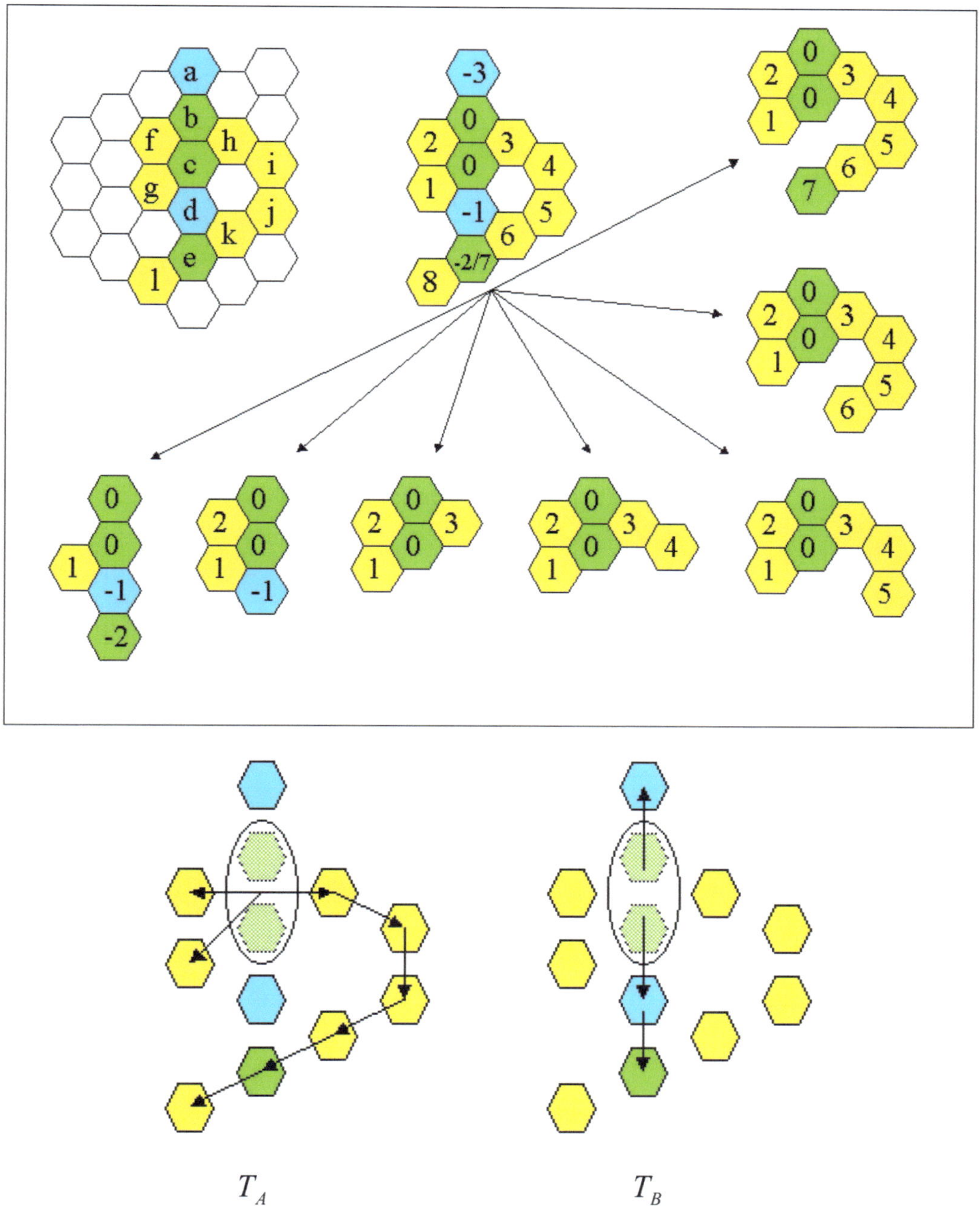

Figure 1B. The parents $A = \{b,c,e,f,g,h,i,j,k,l\}$ and $B = \{a,b,c,d,e\}$ have a common par $C = \{b,c,e\}$. In this example we choose the maximal connected set $D = \{b,c\}$. Observe that the node *e*, belonging to the set *C-D*, has both positive (7) and negative (-2) levels. The virtual root node *r* is made collapsing the two nodes of *D* (represented by the ellipse), and forms the root of the trees T_A (bottom left) and T_B (bottom right).

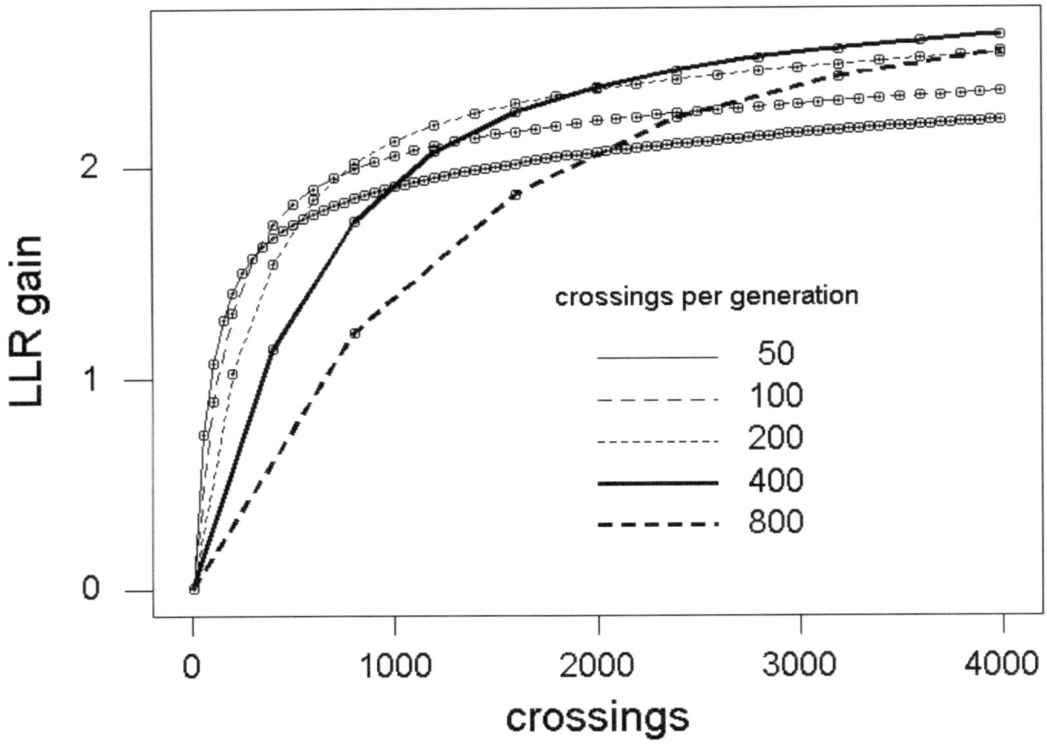

Figure 2. A numerical experiment shows how the number of wel succeeded crossings per generation (wsc_{MAX}) affects the LLR gain. Each little square, representing one generation, consists of the average of 5,000 runs of the genetic algorithm. A total of 4,000 wellsucceeded crossings were simulated for each run, for several values of wsc_{MAX}. In a given curve, with a fixed number of crossings per generation, the LLR value increases rapidly at the beginning, slowing further in the next generations. The optimal value for wsc_{MAX} is 400, in this case. Had the total of well-succeeded crossings been 1,000, the optimal value of wsc_{MAX} should be 200, as may be seen placing a vertical line at the 1,000 position.

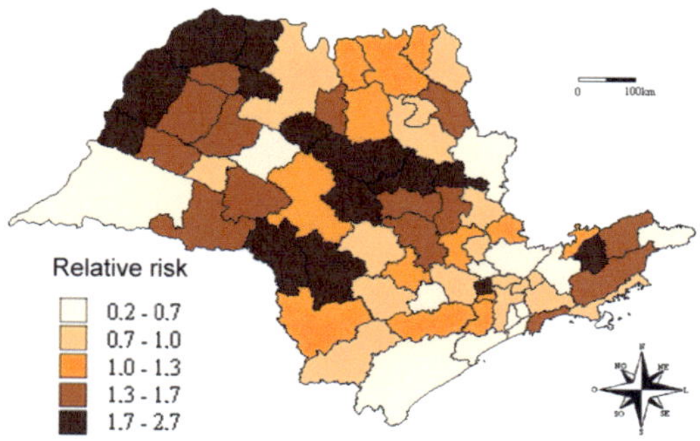

Figure 3A

Figure 3B

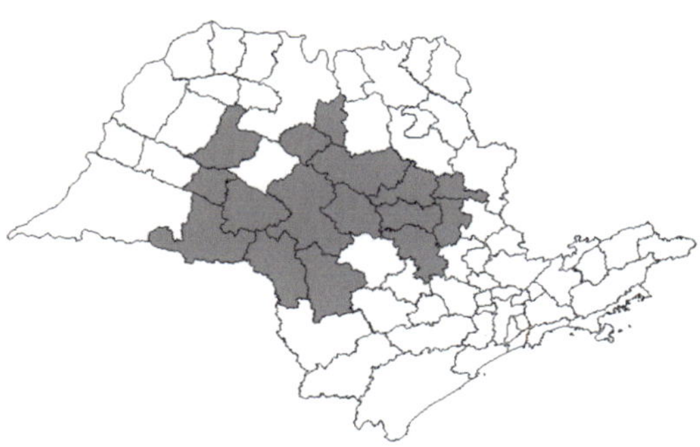

Figure 3C

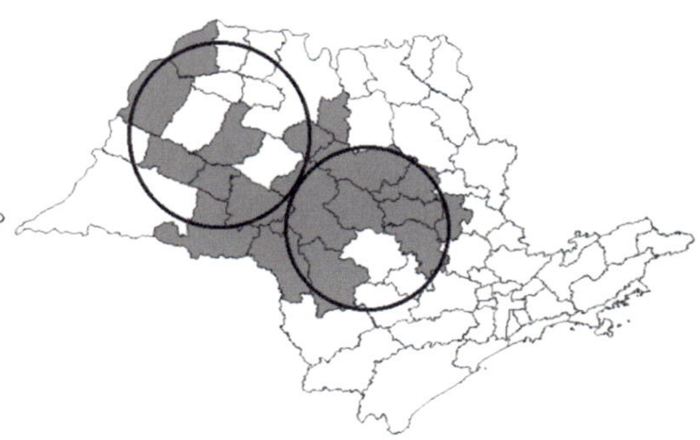

Figure 3D

Figure 3: The clusters of high incidence of breast cancer in São Paulo State, Brazil, during the years 2000-2003, found by the genetic algorithm. The map in Figure 3A displays the relative incidence of cases in each region. The maps 3B, 3C and 3D show respectively the clusters with penalty parameters a=1, a=0.5, and a=0. The primary (right) and secondary (left) circular clusters found by SatScan are indicated by the two circles in Figure 3D, for comparison.

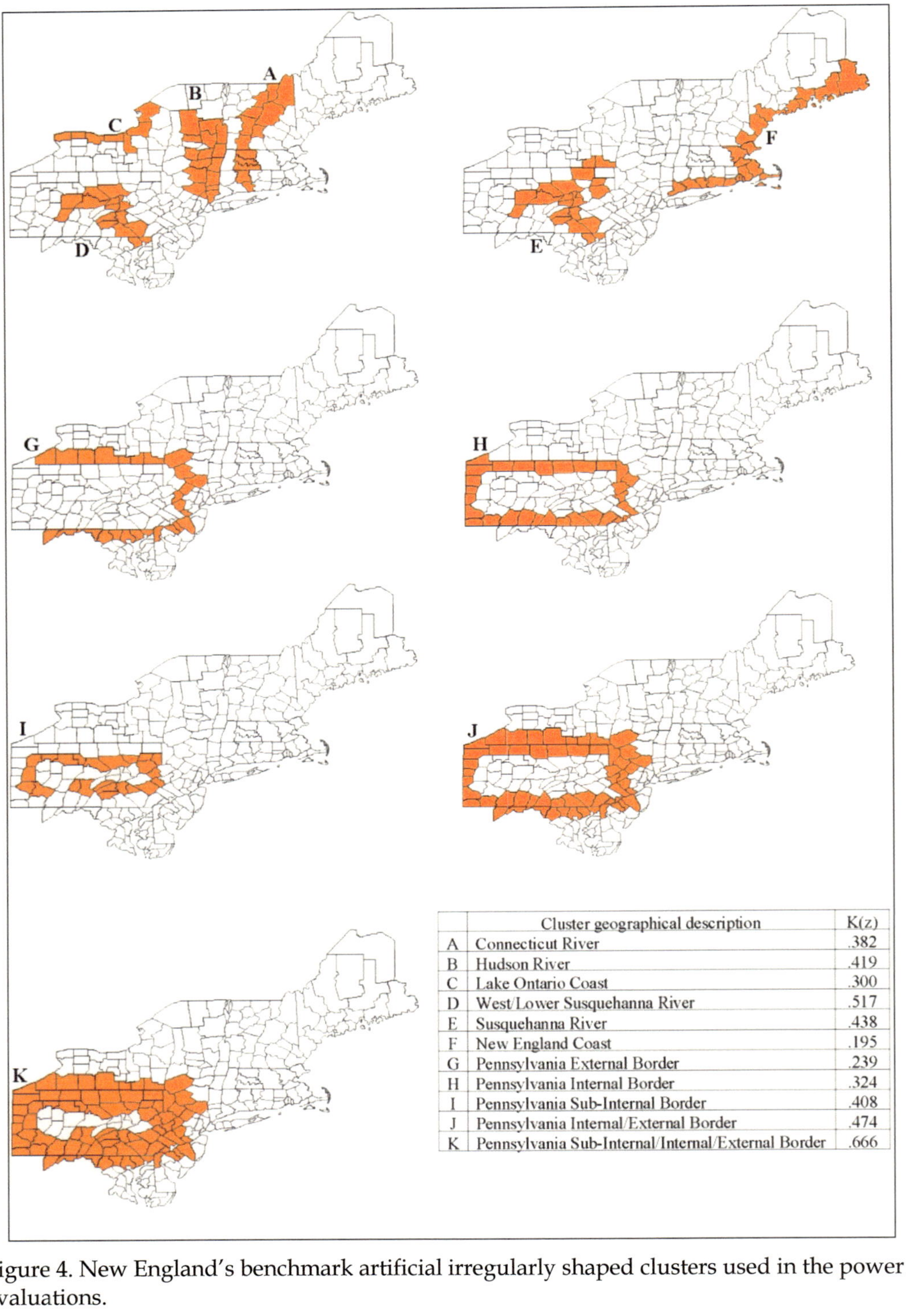

	Cluster geographical description	K(z)
A	Connecticut River	.382
B	Hudson River	.419
C	Lake Ontario Coast	.300
D	West/Lower Susquehanna River	.517
E	Susquehanna River	.438
F	New England Coast	.195
G	Pennsylvania External Border	.239
H	Pennsylvania Internal Border	.324
I	Pennsylvania Sub-Internal Border	.408
J	Pennsylvania Internal/External Border	.474
K	Pennsylvania Sub-Internal/Internal/External Border	.666

Figure 4. New England's benchmark artificial irregularly shaped clusters used in the power evaluations.

20

Practical Considerations for Simulated Annealing Implementation

Sergio Ledesma, Gabriel Aviña and Raul Sanchez
School of Engineering - University of Guanajuato, Mexico

1. Introduction

Nowadays, there are many optimization problems where exact methods do not exist or where deterministic methods are computationally too complex to implement. Simulated annealing may be the answer for these cases. It is not greedy in the sense that it is not fool with false minima, and is pretty easy to implement. Furthermore, because it does not require a mathematical model, it can be used to solve a broad range of problems.
Unfortunately, mapping a real problem to the domain of simulated annealing can be difficult and requires familiarity with the algorithm. More often than not, it is possible to encode the solution (solve the problem) using several approaches. In addition, there are other factors that determine the success of failure of this algorithm. This chapter reviews how to plan the encoding of the solution, and discusses how to decide which encoding is more appropriate for each application.
Several practical considerations for the proper implementation of simulated annealing are reviewed and analyzed. These include how to perturb the solution, how to decide a proper cooling schedule, and most important, how to properly implement the algorithm. Several cooling schedules are covered, including exponential, linear and temperature cycling. Additionally, the impact of random number generators is examined; how they affect the speed and quality of the algorithm. Essentially, this chapter is focused for those who want to solve real problems using simulated annealing for artificial intelligence, engineering, or research.
An illustrative example is solved using simulated annealing and implemented in a popular programming language using an object-oriented approach. This chapter offers a great opportunity to understand the power of this algorithm as well as to appreciate its limitations.
Finally, it is reviewed how is possible to combine simulated annealing with other optimization algorithms (including the deterministic ones) to solve complex optimization problems. In particular, it is discussed how to train artificial neural networks using simulated annealing with gradient based algorithms.

2. Simulated annealing basics

Simulated annealing is an optimization method that imitates the annealing process used in metallurgic. Generally, when a substance goes through the process of annealing, it is first heated until it reaches its fusion point to liquefy it, and then slowly cooled down in a control manner until it solids back. The final properties of this substance depend strongly on the cooling schedule applied; if it cools down quickly the resulting substance will be easily broken due to an imperfect structure, if it cools down slowly the resulting structure will be well organized and strong.

When solving an optimization problem using simulated annealing the structure of the substance represents a codified solution of the problem, and the temperature is used to determined how and when new solutions are perturbed and accepted. The algorithm is basically a three steps process: perturb the solution, evaluate the quality of the solution, and accept the solution if it is better than the new one.

To implement simulated annealing, it is usually necessary to generate huge amounts of random numbers. Unfortunately, typical random generators included in programming languages are of low quality, and are not useful for simulated annealing. These random sequences have a finite length and may have correlation. Choosing an appropriate random generator requires specific knowledge of the problem; basically it is important to establish the amount of random numbers that will be required and the speed of the generator (some problems may require quality or speed; some others will require both quality and speed). (Press et al., 2002) provides a comprehensive review on the subject and includes actual code to implement high quality random number generators.

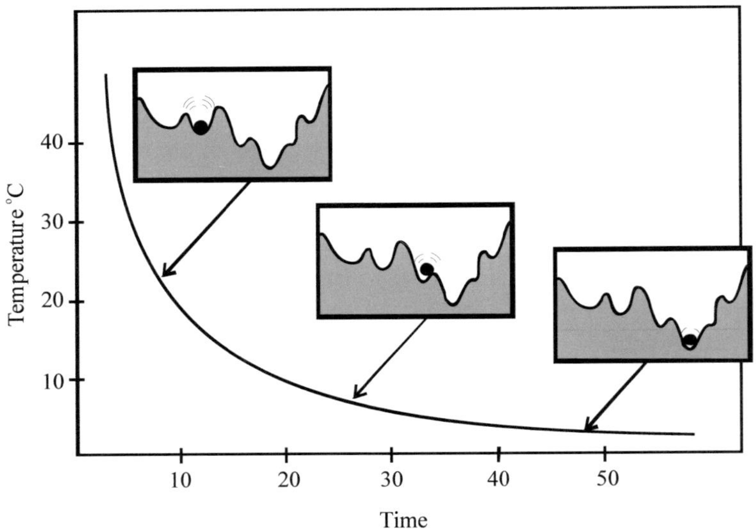

Fig. 1. The method of simulated annealing.

The method of simulated annealing can be easily understood by observing Fig. 1 which shows a hermetic box with an internal uneven surface (with peaks and valleys), and a ball resting on this surface. The objective is to move the ball to a position as close as possible to the bottom of the box. At the beginning of the process the temperature is high and strong perturbations are applied to the box allowing the ball to easily jump over high peaks in search of the bottom of the box. Because of the high energy applied, it is possible for the ball to go down or up easily. As time goes by, the temperature decreases and the ball has less energy to jump high peaks. When the temperature has decreased to the point when the ball is able to jump only very small peaks, the ball should be hopefully very close to the bottom of the box and the process is completed. As it can be from this example, many things can go wrong with simulated annealing; these problems and how to avoid them will be discussed in Section 4.

3. Advantages of using simulated annealing.

3.1 A mathematical model is not required

As odd at it sounds, some problems in real life do not have an exact model, or sometimes, the model is too complicated to be useful. In other cases, there is so little information about the problem that existing models cannot be appropriately used. For these cases, simulated annealing may be perfect as long as two basic operations can be implemented: perturb and evaluate. Thus, if a solution can be designed so that it can be perturbed and evaluated, then the problem can be solved using simulated annealing for sure.

3.2 The problem has many solutions and some of them are not optimal

Unfortunately, some problems have their solution surrounded by non optimal solutions (false minima), and typical optimization algorithms may have a bad time trying to escape from these false solutions. Consider a problem that could be described as a system of non-linear equations, clearly, the mean-squared error may be used to measure the quality of the solution.

For these problems, the mean-squared error is compute using the actual output of the system and the desired output of it. Generally, gradient based algorithms are a good choice to minimize the mean-squared error and find a solution, as they required much less time than solving the problem if simulated annealing is used. However, gradient based algorithms require knowledge of the derivative of the error with respect to each unknown and they are useful when the global minimum is clearly defined. On the other hand, simulated annealing does not required derivative information, and it is not easily fooled with local minima.

Before moving our attention to another topic, it is important to mention that simulated annealing and gradient based algorithms can be used together as hybrids algorithms for global optimization. First, simulated annealing is used to find a rough estimate of the solution, then, gradient based algorithms are used to refine the solution (Masters, 1993); note that more research is needed to optimize and blend simulated annealing with other optimization algorithms and produce hybrids.

4. Typical problems when using simulated annealing.

4.1 Initial temperature is too high

Consider again Fig. 1 that described pictorially the process of simulated annealing, at high temperatures the ball has enough energy to jump over high peaks and it can go easily up or down. If the initial temperature is too high, the ball may fall down and reach a position close to the bottom, but it is also very likely that the ball may jump up ending in a position even higher than the initial position. In other words, applying too much perturbation is useless and should be avoided. This raises the questions: how much perturbation should be applied? How long a level or perturbation should be applied?

4.2 Temperature goes down to quickly

As it can be seen from the previous example, at high temperatures the method of simulated annealing is searching for the global minimum in a broad region, and as the temperatures decreases the method is reducing this search region and tries mainly to refine the solution found at high temperatures. This is one of the good qualities that makes simulated annealing superior when the problem at hand has several deep valleys. Simulated annealing does not easily fall down into a deep valley located close by, instead it searches in an ample area trying always to go down and very occasionally up as the temperature allows. On the other hand, typical optimization methods fall quickly into a close deep valley even if it not the deepest valley. Thus, it is important to note that the temperature must go down slowly allowing the method to search thoroughly at each temperature.
There are two typical cooling schedules in the literature: exponential and linear. Fig. 1 shows a typical exponential cooling, as it can be seen from this figure, the process spends little time at high temperatures, and as the temperature decreases more and more time is spend at each temperature, allowing the algorithm to refine very well the solution found at high temperatures. On linear cooling, the temperature decreases linearly as the time increases, thus, the algorithm spends the same amount of time at each temperature. Clearly, linear cooling must be used when there are several deep valleys close by (note the quality of the final solution using linear cooling may not be good). On temperature cycling the temperature goes down and up cyclically refining the quality of the solution at each cycle. As it was indicated in (Ledesma et al., 2007), temperature cycling is beneficial for training of auto associative neural networks. Additionally, it has been pointed out (Reed & Marks, 1999) that a temperature reduction schedule inversely proportional to the logarithm of time will guarantee converge (in probability) to a global minimum, however, in practice this schedule takes too long, and it is often more efficient to repeat the algorithm a number of times using a faster schedule. Other cooling schedules area described in (Luke, 2007).

4.3 Process completes and the solution is not optimal

At the beginning of the process, the temperature and error are high, as time goes by, the temperature decreases slowly spending some time at each temperature and the error should be hopefully also decreasing. However, it is possible that the process completes without finding an optimal solution. Carefully selecting the parameters of simulated annealing may reduce the probability of this to happen, but this can happen. An easy solution to increase the probability of success is to try again and again until a desired error is obtained.

5. Simulated annealing implementation

Simulated annealing is a two steps process: perturb, and then evaluate the quality of the solution. Usually, the algorithm uses the solution error to make decisions about the acceptance of a new solution. Next, some notation will be offered to make a clear presentation. Let represent a problem solution of M variables as

$$\mathbf{X} = \{x_1, x_2, x_3, \dots, x_M\} \tag{1}$$

where $x_1, x_2, x_3, \ldots, x_M$ are to be found by means of simulated annealing. This representation may be useful for most optimization algorithms; however, simulated annealing is a temperature dependent algorithm and the process temperature must be introduced in Equation 1. Let define T as the process temperature

$$T = T_1, T_2, T_3, \ldots, T_N \tag{2}$$

where T_1 is the initial temperature, T_N is the final temperature, N is the number of temperatures, and the values of T are chosen following a specific cooling schedule that is problem dependent. Please note that T has been defined as a discrete variable because usually the temperature does not increase continually.

To improve the performance of the method of simulated annealing, it is usual to spend some time at each temperature by performing a fixed number of iterations before decreasing the temperature. Let K be the number of iterations performed at each temperature, then Equation (1) can be written as

$$\mathbf{X}_i = \{x_{1,i},\ x_{2,i},\ x_{3,i},\ \ldots,\ x_{M,i}\}, \qquad i = 1, 2, 3, \ldots \tag{3}$$

where i is the number of perturbations applied to the solution, and $x_{1,i}$ is the value of x_1 after it is has been perturbed i-times. Thus, at the end of temperature T_1, the number of perturbations applied to the solution is K, and $\mathbf{X}_K$ represents the solution at the end of this temperature. Usually, each solution $\mathbf{X}_i$ must have an error associate with it, let

$$E_1, E_2, E_3, \ldots \tag{4}$$

be the errors of $\mathbf{X}_1, \mathbf{X}_2, \mathbf{X}_3, \ldots$ respectively. Generally, a technique to estimate the solution error must be defined, but typically this technique is problem dependent and full knowledge of the problem is required. Consider for example a problem where five pieces are to be located at discrete positions in the plane x-y, and it is desired that each piece meets some constraints; without a doubt, the error may be defined as the number of pieces that do not meet the constraints. For other optimization problems, the mean squared error may be more appropriate; common sense is required as rigid rules do not exists.

As it can be induced from the previous discussion, there are not regulations that dictate or limit simulated annealing implementation. There are, however, some specific criteria about how to accept a solution once it has been perturbed. One obvious criterion is to accept a solution whenever it has a less error than the previous solution. There is, though, one popular algorithm used to manage simulated annealing. The metropolis algorithm, shown in Equation 5, follows the criterion discussed previously, and is typically used in simulated annealing to compute the probability of acceptance for a perturbed solution.

$$p_a = \begin{cases} e^{\frac{k\,\Delta E}{T}} & \Delta E > 0 \\ 1 & \Delta E \le 0 \end{cases} \tag{5}$$

where ΔE is the difference between the solution error after it has perturbed, and the solution error before it was perturbed, T is the current temperature and k is a suitable constant. A plot of Equation (5) is presented in Figure 2; it can be observed that when ΔE is negative the solution is always accepted. However, the algorithm may accept a new solution even if the solution has not a smaller error than the previous one (a positive ΔE), and the probability to do this decreases when the temperature decreases or when ΔE increases. Consequently, at high temperatures the algorithm may wander wildly accepting bad solutions; as the temperature decreases, the algorithm is more selective and accepts perturbed solutions only when the respective ΔE is small. This is the theory behind simulated annealing and should be clearly understood to properly implement the algorithm.

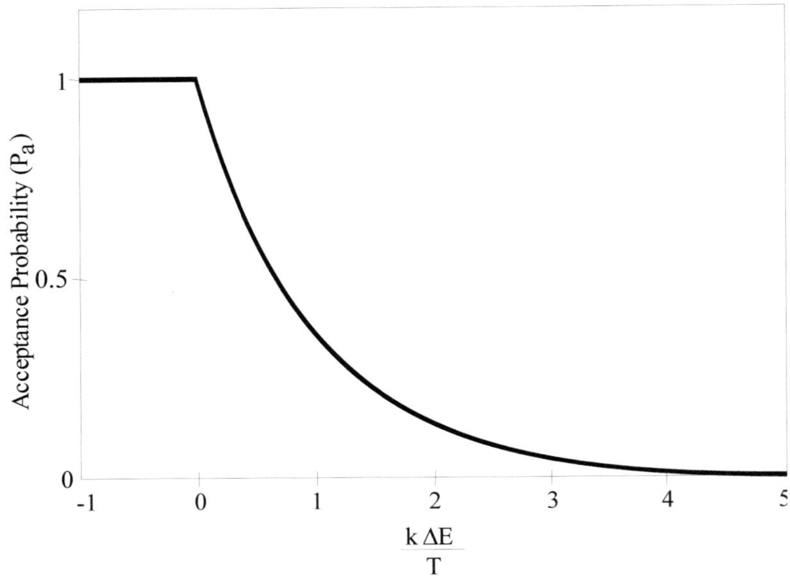

Fig. 2. Probability of acceptance following the Metropolis algorithm

Consider now Figure 3 which shows the probability of acceptance as a function of ΔE for several values of k/T. From this figure, it can be seen that the constant k plays an important role on the algorithm success; if k is equal to T, the algorithm will accept solutions with high probability even if ΔE is not small. This is not good as the method will spend great time trying with bad solutions; even if an excellent solution is found, the method will easily discard it. Generally, a medium ration k/T is desired at the beginning of the process. The authors suggest estimating the value of k as a previous step of the annealing process. This can save a lot of time, as there is not unique value of k that can be used for all optimization problems.

6. Estimating k

When an optimization problem is not properly solved using simulated annealing, it may sound suitable to increase the number of temperatures and the number of iterations at each temperature. Additionally, it may sound logical to start at a high temperature and end with a very low final temperature. However, it is most recommended to carefully choose the simulated annealing parameters in order to minimize the number of calculations and, consequently, reduce the time spend on vain perturbations.

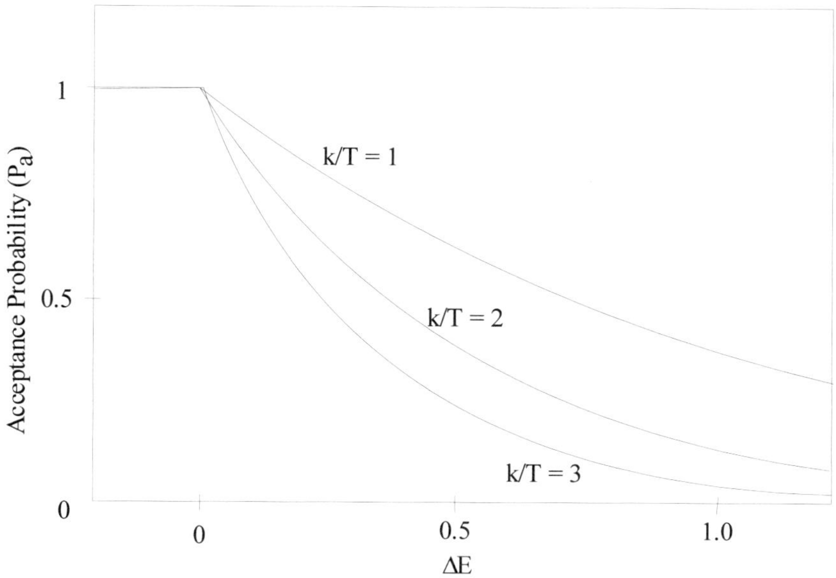

Fig. 3. Probability of acceptance for several values of k/T.

At the beginning of annealing, it is necessary to have an initial solution to start working with. Let $\mathbf{X}_0$ be the initial solution before applying any perturbation to it, and E_0 the error associated with $\mathbf{X}_0$. Typically, $\mathbf{X}_0$ may be created by assigning random values to $\{x_1, x_2, x_3, \ldots, x_M\}$, however, in most cases, it is strongly recommended to use the problem requirements to create $\mathbf{X}_0$., this will warranty at least a good starting point.

As it was described before, the constant k plays an important role on simulated annealing for global optimization. In this section, the authors suggest a simple method to estimate k using the essential operations of simulated annealing (perturb and evaluate). After inspecting Equation 9, it is clear that the value of k must be estimated using the initial temperate and the delta error. An estimate for ΔE can be computed from

$$\Delta E = \sigma_E \tag{6}$$

which can be estimated as

$$\Delta E \approx \frac{1}{Q-1}\sum_{i=1}^{Q} E_i - \frac{1}{Q(Q-1)}\sum_{i=1}^{Q} (E_i)^2 \tag{7}$$

that is, the sample variance of E when the solution $\mathbf{X}_0$ has been perturbed Q times. In practice, Equation 7 is an excellent estimator of the initial value of ΔE as long as Q is at least 1000 or more. It is important to mention that an exact value of ΔE is not required as this value is used only to a get rough estimate of k; this implies that a big value for Q is not necessary.

Once an estimate for the delta error of the solution has been found, finding an estimate for k is straightforward as Equation 5 can be directly used to solve for k. However, an initial value for the probability of acceptance needs to be defined. It is clear that the initial probability of acceptance must not be close to one, neither must be close to zero. A value between 0.7 and 0.9 is recommended. A probability of acceptance bigger than 0.9 has not practical purpose as the algorithm will accept too many bad solutions. On the other hand, a value that is less than 0.7 will rob the algorithm the opportunity to search abroad, loosing one of the main advantages of simulated annealing. In general, an initial value for the probability of acceptance should be 0.8. Thus, an estimate of k can be express as

$$k = \frac{T_0 \ln(0.8)}{\sigma_E} \qquad (8)$$

where an estimate for the standard deviation of the solution error can be computed using Equation 7. The performance of the algorithm is dramatically increased when Equation 8 is used because unnecessary and vain perturbations are not computed; instead the algorithm uses this precious CPU time on doing actual work.

7. Implementing simulated annealing

For now, the reader should have a sense of how simulated annealing works. However, the reader may have some doubts on how to implement it. As it was established before, common sense is required for proper implementation of the algorithm as there are not hard rules. This section describes how to use a programming language to correctly implement simulated annealing. Figure 4 shows the UML diagram for a class to implement simulated annealing. At the top of the diagram the class name (SimulatedAnnealing) is shown, the second block contains the member variables and the third block the member functions. The member variables' names are self explanatory. However, note that k and finalTemp are declared as private as the class itself will compute these values from the other setup parameters. The only public function is Start, it should be called once we are ready to start the annealing process.

SimulatedAnnealing
+numTemps : int +numIterations : int +initialTemp : double -finalTemp : double +isCoolingScheduleLinear : bool +cycles : int -k : double
+SimulatedAnnealing() +~SimulatedAnnealing() +Start(Solution& solution, Solution& wk1, Solution& wk2, double goal) : double -GetTemperature(int index) : double -IsAcceptedByMetropolis(double temperature, double deltaError) : bool -Anneal(Solution& solution, Solution& wk1, Solution& wk2, double goal) : double -EstimateK(Solution& solution, int N) : double

Fig. 4. UML diagram for a class to implement simulated annealing.

The class of Figure 4 makes reference to the abstract class Solution depicted in Figure 5. The class Solution contains the actual implementation of the problem that maps the real problem to the solution coding. Figure 5 describes two classes: Solution at the top and NumEq at the bottom. The class NumEq will be discussed on the next section, for now, just note that NumEq implements the pure abstract functions of the class Solution: operator=, OnInitialize, OnPerturb and OnComputeError. These are the four functions that need to be implemented to solve a global optimization problem by simulated annealing. Note that these functions corresponds to the basic operations required by annealing (perturb and evaluate) plus two extra more: OnInitialize to initialize the solution, and the operator= that is useful whenever a solution needs to be copied from one variable to another one. It is important to mention that for some optimization problems, it may be inefficient to implement the operator= as this operator consumes a considerable amount of CPU time; for this cases other techniques to store and manipulate the solution may be used.

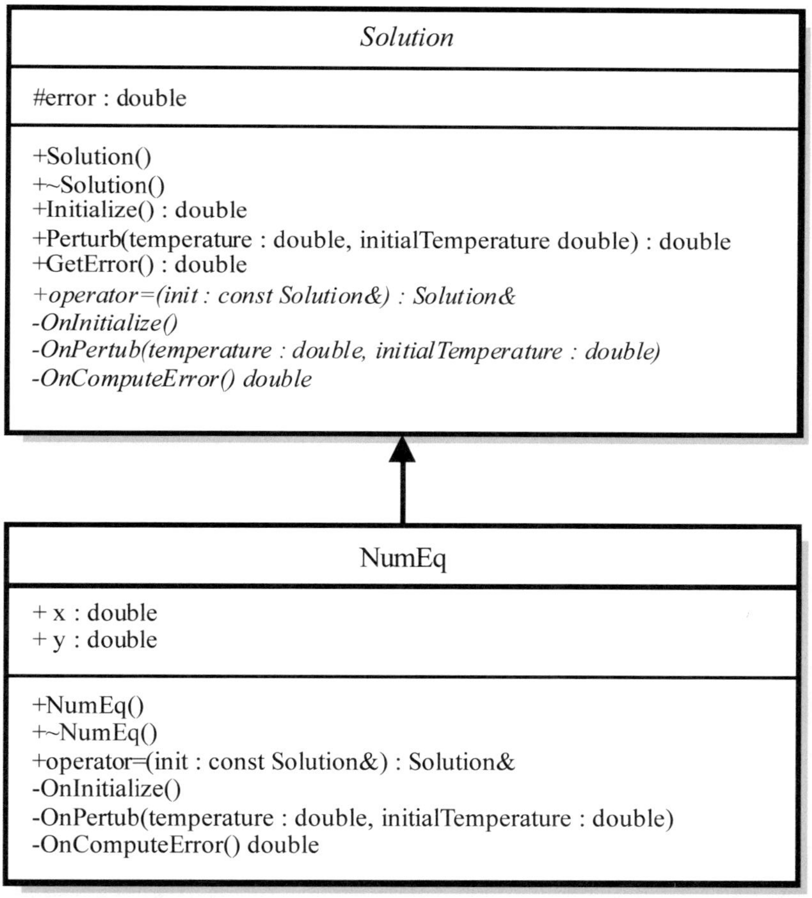

Fig. 5. UML diagram of a class to implement the solution of an optimization problem.

Figure 6 and 7 show a typical implementation using the C++ language for the Simulated Annealing class. The class may be implemented in others programming languages such as Java or C# with minor changes. Let now discuss briefly the implementation of this class.

There are several private functions on this class and are used only by the class itself. The function GetTemperature() is called every time the temperatures changes, its implementation is straightforward once the cooling scheduled has been defined; on the shown code there are two cooling schedules: exponential and linear. The function IsAcceptedByMetropolis() implements the metropolis algorithm of Equation 5, returns true when the perturbed solution must be accepted, and returns false otherwise. The function EstimateK() implements Equation 8. All the magic of the process is implemented in the function Anneal(), which is called several times if temperature cycling is used (i.e., the variable 'cycles' has a value bigger than one).

To use the SimulatedAnnealing class described, the function Start() must be called, this function requires three variables of the class Solution, namely 'solution', 'wk1' and 'wk2' ('solution' is the variable where the actual solution is stored; 'wk1' and 'wk2' are working solutions to perform the annealing process.) In the next section, it will be discussed how to use the SimulatedAnnealing class to solve a simple optimization problem.

SimulatedAnnealing.h

```
#pragma once
#include "Solution.h"
class SimulatedAnnealing
{
public:
        SimulatedAnnealing(void);
        ~SimulatedAnnealing(void);
        int numTemps;
        int numIterations;
        double initialTemp;
        bool isCoolingScheduleLinear;
        int cycles;
        double Start(Solution& solution, Solution& wk1, Solution& wk2, double goal);
private:
        double GetTemperature(int index);
        bool IsAcceptedByMetropolis(double temperature, double deltaError);
        double Anneal(Solution& solution, Solution& wk1, Solution& wk2, double goal);
        double EstimateK(Solution& solution, int N);
        double finalTemp;
        double k;
};
```

Fig. 6. Header file using C++ to implement the SimulatedAnnealing class of Figure 4.

SimulatedAnnealing.cpp

```
#include "SimulatedAnnealing.h"
SimulatedAnnealing::SimulatedAnnealing(void)
{
        numTemps=100;
        numIterations=100;
        initialTemp=100.0;
        finalTemp=0.0001;
        isCoolingScheduleLinear=false;
```

```
        k = 10;
        cycles = 4;
}

SimulatedAnnealing::~SimulatedAnnealing(void)
{
}

double SimulatedAnnealing::Start(Solution& solution, Solution& wk1, Solution& wk2, double
goal)
{
        for(int i=0; i<cycles; i++)
        {
                if (Anneal(solution, wk1, wk2, goal)<=goal) break;
        }
        return solution.GetError();
}

double SimulatedAnnealing::EstimateK(Solution& solution, int N)
{
        double E = 1.0;
        double sum = 0.0;
        double sums = 0.0;

        for(int i = 0; i<N; i++)
        {
                E = solution.Perturb(initialTemp, initialTemp);
                sum+=E;
                sums+=(E*E);
        }
        double variance  = sums/(N-1) - (sum*sum)/(N*(N-1));
        return -log(0.8)*initialTemp/sqrt(variance);
}

double SimulatedAnnealing::Anneal(Solution& solution, Solution& wk1, Solution& wk2, double
goal)
{
        double error = solution.Initialize();
        if (error<=goal) return error; //We are alredy done. Unlikely!
        k = EstimateK(solution, 1000);
        wk1 = solution;
        wk2 = solution;

        finalTemp = goal;
        //
        bool hasImproved = false;
        double temperature, deltaError;
        int i;

        for (int n=0; n<numTemps; n++)
```

```
        {
                temperature = GetTemperature(n);
                hasImproved = false;
                //_________________________________________ Iterate at this temperature
                for (i=0; i<numIterations; i++)
                {
                        deltaError = wk1.Perturb(temperature, initialTemp) - error;
                        if (IsAcceptedByMetropolis(temperature, deltaError))
                        {
                                wk2 = wk1;
                                hasImproved = true;
                                if (work1.GetError()<=goal) break;
                        }
                }
                if (hasImproved==true) // If saw improvement at this temperature
                {
                        wk1 = wk2;
                        solution = wk2;
                        error = solution.GetError();
                        if (error<=goal) break;
                }
        }
        return solution.GetError();
}

bool SimulatedAnnealing::IsAcceptedByMetropolis(double temperature, double deltaError)
{
        if (deltaError=<0) return true;
        return Random(0.0, 1.0) < exp(-k*deltaError/temperature);
}

double SimulatedAnnealing::GetTemperature(int index)
{
        if (isCoolingScheduleLinear)
        {
                return initialTemp+index*(finalTemp-initialTemp) / (numTemps-1);
        }
        else
        {
                return initialTemp*exp(index * log(finalTemp/initialTemp) / (numTemps-1));
        }
}
```

Fig. 7. Source file using C++ to implement the SimulatedAnnealing class of Figure 4.

Figure 8 shows the header file for the Solution class using C++, Figure 9 shows the respective source file. As it can be seen from these figures, the Solution class is abstract as it has four abstract functions. Consequently, to create an object from the Solution class, a new derived class must be created and must implement: the operator=, OnInitialize(), OnPerturb() and OnComputeError(). Observe carefully the implementation of this class;

note that some functions are designed by pairs. For example, Perturb() calls internally the functions OnPeturb() and OnComputeError(). Similarly, Initialize() calls the functions OnInitialize() and OnComputeError(). As it will be seen in the next section using the Solution class to solve an optimization problem is pretty simple.

Solution.h

```
#pragma once

class Solution
{
public:
        Solution(void);
        ~Solution(void);
        double Initialize(void);
        double Perturb(double temperature, double initialTemperature);
        double GetError(void);
        virtual Solution& operator =(const Solution& init) = 0;
protected:
        double error;
private:
        virtual void OnInitialize(void)=0;
        virtual void OnPerturb(double temperature, double initialTemperature)=0;
        virtual double OnComputeError(void)=0;
};
```

Fig. 8. UML diagram for a class to implement the solution.

Solution.cpp

```
#include "Solution.h"

Solution::Solution(void)
{
        error = 1.0;
}

Solution::~Solution(void)
{
}

double Solution::GetError(void)
{
        return error;
}

double Solution::Initialize(void)
{
        OnInitialize();
        error = fabs(OnComputeError());
        return error;
```

```
}

double Solution::Perturb(double temperature, double initialTemperature)
{
        OnPerturb(temperature, initialTemperature);
        error = fabs(OnComputeError());
        return error;
}
```

Fig. 9. UML diagram for a class to implement the solution.

8. Numerical example

Simulated annealing can be used to solve a broad range of optimization problems in artificial intelligence and other areas. However, it would be inappropriate to solve a complex problem to illustrate how to use simulated annealing. Thus, the two variable function of Equation 9 will be use for instructive purposes. Note that other optimization methods are more appropriate to solve this second order equation, and this section is only trying to set the basics for proper use of simulated annealing.

$$f(x, y) = x^2 + y^2 + 5xy - 4 \tag{9}$$

To get a better sense of the behavior of Equation 9, Figure 10 shows a plot of this equation. Let suppose that the goal is to find the values of x and y that minimize f(x, y). Clearly the solution is any point (x, y) that lies on the circle that intersects f(x, y) with the plane z = 0. Observe that simulated annealing is generally used when the solution has many variables, and finding or visualizing the solutions in these cases is much more difficult than interpreting the 3-D plot of Figure 10.

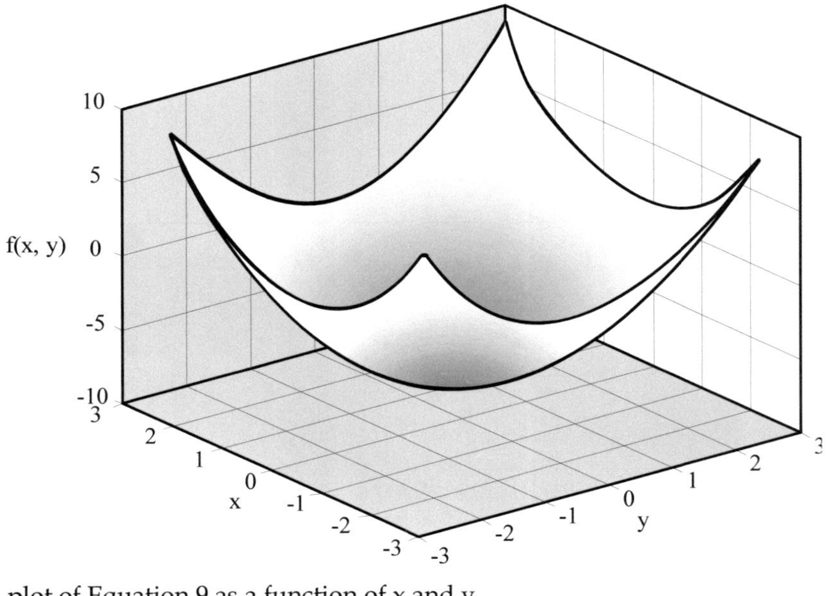

Fig. 10. A plot of Equation 9 as a function of x and y.

Consider Figure 11 that shows how simulated annealing works. At the beginning of the process the temperature is high (approximately 40 degrees in the figure) and the solution is perturbed so that it may lie on any of the points inside the dark circle. As the temperature decreases, the perturbation amount is reduced and the circle radius also decreases. At this temperature, the algorithm refines the quality of the solution previously found; note that solutions with high errors are not longer accepted (only solutions that reduce the error are accepted.) In other words, at low temperatures the algorithm moves the error down when the error is plot against x and y. Observe that the same number of iterations is used at each temperature while the exploring area is reduced; this increases the likelihood of finding the minimum.

Monitoring the progress of the process is important. For example, if the algorithm is not close to the minimum by the time the temperature has decreased considerably; simulated annealing will likely fail as the exploring area will be relatively too small. If this happens, it is better to restart the algorithm instead of performing useless iterations. One quick solution would be to increase the number of temperatures. Some will argue that the number of iterations should also be increased; however, it is important to note that it is not good idea to spend a lot of time at each temperature as the probability of acceptance will not change, if the temperature does not change either. Alternatively, if the temperature decreases slowly, the probability of the acceptance will gradually reduce, and the likelihood to accept a bad solution will be reduced as well.

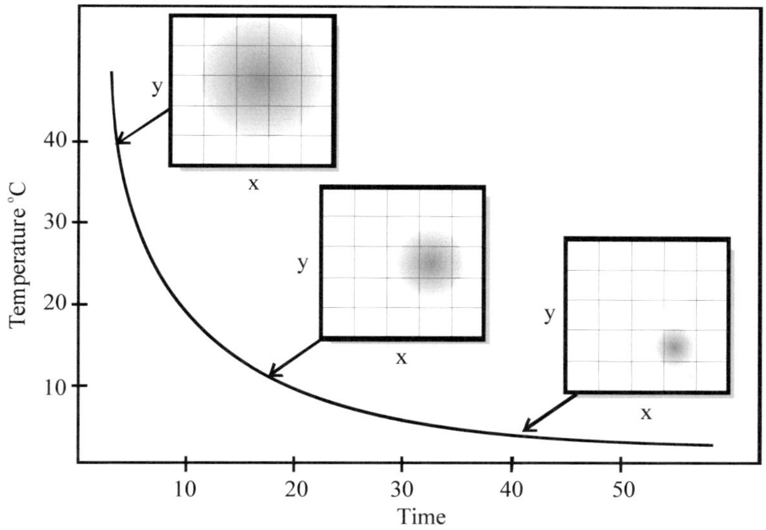

Fig. 11. Exploring area (represented as a gray circle) at each temperature.

Once a global view about how to minimize Equation 9, through the use of simulated annealing, has been presented, let actually show how to solve this particular problem. First, a new class derived from Solution must de created. Figure 12 and 13 show the header and source file for the class NumEq that is used to solve Equation 9; the respective UML diagram is shown at the bottom of Figure 5. Note that for this specific optimization problem, there are two variables of type double to store the solution 'NumEq.x' and 'NumEq.y'. The realization of the function OnComputeError() is straightforward as it directly implements Equation 9. The implementation of the function OnInitialize() is simple; it only assigns

random values between -10 and 10 to 'x' and 'y'. For other optimization problems, it is important to use common sense to implement the function OnInitialize(); if the problem does not provide enough information to do this, at least a valid initial value must be used.
Let know discuss the function Pertub() which is used to perturb the solution. Unfortunately, there are several ways to perturb a solution. It is recommended to try first the simplest way to perturb the solution; if this does not work, more sophisticate perturbation techniques may be used. Additionally, some practitioners prefer to perturb the solution a lot a high temperatures and reduce the degree the perturbation as the temperature decreases, this is what it is used on the example shown. However, it is important to mention that in some cases it is not possible to control the amount of perturbation, and for these cases the function Perturb() always applies the same amount of perturbation for each temperature.
By observing the function Perturb() in Figure 13, it can be observed that to perturb the solution, the value of 'x' is added to a random value which maximum amplitude is proportional to the current temperature. This method works really well, however, this approach may shift the solution too much, and 'x' may end in a region of invalid values. To alleviate this problem, an easy practice is to clip the solution values after perturbing. Alternatively, Figure 14 shows another way to perturb the solution; first a perturbation ratio is computed, then the new value of the variable is obtained by adding a proportional part of the old value plus a random variable; this method does not require clipping as the perturbation applied is blended naturally with the previous solution value. The authors have seen no evidence that one method is better than the other. However, it is important to note that when using the second method, the initial temperature is used only to compute the perturbation ratio and its value is not critical. Before leaving the discussion about how to implement the function Perturb(), please note that this function was specifically implemented using the knowledge that the values of 'x' and 'y' were in range from -10 to 10; other optimization problems may require a different implementation for this function.
The last function to discus is the operator=() which is used to copy a solution to another variable. This function must simply copy the solution variables from the source to the destination, specifically the variables: 'x', 'y' and 'error' in Figure 13.

NumEq.h

```
#pragma once
#include "Solution.h"

class NumEq : public Solution
{
public:
        NumEq(void);
        ~NumEq(void);
        double x, y;
        Solution& operator =(const Solution& init);
private:
        void OnInitialize(void);
        void OnPerturb(double temperature, double initialTemperature);
        double OnComputeError(void);
};
```

Fig. 12. Header file of the class NumEq to solve Equation 9.

NumEq.cpp

```
#include "NumEq.h"

NumEq::NumEq(void)
{
}

NumEq::~NumEq(void)
{
}

Solution& NumEq::operator =(const Solution& init)
{
        NumEq& eqInit = (NumEq&)init;
        x = eqInit.x;
        y = eqInit.y;
        error = eqInit.error;
        return *this;
}

void NumEq::OnInitialize(void)
{
        x = Random(-10.0, 10.0);
        y = Random(-10.0, 10.0);
}

void NumEq::OnPerturb(double temperature, double initialTemperature)
{
        x = x + Random(-temperature, temperature);
        y = y + Random(-temperature, temperature);
        //______________ Clip values to avoid wandering too far
        if (x>10.0) x = 10.0;
        if (x<-10.0) x = -10.0;
        if (y>10.0) y = 10.0;
        if (y<-10.0) y = -10.0;
}

double NumEq::OnComputeError(void)
{
        return x*x+y*y+5.0*x*y-4.0;
}
```

Fig. 13. Source file of the class NumEq to solve Equation 9.

```
void NumEq::OnPerturb(double temperature, double initialTemperature)
{
        const double ratio = temperature/initialTemperature;
        x = (1.0 - ratio)*x + ratio*Random(-10.0, 10.0);
        y = (1.0 - ratio)*y + ratio*Random(-10.0, 10.0);
}
```

Fig. 14. Alternative method to perturb the solution.

Once a new class has been derived from Solution, it is possible to use the new class to solve the optimization problem of Equation 9. Figure 15 shows the actual code for the main function to do this. First, three variables of type NumEq are created; the variable 'solution' is where the final solution will be stored; 'wk1' and 'wk2' are working solutions. Next, a variable of type SimulatedAnnealing is created and configured, here, other configuration parameters may be set. The shown code sets only the initial temperature and the number of temperatures. Finally, the annealing process starts by calling the function Start(), and at the end, the values of 'x' and 'y' (which are the solution) are displayed.

Example.cpp

```
#include "SimulatedAnnealing.h"
#include "NumEq.h"

int _tmain(int argc, _TCHAR* argv[])
{
        NumEq solution, wk1, wk2;
        SimulatedAnnealing sa;
        sa.initialTemp = 10;
        sa.numTemps = 2500;
        cout<<"\r\nError = "<<sa.Start(solution, wk1, wk2, 0.00001);
        cout<<"\r\nx = "<<solution.x;
        cout<<"\r\ny = "<<solution.y;
        return 0;
}
```

Fig. 15. Main function to solve the problem of Equation 9.

Before moving into the next section, note that the classes SimulatedAnnealing and Solution are generics and can be used to solve any global optimization problem by simulated annealing.

9. Solving problems using simulated annealing

9.1 The traveling salesman problem

The traveling salesman problem is a classical problem in artificial intelligence, where a seller has to visit N cities that are located at given positions, and finally he has to return to his city of origin (Press et al., 2002). For this problem, each city has to be visited only once and the resulting path should be as short as possible. Press et al. shows actual code using the C++ language to solve this problem and provides several tips worth trying to set the parameters of the algorithm. There, the problem is solved using the two basic operations described in this chapter: perturb and evaluate. The operation of perturb is performed by using two different type of perturbations. To evaluate the quality of the solution the path length is used. Press et al. ends the subject of simulated annealing by introducing a hybrid algorithm using the downhill simplex method.

9.2 The N-Queens problem

The N-Queens problem is a famous problem that has been attacked by a wide variety of search algorithms (Jones, 2005). It is defined as the placement of N queens on an N-by-N board such that no queen threatens any other queen using the standard rules of chess. This problem may be planned and solved by simulated annealing (Jones, 2005). The method used by Jones is similar to the method proposed here; however, our method is object-oriented and promotes code reuse.

9.3 Artificial neural network training

In (Masters, 1993), it is suggested to use simulated annealing for neural network training. Masters suggest a hybrid algorithm that combines simulated annealing with typical gradient based algorithms. Simulated is used only for initialization, and gradient based algorithms are used to refine the quality of the solution. Additionally, Masters suggest using simulated annealing in combination with other deterministic methods, for example regression to estimate the output weights of a neural network and perturb only the hidden weights. For artificial neural network training the implementation of simulated annealing requires a good random number generator, see (Press et al., 2002) to see code to implement such type of generators. The authors have suggested simulated annealing using temperature cycling for neural network training (Ledesma et al., 2007).
The free software Neural Lab is a powerful tool to simulate artificial neural networks, and it can be downloaded from http://www.fimee.ugto.mx/profesores/sledesma/. Neural Lab implements simulated annealing for neural network training using temperature cycling and several hybrid algorithms.

10. Conclusions

Simulated annealing is a powerful algorithm to solve global optimization problems. It has been successfully used in artificial intelligence (Russel & Norvig, 2002), and real life problems that do no have an appropriate model. There are still many aspects of simulated annealing open for research, including how to reduce the running time of the algorithm, how to optimize the cooling schedule and how to adapt the algorithm as the temperature and error change. The authors have presented several practical considerations that will help the reader to use simulated annealing to solve real life problems.

11. References

Jones, M. T. (2005). *AI Application Programming* (2nd edition), Charles River Media, ISBN 1-58450-421-8, Massachusetts, U.S.A.

Luke, B. T. (2007). Simulated Annealing Cooling Schedules, available online at http://members.aol.com/btluke/simanf1.htm, accessed June 1, 2007.

Ledesma, S., Torres, M., Hernandez, D., Avina, G. & Garcia, G. (2007). Temperature Cycling on Simulated Annealing for Neural Network Learning, Proceedings of MICAI, pp. 161-171, ISBN 978-3-540-76630-8, Mexico, November 2007, Springer-Verlag Berlin Heidelberg, Aguscalientes.

Masters, T. (1993). *Practical Neural Network Recipes in C++*. Academic Press, Inc., ISBN 0-12-479040-2, California, USA - London, UK.

Masters, T. (1995). *Advanced Algorithms for Neural Networks.* John Wiley & Sons Inc., ISBN 0-471-10588-0, New York, USA.

Press, W. H., Teukolsky, S. A., Vetterling, W. T., & Flannery, B. P. (2002). *Numerical Recipes in C++: The Art of Scientific Computing* (Second Edition), Cambridge University Press,

ISBN 0-521-75033-4, Cambridge, New York, Melbourne, Madrid, Cape Town, Singapore and Sao Paulo.

Reed, R. D. & Marks II, R. J. (1999). *Neural Smithing: Supervised Learning in Feedforward Artificial Neural Networks*, the MIT Press, ISBN 0-262-18190-8, Massachusetts, USA.

Russel, S. J. and Norvig, P. (2002). *Artificial Intelligence: A Modern Approach (2nd edition)*, Prentice Hall, ISBN 81-203-2382-3, New Jersey, U.S.A.